The Anthropology of the Enlightenment

Helen Baker
Endowment

Presented to
Juniata College Library
by Her Family

The Anthropology of the Enlightenment

Edited by Larry Wolff and Marco Cipolloni

STANFORD UNIVERSITY PRESS

STANFORD, CALIFORNIA

2007

In memory of Morton Klass,
inspirational anthropologist, 1927–2001

Not to disclose to any nation the state of our
religion, but to pass it over in silence, without any
declaration of it, seeming to bear with such laws and
rites, as the place hath, where you shall arrive.
—Hakluyt, *Voyages and Discoveries*, "Ordinances
  for the Direction of the Intended Voyage for
  Cathay, 1553"

Those who worshipped a bull never tried to compel
those who worshipped a monkey to change their
religion.
—Voltaire, *Philosophical Dictionary*, "Apis"

But are they really superstitions?
—Claude Lévi-Strauss, *Tristes tropiques*

—Larry Wolff

*Dedicated to the "Bronco" network, in the spirit
of worldwide independence, friendship, and freedom.*

Meanwhile the steamers which divide horizons prove
Us lost . . .
—Derek Walcott, "Prelude"

but out of what is lost grows something stronger
(. . .) strong as the wind, that through dividing canes
brings those we love before us, as they were,
with faults and all, not nobler, just there.
—Derek Walcott, "Sea Canes"

There were giants in those days.
In those days they made good cigars . . .
—Derek Walcott, "Volcano"

we can sit watching grey water,
and in a life awash
with mediocrity and trash
live rock-like . . .
—Derek Walcott, "Winding Up"

I had no nation now but the imagination.
—Derek Walcott, "Shabine Leaves the Republic"

—Marco Cipolloni

Stanford University Press
Stanford, California
© 2007 by the Board of Trustees of the Leland Stanford Junior University.

Printed in the United States of America on acid-free,
archival-quality paper

Library of Congress Cataloging-in-Publication Data

The anthropology of the Enlightenment / edited by Larry Wolff
and Marco Cipolloni.
  p. cm.
Includes bibliographical references and index.
ISBN 978-0-8047-5202-2 (cloth : alk. paper)—ISBN 978-0-8047-5203-9
(pbk. : alk. paper)
  1. Anthropology—History—18th century. 2. Anthropology—Philosophy.
3. Enlightenment. I. Wolff, Larry. II. Cipolloni, Marco.

GN17.3.E85A58   2007
301.09'033—dc22   2007007298

Typeset by Westchester Book Group in 10/12 Sabon

Contents

Preface

Larry Wolff and Marco Cipolloni

The modern enterprise of anthropology, with all of its important implications for cross-cultural perceptions, perspectives, and self-consciousness emerged from the eighteenth-century intellectual context of the Enlightenment. If the Renaissance discovered perspective in art, it was the Enlightenment that articulated and explored the problem of perspective in viewing history, culture, and society. If the Renaissance was the age of oceanic discovery—most dramatically the discovery of the New World of America—the critical reflections of the Enlightenment brought about an intellectual rediscovery of the New World and thus laid the foundations for modern anthropology. The contributions that constitute this book present the multiple anthropological facets of the Enlightenment, and suggest that the character of its intellectual engagements—acknowledging global diversity, interpreting human societies, and bridging cultural difference—must be understood as a whole to be fundamentally anthropological.

The Enlightenment not only defined the word and conceived of the subject "anthropology" but also, in one of its most potent coinages, gave the lexicons of many European languages the new word and concept "civilization." First used by the physiocrat economists as they sought to convey the benefits that society would find in economic growth and progress, the word "civilization" came to sum up the European identity of enlightened men and women who comparatively and self-confidently assumed the superiority of their own way of life. To this day "civilization" provides the motto and matter of Western identity, constituting the self-assumed Occidental mantle of "Western civilization."

In the eighteenth century, when "civilization" was first named, the word's most potent effect was in authorizing a perspective on the allegedly less civilized, even the utterly uncivilized: societies to be civilized, or to become more civilized. By the light of civilization, it was possible to discern a whole ordering of societies, around the globe and across the centuries: societies backward, primitive, savage, or barbarous. Indeed, the very concept of civilization presupposed a condition of uncivilized origins and more- or less-civilized stages on the path toward the ultimate Occidental goal. The philosophy of the Enlightenment was deeply preoccupied with discerning and describing the series of those stages, and the concept of civilization thus became indispensable for the articulation of any anthropological perspective.

That perspective, however, could also be turned against the ideal of civilization. Rousseau, for instance, could conclude, without ever visiting the Caribbean, that the Carib was perhaps happier than a Frenchman; while Diderot, without ever visiting Tahiti, would compose brilliant fiction to address the question of whether the sexual customs of the Tahitians might be ultimately as conducive to contentment as those of Christian Europeans. The anthropology of the Enlightenment—discovering the primitive worlds of exotic savages in remote lands—was also capable of harvesting the insights of anthropological perspective, and bringing them to bear with critical intensity on the customs and values of society in Europe. For the philosophes of the eighteenth century, the anthropological agenda pointed the paradoxical path, through the barbarous domains of primitive peoples, to the sophisticated self-doubts of modernity and Europe.

In this book, we seek to excavate the origins of anthropology in the eighteenth century, the first modern intellectual efforts to observe, understand, and analyze other cultures or—in the language of contemporary cultural theory—the Other. An enormous share of cultural theory, in fact, focuses on this very issue of "otherness." The Other came to the forefront of modern intellectual debate with the pioneering works of *Orientalism* by Edward Said in 1979 and *The Conquest of America* by Tzvetan Todorov in 1982, which theorized on European cultural encounters with Asia and America, the East and the West, respectively. The prominence and prevalence of this academic discussion, in the decades since then, makes it now seem all the more important to take scholarly stock of just *how* Europe came to confront intellectually, describe systematically, and analyze critically other cultures beyond Europe. This book on the anthropology of the Enlightenment proposes precisely that: to identify the intellectual and cultural foundations of the European encounter with peoples perceived as alien, exotic, primitive, savage, or barbarous—fundamentally different in ways that demanded critical analysis from enlightened observers. That discourse sought to understand those peoples in their own social and cultural contexts, that is, anthropologically.

This book is—indeed, must be—an interdisciplinary enterprise, and the contributors come from the diverse fields of history, literature, philosophy, and anthropology. We the editors have brought together our own two fields—the historical study of cultural relations and perceptions between Eastern Europe and Western Europe, and the cultural study of historical relations and perceptions between Spain and Spanish America— the better to pursue the anthropological perspective of the Enlightenment, looking eastward and looking westward. Our contributors have given the book a global range, reflecting the far-flung interests of the Enlightenment in the eighteenth century, when the comprehensive mapping and exploration of the Pacific Ocean in the age of Captain Cook made possible an appreciation of the global dimensions of geography and anthropology.

Larry Wolff's introduction explores the intellectual history of anthropology in the Enlightenment, considering Montesquieu and Swift, Voltaire and Rousseau, Fortis and Cook, Herder and Sade, and analyzing the complementary principles of enlightened anthropology: the philosophical spirit of cultural perspective and the ethnographic endeavor of scientific description. Marco Cipolloni's conclusion examines the relation between the Renaissance and the Enlightenment, especially with regard to the New World of America: how the age of Renaissance discovery modulated culturally into the age of Enlightenment anthropology, and how Enlightenment anthropology bequeathed its legacy to the modern anthropology of the nineteenth century. He analyzes the anthropological significance of the discursive relation between the Old Wor(l)d and the New Wor(l)ds, in the crucial European encounter with the Americas.

The contributions to the volume are divided into three principal parts. The first part focuses on anthropology as a philosophical subject, used especially in writing philosophical history: Gibbon on the barbarians of the ancient world, the philosophes on China, Diderot on empire, Herder on India, William Robertson on the Aztecs and Incans, and Adam Smith on hunters and gatherers. In this mode, enlightened anthropology speculatively explored earlier and primitive stages of human development, and compared historical developments across different parts of the globe. The second part of the book focuses on direct ethnographic encounters between Europeans and the supposedly primitive peoples who became the objects of early anthropological observations: in the Pacific, in Greenland, in the Russian Empire, and in Haiti. The third part focuses on enlightened conceptions of human nature, considering how human nature came to be understood anthropologically in its various social and cultural contexts: the cultural meaning of dreams, the social context of law, the significance of environment for transplanted colonists, and the psychological implications of the eighteenth-century theory of "animal economy."

These divisions of the volume thus highlight our principal arguments for understanding the Enlightenment as the crucial intellectual matrix for the emergence of the modern anthropological perspective on human society.

The contributions suggest the rich variety of anthropological discourses and endeavors in the age of Enlightenment. Our book cannot offer a complete and comprehensive account of every anthropological aspect of the Enlightenment precisely because, as the book itself seeks to demonstrate, the Enlightenment was fundamentally anthropological in all of its aspects and preoccupations. The whole character of the Enlightenment was profoundly conditioned by the essential and pervasive importance of the anthropological impulse.

Contributors

Sunil Agnani is currently completing a book entitled *Enlightenment Universalism, and Colonial Knowledge: Denis Diderot and Edmund Burke, 1770–1800*. He completed his doctorate at Columbia University, and then joined the Princeton Society of Fellows before starting as an assistant professor in the English Department at the University of Michigan.

Jean-Philippe E. Belleau is an anthropologist who teaches Latin American studies at the University of Massachusetts at Boston. He is also a researcher at the ERSIPAL (Équipe de Recherche: Société, Identité et Pouvoir en Amérique Latine), Institut des Hautes Etudes d'Amérique Latine, Université Paris-III Sorbonne Nouvelle.

Mary Baine Campbell teaches medieval and early modern literature and culture at Brandeis University. Her books include *The Witness and the Other World: Exotic European Travel Writing, 400–1600* (1988) and *Wonder and Science: Imagining Worlds in Early Modern Europe* (1999), as well as two volumes of poetry. She is currently at work on a book about early modern dreams.

Giulia Cecere has recently completed her Ph.D. in the School of History and Archives at University College Dublin thanks to an Irish Research Council postgraduate scholarship. Her Ph.D. thesis is entitled "Maps, Frontiers, and Cultures: Defining Europe's Eastern Boundaries in the Eighteenth Century." Her current research project is "The Representation of the Characters of Populations in Early Modern Europe."

Marco Cipolloni is professor and chair of Spanish Language and Culture at the University of Modena and Reggio Emilia. He received his Ph.D. from the University of Bologna in 1993, and is the author of many books and articles on Spanish and Latin American intellectual history, theater, and cinema. His works include *Il sovrano e la corte nelle "cartas" della conquista* (1991), *Tra memoria apostolica e racconto profetico: il compromesso etnografico francescano e le "cosas" della Nuova Spagna* (1994), *Ritratto dell'artista come gringo viejo* (2000, on Saura's cinematic portrait of Goya), and the critical edition of the *Teatro completo* of Miguel Angel Asturias (2004).

John Gascoigne is professor of history at the University of New South Wales, Sydney. His books include *Joseph Banks and the English Enlightenment: Useful Knowledge and Polite Culture* (1994), *Science in the Service of Empire: Joseph Banks, the British State and the Uses of Science in the Age of Revolution* (1998), and *The Enlightenment and the Origins of European Australia* (2002).

Nicholas A. Germana is a lecturer in history at Keene State College, New Hampshire. He received his Ph.D. in European history from Boston College in 2006. His dissertation was entitled "The Orient of Europe: The Mythical Image of India and Competing Images of German National Identity, 1760–1830."

Michael Harbsmeier studied anthropology and teaches history at the University of Roskilde in Denmark. His books include *Wilde Völkerkunde: Andere Welten in deutschen Reiseberichten der frühen Neuzeit* (*Savage Anthropology: Other Worlds in Early Modern German Travel Accounts*, 1994) and *Stimmen aus dem äussersten Norden* (*Voices from Ultima Thule*, 2001). He is currently working on a comparative study of accounts of Europe by travelers from other parts of the world.

Neil Hargraves is lecturer in history at Newbattle Abbey College, Scotland. He has published several articles on various aspects of eighteenth-century historiography, and is currently working on a book on the concept of character in eighteenth-century social and historical thought. He is also researching the idea of resentment in historical narrative.

Philippe Huneman is a philosopher of science at the IHPST (Institut d'Histoire et de Philosophie des Sciences et des Techniques), CNRS (Centre National de la Recherche Scientifique), Paris. He is the author of *Bichat: la vie et la mort* (1998), and editor of *Understanding Purpose: On Kant and Biology* (forthcoming). He has published several papers on Kant and on philosophical problems of evolutionary biology. He currently works on causation, adaptation, and emergence.

Michael Kempe is an assistant in the History Department at the University of Gallen, Switzerland. He has coedited a special issue of *Environment and History* entitled *Coping with the Unexpected: Natural Disasters and Their Perception* (2003). His current post-doctoral research is a book project titled *Curse of the Sea: Piracy and International Law in Early Modern Times*. His research areas include history of science, legal history, and environmental history.

Jonathan Lamb is the Mellon professor of the humanities at Vanderbilt University. His books include *The Rhetoric of Suffering: Reading the Book of Job in the Eighteenth Century* (1995) and *Preserving the Self in the South Seas* (2001). He is currently at work on a book entitled *The Things Things Say*.

Christian Marouby is professor of French at Mills College. He has most recently published *L'économie de la nature: essai sur Adam Smith et l'anthropologie de la croissance* (2004). His current research centers on the question of limits in the late eighteenth and early nineteenth centuries.

Anthony Pagden is distinguished professor of political science and history at UCLA. His books include *European Encounters with the New World* (1993), *Peoples and Empires* (2001), and *La ilustración y sus enemigos* (2002), and, as editor, *The Idea of Europe from Antiquity to the European Union* (2002). He is completing a study of the conflict between East and West in the European imagination from the Persian Wars until the present.

J. G. A. Pocock is professor emeritus of history at Johns Hopkins University. His books include *The Machiavellian Moment: Florentine Political Thought and the Atlantic Republican Tradition* (1975), *Barbarism and Religion, I: The Enlightenments of Edward Gibbon* (1999), *Barbarism and Religion, II: Narratives of Civil Government* (1999), *Barbarism and Religion, III: The First Decline and Fall* (2003), *Barbarism and Religion, IV: Barbarians, Savages and Empires* (2005), and *The Discovery of Islands: Essays in British History* (2005).

Larry Wolff is professor of history at New York University. His books include *Inventing Eastern Europe: The Map of Civilization on the Mind of the Enlightenment* (1994) and *Venice and the Slavs: The Discovery of Dalmatia in the Age of Enlightenment* (2001). His current research concerns Habsburg Galicia.

INTRODUCTION

CHAPTER ONE

Discovering Cultural Perspective

The Intellectual History of Anthropological Thought in the Age of Enlightenment

Larry Wolff

Montesquieu's *Persian Letters* was published anonymously in 1721, and quickly attracted a readership in France. Though the work was later revealed to be fiction, it was initially received as a true account given by Persian travelers in France, comparing their own customs and beliefs to those of the French. Part of the book's appeal lay in its Persian exoticism—especially the representation of Persian harem life—which fed a fashionable French fascination with the Middle Eastern world, already stimulated between 1704 and 1717 by the publication of Antoine Galland's French translation of the *Thousand and One Nights*. The subtler part of the impact of the *Persian Letters*, however, lay in its airing of an allegedly objective, because external, critique of French society, as the Persians reported upon those aspects of life in France that seemed perverse, irrational, or repellent to them. It was this criticism of French, and more generally European, society that made the *Persian Letters* into one of the founding works of the Enlightenment.

Montesquieu's Persians wrote their letters as anthropological observers of French customs, while their experience of France led them to become anthropologically perplexed about their own Persian assumptions. Usbek, as a visitor in the land of charcuterie, wondered in Letter 17 why pork was forbidden to Moslems, and concluded that "things in themselves are neither pure nor impure." When he wrote in Letter 26 to Roxana in the harem of Isfahan, he reported on the immodesty of French women: "If you were here, Roxana, you would certainly feel outraged by the dreadful ignominy into which your sex has fallen. You would flee from this hateful place, longing for the welcome seclusion which brings innocence."[1] Montesquieu was well aware that French women, reading his book, would be reciprocally outraged at the repressive seclusion of Persian women in the harem.

In the *Persian Letters*, Montesquieu established the principle of cultural relativism as one of the fundamental intellectual features of the Enlightenment. In Letter 59, addressed to Usbek by Rica, his fellow Persian, the principle was fully elaborated:

> It seems to me, Usbek, that all our judgments are made with reference covertly to ourselves. I do not find it surprising that the negroes paint the devil sparkling white, and their gods black as coal, or that certain tribes have a Venus with her breasts hanging down to her thighs, or in brief that all the idolatrous peoples represent their gods with human faces, and endow them with all their own impulses. It has been well said that if triangles had a god, they would give him three sides.[2]

Here Montesquieu posed questions that anticipated the spirit of modern anthropology: concerning the religious worship of different peoples, of diverse races and tribes. He answered the questions with reference to the coherence of each cultural group, suggesting a correspondence between their gods and themselves. Affirming that "all our judgments are made with reference covertly to ourselves," Rica proclaimed the principle of cultural relativism. Envisioning the three-sided god of the triangles, Montesquieu even adumbrated some of the patterned cultural analysis of structural anthropology. Above all, however, in outlining a philosophical schema of multiple cultures—each coherent in itself, with customs determined only by reference to itself—Montesquieu pointed the way toward an anthropological outlook in the Age of Enlightenment.

RELATIVE PERSPECTIVE: MONTESQUIEU AND SWIFT

"If one has to begin somewhere, or rather with someone, it must be with Montesquieu," wrote the anthropologist Sir Edward Evans-Pritchard in his lectures on the history of anthropology. Evans-Pritchard focused on the *Spirit of the Laws*, published in 1748, to demonstrate Montesquieu's anthropological interest in "the idea of social structure and of dominant values which operate through the structure."[3] The word "anthropology" only gradually acquired its modern meaning over the course of the eighteenth century, until in 1788 Alexandre-César Chavannes published his book, *Anthropology, or the General Science of Man* (*Anthropologie ou science générale de l'homme*). In fact, the original meaning of anthropology involved the attribution of human qualities to God, precisely as described by Rica in Letter 59 when he wrote about the black gods of black Africans. The discipline of anthropology would not fully emerge until the nineteenth century, with such figures as Lewis Henry Morgan, E. B. Tylor, James Frazer, and Franz Boas. The relevant writers of the eighteenth century were philosophes like Montesquieu, whose reflections on society articulated the intellectual premises of the still-inchoate anthropological discipline. The cultural relativism of Montesquieu in the *Persian Letters* in the 1720s would, in some sense, prepare the anthropological ground for Margaret Mead's *Coming of Age in Samoa* in the 1920s.

A sensational success in France, the *Persian Letters* were translated into English almost immediately, and published in London in 1722. Jonathan Swift published the English-language sensation *Gulliver's Travels* in 1726, also articulating the principle of cultural relativism, and ready to be immediately translated into French. *Gulliver's Travels* was the fictional account of a voyage of discovery, with Captain Gulliver as the anthropological guide to a variety of imaginary societies remote from Europe. Swift presented the contrasting cultures of Lilliput and Brobdingnag, each coherent and consistent as perceived from an outsider's perspective, and all the more so by comparison with one another. Lilliput was shown on a fictive map as an island in the Indian Ocean southwest of Sumatra; Brobdingnag was attached to North America, somewhere in the neighborhood of Alaska. As measured from Gulliver's perspective, Lilliputians were tiny creatures, living in a miniature society. The Brobdingnagians were giants, towering over Gulliver, just as he towered over the Lilliputians.

Roughly half a century later, Samuel Johnson, speaking to James Boswell, would dismiss as trivial the play of perspective in *Gulliver's Travels*: "When once you have thought of the big men and little men it is very easy to do all the rest."[4] Johnson's remark was perhaps a measure of how much the play of relative perspective had come to be taken for granted during the decades of the eighteenth century. When Voltaire composed the tale *Micromegas* in the 1750s, concerning interplanetary disparities in size and understanding, he did not consider the issue beneath his intellectual notice. Indeed, one might argue that once Swift had thought of the big men and the little men, and once Montesquieu had thought of the French and the Persians, then "all the rest" would dominate the intellectual agenda of the Enlightenment for the rest of the eighteenth century. "All the rest" was precisely the anthropological problem of how such differing groups of people viewed each other reciprocally from their different perspectives.

The mock geography of the maps included in *Gulliver's Travels* was complemented by a mock anthropology that showed Swift attuned to issues of comparative culture. Lilliputian writing, for instance, was described as "very peculiar, being neither from the left to the right, like the Europeans; nor from the right to the left, like the Arabians; nor from up to down, like the Chinese; nor from down to up, like the Cascagians; but aslant from one corner of the paper to the other, like our ladies in England."[5] Just as Lilliputians might seem small from the perspective of Captain Gulliver, so their writing might look peculiar from the perspective of a male Englishman. Swift was aware that the customs of culture could be the basis for comparing peoples worldwide, including completely invented peoples like the Lilliputians. When Swift described the militant enmity between the islands of Lilliput and Blefuscu, the comical point of discord was their irreconcilable customs for cracking eggs, whether at the larger or the smaller end. Swift surely intended this fierce dispute as a satire on the triviality of theological arguments in contemporary Europe, but by representing larger issues of belief in terms of everyday customary practices, he showed himself also sensitive to the anthropological implications of symbol, structure, custom, and ritual for the foundations of culture and identity.

The relative measure of big men and little men was thus by no means the only cultural counterpoint in *Gulliver's Travels*, which confronted Captain Gulliver in the concluding voyage with the contrasting societies of the Houyhnhnms and the Yahoos. The Houyhnhnms were horses that inhabited an island off the coast of Australia, but horses of such philosophic intelligence, such social and political composure, that Gulliver could scarcely believe in their equine appearance: "The behavior of these animals was so orderly and rational, so acute and judicious, that I at last concluded, they must needs be magicians, who had thus metamorphosed themselves upon some design." The rational qualities of the Houyhnhnms were all the more evident for the fact that the island also included inhabitants of another species with a contrasting culture, the Yahoos. Gulliver regarded them as disgusting savages, little better than beasts, but also had to recognize them as humans related to himself. "When I thought of my family, my friends, my countrymen, or the human race in general," he remarked, "I considered them as they really were, Yahoos in shape and disposition, perhaps a little more civilized."[6] Gulliver, by his travels, had learned something about the human race in general, and something about the range and variety of more- and less-civilized societies.

Gulliver could appreciate the supercivilized condition of the Houyhnhnms, just as he could appreciate the utterly savage conduct of the Yahoos, precisely because the contrast illuminated the importance of perspective for evaluating culture. Like the polarization of perspective between Europeans and Asians in the *Persian Letters*, so the comparative appreciation of more civilized and more savage societies in *Gulliver's Travels* was fundamental for the emergence of anthropological analysis. If Swift did not use the abstract noun "civilization" to describe the society of the Houyhnhnms, it was only because in the 1720s that word had not yet been defined according to its modern meaning. By the 1750s, it would be already current, and profoundly implicated in the anthropology of the Enlightenment.

Lady Mary Wortley Montagu, returning to England in 1718 after years abroad, noted that the experience of other cultures would make her inevitably more critical of English customs:

After having seen part of Asia and Africa and almost made the tour of Europe I think the honest English squire more happy who verily believes the Greek wines less delicious than March beer, that the African fruits have not so fine a flavour as golden pippins . . . and that, in short, there is no perfect enjoyment of this life out of Old England. I pray God I may think so for the rest of my life, and since I must be contented with our scanty allowance of daylight, that I may forget the enlivening sun of Constantinople.[7]

The experience of travel in the Age of Enlightenment would increasingly become the stimulus to question cultural presumptions, and to place the traveler's own native customs and satisfactions—whether narrowly English or more broadly European—in the critical context of multiple and various cultures. Captain Gulliver, returning to England around the same time, though in a fictional dimension, was even more emphatic:

Although since my unfortunate exile from the Houyhnhnm country, I had compelled myself to tolerate the sight of Yahoos . . . yet my memory and imagination were perpetually filled with the virtues and ideas of those exalted Houyhnhnms. And when I began to consider, that by copulating with one of the Yahoo species, I had become a parent of more, it struck me with the utmost shame, confusion, and horror.[8]

The relative comparison of cultures had destabilized Gulliver's relation to his own, leaving him in a condition of anthropological ambivalence.

It has long been accepted that the discovery of artistic perspective was one of the hallmarks of the Renaissance. The representation of objects in relative and proportional size, depending upon their perceived three-dimensional depth in a two-dimensional painting or drawing, was more than just a matter of arranging "big men and little men" within a landscape, but involved a revolution in reflections on human perception and its relation to physical space. The Enlightenment may be correspondingly characterized by the discovery of cultural perspective, with its revolutionary destabilization of the eighteenth-century observer who found herself returning not to Old England, but rather to a new kind of anthropological space, globally demarcated by the principle of cultural relativity, imbued with the unfamiliar flavors of Greek wines, African fruits, and Houyhnhnm virtues.

The Renaissance age of oceanic discovery already made possible the comparison of the Old World and the New World, and permitted the first intimations of relative perspective. Perhaps the most famous Renaissance instance was Montaigne's essay on cannibals in the New World and his own encounter in France with a native of Brazil: "I do not believe from what I have been told about this people, that there is anything barbarous or savage about them, except that we all call barbarous anything that is contrary to our own habits."[9] If such judgments were still rare and striking in the age of Montaigne, they became widespread, even fashionable, in the age of Montesquieu. The Pacific voyages of Captain Cook in the eighteenth century were conducted with the more or less purposeful intention of making anthropological comparisons in the study of human society.

Tzvetan Todorov has written about the cultural dynamics of these anthropological perspectives in France: *Nous et les autres: la réflexion française sur la diversité humaine* (*Us and the Others: French Reflection on Human Diversity*), published in 1989. Todorov suggests that Montaigne's argument concerning cannibals invoked an "ethical and negative" meaning of the term "barbarian," rather than a culturally comprehensive and implicitly anthropological sense. For Todorov, Montesquieu in the *Persian Letters* articulated the fundamental problem of observing human society: "The condition of successful knowing is thus non-belonging to the society described; that is to say, one can not at the same time fully live in a society and know it."[10] Historiographical interest in the anthropology of the Enlightenment dates back at least to Peter Gay's volume, *The Enlightenment, An Interpretation: The Science of Freedom*, which was published in 1969 and proposed that the social sciences in general had their origins in the eighteenth century: "The prehistory of the social sciences had its beginning in the emergence of cultural relativism, the bittersweet fruit of travel."[11] While Gay focused on the development of sociology, political economy, and history among the social sciences, Michèle Duchet published a book in 1971 that specifically addressed anthropological thinking and focused on the French philosophes: *Anthropologie et histoire au siècle des lumières* (*Anthropology and History in the Century of the Enlightenment*). A 1992 symposium held in Wolfenbüttel resulted in an important German volume, published in 1994, on "anthropology and literature" in the eighteenth century.[12]

Todorov's attention to "us and the others," while related to Duchet's project in its subject matter, was in its theoretical concerns also aligned

with Edward Said's *Orientalism*, which was published in 1979 and became an instant landmark in cultural theory with profound relevance for
the history of anthropology.[13] While Montesquieu, in Todorov's analysis,
may have intimated that it was impossible to know a society from within
it (thus positing the need for an external anthropological observer), Said
took the theoretical position that it might be no less difficult to try to
study a society from the outside. In Said's view, the West, over the course
of several centuries, had sought knowledge of Asia and the Middle East in
the compromised context of imperial ambition, and had therefore ended
up fictively constructing the Orient rather than factually learning about
Asia. The dynamics of Orientalism were such that the observer, in spite of
the best empirical intentions, would find himself implicated in the attribution of "otherness" to the Orient as part of the vindication of imperial
purposes. In a related spirit of cultural criticism, Todorov applied the concept of the Other to the New World in the age of discovery in his book, *La
conquête de l'Amérique: la question de l'autre* (*The Conquest of America:
The Question of the Other*), published in 1982.[14] The paradigm of
otherness—as formulated by Said, and as elaborated by Todorov—offers
an interpretation of the intellectual processes of Western culture in the
face of exotic and opaque lands and peoples. In Said's cultural theory,
the fantasist constructions of the Orientalist and the ultimate elusiveness
of the Other implicitly suggest the virtual impossibility of meaningful
anthropology.

Said dates the origins of Orientalism to the eighteenth century, and in
particular to the Sanskrit studies of William Jones and Abraham Hyacinthe Anquetil-Duperron. It is perhaps noteworthy that Said never mentions Montesquieu's *Persian Letters*, an interesting silence inasmuch as the
fictive nature of the work so perfectly fits the argument of *Orientalism*,
concerning the Occidental construction of the Orient as fantasy. Yet, Said's
arguments also assume a high degree of ingenuousness on the part of the
Western observers, the Orientalists, who allegedly did not understand that
they were participating in a project of cultural construction and imperial
domination, and who never suspected that their claims to "know" the Orient were epistemologically hopeless. In this regard, Montesquieu's *Persian
Letters*, though in some sense a work of Orientalist invention, may be interpreted as inconsistent with Said's argument. In the *Persian Letters*, the
problem of perspective was never naively evaded. Montesquieu was self-
consciously concerned with the intricacies of perspective and the obstacles
and opacities that complicate an observer's appreciation of an alien culture. It is precisely this attention to the problem of cultural perspective that
also makes it possible to interpret the *Persian Letters*, and the Enlightenment more generally, as incipiently anthropological.

FROM "ORIGINAL MAN" TO "CIVILIZED MAN":
VOLTAIRE AND ROUSSEAU

In the 1750s, the French physiocrats, particularly Victor Riquetti, the Marquis de Mirabeau, began to use the brand new word "civilisation" in economic discussions about the increase of commerce and wealth. At the same time, as Norbert Elias has proposed in his *History of Manners*, the term "civilisation" began to be associated with the refinement of manners pertaining to a "civilized man" (*civilisé* or *policé*) and accompanying the increase of wealth. From that time on, the word "civilisation"—spelled with an "s" in France and Britain and with a "z" in America—has maintained an extraordinary ideological weight as the standard for measuring and comparing societies and cultures around the globe. While the modern conception of civilization recognizes its plurality, as in Samuel Huntington's account of the "clash of civilizations," the Enlightenment coined the term in the singular mode, as a standard that could be applied to all human societies according to its relative degree of presence or absence: in the words of the Marquis de Salaberry in Constantinople in 1790, "the more or less of civilization" ("le plus ou moins de civilisation"). This relative concept of civilization was used to order intellectually the relation among the different parts of Europe in the eighteenth century, namely in the differentiation between Eastern Europe and Western Europe, but also to establish hierarchically Europe's cultural priority with respect to the rest of the world.[15]

This evaluation of societies according to a standard of civilization was essential for the emergence of anthropology. The advent of the neologism "civilisation" in the 1750s also coincided with the publications in 1754 of Voltaire's *Essai sur les moeurs* (*Essay on Customs*) and Jean-Jacques Rousseau's *Discours sur l'origine de l'inégalité* (*Discourse on the Origin of Inequality*); Voltaire's essay made customs or manners (*moeurs*) into the central issue of historical progress, while Rousseau's discourse called into question the whole notion of historical progress, speculatively posing the anthropological issue of the "state of nature" and the origins of human society. Rousseau's discourse, in particular, would become a touchstone for social, political, and anthropological reflection in the modern world.

The *Encyclopédie*, one of the great philosophical projects of the Enlightenment, edited by Denis Diderot and Jean Le Rond d'Alembert, began to be published in 1751, and the first volume, starting with the letter A, included a very brief article on "Anthropologie." It was classified as a theological term, and was supposed to signify the attribution of human qualities to God—an attribution testifying to the "weakness of our intelligence." The article thus offered a bit of anticlerical humor at the expense of religion, which was mocked for encouraging people to believe that "God operates as if he had hands, eyes, et cetera." Yet, the *Encyclopédie* noted that the term "anthropologie" was also being used to signify "the study of man" in writings about "animal economy," which sought to provide an integrated human physiology that included the cognitive aspects of being.[16] Thus, in the 1750s, there was already a hint in the first volume of the *Encyclopédie* that the meaning of the word "anthropology" was being revised in the context of the Enlightenment.

In the article on "Culture," however, the *Encyclopédie* revealed that the eighteenth-century meaning of the word was still very remote from its modern significance: "culture" was *culture de la terre*, in other words, agriculture. In English, Samuel Johnson's celebrated dictionary of 1755 was entirely consistent with the French *Encyclopédie*: "CULTURE: The act of cultivation; the act of tilling the ground; tillage." A secondary meaning contained perhaps the seeds of future lexicography: "Art of improvement and melioration." The principal reference might be to the improvement of the soil, but the word was theoretically applicable to other arenas of amelioration. The verb "to culture" was so absolutely agricultural that one of its definitions was "to manure."[17] In the 1730s, however, Voltaire allowed for the possibility of another meaning in his *Century of Louis XIV*. He wrote, to be sure, about *culture de la terre*, but also about *culture de l'esprit*, culture of the mind or spirit. In fact, he used the term in a notably modern sense: "The extreme ease which has been introduced into social intercourse, affability, simplicity, and the culture of the mind (*culture de l'esprit*) have turned Paris into a town which is probably far superior, as regards civilized living (*la douceur de la vie*), to Rome and Athens in the days of their splendor."[18] The eighteenth-century lexicon thus witnessed the gradual emergence of such terms as "anthropology," "culture," and "civilization," in some resemblance to their modern meanings.

In *Micromegas*, in 1752, Voltaire presented his parable of relative size, big creatures and little creatures, in uncertain correlation to greater or lesser degrees of culture of the mind. The giant Micromegas came from another solar system, while a relatively smaller "dwarf" came from the planet Saturn and himself appeared as a giant on earth, by comparison with humans. Micromegas reflected anthropologically on the universe's "profusion of varieties with a sort of wonderful uniformity," meaning that "all thinking beings are different, and at bottom they are all alike by the gift of thought and of desires." As travelers from outer space, Micromegas and the Saturnian "dwarf" were in a position as objective outsiders to pursue the anthropological study of human beings: "We must try to examine these insects, we will reason about them afterward."[19] Empirical observation would form the basis of this alien study of mankind, this anthropology.

When *Micromegas* was published in 1752, it appeared together with the "plan" for a history of the human spirit. In 1754 that work was published as a "universal history," and in 1756 as the history of the "customs (*moeurs*) and spirit of nations": *Essai sur les moeurs*. The emphasis on human variety would endow the work with an anthropological sensibility, evident from the beginning, as Voltaire addressed the issue of racial difference: "What is most interesting for us is the perceptible difference in the species of men who inhabit the four known parts of our world. Only a blind man could doubt that the Whites, the Negroes, the Albinos, the Hottentots, the Lapps, the Chinese, the Americans, are entirely different races."[20] Voltaire had no firsthand knowledge of any part of the world except Europe, so his were the anthropological observations of a relatively blind observer.

In spite of the differences that he supposed to exist, Voltaire was equally confident that the varieties of mankind were also alike in "uniformity." In his discussion of "savages," he affirmed that "all men live in society," and that every savage—"a Morlaque, an Icelander, a Lapp, a Hottentot"—lived in the social context of the family. Voltaire furthermore polemically offered an image of savages in society—"gathering on certain days in a sort of barn to celebrate ceremonies of which they understand nothing, listening to a man dressed differently from them whom they don't understand at all"—such that the terms would also describe churchgoing Catholic Europeans.[21] Indeed, for Voltaire, with his anticlerical temperament, there were no cultural customs or values that seemed more savagely barbarous than those of Roman Catholicism, as practiced on his own continent in his own times. Reviewing the role of Christianity in European history, he reminded his readers: "You have seen among these ridiculous barbarisms, the bloody barbarism of the wars of religion."[22] As in *Micromegas*, there could be a triple play of perspective, the Hottentot seeming savage from the perspective of a Christian European, but the Christian seeming no less savage from the perspective of the enlightened philosophe.

Yet, in spite of the barbarism of Christianity and the fact that "this whole history is a heap of crimes, follies, and misfortunes," Voltaire permitted himself some small degree of cultural appreciation for his own society: "It must be that our part of Europe has possessed a character in its customs and genius that is not to be found in Thrace, where the Turks established the seat of their empire, or in Tartary, out of which they once emerged." This constituted a frank affirmation of European priority, compared to the Ottoman Empire, and was even more specific in its designation of "our part" of Europe, that is, Western Europe. The Orient, more generally, served as a foil for Voltaire in his attempts to generalize about European customs: "The greatest difference between us and the Orientals is the manner in which we treat women."[23] Voltaire had never traveled east of Berlin, and his Oriental erudition was no more empirical than that of Montesquieu, but both Frenchmen agreed that social customs concerning the relations of the sexes were fundamental for defining the characters of different societies. Like Montesquieu, Voltaire also mentioned the presence of eunuchs accompanying women in the seraglios of the Orient. For Voltaire, this was one mark of the anthropological difference between Europe and the Orient, though Montesquieu, even more sensitive to the play of perspective, had permitted his Persians to suggest that European priests, as celibate men monitoring female morality, were the counterparts of Persian eunuchs.

Claude Lévi-Strauss, in *Tristes tropiques*, declared that Jean-Jacques Rousseau was "the most anthropological of the philosophes: although he never traveled to distant lands."[24] Lévi-Strauss thus offered a fundamental affirmation of the importance of the Enlightenment for the discipline of anthropology. Rousseau, in fact, was not just the most anthropological of philosophes, but also the most philosophical of anthropologists, for the very reason that he did not travel to distant lands. His reflections were almost purely philosophical, untempered by empirical observation. At the center of his famous discourse concerning inequality stood the figure of the savage, endlessly fascinating to Rousseau. Sometimes the savage was described as a Carib, though Rousseau never sailed to the Caribbean except in his philosophical imagination. Like Voltaire, who wrote speculatively about the customs of the Orient to better appreciate the culture of Europe, Rousseau imaginatively discovered man in the state of nature as the chronologically remote point of perspective from which to evaluate and condemn modern society with its cruel inequalities. Rousseau's philosophical construction of the Caribbean "Other" provided the analytical instrument that he needed in order to study contemporary social structure, with its character of egregious inequality.

"Oh man (*O homme*)," wrote Rousseau, apostrophizing his enlightened public, but also denominating his anthropological subject. "The times of which I am going to speak are very remote—how much you have changed from what you were! It is, so to say, the life of your species (*espèce*) that I am going to describe (*décrire*)."[25] In fact, "description" might seem a strange way to denominate Rousseau's peculiar clairvoyance, by which he confidently claimed to intuit the social structure of a remote prehistoric age, in order to trace, intuitively, the various stages of human development toward the inequalities of modern society. The empirical aspect of anthropology was altogether alien to Rousseau, whose crucial anthropological contributions as a philosophe were altogether matters of theory.

In contrast to Hobbes, Rousseau believed that the state of nature was fundamentally peaceful. He proposed, for instance, that savages were not necessarily violent in the venting of their sexual passions: "The Caribs, who of all people existing today have least departed from the state of nature, are precisely the most peaceful in their loves, and the least subject to jealousy, despite their living in the kind of hot climate which always seems to inflame those passions."[26] Caribbean society, decimated by disease in the aftermath of Columbus and transformed by more than two centuries of Spanish imperial rule, remained almost pristine in Rousseau's anthropological imagination. Thus, he could elaborate his theory of the state of nature, and designate the Caribs as a peaceful point of reference for analyzing the contrasting violence of modern European society. "What a spectacle for a Carib would be the arduous and envied labours of a European minister!" Rousseau exclaimed. "How many cruel deaths would not that indolent savage prefer to the horrors of such a life, which often is not even sweetened by the satisfaction of doing good?"[27] Just as Montesquieu had envisioned the Persian perspective on France, so Rousseau imagined the Caribbean perspective on Europe.

The problem of cultural perspective for Rousseau thus acquired a chronological dimension as he gazed across the wide ocean and into the remote depths of time in order to discover his anthropological subjects. The project of "discovering and tracing the lost and forgotten paths which must have led men from the natural state to the civil state" depended upon the gaze of the philosophe and his capacity to recognize the condition of men in the state of nature: "since original man (*l'homme originel*) has disappeared by degrees, society no longer offers to the eyes of philosophers anything more than an assemblage of artificial men."[28] Thus, the empirical method of the eye would never reveal "the lost and forgotten" state of nature, which could only be reconstructed by the philosophical gaze, focusing on the "original man" who had been disappearing by degrees over the course of centuries. If the anthropology of the Enlightenment concerned the discovery of cultural perspective, then Rousseau's "original man"—the savage, the Carib—represented the vanishing point of perspective in its representational dynamics.

Though Rousseau never left Europe himself, he believed that traveling to observe primitive peoples might enable the modern observer to obtain a better glimpse of the prehistoric past, and the human stages of development between savagery and modernity. Yet, he emphasized that the empirical observations of the traveler would be worthless unless assisted by the philosophical perspective of the Age of Enlightenment:

In the two or three centuries since the inhabitants of Europe have been flooding into other parts of the world, endlessly publishing new collections of voyages and travels, I am persuaded that we have come to know no other men except Europeans; moreover it appears from the ridiculous prejudices, which have not died out even among men of letters, that every author produces under the pompous name of the study of man nothing much more than a study of the men of his own country.[29]

Rousseau's reference to "the pompous name of the study of man" suggested that the word "anthropology" was ready to be coined and adopted, as indeed it was over the course of the next generation.

The "study of man" was already clearly recognized as a branch of knowledge in itself, and Rousseau reflected upon the problems of perspective that complicated and vitiated its pursuit. The traveler reporting upon alien peoples could rarely rise above his own prejudices to produce a philosophically acceptable account of another society. In fact, Rousseau's concerns anticipated the methodological challenge of modern anthropology, and even perhaps the paradoxical dilemma of Orientalism that was identified by Said, who found the Occidental observer scarcely capable of extricating himself from his own cultural complex of Oriental fantasies. Rousseau's frank recognition of the problem of perspective suggested the seriousness of the Enlightenment's engagement with anthropological concerns. The philosophe understood that only the most critical sensitivity to the prejudices of the Self could allow for any meaningful observation and representation of the Other.

The problem, as Rousseau saw it, was that "philosophy does not travel," and he himself—no traveler—relied upon his own philosophical insight when it came to comprehending the Caribs. Even so, he proposed the ideal of the traveling philosopher as the key to anthropological knowledge:

Suppose a Montesquieu, a Buffon, a Diderot, a Duclos, a D'Alembert, a Condillac, and other men of that stamp were to travel to instruct their compatriots, observing and describing as only they know how, Turkey, Egypt, Barbary, the Empire of Morocco, Guinea, the land of the Kaffirs, the interior and the East coast of Africa, the Malabars, China, Tartary and above all Japan, and then in the other hemisphere, Mexico, Peru, Chile, and Magellan lands, not forgetting the Patagonias true and false, Tucamen, Paraguay if possible, Brazil. Finally the Caribbean islands, Florida and all the savage countries—the most important voyage of all, and the one that would have to be undertaken with the greatest possible care.[30]

For Rousseau, a man of many philosophical fantasies, this was among the most fantastic: to imagine Montesquieu in Africa or Diderot in Mexico. The last and most important mission—Florida and the Caribbean—Rousseau might even have been reserving for himself, as his own fantasy voyage, since the savages, he supposed, would offer the most precious insights into the state of nature. Rousseau's extraordinary program of dispatching philosophers from Europe to Asia, Africa, and America demonstrated his readiness to contemplate an anthropological approach to the study of human society, based on empirical observation and philosophical perspective.

Rousseau's project of rediscovering "lost and forgotten paths" in order to understand the human passage "from the natural state to the civil state" was pursued in greater detail, and with more studious empiricism, within the Scottish Enlightenment. Adam Ferguson, John Millar, and Henry Home, Lord Kames, all attempted to trace the stages of development of human society from savagery to civilization. In 1766 Ferguson published *An Essay on the History of Civil Society*, attempting to delineate the stages of primitive human society from hunting and fishing to pastoral herding to agriculture, with emphasis on the idea of "progress" from one stage to the next. Evans-Pritchard notes that "Ferguson's book illustrates many of the basic assumptions we find in modern social anthropology."[31] Peter Gay emphasizes rather Ferguson's contribution to modern sociological thinking, and notes his explicit rejection of conjecture and speculation as practiced by Rousseau in the discourse on inequality.[32] Similarly important for classifying and evaluating the stages of human development were Millar, whose *Origin of the Distinction of Ranks* was published in 1771, and Kames, whose *Sketches of the History of Man* appeared in 1774. Adam Smith's *The Wealth of Nations*, published in 1776, was similarly imbued with this same Scottish interest in the stages of human society.[33]

George Stocking, evaluating Kames's place in the history of anthropology, has noted his ambivalence about savagery and also about progress, both of which suggested positive as well as negative aspects. Stocking stresses the Scottish background of the Scottish philosophes: "There was the ambiguity of Kames' own experience—the sense of loss as well as profit involved in the progress Scotland had experienced in Kames' lifetime. This was stronger perhaps in Ferguson, who had a Highland background and still spoke Erse as well as the Scottish English vernacular."[34] Thus, while the Scottish philosophes explored the stages of "progress" in human society from "savagery" to "civilization," they also preserved an element of critical philosophical perspective in the evaluation of those terms. David Spadafora, writing about *The Idea of Progress in Eighteenth-Century*

Britain, has noted that, among the Scots, David Hume was particularly sensitive to the contrasting courses of progress and decline in the arts and sciences, producing a skeptical perspective on the teleology of civilization.[35] In Scotland in 1776, Adam Smith traced the progress of economics from hunting, herding, and agriculture to contemporary commerce in *The Wealth of Nations*. That same year in England, Edward Gibbon published the first volume of his *Decline and Fall of the Roman Empire*, following the historical vector that pointed toward the triumph of the barbarians.

The Scottish philosophes explored the stages of human progress in a spirit of concerned empiricism, studying in detail the reports of global travelers, and eschewing the speculative approach of Rousseau. They did not, however, set out to explore other continents and observe primitive peoples, as in Rousseau's fantasy of the traveling philosopher. Ferguson's early experience in the Scottish Highlands may have conditioned his philosophical perspective on human societies, but it did not inspire him to undertake voyages of ethnographic investigation to the Andes or the Himalayas. Nevertheless, the anthropological reflections of the Scots and the more philosophically speculative insights of Rousseau influenced travelers over the course of the next generation. There were philosophes who actually did undertake enterprising travels, and there were travelers who became philosophical in their observations under the cultural sway of the Enlightenment. This joining of empirical investigation with the philosophical theory of human society encouraged the emergence of anthropology.

PHILOSOPHICAL EMPIRICISM: FORTIS AND COOK

Alberto Fortis, the Paduan philosophe, played a pioneering role in bringing these elements together in his study of the customs of primitive society, directly observed by himself and analyzed with reference to the philosophy of the Enlightenment. His *Viaggio in Dalmazia* (*Voyage in Dalmatia*), published in Venice in 1774, involved an adventurous journey into the Dinaric Alps, the highlands of Dalmatia, and resulted in a chapter on the primitive Slavic highlanders called "The Customs of the Morlacchi." Voltaire had listed the "Morlaque" almost randomly alongside the Lapp, the Icelander, and the Hottentot as representative savages in the *Essai sur les moeurs*, but Fortis gave a full and particular account of the Morlacchi—indeed, defined them anthropologically, according to their social customs. International interest in Fortis's chapter on the customs of the Morlacchi stimulated the translation of the whole book into English, French, and German.

Fortis was a natural historian, particularly interested in geology, and natural history was inevitably involved in eighteenth-century anthropological

issues. In their work of classification, the most important natural historians of the century, like Linnaeus and Buffon, had tried to come to terms
with the variety of the human species. Linnaeus traveled to Lapland as a
naturalist in 1732, and if he was most interested in botanical life, he was
also, according to Lisbet Koerner, ethnographically attentive to the Lapp
or Sami population of northern Sweden; the frontispiece of his *Flora Lap-
ponica* in 1737 included the human figure of a Lapp as part of the landscape with reindeer and fir trees.[36] Buffon affirmed the unity of the
human species, even as he described its variety of "races," making the comparison, but insisting on the absolute difference between the orangutan
and the Hottentot. Michele Duchet has observed that "the anthropology
of Buffon appeared thus as the product of natural history taken in its
entirety."[37]

Fortis also represented the customs of the Morlacchi as the anthropological aspect of natural history when he attempted to write his comprehensive account of Dalmatia. *Voyage in Dalmatia* sought to give a complete description of customs: for instance, songs, dances, foods, superstitions, marriage, and friendship. Fortis was, at the same time, sensitive to
comparison between civilized Italian life and primitive Morlacchi customs:

> Friendship, so subject to change among us, even for the smallest motives, is most
> constant among the Morlacchi. They have made of it almost a point of religion,
> and this sacred bond is formed at the foot of the altars. The Slavonic ritual has a
> particular benediction for solemnly conjoining two male friends, or two female
> friends, in the presence of all the people. I found myself present at the union of
> two girls, who made themselves *posestre* in the Church of Perussich. The content-
> ment that shone in their eyes, after having formed that sacred bond, proved to
> those present how much delicacy of sentiment may be found in unformed spirits,
> or, to say it better, spirits uncorrupted by the society that we call civilized (*che noi
> chiamiamo colta*).[38]

The play of perspective was complex, with Fortis first employing his
own understanding of friendship "among us"—to contrast with the
Morlacchi—but then making the customs of the Morlacchi into an occasion for discovering the reciprocal perspective, reflecting back upon
"the society that we call civilized." In Fortis's ironic recognition that
"civilized" may be no more than a self-assumed designation lay not only
the philosophical lesson learned from Rousseau, but also a powerful
sense of cultural relativism. This relativism was all the more anthropological for the fact that Fortis, unlike Rousseau, was guided by empirical research, the study of primitive customs witnessed directly by himself in the church of Perussich among the Morlacchi in the mountains
of Dalmatia.

The balance of philosophy and empiricism was similarly evident in Fortis's reflections on relations between the sexes among the Morlacchi, which he interpreted in terms of Scottish theory concerning the stages of mankind. As the Morlacchi pursued a largely pastoral economy in the mountains, it was evident to Fortis that they belonged to the pastoral stage of the development of human societies:

The innocent and natural liberty of the pastoral centuries are maintained still in Morlacchia; or at least there remain the greatest vestiges in the places most remote from our establishments. The pure cordiality of sentiment is not restrained there by considerations, and gives clear exterior signs without distinction of circumstances. A beautiful Morlacchi girl meets a man of her village in the street, and kisses him affectionately, without thinking of mischief. I have seen all the women and girls, and the young and old men, from more than one village, kiss each other as they arrived in the squares of the churches for festival days. It seemed that this people was all of one sole family.[39]

Thus, the anthropological traveler worked from his own observations ("I have seen all the women and girls") to the theoretical reconstruction of an earlier stage ("the pastoral centuries") in the human history of social structure. Fortis's notion of "natural liberty" was probably influenced by Rousseauist reflections concerning the "state of nature"; that state may have been a purely philosophical model of the remote past, but Fortis argued for the value of anthropological research in recovering empirical "vestiges" that corroborated theoretical hypotheses.

Fortis's anthropological study of the Morlacchi clearly took place in an imperial context, as he received some sponsorship from the Venetian Republic for his study of the province of Venetian Dalmatia, and the resulting book was then published in Venice. As a natural historian, he surveyed Dalmatia's natural resources, and suggested their relevance to the economy of the Venetian Republic as a whole; by the same token, his reflections on the customs of the Morlacchi were clearly intended to provide some guidance concerning issues of imperial administration. This was not the only instance in the eighteenth century of an anthropological project aimed, at least in part, at imperial purposes. In the Russian Empire, Catherine the Great sponsored several major ethnographic expeditions to investigate the peoples of her far-flung realm; whether in the Caucuses or in Siberia, those peoples were often perceived as primitive in their customs, like the Morlacchi of Venetian Dalmatia. The St. Petersburg Academy of Sciences commissioned such anthropological enterprises, and the German natural historian Peter Simon Pallas played a particularly extensive part in exploring everything from geography to ethnography across the Russian Empire. During the nineteenth century, the discipline of anthropology evolved alongside the expansion and consolidation of European empires in Asia and Africa. Edward Said, writing about Orientalism, suggests that the Western pursuit of knowledge concerning Asia was almost inevitably entangled in the affirmation of imperial power. By the same token, anthropological knowledge about the customs of primitive peoples could serve the purposes of power in imperial administration, and though the linkage was not always explicit, there were notable instances already in the eighteenth century, such as Fortis's account of the Morlacchi in Venetian Dalmatia.

The most extensive ethnographic investigation of the eighteenth century was undertaken by Captain James Cook during his three voyages of oceanic exploration in the Pacific between 1768 and 1779, roughly contemporary with Fortis's far more limited voyage in Dalmatia. Cook's mission was at once geographical in its mapping of the Pacific islands, scientific in its attention to natural history, anthropological in its detailed accounts of island customs, and political in its alertness to the possibility of British imperial claims. Each expedition was staffed by a scientific team, with an emphasis on natural history, including such naturalists as Joseph Banks on the first voyage, and Johann and Georg Forster, father and son, on the second voyage. However, just as it was for Fortis in Dalmatia, natural history involved attention to human societies as well as the flora and fauna. Cook was always attentive to island customs in his journals, while the expeditions also included artists to record their representations of Pacific landscapes, plants, animals, and peoples.

Cook, as anthropological observer, was detailed in his empirical records, but also philosophically influenced by the cultural reflections of the Enlightenment. In Tahiti in 1769, he discovered tattooing: "Both sexes paint their bodys *Tattow* as it is called in their language, this is done by inlaying the Colour of black under their skins in such a manner as to be indelible. Some have ill design'd figures of men, birds, or dogs, the women generally have this figure Z simply on every joint of their fingers and toes." A century and a half before Margaret Mead on Samoa, Captain Cook in Tahiti reflected on adolescent female sexuality: "The young girls when ever they can collect 8 or 10 together dance a very indecent dance which they call *Timorodee*, singing most indecent songs and using most indecent actions in the practice of which they are brought up from their earlyest Childhood."[40] In Australia in 1770, he closely observed that "the men wear a bone about 3 or 4 Inches long and a finger's thick, run through the Bridge of the nose" or that, without knowledge of metalworking, the aborigines might attach sharks' teeth to the tips of their darts as weaponry. Yet, in Australia, Cook not only observed but also philosophized:

From what I have said of the Natives of New-Holland they may appear to some to be the most wretched people upon Earth, but in reality they are far more happier than we Europeans; being wholly unacquainted not only with the superfluous but the necessary Conveniences so much sought after in Europe, they are happy in not knowing the use of them. They live in a Tranquillity which is not disturb'd by the Inequality of Condition: The Earth and sea of their own accord furnishes them with all things necessary for life.[41]

The reference to inequality suggested that Cook had read, or at least heard of, Rousseau's discourse. Influenced by the ideas of the Enlightenment, Cook in some sense made his voyage into that traveling philosophical expedition envisaged by Rousseau.

The relevance of Cook for the future of anthropology is still evident in the fact that anthropologists in the 1990s contentiously debated the significance of his voyages, as in the controversy surrounding Cook's discovery of Hawaii in 1778 and his death at the hands of the Hawaiians in 1779. When Marshall Sahlins proposed that Cook was regarded as the god Lono by the Hawaiians, Ganath Obeyesekere, in *The Apotheosis of Captain Cook: European Mythmaking in the Pacific* (1992), rejected that conclusion as reflecting Western fantasies of divinity, to which Sahlins promptly replied with the book *How "Natives" Think: About Captain Cook, for Example* (1995). In 2003 the anthropologist Nicholas Thomas published an account of Cook's voyages, remarking of Cook that "he was not an anthropologist—anthropology was anyway still a branch of natural history, and not yet named, at this time—but his way of thinking was proto-anthropological."[42] The proto-anthropology of Cook was the anthropology of the Enlightenment.

One of the philosophes whom Rousseau envisioned as an anthropological traveler was Diderot. In fact, Diderot traveled as far as St. Petersburg to visit Catherine the Great, but though he was perhaps less intimidated by travel than some other philosophes, he never really made an anthropological voyage. Traveling to pay one's intellectual respects to a powerful tsarina was not the same as voyaging to study the customs of primitive peoples with bones through their noses. Yet, Diderot followed with tremendous vicarious interest the contemporary voyages of Pacific exploration, which included not only the English voyages of Cook but especially the French expedition of Louis-Antoine Bougainville, who visited Tahiti and claimed the island for France in 1768.

Bougainville wrote an idyllic description of Tahiti in his *Voyage autour du monde* (*Voyage Around the World*), published in 1771, and Diderot proceeded to create a fictional "Supplement to the Voyage of Bougainville." At the heart of the fiction was the tale of the encounter between two sexual moralities on Tahiti: the island freedom of the Tahitians versus the Christian qualms of a European chaplain. In the frame of the story, two Europeans, labeled only as "A" and "B" discussed with one another the philosophical lessons to be learned from Tahiti, especially concerning morality and civilization. "A" asks "What useful conclusions can we actually draw from the outlandish morals and manners of an uncivilized people?" while "B" supposes that "the most primitive people, the Tahitians, seem to have come nearer to good legislation than any civilized nation." "A" is compelled to reflect upon his own society's prohibitions concerning sex: "How does it happen that an act so solemn in its purpose and urged upon us by Nature by the strongest of all attractions—that the greatest, sweetest, most innocent of pleasures—has become for us the greatest source of depravity and evil?" "A" even wonders, "ought we to civilize Man, or should we leave him to his instinct?"[43] Diderot's story, published for a small public in the *Correspondance Litteraire* in 1773–74, demonstrated the intimate relation between empirical study of human society and philosophical reflection in the Age of Enlightenment. Bougainville's writings, like Cook's journals, were themselves implicitly philosophical, conditioned by the values of the century, but Diderot's "Supplement" showed how much was philosophically at stake in contemporary anthropological investigations.

It was not simply that the Tahitians provided a relative perspective on European customs, like Montesquieu's Persians in France, but further that the relative counterpoint of differing customs rendered all morality problematically uncertain. Rousseau might have preferred intuitive and definitive pronouncements, but Diderot recognized that reports of primitive customs were more likely to provoke difficult discussions, like those between "A" and "B," than straightforward resolutions. The anthropological agenda of the Enlightenment—with its philosophical reflections on the state of nature and stages of society, and its empirical investigations of peoples from the mountains of Dalmatia to the islands of the Pacific—discovered a constellation of cultures, all based on different sets of customs. Each provided a new perspective for viewing the others—indeed, for viewing the complete constellation—and the multiplicity of perspectives, no less than the variety of cultures, encouraged the emergence of an anthropological discourse based on the principle of cultural relativism.

GLOBAL PERSPECTIVE: HERDER AND SADE

P. J. Marshall and Glyndwr Williams have noted that "reports about the peoples of the world were acquiring a new value as the raw material for the attempts to analyse man and nature that came to be known as the European Enlightenment."[44] In this view, the anthropological impulse was not just a part of the Enlightenment, but actually shaped its character and content. In their book, *The Great Map of Mankind: British Perceptions of the World in the Age of Enlightenment*, Marshall and Williams took their title, and their epigraph, from Edmund Burke's correspondence: "Now the Great Map of Mankind is unrolled at once; and there is no state or Gradation of barbarism, and no mode of refinement which we have not at the same instant under our View. The very different Civility of Europe and of China; the barbarism of Tartary, and of Arabia. The Savage State of North America, and of New Zealand."[45]

Burke was thus able to achieve a global perspective, in which China and Europe could be evaluated comparatively as different forms of civility, though not necessarily with the Orient as the Other. He subscribed to the Scottish stadial view of societies, that is, societies conceived according to stages of development existing at different levels of organization. Burke noted that, in the eighteenth century, all those stages could be observed synchronously—from savagery to civility—such that distinct chronological epochs were simultaneously evident in different geographical terrains. Writing in 1777, while Cook was traveling on his third voyage, Burke invoked New Zealand where Cook had observed savage society, and Burke recognized that his present moment offered a historically unprecedented, globally comprehensive, anthropologically comparative conception of human society. This too was a matter of perspective, for the Enlightenment, unrolling the map of mankind, produced a special projection of the spherical globe, such that all human societies were made simultaneously available to the enlightened gaze.

In the late Enlightenment, the most important anthropological philosophe, embracing in his writings the complete map of mankind, was Johann Gottfried von Herder. Cultivating the concept of the *Volk*—the people or nation—as the fundamental grouping of human society, Herder affirmed and explored the tremendous variety of human cultures, without actually ever leaving Europe. In Herder's collections of *Volkslieder* of 1778 and 1779, he pioneered the folkloric study of cultures, including songs from Scotland to Lithuania. "The songs are the archive of the people (*das Archiv des Volks*)," wrote Herder, with keen sensitivity to the significance of folklore. In the volumes of his *Ideas for the Philosophy of the History of Mankind* (*Ideen zur Philosophie der Geschichte der Menschheit*), published between 1784 and 1791, he provided the philosophical elaboration of Burke's hypothetical map. "Let us accompany Cook on his last voyage," wrote Herder, preparing to discuss the role of women in different societies. Drawing upon a global perspective, he affirmed that "the Happiness of Man is in all Places an individual Good; consequently it is everywhere climatic and organic, the Offspring of Practice, Tradition, and Custom." This anthropological principle—with its emphasis on the diversity of social practices, traditions, and customs—was at the same time subordinated to the axiom that "notwithstanding the Varieties of the human Form, there is but one and the same Species of Man throughout the Whole of our Earth."[46] Notably, Herder denied the significance of racial differences within the human species.

The controversy concerning race and its significance in the late Enlightenment reflected the growing prominence of anthropological issues. Immanuel Kant, whose major philosophical accomplishments are not generally associated with either race or anthropology, actually lectured on anthropology as a professor at Königsberg and, unlike his student Herder, believed in the biological importance of racial difference. In 1798 Kant published his lectures as *Anthropology from a Pragmatic Point of View* (*Anthropologie in pragmatischer Hinsicht*), noting that this course of lectures, together with another on geography, were distinct from pure philosophy because they involved "knowledge of the world" and offered illustrative examples. Yet, though he claimed the name "anthropology" for his course, Kant began with a lengthy discussion of human cognitive powers, suggesting that for him the study of man was more a matter of the human mind than of human society. The references to the variety of cultures were, at best, casual: "We pay human understanding no great honor if we live for the day (without foresight or care—like the Caribbean, who sells his hammock in the morning and in the evening is surprised that he does not know how he will sleep that night)." Königsberg on the Baltic was a long way from the Caribbean. Kant cited the Celts with similarly scant cultural concern when arguing that presentiment was chimerical: "This class of enchantments also includes the second sight of the Scottish Highlanders." The second part of Kant's *Anthropology* offered a very brief outline of some social factors, including "the character of nations" and "the character of races," leading to a concluding section on "the character of the species." Though Kant boldly employed the name, Herder's writings came much closer to the modern sense of anthropology, as noted by John Zammito in his book, *Kant, Herder, and the Birth of Anthropology* (2002). Zammito concludes that Herder's work on the history of mankind constituted "one of the great monuments of eighteenth-century ethnography and ethnology," while, "in comparison, the second part of Kant's *Anthropology* makes a poor impression."[47] Yet, even in their different philosophical approaches, Kant and Herder demonstrated an increasingly urgent commitment to the study of human beings in the Age of Enlightenment.

   Herder's emphasis on the cultural significance of the *Volk* brought out the anthropological aspect of every subject that he treated. While Gibbon was anthropologically interested in the barbarians of ancient history, including the Slavs, in his *Decline and Fall of the Roman Empire*, Herder, by contrast, presented the Slavs as an anthropological presence in the contemporary world. Gibbon envisioned the lives of the ancient Slavs in a chapter titled the "State of the Barbaric World," presenting the "Tribes and Inroads of the Sclavonians":

> Their huts were hastily built of rough timber in a country deficient both in stone and iron. Erected, or rather concealed, in the depth of forests, on the banks of rivers, or the edge of morasses, we may not perhaps, without flattery, compare them to the architecture of the beaver, which they resembled in a double issue, to the land and water, for the escape of the savage inhabitant, an animal less cleanly, less diligent, and less social, than that marvellous quadruped.[48]

The ironic comparison between the Slavic savage and the diligent beaver was only flippantly anthropological, and Gibbon seemed indifferent to the fact that the Slavs of ancient history could also be related to their Slavic descendants in eighteenth-century Europe. Herder, on the other hand, wrote about the "Slavic Peoples" (*Slawische Völker*) in the anthropological present tense, describing their domain "from the Don to the Elbe, from the Baltic to the Adriatic," as "the most monstrous region of earth which in Europe *one* Nation for the most part inhabits still today." He called for anthropological investigation of Slavic folklore, to preserve "the progressively disappearing remains of their usages, songs, and sagas."[49] Thus, the question of the Slavs, which was entirely a matter of ancient history for Gibbon, was transformed in Herder's vision into an anthropological subject of study.

   Isaiah Berlin actually argued in 1965 that Herder's emphasis on the variety of human societies put him fundamentally at odds with the universalist impulses of the Enlightenment. When Peter Gay in 1969 wrote about the Enlightenment and the creation of the social sciences, Herder was scarcely mentioned. Yet, Herder's anthropological impulse was entirely consistent with fundamental concerns of the Enlightenment, as articulated in the writings of Montesquieu and Rousseau. Herder's status as a philosophe, rather than an anti-philosophe, appears unequivocal when it is recognized that anthropology was created in the eighteenth century as an enlightened project. "For Herder, to be a member of a group is to think and act in a certain way, in the light of particular goals, values, pictures of the world," wrote Berlin, "and to think and act so is to belong to a group." The recognition that human beings receive their character from their social and cultural contexts was profoundly anthropological. According to Berlin, Herder believed that "the ways in which a people—say the Germans—speak or move, eat or drink, their handwriting, their laws, their music, their social outlook, their dance forms, their theology, have patterns and qualities in common which they do not share, or share to a notably lesser degree, with the similar activities of some other group—the French, the Icelanders, the Arabs, the ancient Greeks."[50] With the concept of the *Volk*, and his emphasis on the globally manifold variety of uniquely coherent cultures, Herder brought the anthropological inclinations of the Enlightenment to the threshold of the nineteenth century, and paved the way for the articulation of anthropology as an academic discipline.

During the years when Herder was publishing his volumes on the history of mankind, anthropological manifestations were evident in many intellectual arenas and various literary genres all over Europe. In 1787 the American adventurer John Ledyard, who had previously sailed with Captain Cook on the third voyage, made an anthropological expedition under the sponsorship of Thomas Jefferson, then the American minister in Paris. Ledyard proposed to travel on foot across Siberia, closely studying the "Tartars" of the region, and then to cross the Bering Straits to North America and pursue a comparative study of the Native Americans. He claimed to have discovered an anthropological resemblance between the Siberian Tartars and the North American Indians, and wrote to Jefferson excitedly from Siberia: "I shall never be able, without seeing you in person and perhaps not even then, to inform you how universally and circumstantially the Tartars resemble the aborigines of America: they are the same people."[51] Anthropological analysis was applied on a global scale, based on Ledyard's empirical experience as a world traveler. His project was also implicitly imperial, for just as Russia ruled over the peoples of Siberia, the American Republic would eventually exercise its rule over the Indians of the West. Catherine the Great actually had Ledyard arrested in Siberia and expelled from the Russian Empire, so he never completed his intended journey. The Russian state thus affirmed its own ultimate authority over the practice of anthropology upon Russian subjects; Catherine sponsored her own ethnographic expeditions. Pursuing American interests, Jefferson, as president of the United States in 1804, sent Meriwether Lewis and William Clark to explore the lands and peoples of the American Northwest.

Ledyard, at Kazan on the Volga, articulated the anthropological agenda that conditioned his observations of the Tartars: "The nice Gradation by which I pass from Civilization to Incivilization appears in every thing: their manners, their dress, their Language, and particularly that remarkable and important circumstance of Colour."[52] Much preoccupied with race, Ledyard made facial measurements and collected skulls as he traveled; this same approach characterized the contemporary work of Johann Friedrich

Blumenbach, the German natural historian who constructed human classifications based on supposed racial differences, and anticipated the later development of physical anthropology with his collection of skulls. Ledyard believed that racial factors had to be correlated with cultural considerations such as manners, dress, and language. He saw himself as a man of science, and his global experience in the Pacific enabled him to envision a global framework—"from Civilization to Incivilization"—for evaluating the varieties of mankind. In his journal, Ledyard coined the expression "Philosophic Geography" to describe his study of the world, guided by the principles of the Enlightenment; his approach might also be labeled "Philosophic Anthropology."[53] The "great map of mankind" was, for Ledyard, not just a patchwork assortment of diverse cultures, but a patterned arrangement according to principles of race, customs, and civilization. In Siberia in 1787, he applied himself to the meticulous measurement of the facial features of his human subjects, but he could also step back for a broad global perspective on the complete catalogue of human societies.

In 1788 Giustiniana Wynne, an enlightened Venetian writer, created an anthropological novel for the international literary public. She took Fortis's chapter on the "Customs of the Morlacchi" as the substance of her novel, *Les Morlaques*, which was written in French and modeled on the sentimental fiction of Rousseau, but packed with details concerning the customs of the primitive mountaineers of Dalmatia. She promised her readers "the image of nature in primitive society, such as it must have been in the most remote times, and such as it has been found among the inhabitants of the most unknown islands of the Pacific." Even with her pen focused on Dalmatia she could not keep her mind from wandering to the voyages of Captain Cook. *Les Morlaques* presumed the existence of a reading public interested in anthropological data:

The natural course of ordinary events in a Morlacchi family will make us acquainted with the customs and usages of the nation in a manner more sensitive than the cold and methodical relation of the voyager. It has not been thought necessary to have recourse to the romantic or marvelous. The facts are true and the national details faithfully exposed . . . This is perhaps the most agreeable way to give an accurate idea of a people who think, speak, and act in a manner very different from ours.[54]

Les Morlaques in 1788, incorporating the "customs and usages of the nation" ("moeurs et usages de la nation"), constituted a kind of fictional culmination of the anthropology of the Enlightenment.

Three years later, in 1791, another novel, radically different in style, introduced a whole new approach to the literary exploitation of anthropological detail. The Marquis de Sade's *Justine*, a contribution to the creation of modern pornography, made use of anthropological material to argue sophistically against conventional sexual morality. For Sade, anthropology seemed to offer an endorsement of the unrestrained pursuit of sexual satisfaction, however brutal. One of Sade's sadistic spokesmen in the novel defended the mistreatment of women with reference to allegedly anthropological examples:

In America I find a naturally humane race, the Eskimos, practicing all possible acts of beneficence amongst men and treating women with all imaginable severity. I see them humiliated, prostituted to strangers in one part of the world, used as currency in another. In Africa, where without doubt their station is yet further degraded, I notice them toiling in the manner of beasts of burden, tilling the soil, fertilizing it and sowing seed, and serving their husbands on their knees only. Will I follow Captain Cook in his newest discoveries? Is the charming isle of Tahiti, where pregnancy is a crime sometimes meriting death for the mother and almost always for the child, to offer me women enjoying a happier lot? In the other islands this same mariner charted, I find them beaten, harassed by their own offspring, and bullied by the husband himself who collaborates with his family to torment them with additional rigor.[55]

Sade, born in 1740, was far from a typical philosophe, but he was sufficiently a man of his generation to have followed the voyages of Captain Cook with interest, even arousal.

The perverse application of anthropology as the apologia for sexual brutality demonstrated Sade's philosophical penchant, in this regard as in others, for taking the logic of the Enlightenment to paradoxical extremes. He made the ideal of the noble savage into the model for the sexual criminal. Montesquieu had dramatized the oppressiveness of harem life in Persia, Voltaire had concluded that "the greatest difference between us and the Orientals is the manner in which we treat women," and Diderot had suggested that the customs of Tahiti called into question the sexual morality of Europe. Sade took all these enlightened reflections into account and followed them to their most extreme anthropological conclusions as he pornographically celebrated and philosophically vindicated the sexual practices of a sadistic monster.

In his 1795 *Philosophy of the Boudoir*, Sade continued to dabble in anthropology, mounting a defense of "cruel pleasures" in mocking tribute to the spirit of Rousseau: "cruelty exists among savages, so much nearer to Nature than civilized men are; absurd then to maintain cruelty is a consequence of depravity."[56] Sade structured the anthropological argument as a sort of syllogism in which the logic of the Enlightenment was followed to the point of perverse absurdity. Incest was anthropologically vindicated: "The most primitive institutions smiled upon incest; it is found in society's origins: it was consecrated in every religion, every law encouraged it. If we traverse the world we will find incest everywhere established. The blacks of the Ivory Coast and Gabon prostitute their wives to their own children."[57]

Burke's great map of mankind was unrolled in Sade's pornography as an illustration of globally pervasive perversity, with the philosopher traversing the world in order to vindicate his every sexual whim. Sodomy, for instance, was pronounced to be globally ubiquitous and therefore an undeniable aspect of nature. Sade's anthropological affirmation that there was nothing unnatural about sodomy could be read as an enlightened defense of homosexuality: "The greatest of men lean toward sodomy. At the time it was discovered, the whole of America was found inhabited by people of this taste. In Louisiana, amongst the Illinois, Indians in feminine garb prostituted themselves as courtesans. The blacks of Benguela publicly keep men; nearly all the seraglios of Algiers are today exclusively filled with young boys."[58] He cited the classical world, of course, and the prevalence of sodomy in ancient Greece and Rome, but his sexual fantasies also ranged across the anthropological map of America and Africa.

In his *Histoire de Juliette*, published in 1797, Sade's anthropological imagination ran rampant: "We dare not fuck our own children even though there are few more delicious pleasures; in Persia, intrigues are exclusively of that variety, and 'tis the same in three quarters of Asia . . . We consider the prostitution of our wives a very great indelicacy: in Tartary, in Lapland, in America it's a courtesy, it's an honor to prostitute your wife to a stranger."[59]

Sade seemed to relish an almost parodic relation to such works as Montesquieu's *Persian Letters*, drawing the lesson of cultural relativism and suggesting that European sexual morality might seem unnatural from the perspective of other cultures. "The Indians of Mount Caucasus live like brute beasts, they couple indiscriminately," wrote Sade, extending his anthropological range. "The women of the Isle de Hornes prostitute themselves to men in broad daylight." He mentioned Mingrelians and Georgians: "these folk abandoned to joy, incest, rape, child-murder, prostitution, adultery, assassination, thievery, sodomy, sapphism, bestiality, arson, poisoning, rape, parricide." The New World was similarly on Sade's agenda: "American women appreciate being fucked by monkeys."[60] Rousseau's Caribs and Cook's Tahitians were cited approvingly for having sex with young children, while Sade seemed even to have been aware of Fortis's "Customs of the Morlacchi" and their alleged contempt for women:

Such is that scorn amongst the Croats, more particularly known to geographers as Uskoks and Morlacks, that when they refer to their wives, they employ the same coarse expression the vulgar commonly use in connection with a vile animal. They never suffer them in their beds, women in that part of the world sleep on the bare ground, without a murmur and with utmost alacrity do as they are told, and are mercilessly beaten at the least hint of disobedience.

Indeed, Fortis had observed about the Morlacchi that "those few who possess a bed, upon which to sleep in the straw, do not there put up with their wives, who must sleep on the floor," and even that the women "do not mind some beating by their husbands."[61]

Sade often distorted, exaggerated, and bizarrely elaborated upon anthropological reports, sometimes perhaps inventing them altogether, but he also was demonstrably familiar with some of the ethnographic literature of the Enlightenment. The line between true reports and utter falsehoods would have been difficult for his readers to discern, as they were in any event likely to be focused on the pornographic sex. Yet, the notable presence of anthropology in Sade's novels demonstrated its philosophical potency and pervasiveness in the Age of Enlightenment. The great map of mankind, charted by Cook, fingered by Burke, and elaborated by Herder, was available to any interested writer or reader by the end of the eighteenth century, and could be represented or interpreted with dramatic philosophical implications.

CONCLUSION: PHILOSOPHICAL AND
ANTHROPOLOGICAL PERSPECTIVE

Voltaire, in his *Philosophical Dictionary* of the 1760s, launched a scathing attack on Roman Catholicism in an article on transubstantiation. That article began with a narrative frame that made the miracle of transubstantiation into a matter of perspective:

The Protestants, and most of all Protestant philosophers, regard transubstantiation as the uttermost limit of monkish impudence and lay imbecility. They are quite unrestrained about this belief, which they call monstrous. They do not even think that a single sensible man could embrace it seriously after reflection. It is, they say, so absurd, so opposed to all the laws of physics, so self-contradictory that not even god could perform this operation.[62]

Voltaire published the *Philosophical Dictionary* anonymously, fearing prosecution for such blasphemous views. Yet, even under the cloak of anonymity he further protected himself by attributing the arguments against transubstantiation to unspecified Protestant enemies of the Roman Catholic Church. Indeed, ever since the sixteenth century, there had been Protestants who rejected one or another of the sacraments and miracles of Roman Catholicism, and Voltaire's attribution was thus perfectly plausible as well as strategically self-exculpatory. Yet, the framing of the article on transubstantiation from a Protestant perspective was also fully consistent with the Enlightenment's anthropological discovery of the power of perspective, dating back to Montesquieu's *Persian Letters* and Swift's *Gulliver's Travels* in the 1720s. Voltaire fully appreciated in the 1760s that customary practices and beliefs that were entirely accepted without discussion in the cultural context of the Roman Catholic world—like communion and transubstantiation—might seem completely absurd if viewed from an external cultural perspective. Voltaire's article on transubstantiation clearly demonstrated that problems of perspective were not only relevant to Persian fictions and Pacific voyages but were central to the whole enterprise of the Enlightenment.

In a chapter entitled "French Anthropology in 1800," George Stocking noted that attention to anthropological issues was already sufficiently developed to allow for the founding in 1799 of the Société des Observateurs de l'Homme, whose secretary offered a toast in 1800 to "the progress of anthropology." The society created a lecture series on "The Natural History of Man," and attempted to sponsor an expedition to Australia, but became caught up in Napoleonic politics and ceased to exist in 1804. Much later, in 1869, the French anthropologist Paul Broca looked back on the short-lived society, and judged that "anthropology had not yet a sufficiently firm foundation."[63] The modern discipline of anthropology would not fully establish itself in academic life until the nineteenth century, under the auspices of men like Broca in France and Edward Burnett Tylor in England. Yet, it was also clearly true that the intellectual principles and projects of "anthropology" had been very extensively articulated and elaborated by the end of the eighteenth century, and that the future "progress of anthropology" was already anticipated and prepared.

The firmest intellectual foundations of anthropology were discovered in the analysis of cultural perspective that characterized the philosophy of the Enlightenment. Just as the Renaissance pioneered the development of artistic perspective, so the Enlightenment pioneered the development of cultural perspective. In the *Persian Letters* of the 1720s, Montesquieu explored the radical intellectual dislocation of imagining how French society appeared from a Persian perspective. In the 1750s, Rousseau envisioned in his discourse on inequality a similar play of perspective across chronological eras, not only viewing savage man from the perspective of civilization, but civilized man from the imagined perspective of savagery. The whole chronological history of mankind, in its successive stages, became a problem of perspective as Rousseau and the Scottish philosophes looked back across the epochs to the vanishing point at the origin of human society, where savage men and women faded into the chronological horizon, dissolving into the state of nature. In the 1780s, Herder formulated the concept of the *Volk*, emphasized the variety of human societies, and explored the crucial comparative perspective from which they were all simultaneously visible on the great map of mankind. With the elaboration of cultural perspective, in its many dimensions, the Enlightenment established the intellectual foundations of modern anthropology.

PART ONE

Philosophical History and Enlightened Anthropology

CHAPTER TWO

Barbarians and the Redefinition of Europe

A Study of Gibbon's Third Volume

J. G. A. Pocock

We shall occasionally mention the Scythian or Sarmatian tribes, which, with their arms and horses, their flocks and herds, their wives and families, wandered over the immense plains which spread themselves from the Caspian Sea to the Vistula, from the confines of Persia to those of Germany. But the warlike Germans who first resisted, then invaded, and at length overturned, the western monarchy of Rome, will occupy a much more important place in this history, and possess a stronger, and, if we may use the expression, a more domestic, claim to our attention and regard. The most civilized nations of modern Europe issued from the woods of Germany, and in the rude institutions of these barbarians we may still distinguish the original principles of our present laws and manners.—Edward Gibbon[1]

In these sentences, which introduce the ninth chapter of *The History of the Decline and Fall of the Roman Empire,* Edward Gibbon begins his presentation of "barbarism" in the sense that will dominate his history and lead him at last to summarize its theme as "the triumph of barbarism and religion."[2] The preceding chapter deals with the Persians, a civilized people, "barbarian" in the classic sense that their native language is not Greek (the Greeks were the French of antiquity). They were "the barbarians of the east," but here we have to deal with "the barbarians of the north,"[3] a very different phenomenon, "barbarian" in another sense and playing a different role in history. They are defined primarily as Germans, and we are presented at the same time with a concept of "Europe," as civilized and modern, but barbarian and German in its origins. This is a distinctive, if already far from new use of the term "Europe," and the purpose of this chapter is to pursue the convergence of "barbarism" and "Europe" until both terms take on meanings cardinal, but not primordial, to our sense of history.

The northern barbarians are Germans and occupy a geographic space termed "Germany." Behind them and beyond, however, are other peoples, here termed "Scythian" or "Sarmatian," and occupying a further space, not given a single name but defined, from east to west, as spreading from the Caspian to the Vistula and from Persia to Germany. These peoples have no domestic claim to our attention; they play no formative role in our history, which is European, yet they will prove to have been of great if sterile importance. When considered together, the two spaces that the Germans and Scythians occupy will delimit the map of "Europe" as it is and has long been known to us: the map of a subcontinent or peninsula, protruding west from the Eurasian landmass into the northern Atlantic, bounded by the Mediterranean Sea to the south and the Baltic to the north, but lacking any coast or frontier on its eastern side, where the Scythians wander with their flocks and herds. This "Europe" is clearly not identical with the space comprising the two Mediterranean basins, the Nile and Euphrates river valleys, in which the Roman Empire has been established and in which the term "Europe" was much earlier invented. It had first denoted the lands lying west and north of the Hellespont and Bosphorus, and the expanding horizon of ancient geographers had realized that these opened out into unknown lands of great extent, to which a diversity of names had been given. This chapter draws attention to the complex process by which "Europe" migrates from the Hellespont to take on the meaning it has for us, and the meaning Gibbon had in mind when he wrote of "the most civilized nations of modern Europe" and their barbaric and German origins.

We must return to the two zones of barbarism mentioned by Gibbon. The eastern Scythians and Sarmatians are pastoral nomads wandering over an immense plain. The Germans, however, to whom Gibbon is about to devote a chapter, are forest transhumants pasturing their cattle in clearings they have made for themselves in the equally immense woodlands watered by the rivers flowing from the Alps into the Rhine, Elbe, and Danube valleys. Into this terrain the true nomads of the steppe seldom venture and do not long remain; but the cattle-herding Germans have not yet become agriculturalists and lack the sense of law, sociability, and even individuality that only the neighborhood of cultivators can provide.[4] It is here, rather significantly, that we may place Gibbon's remark that ancient and barbaric Germany, east of the provinces subject to Rome, "extended itself over a third part of Europe."[5] If, as the accompanying language can be made to suggest, the remaining two thirds lie west of the Rhine to the Atlantic and south of the Danube to the Mediterranean, then the "immense plain" as far as Persia is excluded from Europe, and that term is confined to the lands in which modern civility has taken shape. Where, then, can we place the eastern borders of ancient or modern Germany?

To understand why there has never been a clear answer to the latter question, we may return to Gibbon's language and observe how it became transformed as his chapters succeeded one another, especially as the themes of chapter 9 were taken up again in chapter 26, published five years later. By that point, the account of "Scythian and Sarmatian" nomadism had been extended by two major theses. Joseph de Guignes's great *Histoire des Huns, Turcs et Mogols* (1756–58)[6] had set up the image of a chain of nomad peoples extending as far as the inner Asian frontiers of China, in such a way that conflicts as far away as Shansi and Kansu could set off snowball effects whose repercussions would be felt on the Oxus frontier of Persia or the Danubian frontier of Rome. Adam Smith's Glasgow lectures, still unpublished in 1776, and his *Wealth of Nations*, published almost simultaneously with Gibbon's first volume, had given the "shepherd stage" in "the progress of society" a dynamic importance[7] that lent force to the equation of shepherd, nomad, and barbarian. Gibbon admired de Guignes and counted Smith a friend; it is noteworthy, however, that he did not follow Smith in making the shepherd the original appropriator who had moved mankind out of the "savagery" of the hunter-gatherer. The *Decline and Fall* does not distinguish between "barbarian" and "savage," but uses the terms interchangeably—following earlier schemes of the progress of society[8]—as denoting a stage of vagrancy preceding stationary cultivation, social space, and the exchange of goods, words, and ideas. Scythians and Huns, Germans and Goths were alike "savages," and the latter might owe their origin to "wandering savages of the Hercynian woods," engaged in hunting and beginning to clear the forests of woodland Europe, supposed in the generation preceding Gibbon's to have grown up after the Great Flood and been resettled by the posterity of Noah moving west—Gomer, the son of Japhet, being the ancestor of agricultural peoples, and his brother, Magog, the ancestor of herdsmen and shepherds. Gibbon had abandoned the Noachic genealogies, but there was only Scottish historical sociology to put in their place, and the two were in fact compatible.

If Gibbon's scheme lacked the theoretical depth of Smith's, it furnished a comprehensive historical narrative. In chapter 10, he allowed for an eastward movement of Germanic peoples, settling the Goths in Ukraine, where they became a pastoral culture of the open plains.[9] Here he was situating them in a historical geography, connected with the great rivers from the Vistula to the Volga, which almost link the Baltic and Black Seas and almost provide Europe with the water frontier every continent should have, on its eastern side. This geography furnishes a means of linking the Gothic invaders of Rome's eastern provinces with the Franks, Burgundians, Saxons, and Vandals who had crossed the Rhine and assailed Gaul and Britain. As far back as Snorri Sturluson in the thirteenth century, Odin had been a Trojan leading his Asian Aesir to the Baltic,[10] and Gibbon long kept in mind a humanist version of the same story, in which Odin was a Dacian migrant who had founded a Gothic kingdom in faraway Sweden.[11] He never came to believe this, but there was a need to reconcile an ancient vision of the "Goths" as northern invaders, and Scandinavia as the womb of nations, with the more authentic history of their emergence from Ukraine to invade the Danubian provinces. By chapter 26, he had that story in hand.

Forces not exerted by Chinese power, but originating on its western frontier—Gibbon has little to say about its history following the disintegration of the Han—lead to a Hun assault that drives the Goths from Ukraine across the Danube, with catastrophic results for Rome. There is now a recurrent pattern of steppe disturbances driving pastoral peoples, first into forest Europe and then into the civilized provinces, but this pattern must be set among other, sometimes contrary, developments. Much earlier in history, Augustus's attempt to move the German frontier eastward is less significant for the disaster of the Teutoburgerwald than for his establishment of provinces on the Danube, from its source near the Alps to its mouths on the Black Sea.[12] Collectively known as the Illyrian provinces, these are crucial both to Roman history and to Gibbon's conception of Europe. Their strategic role is to provide a defensible frontier for the provinces growing out of the original "Europe"; their strategic weakness is that they cover the passes of the eastern Alps, through which usurpers or barbarians may descend into Italy itself. After a crisis in the third century—occasioned partly by usurpers, partly by a rather improbable invasion by seaborne Goths, whose light craft infest both the Black Sea and the Aegean[13]—a chain of emperors, Illyrian in either their origin or their power, inaugurate a momentous eastward movement of the centers of Roman empire, which encounters the westward movement of barbarism in a pattern of reflux. As the energies of the Italian city are at last exhausted, the capital migrates from Rome to Constantinople. Gibbon does not accept the argument that Constantinople neglected the western provinces and helped cause their loss, but he does rather significantly remark that "the boundary in Europe," between Illyrian provinces under western and eastern military control, "was not very different from the line which now separates the Germans and the Turks."[14] The frontiers of European history are being drawn for the future.

The Danube valley is an important key to Gibbon's concepts of both Roman Empire and Europe (two terms never interchangeable). When organized into provinces under military control, it protects the northern frontier of the eastern half of the empire, but if that control lapses into either civil war or barbarian invasion, it offers a route into either Greece or Italy. The Huns drive the Goths across the lower Danube; seeking settlement and even Romanization, the latter are badly handled and defeat the emperor Valens, killing him at Adrianople in A.D. 379. This is a disaster but not a collapse; Theodosius contains the Goths as armed allies of the empire, but when they are again mismanaged under his sons, Alaric leads them to plunder Greece and loot Athens before setting out on the road to the Alpine passes and Rome. "A Christian and a soldier," to quote Gibbon,[15] Alaric is more a warlord within the empire than a barbarian invading it. His invasion of Italy is the product of a complex power struggle involving the western emperor and his warlord general, Stilicho, and the Gothic sack of Rome in A.D. 410 draws its vast significance from things happening independently of it. Another chain of pressure originating on the Chinese borders—Gibbon says he cannot trace it through all its links[16]—produces a formidable buildup of barbarians including Vandals on the southern shores of the Baltic, and the locus of eastern pressure shifts north of the Danube. One group of these peoples invades Italy, and under their leader, Radagaisus—"a savage," says Gibbon[17] (unlike Alaric)—is destroyed at Florence, but other forces of the same origin cross the Rhine at the end of A.D. 405, nearly five years before Alaric's sack of Rome, which derives much of its significance from what has happened already. The collapse of the Rhine frontier, Gibbon says, "may be considered as the fall of the Roman empire in the countries beyond the Alps,"[18] Britain and Gaul, Spain and Africa; and we shall need to consider a reshaping of the concept of Europe in consequence of it. This is an achievement of barbarians, notably Vandals; and it is important to note that the Goths are caught up in it, while the Franks resist it as allies of Rome.[19] The imperial system is disintegrating, but the various barbarians are still to be distinguished by their relations to it as successor states; and after A.D. 405–410, the history of this process moves perceptibly to the farther west, a circumstance important in the historiography of "Europe."

There is an anomaly here in the history of vocabulary. Because Goths are recurrently central to the story—at Adrianople in A.D. 379 and at Rome in A.D. 410—the adjective "Gothic" has been used for western Romano-barbaric culture in general and to identify "the Goths" with the fall of the empire.[20] In fact, however, the Visigoths and Ostrogoths are neither the most durable nor the most successful of the peoples termed "barbaric." They establish a kingdom in southern Gaul, which is destroyed by Clovis the Frank; another under Theodoric in Italy, which is destroyed by Justinian's generals and replaced by that of the Lombards; and a third in Spain, which most momentously of all is destroyed by Muslim Arabs advancing through Africa. As we read Gibbon's third volume, we are increasingly aware that he is laying the foundations of a history of the western provinces that are to become kingdoms and create the history we term medieval, modern, and European; that term itself moves west with the barbarians driven by forces originating in China. The usurper Maximus, last of the provincial generals who claim the purple, briefly controls Spain, Britain, and Gaul, "three ample countries," says Gibbon, "which now constitute the three most flourishing kingdoms of modern Europe."[21] This is twenty years before the disasters of A.D. 405–10, and Maximus is not the key to the history of those kingdoms, which must include how the barbarian Franks and Alamanni gave their names to modern France and Germany. With the withdrawal of the imperial garrisons after A.D. 410, Britain vanishes for centuries from Roman and even recorded history;[22] there is the problem here of an insular and archipelagic barbarism that the Chinese thesis does nothing to explain, and Gibbon knows it would be no light matter to restore Britain to the Frankish or Gothic history that lies ahead of him. (A fierce debate about the Irish origin of the Scots is taking shape.) There is quite another story to be told here: that of the movement of the people called Vandals through Gaul and Visigothic Spain to the Roman province of Africa, where under their king Genseric they set up a naval and piratical power that does more to destroy communications between the western and eastern empires than any Goth can achieve.[23] We know that Gibbon knows this kingdom was destroyed by Belisarius and Justinian, but it is hard to read his account of the disintegration of Roman Africa without attributing to him a further foreknowledge of the Arab conquest, which destroyed the unity of the Mediterranean forever, by incorporating the whole of its African coast in the history of Islam. Here we move out of the history of barbarism and religion altogether; whatever the Muslim Arabs are, they are not barbarians (though the Berbers, whom Gibbon calls "Moors," are "a crowd of naked savages" at the time of the Vandal invasion).[24] Western history is to be rewritten from the time Islam places it under siege.

Genseric's Vandals sack Rome a second time,[25] two years after the death of Attila, whose Huns make the furthest penetration west of any nomad people whose wars and migrations can be traced to the Chinese borders. The *Decline and Fall* recounts Attila's history at length, since Gibbon is supplied with narratives that require repetition, but insists that his achievements were transitory and destructive. Other than the foundation of Venice, a by-product of his destruction of Aquileia,[26] Attila leaves his mark on Western history in only one way: the devastation of the Danube valley, interestingly described as "the whole breadth of Europe, as it extends above five hundred miles from the Euxine to the Adriatic"[27]—language that implies the peninsular Europe, north of the Mediterranean and open to an indefinite extension to the East. Attila's kingdom disintegrates at his death, along fault-lines lying far beyond Europe, where the Geougen compete with the Uighurs from Siberia for control of Transoxania,[28] but the Illyrian provinces are no longer a shield to the empire, and the middle Danube is open to new barbarian peoples. These will often be nomads from the steppe, Avars, Magyars, Bulgars, and Mongols, but there will also be Slavs, originally a people of bogtrotters from the Pripet marshes—like beavers in their habitation, says Gibbon, only not so clean[29]—whose language has since "been diffused by conquest from the confines of Italy to the neighborhood of Japan."[30] The image of Russian empire is here implied, but Gibbon will not recount it. We have reached the point where his work divides in the last three volumes, published in 1788, when he resolves to leave aside the history of the medieval West, already recounted by others, and pursue the millennium of eastern history to 1453. But his third volume, published in 1781, reaches the end of empire in the West, and this is the story of the refoundation of Europe by the barbarian occupants of the Latin-speaking provinces bordering the Atlantic. It is the history of what befell Goths, Franks, Lombards and Anglo-Saxons, as they moved west, leaving behind them the open lands as far as China in which their motion had originated. It is also the history of how they acquired that "domestic claim to our attention" quoted at the outset of this chapter.

As barbarian power takes shape in the western provinces, it becomes foundational to a new culture, combining barbarian elements with others persisting from late antique Rome. A crucial step is the conversion of barbarians to Christianity, specifically in the Trinitarian or Catholic form shaped in the great controversy with Arianism.[31] That Goths are Arians is a principal issue in the Roman destruction of their kingdom in Italy and the Frankish destruction of their kingdom in Aquitaine. These processes point to the central step in the formation of the Latin Middle Ages. Justinian leaves Italy open to the triangular power struggle between the exarchate in Ravenna, the Lombard kingdom in Pavia, and the papacy in Rome, and it is when the last-named forms an alliance with the Frankish kingdom in Gaul and erects it into an empire, says Gibbon, that "modern history," defined as that which is not ancient, truly begins.[32] This is perhaps the final "triumph of barbarism and religion," the creation of an autonomous history in the western provinces, whose loss to empire is conceivably the central event of *Decline and Fall*: a history that is Latin and Frankish, papal and in a new sense imperial, and Catholic in a Trinitarian sense scarcely challenged from within[33] until Enlightenment itself.

Gibbon does not reach these matters until well into his volumes of 1788. The series of 1781 concludes with the "General Reflections on the Fall of the Roman Empire in the West," a process anything but simple. It is not only in the island province of Britain—itself a part of the largest island of an archipelago whose barbarism is hard to derive from the Eurasian steppe—and only in that part of the province that can later be known by the name of England, that it is possible to imagine a complete replacement of Roman provincial culture by Germanic folk customs, and Gibbon is by no means sure that this implies the extermination of the older population.[34] Elsewhere, and above all in Gaul, it is a matter of writing a Roman-Germanic history, less Gothic than Frankish, and this is clearly reflected in the historians he now chooses to follow. There are the barbarian historians themselves—Jordanes for the Goths, Paul the Deacon for the Lombards, Gregory of Tours for the Franks, Bede for the English—but it is in Gibbon's selection of modern authorities that the direction of his thought emerges. There is the French Comte de Buat's *Histoire ancienne des peuples de l'Europe*;[35] there is the Saxon counselor Johann Jakob Mascov's *History of the Ancient Germans*;[36] and as Gibbon penetrates the origins of the French monarchy, the names that appear are those of the Abbé du Bos[37] and others including Mably,[38] whom we know lent more to the Roman-centered *thèse royale* than to the Frankish-centered *thèse nobiliaire* favored by Montesquieu.[39] Gibbon knew very well what he was opening up: a story more Frankish than Gothic, both French and German, in which barbarians became Roman even as Rome fell to the barbarians. Mascov's German history is in fact centered on the Frankish dynasties, Merovingian and Carolingian, leading to the foundation of the medieval empire in which German history ceased to be ancient. We are on the way back to the alliance of the popes and the Frankish kings, and the great themes of medieval history: the struggles between papacy and empire, and the emergence of a French kingdom whose Gallicanism aimed at a power independent of either.

The Montesquieuan motif, however, persists. "The most civilized nations of modern Europe issued from the woods of Germany, and in the rude institutions of these barbarians we may still distinguish the original principles of our present laws and manners." This sentence from the paragraph initially quoted is bound to recall Montesquieu's "ce beau système

a été trouvé dans les bois,"[40] and there is good reason why it should. Yet
the forest Germans described in Gibbon's ninth chapter have not yet arrived at any *beau système* of laws and liberties, for the reason that they
have not yet individualized property in land, which they redivide among
the community at intervals; and until the individual is bound to his neighbor by laws that protect the property of both, he can know himself, his
friend, and his enemy only by the behavior codes of a barbaric sense of
honor.[41] Gibbon gives no account in this chapter of when or how the Germans became civilized through land tenure, and it clearly cannot happen
as long as they remain the vagrant war bands of a *Völkerwanderung*. Dis-
regarding the question of what it is in their forest culture that we recognize as the origin of ourselves, it is evident that the western barbarians acquire property, and with it the opportunity of law and liberty (the liberty
of the *legalis homo*) only as they invade Roman provinces and settle upon
Roman lands. This was notoriously a complex process—the warrior German, imposed on the unwilling Roman master of an estate worked by
servile laborers or tenants—and its character has been vehemently and in-
conclusively debated since the humanist jurists of the sixteenth century.[42]
Nevertheless, there has emerged, and will by no means go away, one of
the foundation myths of Western civilization: a blend of Germanic freedom and Roman legality, in which the settlement of barbarians on Roman estates had generated first allodial, then feudal, and then proprietor-
ial tenures. This was a system of property guaranteed by laws, on which
could be erected all the myths of ancient constitutions and immemorial
customs, and on which the various constitutionalisms of the western kingdoms so long depended. Since it first took shape in the writings of the humanist jurists, this mythology had entailed a complex argument over the
roles of barbarian custom and civil law, respectively. Gibbon's French,
Scottish, and German sources made him lean to the Roman side in this debate; an English Whig, he was not an English or a Frankish ancient con-
stitutionalist. But the contest between barbarian and Roman ideas of law
and property could itself be retailed as a history of liberty, and we are
looking here at the roots of his statement that barbarian institutions were
"domestic" to modern Europe.

The Germanic myth offered a way of retelling a process described in
conjectural history, and making it seem to occur in civil history recorded in
documents and texts. In the former history, vagrant hunters and shepherds
had become stationary cultivators, constituting a social space through which
there could pass exchanges of products and ideas, creating commerce, society, manners, and enlightenment.[43] In the history of barbaric Europe, communities of free tenants might become towns, and cities might be chartered
and enter into commerce with one another. The collapse of the ancient slave

economy, and its resettlement by barbarians one degree removed from savagery, had led to the growth of an economy more dynamically capable of market relations than its predecessor—yesterday's barbarian was today's burgher. Gibbon's history of the western Middle Ages, as we reconstruct it, hinges on the growth of trading cities as the feudal kingdoms of Germany and Italy disintegrated in the struggle with the papacy: a new consequence of the triumph of barbarism and religion. He learned this perception from Lodovico Muratori,[44] and it made a Guelf, not a Ghibelline, historian of him;[45] but the history of the western kingdoms, France, England, and most ambiguously Spain, was more central still. Before pursuing this theme, however, we should pause to consider that we have here another governing myth of our historiography: the history of Europe, beginning from the fall of the western empire, the independent power of the Roman church, and the settlement of the barbarian kingdoms, and continuing through a history "as well ecclesiastical as civil" to the end of the Latin Middle Ages, the wars of religion, and the growth of an enlightened states system based on an increasingly oceanic commerce. All eighteenth-century historiography is based on this grand narrative, and it has done so much to determine our own notions of the historic process that we find it very hard to escape this history of Europe. We tell ourselves not to be Eurocentric, but when we attempt to write the history of civilizations not European, we too often come up with histories Eurocentric at one remove, or limited to the subversion of the European narrative without replacing it.

Gibbon's "General Reflections," placed at the end of his third volume but written years before its composition, situate him at the formation of this history; that is, his account of the collapse of Rome west of the Rhine and south of the Alps leads into an account of a "Europe" too strong and complex to be overthrown by another barbarian horde galloping out of central Asia. In fact, he says (following Voltaire, for once) this is not to be feared or expected, since Romanov Russia and Manchu China are engaged in conquering and garrisoning the steppe, and the age of the nomads is at an end.[46] Gibbon's perception of world history is land-bound and Eurasian; he knows that the Europe proof against barbarism is engaged in conquering the globe through oceanic commerce, but mentions this only incidentally. His Orientalism is real, but really septentrionalism; it is limited to the statement that nomads from the steppe, or Arabs and Turks from the Dar-ul-Islam, do not settle down and found free tenures, and therefore never become more than the palace guards of despots.[47] The history of liberty is exclusively European. But since Gibbon's "Europe" continues to confront a "Scythia" that can never again overrun it—but which Russia is engaged in conquering while becoming or not becoming European—it is situated in the geography of a peninsula without a frontier on its open eastward face. There is a history here that Gibbon does not write, for reasons deeply affecting the history he does write in his later volumes.

Beginning with the transitory empire of Charlemagne, and renewing its efforts in later centuries, this power system, Frankish-German (rather than Gothic), Latin, and Roman (in a sense rather ecclesiastical than civil), shaped in the western provinces of the former empire, faces about and begins to expand eastward, absorbing Saxons and Avars under Charlemagne, and proceeding over time to establish Latin and Catholic civilization in lands now Slavonic. North of that "frontier between Turks and Germans," which is all Gibbon has to say of this matter, there is a frontier between Catholic and Orthodox, Poles and Russians, about which one can say little more than that he does not deal with it. We encounter here the problems of "Central Europe" and "Eastern Europe," about the enlightened perceptions of which Larry Wolff has written interesting volumes.[48] Norman Davies too has rightly perceived that there is a history of Europe to be written with Poland at its epicenter (he is a better historian of Poland than he is of Britain, a product of the westward expansion of Frankish Europe into the Gaelic and Norse archipelagoes).[49] It can all be made to begin from the point at which Gibbon suspended publication of his volumes for seven years, between 1781 and 1788: the redefinition of "Europe" as meaning the social, political, and religious complex created by the westward movement of barbarians into the Atlantic provinces of the Mediterranean empire of Rome. The history of this complex becomes the history of Europe, and very nearly of mankind; it confirms our giving the name of "Europe" to the peninsula between the Baltic and Mediterranean, extended as far into the open eastward lands as it is capable of going. Gibbon importantly develops this perception of history, but there are important senses in which he does not write it.

The paradox of the later volumes of the *Decline and Fall* is that they are conceptually governed by the European history I have outlined—the product of the movement of the barbarians into the western provinces—but that Gibbon chose to leave that history as it had been written by others, and to write another that he did not succeed in making independent of it. The history he chose to write was that of the empire centered on Constantinople, lasting a thousand years after the disasters of the fifth century, but in order to understand his problems in writing it, we have to constantly revert, as he did, to the history he knew but did not write. This was the enlightened history of Europe, magisterially constructed by Voltaire and Robertson,[50] and we need to understand that both the Enlightenment and the Europe in which they shaped their perceptions were the product of a Franco-British confrontation and partial reconciliation, somewhat as the Europe we had until very recently was produced by the reconciliation of France and Germany. The history they wrote was not merely Frankish but Neustrian, situated for the most part west of the demarcation lines that partitioned the Carolingian Empire. From the medieval competition between popes and emperors, and its impact on the *regnum germanicum* and the *regnum italicum*, attention moved to the no less Carolingian kingdom of France, its struggles with the papacy and the kings of England, and the great competition with the Spanish and Austrian Hapsburgs, which broke out in Burgundy and Italy.[51] This collision between superstates was complicated by the growth of the independent Netherlands and by a cycle of wars between the Catholic and Protestant confessions, fought out to a significant degree in Germany; but here we have to note some historiographic consequences. The Wars of the Three Kingdoms in the British Isles, and the subsequent emergence of Great Britain as France's leading adversary in Europe and beyond, necessitated a writing of English and British history into that of Europe,[52] so that France and Britain, their histories and cultures, became predominant in the historiography of Enlightenment. Of the other great cultures formed out of the collapse of the western Roman Empire, the history of Spain became marginalized as the collision between Arabs, Visigoths, and later Castilians, and did not develop an enlightened narrative of its own. That of Germany, necessarily prominent in the history of papalism down to the fall of the Hohenstaufen, became a history of the Holy Roman Empire and the German states system succeeding it; a history of Germany on its western face but hardly ever on its eastern, which is why the history of the *drang nach Osten* is not so much neglected by Gibbon as altogether unknown to him. He knew no German and seems to have had little perception of German culture or its history.

As barbarians become agents in their own civilization, others may play the role of barbarians to them. However, where Rome stood on the defensive along its own frontiers, the Europe of barbarism and religion was an expansive force,[53] and barbarians are seen as colonized by it: Wends, Lithuanians, and Prussians in the continental east, Gaels in the archipelagic west, and Scandinavians—by a more peaceable process—in the north beyond the Baltic. Gibbon was aware of some of these peoples, but they do not figure in his history because this was not the history he was writing. We are left facing his decision to leave the Latin Middle Ages where others had written its history, and pursue the story of the eastern empire instead. Here he faced the great difficulty that there was no equivalent of the Catholic, Protestant, and enlightened macronarrative, leading the history of the barbarized provinces to the growth of secular commercial states, which had come to present itself as the history of Europe and the history of society. He could find no guiding thread in the history of Orthodox

Christianity, and could write it only in terms of the more active and dynamic peoples—from crusading Latins to Ottoman Turks—who had from time to time broken in on it.[54] Some of these peoples were, or had been, barbarians; none were the domestic ancestors of a more civilized present.

The empire ruled from Constantinople retained a European frontier on the lower Danube; north and west of this was the Romano-Germanic order of empire and papacy, and north and east were the western extremities of the Eurasian steppe. New waves of nomads sometimes appear in its history—Avars, Bulgars, and Mongols—and we must sometimes turn to Chinese history to understand what is going on, but in no case are they pushing ahead of them groups of forest peoples capable of entering and transforming the settled world of agrarian and mercantile Europe. The anomalous case is that of the Slavonic peoples, who are neither nomads nor Franks; in central Europe, they form warrior kingdoms that interact with the Romanized Germans thrusting from the west, but this process is not duplicated in the Orthodox East. There is no myth or rhetoric telling how Slavs founded free tenures, systems of law, and urban corporations; only if we look further north again do we encounter the beginnings of Russian history—which Gibbon significantly ascribes to Varangians, Scandinavian colonizers from the Baltic[55]—where the myth of the *mir* or self-governing peasant village will make its appearance in the nineteenth century. It is not to be found in the *Decline and Fall*, however, and belongs to a later macrohistory that came to replace the stadial sequences of enlightened social philosophy: that founded on the paradigm of the Indo-Germanic mark or agnatic community, and the Aryan and Caucasian races who were supposed to have propagated it. Gibbon admired the work of Sir William Jones in Calcutta,[56] the discoverer of Sanskrit and student of ancient Indian law, but did not know where it would lead in the next century.[57] There was a world of Anglo-German scholarship that he did not live to see.

In the very last chapter of the *Decline and Fall*, Gibbon pronounces it a history of the "triumph of barbarism and religion," but by then his eye is once more fixed on the city of Rome and the great phrase is to be read in the context of western, neo-Latin and in that sense, "European" history. In the two volumes of east Roman history, the meaning of each of the two terms is transformed. The central event is the irruption of Islam and the Arab conquests of the eighth century, which changed the map of the world—Mediterranean, Levantine, African, and Eurasian—on a much greater scale than the Germanic invasion of the far western provinces had ever done; and yet, by the time Gibbon wrote, the civilization inaugurated by the latter had outflanked Islam on the global ocean, and he could speak of "the descendants of the northern barbarians" as "the masters of the world."[58] The ancestors of contemporary Islam had destroyed Greco-Latin civilization in Mesopotamia, Egypt, Africa, and for a time Sicily and Spain; they had conquered Persia and transformed the world of the steppe as far as China. However, though Gibbon saw this as the work of religion, he did not see it as that of barbarians. There is indeed an account of the horse- and camel-riding desert Arabs that prefigures much later romanticism,[59] but they are not true nomads. Muhammad is a townsman, and as conquerors, they bring religion and laws and are peoples of the book. Islam fascinates Gibbon as a religion, a "rational enthusiasm"[60] that is a response to Christian theology but does not issue in a secular Enlightenment; nor is it allied with the growth of property, individuality, and commerce, the culture of liberty that is Enlightenment's prerequisite. This has been founded—an inescapable paradox—by Gothic barbarians interacting with papal Catholicism. Their liberty and tolerance are both consequence and cause of commerce and power, but Gibbon is only at the brink of arguing that the freedom of Europeans justifies their rule over others. His Orientalism is largely the contention that peoples east of Europe have not solved the problem of escape from palace-centered despotism, to which Rome succumbed for Roman reasons but which post-barbarian Europe for many reasons avoided.

The east Roman empire was in the end defeated and occupied by Turks, and Turks are among the three peoples supplying the title of Joseph de Guignes's great work. As Gibbon pursues his story, however, he moves with de Guignes away from the original simplicity of nomads recoiling from the Chinese frontier and setting off snowball effects rolling toward the West. Islam changes nomad culture, and does so furthermore in its Persian rather than its Arab form. The Turks come to understand empire, and the Mogul empire in India is Mongol only in name. There is one last venture into Chinese history, where the Yuan dynasty set up by Kubilai helps to explain the disappearance of Genghizid power from Europe, and Timur, portrayed as the last of the nomad scourges of God, is primarily the adversary of the Ottoman state.[61] This survives his victory over Bajazet because it is a state, something nomads have never founded; and behind it lies a history Gibbon glancingly recounts, tracing the rise of armies and bureaucracies founded on the slave household.[62] Turks are certainly despots, because they rule by means including devastation, but they are not barbarians—nomads on the frontier of agrarian commerce—in the technical sense.

We reach a point, then, where the original scenario of "barbarism"—shepherds, foresters, and cultivators; Huns thrusting Goths into Rome; Germans changing Roman society as it changes them; barbarism as the object of "domestic" attention—becomes a story told only in Latin Europe, and Latin European history the only story that can be told coherently. It is possible to carry this reading into the eighteenth-century historiography of Latin Europe's own discoveries and colonies: the two American continents, where the absence of either pastoral nomadism or animal-drawn cereal agriculture allowed it to be assumed that the peoples of both continents were hunter-gatherer savages and nothing more. But the enlightened social philosophers and historians, French and Scottish, among whom Gibbon shaped the *Decline and Fall*, did not construct this narrative solely to justify themselves in ruling others. They were interested in *libertas* as well as *imperium*, and liberty was a key to the understanding of themselves, which they had been seeking for some time.

CHAPTER THREE

The Immobility of China

Orientalism and Occidentalism in the Enlightenment

Anthony Pagden

In 1784, or what he chose to record as the "thirteenth year of the reign of Abd-ul-Hamid, son of Ahmed, emperor of the Turks," after three arduous days' march "in arid solitude where all about I saw nothing but brigandage and devastation, tyranny and misery," the ideologue Constantin François Volney came across the ruins of the city of Palmyra.

There he sat down on a column, much as Gibbon had done two decades earlier in the Capitol, rested his head in his hands, fixed his gaze upon the desert, and meditated on the rise and fall of civilizations. Volney's thoughts, like Gibbon's, dwelt on contrasts—in his case, the contrast between the former grandeur of Palmyra, the city that had once controlled the trade routes between the Mediterranean and the Euphrates, capital of the warrior queen Zenobia, and the desert, "grayish and monotone," that now surrounded it. He was conscious that what lay about him was all that remained of a once great city that had been Roman, Parthian, and Sassanid before falling into Ottoman hands and subsequently into ruins. But Volney's quest was much loftier than Gibbon's. He wanted to know not only why empires rise and fall but also the ultimate cause for the prosperity of nations and "on which principles the peace between men and happiness (*bonheur*) of societies might be established." In pursuit of these elusive goals, his mind wandered off to the sources of all the civilizations of the ancient world both east and west, to Nineveh and Balbeck, Babylon and Persepolis, Jerusalem, Sidon, and Tyr. All now were in ruins.

Thus caught up in his meditations, a thought struck him, "which threw my heart into trouble and uncertainty." All of these places, "when they enjoyed all that of which the glory and the well-being of man is made up," had been inhabited by "infidels"—peoples who, like the Phoenicians, venerated the homicidal Moloch, prostrated themselves before serpents, or worshipped fire, but nevertheless did not imagine their deities to be the only ones, or that peoples who knew nothing of them should be bound by the same beliefs or laws. Such peoples had been great empire builders. In time, however they had all been replaced by the avatars or one of another of the world's great monotheistic religions—Christianity, Islam, or Judaism—and in time, all that they had made had crumbled away. Once, under its "infidel" masters, the city of Palmyra and the oasis on which it had been built had been rich and fertile. But now, Volney observed sarcastically, "that believers and saints occupy these lands, there is nothing but sterility and solitude."[1]

This led him to reflect that, looking around, it was clear what he called the "scepter of the world" had passed from ancient Asia to modern Europe. It was a reflection that made him tremble. For although "it pleased me to recover the past splendor of Asia in Europe," the vision of so much destitution also made him wonder if, one day, future travelers might find, beside the banks of the Seine or the Thames or the Zuidersee, just such "mute ruins" as now lay around him. Those future travelers, too, would "weep alone amidst the ashes of the peoples and the memories of the greatness," as he did now.

Volney was reflecting on the history of the translation of "civilization," from East to West, from Asia to Europe. It was as old as the (written) history of the regions to which it applies—which is to say as old as Herodotus. In one shape or another, the great historical question for Europeans—and now Americans—has always been how and why Europe surpassed, supplanted, and triumphed over Asia, from which Europe itself had originated, and from which all its sciences and philosophy had derived. It is the question that has nagged at generation after generation from Herodotus himself until, let us say, Max Weber's great if incomplete meditation on the European *polis*, *"Die Stadt"* of 1913–14.

The shape and definition of both Europe and Asia have of course varied greatly over time. "Europe" moved steadily westward and northward until it reached the shores of the Baltic and the Atlantic. The geography of Asia, on the other hand—as seen from the West—remained largely unchanged, from the day in 326 BCE when Alexander's army was brought to an abrupt halt on the banks of the Beas River, until the early sixteenth century. The only mental additions were vague regions known as the "lands beyond the Ganges," which included a shrunken India, a vastly enlarged Ceylon, and the "land of the Great Khan," on whose eastern shores Columbus believed he had landed in 1492.

During the seventeenth and the eighteenth centuries, however, all this changed dramatically. There was increased European trade with India—not to mention armed European incursions. There was a steady, if still minuscule, European presence in both China and Japan. The East—the Orient—had thus, by the mid-sixteenth century, been pushed all the way to the China Sea. The mental inclusion of India—Muslim and Hindu India—and China as components of Asia greatly altered the perception of the entire region. For any cultured European of the eighteenth century, the history of the "Middle East" was, in most fundamental respects, a continuation of that of the Achaemenid Empire. Reading Jean Chardin's *Voyages en Perse*, wrote Voltaire, was to "imagine an account from the time of Xerxes."[2] But no one, least of all Voltaire, could have said anything remotely similar of either India or China.

The incorporation of what was vaguely called India, beyond and below Bactria, into a concept of Asia was largely unproblematic. Here, after all, were the semi-mythical lands of the gymnosophists, to whom, as Voltaire put it, "the Greeks before Pythagoras had gone for instruction," the lands that—together with Egypt—were the acknowledged source of both ancient Persian and Greek science and philosophy.[3] Most eighteenth-century self-styled Orientalists were overwhelmingly concerned with the search for the origins of European or—as it would come to be called—"Indo-European" culture. Men, like the long-winded Abraham Hyacinthe Anquetil Duperron, for instance, whom Fernando Galiani once scathingly described as "all that a traveler should be, exact, precise, incapable of creating any system, incapable of seeing what is useful and what not,"[4] came to take a vivid interest in modern Asia (and even toward the end of his life in America) and wrote a passionate defense of both Turkish and Arab modes of government. But what drove him to enlist in the army of the Compagnie des Indes in 1754, as a means of reaching India, was a desire to learn Sanskrit and Pahlavi, in the belief that these languages would give him access to the writings of Zoroaster and through them to the sources of all human culture. The same could be said, for their part, of William Jones, Charles Wilkins, or Nathaniel Halhed. "We [in India] now live," Jones told the members of the Asiatic Society of Calcutta in 1787, "among the doers of those very deities, who were worshiped under different names in old Greece and Italy, and among the professors of those philosophical tenets, which the Ionic and Attic writers illustrated with all the beauties of their melodious language."[5] India was, like the Asia of the Greeks, a part of Europe's own history, remote perhaps, but integral nonetheless.

There was another crucial aspect of the history of Asia that linked what is now loosely called the "Middle East" to India. Both in the relatively recent past had been overrun by nomadic or seminomadic tribes (much indeed as, at an earlier period, had the West). These mostly Arab and Turco-Mongolic peoples had settled and created great empires that, by the late seventeenth century, had engulfed all the lands from the China Sea to Hungary. By that time, the governments established by these peoples, particularly in those areas that had converted to Islam, came to be generally subsumed under the heading of "Oriental despotism."

The term, or at least its popularity, we owe to François Bernier in the seventeenth century, and it was based largely on his experience of Mughal India, but the principles would do, mutatis mutandis, for all three of the great Muslim empires—the Safavid, the Mughal, and the Ottoman. The constituent principles of Oriental despotism are familiar enough (and would have been familiar to Herodotus). Under Muslim rule, allegedly, there was no law. Legislation, beyond the precepts of the *Shari'a*, depended upon the whim of the prince. In such states, believed Montesquieu, there are "no laws, so to speak; only mores and manners."[6] Everything was governed according to custom, unexamined if not simply irrational. The subjects of Muslim despots were not persons bound by a rule of law, as were those of even the most unprincipled European monarch, but they were the despot's property, just as he did not rule over, but actually owned the state. Chattel slavery was a condition for many, but slavery understood as the absence of any freedom to act or express oneself independently of the sovereign's will—what Montesquieu termed "political slavery"—was a condition for all. For this reason, claimed Montesquieu in the *Lettres persanes*, republics were unknown in Asia as they were in Africa, both of which "have always been burdened by despotism"—with the exception of a few towns in Asia Minor and the (perhaps more troubling) exception of Carthage.[7]

In almost every important respect, "Oriental despotism" was a transposition to the Muslim world of an image formed by the ancient Greeks of their would-be Achaemenid conquerors. This made it comfortingly familiar. In the triumphal history of the ancient world, at Marathon—a battle that John Stuart Mill claimed to have been of more lasting significance for British history than the battle of Hastings—and again at Salamis, the small, independent, liberty-loving, law-abiding Greeks had successfully defended themselves against a massive despotic state. Salamis had been the end of the Persian menace. It had also been the beginning of Greek empire building, which would continue to grow until Alexander invaded Persia, burned its capital, and set about uniting the world, as he understood it, into one culture. The success story of Europe, which in the very *longue durée* every educated person in eighteenth-century Europe carried in his or her head, had begun at Salamis and been consolidated by Alexander—which is why Montesquieu dedicated an entire chapter to his deeds in the *Esprit des lois*: he who "thought only of uniting the two nations, of wiping out the distinction between conquerors and vanquished" and had, or so it seemed, "conquered only to be the monarch of each nation and the first citizen of each town."[8] That this was all too obviously not the historical Alexander, but the creation of the imagination of Plutarch, a first-century Greek living under Roman rule, was also largely beside the point. For it was Plutarch's Alexander who had been "sent by the gods to be the conciliator and arbitrator of the Universe,"[9] and who provided the model that every subsequent would-be European empire builder, from Scipio Africanus to Napoleon could honorably seek to emulate.

But there was a problem with this history of Oriental despotism. For centuries these Oriental despots had not merely outpaced the Europeans, they had even taken possession of large areas of the former Roman Empire. Why and how had these primitive tribesmen managed to construct extensive complex and highly sophisticated societies? In 1784 Volney could lament that everywhere he had gone in Egypt and Syria, all he had ever seen was "brigandage and devastation, tyranny and misery."[10] But he was aware—indeed, it was a crucial part of his argument—that three hundred years earlier the great Muslim courts of medieval Spain had been more refined, more sophisticated than anything in Christian Europe, and that so much of the ancient learning on which the Renaissance was believed to have rested—rightly or wrongly—had been transmitted to the West through Arabic translations. A ruler such as Mehmed II, the conqueror of Constantinople, on whom Voltaire heaped unstinting praise, was widely perceived as a man of great culture. Mehmed, who had Herodotus and Livy read to him in Greek and Latin, was, in some sense, the true bearer of the values of the ancient world—values that the Christians of the West, epitomized by the squabbling rapacious crusaders who were the real cause of the collapse of the Byzantine Empire, or the corrupt decadent modern Greeks, had long since abandoned. It was Mehmed, Voltaire pointed out, who had established an academy in Istanbul where ancient Greek—which the modern Greeks had all but forgotten—was taught, together with "the philosophy of Aristotle, theology, and medicine."[11]

All of this sat uneasily with the image of an "Oriental" or any other form of despotism. A century later, after Napoleon's brief attempt to replicate the deeds of Alexander in Egypt, and the virtual collapse of the Ottoman Empire—when the Islamic world had retreated to what we now call the "Middle East," a remote, abandoned, underdeveloped corner of the globe—the Islamic Renaissance could be argued away by Ernst Renan as an aberration, the work of Christians, Jews, Ismailis, Zoroastrians, and (since some of the great Islamic scholars, like Averroës and Avicenna, had been indubitably Muslims) "Muslims, inwardly in revolt against their own religion."[12]

In the eighteenth century, however, Islam, at least as represented by the Sublime Porte, was still a constant and powerful presence in Europe. True, the Ottomans were clearly in decline by the middle of the century; their fleets no longer menaced the coasts of southern Italy and Spain as they had once done, but the memories of the year 1683, in which an Ottoman army had stood before the gates of Vienna, still lingered in the European imagination. For many of the less-hostile observers of the East, it seemed as if the widespread European perception of the Orient, as of so much else, could only be explained by enduring prejudices bred of Christian superstition, which sought to cast all that was superficially different as utterly alien. What, asked Voltaire time and again in the *Essai sur les moeurs*, would a Persian or Turkish chronicler have made of the European feudal system? Does that seem anything less like the possession of the subjects by their sovereign than what actually prevails among Muslims? On any closer examination, not only did all Oriental societies differ quite markedly from one another—as France, say, differed from Venice—but even the most supposedly extreme of them, the Ottoman Empire, could not really be described as "despotic." It was, declared Voltaire, absurd to suppose that "the people are the slaves of the Sultan, that they own nothing of their own, that their goods and they themselves are the chattels of their master. Such an administration would destroy itself. It would be bizarre if the Greeks who have been conquered were not slaves, yet their conquerors were."[13] According to the fifteenth-century chronicler Philippe de Commynes, when Mehmed was on his deathbed, he had asked God's forgiveness for having taxed his subjects too heavily. "Where are the Christian rulers," asked Voltaire archly, "who have demonstrated such repentance?"[14]

In Voltaire's view, one of the strengths (as well as, ultimately, the weaknesses) of the Ottomans was that, unlike the Romans, who had attempted to transform the world into a single nation, the Turks, and the Arabs before them, had not. Neither had they, as the Mongol hordes in China had done, simply allowed themselves to be absorbed by the cultures they had conquered. The Ottoman sultan was indisputably a supreme ruler, but he was one who had not only allowed a great degree of freedom of cultural expression among his subjects, but had ruled them through local potentates. Once the conqueror had triumphed, the government was restored to the conquered.[15] In Voltaire's account, the Ottomans come out looking much more like the heirs of Plutarch's Alexander, than of Xerxes.

The imputation that Muslim societies had no laws beyond the whim of the ruler was also rejected as an absurdity. In 1778 Anquetil Duperron wrote a treatise entitled *Législation orientale*, which set out to demonstrate at great length that "the manner in which despotism has been represented until now," in Turkey, Persia, or India, "cannot fail to give anything but an absolutely false image of the government of these places." In each of these societies, there existed recognizable law codes that bound both ruler and ruled alike, and, crucially, "in these three states, individuals have property in both moveable and immoveable goods which they freely enjoy."[16] He was not alone either in his claims for the relative liberality of Muslim states, or in his indignation at the ill-informed manner in which they were generally depicted in the West. Even so uncompromising a European as Edmund Burke, in his struggle with Warren Hastings, went so far as to declare "the Mahometan law," as one "which is binding on all, from the crowned head to the meanest subject—a law interwoven with the wisest, the most learned, the most enlightened jurisprudence that perhaps ever existed in the world."[17] As for Persia, which, as the direct heir of the monarchy of Xerxes, was in all respects more civilized than either Turkey or India, "there is no monarchy," declared Voltaire, "where there are greater human rights" (*droits de l'humanité*).[18]

If the great Muslim empires were not truly despotic—or at least no more despotic than most European monarchies under the *ancien regime*—if they had until very recently been more than a match both militarily and culturally for most of the societies of Europe, what now explained the steady decline of the East, and steady expansion of the West? Why, as Voltaire phrased it, did we who "seemed to have been born only yesterday . . . now go further than any other people in more than one field?"[19]

Voltaire's question—which was also asked by most of his near contemporaries—was not merely about how Christian Europe had succeeded in outpacing the Muslim East, but rather how the "West" had succeeded in outpacing the "East." It was a question couched not in religious, racial, or anthropological terms, but rather one expressed in terms of a geography that assumed all peoples bore ineluctably the stamp of the environments in which they had been born. The answer, therefore, demanded an examination not only of the Muslim East but also of China.

The slow recognition during the eighteenth century that beyond India lay not the open steppe, but a great urban civilization about which the Ancients had known next to nothing, which changed the conceptual map of the world and greatly modified how the "East" was perceived in the West. Now, as Voltaire told Madame du Chatelet in 1740, in what was to become the "avant-propos" to the *Essai sur les moeurs*, if the new universal history was to trace the passage of civilization from East to West, it would have to begin with "a people who had a history recorded in a language which was already established before we had learned how to write."[20] Compared with them, he reflected elsewhere, the French were merely "men of yesterday, we descendants of the Celts who have barely cleared the forest from our savage lands."[21]

Although China had been incorporated in that vague geographical region known as the "land beyond the Ganges" since the fourteenth century, serious interest in the region had begun in earnest only with the Jesuit attempts to convert the Chinese ruling elites to Christianity in the sixteenth century. Even then, China was still thought to be so remote from the known world that Bishop John Wilkins, in his *Essay Towards a Real Character and a Philosophical Language* of 1668, could speculate that Chinese might be the original language of mankind, since the Chinese were so isolated that they could never have participated in the construction of the tower of Babel. Johann Gottfried von Herder—who seems to have conceived a passionate loathing for the place—described China as "thrust into a corner of the earth, placed by fate so far outside the connectedness of nations,"[22] as to play no significant role in human history.

Whereas the peoples of Asia to the west of the Himalayas were inextricably part of the unfolding history of Europe, those to the east were not. Here was another potential state of nature—much as America had been— only one occupied not by simple savages at the threshold of the historical process, but by highly evolved cultures, more ancient even than those of Eurasia, with technologies and forms of government comparable, and in many respects superior, to those of the Europeans. Yet they were—and this was the conceptual difficulty faced by all—not *sui generis*—like the Amerindians or the Africans and later the Pacific islanders, but, because they lay to the east of Europe, clearly had to be incorporated into an enlarged conception of Asia.

It was Leibniz, particularly in the *Noveaux essais* and the *Novissima sinica*, who established what, for many, was to become the enduring image of the virtues and vices of China. In Leibniz's view, what made China so unusual was that, unlike all the other nations of the world, it alone had adhered, as closely as was humanly possible, to a life governed by the law of nature. Because China apparently lacked any single dogmatic religious creed, let alone the competing sects that had turned Europe into a killing field for much of the sixteenth and seventeenth centuries, and because, like most Sinophiles, Leibniz took Confucianism to be a "religion of reason," China was credited with having succeeded in preserving what any reasonable person must assume to be God's wishes—where all the other world religions, in particular Christianity and Islam, had failed. Not that Leibniz was anything other than a Christian, but he could see, as he put it, that "the government of China would be incomparably better than that of

God, if God were as the Sectarian Doctors, who attach salvation to the chimeras of their party, depict him."[23]

For this reason, although Leibniz claimed that he had nothing against the church sending missionaries to China, "the condition of our affairs, slipping as we are into ever greater corruption seems to be such that we need missionaries from the Chinese who might teach us the use and practice of natural religion."[24] Even by the late seventeenth century, the Chinese had earned a reputation in Europe for being great craftsmen and ingenious designers. For Leibniz, however, their true merit was to be found in their morality. Ethics, he argued, was their true strength, because unlike the European ethical tradition since Aristotle, theirs was an ethics that eschewed metaphysical or theological speculation and adhered to education and conversation. "For the true practical philosophy," Leibniz wrote to Joachim Bouvet, the leader of the Jesuit mission in Peking, "consists rather in these good orders for education, and for the conversation and sociality of men, than in general precepts on virtues and rights."[25]

Leibniz had transformed the Chinese into the natural heirs of Socrates. But by insisting that they excelled in what he called the "precepts of the civil life," rather than metaphysics, he had also established a distinction between them and the Europeans. This made the Chinese into one more example, however exceptional, of the East, and would also serve to explain how, in the long run, Europe had succeeded in outpacing them.[26]

Leibniz's image of China as governed by nature's laws, rather than the laws contrived by squabbling priesthoods, was developed and extended by a number of successive observers throughout Europe. One of the most influential was the physiocrat François Quesnay. In a short treatise, entitled *Despotisme de la Chine*, which first appeared in *Ephémérides du citoyen* in 1767, Quesnay set out to explain another feature of the China phenomenon: the apparent longevity and stability of the Chinese Empire. Since the empires of Europe and Asia, both ancient and modern, had expanded and then collapsed, this had now come to be regarded as "so general that the irregularity of governments is attributed to the natural order."[27] Only the Chinese had apparently managed to defy this order. China's success in this respect, Quesnay believed, could be attributed to the fact that in China the laws of nature were sovereign and obeyed by all without question. In China it was not the government that was "despotic"—as Montesquieu had claimed—but rather nature's laws. And it was not so much morals that the Chinese had mastered, as Leibniz had argued, but rather, according to Quesnay, "the very physical laws of the perpetual reproduction of the goods necessary for the subsistence and the preservation of men"[28]—that is, economics. Only the Chinese had understood that nature's objective for mankind was prosperity. Only China had succeeded in trading military expansion—and the culture that had sustained it—for permanent economic growth.

It had achieved this, Quesnay believed, by taking the example of Cincinnatus quite literally. In this massive empire, agriculture had replaced warfare. And in Quesnay's view, only a truly agricultural nation can "establish a fixed and lasting empire under a general invariable government, subject directly to the immutable order of the natural law." This was why in China the farmer, not the warrior, was the exemplary man. And because the laws of nature were sovereign, rather than those of the status hierarchies of the feudal order, farmers could rise to positions of power and eminence unthought-of in Europe.

Compare this, demanded Quesnay, with the governments of the Western monarchies or the Ottoman sultanate, where the ruler was hemmed in by a court, isolated from his subjects, and his government conducted by a group of men who had come to power through hereditary succession. In China the emperor, as the supreme embodiment of the law, submitted himself to regular criticism by his subjects. In China the mandarinate was open to all who could pass an exam. True, there was an aristocracy, but this was crucially not one that carried an automatic right to public office. Above all, the laws of economics were "generally known among the ethical body of the nation, that is to say the thinking part of the people."

China had succeeded where all European empires had failed, because its ruler was not the representative of a social group, but the supreme embodiment of the law (and as such had to be absolute), while its ruling elites, because they had been chosen for their intellectual and moral qualities, were the selfless agents of the common good.

But although Quesnay's China offered a model of stability and what today we would call "sustainable growth," it could not escape what Leibniz had already identified as a nation's greatest potential weakness. Stability and cohesion, however achieved, were evidently highly desirable, particularly among the warring European nations, but they could only be acquired by abandoning that competitiveness which alone would allow for the progress of the sciences. The Chinese, wrote Leibniz, "certainly surpass us, in practical philosophy that is the precepts of ethics and politics adapted to the present life and use of mortals," but they lack logic, geometry, metaphysics, and astronomy.[29] In short they lack the sciences, and without the sciences no intellectual progress is possible. China, as Montesquieu had argued, had stifled all resistance and all change through the elaboration of a complex system of rites, and the use of a writing system of such complexity that an intellectual was simply he who could master the largest number of characters. China had become frozen in time, stable but immobile.

Quesnay also argued—against Montesquieu, who had insisted that China, like all despotic states, was ruled by fear—that the Chinese emperor's power derived from the love he inspired in his subjects.[30] But love could also be a form of fear: fear of offense, fear of disfavor, fear of dismissal. China was in effect one large family in which, as Voltaire phrased it, "paternal authority has never weakened." According to Voltaire, "the learned mandarins are looked upon as fathers to the towns and provinces, and the king as the father of the empire. This idea, rooted in the hearts of all, makes of this immense state one family."[31] According to Diderot, this was one large family in which every Chinese person was subject to a double tyranny: "paternal tyranny within the family and civil tyranny within the empire."[32] Or as Weber would say later: in China "the fetters of the kin group" had never been broken. The outcome had been an excessive veneration of the past, which—Voltaire again—"makes in their eyes perfect all that is ancient."[33]

This immobility linked the Chinese to the peoples beyond the Himalayas. India, as Voltaire said, had remained unchanged since the time of Alexander.[34] In the lands of the Turks, Persians, and Arabs, culture, the arts, and the sciences had made almost no progress since the great flowering of the Middle Ages, a flowering that had also been built very largely upon Greek sources. Similarly in China, wrote Voltaire, the sciences had become "fixed at the same point of mediocrity where they were amongst us in the Middle Ages."[35]

This brings us back to Volney ruminating among his ruins. If indeed the scepter had passed to Europe by the end of the eighteenth century—then why? Why had Europe risen again from the ruins to which the barbarian invasions had reduced it, while Asia, all the way from the China Sea to the Hellespont, had stagnated and decayed after an initial period of furious imperial expansion? Montesquieu believed that he had found the answer in the climate of the respective regions. Asia has no temperate zone, is locked in a constant struggle between extremes in which weak nations (from the torrid south) face strong nations (from the frozen north): "therefore one must be the conquered, the other the conqueror." (David Hume's observation had been that if it was true that northerners had always plundered southerners, then that had nothing to do with climate, and everything to do with poverty. The north was poor, the south rich.) In Europe, however, the strong had always faced the strong, which provided a situation of balance achieved through almost constant struggle: "which is why liberty never increases in Asia, whereas in Europe it increases or decreases according to circumstance." Although Montesquieu believed that this equation "had never before been observed," it did not win many adherents.[36] Climate was recognized as a social factor, but there were also the populations of modern Greece and modern Egypt to remind one, in Voltaire's words, that "if there was irrefutably proof that climate influenced the character of men, government always had a far greater influence."

Although the Europeans might have started later than the Chinese or the Persians, they had now overtaken both. This was not because of climate or because of some peculiar property of the "Oriental" mind, which inclined it to slothfulness and imitation—although there were those who believed in such inclinations. If human nature was, in Hume's celebrated phrase, "so much the same in all times and places, that history informs us of nothing new or strange in this particular," then the reason for the differences among the various peoples of the world had to be sought elsewhere than in supposed natural dispositions. Nations might indeed have characters, but those were acquired, not innate. What had led to the "scepter of civilization" passing to Europe had been the fact that, unlike their Asiatic neighbors, the Europeans had succeeded in developing the metaphysical and inquiring attitudes toward nature—science, or as Weber would put it more bluntly, "reason"—which had given them greater understanding of, and ultimately mastery over nature.

"We pursue," wrote Herder, "the magic image of a sublime science and universal knowledge, which it is true we shall never attain, but which will hold us in pursuit as long as the constitution of Europe endures." By contrast, even the most successful Asian empire had "never engaged in this contest." "Behind its mountains," he went on, "orbicular China is a uniform and secluded empire; all its provinces, however different its peoples, governed by the principles of an ancient constitution, are in a state not of rivalry with one another, but of the profoundest obedience."[37] And what applied to China applied equally to the Muslim and Hindu worlds, for different reasons.

It came down to this: Europe's success in the modern world was due to a complex balance of opposites. It was competition that had driven Europe on, and on. This was not an especially new idea. The first-century Greek geographer Strabo had suggested similar dynamics. The Roman historian Sallust, followed by Machiavelli, had argued that it was precisely the conflict between the plebeian and patrician classes in Rome that had sustained the Republic. Slavery and undue reverence for the dictates of past generations were the things that stifled innovation and, above all, made the advance of science impossible, for true science depended upon three things: competition, the recognition of the need for interpretation rather than simply repetition, and the free communication between peoples. The Europeans had somehow succeeded in preserving their capacity for liberty and thus invention, even after the fall of Rome. The nomadic horseman who had invaded Europe had been Europeanized, which effectively meant Romanized. Edmund Burke remarked that "the old Gothic customary [law] . . . [had been] digested into system and disciplined by the Roman law."[38]

The Mongols had undergone a similar process in China. Sinicization had drawn them down from their horses. It had then transformed them into Mandarins—cultured, polite, civilized, and immensely moral, as even the weary Henry Ellis who accompanied Lord Amherst to Peking in 1816 was prepared to admit. Sighing, however, he asked: who would not "rather again undergo fatigue and privations among the Bedouins of Arabia, or the Eeliats of Persia, than sail along . . . in unchanging comfort on the placid waters of the imperial canal?"[39] The immobility of the Chinese state had absorbed the power of its Mongol invaders, and in the process had deprived them of what might have driven the Chinese to develop the sciences that, given their long history, would have made them far superior to the Europeans. In India the caste system had performed much the same immobilizing role. Though in Herder's view "more learned, more humane, more useful, more noble" than any of the other religions of eastern Asia, what he calls "the Brahmanical system" had transformed all the arts and sciences into the "secret science of one caste," with the inevitable result that it had remained locked into "deception and superstition."[40]

The Islamicized hordes had swept through the centers of Asian and European civilization until, by the seventeenth century, Suleiman the Magnificent had overreached even the ambitions of Xerxes, and come to a halt just beyond the Danube. But the Ottomans too had lost the energy that had once been theirs. Like the Mongols, the Turks had maintained an empire through the extension of what are now called "tribal conquest states." Unlike the Mongols, however, they had not overrun closed patriarchal societies that might have stripped the Turks of their capacity to change and thus progress. Instead, the peoples conquered by the Ottomans, particularly the Greeks, had been the preceptors of modern Europe, and the Ottomans had, indeed, learned a great deal from Persian and later Byzantine society. But they had not learned enough to move far beyond the raid-and-plunder stage of human history. The Ottoman state had fulfilled the ambitions of its Achaemenid predecessors by much the same means as they. The modern Turks knew nothing, as Voltaire pointed out, about modern economics, extraordinary taxation, or advanced loans. They were not haunted by the specter of public debt. "These potentates," Voltaire wrote, "know only how to accumulate gold and precious stones, as they have done since the day of Cyrus."[41] Safavid Persia might have been a partial exception to this rule, but even in Persia, by the closing years of the eighteenth century, the scene was almost as ruinous as the one Volney had witnessed in Ottoman Syria. And in Persia, too, the sciences, which had once been equal to those of the Greeks, had perished "by the changes in the state."[42]

Why? The answer to this question seemed to lie in the nature of Islam itself. Most eighteenth-century observers took a far more dispassionate view of Islam than previous generations had done. But Islam remained more than a religion; it was also the basis of civil law. And this had prevented the development of anything resembling an independent interpretative position toward religion. Such interpretations of the Koran as did exist were, as Voltaire put it, "little more than a recommendation not to dispute with the wise." Even the word "Islam" itself, as he pointed out, signified resignation, acceptance of the word of God.[43]

Only Europe had finally succeeded in preserving its ancient past in a transformed revitalized world brought about by the barbarian invasions. But even in Europe it had been touch and go. Both Christianity and Islam, which Volney contemptuously described as "those self-proclaimed universal sects" (*"ces sects soi-disant universelles"*),[44] shared not only a common mythology and a common theology but also were similarly governed by a priesthood dedicated to limiting the human desire for innovation and change. Christianity, no less than Islam, had done its best to stifle the energy that barbarian invaders had brought to the remains of Rome. For centuries, during the Dark Ages, Christianity had succeeded in keeping Europe far behind even its Muslim, let alone its Chinese, rivals. In Europe, however, science—or to put it more broadly, "enlightenment"—had finally succeeded in triumphing over the obscurantism that was an integral part of all religion. And it had succeeded in so doing because the church was beset by a fatal flaw. Unlike that of Islam, Christianity's sacred book had not been written as a code of laws. Indeed, Christ had specifically repudiated any link between the secular and the sacred, as had generations of Christian theologians. Furthermore, although the New Testament recorded the words of God, it did not claim to have been dictated by him. It could not, therefore, escape the need for interpretation; and interpretation resulted inevitably in schism and confrontation. The Wars of Religion that had devastated Europe between the mid-sixteenth century and the Treaty of Westphalia had been disastrous in all but one respect—they had finally freed the European imagination from what Jean D'Alembert, in the *Discours préliminaire* to the *Encyclopédie*, described as "all the so-called Science [*Science prétendue*] of the centuries of ignorance."[45] In the genealogy of "Enlightenment"—*le siècle des lumières*—which D'Alembert provided at the beginning of his *Essai sur les éléments de philosophie*, it was Calvin and Luther who, for all their dogmatism, by destroying the authority of the Catholic Church, prepared the way for the rationalization of the seventeenth century, exemplified by Descartes. D'Alembert designated the outcome variously, as the "state of civilization," this "age of reason," this *siècle de philosophie,* an age that was, above all, an age of criticism.[46]

Throughout the East, however, and for very different reasons, criticism had been stifled; "reason" and "enlightenment" had never made any significant headway against entrenched tradition. In the end, if Asia was Europe's "Other," this was because unlike Africa or America, Asia had always been seen as Europe's place of origination. Even China, which had no historical connection with Europe, by virtue of its antiquity and its obviously high level of civilization, belonged to the same cultural orbit. And Asia would always be there, as Volney had seen, to remind the Europeans that if they ever allowed themselves to follow the paths of the "believers and saints," they too could end up like the Asians. Some new race of empire builders would then stand by the banks of the Seine, the Thames, or the Zuidersee, there to "weep alone amidst the ashes of the peoples and the memories of their greatness."[47]

CHAPTER FOUR

'Doux Commerce, Douce Colonisation'

Diderot and the Two Indies of the French Enlightenment

Sunil Agnani

> Let us stop here and place ourselves back in the time when America and India were unknown. I address myself to the most cruel of Europeans, and I say to them: there exist many regions which will furnish you with rich metals, with appealing clothing, with delicious dishes. But read this history and see at what price this discovery is promised to you. Do you, or do you not want it to take place? Does one believe that there could be a creature so infernal as to say: I WANT THIS. Well! There will be no single moment in the future where my question would have the same force.—Denis Diderot, 1780[1]

> What do these forts which you have armed all the beaches with attest to? Your terror and the profound hatred of those who surround you. You will no longer be fearful, when you are no longer hated. You will no longer be hated, when you are beneficent. The barbarian, just like the civilized man, wants to be happy.—Denis Diderot, 1780[2]

First the traveler, then the philosophe: This couplet is as important to the story of eighteenth-century intellectual history as is the revolutionary and the philosopher, or the soldier and the statesman. As a variation on this, I would also add the administrator and the philosophe as another vital pair of complementarities and antagonisms. This study considers two texts by Denis Diderot with a view to investigating the significance of some of these doubles. The first text is rather well known, although it has of late sparked or been reilluminated by scholarship with a greater degree of historical specificity.[3] I refer to Diderot's *Supplément au voyage de Bougainville*, which is set in the South Pacific (though it is a South Pacific of the mind as much as of the seas, and this is part of my consideration). What one finds when looking at the writings of the philosophes is in part a lucid demonstration of the now widely recognized but still debated thesis of Orientalism: the traveler and the administrator undertake to gather and collect information, and this in turn plays a vital role in informing the technologies of management and government.[4] But this is to go straight to the apparently menacing outcome of an initially rather innocent or pure act: I mean the desire, as Diderot remarked in the *Encyclopédie*, to note down and to "collect all the knowledge that now lies scattered over the face of the Earth."[5] It is here that we may locate many of the secondary reflections, as one could call them, upon the initial reports from the field: the famous considerations of natural man by Rousseau in his *Discourse on Inequality*; the various footnotes throughout the work of Kant, even in his aesthetic works, to the Caribs, to Africans, and so on; and Diderot's peculiar and parodic remarks upon Tahiti in the *Supplément*. But all along there are interruptions in this smooth continuum, which connects the traveler or administrator to the philosophe, disrupting the apparent imperatives for empire, land acquisition, or trade.

One of the primary flaws of the debate around Orientalism, at least within the discipline of literary studies, may have been to lay too much emphasis solely upon the question of representation.[6] Constrained by the terms of this debate, I too begin by commenting upon the question of representation in Diderot's work. I hope, however, to attach these observations to a set of keywords in the political lexicon of the period that circulate among the writers of these works. I must first reiterate one link between the question of representation—in this case, of the native or of native society—and political analysis, which pertains more specifically to the concept of hegemony.[7] In order to operate, hegemony requires constant repetition and reiteration; in one formulation, it depends upon coercion and consent (and it is the presence and importance of the latter, consent, which make it amenable to some forms of liberal political thought). I introduce this idea primarily to illustrate what one finds throughout Diderot's later political writings: unwilling to accept the necessity of coercion as an element of colonization, Diderot both attempts to imagine in many different formulations how this project could be undertaken by means of consent, participating in a set of representations that legitimize dominance of one kind, *and* frequently fractures this image. In the *Supplément*, this is evident by his undermining of the truth-claims of Antoine de Bougainville's original text, and in his use of an imagined Tahitian Other to flay the priest and cleric in France.

Composed during the period 1770–73, the *Supplément au voyage de Bougainville* was short and relatively coherent, not widely published in Diderot's lifetime, and circulated as an underground manuscript (perhaps because of its sexually scandalous nature). By contrast, the second text under consideration is much more scattered, anonymous in its initial editions, and only in the mid-twentieth century was Diderot's authorship conclusively verified. I refer to his contributions to the immense and fascinating work known as the *Histoire philosophique et politique des établissements et du commerce des Européens dans les deux Indes* (1770, hereafter *Histoire des deux Indes* or *Histoire*).[8] The ten-volume work was edited by the abbé de Raynal, and went through three editions (1770, 1774, and 1780).[9] This much one can learn from reading the brief selection of material present in a recent edition of Diderot's *Political Writings* (1992),[10] but there are several other aspects of this massive work that are hardly visible from the excerpts presented there. Diderot's involvement in the three editions increased with each publication, and he was said to have thoroughly rewritten the third edition by spending as much as fourteen hours a day at the task. His contributions, by many estimations, amount to approximately one-third of the 1780 edition.[11]

The subtitle to this study aims to lay stress upon the notion of the "two Indies," extending a thought implied by the structure of Raynal's work, which moves at times from Occident to Orient, from north to south. Indeed, the two are not identical images of each other; not exactly twin Indies, not *les Indes jumelles*.[12] Yet the affinity suggested in such a work between *les Indes occidentales* and *les Indes orientales*, in conjunction with a shift between *l'Amérique septentrionale* and *l'Amérique méridionale*, brings out a quality that is quite striking to the contemporary reader: the link between the old colonies and the newer ones in this colonial encyclopedia, or—to put the matter in other terms—the relation established between the New World and the Old World. One sees the same distinction at work in Edmund Burke's writings on India, which are fundamentally shaped by events in the New World: by this I mean events both in North America and in the West Indies. In the writings of both Diderot and Burke, there is ample evidence to sustain Anthony Pagden's helpful distinction in this period between the "new" and the "old" colonies.[13] The old or first colonies refer to those in North and South America, while the new or second colonies refer to the growing importance of Asia to European colonialism in the eighteenth century. We see this axis of comparison everywhere in the *Histoire des deux Indes* (beginning with the organization of the contents of the ten volumes), in travelogues from the period, in administrator's memoirs, and in the movement of such military figures as Charles Cornwallis, leaving Yorktown in Canada for Bengal. In addition to this axis of comparison is the second between North and South America within the New World; one could attempt to enumerate the typologies of this discourse in order to understand their various functions.[14]

This second opposition between North and South America will become increasingly important as comparative reflections of the fate of societies and man in the various regions of the New World proceed in the nineteenth century. This comparison is at work in some of Tocqueville's reflections in *Democracy in America* when he wonders why "no nations upon the face of the earth are more miserable than those of South America," in spite of it enjoying an isolation from enemies and a geographical richness akin to North America.[15] Often this distinction between North and South America becomes a shorthand for several other oppositions having less to do with geography than with religion. One could mention here Voltaire's positive evaluation of the behavior of the Quakers in North America for winning over and persuading the Indians by commerce, in contrast to the methods commonly used, in his view, by the Jesuits in South America.[16]

There are two foci to my examination. The first concerns Diderot's exploration of the possibility of a colonialism that is consensual; I refer to this as *douce colonisation* (the phrase is my own, coined on analogy with "*doux commerce*").[17] The second theme is related to this by the transposition of reciprocal consent to the intimate sphere, where it thereby pertains to *métissage* or breeding. The two elements are also both related to issues of population and settlement. The discussion of procreation, and of population as a form of wealth in the *Supplément*, derives from the larger consideration of the settlement of colonies (part of *douce colonisation* or "soft colonization"). The *Supplément* supplies the occasion to introduce these topics, while the *Histoire* allows for their elaboration and contextualization.

DOUX COMMERCE AND BREEDING

As a word on its own, breeding has many divergent valences, to which the title of this section refers (from manners to animal husbandry to biology). One comes upon the notion frequently when examining the *Histoire*, which is caught in the whirl of discussions around the possibilities of commerce in the period. Yet tied in with this economic debate is an essential relationship to sexuality, and this occurs via a notion of wealth as it is yoked to the emerging idea of population in the period. To summarize: an empty continent, or empty island—to use the example given by the Tahitian native in Diderot's *Supplément*—obviously needs someone to labor upon it (so it was argued, following a logic stated in its clearest form in Locke's *Second Treatise of Government*, the "agriculturalist argument," as it is sometimes named). Wealth, both in the *Histoire* and in the *Supplément*, is often explicitly understood as population—an idea not surprising to scholars of the French eighteenth century, where one finds many writers concerned with the depopulation of one continent (North America) in a manner linked with the depopulation of another (Africa). On the one hand was the accidental ethnocide of disease alongside the intentional effects of conquest (as popularly reported, whether accurately or not, by De Las Casas in an earlier period); on the other hand was the concomitant forced migration of Africans as slave labor. Two continents' native populations, it was argued, were thereby jeopardized.[18]

There are two or three different ways I understand breeding to operate in Diderot's work that may hold more generally in related late eighteenth-century French Enlightenment debates (keeping in mind that this forms a part of the plural Enlightenments that scholars such as Pocock have suggested as a more accurate way of understanding this period). Consider, schematically, the following: (1) What role does breeding play in Diderot's understanding of consensual colonialism? (2) How does Diderot understand the figure of the Creole? (3) What is the relation of wealth to population, and of these two terms to breeding? and finally (4) How does Diderot understand the idea of a "directed" or "rational breeding"? In addressing these questions, it is also important to speculate on how the larger issues of political economy and population are tied into Diderot's thoughts on the intimate relations that are possible between colonizer and colonized.

THE *SUPPLÉMENT AU VOYAGE DE BOUGAINVILLE*

1. With other eighteenth-century writers and thinkers, it is often easy to push aside questions of sexuality. Though Edmund Burke's language and rhetorical presuppositions are everywhere dependent on sexual difference, particularly in his *Philosophical Enquiry into the Origin of Our Ideas of the Sublime and Beautiful*, but even in his *Reflections on the Revolution in France* (as Wollstonecraft was quick to point out in her rather prompt reply, *A Vindication of the Rights of Men*), it is rare that one finds more explicit political pronouncements on these matters in his work. This, however, is impossible to avoid when one turns to Diderot, who everywhere bears some oblique and at times more direct relationship to the theme of libertinage in the French Enlightenment. It should not be

surprising that someone whose first novel, *Les bijoux indiscrets*, concerned physical bodies, sexuality, and the exotic in a humorous and bizarre mixture should return to the question later in his writerly life. (Perhaps it was for this reason that Michel Foucault declared in the opening line of the fourth part of his introductory volume on the *History of Sexuality*, "The aim of this series of studies? To transcribe into history the fable of *Les Bijoux Indiscrets*.")[19]

Indeed, what is striking about the *Supplément* is the centrality of sexuality and gender. Any reading that focuses only on the exotic and the anthropological elements without considering in some cursory way their relation to these aspects will miss what is both most distinctive and peculiar about the work. The *Supplément* is sometimes read as protofeminist, or at least as a hymn to the freer sexual ways of Tahitian society in relation to Europe. Other critics have considered it an expression of Diderot's "anarchic" strain of thought.[20] We should, however, be wary of calling it either feminist or anarchic, while recognizing that the text raises important issues pertaining to colonialism and gender.

The sexual liberation that Diderot presents is part of a male fantasy structure, in addition to the reliance upon an underlying heterosexual matrix. Men are still the sexual keepers of women; what is described is a social structure in which women are passed to men for breeding. What might be seen as liberation is actually the use of female labor and procreation for the "wealth" of society, and we can thereby tie together several terms in this work. The emphasis in the text on the circulation of human bodies as commodities[21] should be linked to the language of French political economy in the period. The focus upon bodies may be a contrast with prevailing physiocratic views of land as a source of wealth, though Diderot's relationship to that school was changing over the course of his life.[22] Is Diderot proposing that labor power in the form of human bodies capable of work is in fact a truer source of labor? If so, this is why such a view should be connected with the colonial fantasy of open land (that is, land to be labored upon), which is quite central to the text. One instance of this is when Orou rhetorically asks the chaplain why we place such an emphasis on population, and answers himself, "if you wish to judge its value [the value of the French male visitors mating with Tahitian women], imagine that you had still two hundred leagues of coastline to navigate, and that every twenty miles the same tribute [of mating] was collected from you. We've vast tracts of untilled soil; we lack hands and asked you for them."[23] The open coastline and vast tracts that must be settled demand a populace to exert labor upon them; that these hands are "asked" of the European visitors is also significant. Thus, in a preliminary way, we can argue that there is some link between population, sexuality, and colonial fantasy; and all of these fit into Diderot's theory of political economy.[24]

2. One should take note of the form of the text, namely the role of parody and comedy in undercutting what otherwise would be a too-serious effort at the gathering of knowledge. Here we can recall the subtitle—or rather the full title—of the work: *Supplement to the Voyage of Bougainville, or Dialogue Between A and B on the Inappropriateness of Attaching Moral Ideas to Certain Physical Actions That Do Not Accord with Them*. The prying apart of the moral idea from the physical action—primarily the negative pall cast upon human sexual activity by Christianity—is the aim of Diderot's critique. There is also a contrast made between the empirical effort of the scientific ethnography and Diderot's parody of it in the form of a pseudo-ethnography. However, if it is overstating the case to call the original an ethnography, it would be more accurate to say that the object of his parody is Bougainville's traveler's tale, with its claim to a truth beyond fiction (though often the genre of the traveler's tale made use of novelistic techniques).

I would also call attention to the genre of the work—the philosophical dialogue—familiar since Plato's establishment of the form. Thematically, too, the *Supplément* echoes aspects of the *Republic*'s discussion regarding the design of the *kallipolis* (the beautiful or ideal city). There Plato argued for the common ownership of women and children, the elimination of notions of "mine and thine"; here, in Diderot's *Supplément*, these efforts are apparently realized.[25] Tahiti as an actual historical referent is bracketed, as it were, by Diderot's clever and humorous use of the traveler's account. The dialogue contains within itself the critique of its claims to veracity, as when Diderot cuts from the conversation between Orou and the chaplain back to A and B. After the chaplain discusses his lapses of restraint with several of the Tahitian women, A and B comment to each other:

A: I warm to this polite chaplain.
B: And I much more to the manners of the Tahitians and remarks of Orou.
A: Though they show a rather European influence.
B: I don't doubt it.[26]

This appears to be a humorous sign of the self-awareness of the work, a wink to the reader that Diderot knows he is making fast and loose with Tahiti as a place, and Orou as its spokesperson. This is also why there is a great emphasis on the many levels of mediation in the text: Orou is said to translate the old man's speech from his vernacular to Spanish, which he knows, and this is transcribed into French.[27] Thus there are two filters between the text we read and the original speech.

The original recedes, and at times is fully inaccessible, as when one speaker says to another: "The chaplain remarks in a third fragment which I've not read to you that the Tahitian doesn't blush."[28] What B has not read to A, but apparently has in his possession, is the *absent* original text.

3. Nature, the term really under investigation, is what Diderot self-consciously makes the center of his philosophical dialogue. For Diderot, the layers of civilization that have accreted in civilized societies over natural man may fall away when he reaches the colonies. The savage and the monk, the natural man and the artificial, Tahiti and Europe—all these are used to lead to the idea of relativism. Or so it seems. It may be that the question—as to which of these oppositions may be better—is itself being thematized in order to interrogate the basis for such a cultural critique. In contrast to later writers on exotic locales, although Diderot emphasizes the heightened physicality of the Tahitians, he does not seem to argue that this comes at the expense of rationality. The dialogue opens with the Tahitian seeming to be fully other-directed, altruistic, sexually free, and uninhibited; to be working basically within a gift economy. But then there is a moment in the dialogue where Orou says, "however savage we are, we know just how to scheme."[29] This follows his explanation for their apparent generosity: "While more robust and healthy than you, we saw at once that you surpassed us in intelligence, and we immediately marked out for you some of our most beautiful women and girls to receive the seed of a race superior to ours. We tried an *experiment* which may still bring us success" [emphasis mine].[30]

This passage depicts a kind of self-improving native who works by directed "breeding." Though eugenic in its etymological sense, it is a self-willed or collectively undertaken decision, and not imposed externally from above (the role of the state is certainly much more central to the twentieth-century understanding of the term). This is Diderot's fantasy of a controlled experiment in interbreeding, in a directed *métissage*—a theme that recurs in the *Histoire des deux Indes*. The idea of a calculating native may be part of a standard stereotype, inasmuch as with the Oriental or savage there was always the possibility of an inversion: the passive Oriental suddenly is represented as wily and conniving; the lazy savage as menacing. Nevertheless, in these passages from Diderot, the native—while healthy and vigorous—is also represented as fully rational. Orou is rather the very picture of a philosophe himself.[31]

With regard to the masculine domination of Tahitian society as portrayed by Diderot, the idea of women as the property of men is addressed directly in the dialogue by A and B: it is in consequence, they remark, of the early introduction of the idea of property that many ill effects follow.

The end of the dialogue, where Diderot initiates a characteristic "call to arms," is a key passage in part because it illustrates a style of expression that appears often in the *Histoire des deux Indes*. Diderot presents a lengthy list of the wrongs of European society in the mouth of B: "Orou explained it ten times over to the chaplain. . . . It's the tyranny of man which converted the possession of woman into property."[32] This critique of woman as property allows Diderot to declaim against the unnecessary practices of modesty and constancy; his genealogy shows these to have been formed as virtues and vices only as a consequence of this flawed beginning. All of this is due, once again, to the falling away from nature: "How brief would be the codes of nations, if only they conformed rigorously to that of nature."[33]

As noted earlier, Diderot, perhaps unsurprisingly, does not question the heterosexual relation between man and woman. This obvious remark yields more insight when we relate it to the political economy that he envisions, wherein sexual activity must be productive, like any other labor. In order to be a man, it is implied, one must procreate. Thus the chaplain, in Orou's eyes, is emasculated because he refuses to mate. When he does succumb, Orou tells him, "My first thought was that Nature . . . had deprived you of the ability to reproduce your kind. . . . But, monk, my daughter told me that you are indeed a man, and robust as any Tahitian."[34]

THE *HISTOIRE DES DEUX INDES*

In shifting from the *Supplément* to the *Histoire des deux Indes*, we move from a literary conte to a work that does not operate by these conventions but itself makes some of the same claims to truth as the text that Diderot parodied and drew upon, namely Bougainville's original *Voyage autour du monde*. Nonetheless, many of the themes and questions that animate the *Supplément* appear in this work; questions merely latent in that work regarding the relation of the economy to sexuality and population are explicitly discussed in the *Histoire*. One of these would be the question of interbreeding with an indigenous population. We therefore find in the *Histoire* several examples that attempt to conceive of an alternative to the outcome of depopulation (of the New World by the activities of the Spanish, and of Africa by the slave trade) and yet carry on the imperative to colonize. Suggesting that European colonizers arrive and intermarry with local populations thus seemed a more "humane" way to civilize and settle a territory. In the *Supplément*, as we have seen, the solution imagined is one in which this activity would be undertaken with the *consent* of the colonized. The Tahitians realize the superiority of their visitors in certain domains, and hope to benefit from this (as we learn in the surprise revelation of their crafty calculations, turning the economy of the gift into the self-interest of the exchange).[35]

The motif of population within Diderot's thought is rather widespread, and brings together many disparate areas of his thinking. Although I focus on its relation to his views upon the ideal form colonialism could take, we see it even in relation to Diderot's views on the church. Writing in the *Histoire* about reforms that should be undertaken to ensure the church's subservience to the state, Diderot writes, "The vow of chastity is repugnant to nature and diminishes the population; the vow of poverty is only that of an inept or lazy person. The vow of obedience to some other power than to the dominant one and to the law is that of a slave or an outlaw."[36] Diderot decries the vows that the clergy must undertake; his argument against the vow of chastity is based both on the naturalist idea of sexuality already discussed and its effect on diminishing population. The core of Diderot's views on the matter of population are, however, most clearly expressed in a passage added to the 1780 edition within a discussion of national character (*esprit national*). Diderot presents a theory of national character as deriving from both variable and constant causes, and further distinguishes the national character from the code of behavior that determines the actions of individuals, who generally will not hesitate to build their "own prosperity through public ruin." Diderot correlates, on the one hand, national character with the nation's capital city in particular; on the other hand, he takes as his figure of the quintessential individualist the person who has traveled farthest from this metropolitan capital. This is the colonist, who loses any trace of national character when he passes "beyond the equator." Instead he is capable of "whatever crime will lead him most quickly to his goal." Diderot concludes that "this is how all the Europeans, every one of them, indistinctly, have appeared in the new world."[37] The opposite, therefore, of the *esprit national* is manifested on an almost mathematical inverse ratio of distance from the capital; in fact, it is this theory that enables Diderot, unlike most other thinkers of this period, to account for the contradiction of the fine phrases regarding liberty at home and the despotic practices undertaken abroad.

But what solution to this contradiction does Diderot propose? We are brought back to the recurring fantasy: "Would it not have been more useful and humane, and less costly, to have taken to these distant regions a few hundred young men and women? The men would have married the women of the country, and the women the native men. Ties of blood, the strongest and most immediate of bonds, would soon have formed a single family out of the natives and the foreigners."[38] The argument operates by an appeal to self-interest alongside a claim to greater moral good (for example, "more useful *and* humane, and less costly"), which is characteristic of the political language of the period (compare Burke's notion of "graft[ing] benevolence even upon avarice").[39] Here this idea is joined to Diderot's idea of rational breeding, undertaken by the colonizer with the colonized. But rather than posing the opposition of the parties to this encounter in dichotomous terms, "the foreigners and natives of the country," Diderot imagines that "a single and uniform family" will be produced by consanguinity.[40] The consequence of this encounter is described in terms demonstrated by the narrative of the *Supplément*. The intimate relationship (*liaison intime*) would lead the primitive inhabitant (*l'habitant sauvage*) to realize that the arts and knowledges that are brought to him (*qu'on lui portait*—the original brings out the form of address more strongly) are superior and would lift him from his state. The manner used by these soft colonizers, or imploring and moderate teachers (*instituteurs suppliants et modérés*), would lead the natives to submit themselves to them "*sans réserve.*" This absence of reserve can serve as an index of the degree of dominance *with* hegemony that Diderot imagines is possible.

What is the outcome of this "*douce colonisation*"? Out of the "*heureuse confiance*" peace would emerge, impossible with the "*ton impérieux*" normally employed by masters and conquerors. Diderot had no doubts that this event would be fully compatible with the mercantile aims of empire: "Commerce establishes itself without trouble between men who have reciprocal needs, and soon they become accustomed to seeing as friends and as brothers those whom interest or another motive leads to their country."[41] (Note the importance of introducing the language of kinship in order to legitimate such an order.) Though the different editions of the *Histoire* express conflicting degrees of optimism on the role of commerce in the development of *les mœurs*, overall it is striking how pervasive this sentiment is.[42] It may seem unusual in hindsight to see commerce as unambivalently furthering the progress of *lumières*, especially after the nineteenth century, the Industrial Revolution, and Marx's language used to describe the extraction and drain that characterize (in some analyses) the colony-metropole relationship.[43] However, it is a familiar echo of Montesquieu's language of *doux commerce*, and the Scottish Enlightenment's discussion of commercial society in the four-stage theory. Moreover, it should be understood within the context of the burdensome structure of French absolutism in the 1770s; in relation to this, commerce is equated with a kind of liberty.[44] It also may owe something to Diderot's response following a visit to Holland in 1773, when he initially expressed the widespread admiration held by many philosophes in the period for the small merchants of that country— an enthusiasm tempered in his later reflections.

Let us return to the passage cited earlier to examine a second consequence that Diderot imagines follows from *douce colonisation*, one that
is perhaps surprising given the tenor of Diderot's other writings on the
subject of religion: "The Indians would adopt the religion of Europe, for
the reason that one religion becomes common to all the citizens of an
empire when the government abandons it to them, and when intolerance
and the madness of preachers does not become an instrument for discord."[45] The view presented here does not seem as relativistic as that presented in the *Supplément*, since both the civilization and the religion of
Europe are assumed to be self-evidently superior but *tainted by their
mingling with force.* Civilization, as he says in the next line, will be
adopted by inclination so long as one does not demand this be adopted
"*par la force.*"[46] Though this passage does not present us by any means
with a consistently anticolonial position, I would still argue against the
views taken by many scholars of Diderot's political evolution that this
greater pessimism about the claims of alterity represents Diderot's aban-
donment of "primitivism" for a more "realist" view. Laurent Versini,
editor of an important recent edition of Diderot's works, neglects the elements of a genuinely radical critique that appear throughout his corpus
of writings.[47] It is for this reason—the internal contradictions—that
Duchet, influenced by French structuralism of the 1960s and 1970s, introduced the term "*écriture fragmentaire*" to describe the *Histoire des
deux Indes.* Further, and more to the point for my argument here, she
notes that it is precisely these inconsistencies of the work that should interest us as much as the statement of a consistent political position. By dis-
missing the philosophes' evident curiosity about the primitive and concern
for various colonies, others have argued that

[b]y the final edition the colonies had become something of a pretext; any Frenchman reading the *Histoire* [*des deux Indes*] in the tense political atmosphere of
the 1780s could not fail to realize that he was being called upon to recognize the
fact that a radical turning point had been reached in the destinies of France and
Europe, and that this active participation was required to usher in a new order.[48]

This argument unnecessarily reduces the implications of the *Histoire* by
reading it within an exclusively European context. To assert that all ten
volumes are merely coded ciphers for a critique actually directed against
French absolutism is unpersuasive.[49] This would presume precisely what
should be examined, namely a political perspective that makes a claim to
liberty within the European context but does not see it as necessary that
this critique should be extended or applied in a more genuinely universal
manner—that is, in Europe's colonies as well. What is, after all, striking
about such a work as the *Histoire* (with its numerous contributors) is that

so many figures in the 1780s and 1790s were beginning to conceive of *the globe*, of the movements of commodities and populaces in this larger frame of analysis, and with their movement the concomitant movement of ideas and cultural practices. And this reflection was undertaken not in a peripheral work of the period, but in fact, as Robert Darnton notes, in one of the period's veritable best sellers.[50]

Certainly the implications of such an *écriture fragmentaire* are everywhere apparent, even—or rather particularly—in the modern edited collections and translations of the *Histoire* that have been made. There is, for example, a final paragraph to the section I have been discussing that is left out of the recent English selection of Diderot's *Political Writings*.[51] After the claim that the Indians would accept the religion and ways of the Europeans provided they were not tainted by force, Diderot writes, "Such would be the happy effects which *the most imperious attraction of the senses* would produce in a colony which is being born. Absolutely no armaments, no soldiers, but plenty of young women for the men, and plenty of young men for the women" [emphasis mine].[52] In an incipient colony, the imperious tone (*le ton impérieux*) of the masters (Diderot's phrase in the earlier passage) is here turned into the most imperious attraction: an overwhelming reciprocal sensual attraction. Arms and soldiers replaced by an abundance of young women for men, and vice versa. Note that here Diderot does not imagine a shipload of male conquerors arriving on this primal scene who would mate with native women (closer to what occasionally did happen), but rather both European men and women pairing off with native men and women. It is as if Diderot wishes to mitigate the force associated with conquest by replacing the antagonism between colonizer and colonized with physical, sexual attraction between male and female on both sides. By recourse to this libidinal economy, he is able to elaborate a more consensual model of colonization. Thus, even Diderot's "principles of colonization"—as the English title for this excerpt would have it—are tied to his idea of rational breeding.

Why Diderot felt compelled to answer this question concerning the legitimate basis for colonization is clear to anyone who has read Raynal's general introduction to the ten-volume edition. Raynal writes: "Europe has everywhere founded colonies; but does it know the principles upon which one ought to found them? Can one not discover by what means and in which circumstances [one ought to]?"[53] Once Diderot felt he had come upon a consistent principle (and perhaps here one could make a link between Diderot's earlier novels on sexual themes and his straightforward proposed "solution" to the dominance involved in the colonial encounter), he was not hesitant to apply it in many contexts. Diderot's dealings with Russia and with Catherine II were quite extensive (including his visit of

1773 to Saint Petersburg), but some remark should be made on the amusing scheme he devised to spread the spirit of freedom among the Russian people, who were at present too accustomed to the despotism under which they labored. In fact, this may be one source of the views he expressed in the 1780 edition of the *Histoire des deux Indes*. In the opening pages of his *Observation sur le Nakaz*, Diderot writes, "The Russian empire occupies an area of 32 degrees in latitude and 165 degrees in longitude. To civilize such an enormous country, all at once, seems to me a project beyond human capacity, especially when I travel along the border and find here desert, there ice, and elsewhere all kinds of barbarian."[54]

The scale of Russia leads Diderot to make several proposals: first, to move the capital to the center of this land mass; second, to appoint someone to civilize one district within it.[55] The third proposal, of particular interest to my argument here, is related to the second:

The third thing would be to introduce a colony of Swiss people, and situate it in a suitable region. Guarantee it privileges and freedom, and grant the same privileges and freedoms to all subjects who entered this colony. The Swiss are farmers and soldiers; they are loyal. I know by heart all the objections that can be raised against these methods; they are so frivolous that I shall not take the trouble to reply to them.[56]

This passage fits more clearly with Diderot's general principle of a noncoercive persuasion of the native, which one finds dispersed throughout his writings on the primitive. This facet of the passage just cited is clearer if we read it alongside section XXXVIII of *Mélanges pour Catherine II*, which is entitled "A Systematic Idea for the Manner of Leading a People to the Sentiment of Liberty and to a Civilized State."[57] There Diderot writes,

If I had to civilize savages, what would I do? I would do useful things in their presence, without saying or prescribing anything to them. I would maintain an air of working for my family alone and for myself.

If I had to build up a nation to [the sentiment of] liberty. What would I do? I would plant a colony of free men in their midst, very free ones, such as (for example) the Swiss, whose privileges I would protect very securely. And I would leave the remainder to time and to the force of example.[58]

Here I will only point toward a more complex question on the general problem of freedom in Diderot's late political thought, which he feels relies upon the principle of imitation, as here with the imitation of the Swiss. Can the former primitive ever be original, or is he or she condemned to only the *imitation* of the free?[59]

Yet in order to return to the question of breeding in relation to an envisioned noncoercive colonial encounter, I should here cite one of Diderot's most explicit considerations of the racial implications of such a policy, found in his discussion "*sur les Créoles*" (in the 1770, 1774, and 1780 editions). The arguments that Diderot gives in favor of this practice explain the striking analogy with the family noted earlier when he remarks that "consanguinity" produces one "large family."[60] Regarding the Créoles, he writes that "[t]he physical advantage of crossing races between men as between animals, in order to retard the bastardization of the species, is the fruit of a secondary experience, one which comes after the utility recognized in uniting families in order to cement the peace of societies."[61] Indeed, earlier his argument that the European male and female settlers should mate with their counterparts had been made from the point of view of utility. That argument provided a sociopolitical reason for interbreeding, which is here supplemented by a biological argument in favor of it. "The Creoles are in general well made. Hardly does one see a single one afflicted with the deformities so common in other climates. History does not reproach them with any of the cowardices, betrayals or baseness which soil the annals of all peoples. Hardly could one cite a single shameful crime which a Creole has committed."[62] Thus, in the improvement of the race is also produced a docile colonial subject, one unlikely to rebel. What better harmonization of interests could one hope for?

This gentle colonialism coexists in the *Histoire des deux Indes* (often on the very same page) with passages that excoriate the crimes of Europe and rail against slavery. Diderot's voice seems to find its most forceful expression from within the security of anonymous authorship, which allows him to adopt a strong, hortatory tone. The countless passages where he switches to the second person, addressing the reader as "*tu*" or "*vous,*" enable him to accuse and to speak in a prophetic mode. If we keep these in mind alongside the arguments proposed in favor of *douce colonisation*, then we can attend to the contradictory nature of this work (as Duchet urges). But I do not make this remark simply to indicate a formal, epiphenomenal aspect of the *Histoire des deux Indes*. It also seems to me that we can thereby examine this work within the complex field of texts and authors that has been addressed by such important studies as Uday Mehta's *Liberalism and Empire*.[63] In the French context, Duchet, for example, writes about "humanitarianism and anti-slavery," and, considering the policy of interbreeding, she argues that wherever there was a crisis in labor—a labor shortage because of the impossibility or impracticality of slavery—interbreeding with the natives was suggested.[64] Interbreeding, in this sense, is one answer to the crisis caused by the growing antislavery movement. Humanitarianism in France is akin to liberalism in Britain; slavery akin to the coercive aspects of empire. Just as arguments against slavery are shown to have a more practical basis in political economy, so too the arguments against empire (for example, Adam Smith's anticolonialism moved between a moral argument and an argument concerning efficiency). Both humanitarianism and political liberalism served as alibis for empire by providing a degree of moral legitimacy.

Of course, within the period, the arguments put forth for the abolition of slavery often took on a moral or even religious character. However, Raynal himself had something to say about this effort at explanation, arguing against those who would "give honor to the Christian religion for the abolition of slavery. We will dare not to be of his opinion. It is when there is industry and wealth in the people that the princes value them as something significant. It is when the wealth of people can be useful to kings against the barons that the laws improve the condition of the people."[65]

And so we begin to close the unusual circle connecting the terms we have traced in the *Supplément* and the *Histoire des deux Indes*; it is commerce that should be extolled for spreading wealth among people and for bringing about the abolition of slavery. This view of commerce, in turn, should be connected with the critique of absolutism implicit in Raynal's observation. It provokes Diderot to bring together this argument regarding commerce with the primary subject of the *Histoire*—namely colonialism: "In these mercantile societies, the discovery of an island, the importation of a new commodity, the invention of a machine, the establishment of a trading post . . . the construction of a port become the most important transactions, and as a result the annals of peoples will demand to be written by *commercial philosophers*, just as they were formerly written by speaking historians" [emphasis mine].[66]

These future commercial philosophes who take the place of "speaking historians" indicate Diderot's search for a kind of writing and insight that would match the radical transformations wrought by these discoveries and innovations. From the language of this passage, one might be tempted to think that Diderot had Adam Smith's *Wealth of Nations* in mind; the paragraph opens with the words "A spirit of trucking and exchanging is being established in Europe,"[67] which recall the famous lines about man's proclivity to truck and barter. However, this passage dates from 1774, before the publication of Smith's work—in fact, Smith frequently cites the *Histoire* as his source in his chapter "Of Colonies."[68] It seems, therefore, that what we have here is an example of the prophetic voice in operation.

The *Histoire des deux Indes* itself, I would suggest, attempts to fulfill the very desire that Diderot expresses in the work. Faced with the scale of the discoveries for European science, Diderot dreams of a method that some would later identify with the modern discipline of anthropology:

The discovery of a new world can alone furnish the food for our curiosity. A vast land lying fallow, humanity reduced to the animal condition, open country without harvests, treasures without possessors, societies without civilization [*police*], men without mores: How could such a spectacle not be full of interest and instruction for a Locke, a Buffon or a Montesquieu! What reading could be as surprising, as moving, as the narrative of their voyage! But the image of raw and wild nature is already disfigured. One must make haste in gathering the half-erased traces, after having described and delivered over to contempt the greedy and ferocious Christians which an unfortunate chance led first to this other hemisphere.[69]

In retrospect, one can see in this statement many of the notable achievements, as well as the constitutive flaws of modern anthropology. The *Histoire des deux Indes* is at times an attempt to be this reflection of John Locke, had he actually visited North America and seen the Indians of the Carolinas, or of Montesquieu had he actually visited Persia and China. And like the later *tristesse* that would strike Claude Lévi-Strauss, there is also an urgency and a haste to undertake this project before the traces of the primitive fade away, only to become objects of nostalgia for European society. This temporal relation to the future is apparent throughout the work; it is that of the future anterior, the will-have-been—in this case, the will-have-been-destroyed, and accounts for the haste. Hence, in posing the question to the European (cited in the first epigraph), whether you still wish that the Americas had been discovered, Diderot writes that "there will be no single moment in the future where my question would have the same force." Natural man was discovered, and in his discovery was lost. The "philosophical fiction" for a moment entered indicative prose, only to vanish back into the imagination.

"THESE NEW HERCULES": TOWARD A TRAVELING PHILOSOPHY

That the dream was not Diderot's alone is clear from another passage to which, it strikes me, the philosophe was responding—perhaps directly. In 1754, tucked away in a lengthy ten-page footnote to an essay that made an effort to answer a question posed by the Academy of Letters at Dijon (the very same academy through which Raynal would later pose his question on the settlement of the New World), a citizen of Geneva complained that:

For the three or four hundred years since the inhabitants of Europe have inundated the other parts of the world, and continually published new collections of voyages and reports, I am convinced that we know no other men except the Europeans; furthermore, it appears, from the ridiculous prejudices which have not died out even among men of letters, that under the pompous name of the study of man everyone does hardly anything except study the men of his country. In vain do individuals come and go; it seems that philosophy does not travel.[70]

So wrote Jean-Jacques Rousseau in the *Discourse on Inequality* as he reviewed the achievements of European travelers, which he asserted were limited mainly to the study of natural sciences. Rousseau wishes that two men, one of great wealth and the other a scientist, would undertake a voyage to study "not always stones and plants, but for once men and morals,"[71] which rather directly corresponds to Diderot's call for a "*philosophe commerçant*" or commercial philosopher. That the primary discovery of such travels thus far was also circumscribed by the vision of the one who sees, as Rousseau here asserts, perhaps also informed the witty aside by one of the speakers in the *Supplément* concerning Orou's remarks that "they show a rather European influence." Yet, to my mind, more interesting than any play of mirrors (between self and self-as-other) is Rousseau's criticism that philosophy did not travel, which Diderot's "traveling philosophy"—described in the passage cited above from the *Histoire*—was meant to supply. Rousseau notes that virtually all the information one has on the two Indies derives from unreliable sources, since "there are scarcely more than four sorts of men who make voyages of long duration: sailors, merchants, soldiers, and missionaries."[72] The first three, according to Rousseau, cannot be relied upon as good observers, while the fourth (missionaries) are more concerned with their "sublime vocation."[73]

For all of these reasons, Rousseau wishes that those who voyaged were of another disposition; in fact, he wishes that Diderot himself (among others) might undertake to travel "as Plato did":

The academics who have traveled through the northern parts of Europe and the southern parts of America intended to visit them as geometers rather than as philosophers . . . we know nothing of the peoples of the East Indies [*des Indes Orientales*] who have been frequented solely by Europeans more desirous to fill their purses than their heads . . . Let us suppose a Montesquieu, Buffon, Diderot, Duclos, d'Alembert, Condillac, or men of that stamp traveling in order to inform their compatriots, observing and describing, as they know how, Turkey, Egypt, Barbary . . . the Malabars, the Mughals, the banks of the Ganges . . . then, in the other hemisphere, Mexico, Peru . . . Let us suppose that these new Hercules, back from their memorable expeditions, then at leisure wrote the natural, moral, and political history [*L'histoire naturelle morale et politique*] of what they had seen; we ourselves would see a new world [*un monde nouveau*] come from their pens, and we would thus learn to know our own.[74]

I have not been able to ascertain whether this passage had any direct effect upon Raynal as he formulated the *Histoire philosophique et politique* . . .

des deux Indes (note the similarity and variation from the title Rousseau proposes above), or Diderot in his capacity as editor and contributor; more striking to me is the sentiment. In its desire to mix philosophy and travel, to produce a more comprehensive and encyclopedic account of "the new worlds" to be seen, these citations attest to the global vision of much eighteenth-century prose, and the desire of many to undertake this "Herculean labor." But, one might ask, to what end?

CONSENSUAL COLONIALISM AS A CONCEPTUAL LIMIT: THE *HISTOIRE DES DEUX INDES* AND THE CONTRADICTIONS OF LIBERAL THOUGHT

The line cited in the first epigraph, "there will be no single moment in the future where my question would have the same force," is an example of the *production* of nostalgia, an affect that necessarily contains within it a temporal element. It is linked to the operation of a future anterior: not simply the will-have-been, but rather (morosely) the will-have-been-destroyed. In this case, the will-have-been-destroyed refers to the tribal cultures of the primitive that Diderot foresees disappearing completely from the earth with the expansion of Europe.

Diderot's views on the possibilities and limits of colonialism as *"douce colonisation"* can be more keenly imagined and hoped for by Diderot precisely because it precedes the classical period of imperialism in the nineteenth century. More on his mind is the reform of the methods employed by Spanish colonists in the New World. Thus arises a turn to breeding, by means of the concept of population—itself derived from debates on political economy in the period. Not only is breeding, or interbreeding, a kind of libidinal sublation of the political conflict presented between colonizer and colonized, but it is also presented as a rational decision on *biological* grounds, whose end result is imagined to be a docile colonial subject—a docility inscribed in biology. In this earlier period, mixture of this sort can be solely considered from a biological viewpoint (at the exclusion of a focus on the psychology of colonialism, more clearly a legacy of modern movements of decolonization). If we are not, however, presented with a glimpse of the interior experience of the colonized, we are given an exterior vision that perceives fragility, a vulnerability of the societies that Europe is encountering.

It is the vulnerability that is expressed as nostalgia in the future anterior. The newness of this sentiment, of the vulnerability of societies and ways of life—many of which have indeed ceased to exist—should be seen as the impetus behind the call for the new genre of prose for which Diderot had no name. In seeking this worldly prose, was Diderot dreaming of anthropology in the modern sense? In any case, one finds here the same paradox noted by Walter Benjamin in his essay on the "oral" tales of Nikolai Leskov: The very possibility of the appreciation of their oral quality was already a sign of the demise of orality itself.[75] Only in its passing away did the shimmer of a fading aura become visible. And so it is here, the birth of an anthropological imagination was only possible when the complete obsolescence of these manifold societies was imagined (glimpsed so early—in 1780); it was also underwritten by a vision of the globe constructed from the geography of many European empires, whose contours are traced in the very form of the *Histoire des deux Indes*: the Dutch, the Portuguese, the Spanish, the French and English colonies. The *Histoire* is therefore a testament to and key document in the prehistory of the modern concept of globalization, in that it envisions both a global form of hegemony and gives inklings of global forms of counterdominance that were to emerge—such as the famous prophetic lines on an imminent rebellion led by a black slave incarnating the figure of Spartacus.[76] Toussaint Louverture was, in fact, rumored to be one such reader of the *Histoire*.[77]

This should be connected with a primary thesis concerning the relationship between liberalism and empire: empire was the *historical space* within which liberalism as a *political practice* and coherent set of political beliefs emerged. What does one do with this apparent contradiction? Is this a contingent historical overlap, or is there some more immanent constitutive flaw to political liberalism? This reading of Diderot aims to trace one set of linkages among consent, hegemony, and dominance—particularly the fantasy of a dominance with hegemony, a submission "without reserve." Consensual colonialism, the expression of this fantasy and also of a conceptual limit, is thus a political formulation that can exist *within* liberalism, and we may thereby have a better sense of the evolution of that other peculiar institution of the nineteenth century, liberal imperialism.[78]

CHAPTER FIVE

Adam Smith and the Anthropology of the Enlightenment

The "Ethnographic" Sources of Economic Progress

Christian Marouby

Several decades ago, British social science historian Ronald Meek traced (in *Social Science and the Ignoble Savage*) the genealogy of a fundamental paradigm of evolutionary anthropology—the model he aptly called the Four-Stage Theory[1]—from its early adumbrations in the classificatory attempts provoked by the European discovery of the Americas to its first mature and lasting formulation, in the early 1750s, by Turgot and Smith. This formulation of a crucial anthropological paradigm by the two major Enlightenment founders of economic theory only highlights the initial connection between the two nascent disciplines: each stage of anthropological development, defined according to an increasingly productive mode of subsistence, is also a stage of economic progress. Or conversely, to emphasize the direction I pursue in the following pages, the theory of economic progress is originally grounded in an anthropology.

Since Meek's pioneering work, it seems we have become ever more conscious of this essential connection between the speculations of early anthropology and the development of economic theory in the Enlightenment. So much so that I would be tempted to say, at the risk of overstating the case, that the late eighteenth-century triumph of the notion of a universal human progress—at once anthropological and economic—may well be one of the most important long-term intellectual consequences of the discovery of the Americas. And yet what has received surprisingly little attention since Meek's compelling demonstration is precisely *what* contemporary anthropology this theory of progress was founded on. Which sources did early economist theorists use among the already considerable "ethnographic" documents available by the mid-eighteenth century? On which of the great contemporary essays and discourses on origins did they primarily draw for their inspiration? And most important, what inflections, what interpretations of these sources enabled them to arrive at what might be called an anthropology of growth?

In any attempt to answer these questions, the work of Adam Smith must occupy a privileged and exemplary position. This is not only because—however fair we may regard the judgment of posterity—Smith has obviously been much more famously influential than any of his French or Scottish Enlightenment contemporaries, so that he alone could lay claim to being considered a "founder of discursivity," but also because the connection between anthropology and economics in his work is not only pervasive but remarkably explicit. Anyone who has opened the *Wealth of Nations* knows that from the very first page we are greeted by the dramatic appearance of "the savage nations of hunters and fishers" who are "so miserably poor, that, from mere want, they are frequently reduced . . . to the necessity sometimes of directly destroying, and sometimes of abandoning their infants, their old people, and those afflicted with lingering diseases, to perish with hunger, or to be devoured by wild beasts."[2] And as this strategic positioning rightly leads us to expect, this is only the first of many references throughout Smith's masterwork.

At each major turning point in his development, Smith again refers to the example of peoples at various stages of progress, and notably the first, the "rudest state" in which humanity can be known to exist, and whose living illustration Smith sees, as so many of his contemporaries, in the "savage nations of America." Nor is this "anthropological" interest limited to the great economic work of Smith's maturity. In the *Lectures on Jurisprudence* that he had taught as early as 1751–52, illustrations drawn from "ethnographic" reports are, if anything, even more abundant and extensive. This is, of course, not the place to retrace the whole genesis of Smith's thought, but to remind ourselves that from the very beginning— as Meek had already shown—anthropological preoccupations are coextensive and even foundational for a theory of economic progress. And this is not only "genetically" so, but also by virtue of a necessity inherent in the universalizing project itself. Smith could have been content with inquiring into "the nature and causes of the wealth" of modern, commercial nations, and that is indeed what he does for the greater part of his great book. But he also wants to give his theory—this is, of course, how he is so much a part of the Enlightenment project—a universal and natural foundation. That is why the notion of economic progress has to be grounded in an anthropology—both in the sense of an empirical description of all the variously advanced peoples on the face of the earth, and in the sense more usually favored in the French use of the word: in a conception of human nature. In the beginning, economic progress must be naturalized.

It is remarkable in the case of Smith that this process is almost transparent. For Smith's anthropology, unlike that of some of his famous contemporaries, is by no means entirely speculative or imaginary. He had evidently read many of the travel narratives and accounts of "savage nations" available in his days, and, most fortuitously for the present project, we have a fairly precise idea of what those are. Thanks, on the one hand, to the explicit bibliographical references by Smith himself in the *Wealth of Nations*, and even more often in his *Lectures on Jurisprudence*, as well as those later identified in the scholarly editions of his work, but also, on the other hand, to the additional information and confirmation provided by the extant catalogue of his personal library[3]—and the overlap between the two lists thus constituted is nearly complete—we are able to establish with a high degree of assurance the corpus of the ethnographic documents Smith had actually read and used (see Appendix). This body of "ethnographic" documentation is not only extensive, but fairly representative of the range of information available in the later Enlightenment, including such major works as those of Charlevoix and Lafitau,[4] who by Smith's own estimation had given "the most distinct accounts" of the populations that are his primary example.[5] Adam Smith's anthropology, which has famously been labeled "conjectural" by Dugald Stewart,[6] would also seem to lay claim to a significant empirical basis.[7]

And yet things are not so simple. While Smith does refer to, and occasionally quotes, a wide range of identifiable ethnographic documents in support of his argument, a comparison between these sources and Smith's own anthropology reveals a pattern of selections, of misreadings or interpretive moves, and of outright omissions that on closer examination appear not only highly visible but also highly significant. One could be tempted to describe such patterns as reading strategies, if the term did not connote a higher degree of systematicity and intentionality than is probably involved. Let us say then, although the term may now be too weak, that the comparison brings out a series of crucial *inflections* of the original sources, unsystematic but by no means random, driven as they are by a theoretical *telos*, since, as shown below, they are governed by a kind of necessity at the heart of Smith's anthropological argument.

The first of these tropes is not so much anthropological as demographic. And it is, as indeed are most of those I outline here, strangely familiar, not only because of its widespread acceptance in the thought of

the long Enlightenment—this is Adam's Smith exemplarity—but because
it has remained remarkably resilient until our own day, at least in the popular imagination. This first inflection is a systematic minimization of the
size of populations at the first or "hunting" stage. "In a nation of hunters
and fishers," asserts Smith in the *Lectures on Jurisprudence*, "few people
can live together, for in a short time any considerable number would destroy all the game in the country, and consequently would want a means of
subsistence. Twenty or thirty families are the most that can live together."[8]
In the first version of the same *Lectures*, he had mentioned "thirty or forty
families," and even ventured a total population estimate: "about 140 or
150 persons,"[9] which he seemed to want to confirm on the next page by
the number of "hunters" engaged in military expeditions: "It is impossible
that 200 hunters could live together for a fortnight. They could not find
subsistence by the chase in so large a body."[10] In the *Wealth of Nations*,
the estimated range is slightly higher: "An Army of hunters can seldom exceed two or three hundred men. The precarious subsistence which the
chace affords could seldom allow a greater number to keep together for
any considerable time."[11] Let us pass over the possible contradictions between these different numbers, and the problems of adducing total population numbers from the size of war parties. Neither do I suggest that
Smith should be confronted with demographic studies of aboriginal populations that were only undertaken in the second half of the twentieth
century—although these show that he was manifestly wrong by huge
margins[12]—but the comparison between his numbers and those found in
his own sources is sufficiently telling.

The most complete and precise on this subject is Arthur Dobbs's book
on the Hudson Bay region, which Smith mentions explicitly in the *Wealth
of Nations*. Dobbs gives a detailed account of the different tribes allied
with the Six Nations of the Great Lakes region—Smith's prime example
for the "hunting" stage—also focusing on the number of warriors or
fighting men. And he does indeed indicate, for the "Iroquise Unihkil-
lyiakow," "about 30 towns, each of about 200 fighting men." This corresponds to Smith's estimate (if we ignore that there are thirty such
"towns" for just this one tribe), but it is also Dobbs's lowest number. For
the other nations, he lists "towns" providing four hundred, six hundred,
and eight hundred "able men," and several supplying one thousand warriors each[13]—obviously only a proportion of much larger populations.
William Douglass, whose *Summary* is repeatedly referenced by Smith,
gives numbers of fifteen hundred fighting men for the Algonquins, and six
thousand for the "Chirakees."[14] There is no need for detailed extrapola-
tions to see that the numbers provided by Smith's own sources are much
greater than the 150 or even 200 he allows as a maximum population for

"hunters," and there must be some powerful motivation on his part to ig-nore, or at least to drastically minimize this evidence. And indeed Smith has already admitted what is at stake here. It isn't a question, as in Buffon (whose support Smith nevertheless seeks out), of demonstrating the al-leged generative weakness of the American continent, nor of seeking to alleviate the bad conscience of Europeans for the depopulation of the same. More fundamentally, the point is for Smith that the mode of subsis-tence corresponding to the first stage *cannot* sustain anything but a tiny population without threatening its own resources. It must be conceived, he has already told us, as inherently "precarious."

But this precariousness depends in turn on a conceptual move that is even more fundamental, a prior inflection that should by rights have come first, since it has been under our eyes from the beginning—except that this figure has since then been so familiar, and has remained such a part of our anthropological imaginary, that it may have become invisible to us. I am, of course, speaking of the reduction of the first stage—we have already seen it a dozen times—to the age of "hunters." That is to say the exclu-sion, or at least the marginalization, of collecting or gathering. Adam Smith, who has advocated and usually practices a "simple and direct style" (which does not exclude a masterful use of rhetorical modes, as Vivienne Brown has shown)[15] is not prone to the kind of troubled textuality—not to speak of the lyricism—we have come to recognize in the writings of Rousseau on the same subjects. And yet the exclusion of gathering is the occasion of a rare but unmistakable moment of textual tension in his work, as if such a reduction could not quite be achieved without leaving a trace. "If we should suppose," Smith begins in one of his *Lectures* in a typical conjectural mode, "10 or 12 persons of different sexes settled in an uninhabited island, the first method they would fall upon for their sus-tenance would be to support themselves by the wild fruits and wild ani-malls which the country afforded."[16] The gathering of "wild fruit" is at first recognized on a par, in an exact parallel with the hunting of "wild animalls." But then in the next three short sentences, Smith thrice denies—the classic figure of denegation—its importance as a mode of subsistence: "The sole business would be hunting the wild beasts or catching the fishes. The pulling of wild fruit can hardly be called an employment. The only thing among them which deserved the appellation of a business would be the chase." As a result of which Smith can safely conclude: "This is the Age of hunters."

There is probably no need to insist on the heaviness of the rhetorical apparatus (their "*sole* business"; "can *hardly* be called"; "the *only thing*"), nor is it perhaps necessary to point out what nexus of powerful cultural dispositions, if not prejudices, operate in this reduction. The well-known privilege of hunting, still highly recognized in the eighteenth century, and the accompanying prestige of a diet based on meat, prevalent to this day in Western societies, make it appear "natural" for Smith and his contemporaries to imagine that the initial mode of subsistence of humanity would have essentially been dependent on hunting, and only marginally on plant stuff, just as they "naturally" conceived of the second stage as "pasturage," instead of cultivation.[17] But the consequences of this reduction for the alleged precariousness of the first stage are momentous. We now know that except in the marginal conditions of subarctic regions, hunter-gatherers the world over relied on the collection of plant foods for more than half, and frequently more than 70 percent of their diet.[18] Of course, there again, Adam Smith cannot be faulted for ignoring studies in economic anthropology that were only undertaken in the 1960s.

But what about his own sources? There is no doubt that hunting and fauna tend to take pride of place in the accounts of natural resources used by native populations—which is hardly surprising given how impressed early Europeans were by the abundance of wildlife in the New World—but side by side with the varieties of game, they also list an equal abundance of vegetable foods, not just available, but heavily relied on for most of the year. Smith cannot have missed, for example, the testimony of the same William Douglass I mentioned earlier: "Their bread-kind are mays, or Indian corn, phaseolus, kidney or Indian beans, several sorts of tuberous roots called ground-nuts; several sorts of berries, particularly several sorts of *vitis idea*, in march, where hunting and fowling is inconsiderable, they carry with them, for subsistence, parched Indian corn called no-cake."[19] Nor could he have overlooked the remarkably complete and precise enumeration to be found in Pehr Kalm's *Travels in North America*, a book he also refers to explicitly in the *Wealth of Nations*. The passage[20] is too rich to be discussed in detail here, but Kalm identifies an extraordinary variety of vegetables, fruits, berries, nuts, and roots, as well as *folle avoine*, a wild grain that was not just collected, but literally harvested. The impression given by such accounts, rather than scarcity, is one of profusion of plant as well as animal resources—a profusion that should seemingly have given Adam Smith some pause, and cannot be so easily dismissed. But as if that were not enough, Smith is in fact confronted, as the attentive reader may already have noticed in the preceding examples, with an even more serious problem for his construction of the first stage, one that forces him into some of the most spectacular denegations of his own anthropological sources.

This problem, only technical in appearance but a veritable thorn in the side of Scottish Enlightenment anthropology, is the undeniable presence

of agriculture among the populations that are its prime example of the
first stage.[21] In this respect, Smith and his contemporaries were out of
luck. All the peoples they knew about, whether in South, Central, or
North America, practiced some form of agriculture. There were authentic
hunter-gatherers in California, but they had not been described, and as
far as the other parts of world where existing cultures would have fit the
first stage, Smith knew of the Hottentots of southern Africa (pastoralists),
but not of the famous !Kung or San of the same region, and the first
sketchy reports on the Australian Aborigines—our other classic example
of hunter-gatherers—only reached Europe with Cook's journals, too late
to serve for his purposes. Adam Smith, therefore, had to make do with the
Americans as his best example—indeed as his only example—of the first
stage. And that is a problem, because according to the "four-stage" theory, agriculture should only appear at the *third stage*. "We find accordingly," Smith observed in the *Lectures*, "that in almost all countries the
age of shepherds preceded that of agriculture," adding that indeed "the
whole of the savage nations which subsist by flocks have no notion of cultivating the ground." But then there is the all-too-visible anomaly of
American agriculture, which all his sources clearly document, in particular the "most distinct accounts" he had found in Charlevoix and Lafitau.
Smith seems for a moment willing to concede the point: "The only instance that has the appearance of an objection to this rule is the state of
the North American Indians. They, tho they have no conception of flocks
and herds, have nevertheless some notion of agriculture." But it is only to
dismiss it in the next sentence with all the rhetorical power he can muster:
"*Their women plant a few stalks of Indian corn at the back of their huts.
But this can hardly be called agriculture.* This corn does not make any
considerable part of their food; *it serves only as a seasoning* or something
to give relish to their common food; the flesh of those animalls they have
caught in the chase." And once again, having saved the rule from the exception, Smith can safely conclude on the natural progression from the
first to the second stage: "Flocks and herds therefore are the first resource
men would take themselves to when they found difficulty in subsisting by
the chace."[22] The rhetorical move, admirably transparent, is almost identical to the one Smith used to marginalize gathering, and it serves the same
purpose. A fact is first acknowledged the better to be dismissed.

Thus, Smith's theory benefits from what might be called the *empirical
effect*, by seemingly taking account of the observations of "ethnographic"
documents, while at the same time going against the evidence of those observations. Even a cursory reading of Smith's sources makes it clear that
the real staple food of those same "North American Indians" was the famous *sagamité*, a corn gruel, and that if anything served to "season it"

and to "give it taste"—as Lafitau had observed, using the very same words we have just seen Smith borrow to say the opposite—it was, on the contrary, the less-common product of hunting.[23] Why such a blatant "misquotation" of what Smith considers one of his best sources? In a sense, what is at stake here, what must be "repressed," is the same as in the first example of rhetorical dismissal: the possibility that plant foods might provide a substantial, perhaps even a dominant part of resources at the first stage. But with the possibility of agriculture, those stakes are much higher. When Smith dismissed gathering as a significant "business," he most probably really thought that "the pulling of wild fruit" could not make a substantial difference to the subsistence base of a "hunting" economy. The possible practice of deliberate plant cultivation by those very populations he considered the model of the first stage had to appear much more threatening to him. It isn't simply that, as we have seen above, the appearance of agriculture before pastoralism would call into question the theory of a universal progression through four distinct stages. That, after all, would only be a "theoretical" problem, and it could be tolerated as an exception, or explained by exceptional local conditions.[24] But for Smith, agriculture is not simply a different and more advanced mode of production, it is the most productive, because "in agriculture," as he writes in the *Wealth of Nations*, "nature labours along with man," adding that "the most important operations of agriculture seem intended, not so much to increase, though they do that too, as to direct the fertility of nature towards the production of the plants most profitable to man."[25] One could well wonder why the "fertility" of nature, or as he writes in an earlier chapter, "the spontaneous productions" that she brings forth "with such profuse abundance"[26] are not recognized by Smith as equally "profitable" to the activities of gatherers, and contributing to making the first stage a condition of natural affluence. In any case there is no doubt that for him to admit that the "savage nations of America" practiced agriculture would change everything: it would make it impossible to maintain the thesis of their "precarious subsistence." For this reason alone, it must be dismissed.

However, this dismissal, like that of gathering, has another consequence, or perhaps another cause. Whether intentional or not, it betrays yet another cultural disposition, or prejudice, equally long-standing, if not, thankfully, as persistent in Western modernity as those we have already seen to operate, but at least as momentous: the tendency to marginalize the productive (as opposed to reproductive) function of women. The attentive reader will no doubt again have noticed that in the preceding passage, it was "their women" who "plant[ed] a few stalks of Indian corn at the back of their huts," a gender division of labor that can only contribute to further discrediting the economic value of their activity, which, Smith concluded, "can hardly be called agriculture." Concentrating on economic analysis proper, Kathryn Sutherland has documented a systematic tendency in the *Wealth of Nations* to underestimate the importance of women as producers.[27] Our present focus on anthropological assumptions would only reinforce her argument, for Adam Smith's sources make it abundantly clear that women, and women almost alone, were responsible for the cultivation of the "fields," and for much else besides. For example, as Charlevoix observed in the second of Smith's "most distinct accounts of the manners of those nations": "Besides the care of the household, and the provision of wood, the women are almost always solely charged with the cultivation of their fields."[28] Indeed many observers, like Charlevoix, complain that women bear the brunt of productive activity, and work much harder than the men: "As for the men, they glory in their idleness, and in effect pass more than half of their lives doing nothing, convinced that daily work degrades a man, and is an obligation only for women"[29]—an observation whose implications should have alerted Smith, and which I discuss below.

Regarding the question of the gender division of labor, which can now be extended back to the dismissal of gathering, Adam Smith's sources are perfectly consistent with what we know of the respective contributions of men and women among hunter-gatherers. Human societies are capable of almost infinite variations, and there have been instances of men participating in gathering, and even cases, less frequent, of women who hunted. But it remains that the classic pattern—confirmed by innumerable observations; indeed, one of the few "patterns of culture" that seems to authorize generalization—is that in hunting and gathering societies, men hunt and women gather. This is veritably the most ancient division of labor. It is therefore all the more striking to see how Smith, for whom this concept is perhaps the most fundamental of all, interprets his anthropological data. He recognizes the division but dismisses the labor, and for his vision of the first stage, this has the most serious consequence. Whether or not we take into account the anomaly of American agriculture, and however prudent we may want to be as to the relative importance of gathering, we arrive at the same conclusion: by failing to recognize the contribution of women, Adam Smith is not only doing them a grave injustice, but depriving the age of "hunters" of half of its resources.

It must now become clear that a vision of the first stage as a state of *deprivation* is precisely what Smith needs in order to give his economic theory an anthropological basis. The status of this "need" and of this "in order to" is, of course, highly problematic. For all the preceding attention to rhetorical or strategic effects, I have been trying to avoid the suggestion of intentionality, which seems to me undecidable. Neither is it a question of Smith's sincerity—even if it is sometimes difficult to reconcile his interpretations with his sources. Rather it is a question of theoretical necessity, or *telos*. What we see operating in Smith's anthropology is a series of inflections, of tropes, which all tend to the same end. It is in fact the same inflection, and what it seeks to find anthropological evidence for is, of course, an original condition of humanity—the first stage—as subjected to precarity, or better yet, scarcity. In Smith's thought, what Karl Polanyi has famously called the "postulate of scarcity" is the meeting ground between anthropology and economics—both the principle through which economics finds its anthropological grounding, and through which anthropology is plunged into economics. This is not only in the sense that, as Smith repeatedly asserts, rarity alone is a source of (economic) value, but more crucially for the question that interests us here, because scarcity is also, paradoxical as it might seem, the foundation of economic progress: it is the condition that makes stage progression not only necessary, but inevitable.

It is therefore essential for Smith to view the first stage as inherently precarious, as always on the verge of mere survival. Innumerable descriptions echo throughout Smith's work the dismal vision found at the opening of the *Wealth of Nations*. "Bare subsistence is almost all that a savage can procure,"[30] may be, after the several other examples we have already seen, the quintessential formulation of this idea in the *Lectures on Jurisprudence*. Even in the *Theory of Moral Sentiments*, Smith's first book, ostensibly unconcerned with anthropological preoccupations, we find equally dire pronouncements: "The extreme indigence of a savage is often such that he himself is frequently exposed to the greatest extremity of hunger, he often dies of pure want, and it is frequently impossible for him to support both himself and his child,"[31] and again: "Every savage undergoes a sort of Spartan discipline, . . . he is in continual danger: he is often exposed to the greatest extremities of hunger, and frequently dies of pure want."[32] The Smithian first stage is premised on lack. It is a condition that humanity can only survive by escaping onto the next stage. It is precisely, by virtue of its precariousness, a mere *stage* in the course of progress, as will indeed be all subsequent stages, propelled by this original logic of lack. Smithian teleology is a fugal movement, a (hopeless) flight away from an original scarcity, and perhaps even, as we shall finally see, from an ontological lack at the heart of human nature.

But as I have tried to show, if only too briefly, this vision of the first stage does not spontaneously emerge from the "ethnological" sources available to Smith, but must be constructed from them through a series of selections, (mis)readings, and denegations. While Adam Smith's anthropology undeniably leans on ethnographic documentation, while it borrows from actual descriptions to achieve a certain empirical effect, if not legitimacy, it must also, at the same time, *protect* itself from those very sources. In particular, it must find a way to deflect the many indications that would lead to a vision of the original condition of humanity, as I have suggested, as one of abundance, rather than scarcity. One could show that this question is not wholly resolved in the work of Smith, resulting in a certain ambivalence, and moments when he seems unaccountably to recognize such an abundance—as he does recognize that historically the "first stage" has, after all, been by far the most stable and long-lasting period of humanity—and that even occasionally hint at the possibility of another Smithian anthropology.

All the points of contention, or resistance, we have seen so far—minimization of population size, discounting of the input of gathering and of a possible form of agriculture (the contribution of women), and the degree of affluence afforded by the first stage—have to do with measures of productivity, and on this score the debate can only be about the relative degree of *poverty* of the first stage. While Adam Smith's inflections unquestionably push this assessment toward the lowest range of possibilities, no one, in his time or in ours, would deny that the material "wealth of nations" at that stage, and the densities of population it can sustain, are substantially lower than at subsequent ones. A slightly but significantly different question is *why* populations at the first stage do not produce more, why indeed they do not progress to the next, more productive stage faster than they are observed to do. Smith's answer, (tauto)logically, is that they can't, because their mode of production is inherently precarious, at the limit of survival. But the clear implication is that, given a chance, they undoubtedly would, to use one of his most famous expressions, seek to "better their condition." There is, however, consistent throughout all his sources, a whole other series of observations that challenge even more radically the thesis of scarcity, and any attempt to justify it in quantitative terms, by displacing the question altogether.

From the earliest missionary "relations" to the most sophisticated "ethnographies" of the eighteenth century, all concur that "the hunters" spend an inordinate amount of time feasting, sleeping, or doing nothing. Most of these comments are far from flattering: "Like the wild Irish," Douglass writes tellingly, "they dread labour more than poverty; like dogs they are always either eating or sleeping, excepting in traveling, hunting, and their dances."[33] Even the most favorably disposed complain of the Indians' laziness, as we already saw with Charlevoix's observation that men "glory in their idleness, and in effect pass more than half of their lives doing nothing." Among Smith's "most distinct accounts," the clearest and most explicit testimony can once again be found in *Moeurs des sauvages américains*, where in a long, pointed passage Lafitau also remarks on "the laziness, the indolence, the loafing" ("la paresse, l'indolence, la faineantise") that characterize the "Sauvages de l'Amérique," so that "they are the most unoccupied people in the world; and if one makes an exception for certain small things that do not require much time, and still less constraint and application, they are almost always with arms crossed, doing nothing else but holding assemblies, singing, eating, playing, sleeping, and doing nothing."[34] For Charlevoix and Lafitau, and the many representatives of a "primitivistic" current in the Enlightenment—a current that deserves much better than its usual reduction to the myth of the "noble savage," drawing as it does on the stoicism of antiquity and on the seventeenth century "moralists" well known to Smith—this is only the first step in a reversal that will see in American Indians models of moderation, contentment, and indifference to material pursuits. But one need not go so far to realize that even the most negative formulations Smith may have found in his sources present for his theory a formidable problem, for one cannot logically maintain—even if such a contradiction is one of the most common in the discourse on the savage—that populations at the first stage live on the brink of survival, that "bare subsistence is almost all a savage can procure," and *at the same time* that "they are the most unoccupied people in the world" and "in effect pass more than half of their lives doing nothing." Between these two propositions, there is not simply a question of degree, or interpretation, but of complete incompatibility. Either their mode of subsistence is barely sufficient to insure their survival and they must exert constant efforts not to die of starvation (Smith's dominant thesis), or they spend half of their life "*sans rien faire*" because their minimal needs are met in a relatively short time. They have "great intervals of leisure," as Smith astonishingly recognizes in his essay "Of the Imitative Arts,"[35] because they are in fact easily satisfied. But in that case, the logic of lack—the "postulate of scarcity" in which we have seen him so thoroughly invested—collapses altogether.

Of all the subjects of confrontation between Smith and his sources, this is the most intriguing. Unlike the cases we have previously seen, it leaves no sign of resistance. Indeed as I have just shown, Smith is even on rare occasions willing to recognize "great intervals of leisure" at the first stage. It is true that the only two explicit statements of such an admission occur, perhaps significantly, in marginal works, the second (and earliest) in the *Lectures on Rhetoric and Belles Lettres*. But we can even find such an inference inside the *Wealth of Nations* itself. In the first chapter of book V, "On the Expense of Defense," Smith goes back to the four-stage theory as an explanatory principle, to clearly acknowledge that as society progresses through each successive stage, the amount of leisure *diminishes*: "A shepherd has a great deal of leisure; a husbandman, in the rude state of husbandry, has some; an artificer or manufacturer has none at all."[36] Although frustratingly (perhaps significantly) Smith has in this case, contrary to his usual practice, skipped over the first stage—so that we have no proof, even though the inference is inescapable that "a hunter" should have even more than "a great deal of leisure." But that is all we get. Has Smith seen the problem, the contradiction? On this subject, we cannot speak of deflection, even of denegation, but only of a kind of blindness. And indeed a cynical view of the relation between Smith's anthropology and what I have called his ethnological sources is that he sees only what he wants, what is convenient for his theory. I prefer to refrain from such a view in favor of a more complex, perhaps dialectical, perhaps even unconscious relation between theory and the empirical "evidence" of the ethnographic sources. What we find in Smith is a striking example of the weight of the theoretical over the empirical, but without the theory ever becoming entirely theoretical. Rather, Smith's theory of stage progression is grounded in an anthropology that is itself partly a projection of the very theory it is intended to support. It is only imaginary in the particular Lacanian sense of a specular or projective anthropology—or perhaps, paraphrasing the title of a book that has become famous in another field, we could speak, in Smith's case, of an "imagined anthropology." But certainly, however fortuitous Dugald Stewart's term may have turned out to be, it never is a purely "conjectural" anthropology. Unlike Rousseau, Smith is not attempting to imagine a state "that no longer exists, that may not have existed, and that will probably never exist,"[37] but a stage through which every society has actually passed, and at which several "savage nations" can still be shown to exist—hence the constant confusion, or interchangeability in his anthropology, between "the age of hunters" and "the savages of America," however the latter may be reduced to the former. Adam Smith's first stage, "imaginary" as it may be, is never meant to be understood as a hypothetical state of nature, but corresponds closely to Rousseau's *second* stage, after the first "revolution," following the first socialization, after, so to speak, the first gatherings of gatherers.

There are in fact only two instances in the whole of his work when Smith really engaged in conjecture. The first, at the beginning of the "Considerations Concerning the First Formation of Languages," is too inconsequential for our subject, but the second, in the *Lectures on Jurisprudence*, is of the greatest import, since it is the only time when Smith does seek, in the purely conjectural mode, to imagine human beings in the state of nature, thereby giving us a crucial glimpse of his "anthropology" in the French sense, and perhaps the key to his anthropology *tout court*. The remarkable passage, only a few pages long, begins with a proposition

that first seems entirely compatible with Rousseau's notion of perfectibility: "Man has received from the bounty of nature reason and ingenuity,
art, contrivance, and capacity of improvement far superior to that which
she has bestowed on any of the other animalls." But already the end of
the sentence reveals a profound discordance with the Rousseauist vision
of the natural condition of man: "but [man] is at the same time in a much
more helpless and destitute condition with regard to the support and
comfort of his life."[38] And this is the theme that Smith develops in the rest
of the passage. Unlike the other animals, who find in nature everything
they need, and in the condition that best suits those needs, man, "of a
more delicate frame and more feeble constitution, *meets with nothing so
adapted to his use that it does not stand in need of improvement and
preparation to fit it for his use.*"[39] Smithian man is originally dysfunctional. He is naturally unadapted to the natural world in which he originates. Like every human at the beginning of life, man is born nonviable—
but this is because a deficient mother nature produces nothing entirely
suitable to his nature, nothing, Rousseau would say, that does not need
not be "supplemented" if he is to survive.

Smith proceeds to illustrate this notion with regard to the three fundamental human needs of food, clothing, and shelter, natural but dependent
on artifice for their satisfaction. Raw food, as can be seen from the frequent "diseases arising from indigestion" among the "savage nations"
who make do with "undressed victualls," is not well adapted to man's
"feeble and puny stomach," so that he must "apply fire to the preparation
of his food." Similarly, the "naturall temperature of the air" is perfectly
adapted to the condition of animalls," but "even this soft and subtle fluid
is too severe for his tender and delicate frame" and he must create "around
his body a sort of new atmosphere, more soft, warm, and comfortable
than the common circumambiant air" by wrapping his body in clothes and
building houses. Thus, for Smith, natural man is not only, as for Rousseau,
endowed with perfectibility, but from his original condition under the *obligation* to make use of this faculty to perfect the natural world; his very
survival depends on it. "These are contrivances," insists Smith, "which
none of the other animalls perceive the need of, but men can hardly subsist
without them."[40] In this anthropology, the very nature of man compels
him from the very beginning, to borrow once again Smith's famous dictum, to "better his condition" in order to escape from it, or else not to be
at all. The Smithian state of nature is not, as for Rousseau, a condition
"that no longer exists, that may not have existed, and that will probably
never exist"—it is a condition that *can hardly have existed at all.*

But it is also a condition from which all subsequent stages nevertheless inherit, as we have seen with the "age of hunters," the fundamental

premise of an ontological lack. For the logic of lack does not end with man's original needs. Once propelled out of the state of absolute deprivation that Smith posits as our natural condition, it reveals an uncanny ability to proliferate infinitely from stage to stage to the highest human achievements. "The same temper and inclination," says Smith, "which prompted [man] to make these improvements push him to still greater refinements."[41] Indeed it is "to supply the wants of *meat, drink,* cloathing, and lodging," he continues a little further, that "allmost the whole of the arts and sciences have been invented and improved," even those perfected to gratify "frivolous distinctions and preferences."[42] The "*same temper and inclination,*"! But a moment ago it was not a question of "inclination," nor of "refinements" and "niceties," but of bare survival. And yet it was on this continuity between the original needs of mankind and all further technological and cultural progress that Smith would now insist, in one of those spectacular rhetorical developments of which he was a past master—agriculture, forestry, all the different "arts" that transform the products of nature, and then all the traders and merchants that carry and distribute them, and consequently shipbuilding and the art of navigation. "Geometry, arithmetick, and writing" that "have all been invented originally to facilitate the operation of the several arts," as well as all the social institutions that guarantee and encourage their successful development. "Even law and government have these as their finall end and ultimate object . . . Even wisdom and virtue in all its branches derive their lustre and beauty with regard to utility merely from their tendency to provide for the security of mankind." So that, Smith concludes, "in a certain view of things all the arts, the sciences, law and government, wisdom, and even virtue itself tend all to the same thing, the providing of meat, drink, raiment, and lodging for men."[43] This is an impressive culmination, even in the abbreviated version I have presented here; to do full justice to the passage, let alone to replace it in the full context of the Smithian reflection on human motivations, would take us far beyond our present scope.

One must emphasize, however, that within a few pages, a crucial if unacknowledged shift has taken place in Smith's account of human development. Humanity has imperceptively moved from the register of needs— indeed, of absolute physiological needs—to that of desires, even of the most sublime human aspirations. But perhaps most important, this shift is not presented as discontinuous—as it is, again famously, in Rousseau's account of the first "revolution"—but on the contrary as taking place in complete continuity. This very particular mode of continuity might be labeled, in the language of psychoanalysis, *anaclitic*: desires *lean* on needs, they remain "propped up," if not propelled, by those original needs from which they thereby inherit their energy—even if this energy was initially the purely negative impulse of physical "wants"—in the form of an inexhaustible drive to progress. This vision of the transition from a state of nature conceived as originally dysfunctional, but from which *for this reason* all human development necessarily ensues, may well be Adam Smith's most original contribution to the anthropology of the Enlightenment. And there is no doubt that it is, in Dugald Stewart's terms, wholly "theoretical and conjectural." But then the only pure conjecture in Smith's conjectural history is the very principle on which it is founded. It is also that *a priori* assumption that makes Smith's anthropology, before and beyond any empiricism, a theory of economic progress.

APPENDIX: ADAM SMITH'S
"ETHNOGRAPHIC" SOURCES

Works Explicitly Referenced by Smith or Identified
in Scholarly Editions

Direct references in the *Lectures on Jurisprudence* (hereafter *LJ*) and the *Wealth of Nations* (hereafter *WN*) are designated by "Ref." References identified by later editors are designated by "Ed." Pages numbers refer to the Glasgow edition.

Buffon, George Louis Leclerc: *Histoire naturelle* (1750)
(Ref.—*WN*, p. 243; Ed.—*WN*, p. 560)
Carreri, John Francis Gemelli: *A Voyage Round the World* (1704)
(Ref.—*WN*, p. 568)
Charlevoix, François Xavier: *Histoire et description de la nouvelle France, avec le journal historique d'un voyage dans l'Amérique septentrionale* (1744)
(Ref.—*LJ*, pp. 20–21, 106, 201; *WN*, p. 571)
Charlevoix, François Xavier: *Histoire de l'Isle Espagnole ou de Saint Domingue* (1730)
(Ed.—*WN*, p. 560)
Dobbs, Arthur: *An Account of the Countries Adjoining to Hudson's Bay* (1744)
(Ref.—*WN*, p. 744)
Douglass, William: *A Summary, Historical and Political, of the First Planting, Progressive Improvements, and Present State of the British Settlements in North America* (1747–1750)

(Ref.—*WN*, pp.175, 317, 326; Ed.—*LJ*, p. 214; *WN*, pp. 327, 744, 941)

Frézier, Amédée François: *A Voyage to the South-Sea and Along the Coasts of Chili and Peru* (1717)
(Ref.—*WN*, pp. 186, 222)

Gumilla, J.: *Histoire naturelle, civile et géographique de l'Orénoque* (1758)
(Ref.—*WN*, p. 563)

Juan, Jorge, and Ulloa, Antonio de: *A Voyage to South America* (1752)
(Ref.—*WN*, pp. 164, 186, 188, 205, 222, 576; Ed.—*WN*, pp. 220, 247, 268, 574)

Kalm, Pehr: *Peter Kalm's Travels in North America* (1770)
(Ref.—*WN*, p. 240)

Kolben, Peter: *The Present State of the Cape of Good-Hope: Or a Particular Account of the Several Nations of the Hottentots* (1731)
(Ref.—*LJ*, p. 583; Ed.—*LJ*, p. 352)

Lafitau, R. P. Joseph-François: *Moeurs des sauvages Américains, comparées aux moeurs des premiers temps* (1734)
(Ref.—*LJ*, pp. 106, 201; Ed.—*LJ*, p. 439)

Poivre, P.: *Voyages d'un philosophe, ou observations sur les moeurs et les arts des peuples de l'Afrique, de l'Asie et de l'Amérique* (1768)
(Ref.—*WN*, p. 173; Ed.—*WN*, pp. 679, 680)

Raleigh, Sir Walter: *The Discovery of the Large, Rich, and Beautiful Empire of Guiana with a Relation of the Great and Golden City of Manoa (Which the Spaniards Call El Dorado)* (1596)
(Ref.—*WN*, p. 563)

Raynal, Guillaume Thomas: *Histoire philosophique et politique des établissements et du commerce des Européens dans les deux Indes* (1775)
(Ref.—*WN*, p. 226; Ed.—*WN*, pp. 225, 227, 444, 511, 575, 589, 626)

Other Works in Adam Smith's Library

Cook, James: *An Account of the Voyages Undertaken by Captains Byron, Wallis, Carteret, and Cook,* version de John Hawkesworth (1773)

Cook, James: *A Voyage Towards the South Pole and Round the World* (1777)

Cook, James: *A Voyage to the Pacific Ocean* (1784)

Dampier, William: *A Voyage Round the World* (1697)

Dampier, William: *Voyage to New Holland* (1703)

Hakluyt, Richard: *The Principal Navigations, Voyages, Traffiques and Discoveries of the English Nation* (of which the most important part, the voyages of Walter Raleigh, already appear in our first list) (1599)

Lafitau, R. P. Joseph François: *Histoire des découvertes et conquestes des Portugais dans le nouveau monde* (1734)

Pauw, Cornélius de: *Défense des recherches philosophiques sur les Américains* (1771)

CHAPTER SIX

Beyond the Savage Character

Mexicans, Peruvians, and the "Imperfectly Civilized" in William Robertson's 'History of America'

Neil Hargraves

William Robertson's dual portrait of the Mexicans and Peruvians in his *History of America* (1777) is situated within a wide-ranging history that encompasses a conjectural account of the history of enterprise and navigation (book I); narratives of conquest, discovery, and civil war (books II, III, V and VI); a dissertation on the political economy of Spanish America (book VIII); and two "philosophical" treatises on the nature of America and the Americans (books IV and VII). The structural complexity of the resulting work has made *America* difficult to approach *in toto*. Contemporary critics were either puzzled or dazzled by its heterogeneity. The Abbé de Mably, for example, saw it as confused and poorly structured. He deplored in particular the retrospective "characterizations" of the Americans, seeing them as misplaced (they should have been positioned, in Sallustian fashion, at the beginning of the history).[1] Edmund Burke, however, was impressed by its ambition: in addition to profound philosophy and patient research, Robertson's pen was able to encompass the realms of poetry, fable, the "adventure of travel," natural history, and, of course, protoanthropology; in Burke's famous words, it unrolled the "great map of mankind."[2] Given this diversity, Robertson's treatment of the Mexicans and the Inca can be viewed through three distinct lenses. First, he provides formal social "characters" of both peoples in book VII, at the conclusion of his narrative of the discovery and conquest of the Spanish colonies. Book VII thus functions as a space cleared in the history specifically for the contemplation and investigation of social forms: it invites the reader to reflect upon the narrative, and in a sense is intended to clarify the narrative presentation of the Mexicans and Peruvians. Second, there is the picture of the Americans that emerges from the preceding narratives themselves (books V and VI). Third, book VII also functions, in the larger scheme of *America*, as an appendix or continuation of the monumental and ambitious account of the "condition and character of the Americans" on the eve of Columbus's landfall, which is the kernel of book IV of *America*. Book VII thus serves as a kind of coda or addendum to the character of the generic "American" that Robertson had already established. Robertson's portrayal of the Mexicans and Peruvians thus opens up a wide range of questions concerning the relationship between narrative and philosophical history, the formation of social character and its relationship to the progress of society, the problems of the representation of and the evidence for social character, and the depiction of cultural interaction in eighteenth-century historiography.

Burke praised particularly Robertson's mastery of "gradation" in his depiction of the American peoples, a point that the contemporary success of (and subsequent concentration on) book IV has tended to obscure. Thus, in *America* we "are brought acquainted with man in every state of his existence . . . and behold nations in every stage of their progress, from infancy to adolescence." This required "the nice discrimination of those shades that mingle perceptibly in so many different gradations of savage life."[3] This is an echo of Robertson's own programmatic statement on the nature of the "history of the human mind," in which he declared that "we must contemplate man in all those various situations wherein he has been placed. We must follow him in his progress through the different stages of society, as he gradually advances from the infant state of civil life toward its maturity and decline."[4] The challenge for the construction of *America* lay in relating the different peoples encountered in the narrative, from the Spanish themselves to the Caribs, the Tlascalans, Cholulans, Mexicans, and Peruvians, to a common framework of comparison, and in encompassing them within a common language of description. In a situation where the different peoples were essentially "incommensurable," to adopt Anthony Pagden's term,[5] this placed great demands on Robertson's ability to produce a "philosophical" history that accurately reflected the complexity of the human mind and character.

Book IV, by contrast, in synthesizing the native American to a single largely undifferentiated "character," appeared to many to be a falsification, a needless *reductio ad unum*. Bryan Edwards, historian of the West Indies, condemned Robertson's attempt to establish it as a "fixed principle" that all the American savages have "the same character."[6] Edwards linked this to Robertson's qualified (and limited) espousal of the notorious "de Pauw" thesis concerning the physical degeneracy of the American.[7] Book IV is the clearest example of Robertson's determination to push his historiography beyond the limits of his immediate narrative subject, and it is on that work that Robertson's status as a pioneer of anthropology, such as it is, has rested.[8] Although robustly condemned by critics such as Thomas Jefferson, Robertson's picture of the native American was persuasive and eloquent enough to continue to be cited seriously by later anthropologists—such as Lewis Morgan—until the late nineteenth century.[9] The *Monthly Review* confidently predicted that "future times will probably refer to it as that part of his works which gives the best idea of his genius" and as "the most finished of all his productions."[10] It was a powerful intervention in a wide-ranging and overlapping set of debates concerning the nature of savagery, the nature of America, and the nature of mankind.[11] The drive to create a unitary picture of the American was in part dictated by Robertson's formal commitment, stated more explicitly in book IV than in any of his other writings, to Scottish four-stage theory: the character of the savage American thus becomes an attempt to marry the ideal and synthetic stadialism of Adam Smith or John Millar, with empirical evidence and verifiable "proofs," Robertson's stock-in-trade and the foundation of his reputation as a historian.[12] Book IV was also a great piece of advocacy. The geologist John Playfair, writing to Robertson's son, praised its skill in "delineating the character of the savage," compared with Raynal's "ill-defined" and "incomplete" image: "Your father's pencil to all the energy and expression of the abbe's, adds the accuracy of real perspective, and that judicious selection of circumstances, which adds a relief to the whole. It is conducted with all the skill of the philosophic historian who is neither to be mislead by the misrepresentation of facts, nor seduced by the spirit of system."

Playfair admitted himself cured by Robertson of the "excessive admiration" that, under the influence of Rousseau, he had previously entertained for the savage state.[13] It is significant therefore that book IV was cast in the form of a "character," a crucial tool in eighteenth-century philosophy, literature, and historical writing. It was indeed both a forensic exercise in character reconstruction, and a piece of character "painting." Through the medium of the character, Robertson attempted to create a unity, and an organic appearance of unity, out of the diverse materials on and various appearances of the American. This was why he deliberately eschewed the technique of Raynal/Diderot and Charlevoix, of scattering characterizations of individual tribes throughout the narrative, a technique that led to what Playfair called "vague and indeterminate" pictures, and frustrated the "philosophical" attempt to simplify, order, and classify the principal characteristics of the American.[14]

Playfair's praise of Robertson as a philosophical *historian* is also significant. Robertson's ability to keep these two roles in harmony was crucial to his authority in a subject that, in the opinion of many, had been tarnished by the dogmatic systems of philosophers. As the *Critical Review* wrote, Robertson had sedulously and skillfully avoided the "rage of theory" and "passion for system," which were the "disease of modern philosophy." It was through his identity as a historian rather than philosopher that Robertson would inoculate the study of the New World from the errors of the past: "If certainty is anywhere to be sought after, it is in historical researches."[15] Even critics of Robertson, such as the Spanish Jesuit Juan Nuix and the Mexican antiquarian Francisco de Clavigero, were willing to concede that Robertson in his capacity as historian was far preferable to "*pretendidos filosofos y politicos*" such as Raynal/Diderot or de Pauw.[16] This was part of Robertson's carefully stage-managed pose of impartiality, which lent his pronouncements a special weight and power.[17] Thus, the curious sight of two antagonists on the subject of the American and savagery, Josiah Tucker and James Dunbar, both appealing to what Tucker called Robertson's "excellent and impartial history" to shore up their own somewhat polarized positions. Dunbar, countering what he saw as Tucker's willful misreading of Robertson, claimed that "Dr Robertson's description of savage life, though not indulgent, is credible and consistent."[18] Robertson's integrity as a historian, his perceived mastery of the sources, and his skill in reading and picturing "character," all granted his synthetic character a particular authority. In creating this template of the savage from disparate sources, and in fixing principal features of savage life in place, collecting together and tethering diverse appearances, Robertson had in fact manufactured a piece of evidence, and carved out a locus for discussion by philosophers on the nature of American and savage life. This fiction of American character served to amalgamate a multiplicity of competing characters into one.

Book IV is explicable therefore as a "character," a device that enabled Robertson to compress and organize his diverse materials. Louis van Delft has shown how the device of the character was crucial in the conceptualization of early anthropology. Initially functioning as a space for moral evaluation, the Theophrastan character as it flourished in the seventeenth century enabled certain features of human behavior to be examined and, when characters were placed in relation to each other in the form of a "gallery" or "map," compared.[19] As van Delft argues, character as a heuristic device enabled definition, distribution into classes, generalization, and the imposition of order on the profusions and proliferations of human nature. Of course, the Theophrastan character was closed, bounded, static, and essentially one-dimensional: this was part of its purpose, to clarify, simplify, reduce—although hopefully without any essential distortion—"in little comprehending much."[20] Van Delft, however, also shows how by the eighteenth century a more open-ended, dynamic, evolutionary concept of character was being developed, by writers such as Marivaux, and greater attention was being paid to the possibility for change, nuance, transformation, and mixture.[21] Van Delft is particularly interesting on the metaphorical associations of character, with typography and bibliography (reading the book of nature), anatomy (creating an anatomy of mankind), portraiture (the gallery of virtues and vices), and cartography (charting the map of mankind).[22] These metaphors fed into the writing of both conventional and philosophical history in the eighteenth century, and informed historical discussions of character. Book VII of *America* is a fascinating exercise in dual character construction, which reveals something about the applications of the concept of character as a tool for understanding or at least popularizing the ideas of philosophical historians and protoanthropologists. For Robertson, character was at once a historical artifact, a piece of evidence, a narrative device, the summation or encapsulation of a narrative, a means of linking the individual and the collective, and a system of interlocking relations. All of these are apparent in Robertson's study of the Mexicans and Peruvians through his combination of narrative, philosophical, and quasi-antiquarian history.

Given the complex structure of *America*, Robertson's character of the American did not simply reside in the specialized space of book IV or book VII, but also in the more dynamic, open, and democratic (in the sense of being partly constructed by the reader) shifting glimpses provided by the narrative.[23] Here, Robertson faced the acute problem of how to encompass the American within the narrative portions of the history. Narrative—the locus of action—was seen to be an arena in which the American, *because of* his defects of character, could not compete. Thus, as Washburn has pointed out, in the emerging national histories of the United States, the native American was marginalized from the narrative, treated either separately or occasionally as a footnote. The American thus became the province of the anthropologist rather than the historian.[24] In a different context, Knud Haakonssen has detected a rigid methodological distinction in James Mill's *History of British India*, the radical separation of two types of history according to the level of cultural development: the Indians were not permitted to come into the orbit of Mill's narrative, being exiled to the dissertations and appendices of static "character" construction.[25] These "peoples without history" were so because they lacked the capacity for purposive and sustained action. Thus, book IV is a commentary on the failure of the Americans to engage in equal terms with the

Spanish. With no meaningful interaction possible between the Americans and the Spanish in book III, Robertson even disclaims his office as a historian: "in a contest between naked savages and one of the most warlike of European nations, where science, courage and discipline on one side, were opposed by ignorance, timidity and disorder on the other, a particular detail of events would be as unpleasant as uninstructive." The early stages of *America* frustrate Robertson's ideal of narrative history, one where "minds are most violently agitated, and . . . powers and passions are called forth" by the rivalry of two equal forces.[26]

Yet the Americans did force their way into the narrative, with problematic consequences for Robertson's template of savage character. Indeed, Bryan Edwards saw a fundamental inconsistency between Robertson's narrative depiction of the Americans and his philosophical synthesis of their character, thus underlining the difficulty of attempting to view the same object under very different lights. Narrative and theory were distinct operations, and the attempt by Robertson to fuse them together led him into frequent "repugnancy and contradiction." Turning from book IV to Robertson's own narrative, Edwards observed that "exceptions present themselves to every general conclusion until we are burthened with their variety."[27] Alexander Du Toit has recently emphasized the extent to which the narrative depiction of the Americans places them in a classical republican discourse that bears little relation to the stadial character that emerges from book IV, and connects this with the tradition of civic thought in Scotland.[28] Although this may be true, there is a more general point to be made here: the language of character in the narrative tended to be different from that employed in formal set-piece characters. Narrative conventions tended (in the eyes of many critics, and perhaps Robertson himself) to overrepresent, to stretch the qualities of the native American, or else failed to capture them at all. Books IV and VII, as "characters" of the Americans, embodied Robertson's recognition that the narrative could not reveal the character of the savage American with the same clarity that it could disclose the character of a purposeful actor; that, in fact, narrative history could distort or obscure this kind of character. The tendency of narrative is to inflate and individualize them; the purpose of "philosophy" is both to constrain and to generalize.

The cases of Mexico and Peru are crucially, if ambiguously, different. The "history of events" is intimately shaped by the character of the Americans with whom the Spanish interacted. Book IV inhabits a junction in the history between two phases of narrative: the second phase is determined by the "knowledge of a people, who, if compared with those tribes of America with whom they [the Spanish] were hitherto acquainted, may be considered as highly civilised," which results in a "history of events extremely different from those which we have already related."[29] The implication here, however, is that books V and VI, the narratives of the conquest of Mexico and Peru, are fuller, more interactive narratives, closer to the model of European history that Robertson lauded as the ideal. Thus, it should follow that the character of the Mexicans and Peruvians, as participating actors, would possess a greater narrative identity and emerge more clearly. Yet, in a sense, this creates even greater problems of representation. The improvement of the Mexicans and Peruvians is only partial. At times the old pattern reasserts itself, and the narrative threatens to descend into a nightmare of unrecountable unilateralism: "no power of words can render the recital of a combat interesting, where there is no equality of danger; and when a narrative closes with an account of thousands slain on one side, while not a single person falls on the other, the most laboured descriptions . . . command no attention."[30] To what degree the Mexicans and Peruvians are in fact capable of sustaining an equal narrative is therefore unclear.

Robertson grounds his discussion in a critique of the Spanish sources, rooted in a fundamental failure of observation.[31] Cortes and his followers, illiterate and "rapacious adventurers" lacking "sagacity or precision," were so entirely absorbed in their one object—the "ardour of plunder"— that they "seemed hardly to have turned their eyes towards any other." They lacked the "qualities requisite for observing the striking spectacle presented to their view." Thus, "the accounts given by them of the policy and order established in the Mexican monarchy are superficial, confused and inexplicable." In addition, their "barbarous researches" were warped by superstition and "fanatical zeal." Everything concerning the subject is therefore obscure and uncertain. The real danger, however, lay in the lazy adoption by later historians of such terms of description. The absence of a vocabulary to describe the rulers of an intermediate state such as Mexico, easily led careless Spanish historians into calling Montezuma an "emperor," his residence a "palace," and his household a "court." Thus, the "colours with which De Solis delineates the character and describes the actions of Montezuma . . . are the same that he must have employed in exhibiting to view the monarch and institutions of a highly polished people."[32] As Robertson pronounces:

> There is not a more frequent or a more fertile source of deception in describing the manners and arts of savage nations, or of such as are imperfectly civilized, than that of applying to them the names and phrases appropriated to the institutions and refinements of polished life.
>
> Under such appellations they acquire, in our estimation, an importance and dignity which does not belong to them. The illusion spreads, and giving a false

colour to every part of the narrative, the imagination is so much carried away with the resemblance, that it becomes difficult to discern objects as they really are.[33]

Yet Robertson's own narrative is not so austere. This is partly due to his narrative technique: as Brading has observed, Robertson's narrative account—like that of Gibbon—often takes the form of paraphrase.[34] Thus, its treatment of the Mexicans and Peruvians is uneven and occasionally contradictory, both because of the instability of the terms used, and also due to Robertson's elaborate modulation of perspective. Robertson of course uses the narrative for dramatic effect, alternately adopting the viewpoints of the Spanish or the Americans. In doing so, he commits many of the category mistakes that he condemns in the Spanish sources. Thus, he contrasts the Spanish, a "handful of adventurers," with the "powerful kingdom" and "great empire" in which they are marooned.[35] Montezuma is clearly represented as a puissant monarch, in contradistinction to a "petty cazique"; he exhibits a "transport of rage natural to a fierce prince" rather than necessarily typical of a savage. Montezuma is slotted into familiar, universal and cross-cultural categories: he is a tyrant, with a tyrant's hauteur, cruelty, and suspicion, displaying "what might have been expected from a haughty prince in possession of extensive power," although possessing an "unexampled rigour."[36] In adopting the perspective of the Tlascalans, to whom Montezuma is a domineering overlord, he is magnified in the eyes of both the Spanish and the reader. The Mexicans are a "warlike and enterprising" people. The language of description that Robertson applies is largely unmoored to any specific cultural setting, except when he steps in to explain the baffling lack of response displayed by Montezuma to the Spanish challenge. Later, Montezuma is even depicted in a sentimental register, that ultimate signifier of modernity, as an unfortunate (and tearful) monarch in the manner of Robertson's depiction of Mary Stuart.[37]

The reading of character is itself at the heart of Robertson's narrative. Even in the unprofitable and distasteful description of "unequal" warfare, Robertson is eager to draw out from the encounter those circumstances that "throw light upon the character of both the people of New Spain, and of their conquerors."[38] He dramatizes and indeed enters into the essential inability of the Americans to read the character of the Spanish, tracing their attempts to decode the unfamiliar and contradictory signs presented by Cortes and his followers: "They were at a loss, however, in what manner to address the strangers, what idea to form of their character, and whether to consider them as beings of a gentle or of a malevolent nature. There were circumstances in their conduct which seemed to favour each opinion . . . This uncertainty was apparent in the mode of addressing the Spaniards."[39]

The tendency of Robertson's narrative is at times to diminish the differences between the Spanish and the Americans. Indeed Alexander du Toit has noted the strange resemblance of Spaniard and American that is created by Robertson's use of narrative conventions and designations, for example, in ascribing European martial virtues to a character such as Guatimozin, deliberately distancing him from the "sullen fierceness of barbarian," while implicating the Spanish in savage or barbarous behaviors.[40]

The slipperiness of the language here makes it easy to blur the essential distinctions between savage and civilized. A parallel between American and Spanish is established, however, not simply by incorporating them within an identical language of character, but also by deliberately constructing a symmetry of action and response between his interactors (a characteristic of Robertson's narrative structure in the earlier, altogether more conventional *History of Scotland*).[41] Thus, the wonder and astonishment that each provokes in the other, a motif that Robertson adopts from the sources such as Diaz but which he uses with a particular emphasis and insistence.[42] At first, both the Spanish and the Americans are locked into a mutual gaze, vividly (and literally) exemplifying Hume's dictum, "Thus all mankind stand staring at one another."[43] Yet the thrust of the narrative, dictated by the energy and ambition of Cortes, quickly disrupts this static tableau of mutuality, and the Spaniards and the Americans rapidly diverge—the former into pragmatic calculations of how best to survive and prosper from this situation, the latter into a religious struggle to reconcile this encounter with their worldview.[44] The effect on the Spanish of this "romantic" challenge to their imagination is, in Robertson's pathological language, to inflame their wants and desires or to "intoxicate" them.[45] At any rate, it enlarges their ambitions and stimulates them to action. In a sense, the "illiterate adventurers" are presented by Robertson as impervious to reflection and therefore to challenge, while the Mexicans labor to study and comprehend the meaning of the Spanish arrival. This "astonishment" scarcely detains the Spanish, while it effectively paralyzes the Americans: the Mexicans are depicted repeatedly as rendered passive and hushed by their "silent amazement"; Montezuma in his humiliation is struck "dumb with astonishment."[46]

The other master motif is that of "ascendancy." Robertson imports this device from more conventional political narrative, such as his own *Charles V*, where it was used to depict the way in which an *homme politique* through his superior knowledge of character and motivation could manipulate and outmaneuver more "traditional" and less politically adept characters. By applying it to the relationship between two cultures and two peoples, and making it the explanatory factor for the subjugation of mighty empires, Robertson creates suggestive analogies between the operation of individual and collective characters. The notion of "ascendancy" provides a way for Robertson to present the mystifying collapse of the political will of the Mexicans and Peruvians in explicable and familiar terms, without requiring further or more searching explication. However the "ascendant" is a particular product of Cortes's "capacity" rather than a more general assertion of Spanish superiority to the Americans.[47] It is an explanation in terms of character interaction, discernment, and manipulation. This mode of explanation is interesting in that it locates the causes of Mexican and Peruvian defeat in the history of the mind rather than in physical, technological, or even moral (as we would understand it) causes.[48]

Of course, narrative permits development, and Robertson wrestles with the potential of the Mexicans and Peruvians to adapt to the Spanish and begin to effect a transformation in their behavior.[49] He dramatizes Cortes's "wonder" at the swift transition of the Mexicans from tame and passive subjects to a people of "implacable ferocity."[50] This is part of the conventional picture of the savage as unstable and fickle, lacking indeed a settled identity. However, this new and striking manifestation of the savage is in some ways represented positively, as patriotic, "gallant," and associated with key Robertsonian virtues such as vigor, courage, ardor, and generosity.[51] Yet such language is not sustained: increasingly the Mexicans are depicted as a frenzied mass, a furious and elemental "multitude," a "torrent," swept up into "irresistible violence."[52] They are stripped of those individual, human characteristics that had occasionally illumined them (Guatimozin is the notable exception). The Mexicans are depicted as a natural force, and in a nightmare vision, Robertson shows how this fury was able to obliterate all distinctions: "In a moment the confusion was universal; horse and foot, officers and soldiers, friends and enemies, were mingled together; and while all fought, and many fell, they could hardly distinguish from what hand the blow came."[53] This is neither the unequal one-sided slaughter nor the complex interactive game of war that Robertson had posited as the two narrative alternatives; rather, it is something altogether darker and less accountable. The Mexicans in the hour of victory are effectively rendered alien and horrifying: in depicting their "barbarous triumph," Robertson converts them from almost equal and semantically similar antagonists into something altogether more degraded, regarded entirely from the Spanish perspective (and thus embroidered with Spanish imagination).[54]

The Peruvians show themselves capable, to an extent unseen in the previous encounters in the New World, of adapting themselves to European forms of action, of observing closely and successfully imitating them: "though they displayed not the same undaunted ferocity as the Mexican warriors, they conducted some of their operations in a manner which discovered greater sagacity, and a genius more susceptible of improvement in the military art. They not only observed the advantages which the Spaniards derived from their discipline and their weapons, but they endeavoured to imitate the former, and turn the latter against them."[55] In one peculiar section, Robertson links the Peruvian Empire to European empires, emphasizing the nature of the Peruvians as a civilizing people with echoes of Britain's civilizing mission in India (although linked with Asian despotism); their conquests are also in part the product of the operation of ascendancy.[56] Atahualpa is contrasted implicitly and explicitly with Montezuma, and represented as capable of outperforming the Spanish in the game of mutual observation and unmasking: "the Inca quickly discovered their ruling passion."[57] He is "a prince of greater abilities and discernment than Montezuma, and seems to have penetrated more thoroughly into the character and intentions of the Spanish."[58] In a striking reversal, Pizarro is made to feel the object of a "barbarian's scorn."[59] The Spanish are shown to be "astonished" by the power, wealth, and "deportment" of the Peruvian Empire.[60] The Peruvians are also observant to improve any circumstance, such as the ambiguous return of Almagro to Peru, to their own advantage. Thus, events join Peruvians and Spaniards together in a community of observation and calculation: "The Spaniards and Peruvians fixed their eyes upon him with equal solicitude."[61] This seems to create the conditions for a reciprocal narrative. Yet Robertson swiftly undercuts this promising sign of purposeful vigor and sagacity on the part of the Peruvians: these "essays to imitate European arts and to employ European arms" are no more than "imperfect," and Atahualpa is ultimately unmasked as a "credulous prince."[62] The Peruvians henceforth disappear from the narrative, except as instruments of labor or as silent, spectral spectators of actions in which they cannot participate. This is illustrated vividly if mystifyingly in the defeat of Almagro at Cuzco:

The Indians, instead of executing the resolution which they had formed, retir'd quietly after the battle was over; and in the history of the New World, there is not a more striking instance of the wonderful ascendant which the Spaniards had acquired over its inhabitants, than that after seeing one of the contending parties ruined and dispersed, and the other weakened and fatigued, they had not courage to fall upon their enemies, when fortune presented them with an opportunity of attacking them with such advantage.[63]

Overall, the narrative raises a variety of questions concerning the identities of the Mexicans and the Peruvians that it cannot really address. Robertson attempts to explain the inconsistencies of, for instance, Montezuma, by relating him to a specific social context: "But though his talents might be suited to the transactions of a state so imperfectly polished as the Mexican empire, and sufficient to conduct them while in their accustomed course, they were altogether inadequate to a conjuncture so extraordinary, and did not qualify him either to judge with that discernment, or to act with the decision, requisite in such an emergency."[64]

Like Atahualpa, Montezuma is unmasked, and condemned for failing to play a role—the great prince, the sagacious politician—for which he is cognitively unequipped. The inconsistencies of the Mexicans and the Peruvians created in the narrative are assimilated to the abrupt transitions, the instability of identity, which is a defining feature of the savage. Moreover, there remain the crucial differences between them, which have been elided by a narrative that reduces them both to the same condition, subordination through a combination of force and the mysterious enchantment of "ascendancy." Yet the effect of the narratives of books V and VI is to create an uncertainty concerning their characters, and the operation of social character. It is this that book VII exists to remedy.

Since the Mexicans and the Peruvians are both distinct from savages, neither of them fit the generic character template of the American. Thus, book VII serves as a secondary characterization: hanging off the framework provided by book IV, but moving beyond it. Book VII also represents a descent into the particular, a generic shift from the broad comparative philosophical stance of book IV to a more narrowly "antiquarian" approach. As Robertson the skeptical empiricist proclaims: "it is not by theory or conjectures that history decides with regard to the state or character of nations. It produces facts as the foundation of every judgment which it ventures to pronounce."[65] This is despite Robertson's own dismissal of mere antiquarians—Clavigero a "credulous bigot," Garcilaso de la Vega a fabulist—and his clear discomfort in dealing with particularities about which he has no firsthand knowledge: this perhaps explains his uncharacteristic desire to demolish Clavigero's attacks detail by detail in his revisions of 1789.[66] As intermediate peoples, the Mexicans and Peruvians are placed outside the strict typology of stadial theory, itself notoriously weak in explaining the transitions from stage to stage and the motors that drive this change.[67] Indeed, the distinction that Robertson applies is the broad one between "civilized" or polished and the rude or barbarous—a simplified and imprecise two-stage schema: "to allot them their proper station between the rude tribes in the New World, and the polished states of the ancient, and to determine how far they had risen above the former, as well as how much they fell below the latter."[68]

The notion of progress itself is also brought into question, since Robertson is unable to determine whether the Mexicans and Peruvians are in fact progressing, declining, or merely static. Instead, their development is so uneven, peculiar, and perhaps unnatural that it is "national manners"—particular, contingent, and ultimately inexplicable—that usurps the place of the progress of society and indeed replaces the examination of "political institutions."[69] Above all, book VII investigates the nature of social character, and implicitly asks the crucial question: How is the character of a particular people or society formed and diversified? The dominant motifs for book VII are those of imperfection and "singularity." It sets out the *singularity* rather than the typicality of the Mexicans and Peruvians, their essential deviation from any natural course of development.

Book VII adopts a two-stage analysis in its attempt to establish the extent of the intermediacy of Mexicans and Peruvians on the scale of rudeness and refinement. Robertson's attitude toward both peoples is, initially at least, studiedly ambiguous. In some ways, he sees them knocking at the limits of their situation; in others, they are thrown back to the very heart of book IV and seem incapable of advancing to meet the requirements or expectations of a more polished state.

They represent the human species in a very "singular stage of its progress." Viewed from a certain angle, both "may be considered as polished states."[70] From a purely political perspective, they are both considerable empires, and merit comparison with advanced oriental despotisms. Referring to the "facts," however, Robertson admits that perspectives vary: "some occur that suggest an idea of considerable progress in civilization in the Mexican empire, and others which seem to indicate that it had advanced but little beyond the savage tribes around it. Both shall be exhibited to the view of the reader."[71] While appearing at first to endorse the notion of the Mexicans as polished, Robertson then wheels around and reexamines this position. The signs of civilization are, following Jose de Acosta's scheme, the possession of property, the number and greatness of cities, the separation of professions, the distinction of ranks, the peculiarly advanced state of government and police, and the improvement of arts and sciences.[72] Conversely, the signs of Mexican savagery are their destructive mode of warfare, their possession of the typical savage trait of desire for vengeance, the poverty of their arts (here Robertson questions the evidence of their "superior refinement in arts"), and more broadly their "ferocity of character." By grounding this argument in terms of character and manners, Robertson shifts its focus away from the possession or otherwise of particular institutions, and more toward the spirit or "genius" that informed those institutions: in a sense, away from social facts and toward internal principles, which it is the historian's special role to interpret.[73]

Religion is a fascinating example of this interplay between institutions and manners, or rather between outward signs of improvement and the

possession of a countervailing "national" character. A crucial sign of civilization, the possession by the Mexicans and Peruvians of regular, powerful, and elaborate "systems" of superstition is, like their "despotic" government (to which they are closely causally linked), a means of partially
admitting their advancement beyond savagery while associating it with
images of corruption, perversion, and degradation, which seem to negate
altogether the tendencies of progress.[74] Despite its indeterminacy in
Robertson's sociological scheme, religion has a crucial impact in defining
the Mexican: "To what circumstances it was owing that superstition assumed such a dreadful form among the Mexicans, we have not sufficient
knowledge to determine. But its effect is visible, and produced an effect
that is singular in the history of the human species."

Religion operates to confuse the simple relationship between the natural
progress of a society and its actual character: "the genius of their religion
so far counterbalanced the influence of policy and arts, that notwithstanding their progress in both, their manners, instead of softening, became more
fierce." Indeed, such was the peculiar effect of this superstition that it
ceases, in fact, to be an effectual sign of civility: "from the extravagance of
their religious notions, or the barbarity of their rites, no conclusion can be
drawn with certainty concerning the degree of their civilisation."[75] Robertson draws a clear distinction between the "degree of . . . civilisation" and
"the character of the people."[76] The Mexican religion confirms and gives
added force to their "ferocity," the mark of their American savagery (although a word also applied insistently to the Spaniards), but also makes it a
peculiarity beyond a social or institutional context—it becomes an essential
component of an independent character. Or rather, since Robertson seems
unable to judge precisely, it harmonizes with this character, is bent to it.

This ferocity, whatever its precise origin, determines their manners in a
way that the signs of progress do not. It also escapes the prison of stadial
typology. Their ferocity is not simply an extreme manifestation of the
savage character, but in some respects moves beyond the savage character
altogether: "The manners of the people in the New World who had made
the greatest progress in the arts of policy, were, in several respects, the
most ferocious, and the barbarity of some of their customs exceeded even
those of the savage state."[77] This conjunction of refinement and a form of
ultrasavagery perhaps implies a *progress* (or progression) of savagery itself, although it is clearly not a positive or enlightened progress. It is this
unaccountable ferocity that explains the disordered shape of the narrative:
how the Mexicans are able to mount a challenge to the Spanish, but also
why they collapse so spectacularly.

Book VII, itself a bifurcation of Robertson's overall treatment of the
American, is further bifurcated by Robertson's separate but parallel

treatment of the Peruvians. Superficially, the Mexicans and Peruvians are similar, the key difference being the apparently greater refinement of the Peruvians. As with the Mexicans, Robertson seeks in book VII to re-align their character with their "savage countrymen," and therefore to revise the estimates of their state of civilization.[78] Yet, in purely social terms, they are clearly the most improved of all Americans, and in his analysis, Robertson makes comparatively little attempt to demolish the claims of the Peruvians to genuine signs of civility and polish, although the same arguments concerning the lack of antiquity and the absence of such elemental skills as writing are still applied. They are to be contrasted with the Mexicans, particularly in having shed (if they ever possessed it) any remnant of savage "ferocity." Yet the Peruvians were not corrupted by improvement: quite the opposite, their "simple manners" succeeded in converting despotism into a beneficial institution.[79] Instead, the Peruvians represent an alternative and quite different picture of American savagery: their counterparts are the gentle, meek, subservient natives of Las Casas, from whose feeble simplicity they should, in strictly social and progressive terms, be most removed. Thus, their character exhibits a fresh species of singularity, for which Robertson tentatively advances two causes. It is, once again, their "spirit of superstition," which formed them to "a national character, more gentle than that of any people in America."[80]

Yet religion may not be the sole or determining cause of this "gentleness of character"; it is as apparent in their civil institutions, and may be linked to the "singular" state of their institutions of property.[81] Whatever the precise causes, their society forms a remarkable unity, with all circumstances tending to reinforce this national character. As with the Mexicans, Robertson turns their potentially positive characteristics away from any positive association, by using the form of "characterology" to condemn this as a weakness, a lacuna, a "fatal defect." Their gentleness is an "unmanly softness," not only a moral lack but also one puzzlingly at odds with their stage of society. Robertson emphasizes the anomalous nature of the Peruvians: "there is not an instance in history of any people so little advanced in refinement, so totally destitute of military enterprize."[82] Here they stand in contrast not only to the Mexicans but also to the "Chilese," who are depicted in book VI as the very pattern of a noble and martial American savagery that had been marginal hitherto (and subsequently) to Robertson's discourse and who stand as a reproach to Peruvian passivity.[83] Thus, classical republicanism combines with the de Pauw thesis to condemn the Peruvians, while Robertson refuses to legitimate their "softness" as a sign of civilization (which had been one of the achievements of Scottish Enlightenment social thought, as Christopher

Berry has noted).[84] "This character hath descended to their posterity," Robertson concluded damningly: the modern Peruvians are "now more tame and depressed than any people of America. Their feeble spirits, relaxed in lifeless inaction, seem hardly capable of any bold or manly exertion." The most civilized people in America had failed utterly to adapt to the conditions of modern civility. In this, interestingly, they paralleled the Creole descendants of the Spanish, depicted by Robertson in book VIII.[85]

Thus, between them, the Peruvians and the Mexicans represent the two halves of the dichotomy of savage character, and serve to expose its contradictions. They both emerge not only as anomalous but also as extreme: the Mexicans carry the savage identity of ferocity to its furthest extent, indeed to an inhuman excess, while the Peruvians extend the passivity of savagery to an absurd feebleness. They are, for Robertson, images of imperfection, existing uneasily alongside more defined categories: existing indeed beyond savagery, but in an ironic and "singular" way. Above all, Robertson uses the language of character as a means of circumscribing and limiting the qualities of the Mexicans and Peruvians, denying them a facile claim to civility; yet, at the same time, character emerges from outside the typology of philosophical history as an independent force, questioning and overturning rigid social categories. It is the strange autonomy of character in the *History of America* that gives his anthropology a rich and suggestive complexity that Robertson himself struggled to contain.

CHAPTER SEVEN

Herder's India

The "Morgenland" in Mythology and Anthropology

Nicholas A. Germana

Johann Gottfried Herder was the progenitor of two related but radically contrasting traditions. First, he coined the term *Volk*, which became the catchword of nineteenth- and twentieth-century German racism. His emphasis on the value of German culture in the eighteenth century, while not entirely devoid of chauvinism, became a hostile, exclusive nationalism in the decades that followed. Second, Herder was one of the great neo-Humanist thinkers of his era, and his focus on the literary traditions not only of Germans, but of other central and eastern European peoples as well, sparked an interest in folk culture throughout Europe. Among the cultures Herder was most captivated by throughout his career was that of the so-called Morgenland.

Herder's conception of the Morgenland, like those of his contemporaries, changed significantly from the 1760s into the first decade of the nineteenth century. His interest as a Lutheran minister began within his own religious tradition, and his early interest lay primarily in Hebrew poetry. The tradition of biblical scholarship was quite advanced in Germany, especially in Protestant areas, and had been since the Reformation. However, with the "rediscovery" of Persian and Indian literary sources in the 1770s and 1780s, Herder began to turn his attention eastward toward South Asia.[1] By the late 1780s and 1790s, Herder's Morgenland was often understood to be India. While his influence on the Early Romantics has been studied with regard to language[2] and nationalism,[3] Herder's example of looking to India for inspiration has been largely ignored.

The focus of this study is on Herder's increasing interest in India from the 1760s right up to the time of his death in 1803, and the uses of the "mythical image" of India in his work.[4] For German thinkers, this image was sometimes as much about their own sense of German identity as it was about India or Indians. Despite the pluralism of Herder's thought, and despite his frequent criticisms of Western imperialism in contemporary India, his image of India, as we shall see, was inseparable from the most central concern of his career: the elevation of German culture to a new and higher place of honor and respect.

Herder's impact went well beyond the Early Romantics to affect German culture in a deeper and more practical way. His thinking on history, culture, and humanity was influential in the development of four new academic disciplines in the late eighteenth and early nineteenth centuries—anthropology, comparative philology, comparative mythology, and *Germanistik*. Though comparative mythology failed to take root in the university, the other disciplines went on to play a central role in the formation of German identity in the nineteenth century. This study focuses primarily on anthropology as a new field of study in relation to Herder's interest in India and the Orient.[5] The other disciplines named above have a common source in the new anthropological emphasis of Herder's works in the latter half of the eighteenth century.

FRAGMENTS ON RECENT GERMAN LITERATURE (1767)

In 1767, three years after leaving Kant's tutelage in Königsberg, Herder published three collections of critical fragments entitled *Fragments on Recent German Literature*. In this essay, Herder sought to carry out an application of the "genetical method" that he had first articulated in an unpublished essay "On the History of Lyrical Poetry" (1764 or 1766–67).[6] This method was inspired by Kant's *Universal Natural History and Theory of the Heavens* (1755), a work that had a deep impact on Herder's historical thinking.[7]

In the first fragment, Herder remarked that "our nursemaids, who train our tongues, are our first teachers of logic."[8] He then announced the *anthropological* focus of the *Fragments*: "The *genius* of its language therefore is the genius of a nation's literature." This anthropological project required a new methodological approach: "How much can be explained on the basis of their environment and their language organs? On the basis of historical evidence, to what extent can the richness and poverty of their language be said to have grown out of their way of thought and life?"[9]

As John Zammito argues, this literary approach to understanding the nature and character of different peoples put Herder at the forefront of a new science in the eighteenth century—anthropology.[10] Herder's emphasis on a historical approach to culture and its development marks one of the earliest efforts in the development of anthropology as a field of inquiry, and eventually as an academic discipline. This approach to anthropology, that is, an examination of language as the best way to understand the history and nature of a people, would dominate the field into the nineteenth century. Philology and linguistics were inseparable from anthropology until race became a determining factor, and eventually *the* determining factor. This transition did not happen overnight, and the struggle between linguists and racial anthropologists became heated in the middle of the nineteenth century until Darwinian evolutionary biology decided the contest in favor of the latter.[11]

In the *Essay on the Origins of Language* (1770), Herder explained in greater detail how exactly primitive human beings might have first learned to articulate themselves through language. Here in the *Fragments*, he cites two specific formative influences—the irresistible force of the passions and intimate proximity to nature. Since the function of language is to communicate, and since early man had only just begun to employ it, Herder concludes that most of his words would have been used to describe (1) states of emotion, and (2) natural objects. For the former, it would be necessary to employ metaphors, and for the latter, some kind of imagery that was intended to bear some resemblance to the object in question. Consequently, he argues that "the earliest languages, therefore, must have been full of images [*bildervoll*] and rich in metaphors [*reich an metaphern*]."[12]

Herder's theory of the development of language is, as Zammito points out, both "*onto*genetic as well as *phylo*genetic."[13] He relates the development of language at the level of the individual to that at the level of the species. This assumption—that earlier historical stages of human life resemble earlier stages in the development of the human individual—was not new in Herder; it goes back at least as far as efforts by Europeans to understand who the Amerindians were in the sixteenth century.[14] What is innovative in the eighteenth century is the Rousseauist praise and admiration for this "childlike" state. As shown below, this aspect of Herder's thinking made India a very attractive subject for him, and gave him a surprising opportunity to compare and connect ancient Indians with ancient Germans.

Due to its abundant imagery and wealth of metaphors, Herder concluded, "this youthful age in the life of language was exclusively *poetic* [*bloß das poetische*]."[15] As mankind matured, however, language was refined and transformed from poetry into prose. Prose, Herder argued, is the style of thinking and communicating that is most suitable for philosophical reflection. Herder's praise for the more poetic, less philosophical language of earlier humans shows a much stronger connection to Rousseau than it does to Kant, especially the Kant of "What Is Enlightenment?" (1784). In that work, Kant argued that Enlightenment is synonymous with the maturation of mankind, akin to the growth and development of the human individual from dependent childhood to autonomous manhood (ideally, at least). Herder doesn't claim or even imply that the development of language into a more mature phase is a positive thing. In fact, he openly laments what that process inevitably leaves behind—"Advanced age knows, instead of beauty, only *correctness*," and "[t]he more language becomes art, the more it removes itself from nature."[16]

In the seventh fragment, Herder compared modern European languages, German included, with what he considered "the *most ancient* language[s]" known to man, Hebrew and Arabic. The differences between these early poetic languages and modern prosaic languages are "as pronounced as that between the way of life in that region and our own."[17] Herder thought the ancient languages were more concrete, with more abundant references to objects in nature and everyday objects like livestock, plants, and other things closely associated with the pastoral life. Modern language is poorer from its lack of concrete words anchored in everyday experience: "The ancients, on the other hand, dealt with coins of gold; they spoke through images, whereas we, at best, speak with images."[18]

Herder went on to use Arabic as an example of how ancient languages were rich in synonyms, while modern European languages, more exact and precise, had far fewer:

> The Arabian poet, who has at his disposal five hundred words to say lion, words that connote varying conditions such as young, hungry lion, etc., is able to paint with a word, and thus is able to achieve, by means of these images captured in one sweep, setting them one against the other, more *manifold* expression than we, who are able to create distinct variation only by adding modifiers.[19]

Through this examination of the historical development of language, Herder did two things. First, he demonstrated a profound difference between the richer, poetic language of the ancients and the more precise, less-colorful prose of modern European languages. He also put together some of the key pieces that constitute the "mythical image" of the Orient. The people of the Morn, the *Morgenländer*, stand in an ideal, childlike relationship to nature and consequently to language. Their language is a window into their souls.

If Oriental languages served to illustrate Herder's ideal of childlike purity, French epitomized modern, sterile, philosophical language. Herder purposefully joined German with the Oriental languages in opposition to French. In the thirteenth fragment, he came back to the strength of the German language, particularly in relation to French. The German language, he concluded, is closer to its original form and, consequently, has not developed entirely away from its original richness. The closer a language is to the original, he claimed, "the freer it will be."[20] He continued, "[a]ll of this is confirmed by the French language," which has developed into a clearer "language of reason." As a result, however, the French language has surrendered its wealth of synonyms and inversions. It has become more precise and therefore more rigid. Herder was able to "conclude at once that its order is inferior to our own, because ours provides greater room to adjust its order to each purpose."[21] He continued this critical evaluation of French in the conclusion to the first collection of *Fragments*, entitled "On the Ideal of Language." He conceded to the Francophile the claim of refinement, but found the language poorer for it: "Now, just as a handsome polite person, clear and rational in conversation, is more readily suffered in social intercourse than a profound and quiet man, the French language has gathered for itself, over the German, the predicate of intellect, though our own might claim the title of a *language of higher reason*."[22]

The second collection of the *Fragments* was also published in 1767, and took as its central theme "On the means of rousing genius in Germany." Having established the affinity between German and the Oriental languages, Herder devoted the bulk of the collection to a consideration of German "orientalizing poetic art" in comparison with "the originals upon which it is based."[23] Here is where he also makes his strongest case for a cosmopolitan nationalism, a German cultural nationalism grounded not in exclusiveness, but in the appropriate inspiration by other cultures. "Oriental," particularly Hebrew, literature was the central source of his inspiration.

As far removed from the worlds of the Hebrews and Arabs as they were, Herder argued that German poets could take inspiration from the national spirit, from the patriotism of the ancient poets. The Hebrews, in particular, stand out for the strength of their national character: "In the initial formation of each people, patriotism enflames the veins, but in none has this sanguine ferment prevailed as long as it has in this one."[24] The national spirit of their poetry is intimately connected to what Herder called their "national prejudices."[25] Among the "national prejudices" of the Morgenländer, Herder included their proclivity for fantastic tales and fables. This early stage in human development, the childhood of mankind, was an era when imagination reigned. For the Enlightenment, this faculty was indicative of inferior minds, and their religious rituals and fables were denigrated as superstition and ignorance. Following Rousseau, and presaging the Romantics, Herder held up the products of this early phase as artifacts of a richer, more creative era in human history.

In fragment 7 of the second collection, Herder suggested the best way for modern Germans to feel the proper influence of Oriental poetry, that is, through the act of translation. Simply imitating the works of the Morgenländer would be insufficient. Instead, Germans would do better to devote themselves to "oriental philology," to a comprehensive study of Oriental languages. Such an endeavor, he argued, "will cast poor and stupid mimics to the winds."[26] Intimate familiarity with the "beauty and genius" of other nations will result in the recognition of the beauty and genius within one's own—"it is a model of emulation that remains original."[27] Herder himself would later take this advice to heart as he offered some minor "explications" (the translations were not his own) of some Sanskrit texts. August Wilhelm and Friedrich Schlegel were among the first Germans to take this approach to Indian texts in the decades after 1800.

THE OLDEST DOCUMENT OF THE HUMAN RACE (1774)

A number of unpublished texts from the late 1760s and early 1770s, including one on the "*Archäologie des Morgenlandes*" (1769), resulted in the publication of *Die Älteste Urkunde des Menschengeschlechts* in 1774. The titles of these works indicate the direction of Herder's investigations. Under the influence of Johann David Michaelis, the leading Hebrew scholar in Germany, as well as Johann Joachim Winckelmann, Herder was looking at literature and mythology as "documents" that modern scholars could use to understand primitive cultures, and, even more important, to *compare* them.

In the *Älteste Urkunde*, Herder was looking for structural connections between the mythologies and/or languages of these different cultures. For example, he conjectured that the seven syllables of the Greek alphabet are the product of cultural influence from Egypt, and he connected them with the seven main gods of ancient Egypt.[28] He speculated that there was a connection between Egyptian and Chinese cultures based on their common use of visual symbols (hieroglyphs and pictographs) instead of an alphabet.[29] He also argued that the same sensual themes of heaven/earth and day/night can be found in the religious texts of the various Oriental cultures.[30] However, he asked, if such striking similarities exist between these cultures, why is this the case? Is it because the oldest among them received revelation (*Offenbar*), and then transmitted it to the other cultures over time, like a historical/cultural game of telephone? As with the advent of human language, Herder concluded that this was not the case. Rather, each culture, and consequently its productions, was formed by the collective work of both endogenous and exogenous forces. Doubtless, all of these early peoples preserved in their language and traditions some trace of man's primordial religious experience. That experience was then shaped by internal necessities and proclivities, as well as external influence of other cultures. Consequently, Herder saw a deeper unity behind the remarkable diversity among these cultures; he saw "One and the same image [*Bild*] in different forms [*Gestalten*]."[31]

In addition to referring to India, albeit in passing, the *Älteste Urkunde* points toward Herder's work of the 1780s in another way. His main source of information on Persian religion came from Abraham Anquetil Duperron's rendering of the *Zend-Avesta* (1771). Duperron's translation marked an important breakthrough in the study of the Persian language, and would have important consequences on the later breakthrough into Sanskrit by both himself and Sir William Jones.[32] Herder's reading of the *Zend-Avesta* is an indication that he was reading the most cutting-edge material on Oriental languages being done in Europe at the time. It also signaled the beginning of the movement of Herder's image of the Morgenland further east.

AUCH EINE PHILOSOPHIE DER GESCHICHTE ZUR BILDUNG DER MENCHHEIT (1774) AND IDEEN ZUR PHILOSOPHIE DER GESCHICHTE DER MENSCHHEIT (1784–1792)

By the mid-1770s, Herder had committed himself to a more ambitious project—a comprehensive history of human cultures. His *Ideen zur Philosophie der Geschichte der Menschheit* took the project to its extreme by attempting to trace the history of man through the natural history of the world beginning with its formation and climates and its habitation by the first plants and animals. For the purposes of this chapter, what is most important about these broadly historical works is their attempt to trace the influence of one culture on another as they developed over time. In both works, the Orient has the pride of place as the part of the world where humankind began its divinely guided journey. In the

1770s, Herder's Orient was constituted primarily of what we call the Middle East, extending as far east as Persia. By the 1780s, however, as British colonial officials and scholars began to unearth ancient Indian documents, Herder's Orient shifted further eastward. This eastward shift of the "Orient" was not Herder's doing alone, but was part of a general trend in European Orientalism.[33] As a consequence of this trend, ancient Indian culture came to represent the childlike ideal that is so central to the mythical image. It is even more important, however, that Herder's representation of India and the Orient was inextricably tied to his political philosophy and his attitude toward the condition of the Holy Roman Empire in his day.

Auch eine Philosophie, a self-deprecating title indicating that it is just "another" attempt at such a project, was published in 1774. It contains the most forceful expression of Herder's pluralism as it is celebrated by Isaiah Berlin, as well as unequivocal condemnations of European imperialism and "enlightened" despotism. As with earlier works, there is a tension between Herder's insistence on the equality of all cultures and his belief that Christianity is the most humane and important development in human history. He reconciled his pluralism with his belief in some kind of progress through recourse to Providence, to a teleological understanding of history.

In *Auch eine Philosophie*, Herder identified three distinct stages in the development of human history that correspond to the development of human beings. The ancient Orient marks the childhood (*Kindheit*) of mankind, while the age of the Egyptians, Phoenicians, and Greeks marks the boyhood (*Knabenalters*), and the Romans signal the manhood (*Mannesalter*) of the human race. Herder pictured Providence (*Vorsehung*) guiding the development of human culture from its birthplace near the Euphrates, Oxus, and Ganges Rivers, down to the Nile and on to Greece and Phoenicia.[34]

As the birthplace of human culture, the Orient is also the birthplace of human religion, the "rightly chosen soil of the gods!" (*recht auserwählter Boden Gottes!*).[35] Herder praised the Morgenländer for their "childlike devotion" (*kindliche Ergebung*) to their gods. In fact, he concluded that in these earliest societies, religious devotion was inseparable from the form and means of government. He speculated that as a rule, "the oldest philosophy and form of government in all lands must have naturally originated in theology."[36] He derided his fellow Europeans for their misunderstanding of ancient Oriental societies. They were not simply passive subjects of "oriental despotism"; rather, their obedience came from reverence for *Vaterautorität* (the authority of the father)—it was an expression of genuine religious sentiment. Herder identified a primitive universal monotheism in the varied polytheistic cultures of Greece, Egypt, and the Orient. Wilhelm Halbfass has shown that this Deism was a common element in Enlightenment views of India and the Orient.[37] Particularly for someone as favorable to Rousseau as Herder was, this vague, primitive Deism was highly regarded as childlike and pure.

Herder's chastisement of his contemporaries' attitudes toward "oriental despotism" is important for two reasons. First, for the purposes of the historian or literary scholar, it makes Herder's inclusion in the Saidian category of an "Orientalist" problematic. He did not associate despotism with ancient Oriental cultures, but rather, with his own. This leads to the second point. Like Montaigne (whom Herder admired greatly) in his essay "On Cannibals," Herder was clearly using this image of the pure, childlike Morgenländer to reflect back negatively on contemporary European culture. He argued that despotism was introduced to the Orient by foreign conquerors, by which he meant Muslims and Europeans. The purity of the innocent Oriental was spoiled by the "cold" thought and ways of the European.[38] This strong aversion to European colonialism remained with Herder throughout the rest of his life. In the third installment of the *Ideen zur Philosophie der Geschichte der Menschheit* (1787), he proclaimed that the European colonizers appear "impure, dark, and wild" in comparison to the virtuous Indians.[39] In the tenth collection of the *Humanitätsbriefe* (1797), he referred to Bartolomé de Las Casas's accounts of the Spanish conquest of the West Indies.[40] Herder clearly employed the same rhetorical strategy used by Las Casas in his *Short Account of the Destruction of the Indies* (1542), by ironically making the pagan natives out to be ideally submissive, Christlike people, while portraying the European invaders as the brutal and immoral savages. In the 1790s, he used the same strategy to compare Germans with their European neighbors.

Herder's critique of his contemporaries on the issue of "oriental despotism" reflected his own deep dissatisfaction with the state of Europe, and Germany in particular, in his time. He juxtaposed for the reader the innocent and reverent world of the ancients with the stifling forms of monarchy that reigned in Europe. As human culture spread historically from the ancient Oriental river civilizations to Egypt and on to Greece and Rome, Herder noted that one of the most conspicuous signs of the "aging" process was the evolution of more sophisticated forms of governance. When mankind reached its *Mannesalter* during the Roman Empire, its most salient feature was the dominance of the state.[41] In his own day, Herder complained that all-powerful and intrusive governments stifled the human potential for self-governance (*Selbstgerechtigkeit*), personal growth and development (*Selbstwürde*), and self-determination

(*Selbstbestimmung*).[42] In 1780, he had outlined what he believed to be the appropriate, limited, sphere of government in another prize-winning essay, "On the Influence of Government on the Sciences, and of the Sciences on Government." The arts and sciences are better able to flourish, he argued, when government interfered as little as possible.[43] These criticisms echoed Montesquieu's critique of despotism and anticipated Wilhelm von Humboldt's passion for *Bildung*.

As culture spread and mankind aged, the growth of despotic government was accompanied by a denigration of the pure religious principles that inspired the "*kindlichen Religionsgefuhl*" of the Morgenländer: "The religion of the ancient world, which had come from the Morgenland through Egypt, to Greece and Rome had lost its aroma (*verduftetes*) and become powerless."[44] From early on, Herder associated flowers and their powerful aroma with the richness of Oriental culture.[45] In introducing the inhabitants of Northern Europe, Herder contrasted their cold climate with the "*Aromatischen Treibhause Osts*"—the aromatic hothouse of the East.[46] This chronology is consistent with Herder's ideas about the "aging" of language from poetry to philosophical prose. As mankind grew out of its childhood and into maturity, the richness and naturalness of poetry was replaced by cold, rational, philosophical prose.

Herder saw in the religions of the Northern European peoples the remnants (*Reste*) of Oriental culture refashioned in the "Northern character" (*Nordische Art*). He didn't address the question of transmission, of how there could have been an Oriental cultural influence on the various peoples of Northern Europe. The people that inhabited this region, according to Herder, were very different from the Morgenländer as a result of climatic and other differences, but they shared one all-important quality— their wildness. Drawing on the portrayal of the ancient Germans in Tacitus, Herder described the ancient Northern Europeans as "*Wilden*" (wild people), a term he also liberally employed when describing the Morgenländer.[47] Their wildness, their innocence, and their closeness to nature made them ideally suited to reinvigorate the true spirit of the Oriental religions, and, indeed, they brought that spirit to its highest fruition in human history, European Christianity. The idea that ancient Germans received a special cultural transmission from the Orient would reach its greatest prominence in the Heidelberg Romantic circle, particularly in the works of Friedrich Creuzer, the brothers Grimm, and Joseph Görres.

Herder used the Orient as an ideal mirror in which he could see the reflection of Germany. It was very much an ideal mirror because it reflected back to the viewer precisely what he wanted to see. Herder was grinding two axes in *Auch eine Philosophie*. First, he was making a statement about his hatred of European despotism, whether in the form of imperialism abroad or "enlightened" monarchy in Europe. The Morgenländer were driven to their great achievements not by the force of a tyrant, but by their religious reverence for *Vaterautorität*. Second, Herder was elevating the German people to a much higher place in history. He associated true Christianity with the purity of the Northern European peoples. Compared to the glory of Rome (and, one might add, France), the northern tribes had no vast empire and no inexhaustible wealth, but their very wildness made them ideally suited to rejuvenate the religious spirit of the ancient East, and with it mark an unprecedented advancement in the history of mankind. One can see here the same sentiment expressed by A. W. Schlegel: "If the regeneration of the human species started in the East, Germany must be considered the Orient of Europe."[48]

Susanne Zantop was one of the few scholars to recognize the *identification* of many German thinkers with colonized peoples.[49] In *Colonial Fantasies*, Zantop argued that Herder and other German thinkers emphasized Germany's political weakness as a way of asserting moral and spiritual superiority. In the collection of the *Humanitätsbriefe*, Herder published a poem on the topic of *Deutsche Nationalruhm*—German national glory. In this poem, he proclaimed that the glory of the Germans lay in their moral greatness, a quality shared by all colonized, subjugated peoples:

> "Morality of ancient times! How did we
> Lose our national glory,
> And become German negroes?"

> Well! The first glory
> Of the Nation is Innocence; never to
> Bathe the hand in blood, to
> Force it to be forgotten,
> As one's own blood.

> The second glory is moderation.
> The Hindus' and Peruvians' pain,
> The rage of Blacks, the roasted Montezuma
> Of Mexico, all call to heaven still
> Begging to be avenged!
> Believe me, friend, no Zeus with this choir
> Of gods will visit a people that,
> Burdened with guilt, blood, and sins
> And gold and diamonds, sits down to dine!
> He joins instead the frugal meal
> Of quiet Ethiopians and Germans.

> (*"Moral der alten Zeiten! Doch wohin
> Sind wir verirrt von Nationalruhm
> Zu Deutschen Negern?"*

> *Wohl! Der erste Ruhm*
> *Der Nation ist Unschuld; nie die Hand*
> *Im Blut zu waschen, auch gezwungen es*
> *So zu vergießen, als sein eignes Blut.*
>
> *Die zweite Ruhm ist Mäßigung. Es ruft*
> *Der Hindus und der Peruaner Noth,*
> *Die Wuth der Schwarzen und der Mexicaner*
> *Gebratner Montezuma rufen noch*
> *Zum Himmel auf, und flehn Entsündigung!*
> *O glaube, Freund, kein Zeus mit seinem Chor*
> *Der Götter kehrt zu einem Volke, das*
> *Mit solcher Schuld- und Blut- und Sündenlast*
> *Und Gold- und Demanlast beladen schmauf't*
> *Er kehrt bey stillen Aethiopiern*
> *Und Deutschen ein, zu ihrem armen Mahl.)*[50]

For Herder, the Germans stood side by side with other colonized peoples of the world. In the third volume of the *Ideen* (1787), Herder lamented the conquest of the wild, independent German peoples, first by Nordic invaders, then by Christian Franks under Charlemagne. Prior to that time, the Germans had lived in isolation longer than any other European people, which accounted for their "wildness" and the other noble attributes they shared with the Morgenländer (as we saw in *Auch eine Philosophie*), as well as Native Americans.[51] He repeated this lamentation in the *Humanitätsbriefe* ten years later in the context of another condemnation of European imperialism.[52]

Herder also made direct references in the *Ideen* to the characteristics that the German people have in common with the Morgenländer. For example, when comparing the Indians to the "impure, dark, and wild" Europeans, he stated that one of the defining qualities of the Indians is "*keuschheit*" (purity).[53] In describing the Germans, also as victims of European imperialism, Herder claimed that the women of all German peoples ("*allen Deutschen Stämmen*") are industrious, trustworthy, honorable, and pure (*keusch*).[54] These are the shared qualities of honorable, oppressed peoples.

In the *Ideen*, Herder devoted several pages to a consideration of the role of the Brahmin caste in India. Most notable in his thinking about Brahmins was Herder's respect for the role they play as preservers and transmitters of Hindu culture. He recognized the prominence of Hindu Brahmins, not just in religious matters, but in Indian politics as well.[55] Herder concluded that the "Brahmin establishment" (*Einrichtung der Bramanen*) was beneficial to Hindu culture because it preserved traditions that bound the people together as a *Volk*, and helped preserve the morality of the people, which stood in such marked contrast to the sinful Europeans. He attributed to the Brahmin caste itself a morality that was unquestionably "pure and lofty" (*rein und erhaben*).[56]

The role of Brahmins as preservers and transmitters of culture was especially important, Herder argued, because the Hindus did not preserve their culture, as the Greeks later would, in history. The rich mythology of Hinduism treats the origins of the world, their people, and the various castes that make up Hindu society, in an entirely ahistorical way.[57] In the fourth collection of his *Zerstreute Blätter* (1792), Herder took a Winckelmannian approach to the problem of Indian history by turning to an analysis of Hindu monuments and art, in which he found evidence of a pervasive religious culture that was both "local and national." This religious culture had its origins near the Ganges, and consequently (though Herder didn't put it this way), with the Brahmin caste that claimed that region as its birthplace.[58] In the *Ideen*, Herder concluded that every people in their childhood needs to have some kind of Brahmin class. He found parallels in the Mandarins of China and the Lamas of Tibet.[59]

Ronald Inden has argued that many European thinkers viewed the foundation of Indian society as "essentially idealistic (that is, apolitical)."[60] In this view, caste is the defining institution in Indian society. Friedrich Schlegel, Novalis, and Hegel all held similar views about the apolitical nature of ancient Indian culture. For Hegel, in particular, this was evidence of India's low place in the teleological unfolding of world history. Given Herder's aversion to centralized government, however, he saw the cohesiveness provided by the Brahmin caste as a good thing, and an essential element in the growth and spread of Hindu culture.

Herder was not entirely uncritical of the Brahmins, however. There is a fundamental problem with one class in society having complete control over all religious and political matters, all of the arts and sciences. When Herder said that all peoples in their childhood needed a Brahmin class, he had to be conscious of Kant's "What Is Enlightenment?," which was published three years earlier. Enlightenment, Kant famously proclaimed, is man's release from self-incurred tutelage. Despite many disagreements with his former mentor, Herder too had a teleological view of history, as we have seen. Continued domination of the Indian *Volk* by the Brahmins inevitably made them "ripe" (*reif*) for "subjugation" (*Unterjochung*).[61] It is interesting here that Herder did not focus on the actual domination of the Brahmins over their countrymen. Instead, he claimed that their *Herrschaft* made the people "ripe" for subjugation, presumably at the hands of others. *Herrschaft* has the connotation of legitimacy, as in the rule of lords over vassals in the European Middle Ages. *Unterjochung* connotes a more humiliating experience of subjugation—literally, to be put under a yoke. Even in this criticism of the Brahmins, Herder subtly turned the accusation of despotism back on the Europeans.

The first volume of the *Ideen* was published in the fateful year 1784. That same year the Asiatick Society of Calcutta was founded by a group of British imperial officials; most prominent among them was the jurist and Persian scholar Sir William Jones. With the sanction of Governor General Warren Hastings, the society was established to uncover and translate native literary sources that would assist the East India Company in its administration of the regions they controlled in India. The Asiatick Society was, therefore, a quintessentially "Orientalist" institution from its inception. In the years that followed the society's foundation, members, and associates turned out translations of important sources that opened up Indian culture to the West for the first time.

Herder kept himself abreast of the most recent European scholarship on the Morgenland. As seen above, in the 1770s, his image of Persia and Zoroastrianism came from Anquetil Duperron's translation of the *Zend-Avesta*. In the *Ideen*, his sources on Indian thought and culture included some of the most prominent Orientalist scholars from Britain and France, such as Alexander Dow, Nathaniel Halhed, John Holwell, Sir James Mackintosh, and Pierre Sonnerat. In the late 1780s and early 1790s, Herder's image of India became increasingly shaped by the new work being done by the Asiatick Society and its members. In particular, he became passionately engaged with Charles Wilkins's translation of the *Bhagavad-Gita* (1785), and Jones's translation of the fifth-century Indian Sanskrit drama *Shakuntala, or the Fateful Ring* (1789).[62] More than any other single source, *Shakuntala* helped shape the mythical image of India for Herder and his contemporaries. Jones's translation of the play into English, followed in 1791 by Georg Forster's translation from the English into German, inaugurated what Raymond Schwab has called the "*Shakuntala* Era" in Europe.[63]

Forster sent Herder a copy of his translation in May 1791.[64] Herder was so taken by the play that, the following year, he published a passionate review in the fourth collection of his *Zerstreute Blätter*. This collection contained Herder's most enthusiastic writings on India. In addition to the essay on *Shakuntala*, the collection also included the *Denkmale der Vorwelt* essay referred to above (and considered again below), and the poetic work *Gedanken einiger Bramanen*. This last work consisted of reworkings of Indian themes found in Abraham Rogers's Latin translations of the poetry of Bhartrihari.[65] It is noteworthy that when Peter von Bohlen published a German translation of Bhartrihari in 1833, he chose to keep four of Herder's renderings, despite the fact that Herder never had access to the Sanskrit originals, nor would he have been able to read them if he had.

Whatever other sources Herder drew from, it was unquestionably *Shakuntala* that most informed his image of India. He felt certain that this drama provided an insight into the "philosophy and religion, the way of life and the morals of the Indians" that could not be found anywhere else.[66] He marveled at the sight of an "earlier age of innocence, where gods and men live [together]."[67] Herder even lamented that Europeans were not in possession of more literary works like *Shakuntala*, which was so much more informative than the "never-ending religious books" of the Vedas, Upavedas, and Upangas.[68] In order for his contemporaries to have such an appreciation for the drama, however, Herder cautioned that it was necessary for them to read the play with the "delicate consideration, stillness, and care" of the Indian, rather than the "fleeting curiosity" of the European.[69]

Shakuntala begins with a traditional benediction to Siva and a prologue between the "actor-manager" and an "actress." Goethe planned a stage production of the play, and Raymond Schwab claims that the brief prologue to *Shakuntala* was the inspiration for the "Prologue in the Theater" at the beginning of *Faust*.[70] The story line of the play involves the great love between an Indian king, Duschmanta, and a Brahmin's daughter, Shakuntala. The importance of *Shakuntala* for Herder is clear from his comparison of the play with the works of Shakespeare and Ossian (whose authenticity was still without question for him). He was particularly pleased to report that no less an authority than Sir William Jones had drawn the connection between Kalidasa and the English Bard.[71] Ossian and Shakespeare had been held up by Herder as prime examples of national literary genius in the *Alte Volkslieder* and other works from the mid-1770s. Once again, Herder gave India the primacy of place when he claimed that the oldest and most beautiful (*schönsten*) fables originated there. The Indians' "delicate feel for fairy tales (*feine Märchengeist*)," he continued, is clearly evident in their mythology.[72]

Keeping with his claims about the centrality of flowers in Indian symbolism, Herder emphasized the prominence of flowers in the play. In *Denkmale der Vorwelt*, Herder explained that Indian mythology is "entirely a metaphysics of flower and plant life" (*so ganz eine Metaphysik des Blumen- und Pflanzenlebens*), and that "every flower teaches us this system (the Indians love flowers)."[73] Shakuntala exemplifies this aspect of Indian culture by her great affection for and closeness to the flowers and trees in the sacred grove. When Duschmanta first sees her, she is watering the trees and talking to them. Herder noted that her tone as she speaks to the flowers is the loving tone of a sister—"*Tief ist das Gefuhl.*"[74] The flower symbolism in *Shakuntala* reinforced Herder's long-held opinion that the more innocent, childlike Morgenländer shared a relationship with nature that was lost to prosaic modern man.

The essay *Ueber Denkmale der Vorwelt* has two parts. The first part of the essay contains Herder's thoughts about how to best approach the topic, and his observations concerned Greece, Persia, and Egypt, as well as India. The second part of the essay is concerned almost exclusively with Indian monuments. As indicated above, *Denkmale der Vorwelt* reflects the important influence of Winckelmann on Herder's thought. It is remarkable among Herder's works because it deals with plastic art, sculpture, and architecture, rather than with literary productions. The image that Herder seized on as most central to Indian art is, as we have seen, the flower. He noted that in Indian art Brahma appears on a lotus, and Krishna pays tribute to his beloved Lakshmi by adorning her with flowers.[75] Interestingly, Herder's main source for the importance of flowers in Hindu symbolism was not from the plastic arts, but from Jones's and Forster's introductions to *Shakuntala*.

Herder took it as one of his main tasks in the essay to refute (*widerlegen*) contemporary criticisms of Indian art. A common criticism of Indian art at the time was that it was grotesque, that brightly colored, four-armed, highly ornamented icons could never be beautiful like the ideal, humane forms that characterized Greek iconography. The distracting, fantastic images of Hindu deities were among the main reasons why the classicist Goethe could not embrace Herder's fascination with India.[76] Herder explained the sensational images of the Hindu deities as a product of their youthful sensualism; consequently, he held them in high esteem. The Indians alone among the nations of the earth put their "sensual desire" (*sinnliche Wohllust*) to the service of reverence for the gods.[77] The fantastic representations of Hindu gods are not evidence that the ancient Indians were incapable of reproducing realistic works of art. Herder cited Karsten Niebuhr's assessment that Indian representations of elephants are in fact superior to those done by the ancient Egyptians.[78]

Another criticism of Indian art, from a Grecophile perspective, was that the Hindu gods, despite being so colorful, lacked liveliness. Herder refuted this argument with a claim that would be revived by Friedrich Creuzer two decades later, causing great controversy in Germany. Herder argued that Hindu gods, unlike Greek gods, were *not* personifications, but rather embodiments of previously existing religious "symbolic concepts" (*symbolischen Begriffe*).[79] Brahma, for example, embodies the creative principle of the Divine, Vishnu embodies sustenance, and Siva destruction. These deities are intended to represent aspects of the One divine force or reality that permeates all of existence. The Greek gods, by contrast, were given human qualities and lives, reflecting less concern with religious symbolism.[80] The more anthropomorphic gods of the Greek pantheon reflected a focus on man, while the fantastic imagery of the Hindu gods reflected a deep religious sentiment. Herder attributed this predominantly religious quality of Indian art to the dominance of the Brahmin caste in all aspects of Indian life.[81]

Herder's contention that the ornamentation of Indian art reflects its expression of religious symbolism is associated with his larger claim that Indian art and literature are deeply philosophical. This bold claim, that these "primitive," pagan people articulated philosophical systems at such an early date was influential in shaping Friedrich Schlegel's image of India. Hegel grudgingly admitted that the ancient Indians had constructed philosophical systems, while simultaneously insisting that they were hardly worthy of the proud name of philosophy as it had reached its apex in the modern West.

Herder then went on to summarize the main points of the Hindu philosophical system as expressed in Indian art. First, he continued a theme that we have seen before by arguing that Hinduism is grounded in a latent monotheism. Creation, sustenance, and destruction are the three forces that permeate the universe, but they are all aspects of the same divine reality. Second, Herder briefly addressed the importance of *Seelenwanderung*, or reincarnation. Here he cited passages from Wilkins's 1785 English translation of the *Bhagavad-Gita*. He offered another reason for the style of Indian art by arguing that the Hindu belief in reincarnation causes them to see the body as a mere "collection of elements" (*Zusammengefeßtes von Elementen*).[82] Third, in a line of reasoning similar to the first one, he pointed to the Hindu idea of Brahm (Brahman). As opposed to the deity Brahma, Brahm is the primordial One out of which the multitude of beings in the universe originate and to which they return. The gods represent aspects of this original, amorphous unity.[83]

Herder's excitement and enthusiasm are evident in this passage, which includes a German translation of Krishna's address to Arjuna, taken from Wilkins's *Bhagavad-Gita*: "no thing is a part of Him, all things are in Him; they are expressions of Him" (*kein Ding ist ein Theil von Ihm, alle Dinge sind in ihm; sie sind sein Abdruck*).[84] Herder concludes the essay with two more of his own translations from Wilkins, expressing the same idea of the unity of all being, and of the individual's personal relationship with the Godhead. These excerpts constituted the first translations of the *Bhagavad-Gita* into German.

THE LEGACY OF HERDER'S "MORGENLAND"

There are few, if any, issues that engaged the Early Romantics that were not first dealt with by Herder. Their fascination with language, fables and folktales, mythology, and nationalism, can all be traced back to the influence of Herder. As we have seen, the same is true of the Early Romantic obsession with India. Herder's image of India is significant for two main reasons: the first pertaining to debates that were raging in his own day, the second pertaining to debates about German identity that would take center stage in the first two or three decades of the nineteenth century.

Herder's main interest in India, and his interest in other cultures generally, was always subordinated to his desire to honor German culture and encourage its growth. From his earliest essays in the 1760s, Herder argued that German "oriental" writers should look to the poetry of the Morgenland as a source for inspiration in their attempts to create German literature. Herder's "pluralism" was the product of his desire to assert the value of German *Kultur* (culture) at a time when French culture was heralded as the model to be emulated by all civilized peoples. If every culture is unique and special, then no one culture can claim to be the model for all mankind.

In the 1760s and 1770s, the Morgenland Herder spoke of was primarily the Orient of the ancient Jews, and the literature with which he was primarily concerned was the Pentateuch. It was not by accident that Herder chose the ancient Near East as the place where his Garden of Eden would be set. Not only was this region the birthplace of Judaism and Christianity, but the ancient Morgenländer were ideally suited to play the role of the Rousseauist "noble savages." Herder's Rousseauist romanticism led him to embrace the "childlike" figure of the ancient Oriental and celebrate his innocence and purity. Later thinkers accepted the same characterization of the Indian as childlike and close to nature. Novalis embraced the idea and praised this quality, while Hegel held it in disdain. Like Rousseau, Herder also intended to show contemporary Europeans how corrupt their advanced state of civilization had become. While the Orient was held up by Herder as a source of inspiration, it was always—either explicitly or implicitly—in contrast to French culture.

From the mid-1780s on, Herder's Morgenland moved further east until it reached India. India was particularly appealing to Herder because it allowed him to simultaneously compare Germany with the childlike, wild innocence of the Indians, and contrast it with the brutal imperialism of the French and British. Herder's image of India was depoliticized and emphasized the centrality of religion and the Brahmin caste. This image reflected

Herder's idealized image of Germany or, rather, his image of an ideal Germany. *Kultur* was what made Germany great, not politics. Germany's political weakness, like that of ancient India, was not simply accompanied by, but was the cause of its cultural greatness.

Herder opened the door for the Early Romantics by introducing them to his image of India, but his greatest influence was felt in German universities in the first two decades of the nineteenth century. Four new disciplines came into existence at this time that can be traced directly back to Herder's work and bear the stamp of his passion for India—anthropology, comparative mythology, *Germanistik*, and comparative philology. Friedrich Creuzer's work on comparative mythology was anticipated in *Älteste Urkunde des Menschengeschlechts* and *Auch eine Philosophie*. Although this discipline did not take root, as did the other three, its impact was forceful and controversial. Like Creuzer's comparative mythology, *Germanistik* was most closely associated with the Heidelberg Romantics. The brothers Grimm and the controversial Joseph Görres, as well as Clemens von Brentano, contributed to the excavation of German folklore begun by Herder.[85] Like Herder, and A. W. Schlegel, these thinkers traced the origins of German folktales and mythology back to India. Friedrich Schlegel went even further by suggesting a linguistic—and, by implication, racial—lineage. Finally, Bopp's comparative philology was inaugurated with his study of Sanskrit grammar in 1816. Bopp himself was deeply influenced by Herder, and his emphasis on a comparative approach to languages is clearly rooted in Herder's work on the same subject dating back to the 1760s. Bopp taught Sanskrit to Wilhelm von Humboldt, and later became the first scholar to offer courses in Sanskrit at the University of Berlin, following his appointment as chair of Oriental Languages in 1821.

Finally, each of these disciplines was grounded in a new scholarly approach to all of the academic fields that we associate today with the "humanities"—anthropology. John H. Zammito has treated this subject in detail in his recent book *Kant, Herder, and the Birth of Anthropology*. Herder's primary interest was in the nature of human society and culture, and in his works he began to lay the foundations for the discipline of anthropology that we know today. The sources he consulted were primarily literary, and occasionally in the plastic arts, whereas nineteenth-century anthropology would be grounded in archaeology and biology. Once again, we can see that Herder's interest in Oriental cultures was one of the driving forces behind his explorations and experiments in this field.

PART TWO

Ethnography and Enlightened Anthropology

CHAPTER EIGHT

The German Enlightenment
and the Pacific

John Gascoigne

The distant mirror of the Pacific gave varying reflections from different European vantage points. As the "new world" of the Pacific[1] came into closer view in the period after the end of the Seven Years' War in 1763, so too it was drawn into enlightened discourse on the proper functioning of human society. Where previously America had largely provided the human laboratory for exploring the beginnings and development of social institutions (as Locke had written, "in the beginning all the World was *America*"),[2] by the late eighteenth century, the Pacific was providing a fresher alternative.[3] For the French philosophes, the reports brought back from the Pacific provided further fuel to attack what they considered the artificiality of their social institutions and the baleful influence of religious dogma—such, for example, formed the essential themes of Diderot's *Supplement to the Voyage of Bougainville*.

Where the French Enlightenment challenged the existing structures in church and state, in its English and Scottish manifestations, the Enlightenment tended to seek the path of improvement. New knowledge, such as that from the Pacific, helped shape theories about the way in which society could change and develop without major rupture. English voyagers in the Pacific were also not quite as quick to paint Pacific societies in the glowing colors of French explorers such as Bougainville or Philibert Commersen, the naturalist who accompanied him: James Cook and Joseph Banks certainly admired much of what they saw in the Pacific—and, above all, Tahiti—but they did not shy away from underlining such less-palatable features of Polynesian society as infanticide, frequent warfare, and, in places, cannibalism.

The British tendency to look more cautiously than the French at the new world of the Pacific and to be less inclined to use explorers' accounts as a stick with which to beat their own society largely suited the more cautious world of the German *Aufklärung*—a movement that helped to give identity to the bewildering array of the German-speaking lands. "Germany? But where is it?" asked Goethe and Schiller in 1797, "I don't know how to find such a country."[4] True, the German-speaking world had no clear political expression apart from the ramshackle Holy Roman Empire, but it valued its traditions and separate identity, and few sought to reconstruct anew the institutions in the manner urged by some of the French philosophes.[5] Rather, the hope of most of the *Aufklärer* was that the ancient German institutions could be reshaped by a process of growth and development[6]—very much in the manner urged by many of the leading lights of the English and Scottish Enlightenments.

This affinity between Germany and Britain helps to explain the increasing interest in British thought in the last quarter of the eighteenth century, at the time when the German Enlightenment was developing its characteristic forms. French thought—and, above all, the work of the ubiquitous Rousseau—remained important, but its dominance was increasingly challenged. This was perhaps because the later French Enlightenment developed along more radical and less evolutionary lines than those embodied in the earlier work of a figure such as Montesquieu, whose sympathy for tradition and espousal of reform rather than revolution had long endeared him to German thinkers.[7] The English intellectual influence was strengthened by the Hanoverian connection with the British monarchy, particularly as the University of Göttingen (founded in 1737) came to play an increasingly important role in German intellectual life. And, of course, growing British trade meant that more and more of the world—including the German lands—came into contact with the British, as Kant could testify at the busy port of Königsberg with its many British ships and trading houses.

For politically divided Germany, Britain provided one of its major arteries to a larger world. There was no German state to finance the expeditions that took the British—or the French or Spanish—to the Pacific, bringing back in their wake detailed journals or packing case after packing case full of specimens of natural history displaying the richness and diversity of the three kingdoms of nature in its Pacific dimension. Though the Hapsburg Empire under Joseph II did contemplate a Pacific voyage, it lacked the resources to do so.[8] If the Germans were to join in the study of the Pacific, this had to be done largely through British intermediaries— something that further strengthened the tendency in the German lands to see the Pacific through British eyes.

From the British point of view, there were considerable advantages in involving Germans in their expeditions as subjects of states that were not likely to pose a challenge to British imperial designs. Furthermore, Germany provided university-trained experts in abundance, by contrast with the much more limited university presence in Britain itself. In England there were only the two largely clerical universities of Oxford and Cambridge; Scotland, by contrast, had four universities that, like those of Germany, developed in the eighteenth century strong traditions of professorial teaching and intellectual innovation. But the Scottish universities were a Lilliputian world compared with the relatively vast network of German universities, the scale of which reflected the diversity and lack of unity of Germany itself, for each princedom or principality took pride in having its own university. German culture, to an extent unparalleled elsewhere in Europe, drew strongly on university roots. This further strengthened the cautious character of the German Enlightenment since university professors (particularly those enjoying the status and privileges of German professors) were unlikely harbingers of revolution. The German universities looked on knowledge as a tool for improvement and reform and a means of revitalizing the institutions of church and state—not as an instrument for the demolition of the network of distinctive German traditions of which they formed a part.

The growing links between Germany and Britain in the late eighteenth century meant that a number of Germans were drawn into the British penetration of the Pacific. Thanks to its universities, Germany could provide experts in the rapidly growing field of natural history, as well as those with strong philological or medical qualifications. Moreover, the fruits of Pacific investigation could be subjected to professorial scrutiny in the German universities to an extent not possible in Britain, where much of the intellectual life continued to be conducted in the club-based world of such London institutions as the Royal Society or the Society of Antiquaries.[9] In Britain the political and social dominance of a landowning gentry class was reflected in an intellectual culture where the amateur with private means pursued what was of interest to him (the masculine pronoun was almost always appropriate) and his class. In Germany the number of universities meant that knowledge had become more institutionalized and professionalized, particularly as new universities, such as Göttingen, had begun to foster a research culture in which professorial advancement was linked to publication.[10]

France, too, had developed a core of professional savants through its academy and other bodies, which helps to explain why France, in contrast to Britain, had little need of German graduates in its exploration of the Pacific and other parts of the world. In France, however, such savants were employed in institutions more directly under the sway of the state than the German universities; in France, too, the polarization between such state savants and salon-going, unsalaried philosophes was a further catalyst to push Enlightenment thinking in more radical directions.

The German response to the "new world of the Pacific" in the late eighteenth century was very closely linked to that particularly German institution, the university—and especially to one particular university, that of Göttingen. Göttingen's links with the British royal house gave it ready access to British accounts of exploration, and its emphasis on professional education meant a strong medical faculty that provided fertile ground for the study of natural history. Its relatively recent origins meant, too, that the traditions of *Schulphilosophie* (university instruction in philosophy that continued the traditions of scholasticism), with its highly systematic, pedagogically organized overview of knowledge, were much less entrenched. The study of philosophy there was more likely to respond to more contemporary concerns such as the study of ethics, which, in turn, provided a stimulus for the study of other cultures and the beginnings of anthropology.[11] Travel had long been a particular preoccupation of the Göttingen professors: the great Albrecht von Haller—who established the fame of the medical faculty there as professor of anatomy, botany, and medicine from 1736 to 1753—promoted a reading circle devoted to travel literature, members of which included the distinguished Göttingen philologist, Johann Reinhold David Michaelis.[12] Out of such preoccupations emerged Michaelis's instructions for an expedition to Arabia (1761–69), sponsored by the Danish crown but including such Göttingen graduates as Carsten Niebuhr. Michaelis's *Fragen* (*Questions*) represented the best distillation of the work on the study of other cultures then available.[13]

In the period at the end of the Seven Years' War in 1763, when European exploration of the Pacific was gathering pace, Göttingen became even more concerned with the intellectual repercussions of European contact with vastly different cultures. Such issues were discussed regularly at the Königliche Sozietät der Wissenschaften (Royal Society of Sciences) and figured in the *Göttingischen Anzeigen von gelehrten Sachen* (*Göttingen Newspaper on Scholarly Affairs*).[14] Significantly, it was at Göttingen that the terms "Ethnographie" and "Völkerkunde" ("Ethnology") first emerged, being coined by August Schlözer, who took up a chair there in 1769—Schlözer claimed paternity of the concept of *ethnograpisch* in the course of a debate with Herder in 1772–73.[15]

Before taking up his post at Göttingen, Schlözer had been in St. Petersburg—a reminder that, along with the British Empire, early German theorists of ethnology drew extensively on the exploration made possible by the resources of the Russian Empire.[16] Furthermore, the need of the Russians for foreign experts to describe in scientific form the resources of their vast territories was much more acute than in the British case, and it was principally to the graduates of the German universities that the Russians turned—generally with a much stronger expectation of a direct return to the needs of government than the British displayed in the distant Pacific. Among such German experts employed in Russia was Johann Reinhold Forster who, along with his son, George, did most to implant in Germany an interest in the late eighteenth-century European encounter with the Pacific. Bored with the life of a clergyman in a small German-speaking enclave within the largely Polish-speaking lands near Danzig, Johann Reinhold Forster readily responded to the invitation in 1765 to undertake an investigation of the German-speaking colonies on the River Volga. But he only remained until 1766: foreshadowing his later experiences with the British government, Forster fell out with his Russian employers, who objected to his findings about the poor treatment of the German colonists. Nonetheless, his experience (and that of his eleven-year-old son, George, who accompanied him) in dealing with different cultures probably played some role in preparing him for his later voyage to the Pacific.

Johann Reinhold Forster's familiarity with both the Poles and the different peoples of Russia is a reminder of the extent to which Germans were often exposed to a greater range of cultures than other Europeans—which may have helped to interest them in the infant discipline of anthropology. Lacking a single state of their own, Germans frequently lived alongside other peoples and languages, which may have inclined them to be sympathetic to cultural diversity and more skeptical than the French of universalizing models of human society. As Koerner suggests, Herder's emphasis on the uniqueness and value of each culture no doubt owed much to his upbringing on the Eastern Baltic, where he was exposed to a range of cultures and languages.[17] This anthropological interest in other cultures was characteristic of the Enlightenment in the German lands, as elsewhere. When the *Berlinische Monatsschrift* was established in 1783—the year before it published the celebrated articles by Kant and Mendelssohn on the subject "What is Enlightenment"—it set as one of its goals inclusion of articles on "Description of peoples and their customs and institutions, preferably from countries close to us."[18]

The Forsters, father and son, both combined travel in the distant Pacific with firsthand observations of societies on the periphery of the German-speaking lands: along with his experiences as a child when his father lived in largely Polish-speaking lands and his subsequent time with his father in Russia, George Forster served a reluctant term as a professor at the University of Vilna from 1784 to 1787. Ironically, he was released from (what he considered to be) this exile by the offer of serving the Russian government like his father before him. Like the British, the Russians also were expanding into the Pacific and George's experiences serving the British Empire in his forays into the Pacific made him a natural choice in 1787 to serve as a scientist on a proposed four-year imperial Russian expedition, the main goal of which was to consolidate Russia's position in the Pacific. In the event, the chosen vessels were commandeered for the war against the Turks, but George Forster was nonetheless released from his post at Vilna to take up a more congenial position as the university librarian at Mainz.

Johann Reinhold Forster's response to the failure of his plans to work in the service of the Russian Empire was to turn to the British Empire. In doing so, he called on the international freemasonry of natural historians, and it was thanks to such natural historians as Daines Barrington, Thomas Pennant, and Daniel Solander that he first became established in Britain, gaining the post of tutor in modern languages and natural history at Warrington Academy—a position he held from 1767 to 1770. Naturally, he drew on his recent experiences in Russia to help underline his credentials in the field of natural history. The first of a series of natural history papers presented to the Royal Society was devoted to the natural history of the Volga[19]—a work that made plain his admiration for the "celebrated Linnaeus" and provided the first Linnaean account of the flora and fauna of eastern Russia.[20] Forster, then, expanded the territory made accessible to European science through the use of the Linnaean classificatory system—thus continuing the Linnaean tradition of scientific exploration and the mission of bringing classificatory order to more and more of the globe. The extent to which Forster's conception of the scope of natural history included the study of human society was underlined by the considerable collection of artifacts he brought with him—the sale of which was to provide a much needed source of income, just as, subsequently, the Forsters attempted to capitalize on the vast collection of Pacific artifacts they built up on Cook's second Pacific voyage.[21]

Though Johann Reinhold Forster had graduated in theology at the University of Halle, his primary interest had been medicine[22]—the faculty that provided the main institutional foundation for the study of natural history. (Appropriately, he belatedly received a doctorate in medicine at Halle in 1782, following his appointment there as professor in 1779 with particular responsibilities for natural history and mineralogy.) He reared his promising son, George (who also subsequently received a doctorate in medicine), in the study of natural history—a field that became the central intellectual core of the two men's careers and interests. In 1789, five years before his death, George Forster was to remark that "Natural history in its broadest sense and particularly anthropology have been my pre-occupation hitherto. What I have written since my voyage is for the most part closely related to these."[23] Though both Forsters benefited considerably from the institutional support provided to natural history by the medical faculties within the German universities, neither of them had much enthusiasm (or expertise) for the clinical practice of medicine. In 1785, while at the University of Vilna, George Forster candidly admitted that "I don't very much like practical medicine, [but] like very much natural history . . . above all because it leads so immediately to the good and true philosophy of man"[24]—a remark that underlines the extent to which the study of humankind was an integral part of the Forsters' conception of natural history.

For both father and son, the dominant deities in natural history were Linnaeus, who brought order, and Buffon, who brought majesty and purpose to the study of nature—a pursuit that was still establishing its scientific credentials. When George Forster published his account of Cook's second voyage, he was at pains to disabuse those who regarded the natural history that both he and his father pursued as mere specimen hunting. His father was sent to the Pacific, insisted the young George, with loftier ambitions than "being a naturalist who was merely to bring home a collection of butterflies and dried plants"; on the contrary, he was expected to provide "a philosophical history."[25] Like their great mentor, Buffon, the Forsters saw in natural history a means of making sense of nature, of illustrating the way in which the different facets of the terraqueous globe were interrelated and interdependent. In particular, the Forsters sought to locate humankind firmly in its natural setting and to demonstrate the extent to which human beings were an integral part of their environmental setting. Hence the grandiloquent opening of Johann Reinhold Forster's scientific reflections on Cook's voyage, *Observations Made During a Voyage Round the World*: "My object was nature in its greatest extent; the Earth, the Sea, the Air, the Organic and Animated Creation, and more particularly that class of Beings to which we ourselves belong."[26]

On a more microcosmic scale, George Forster later used that most distinctive feature of Tahitian flora, the breadfruit tree (the plant that launched Bligh's *Bounty* and *Providence* expeditions) to illustrate the interconnectedness of the human world and that of the vegetable kingdom in Tahiti—an approach that foreshadows present-day understandings of ecology.[27] "The history of the products of the soil," wrote Forster, "is closely interwoven with the fate of mankind and its emotions, ideas and actions. The realm of nature borders the domain of every science, and it is impossible to review the former without examining the latter."[28]

By taking such a wide view of the scope of natural history, the Forsters were responding to Buffon's admonition to rise above their traditional role of collectors of data and to aspire to provide generalizations about the workings of nature. The naturalist, urged Buffon, should seek "combination of observations, the generalisation of facts."[29]Appropriately, on their return from their voyage with Cook, Johann Reinhold Forster made the pilgrimage to visit Buffon and gave him a set of botanical specimens from the South Seas.[30] Buffon reciprocated by acknowledging the Forsters' contribution of some of the zoological specimens discussed in the sixth supplement of the *Histoire Naturelle*.[31] Later, George Forster was to promote the diffusion of Buffon in the German-speaking lands through his translations—notably the sixth volume of the great *Histoire Naturelle*.

Such an elevated Buffonian sense of the nature and scope of natural history was proclaimed by Johann Reinhold Forster in the lectures he gave while at the Warrington Academy. Though the academy—which was intended for the education of Protestant dissenters excluded from Anglican Oxford and Cambridge—was small and poorly endowed, it offered Forster his first opportunity to focus on what had been and would increasingly become his true intellectual love, the study of natural history. "The manner in which we propose to treat *Natural History*," he told his audience in his first set of natural history lectures (chiefly devoted to mineralogy), "is a *Scientific way*." It was his intention to ensure that "all things may be arranged in such a manner, that we may see their *Order*." Like Buffon, he drew a parallel between the role of the civil historian concerned with what Buffon termed "the epochs of the revolutions of human affairs"[32] and the role of the natural historian. Both, wrote Forster with an affirmation of the empiricist rigour that was to remain a feature of his work, had a duty of "veracity," but the lot of the natural historian was more difficult since he was obliged to "give such definitions or descriptions of the Natural bodies, that no body may be mistaken."

Out of such a truly scientific approach to the subject emerged both practical advantages and a more soundly based religion, for the natural historian could "by reflecting at [sic] the Nature and Properties of these bodies" demonstrate "the proper use and best which can be made of them, for human Society," as well as establishing that "Nature is the great book, on which the Deity with indelible Characters, has written its immense and adorable Attributes."[33] In the lectures that followed on entomology, he was at pains to rescue natural history from the condescension of those who dismissed it as the pursuit of mere "*fly-catchers*" whose "knowledge is confined to a very minute and trifling object." Again, he insisted, the study of nature brought with it a lofty sense of the order and interconnectedness of nature and, by doing so, strengthened a sense of the grandeur of the "great Works of the Architect of the Universe" and the "providential care for each of the minute parts . . . of his Creation."[34]

However, Forster's young audience evidently did not warm to these rhapsodies about the merits of natural history: Forster complained in a letter to the naturalist Daines Barrington in 1768 about "the Follies and Tricks of Young Monkeys, who are quite licentious and under no discipline and tease me with their Tricks to death."[35] It must have been with great relief, then, that Forster took up the offer to accompany Cook as a scientific observer on his second great voyage of 1772–75, the main aim of which was to establish once and for all whether there was a great South Land to balance the land masses of the northern hemisphere. For Johann Reinhold Forster and his son, George—who continued to accompany his peripatetic father, from whom he picked up an education as best he could along the way—the new world of the Pacific offered fertile ground to establish the significance of natural history as a pursuit worthy of the Enlightenment by shining the light of science on the dark corners of the earth. The fact that the Pacific was, in European terms, largely virgin territory made it a particularly important instance of the capacity of enlightened thinking to make comprehensible a major section of the globe. In the spirit of Linnaeus, the Forsters set out with the goal of making the natural order more comprehensible by the use of classification. It was a goal that complemented the activities of Cook, who sought to make the Pacific more manageable (and exploitable) by the use of maps that could use mathematical coordinates to render a whole range of geographical features in forms familiar to the European mind.[36]

The Pacific offered whole new categories of specimens from the three kingdoms of nature, animal, vegetable, and mineral, together with the possibility of linking such findings more closely to the study of humankind and its behavior. Making the most of such opportunities, the Forsters brought back large numbers of specimens reflecting both the natural and human worlds of the Pacific together with lengthy classificatory lists. Johann Reinhold Forster proudly noted in his account of the artifacts that he had collected that in addition, "Our Herbarium amounts to 6–700 extremely rare species of which hardly any specimens are found in the collections of Europe and of which 2–300 have never been seen or described by any other botanist."[37] The extent to which Forster saw himself as self-consciously continuing a Linnaean tradition is reflected not only in his use of Linnaean nomenclature but also in that he bound a copy of Linnaeus's 1762 *Instructiones Peregrinatoris* (*Instructions for a Traveler*)[38] in with his own observations on travel.

The Forsters could bring to this encounter with a new quarter of the globe an intellectual rigor strengthened by the German university system.

Though Johann Reinhold Forster's student days at the University of Halle from 1748 to around 1751 came at a less than distinguished period in that university's history, at least some attention was given there to the study of natural history and, elsewhere in Germany (and, in particular, at Göttingen), the many German medical faculties did much to promote natural history. Natural history was one incentive to cultivate an early form of anthropology; another was the strong philological traditions of the German university system that Johann Reinhold Forster had imbibed at Halle[39] and passed on to his son.

As students of both the ancient and modern languages, the Forsters naturally brought to their Pacific explorations a fascination with the new languages they encountered and attempted to use such linguistic material to answer larger questions about patterns of migration and cultural transmission within the Pacific. As Johann Reinhold Forster wrote in his *Observations Made During a Voyage Round the World*: "I took particular care in collecting the words of every peculiar nation we met with, that I might be enabled to form an idea of the whole, and how far all the languages are related to each other."[40] The Forsters grasped every opportunity to collect information on the languages of the Pacific islands, compiling word lists on every island where Cook landed[41] and busily questioning Odiddy, a Tahitian who accompanied Cook's voyage for part of the way, about the Tahitian language.

On the basis of such linguistic studies, he concluded that there was a link between the Polynesian languages and Malay though, he suggested, this probably went back to their descent from a common, more ancient language. Hence, he concluded (in line with modern scholarship) that the pattern of migration into the Pacific had been down from Southeast Asia and then eastward.[42] In a comment that underlies the fact that Johann Reinhold Forster's scientific investigations were also expected to serve imperial ends, he suggested that his linguistic work "may one day or other become usefull, if the Europeans especially should chuse to make settlements in the Islands or at least to erect here a new branch of commerce."[43]

The Forsters' fascination with the languages of the Pacific was of a piece with their strong belief in the interconnectedness of all aspects of human society and, beyond it, of nature as a whole.[44] Long after his Pacific voyage, George Forster continued to ponder the effects on human society of its being rooted in a particular place. In the fateful year of 1789, five years before his death, he argued for a distinction between all the local factors that shape society (*"lokale Bildung"*) and those characteristics that all humanity shared (*"allegemeine Bildung"*)—hence the title of the address "Über Lokale und Allgemeine Bildung."[45] The origins of such a position are evident in the way in which on their Pacific voyage both father and son devoted a great deal of detail to building up a strong impression of the particular characteristics of the widely different locations they encountered. Their accounts of the voyage conveyed a sense of the way that such characteristics helped to shape human societies—one of the primary manifestations of which was language. They partially agreed with Montesquieu and other theorists about the importance of climate in creating human variations, but qualified this with an emphasis on the way the particular features of a society, its location and cultural adaptations, also played an important role in explaining differences.[46] This strong sense of the integral links between all aspects of nature and of human society led to a strong suspicion of theory—or, at least, theories that did not allow for a great deal of variation.

Hostility to theorizing was strengthened by their well-developed empiricism[47]—an empiricism natural to travelers who were continually being presented with new information, particularly in relation to the remarkable fecundity of human invention and the cultural artifacts it produced.[48] The preface of Johann Reinhold Forster's *Observations Made During a Voyage Round the World* dismissed existing attempts to arrive at "The History of Mankind" as having led to "systems formed in the closet" contrasting this with his own work in which "Facts are the basis of the whole structure."[49] His son dutifully echoed such views in his preface to the *Voyage Around the World*, describing it as a work in which human nature is "represented without any adherence to fallacious systems."[50] Such affirmations of empiricist rigor may also have owed something to their close links with the English and their Baconian scientific traditions.

Both these characteristics—an emphasis on the interconnectedness of nature and a strong empiricism—later manifested themselves in George Forster's controversy with Kant in 1786 over the extent to which the human race could be divided into well-defined races. Forster responded in 1786 to Kant's "Bestimmung des Begriffs einer Menschenrace" ("Definition of the Concept of a Race," 1785) and "Mutmasslicher Anfang der Menschengeschichte" ("The Probable Beginning of the History of Mankind," 1786) with his own "Noch etwas über die Menschenrassen" ("More About the Races of Man"). Kant proposed that humankind had separated into different races as a consequence of environmental factors (and, above all, climate) operating on innate predispositions ("*Kerme*" or "germs") that had existed in the original race. He postulated that this original race was white but that it had since given rise to the black, yellow, and red races. The races thus produced could interbreed—an important point given Kant's emphasis on the unity of humankind—but once interbreeding took place, it was not possible to produce the pure strains of races as characterized by skin color, even if the parents moved to totally different environments—an indication that climate alone was not responsible for variations in skin color. For Kant, then, what distinguished one human race from another was the ability to produce offspring who did not display the characteristics of a mixed race, the inevitable outcome if parents of different races mated.

Forster responded to Kant with considerable respect, opening his essay with an acknowledgment of the way that the spread of the *Berlinische Monatsschrift* (in which Kant's essays were published) to distant Vilna—where Forster was then reluctantly situated—was an indication of the diffusion of the "Aufklärung." However, Forster did become rather indignant in response to Kant's suggestion that it was not possible clearly to establish the color of the South Sea islanders, especially as they had not produced offspring within the different climatic conditions of Europe. Forster responded from his firsthand knowledge together with the observations of previous Pacific explorers to illustrate the extent to which such characteristics as skin color were subject to all manner of variations. "In the New Hebrides," pointed out Forster, "both Bougainville and ourselves saw black, black-brown and dark-brown men." Such variations he saw as being complicated still further by the gradual workings of climate.[51] Such subtle shades of variation he thought undermined Kant's attempt to arrive at clear categories to distinguish one branch of humanity from another. Moreover, Kant's contention that races could be distinguished on the basis of the color of their offspring could be undermined by the way that light-skinned children could result from the union of black and white (especially if the father and mother's own skin color was in the middle of the wide spectrum of shades between white and black).[52]

Forster also sought to refute Kant by drawing on the anatomical work of Thomas Soemmerring, a very close friend and sometime colleague when Forster taught at the Collegium Carolinum at Kassel from 1778 to 1784. In 1784[53] Soemmerring had shown that, when compared with other members of the animal kingdom, the differences between black and white humans were almost literally skin deep. Though Soemmerring himself thought the differences were still substantial enough clearly to differentiate black and white races, Forster was inclined to regard the division of the humankind into distinct races with some skepticism, arguing for a high degree of continuity among all the different manifestations of humankind. Again, his inclination was to stress interconnectedness rather than difference and, in doing so, to question the quest by Kant and others to arrive at clear categories to explain human variation.

Moreover, he questioned other basic methodological positions taken by Kant, in particular his influential division of natural history into two branches: one ("*Naturgeschichte*") concerned with the description and classification of nature, and the other ("*Naturbeschreibung*") taking as its goal the distillation of general principles and fundamental interrelationships from the ever-increasing bodies of data being accumulated by natural historians. Forster's fundamental concern with the extent of variation in nature and the close links between all its different aspects made him skeptical of such a distinction. Any principles arrived at through a form of natural history devoted to the Kantian program of *Naturbeschreibung* were, in Forster's view, likely to be overwhelmed by the extent of natural variation[54]—variation that his own strongly empirically based work as a natural historian encountering the Pacific had made manifest to him.

Though Forster might dismiss the Kantian explanation for human variation, he still did have to provide some explanation for human differences—even if he was reluctant to erect hard and fast categories, such as concepts of different races. The important work of his friend, Soemmerring, may have underlined the gulf between animals and humans, but it had also placed considerable stress on the differences between blacks and whites in a number of anatomical respects, such as variations in bone structures. George Forster did not attempt to arrive at a definitive position to deal with this problem—indeed, in his debate with Kant, he suggested that a solution was best left to time and to the further accumulation of empirical information. However, in this essay, he did suggest that humankind did not have one single origin and that human variation could be therefore explained by its diverse beginnings.[55] Though this position of polygenesis could be used by apologists for slavery to justify the subordinate position of blacks as having a separate origin from whites, this was certainly not George Forster's intention since the overall burden of his work was to emphasize the unity and equality of humankind;[56] rather, his intention was to emphasize the extent of human variation and the way that such variation undermined any firm basis for the division into separate races.

However, polygenesis was a radical position in a society where the dominant Judeo-Christian tradition emphasized monogenesis: the common origin of all humankind from one pair of ancestors, Adam and Eve, and the fact that, as a consequence, human beings were, in the biblical phrase, "of one blood." This questioning of such a basic tenet of Christianity as the common Adamite origin of humankind was of a piece with what appears to have been George Forster's dismissal of Christianity more generally— particularly after he left Kassel for Vilna in 1784. Contemporaries remarked, for example, on the fact that he did not have his children baptized.[57] Taking up this monogenesist position also marks the growing divergence between father and son, Johann Reinhold Foster having written in his *Observations* (1778) that holy writ established it as "a fundamental position, that all mankind are descended from one couple."[58]

However, George Forster's writings contain little in the way of a direct attack on Christianity in the manner of some of the French philosophes. One of the features of the German Enlightenment (as of the English-speaking Enlightenments of the British Isles, North America, and Australia) was a tendency to work within the established institutions of society rather than to attack them directly. George Forster reflected the German *Aufklärer* in his inclination to remain within a system in which Enlightenment discourse was largely carried on within universities that were closely tied to the institutions of church and state. He might have had private reservations about religion, but it was inconsistent with his role as a professor to make these a source of controversy. Ironically, his last position was to be an employee of the prince-bishop of Mainz—a sympathizer with Enlightenment principles—as his university librarian.

Nonetheless, George Forster's account of his great Pacific voyage—though published in 1777 when he was only twenty-three—indicates some of the anticlerical impulses of the Enlightenment. References to the role of Providence are conspicuously few,[59] and where indigenous religions are discussed, there is a strong animus against "priestcraft"—something that could reflect both Protestant and Enlightenment sympathies. In Deistic fashion, George Forster argued that there was a true, simple and universal religion that had been corrupted by the machinations of a priestly class. His observations of Tahiti prompted him to observe that the fundamentals of their religion corresponded to that "simple and only just conception of the Deity, [which] has been familiar to mankind in all ages and in all countries." However, as a consequence of "the excessive cunning of a few individuals, those complex systems of idolatry have been invented, which disgrace the history of almost every people."[60] A visit to Tonga prompted a similar outburst: "religion is veiled in mysteries, especially when there are priests to take advantage of the credulity of mankind." Always on the lookout for the beginnings of luxury, George Forster speculated that the undermining of the simplicity and equality of Pacific societies was likely to be carried out "under the cloak of religion, and that another nation will be added to the many dupes of voluptuous priest-craft."[61]

George Forster did appear to have drawn a distinction between priest-craft and true, enlightened Christianity, for another attack on "the influence of priestcraft, whose great aim is ever to veil religion in mystery" was followed by an affirmation that true Christianity "does not wear the mysterious cloak . . . and throws a pure and steady light around. It admits of no mystery, and its true and venerable ministers have at all times assured and convinced us, that they reserved no private knowledge for themselves."[62] Forster's conception of true Christianity bears a remarkably close resemblance to the original pure religion of all humankind that preceded the Christian dispensation, and its lack of ritual and minimal role for its clergy help to explain George Foster's subsequent straying from the faith of his father.

By contrast, his father's accounts of his travels do have a more overtly Christian content, though Forster, too, expressed a measure of scorn for "priestcraft." Like his son, he regarded true religion as characterized by what he called "a noble simplicity, which the true adoration in the spirit and truth requires." However, his observations of Tahitian religion led him to add that "the greater part of mankind, when left to themselves, in their religious principles, and modes of worship, have always more or less deviated" from such religious simplicity. Humankind, then, needed guidance not to leave the path of true religion and, for Forster senior, that guidance came from "the Christian dispensation; wherein the ideas of the Deity are pure . . . excluding all priest-craft from its true and genuine votaries."[63] Johann Reinhold Forster's emphasis on religious simplicity and opposition to "priestcraft" and ritual would have caused little controversy in Protestant Germany and may have owed something to his own theological training as a reformed clergyman (though, interestingly, his formal involvement with the church seems to have faded away after leaving his parish near Danzig for Russia in 1765).[64] In his journal, he did on occasions appeal to specifically Protestant principles, arguing that these should prompt a clear departure from the colonizing practices of the popish Spanish and their "blind Zeal for their religion, conducted by bigoted ignorant Friars." By contrast, when it came to the treatment of the South Sea islanders, "Protestants, who boast the principles of reformation, should show them by their humanity and reformed conduct."[65]

What was, however, rather more controversial was the extent to which he thought it was possible to arrive at religious truth without the guidance of Revelation. For, in his *Observations,* he conceded that the Tahitians had retained much that was good despite the fact that they were innocent of the Gospel: that their religion "is in my opinion less cruel, and not so much clogged with superstition as many others, which were or still are in use among nations who are reputed to be more civilized and more improved."[66] Moreover, in the privacy of his journal, he observed that "they exercise all the Social virtues to one another, which are usual among the civilised nations. Charity, the main spring of all morality and virtue, is no where more exercised than among these people."[67] It was just this issue of the extent to which true virtue required Revelation that had, back in

1723, led to Christian Wolff being forced out of a then strongly Pietist Halle, for he had argued that the high morals of the Confucian Chinese were based on human reason rather than on Divine Revelation. Wolff had returned to a less strictly orthodox Halle in 1740 (dying there in 1754), but the aged Wolff is unlikely to have any very direct effect on Johann Reinhold Forster while he was a student there from 1748 to about 1751. Still Wolff's presence indicated a tolerance of religious liberalism that was strengthened by the rationalizing theology of Wolff's pupil, Siegsmund Baumgarten, whose theological lectures attracted crowds of students.[68]

Whether from his Halle background or simply as a consequence of having observed such a diversity of human behavior, Johann Reinhold Forster was prepared to distinguish very markedly between morality and religion, even to the extent of accommodating a remarkable degree of moral relativism. Thus, he rebuked his fellow travelers, who decried the practice of cannibalism among the New Zealand Maoris for attempting "to punish the imaginary crime of a people whom they had no right to condemn," adding that "the action of eating human flesh, whatever our education may teach us to the contrary, is certainly neither unnatural nor criminal in itself."[69]

Johann Reinhold Forster was, then, at least in some times and places, willing to judge the Pacific societies he encountered in their own terms without the use of a Western measuring rod. Both he and his son were also ambivalent about the extent to which Enlightenment conceptions of progress and improvement corresponded to what they observed in their travels and, in particular, at Tahiti. By the standards of Western development, Tahiti had quite some distance to travel down the path of progress but, nonetheless, in the eyes of the Fosters and other Pacific explorers, had many virtues that had been lost or obscured in Europe. There, wrote Johann Reinhold Forster in his travel notes, was a society in which "the Inhabitants are happy enough to have none of the artificial Wants which Luxury, Avarice and Ambition have introduced among the Europeans."[70] In his *Observations*, he even questioned whether the price of European knowledge of these societies was too high, for such contact was likely to lead to the demand for European luxuries: "If the knowledge of a few individuals can only be acquired at such a price as the happiness of nations, it was better for the discoverers, and the discovered, that the South Sea had still remained unknown to Europe and its restless inhabitants."[71]

Here again, then, appears to be the familiar phenomenon of the European traveler projecting onto the Pacific the myth of a Golden Age and, in the manner of Bougainville and Commersen, decrying in Rousseauist fashion the passage from nature to culture and with it the corrupting hand of civilization. And, yet, the Forsters were critical of Rousseau and

what they perceived as his excessively negative portrayal of the consequences of the evolution of human society[72] along such familiar stages as
the progression from hunter-gatherer to pastoral, thence to agriculture
and, finally, to a commercially based society. In his *Voyage*, George
Forster expressed reluctance to promote the views of "Rousseau, or the
superficial philosophers who re-echo his maxims."[73] Johann Reinhold
Forster conceded that the South Sea islanders might appear "to be happily
situated, something like what is said of the golden age, they may live almost without labour" but, he continued, "certain evils in great measure
counterbalance this seeming happiness, the faculty of the mind are [*sic*]
blunted, if the body is so enervated by indolence."[74]

Nonetheless, as West had illustrated in relation to George Forster's account of Tahiti,[75] there was a profound ambivalence in the Forsters' view
of the stadial progress so beloved of the Scottish social theorists of the
eighteenth century. The underlying framework of the Forster's accounts
of the Pacific is shaped by the idea of an evolutionary growth of society
toward civilization as largely perceived in European terms. But, particularly when it came to Tahiti, the Forsters were obviously rather uncertain
whether such an upward climb fully equated with the advance of morality
and human happiness—which raised worrying issues about the stadial
model so basic to their outlook and that of many of their fellow *aufklärer*.
To some extent, Johann Reinhold Forster tried to square the circle by offering a scientific explanation of why in Tahiti particularly there was so
much of value, even though it was a culture well removed from the civilizing impulses of Europe. In the manner of "the great Mr. de Montesquieu,"
he suggested that perhaps there was a climatic explanation: that by an inverse law, the Tahitians in their low latitudes bore out the contention
"that the human species when unconnected with the highly civilized nations, is always found more debased in its physical, mental moral and social capacity, in proportion as it is removed from the tropical regions."
But Forster was honest enough to concede that this did not fully explain
why Tahiti of all the societies they had encountered near the Equator was
particularly blessed and he had to lamely conclude that there must be
"some other cause of this remarkable circumstance."[76]

Such occasional backslidings into the language of the Noble Savage
aside, the Forsters shared with their German (and Scottish) contemporaries a preoccupation with the question of what were the wellsprings of
prosperity and ordered civilization—an intellectual agenda that colored
their whole encounter with the Pacific. The scholarly Forsters also brought
to their subject that interest in universal history which the German Enlightenment did so much to promote and, with it, a conviction that civilization was a cumulative phenomenon. As Johann Reinhold Forster put it

with italicized enthusiasm immediately after the section on Tahiti cited above: "All the ideas, all the improvements to sciences, arts, manufactures, social life, and even morality, ought to be considered as *the sum total of the efforts of mankind ever since its existence*"—all of which made the case of Tahiti, which had had so little contact with other cultures, all the more perplexing to Forster.

But his puzzlements about Tahiti did not weaken Johann Reinhold Forster's resolve to use his Pacific travels to illustrate the great theme of the advance of civilization: as he put it at the end of the preface to his *Observations*, it was his goal to show "by what steps they [human beings] may gradually emerge from the darkness of barbarism, and uniting in social compacts, behold the dawn of civilization." Conversely, his work also would provide salutary warnings about the way in which civilization could also go into reverse and "by what accidents and misfortunes men may, for want of mutual support, degenerate to savages." The intellectual equipment that came most readily to hand in giving substance to such a view was the stadial language of the French and Scottish social theorists. Johann Reinhold Forster's general reflections on the societies of the South Seas led him to conclude, for example, that "mankind, in a pastoral state, could never attain to that degree of improvement and happiness, to which agriculture, and the cultivation of vegetables, will easily and soon lead them."[77]

In a similar vein, George Forster concluded his *Voyage* with a hymn to progress urging his readers to reflect on the way his work illustrated the "blessings which civilization and revealed religion have diffused over our part of the globe" and the extent to which his fellow Europeans should give thanks for "distinguished superiority over so many of his fellow creatures, who follow the impulse of their senses, without knowing the nature or name of virtue."[78] In 1778, the year after this book was published, George moved to Kassel to take up a professorship of natural history and there marked his admission to the Société des Antiquités de Cassel with an "Antrittsrede" ("Inaugural Speech") in which he drew on his Pacific experiences to again underline his un-Rousseauian belief in the merits of the advance of civilization. For the young Forster, the same dynamics that he had observed in the Pacific had been at work in human history as a whole, and the self-evident merits of progress would mean that all humankind would eventually share a common culture: "Civilization arrives a little nearer by the same degrees in all lands, it is only the epochs which are different." Cannibalism had existed in the ancient world but had died out as it had in Tahiti and so, Forster was confident, it would eventually do so among the Maoris of New Zealand. He also drew on the familiar scale of human ascent from the Tierra del Fuegians to Europeans—pausing to praise the society that he addressed as an example of the contemporary enlightened

spirit abroad within Europe.[79] Despite such cultural condescension underlying the speech—and Forster's work as a whole—was a strong belief in human equality since all peoples were linked in a common history and would
eventually arrive at a common civilization, even if such a civilization might
bear a remarkable resemblance to eighteenth-century Europe.

George Forster's time at Kassel from 1778 to 1784 brought him in regular contact with colleagues at the nearby University of Göttingen (from
which he received an honorary doctorate), and he was a close friend of
Georg Lichtenberg, with whom he edited the *Göttingisches Magazin der
Wissenschaften und Litteratur* from 1780 to 1784.[80] Such academic connections were cemented in 1785 by his marriage to Therese, the daughter
of Christian Heyne, a prominent classical philologist—a union that, like
so many chapters in the life of the ill-starred George, ended badly, with
his becoming part of a *ménage à trois* with his wife's lover. It was a marriage that linked George Forster with some of the leading figures in Göttingen, including the great naturalist and professor of medicine Johann
Blumenbach, who was a brother-in-law of Heyne. George Forster was
drawn to Blumenbach by common intellectual sympathies as well as these
dynastic connections. When, in 1786, Forster came to draw together his
long-gestating textbook on natural history, he conceded to Soemmerring
that it was difficult to improve on Blumenbach's treatment in his *Hand-
buch der Naturgeschichte* (*Handbook of Natural History*—first edition,
1779; twelfth edition, 1830). This was true particularly in relation to
physiology (and especially in its connections with anatomy)—hence, he
acknowledged that the overall treatment would remain "tolerably Blu-
menbachisch."[81] Both Forster and Blumenbach also agreed on the extent
to which physical anthropology should form a part of natural history;
predictably, one of Forster's underlying themes was the interconnectedness of all of natural history (including physical anthropology) and, indeed, of all the different sciences.[82] He was also sympathetic to one of
Blumenbach's key notions, the concept of the "*nisum formatiuum*,"[83] a
formative force at work in nature. Both figures also shared a common opposition to the way that Kant attempted to define the division between
species on criteria based on breeding—the thrust of Blumenbach's approach, by contrast, was to attempt to define species by a range of common morphological features, the so-called Totalhabitus.[84] When, for
example, he came to consider human beings, Blumenbach attempted to
distinguish the different human races by skull structure along with other
characteristics.

However, there were also important differences between the two, for
Blumenbach did follow Kant in accepting the notion that there were distinct human races[85]—something which, as Forster's exchange with Kant

makes clear, was not consistent with Forster's emphasis on the gradual variations in nature. Forster's sympathy for polygenesis was also at variance with Blumenbach's robust defence of monogenesis—a position that led one of Blumenbach's English admirers to pen the following verses, entitled "On a Collection of Skulls from Different Nations":

> Blumenbach's penetrating Thought
> Through Nature manifold has sought
> The various Races of Men has trac'd
> And on his Shelves in Order plac'd. . . .
> Yet all of ev'ry Age and Land
> The Work of an Almighty Hand,
> One Flesh and Blood unites them all
> One God, and Father, each May call.[86]

Though at Halle from 1780 to his death in 1798, Forster senior also had considerable contact with the Göttingen professors, especially Johann Michaelis (with whom he corresponded from soon after his graduation at Halle, the university attended by both Forster and Michaelis) and Blumenbach, whose anthropological work Forster had praised in the preface to his *Observations*.[87] Soon after his arrival in Halle, Johann Reinhold Forster began a long and scientifically fruitful correspondence with Blumenbach, whose popular *Handbook of Natural History* became the textbook for Forster's courses.[88] Drawing on his rich collection of Pacific specimens, Forster could reciprocate for Blumenbach's scientific courtesies by providing him with geological samples from the *Resolution* voyage.[89]

More significantly, Forster's Pacific observations led Blumenbach to propose that, in addition to the existing classification of humankind into Caucasian, Mongolian, Ethiopian, and American, there should be a fifth—the Malay. Hence, he wrote in the revised 1781 edition of his *De Generis Humani Varietate Nativa* (*About the Innate Variety of Human Kind*)—originally his Göttingen MD thesis of 1775:

Finally, the new southern world makes up the fifth . . . Those who inhabit the Pacific Archipelago are divided again by John Reinhold Forster into two tribes. One made up of the Otaheitans, the New Zealanders, and the inhabitants of the Friendly Isles, the Society, Easter Island, and the Marquesas, and c. men of elegant appearance and mild disposition; whereas the others who inhabit New Caledonia, Tanna, and the New Hebrides, and c. are blacker more curly, and in dispositions more distrustful and ferocious.[90]

Thus, this prefigured the subsequent division by the French explorer Dumont D'Urville of the Pacific peoples into Polynesians and Melanesians. The third edition of 1795 supplemented these comments on the fifth

(Malay) division of humankind with further details gained (as Blumenbach effusively acknowledged) from Joseph Banks[91]—to whom he dedicated the volume as a whole.

Both Forsters continued to keep the German-speaking world informed of British activities in the Pacific through their translations. From 1790 until his death, Johann Reinhold Forster acted as editor of the *Magazin von Merkwürdigen neuen Reisebeschreibungen aus Fremden Sprachen* (*Magazine of Curious Travel Accounts in Foreign Languages*, sixteen volumes, 1790–1800). This series provided an abridged account in German of Captain Hunter's voyage to Australia, including lengthy notes by Forster on the Pacific background. A posthumous translation by Forster of Vancouver's travels also appeared in this series.[92] Earlier, in 1784, Johann Reinhold Forster had provided a justification for such voyages of discovery in his *Geschichte der Entdeckungen und Schiffahrten in Norden* (*History of the Voyages and Discoveries Made in the North*), which was dedicated to Catherine the Great as a tribute to Russia's role as a promoter of exploration and in a vain bid to obtain membership of the St. Petersburg Academy. Though such explorations might be prompted by commercial motives, they served enlightened ends, for they "seem to have greatly contributed to the promotion of knowledge, and to the introduction of milder manners and customs into society." Indeed, Forster concluded with an affirmation that there was a Providential purpose at work in such voyages and the general expansion of European society that accompanied them. Exploration revealed something of "the wisdom of a supreme being, who dispenses his benefits over the whole universe, and manifests the utmost sagacity and intelligence in the accomplishment of his purposes."[93]

Johann Reinhold Forster's view of the ways that civilization and progress were promoted by exploration could be well contained within the generally unthreatening bounds of the German Enlightenment. His view of the advance of civilization was positive but nonetheless content with gradual improvement, and his *Weltanschauung* still kept a considerable place for the workings of Providence. By contrast, his son brought to his account of the upward march of civilization a degree of enthusiasm and a secularism that was less comfortably contained within the *status quo*. George Forster so brightly portrayed the benefits of the spread of civilization and the Pacific exploration—which formed a conspicuous example of such progress—that the drab realities of the society around him must have been even more evident.

Like his father in his edition of Hunter's journal, George Forster predicted a bright future for the infant colony of New South Wales. In 1786 he published his "Neuholland und die brittishche Colonie in Botany-Bay"

("New Holland [Australia] and the British Colony in Botany-Bay [New South Wales])" in response to the plans for a penal colony there—plans that did not eventuate until 1788, an indication of how *au courant* Forster was in matters relating to the British in the Pacific, even while at Vilna. For Forster, the British were extending the reach of civilization just as they had in America, and New Holland was likely to become "the future homeland of a new civilized society which, however mean its beginning may seem to be, nevertheless promises within a short time to become very important." It was a colony that offered the opportunity of realizing Enlightenment hopes for the rehabilitation of the socially deviant through exposure to a new environment. Thus, a convict there could "cease to be an enemy of society whenever he regains his full human rights."

In his *Voyage*, George Forster's recent contact with the Pacific had tempered to some extent his affirmations of the merits of the advance of progress along the path to European conceptions of civilization. By the time he came to write this essay, however, he took a strongly teleological view of human development. Where Cook and Banks had written sympathetically of the Australian Aborigines as untroubled by European preoccupation with luxuries, Forster in his "Neuholland" dismissively argued that "Among all the races which may claim to be called human, that which inhabits New Holland is the most wretched," noting in stadial fashion that they lived "without agriculture." Their way of life, he conceded, "is also in the end a path to civilization," but he saw it as a particularly long and uncertain path. In the manner of Kant, Forster took the strong anti-Rousseauian view that it was only in the conditions of civilization that Man "begins to achieve the potential with which he has been endowed in the form of his faculties, and becomes a truly human being." It followed, then, that the spread of civilization—of which the Botany Bay venture was a part—was "in the interests of mankind, and population of the whole earth with civilized inhabitants is the great goal, which we above all see before us as worthy of our efforts." He concluded the essay with an encomium to Cook—whose exploration had prompted the new colony—as a second Columbus, and, like him, one who "defines a second similar epoch in our day."[94]

This theme of Cook as a world historical figure was developed in an essay that George Forster wrote the following year (1787), entitled "Cook der Entdecker" ("Cook the Discoverer"), which formed the preface to his German translation of the official account of Cook's third Pacific voyage. Again the spread of European influence around the globe is very much linked to the spread of the Enlightenment: he warmly commends Cook as one who "has advanced his century in knowledge and enlightenment" and with it, "a golden future of general advanced knowledge." The advance of civilization to which Cook had so signally contributed Forster connected with a more general dynamic of progress that had brought with it the recognition of "the universal rights of man"—a process that he hoped European contact with the Pacific would serve to stimulate further, particularly since "enlightenment . . . advances from experience to experience without limits."

The spread of civilization could also be hastened by the foundation of European colonies in the Pacific—Forster recommending, for example, that the British send settlers to the north island of New Zealand. Such opportunities had been made possible through Cook's initiative and courage, which now served to promote "the general enlightenment of all civilized peoples." In an almost millenarian passage, Forster held out the hope that Cook's voyages ushered in a new age for humankind with "general enlightenment, [and] the joint advance of our whole kind towards a certain goal of perfection"; this he saw as enabling the "wiser Europeans" to "finally assail the old Asiatic obstinacy as well as the invincible refractoriness directed against all progress of enlightenment." Within Europe and beyond, "the limit of progressive enlightenment lies beyond our horizon," but its fruits were becoming manifest as "Tolerance and freedom of conscience announce the victory of reason and pave the way for the freedom of the press and the free study of all conditions which are important to man in the name of truth."[95]

Such chiliastic zeal for the progress of Enlightenment helps to explain why George Forster greeted the French Revolution with enthusiasm as a way of hastening the march of progress. In his view of human history, the steady growth of civilization was ineluctable, but the possibility of rapidly overcoming some of the obstacles in its way must have been intoxicating indeed. When the French Revolutionary armies conquered Mainz and the prince-bishop fled, Forster responded enthusiastically to the prospect of being able to play a part in the establishment of a republican and democratic form of government—even though his trip to Paris (where he died) led to disillusion about actual Jacobin practice.[96] But even during the Revolution, Forster was sufficiently still in sympathy with the character of the German Enlightenment to urge German rulers to introduce reforms from above and bring about change without wholesale revolution. As he put it in 1792: "One could take advantage . . . of the events in France without having to pay too steep a price for that which is good in them; the French volcano could make Germany secure before the earthquake."[97] But, of course, such a *via media* was illusory in the face of the polarization between defenders and opponents of the old regime that the French Revolution brought in its wake.

The Anglophile professors at Göttingen were generally more cautious in their political views and had considerably more reason to be content with the *status quo* than the peripatetic and generally impecunious George Forster. Both he and his father, however, brought welcome contact with the larger British world and firsthand knowledge of the exciting new world of the Pacific. Ironically, the Forsters themselves had almost systematically destroyed their highly placed contacts within England as a consequence of the wrangling over who should receive the royalties for the official account of Cook's second voyage. Johann Reinhold Forster's vain attempts to secure this lucrative publication for himself culminated in his commissioning young George to publish the egregiously ill-judged *A Letter to Lord Sandwich*, in which he accused Lord Sandwich (the first lord of the Admiralty) of being motivated by "revenge and *private pique*," the prominent naturalist Daines Barrington (a member of a well-connected aristocratic family) of not keeping his word, and the king himself of being guilty of "neglect[ing] a duty" in not responding to the Forsters' petition.[98]

That great disposer of the scientific riches of the British Empire, Joseph Banks, was not included in this fusillade, but the Forsters perceived a growing coldness from him. It was not surprising: Banks was a close friend of Sandwich and he would also no doubt have heard some of the envious remarks that Johann Reinhold Forster made about him. Banks also grew increasingly pressing about the 250 pounds that Johann Reinhold Forster owed him—though when Forster died, he forgave his penniless and long-suffering widow the debt following the intervention of Blumenbach.[99] In her effusive thanks to Banks, Forster's daughter went so far as to acknowledge that her late father "with all the great Qualifications of his head and heart, still was but too often deficient in point of Prudence and cool Discrimination."[100] As Hoare aptly puts it, Blumenbach in effect was to replace the Forsters as the recipient of a steady stream of scientifically significant natural history specimens made possible by Banks's position as president of the Royal Society and chief organizer of Britain's voyages of scientific discovery.[101] The one prominent member of the British natural history community with whom the Forsters maintained contact was the Welsh naturalist Thomas Pennant,[102] to whom George Forster poured out his heart in 1787 from Vilna, bemoaning the unwisdom of having sought "to claim as a debt [from Lord Sandwich], what on the other side was considered as the favour of a voluntary choice" and, more generally, the doleful effects on his own career of his father's actions, including the fact that "Sir Joseph's [Banks] mind appears to have been alienated from me."[103]

The Forsters may have undermined their links with the British scientific and political establishment, but they nonetheless brought with them to Germany both firsthand knowledge of the Pacific and a rich store of

Pacific natural history specimens. These included an extensive collection of ethnological artifacts, some of which the Forsters bestowed on Göttingen.[104] The university's store of Pacific artifacts was greatly expanded in 1782 when, thanks to the initiative of Blumenbach, the university received from George III a gift of more than 350 items deriving from the second and third voyages of Cook.[105] In 1799 these were supplemented (again thanks to Blumenbach's political skills) by a further 160 objects through "the purchase of the specified collection of South Seas curiosities left by Professor Forster of Halle."[106]

Quite apart from the Forsters, the Göttingen professors had their own British contacts from whom they eagerly sought further information generally about the Pacific and Cook's voyages. George Forster's friend, the polymath Georg Lichtenberg, had come to know many of the major figures involved in Pacific voyaging, including the botanist Daniel Solander, the artist William Hodges, Banks, and the Tahitian Omai— from these he brought back from his second trip to London in 1775 accounts of Cook's second voyage.[107] Lichtenberg's interest in Pacific voyaging led him to write a biographical account of Cook[108] that drew on information from this circle together with the Forsters—a work to which George Forster approvingly referred in his essay on "Cook the Discoverer" and which he praised in a letter to Banks as doing "the most ample Justice to his [Cook's] Life and Character."[109] The Orientalist Johann Michaelis grasped every opportunity to collect information about indigenous peoples and particularly those of the Pacific; he was fascinated by the role of languages and the extent to which it reflected the opinions of a people.[110] He had been in touch with Johann Reinhold Forster as far back as 1765 before he set off for Russia, and received from him reports on Cook's first Pacific voyage including a sample of bark "tapa" cloth that Banks had brought back from Tahiti. When Forster himself set out for the Pacific, Michaelis provided him with a list of possible areas of enquiry that had been drawn up for the Danish expedition to Arabia.[111]

Another of Michaelis's Pacific informants was the prominent physician Sir John Pringle, who preceded Joseph Banks as president of the Royal Society (serving from 1772 to 1778). He visited Göttingen in 1766 and in the same year Michaelis secured for him membership of the Göttingen Königliche Sozietät der Wissenschaften. Pringle responded with warm praise of both this society and the university along with commendation on the impact in England of Michaelis's Hebrew scholarship and of the "learned questions drawn up for the use of the Danish Missionaries"— the ethnological agenda that Forster was later to take with him. The return of Samuel Wallis's expedition to the Pacific in 1768 gave Pringle an opportunity to correct earlier reports from the Byron expedition of 1764–66 about the existence of giants in Patagonia, and the return of the *Endeavour* in 1771 prompted a lyrical account of Tahiti and the Society Islands (based largely on Banks's account). These islands, Pringle wrote, "may be most truly called the Fortunate Islands"—though he did qualify this Rousseauian idyll by adding that "Their greatest unhappiness is from war." Pringle was able to give Michaelis advanced intelligence of the fact that Cook's second voyage had proved the nonexistence of a great South Land for, he wrote in 1774 following the return of Furneaux's *Adventure* (the ship that had accompanied Cook's *Resolution* but had become separated), "C. Furneaux has made a most successful circumnavigation, in a very high southern latitude . . . without seeing anything but water, air and sky." He concluded, then, "that the great outlines of our globe are already drawn." Pringle continued his reports during Cook's third voyage: after announcing Cook's arrival in Cape Hope in mid-1775, he expressed the hope that Michaelis would pass on "this account to my good friends of the University that may be curious in such matters." Among the eager recipients of news from the Pacific would have been Blumenbach, to whom Michaelis later passed on a copy of Pringle's treatise on preserving the health of mariners.[112]

In the same letter, Pringle commented sympathetically on David Hume's objection to the notion of eternal punishment as inconsistent with a loving God—though adding that rather than reject the New Testament, Hume should have rejected the teachings of Calvin and Knox. Evidently, then, along with their shared interests in natural history, Pringle and Michaelis had in common a liberal attitude on theological matters. Reacting against the Pietist orthodoxy of his father, Christian Michaelis—partly as result of the rationalizing theological teaching of Baumgarten (who may also have influenced Johann Reinhold Forster)—the younger Johann Michaelis left Halle for Göttingen. There he eventually opted for a chair in philosophy rather than theology to avoid having to subscribe to the Augsburg creed and its declaration of Lutheran orthodoxy.[113]

Together with Michaelis and Lichtenberg, the other main epistolary contact between Göttingen and the English-speaking world was Blumenbach, whose standing and, with it, the number and range of his correspondents, increased up to his death in 1840. Along with the extensive and scientifically important correspondence with Joseph Banks (which has been discussed elsewhere),[114] Blumenbach developed a network of contacts who could pass on to Göttingen some of the scientific riches made possible by the expansion of British imperial power. Blumenbach was ever-anxious for skulls from all parts of the globe to assist his investigations into comparative physical anthropology, and he built up a considerable collection that his family referred to as his "Golgotha," the biblical "place of the skull."

The unearthing of the skull of the Scottish king, Robert Bruce, in 1821, for example, led to an application to the royal librarian "to send a Cast of this Celebrated Skull to the far famed Professor of Göttingen [Blumenbach] whose Museum is the wonder of the World and who is in the habit of receiving such presents from all the crowned Heads in Europe."[115] The methods his correspondents used to obtain these skulls were not overscrupulous and effectively amounted in some cases to grave robbery of indigenous sites. Blumenbach tended to adopt the same insouciance toward the supply of crania from European as well as non-European sources, being supplied in 1820 with a skull of the allegedly distinctive Irish kind, along with one from a church in Kent whose piles of skulls were supposed to go back to Anglo-Saxon times.[116]

Thanks to Banks, Blumenbach obtained skulls from the West Indies, Tahiti, and Australia. Blumenbach also collected notes on Australian Aborigines from early accounts of the British colony of New South Wales by Collins, Tench, and Hunter—accounts that he supplemented with correspondence with early visitors to the colony such as John Bigge.[117] From New Zealand he obtained a skull of a Maori prince through the *aide de camp* of His Royal Highness, the Duke of Cambridge—the *aide* declaring to Blumenbach in 1822 that "you have *friends* in Hanover and *England* sensible of *your* worth."[118] From another part of the Pacific—Peru— Blumenbach obtained a skull in 1825 thanks to the British informal empire of trade in South America, it being sent by the chief commissioner of the Anglo-Chilean Association on an English transport.[119] Four years later another South American skull arrived, this time from Demerara (Georgetown, British Guiana), again via an English contact (whose nephew Blumenbach had helped in Göttingen).[120] British expansion into Southeast Asia led to crania being sent back from Burma, and the colonial administrator, John Crawford, insisted to the officials at the British Museum that these be forwarded on to "the only proper hands, those of Dr. Blumenbach."[121]

Blumenbach's contacts also extended to England's separated brethren in the young United States. He received natural history news from Benjamin Barton, professor of medicine and natural history at the University of Pennsylvania, and (it would appear) a skull that reached him via Michaelis.[122] In 1824 a skull of a Narragansett Indian arrived thanks to a young American who was thankful for "your intercourse and—may I say—friendship while in Göttingen,"[123] followed in 1835 by a cast of the head of the Methodist preacher George Whitefield, which an enthusiastic Massachusetts phrenologist had sent on because it was supposedly "wholly deficient in the organ of *religious sentiment*."[124]

Along with Blumenbach's contacts with the British Empire (and its former transatlantic possessions) went recourse to the nearby Russian Empire for natural history specimens from its increasing territories. Appropriately, these two empires were drawn together in the dedication to the 1795 edition of Blumenbach's magnum opus, *De Generis Humani Varietate Nativa*, both to Banks and the Baron Georges-Thomas de Asch of St. Petersburg, Blumenbach's chief conduit of Russian specimens. Like so many members of the Russian scientific elite, Von Asch was of German origin, having studied medicine at Göttingen under the great von Haller. He sent Blumenbach more than forty skulls, including that of a female Georgian—the Georgians, who were celebrated for their beauty, being the exemplar for the Caucasian racial type.[125] Another Russian source of skulls was Professor Karpinsky of St. Petersburg who, as Blumenbach reported to Banks in 1792, sent four specimens of "the *Mongol* race."[126] Much later, in 1826, Blumenbach drew on the close marriage ties between the Russian imperial house and some of the German princely families to obtain two skulls from Kamtchatka on Russia's Pacific coast as a consequence of the visit of Princess Auguste of Weimar to her mother at St. Petersburg.[127]

Increasing Russian expansion into the Pacific was reflected in some of the other anthropological material that made its way to Blumenbach. The Von Asch ethnographical collection, which was integrated into the Göttingen museum, included a pickaxe from "North America opposite the Chukot Peninsula," which was reminiscent of New Zealand artifacts because the blade was made from nephrite (greenstone).[128] For information on Pacific (and other) languages, Blumenbach could draw on the work of Adam Krusenstern, commander of the first Russian circumnavigation from 1803–1806—the belated realization of the voyage on which George Forster had planned to sail. On his voyage, Krusenstern was accompanied by the Göttingen-trained physician Georg Langsdorff.[129] Another member of this expedition, W. G. Tilenau, consolidated links with Göttingen by a visit there in 1814, leaving some notes on Polynesian bark cloth samples.[130]

Thanks to such activities of the Göttingen professors and, a fortiori, to the work of the Forsters, the Pacific became well established as part of the vibrant late eighteenth-century German debate about the nature of human development and the great Rousseauian questions posed by the transition from nature to culture. In defending his fundamental thesis that each culture is unique with its own inner dynamic that prompts change and evolution, Johann von Herder drew explicitly on the Forsters. In his *Outlines of a Philosophy of the History of Man*, he referred to Johann Reinhold Forster as the "Ulysses" of the Pacific and his *Observations* as a model of its kind—adding the wish that there was a comparable *"philosophico-physical geography* of other parts of the World, as foundations for a history of man."[131]

Herder drew on Forster's Pacific reflections and other travelers' accounts of the Pacific to substantiate his arguments about the way cultures change and evolve: "A few centuries only have elapsed since the inhabitants of Germany were Patagonians; but are so no longer." With his stress on the unique value of each culture, Herder was, however, more disposed than the Forsters to emphasize what was uniquely valuable about particular Pacific societies. When, for example, he referred to the Mallicollese [Malekulans] of the New Hebrides [Vanuatu]—described in the Forsters' accounts of Cook's second Pacific voyage—he pointed out that they "display capacities that many other nations do not possess." Herder painted the Tahitians in the customarily bright colors as leading "a tranquil happy life." In the manner of Montesquieu, he attributed this largely to their climate, whereas the "less temperate" climate of Australia required the Aborigines to "live more hardly, and with less simplicity." Nonetheless, the Aborigine, too, he saw as having developed his own integrated way of life reflecting the worth of each culture: "he has united as many ways of life as his rude convenience required, till he had rounded them as it were into a circle, in which he could live happily after his fashion"—the same, he added, could be said of the New Caledonians and New Zealanders, adding in a rather un-Herderian manner, together with "even the miserable creatures of Tierra del Fuego." These examples drawn from Cook's second voyage he supplemented with material from the third voyage that, no doubt, he read in George Forster's German translation.[132]

For Kant—a voracious reader of travel accounts—the Pacific also served as a social laboratory to test assumptions about human nature and culture. As Kant wrote in his *Anthropology from a Pragmatic Point of View*: "One of the ways of extending the range of anthropology is *traveling*, or at least reading travelogues."[133] He drew on Cook's account of Tahiti, for example, to substantiate his view that wife beating in some cultures was expected by the wives themselves as a manifestation of jealousy of other men.[134] Like George Forster, Kant took the view that humankind required the amenities of civilization to live a fully moral life; consequently, he regarded some of the almost utopian accounts of life in the South Seas with rather more skepticism than Herder.[135] In his review of Herder's work, Kant did go so far as to refer to the "happy inhabitants of Tahiti," but he called into question Herder's view that they could be quite happy in their existing form of culture. For Kant, true happiness or, at least, true human fulfilment came from participation in "the ever continuing and growing activity and culture . . .

whose highest possible expression can only be the product of a political constitution based on concepts of human right, and consequently an achievement of human beings themselves."[136]

The exchange between Kant and Herder is one instance of the way that accounts of the Pacific were drawn into larger German Enlightenment debates about the nature of human society. Not only were the accounts of the Pacific to be significant in shaping discussion about human development, but the approach adopted by the Forsters and the Göttingen professors (and particularly Blumenbach), with its emphasis on basing theoretical speculation on strong empirical foundations, continued to be influential in Germany. The great heir to the Forsters was to be Alexander von Humboldt, who met George Forster while studying at Göttingen in 1789–90 with his brother, Wilhelm (who later drew on the Forsters' accounts of the South Seas languages in his influential work on comparative philology).[137]

George Forster and Alexander von Humboldt were drawn together by their shared scientific and political views, and in 1790 the two were traveling companions on a journey through the Low Countries, France, and England (where Forster introduced him to Banks).[138] Quite self-consciously Alexander von Humboldt saw himself as continuing along the same trail that George Forster had blazed by utilizing the genre of the travel account to explore the interrelationship between all the different elements of a particular location: its natural history and the manifestations of human culture. As Humboldt put it in his great *Kosmos* (1845–62): "Through my famous teacher and friend George Forster, began a new era of scientific expeditions, the purpose of which is comparative ethnology and geography." Humboldt even drew a parallel between the way George Forster had been invited to serve as a scientific observer on a Russian expedition and the way "I was invited by the Emperor Alexander in 1812 to undertake an expedition through the interior of Asia"[139]—another reminder of the important links between German science and Russian imperial expansion.

While many of Humboldt's nineteenth-century scientific contemporaries devoted themselves to refining further their particular scientific specialties, Humboldt maintained something of the integrated worldview that had characterized the Forsters' writings on the Pacific.[140] His monumental *Kosmos* was probably the nearest the nineteenth century came to presenting a total view of nature and its interrelationship with humankind. Though von Humboldt did not have firsthand experience of the Pacific beyond the shores of South America, he incorporated into this remarkable scientific *summa* ethnographical accounts of the South Seas, which he saw as allowing European scientific observers to arrive at more securely based generalizations, since they had previously been restricted to "a small portion of the earth." Like his master, George Forster, he was skeptical of the systems of racial classification—whether that of Blumenbach, with its five races, or the more recent one of the English anthropologist, James Pritchard, with seven races: of both he wrote "we fail to recognise any typical sharpness of definition, of any general or well-established principle, in the division of these groups."[141] As with Forster's querying of the Kantian racial divisions, it was a position that reflected an emphasis on the interconnectedness of all of nature together with the wariness of generalizations that follows naturally from the accumulation of empirical data through extensive travel.

Thanks to George Forster's influence, then, Humboldt in some ways carried into the nineteenth century some of the approaches and concerns of the German Enlightenment with its belief in the integration of all knowledge and its preoccupation with the universal history of humankind and the stages of its development. For eighteenth-century Europe, the "new world of the Pacific" was fertile ground for such conjectures, and Germany participated in this European-wide reflection on the significance of the data brought back by Pacific explorers. It did so both by the involvement of some Germans (notably the Forsters) in British and, to a lesser extent, Russian expeditions and through the focused research made possible by its universities (notably Göttingen). While imperial powers like Britain, France, Spain, and Russia looked to Pacific expeditions to promote both the Enlightenment and empire, the German involvement in the Pacific had, perforce, given Germany's fragmentation, to be much more restricted to the rewards brought by the pursuit of Enlightenment science and anthropology. When Germany again focused closely on the Pacific, it was in the Wilhelmite period, when a newly united nation joined other imperial powers in an expansion into the Pacific, in which the relative detachment of the Enlightenment was replaced by the more familiar goals of empire.

CHAPTER NINE

Persian Letters from Real People

Northern Perspectives on Europe

Michael Harbsmeier

The exotic observer from beyond Europe—China or Persia, for instance—is certainly one of the most fascinating figures of the European Enlightenment. Many interesting chapters in the history and prehistory of this figure have been written already, but there is still no study of how real people originating from other parts of the world have had a share in fashioning at least some of the images of the non-European outside observers so important for early European sociology and auto-ethnography. I begin with a very concrete example from Greenland in order to arrive at a better understanding of how real exchange and interaction between Europeans and some of their Others have been involved in articulating the perspective of the observer-from-elsewhere in eighteenth-century Europe.

POOQ AND QIPEROQ

The first two Greenlanders voluntarily undertaking a voyage to the Danish capital arrived in Denmark in October 1724.[1] The two young men, Pooq (later baptized as Christian) and Qiperoq, had been persuaded by the Danish missionary Hans Egede to pay a visit to the Danish king and capital as part of a campaign by the newly founded Greenlandic Company of Bergen and its director, J. A. Refdal, to obtain further support from King Frederik IV. Having departed from Godthaab on board the ship *Cronprintz Christian* in August, and after an intermediate stopover in Bergen, they arrived in Elsinore, north of Copenhagen, during the night between October 10 and 11. Already the next morning they were invited to Fredensborg castle to take part in the celebration of the king's birthday. Two weeks later, they were again called to the court, and this time, at the celebration of the birthday of Prince Charles, "the king did not content himself with looking at the Greenlanders"; he also wanted them to "demonstrate their skills." Thus, the two Greenlanders paddled their kayaks on Lake Esrom and started to practice "the exercises of their country both rowing their Greenlandic boats and shooting and throwing their javelins at the ducks, that had been set out in the lake for that purpose." With royal permission, an even greater spectacle was held in the very center of Copenhagen on November 9 from two to five o'clock in the afternoon: surrounded by a fleet of Danish sailing ships displaying huge images of the wealth and curiosities of Greenland on their mastheads (whale, walrus, narwhal, salmon, and polar bear skins), the two young Greenlanders once again paddled their kayaks with only one paddle, turning around in their boats, and, to the joy of the onlooking crowds, bringing down with their spears the ducks that had been put out for this great colonial spectacle. Having thus constituted one of the great events of the year in Denmark, they both returned to Greenland on December 3. Pooq arrived in April 1725, while Qiperoq died on the way, and was buried in Bergen in February.

Only four years later, another four Greenlanders arrived in Copenhagen, this time the visit was conducted by the eldest son of Hans Egede, Paul Egede. Already baptized in Greenland with the name Christian, Pooq once again was part of the show, this time accompanied by his wife, Christina, and two other Greenlanders, Carl Daniel and Sophia Magdalena. Arriving on October 2, 1728, this group also was invited to the court the next day, and again there was held a spectacular parade for the public. During the following months, the public of Copenhagen had the opportunity, for a fee, to take a closer look at the exotic Greenlanders at the royal castle. Before the Greenlanders could return home, however, they all died of smallpox during the spring: Sophia Magdalena on April 12; Christian (Pooq) on May 1; Pooq's wife, Christina, and their little daughter, as well as Carl Daniel, during the course of May 1729.[2]

Having come to power in 1731, King Christian VI did not want to continue the colonial policies of his predecessor. A number of Danish officials were thus called home—bringing with them yet another series of Greenlanders to Copenhagen. Hans Egede, who decided to stay in spite of the withdrawal of royal support, protested on the grounds of the smallpox tragedy two years before, but this did not prevent Claus Paars and other officials from taking their Greenlandic servants with them to Denmark. Two of these, Claus Paars's young servants, Friderich Carl and Anna Sophia Magdalena, were presented at court—dressed in European clothes of the nobility—on the occasion of the queen's birthday, but there does not seem to have been any public spectacle. The following year, King Christian VI issued the order that henceforth no further native Greenlanders should be brought to Denmark unless by the explicit command of the king. This was too late, however, to prevent the tragedy that was to follow: four of the Greenlanders died, presumably of smallpox, and of the two remaining, who were sent back to Greenland in the spring of 1733, only one survived the return passage. That one, according to Hans Egede, brought the epidemic back to Greenland with him, which led to the death of almost half the native population. The boy himself died shortly after—probably of tuberculosis.

The first to live for a considerable number of years in Greenland after having visited Denmark was Pungujôk, who, having been exposed in Greenland, was immune to smallpox: he followed Paul Egede to Copenhagen as assistant and informant for the latter's linguistic studies in 1738. Pungujôk paid no visit to the Danish court, and returned safely to Greenland in June the following year. Encouraged by this experience, Paul Egede again took two young Greenlanders with him when, in 1740, he was forced to give up his missionary work for reasons of bad health. Arnasak and the ten-year-old boy, Tullimak, were received by Christian VI and returned to Greenland the following year. Even less is known about the five young Greenlanders, who in 1746 were brought to Denmark by the missionary Sylow on his retirement. Neither they nor Okako—who on his own initiative came "to discover," as he put it, Copenhagen in 1776—were invited to court or made to perform in any public spectacles.

The impressions of paradigmatic Pooq suggest the possibility of identifying a specifically Northern view of Europe. The first two Greenlanders, Pooq and Qiperoq, are also those whose voices can be traced most clearly in the sources. During their stay in Copenhagen, they were quoted extensively and verbatim by a number of those to whom they were shown and presented. Even more interesting, however, are Hans and Paul Egede's diaries, which tell us in great detail how Pooq reported to his fellow Greenlanders about his experiences after his return.

From the diary of Hans Egede we learn that Pooq, immediately after his return, wanted to marry a girl who had come to the colony during his absence. The first of Pooq's many travel accounts therefore has the form of a marriage proposal, dated June 20, 1725. According to Paul Egede, Pooq was quick to come to the point:

"I have sailed over the dangerous, long-winded sea to the Land of the Big-Beards [Norway]. I have seen many remarkable things. I have seen the great Overlord, the king. I have heard the terrible weapons' sound, inside and outside his great houses.

I have become rich, I own three big chests with valuable things, which is all too much for me alone. I have therefore chosen you as my wife. The reasonable Pavia [Paul Egede], whom you all love, has brought you for me. You are mine and share all my wealth." After that he immediately wanted to go to bed with her; but she shouted: He is mad, protect me! We then had to hold him back, until she, after the custom of the country, could cry herself into readiness for a day or two and run away a couple of times, though she expected that we would find her again.[3]

This marriage proposal was, however, only one version of Pooq's account of his voyage. In an earlier entry, Hans Egede mentioned having heard "the songs, which he had made about his voyage, and what particular sights he had witnessed in our country."[4] Paul Egede later summarized this song as follows:

He had performed his voyage in a song, the content of which was: that he had been for two months on the great sea where no land was in sight, before he came to the Land of the Big-Beards, from there to the great lord, the king's land, where the crowd of people were like mosquitos, the houses inside and outside wonderful and great, and the round tower in particular, which he called a mountain with a snail's spiral all the way to the top. There are no other mountains in the king's land, other than their houses. The king's houses and the houses of devotion [churches] were so high, that one could not shoot over them with a bow.[5]

The most elaborate—perhaps even the definitive—version of Pooq's travel account also goes back to an entry in the diary of Hans Egede from precisely a year later. Before mentioning the songs of Pooq, Egede here described a scene, which his son Paul—who at that time was only eighteen years old—would use thirty-four years later as a model for the further elaboration of Pooq's travel account. Hans Egede's diary entry reads as follows:

25th April. The Greenlanders set up a play and comedy with singing and dancing, that my colleague and several others went to see. Such playing consists of two people standing in front of each other, each with a little drum in his hand, on which they play, singing against each other, and that with which the one reproaches the other he presents in the form of a song. If the counterpart cannot answer this or refute him, then he must yield with shame and be laughed at by all those who listen. One of those, who here competed with another, was very well spoken, so his counterpart had to give up, so another came to try his art on him, but he also had to retreat in dishonor. After that our Pooq let us hear the songs he had made about his voyage and what he had seen in our country.[6]

The full and final version of Pooq's travel account was the result of Paul Egede's attempt to stage his main hero as a participant in the "traditional" song contest, to which his father had made Pooq's performance a mere epilogue or postscript. This most prestigious and authoritative version of Pooq's travel account was printed in 1760 as an appendix to Paul Egede's *Grammatica Grönlandica Danico-Latina*. The trilingual— Latin, Greenlandic, and Danish—"*Colloquium quod cum conterraneis suis instituit Poekus Grönlandus, Hafnia domum reversus*" or "Dialogue Between Pooq Greenlander and His Fellow Countrymen, After His Return from Copenhagen," runs for twenty-five pages in Egede's book; it is followed by a likewise trilingual disputation involving an *angákok*, or shaman. Paul Egede thus managed to change an alleged native song contest in Greenland into an exercise text to be used in a classroom in Europe. The dialogue starts like this:

> *Pooq*: With heartfelt longing I see you.
> *Simik*: You have intrepidly traveled over the big sea.
> *Pooq*: I have found the sea to be so vast that we saw no land for two months.
> *Kyaut*: Now you see the land of the Kablunak. Where is your companion?
> *Pooq*: He died in the spring in the land of the long-bearded.
> *Kyaut*: You have so much to tell about.
> *Pooq*: I have lost my way in my stories because there are so many.
> *Kyaut*: Have you not been in the land of the king, the supreme lord?
> *Pooq*: Yes. We embarked from the bearded ones' land, set course to the south, and arrived on the third day in the land of the king. Before we saw land, we saw high houses and large ships lying at anchor. The land has no mountains and is quite flat.
> *Kyaut:* Marvelous.
> *Pooq*: The house of the king and the churches are higher than all others. Their height cannot be reached with a bow and arrow.
> *Persok:* You have probably been inside of them, you have perhaps also contemplated the king's house.
> *Pooq*: Certainly. When we anchored close to the city, I and my departed friend were picked up by a beautifully painted boat with fourteen oars. When we wanted to row alongside them in our kayaks, we paddled ourselves; but what a crowd of spectators on the shore, like mosquitos in large numbers.[7]

The dialogue continues in much the same way with a description of the "sledge with a house on it which had windows on both sides," of the king's house, "huge as an iceberg" and with an entrance "so large that there could be twenty tents inside," and of the "many kinds of well dressed armed people," bearing weapons not because "they hunt and shoot reindeer and seals," but "to show that the great lord lives in the house"; the "manifold, huge, nicely painted rooms" inside the king's house and "the weapons, that made a terrible noise when fired."[8]

The dialogue further described the food that was served in the presence of the king and queen, food that was "so nicely painted and delightfully made, that I [Pooq] thought it was meant as ornament and not to be eaten"; reflected on "how we and our fellow men are on average good and on average bad, whereas the Kablunat [the Europeans] have no equal, neither in the good nor the bad." The dialogue noted that in Denmark the cannons were ready in case the enemy should attack; the armed men were on guard on the banks and between the houses to look out for fire, which they fought with artificial instruments; and the Danes obtained their food from the land, and from trees. The Greenlanders remarked that Greenland was colder than Denmark, and reflected that they could not live in Denmark, because there were only seals there, and no whales, and because there was no free hunting and fishing there, and because the great lords owned both the animals on land and the fish in the sea.[9]

The Greenlanders of the dialogue further noted that in Denmark whale oil and blubber were "used for lamps which hang outside the houses to give light to the passersby"; that the Danish authorities took care of the common people; and a big house full of old men and women was provided for no cost, as well as a house only for orphans; another for mad people; another for bad women, who had to work against their will; and two or three more houses for other miserable people. "They do not live our way, to share food," observed the Greenlanders of the Danes. "Some are much too rich, have many houses where nobody lives, while others have neither house nor clothes, but walk around like beggars." Poverty in Denmark resulted from the fact that "some are cripples and cannot work, others lazy and do not want to work, while still others destroy themselves with mad-making water." The Greenlanders noted that there were houses with no other business than to sell mad-making water, where the sailors "drink, yell, fight, and are without reason."[10]

At the end of the dialogue, Pooq summarized his experience of the Danish Kablunat:

There are many extremes among the people . . . Among the Kablunat there are so many madmen that they have to be tied up and locked up and remain so for the rest of their lives . . . On the other hand, they are extremely clever people. They can find their way through the wide, huge sea by simply measuring the height of the sun and constantly watching that mobile thing which points to the north. They build those awfully great ships on land and make them move by themselves when they are ready. They can make such artificial machines that can lift ships into the air, move whole houses from one place to another and large stones into the air. They can predict when a darkening will happen and for how long. In short, I have seen so much of their marvelous doings that I became speechless, and had to acknowledge the saying of the ancestors: the Kablunat are capable of everything except the tides.[11]

I have quoted at length from Paul Egede's dialogically staged travel account in order to suggest a comparative view of how differently the voice and the eye of the external observer have been constructed in various parts of enlightened Europe.

COMPARISONS: REAL AND IMAGINARY
VISITORS TO EUROPE

Descriptions of Europe by foreign visitors were obviously nothing new, either at the time of Pooq's first voyage to Denmark in 1724, or at the time of the publication of the complete version of his travelogue in 1760. Gian-Paolo Marana's *L'Esploratore turco e le di lui relazioni segrete alla Porta Ottomana, scoperte in Parigi nel Regno di Luigi il Grande* from 1682 had become influential through the much-expanded English version, *Letters from a Turkish Spy*.[12] Montesquieu's *Lettres Persanes* (1721) in turn inspired a whole series of more or less original imitations and transformations of what by then had become a recognizable genre throughout the rest of the century.[13]

There was a difference, however, between Pooq and many other Asiatic, Turkish, African, or Iroquois ambassadors, princes, spies, and other foreign visitors and observers of the Enlightenment. This difference lay in the degree to which Paul Egede, as a result af his systematic missionary as well as ethnographic and linguistic efforts, was able to stage Pooq's case as that of a visitor who, upon coming home, shared his experiences with his fellow countrymen in a geographically, linguistically, ethnographically, and historically precisely circumscribed, and thus "realistic," setting.

Even when restricting ourselves to contemporary Danish examples, Paul Egede's realism seems rather exceptional. Ludvig Holberg (1684–1754), who (presumably on the basis of conversations with Bishop Paul Egede in Copenhagen) compiled a whole collection of various visiting Greenlanders' comments and questions about European and Danish manners, customs, and religious beliefs, neither describes the precise location and circumstances of the dialogues he quotes, nor gives the names of his heathen critics of civilization.

Even more unspecific and anonymous is the author of the twenty-two-page pamphlet published in Copenhagen in Danish in 1771 under the title *A Greenlander's Description of Copenhagen with Deliberation on the Keeping of the Ten Commandments*. As in Holberg, this Greenlander also functions as a spokesman for a kind of superior reason. Describing the inhabitants of Copenhagen in terms of the discrepancies between their

official and outward Christian beliefs on the one hand and their inner
convictions and actual behavior on the other, this anonymous Greenlander too engages in a lively discussion of a number of the central concerns
of the Danish or Copenhagen public of the time. With reference to the
philosophies of both Epicurus and Spinoza, the Ten Commandments of
the title of the pamphlet serve only as an excuse for describing the generally immoral and improper behavior of the inhabitants of Copenhagen,
especially their excessive drinking and consumption of commodities
originating from other countries and even from outside of Europe. Concerning the fifth commandment on murder, the Greenlandic observer
notes the fact that people "do not kill anybody at the first stroke, but it
is not counted as any sin if one kills one's good friends by a long chain
of biting vexations, deadly frauds, cheatings, slanders and all other sorts of
slow and subtle poisoning. This is called politics ["Politique" in the Danish
original, as if something imported from France] and seen as praisewor-
thy."[14]

Both Holberg's epistle and the anonymous pamphlet just quoted clearly
belong to the European tradition most famously represented in Danish literature by Bishop Erik Pontoppidan's two volumes from 1745, entitled
*Menoza, an Asiatic Prince, who traveled around the world to seek Chris-
tians, particularly in India, Spain, Italy, France, England, Holland, Germany, and Denmark, but only found very little of what he was searching
for: A Treatise containing the unshakable foundations of both the natural
as well as the revealed religion and which warns against the known devia-
tions in doctrine and practice of most Christians.* Pontoppidan's Menoza,
who was to have a major literary career in many different German versions, first passed through the Danish and Moravian missions in Tranquebar, the Danish colony in India, before embarking on his journey through
first the southern and then the northern parts of Europe. There he engaged
in extended dialogues and discussions with representatives of all different
sorts of Christians to clear his mind and that of his readers from all kinds
of misundersandings of natural and revealed religion.

Menoza's and Pontoppidan's spectacular success certainly influenced
both Ludvig Holberg, the anonymous Greenlandic pamphleteer of 1771,
and Paul Egede in his reworking of the notes of his father after the return
of Pooq in 1725 and the publication of the *Grammatica Grönlandica
Danico-Latina* in 1760. On the other hand, however, it was precisely the
Moravian mission in Tranquebar, which, substantially funded by the Danish king, produced an even earlier example of *Persian Letters* from real
people, namely the so-called *Malabarische Korrespondenz*; this consisted
of a large number of letters from a whole series of—alas anonymous—
heathen Tamils about their own religion compared to the preachings and

doctrines of the missionaries. Edited and translated by the Halle missionaries Johann Ernst Gründler (1677–1720) and Bartholomäus Ziegenbalg (1682–1719), these "curious miscellaneous writings" received from "various Malabarian heathens" were published in German in Halle in 1714 and a second series in 1717.[15] These letters may be considered the earliest example of the Danish-German Moravian-Pietist missionary tradition of realism in the staging of the voice of an external, extra-European visitor, observer, and critical commentator.

The missionary genealogy of this authentic variant of the fictional tradition known under the name of *Lettres Persanes* naturally invites comparison with other and earlier missionary traditions. According to the French-Canadian historian Normand Doiron, who has studied what he calls the genealogy of the "eloquence sauvage" through seventeenth-century Jesuit relations, there is, on the part of these missionaries, surprisingly little concern about the precise situations and circumstances for the performance of native American "harangues" or "discourses" spoken by the chiefs and quoted verbatim at length by the Jesuits. Looking more closely at speeches from the years 1633, 1636, and 1639, Doiron demonstrates in detail precisely which of the speeches of Cato the Elder or Titus Livius were made into models for the missionaries' creative attempts at painting idealized portraits of the Native Americans.[16] While the eighteenth-century Pietists would do their utmost to guarantee the authenticity of heathen voices, the seventeenth-century Jesuit missionaries were more eager to have them present the strongest and most convincing arguments and demonstrations. For the Jesuit missionaries, the American chiefs had to follow the rules of classical rhetoric in order to be heard by their European readers. For the Lutheran Pietists, it was almost the other way around: realism depended not so much on the power and persuasiveness of what was said as on the authenticity of the setting and situation and therefore of the quoted voices.

According to Doiron, most of the American speeches were given by chiefs or other offical leaders of their communities. The Greenlanders, however, like Pooq and his brother Qiperoq, spoke in voices that were not authorized by their status in their own societies, but were instead authenticated by their experiences among the missionaries and their voyages to Europe. One of the most famous instances of the Jesuit tradition of *Persian Letters*, Lahontan's *Dialogue curieux entre l'Auteur et un Sauvage de bon sens qui a voyagé*, first published anonymously in Amsterdam in 1703, involved a characteristic break with this same tradition, precisely because Adario, alias Kondiaronk, even though still a chief, does not perform an offical speech of any kind. Instead, he engages in a series of conversations with the author, dealing not with the history of his own country and tribe, but rather with his experiences as a traveler among the

French, who were also the intended readers of the text. Lahontan's dialogue suggests that breaking from classical rhetorical forms was an important step toward realistic representations of the voice of the outside observer.

The Age of Enlightenment offers many interesting parallels to the case of Pooq, other examples of exotic outsiders brought to visit various parts of Europe. I have discussed elsewhere such figures as Omai, Aoutourou, Maheine, and Kadu in the texts of Cook, Forster, Bougainville, Diderot, Kotzebue, and Chamisso.[17] Here I concentrate on a parallel northern example, namely that of the four "Eskimos" whom George Cartwright brought in 1772 from the Canadian Arctic to England, where they called forth almost as much public attention as the South Pacific islanders, like Omai, who arrived soon after from the other end of the world.[18]

Returning from Labrador in November 1772, Cartwright had somehow succeeded in persuading no fewer than five native Inuit to follow him on his way home to London: the young man Attuiock and the youngest of his four wives, Ickcongoque; their youngest, four-year-old daughter, Ickeuna; Attuiock's brother, Tooglavinia; and this brother's wife, Caubvick. Much like the Greenlanders brought to Denmark, the Inuits, all except Caubvick, soon died in England from smallpox.[19] Their stay in England, however, and more particularly the way in which Cartwright understood and described their reactions, was strikingly different from the experiences of the two brothers from Greenland in Denmark half a century earlier.

Cartwright was no missionary, but went to Labrador in order to manage the economic interests of a trading company founded in 1770.[20] His spectacular visitors were not seen as evidence of the progress of Christianization or the wide-ranging power of his king, but rather as objects or even curiosities of natural history. According to his diaries, Cartwright did all in his power to give the general public access to "his Eskimos." When his neighbors complained about the crowds of carriages queuing in front of his residence to get a glimpse with their own eyes of the exotic visitors from the Arctic, Cartwright found a better place to accommodate the many interested visitors inspecting his guests.[21] He also tried to mobilize royal interest in these Canadian subjects, but in vain.

The contrast to the royal reception of Pooq and Quiperoq was even more conspicuous in Cartwright's descriptions of the reactions of "his Eskimos" when confronted with the various sights and curiosities of the British capital. London Bridge, Blackfriars Bridge, even St. Paul's Cathedral in no way called forth the awe and astonishment that Cartwright anticipated. Only after it was explained to them, that these monuments were not created by nature, but were the product of human efforts, did the visitors react according to the expectations of their hosts.[22] Unlike Pooq, however, Cartwright's Eskimos had no intention of telling their fellow countrymen about their experiences: "Upon my asking them how they should describe it to their countrymen on their return, they replied, with a look of the utmost expression, they should neither mention it, nor many other things which they had seen, lest they should be called liars, from the seeming impossibility of such astonishing facts."[23]

Cartwright and the public he successfully addressed were chiefly interested in evaluating these visitors as objects of natural history—so much so, in fact, that Cartwright even made the visitors themselves seem to share this obsession. He described them watching monkeys:

I observed their attention riveted on a small monkey; and I could perceive horror most strongly depicted in their countenances. At length the old man turned to me and faltered out, "Is that an Esquimau?" I must confess, that both the colour and contour of the countenance had considerable resemblance to the people of their nation; but how they could conceive it possible for an Esquimau to be reduced to that diminutive size, I am wholly at a loss to account for; unless they had fixed their attention on the countenance only, and had not adverted to any particulars. On pointing out several other monkeys of different kinds, they were greatly diverted at the mistake which they had made; but were not well pleased to observe, that monkeys resembled their race much more than ours.[24]

On the occasion of a visit to "that excellent surgeon and anatomist, the ingenious John Hunter," Attuiock was represented as sharing another of his host's obsessions, namely cannibalism:

In the afternoon Attuiock walked out of the room by himself, but presently returned with such evident marks of terror, that we were all greatly alarmed, fearing some accident had happened to him; or that he had met with an insult from one of the servants. He seized hold of my hand, and eagerly pressed me to go along with him. I asked the cause of his emotion, but could get nothing more from him than "Come along, come along with me," and he hastily led me into a room . . . in which stood a glass case containing many human bones. "Look there," says he, with more horror and consternation in his countenance, than I ever beheld in that of man before, "are those the bones of Esquimaux whom Mr. Hunter has killed and eaten? Are we to be killed? Will he eat us and put our bones here?"[25]

After the ensuing laughter of the congregated gentlemen, Cartwright explained that these were actually the bones of executed criminals and that Mr. Hunter "might better know how to set those of the living, in case any of them should chance to be broken." This did not satisfy the Inuit: "Attuiock's nerves had received too great a shock to enable him to resume his usual tranquility, till he found himself safe in my house again."[26]

Cartwright's Arctic guests never had the chance to tell their fellow countrymen about their experiences in London. Cartwright, however, predicted that Attuiock and his company would need years to produce a proper account of what they had observed. Cartwright made the travelers' voices express one single message: how much they still had to develop, how much time they would still need to remain abroad, before they would have any chance of appreciating England:

I took Attuiock with me and walked beyond the Tower. We there took a boat, rowed up the river, and landed at Westminster Bridge; from whence we walked to Hyde Park Corner, and then home again. I was in great expectation, that he would begin to relate the wonders which he had seen, the instant he entered the room; but I found myself greatly disappointed. He immediately sat down by the fire side, placed both his hands on his knees, leaned his head forward, fixing his eyes on the ground in a stupid stare; and continued in that posture for a considerable time. At length, tossing up his head, and fixing his eyes on the ceiling, he broke out in the following soliloquy; "Oh! I am tired; here are too many houses; too much smoke; too many people; Labrador is very good; seals are plentiful there; I wish I was back again." By which I could plainly perceive, that the multiplicity, and variety of objects had confounded his ideas; which were too much confined to comprehend any thing but the inconveniences that he had met with. And indeed, the longer they continued in England, the more was I convinced of the truth of that opinion; for their admiration increased in proportion, as their ideas expanded; till at length they began more clearly to comprehend the use, beauty and mechanism of what they saw; though the greater part of these were as totally lost upon them, as they would have been upon one of the brute creation.[27]

These few incidents already make abundantly clear that there was a great difference between the Danes and the Englishmen studying and commenting on the human objects brought home from Greenland in 1724 and from Labrador in 1772. Pooq's travelogues, as transcribed by Hans and Paul Egede, were unique inasmuch as they offered realistic accounts of dialogues and interactions with more than just one single perspective.

CONCLUSION

I have tried to describe and identify an anthropologically realist current in the traditon or the genre of *Persian Letters*. This current may be attributed to a combination of missionary zeal, common to both orthodox Lutheran and Moravian Pietism, and enlightened interests in philology and natural history. I have restricted myself here to texts concerning Greenland and the North. Much of the same pattern, I believe, can be found in numerous travel accounts of the late eighteenth century, including those of the Danish-German traveler to the Middle East, Carsten Niebuhr. His work also, emphatically proto-anthropological, was marked by a combination of interests in Holy Scripture, natural history, and Oriental philololgy. The study of ancient and exotic texts and languages may not have substantially altered approaches to natural history, but it greatly encouraged efforts to understand the voices of living Others.

CHAPTER TEN

Russia and Its "Orient"

Ethnographic Exploration of the Russian Empire in the Age of Enlightenment

Giulia Cecere

The Russian Empire was a complex ethnic and linguistic coagulum that engaged scholars and explorers in strenuous and time-consuming research. In the eighteenth century, the designation of its linguistic origins and ethnic groups proved increasingly crucial for the elaboration of a "map of eastern populations" and recognition of the boundaries between one kind of "civilization" and another. Ultimately, such a map of populations required a certain degree of correlation with political and cultural criteria. Geographical, linguistic, and ethnographic representations were, however, far from being unanimous and showed an ambiguity and heterogeneity that kept challenging contemporaries. Russia did not have a passive role in this process of cultural definition. Instead, interesting voices emerged from the East and had a relevant impact on Western debates. A series of scientific expeditions led to the discovery of territories still largely unknown and the classification of the languages, populations, and resources of its European and Asiatic provinces. Russian expeditions were certainly the most effective means for the discovery of geographical data and for the clarification of issues related to the Slav, Tatar, Cossack, and Mongol peoples and languages. Yet, government policies and ethnographic research did not develop along parallel paths. Against the standardization championed by Russian officials, natural historical findings presented a decentered and pluralistic vision of the new world discovered.

The Russian exploratory process was not a novelty of the eighteenth century. Indeed, from the seventeenth century onward, a series of attempts had been made to discover some of the unknown lands of the Russian Empire, the main *terrae incognitae* being the eastward regions of Siberia, as the first section of this contribution investigates. The opening of some routes and of contacts with indigenous populations was a task first performed by Cossack adventurers. Only under Peter the Great, however, were effective efforts undertaken to give a scientific and regular character to such enterprises. His strong will certainly enhanced new ambitious exploratory projects and the building up of scientific expertise in Russia, predominantly based on foreign personnel. As early as the seventeenth century, but also through the eighteenth century, languages appeared as the major paradigm of the classificatory enterprise. Early accounts were rich in details and judgments, dividing peoples into settled and nomadic as well as stressing their religious creeds.

The second section of this chapter shows that most of Peter's plans were still far from systematic and were only to be accomplished after his death. Moreover, science suffered from a serious lack of support by his successors until Catherine II ascended the throne. Until then, scientific research was dominated by an entourage of foreigners that at times helped to stir up jealousy and quarrels within the scientific establishment and, in some instances, even betrayed the security of the Russian state. The investigation of, and encounter with, native populations was still predominantly filtered through a strong Eurocentric mentality, which involved moral contempt as well as missionary ideals and concealed aspirations to take control of new lands and tributary populations.

With the direct involvement of Catherine the Great, a program of extensive and ongoing research was finally set up in the second half of the eighteenth century, as the third section demonstrates. A series of expeditions were patronized by the Academy of Sciences, under Catherine's tutelage, to survey the territory and population groups of all the provinces of the Russian Empire. Russia gradually recovered possession of its own scientific interests and objectives, becoming the only director of both fieldwork and the publication of its results. Moreover, an increasing number of Russians were occupying the higher echelons of scientific institutions. Investigation itself was then inspired by a more refined kind of anthropological and ethnographic concern. A comparative approach became common, together with a growing sensitivity toward the threat of Russification to the native populations. In addition to their intrinsic complex ethnic, social, and linguistic reality—which proved problematic for Russia to control—the life of Asiatic nomads also appeared as unusual and "exotic" to the readers of the time.

ETHNIC AND LINGUISTIC GROUPS

The expansion of the Muscovite state, especially in the seventeenth century, entailed the protection of the new frontiers, plans for fortified towns, and the search for attractive areas for colonization. Throughout the sixteenth and seventeenth centuries, the conquered areas in the south and in the east had remained outside effective control, but were defensive lines from which Russia's expansion was pushed farther.[1] From Peter to Catherine, the attitude of the Russian government toward indigenous populations underwent a series of crucial changes. It is, however, important to stress that the frontier, as a point of contact between different worlds, was perceived differently by Russia and the subject populations. The relationship was based on an unequal encounter, that is, as Khodarkovsky has forcibly stated: "those who held the instruments of political power also controlled the terms in which that communication took place."[2] The place of encounter itself was a region where several cultures met, such as pagan and shamanistic, Muslim, Buddhist, and Orthodox. These different worlds continued to remain separate long after their initial encounter. By analyzing the perspective of the native people, therefore, one will also have a better understanding of such complex relationships and the motives that stood behind certain events, strategies, and choices. In the eighteenth century, Russia still had a limited knowledge of nomadic society. In general, the government showed little interest in the different mores, customs, and laws of the new subjects, but focused on political, economic, and religious classifications. Moreover, Russian officials appointed in the border regions were both harsh and corrupt. Ethnographic concepts themselves were under construction and developed slowly and regionally. The process of assimilation of the nomadic tribes into the Russian Empire went through thorny issues and phases, and by the end of the eighteenth century, the nomads' domination of the steppe came to an end, with many of them impoverished and subdued by imperial arms. Yet the Russification of ethnic minorities remained problematic even in the nineteenth century.[3] The Bashkirs, for instance, were notorious in Russian history for their strenuous resistance to Russian conquest and negotiated for themselves the status of a distinct military force, known from 1798 as the Bashkir Host. Although Speranskii placed them under the category of rural citizens in 1832, that was only on paper. Not until Russia's conquests in Central Asia, Kuban, and Caucasus in the 1860s would they be totally incorporated and turned into loyal citizens.[4]

The exploratory process saw its instruments refined and its goals widened especially in the second half of the eighteenth century, thanks to the support of Catherine II. Yet, the first scientific research efforts in Russia dated back to Peter's reign. Seventeenth-century Cossack discoveries in Siberia and the numerous embassies to China through overland routes provided material necessary to make Peter's foundations possible.[5] He had conceived of the establishment of scientific personnel and institutions, and the promotion of geographical research. Together with the first cartographic survey (1715–44), important scientific expeditions were patronized by Peter to increase the knowledge of his gigantic domains. Translators were employed and missions organized for the study of languages. Moreover, Russia embarked on the first production of data to define the populations according to geographical criteria, census count, and sometimes even ethnography.[6] Cadastral surveys were significantly pursued in 1719, throughout the 1730s, from 1745, and from 1762, although at different intervals in various provinces and without uniform criteria. Data on languages were considered the most important element of culture together with religion. To a certain extent, cadastres shed light on linguistic and ethnic processes of assimilation, although it is difficult to use them for definite figures. Non-Russians, for example, were classified under different rubrics in different cadastres, while varied criteria intersected, statistics were lost, some peoples resisted, and a number of territories or categories were excluded.[7]

Scholars such as I. Kirilov, V. Tatishchev, and M. Lomonosov called for a better understanding of the ethnic composition of the empire. They were involved in the geographical surveys and were also engaged in exploratory and administrative activities. By 1744 a large number of districts were charted, and cartographic material, together with the results achieved by scientific expeditions, converged to better delineate and recast the spatial conception of Russian lands within a grid based on geographical coordinates. The Urals were identified as the main divide between European and Asiatic Russia. Yet, although fully within the European boundaries, the regions of the middle Volga and the northern Caucasus were still associated with Asia and, like Siberia, became the objects of Russia's eighteenth-century "civilizing mission" and anthropological study. The eighteenth century marked the emergence of a new imperial dimension, grounded pragmatic considerations, and the ideas of the Enlightenment. Alongside the Russians, there were huge populations of non-Slavs. Nearly all the native populations, except for the Tatars, were rural peoples. Tatars and Chuvashes were Turkic linguistic groups, while Cheremises (now Maris), Votiaks (now Udmurts), and Mordvins belonged to the Finno-Ugric family. Since the time of Peter the Great, the government had begun a process of incorporation of these regions into

the Russian Empire by exerting more direct military control and economic and political pressure over the indigenous populations. These were
described by Russian officials as "wild, untamed horses," "wild animals," and "wild, unruly and disloyal peoples."[8]

Peter supported the Orthodox Church's missions for pragmatic reasons, and incentives were offered to those who converted to Christianity,
settled and farmed, or enlisted in the army. Yet, those like the Kalmyks,
who were needed to protect Russia's southern frontier, remained exempt
from sedentary life until the 1860s. Contrasting Catholic and Orthodox
missionary efforts, in 1719 Ivan Pososhkov urged the government to convert the new subjects in the southeastern areas, but also to send missions
to the Kamchatka Peninsula. He significantly stated: "our pagans are like
children."[9] If under the reign of Peter's successors, especially Elizabeth,
violent assaults on the non-Christians increased, Catherine II ended this
period of repressive assimilation and inaugurated the most tolerant period
in Russia's relations with non-Christian subjects since the mid-sixteenth
century.[10] Although she would not judge other peoples' culture and religion, she would regulate them. Her humanitarian ideas were certainly
rooted in the ideas of the Enlightenment, but they also responded to more
pragmatic needs. Reform, the incorporation of new territories, and the
importation of German colonists required the manifestation of tolerance.
From Peter to Catherine, one can also note the emergence of increasingly
specific ethnonyms to classify the peoples of the empire, which also reflected less emphasis on religion and increased stress on languages, origins, places of residence, and ways of life. Many non-Russians, however,
continued to see religion as the most important identity, thus changing
their designation from Chuvash or Votiak to "Tatar" after conversion to
Islam. "Tatar" was employed by non-Russians generically as synonymous
with Muslim, just as "Russian" was identified with Christian. In early
Russian documents, however, "Tatar" referred to the Turkic-speaking
peoples; hence, the Chuvashes, Cheremises, Votiaks, and Mordvins were
called "Tatars," regardless of their religion.

The investigation of eastern regions and populations had been the major preoccupation of a seventeenth-century Tatar author, whose work was
discovered by Strahlenberg in the eighteenth century and became a key
documentary source for later historians and explorers.[11] Abul-Ghazi
(1603–63), a descendant of Genghis Khan, was khan of the Tatars of
Khwarezm, also a historian and editor. In his *Histoire généalogique des
Tartares* (1726), he "mapped" the geographical sites of the populations
between the Russo-Turkish and the Russo-Chinese frontiers.[12] To the
characteristics of each population group there corresponded a relevant
position in an imaginary scale of civilization, with languages and physical

traits used as the major attributes to establish ethnic links and origins. The provenance of ethnic appellations still seemed independent and unverifiable. Although they grew more precise, they would not be standardized until the nineteenth century. A complex nomadic reality was revealed through the descriptions interspersed in the text, which reflected the author's sensitivity to social organizations, frontiers, and ethnic roots. In such a confused region of plains, steppes, mountains, deserts, and plateaus, populations became the only reference points for frontiers and boundaries. Abul-Ghazi highlighted the political status of the population groups, distinguishing those under direct Russian rule from those that had been colonized and paid tribute to the tsar, or were reluctant to accept any interference with their independence.

As the title of his book suggests, Abul-Ghazi's purpose was to retrace the genealogy of the Tatars, who were peoples dwelling in northern Asia and divided into three different "nations": the Tatars, Kalmyks,[13] and Mongols, who were in turn fragmented into an indefinite number of subgroups. He clarified that contemporary Turks had nothing to do with the Turks, or Tatars, who had invaded Asia in the ninth century. By his time, the Turks were just a "mass of Saracens, Arabs, Greeks, Slavs, and other mixed peoples of doubtful origin."[14] Missionaries, he added, had wrongly suggested that all the peoples inhabiting northern Asia were to be gathered under the generic appellation of Tatars.[15] The Tatars' physical traits varied according to their proximity to either the Russian or Turkish borders, assuming features similar to those of their closest neighbors. Muslim Tatars (near Turkey) and Christian Tatars (near Russia) clearly differed from each other. Their languages were indeed affected by the proximity of certain religious and ethnic groups, and Abul-Ghazi offered a wealth of examples throughout his narration.[16] Moreover, in Abul-Ghazi's view, their geographical location reflected the natural border between Russia and Siberia: "Nature has separated Russia from Siberia by a long chain of very high mountains."[17]

Abul-Ghazi never missed the opportunity to highlight frontier disorders and disputes, indicating administrative, jurisdictional, and linguistic clashes. Nomadic life, deep-rooted in the Tatar nature, mirrored underdevelopment and a "confused and fabulous knowledge of that country."[18] The last section of the book, devoted to the Russian conquest of Siberia and the "pagan" population, was concise and cursory, listing the population groups, simply located according to geographical criteria. He vaguely sketched a few physical traits and tribal habitations. Among those peoples, the Samoyeds were considered "the most stupid and poor of the whole of Siberia," as they surpassed in their primitiveness all the other pagan peoples.[19]

Nevertheless, in the first decades of the eighteenth century, linguistic scrutiny was still at an early stage, very much dependent on personal interests and skills. Bering left three accounts, but only one of them has been published entirely.[20] His first journal showed that the team was also involved in ethnographic observation, although of a very general nature. He described some habits, customs, and characteristics of the Tungus, Ostyaks, Yakuts, and Chukchi, especially stressing their idolatrous nature and the need to convert them to Christianity. There was also an attempt at establishing the roots of some of them, mainly based on linguistic hypotheses.[21] More scientific criteria started to be adopted from the 1730s thanks to authors who focused specifically on certain Asiatic regions and devoted equal time to fieldwork and scholarly research. Among the experts on Siberian populations and languages, the Swedish officer Philipp Johann von Strahlenberg stood out. In his book, names of populations and places were explained through an etymological analysis retracing the derivation, variations, and meanings of certain words. His research aimed at bringing order to the nomenclature related to Siberia and to Russia in general, and at recording the solutions put forward by different scholars. For instance, he cited Bayer,[22] who had developed his own theory on the relation of the Russians to the ancient Scythians, the errant nomads of Herodotus who had inhabited the regions east of the Volga and north of the Caspian Sea before moving to the west of the Volga. The debate on the origins of the populations of the Russian Empire was still open and lively, and Strahlenberg advanced his own proposition mainly based on etymological conjectures, which tended to relate the names of populations to the color of their hair. He pinpointed different branches: one with black hair and little brown eyes (Cheremises, Kalmyks, Voguls, Mordvinians, Samoyeds, Lapps, and Finns); the other red-haired with wide-open blue eyes (Bashkirs, Cossack hordes, Ostyaks of Oby and Perm, and Votiaks).[23]

Strahlenberg stressed the common mistake of considering Siberia as part of Great Tatary and explained it as the result of the ancient practice of summarizing all the northern regions of Asia under the generic expression "*Asia extra Taurum.*" In the text, a series of minor classifications helped to visualize the ethnographic complexity of the eighteenth-century Russian Empire. Some of the ethnological and linguistic reflections were drawn from the oral tradition. From his conversations with local inhabitants, who often referred to ancient legends to describe their world, Strahlenberg heard stories such as that of the so-called *Hyperboreis* peoples, maybe the ancestors of the Kanski Tatars, a group comprised within the Samoyeds.[24] Under the class of Tatars, or Turks, Strahlenberg included also the Mongols and Kalmyks, but criticized the European habit of considering all these populations simply as Tatars; that general denomination, in his view, failed to take into account the variety of names of the different tribes and their characteristics.

Strahlenberg believed that the populations of Siberia were far removed from the civilized world and that the Siberians lived in a state of nature in extreme simplicity. Their languages were therefore far more limited than European languages, which were rich, refined, and highly developed. The primitivism of these languages was probably the result of the scarcity of contacts with foreign peoples and historical changes. In the Kalmyk language, Strahlenberg identified the vestiges of ancient Mede and Persian peoples and thus advanced the proposal of using the languages of these northern peoples to investigate ancient migrations. Pagan rites and ceremonies, witnessed and described by Strahlenberg, recalled for him the sacred traditions of the ancient Egyptians and Greeks. Traveling through northeastern Siberia, Strahlenberg found himself in the purported "*Scythie inconnue*," inhabited by Yukagirs, Tschalatzi, Chukchi, Olutorski, Liutori, Koraeiki, Kamtchadali, and Kurilski—about whom ancient authors had left no description. Referring to the "*peuples du Nord*" in general, he professed his enlightened views: "comparing these barbaric nations with the polished peoples of Europe, one must recognize forcefully the well-being of the latter, wherein sciences and arts are enhanced to a high degree and wherein we find many reasons to rectify our customs and make ourselves worthy of the help of our Creator. The representation of such a comparison should also awaken pity for these poor peoples."[25]

His linguistic observations, randomly interspersed in the text, were summarized and analytically examined in his Kalmyk-Mongol dictionary, included at the end of the book, which presented a list of words in these two languages and in translation.[26] He drew a table of the different peoples gathered under the name of Tatars. Regrettably, the material he brought back from Siberia was partly lost, and for this reason, his book contained errors that were later amended in the dictionary.[27] In northern Asia he defined three kinds of different scripts: Turkish, used by the Tatars of Crimea; Kalmyk or Mongol, similar to that of the Chinese Tatars; and Tangut or Tibetan. Strahlenberg is considered one of the first Mongolists, one of the first experts on the populations and languages of the Uralic and Altaic stock; his work foreshadowed the later eighteenth-century achievements of Peter Simon Pallas. Russian linguists still consider Strahlenberg the founder of the Ural-Altaic theory, speculating on the affinity between Ural-Altaic and Indo-European languages, even though, according to Krueger, it is difficult to evaluate Strahlenberg's work.[28] Eighteenth-century Mongolian was very much a language in transition and there are no uniform records left that would enable a thorough reconstruction. The vagaries in Strahlenberg's transcriptions added further confusion, but his dictionary was translated into many languages and made the issue of the Kalmyk-Mongol language more accessible to scholars and researchers of the time. Strahlenberg's work was one of the most often quoted sources by western European and Russian authors alike.[29]

THE FIRST ACADEMIC EXPEDITIONS (1727–1743)

Gerhard Friedrich Müller's account of the second Bering expedition begins with these significant words: "what have we learnt from the voyages of the English and the Dutch on the Glacial Sea or beyond the Nowa Semlia? Nothing which deserves consideration . . . That was the state of things, the honor of doing better was reserved to the Russians, . . . given that the limits of their empire extend up there."[30] He subsequently praised Peter the Great as the initiator of a true scientific exploratory process and the defender of Russia's legacy vis-à-vis western European rivals.[31] Müller and his fellow academicians had been appointed by the Senate to accompany Bering on his second expedition. These missions, contrary to the previous independent ones, were sponsored by the government and entailed official tasks. Apart from pursuing geographical and hydrographical surveys, the explorers were asked to undertake astronomical observations, inquiries into natural history, and the investigation of the history of populations, commerce, customs, military and political organization, and languages. A Russian student, Stepan P. Krasheninnikov, was sent to Siberia in advance to organize the preliminaries for the expedition. He was a physicist and a geographer, and later became professor of botany and natural history in St. Petersburg, and published his account of this mission in 1755.[32] In 1738, Georg Wilhelm Steller, sent by the Academy of Sciences, met them to assist and eventually replace Johann Georg Gmelin, who suffered health problems. Gmelin published the results of his research into Siberian natural history in 1747–49 under the title *Flora Sibirica*.[33] J. E. Fischer was appointed to support Müller, while Jacob Lindenau, later an eminent ethnographer, joined them as a translator.[34]

These accounts were highly descriptive and informative, yet still very partial in comparison with later diaries, as the instructions themselves testify.[35] They also show that travelers were more concerned with collecting and accumulating data rather than the search for principles. Languages seemed a priority for Müller, while Gmelin was interested in customs and religion, as well as being guided by a firm Enlightenment ideology. From this perspective, indigenous peoples were still seen as enveloped in deep darkness, at the opposite extremity of enlightenment.

Müller presented a detailed description of previous expeditions and listed all the documents preserved, some of which had been discovered in the Yakutsk archives in 1737.[36] From the history of the *promishlenniki*, fur tradesmen led by Ignatiev who started surveying the Glacial Sea in 1647 and discovered the population of the Chukchi, Müller moved on to list a number of Cossack expeditions.[37] The most notable enterprise was the conquest of Kamchatka in 1697, thanks to Vladimir Atlasov.[38] Müller was interested in delineating the events linked to the submission of the turbulent Chukchi, which had been attempted by Atlasov himself in his second voyage in 1702, by a certain Popov around 1711, and by a Cossack colonel named Afanasy Shestakov in 1726–27.[39] Through Müller's account, we also learn that Peter had specifically requested General-Admiral Count F. M. Apraksin to report on the sighting of European vessels, and the finding of remains of European settlements and ports.[40] Prince Gagarin had taken part in an expedition to Siberia, Kamchatka, and the Kurile Islands in 1712–13, and from 1721 became the first governor of Siberia. Moreover, with a 1725 *Ukaz*, he planned Bering's first voyage. Müller's *Voyage* is therefore a thorough account of all past and present expeditions to Siberia and refers to and comments on the large number of documentary sources on this subject that he himself used.[41] When the narration focused on Bering's second voyage, Müller himself became one of the protagonists of the Russian discovery project, which he recounted with an abundance of detail. He had developed his own scholarly interest in Siberia through the reading of Witsen on Tartary, and under the influence of Bayer and Paus.[42] He had started to study the populations of the Samoyeds and Kalmyks even before his appointment to Bering's second expedition.

Müller reported that the Russian Academy insisted that scientists send back to St. Petersburg copies of all observations in Latin and Russian. In the event, however, communication proved faulty because of bad road conditions, a dearth of horses and men, and the remote distances. He described the route of each team, and reported their difficulties and results, including the discovery of interesting documents. In Yaroslavl, he was prevented from pursuing his investigation by church authorities who refused to accept the Senate's documents authorizing the expedition to consult archival collections. The church of Nizhnii Novgorod, by contrast, offered assistance that enabled the gathering of further genealogical data. In Kazan, he pursued research on the effect of Russian schooling on Tatar and Chuvash speakers, also compiling a vocabulary of the non-Russian languages of the region. The list included the Tatar, Chuvash, Mordva, Cheremis, and Votiak and was further extended in the following decade.[43]

During the first years of exploration, Gmelin and Müller were full of enthusiasm, but they had grown weary due to discomfort, privations, and perils that undermined both their physical and psychological strength. The expedition's morale was also affected by the tense atmosphere that affected almost all work teams. In Müller's opinion, for example, Delisle de la Croyère wanted to go ahead of his colleagues in order to conceal his incompetence, but by doing so, he only incurred more expense and jeopardized the quality of the expedition's research. Schumacher, secretary to the academy, suspected that both Müller and Gmelin were trying to disparage their colleagues and that it was Krasheninnikov and Steller who were doing all the real work. Moreover, Müller had grown rancorous toward Bering who, he believed, resented the fact that others were intruding on his territory, trying to demonstrate what he himself had already proved. In fact, Bering's official mission was to discover whether the two continents were joined, but the Senate had also asked him to explore the American coast and write reports on trade, thus, in some sense, overlapping with Müller's tasks.[44] Müller considered himself lucky, in the end, to have survived. The deaths of Gmelin and Krasheninnikov in 1755 were considered a consequence of the irremediable deterioration in their health subsequent to the expedition. Bering had died in 1741; in the same year, Delisle de la Croyère had died of scurvy on board ship, and Steller had died of a fever in 1746.[45]

In Siberia, Müller's work became even more tiring and time-consuming but was extremely productive from the historical and geographical points of view.[46] He brought back material on the geography of the settlements, customs, and commerce of the Kamchadals, Koryaks, and Kurils. In Tobolsk, he retraced the trade routes between European Russia and Siberia, and those of the Kalmyk and Buryat caravans. All the documents gathered in these years were later included in a number of historical works such as the *Istoriia Sibirii* (*History of Siberia*, 1768).[47] But Müller also had access to oral sources thanks to numerous interviews with local peoples and travelers. His research on languages and customs would, for example, form the body of his *Commentarii* (1747). The questionnaires and detailed instructions that Müller had prepared were of crucial importance, and were also made available for Fischer's research.[48] As a result of the discoveries made in Kamchatka, the Academy of Sciences of St. Petersburg had a number of maps drawn, and the Russian Atlas (1745) was revised on the basis of the fieldwork carried out in Siberia.[49]

In line with the instructions received in 1733 from the chancellery, Gmelin's *Reise durch Sibirien* (1751) was of a quite different nature, focusing mainly on populations and popular culture. In contrast to Müller's research, there was no evidence of linguistic concern. In Gmelin's account, there was room for anecdotal stories, reports of daily life, the organization of fieldwork, and personal comments.[50] His research into natural history, on the other hand, constituted the source for his four-volume *Flora Sibirica*, which was a natural history of the plants of Siberia. In his travel diary, we also find a great deal on the native populations. Gmelin wrote: "they are extremely ignorant and live in the deepest misery: their state clearly shows that our own well-being corresponds to our enlightenment."[51] The first population described was that of the Chuvash. The scientists discussed them with the *voevoda* of the province, and also summoned two of them to their lodgings to inquire about their customs.[52] In the case of the Yakuts, Gmelin portrayed their traditional costume and compared them physically to the Kalmyks, adding two drawings to show their characteristic traits: their black hair, little eyes, flat nose, and roundish face. The Tatars were considered the most "civilized" of all these peoples, especially those of Muslim creed who were compared favorably with the so-called idolaters. In Tobolsk, the researchers witnessed a Tatar wedding, and Gmelin described the ceremony, costumes, customs, music, and instruments, once again showing an extraordinary interest in popular culture.

Moreover, Gmelin's persistent preoccupation with religious ceremonies suggested a missionary impulse that reflected his Pietist background.[53] The Swedish Johann Bernard Müller already had expressed his concern in 1727 for the conversion of Siberian people to Christianity. The Ostyaks were the subject of his work, entitled *Les moeurs et usages des Ostiakes,* which reported a pitiful shortage of information about Siberia and even more about the Ostyak people.[54] In his view, unfavorable climatic conditions certainly discouraged geographers and explorers from visiting the area between the 57th degree of latitude and the frozen north. The Siberians were grouped under the designation of Tatars, many of whom were pagans, and others Muslim. Both the Ostyaks and the Samoyeds lived in a state of lawlessness, worshipped idols, and did not eat bread, but raw meat, herbs, and roots. They also "drink blood more happily than water."[55] For his part, Gmelin showed similar moral contempt on a number of occasions for some of the local habits and vices, like laziness and drunkenness. Laziness was a vice conventionally attributed to "unenlightened" people. This judgmental attitude was sometimes blended with anthropological curiosity, when Gmelin, for instance, described Tatar circumcision, diseases, or dietary habits.[56] It is clear that this voyage was also playing a role in a program of political propaganda if we look at some comments on the beneficial effects of Russian colonization. About the Yakuts, Gmelin stated for instance: "since these peoples have been subdued by the Russian government, these barbaric customs no longer exist."[57]

Under Anna's reign the academy received little support and could only survive thanks to the help given to Schumacher by the court. Moreover, allegations were put forward that Germans there were paid higher wages and that there was a climate hostile to Russians. After the regency of Ernst Johann Biron, however, there was a wave of anti-German sentiment.[58] The suspicion of and antipathy to foreign members of the academy was further fueled by leaks from foreign participants in the expeditions, and in particular by the deceit of both Joseph-Nicolas Delisle and Gmelin in 1751. Despite the fact that he had committed himself to refrain from publishing any information about the expedition without Russian permission, Gmelin had the first part of his memoirs published in Göttingen. This publication included some allegations about the chancellery's negative role in the expedition, as well as other embarrassing remarks. Not only did Delisle ship a huge amount of secret material to Paris, but he also published maps and reports on the North Pacific that contradicted some earlier charts of the Russian Academy and claimed for Delisle de la Croyère and himself discoveries that were not theirs. Gerhard Friedrich Müller was called to act as a defender of the academy and of Russia. He used a series of works to refute Delisle, and published some maps that served as corrections to Delisle's allegedly fabricated accounts.[59] With his foreign contacts and publications, Müller certainly provided favorable propaganda for the Russian Academy.

Through the wealth of manuscript material that Delisle had managed to smuggle into France, a good portion of which is now preserved in the Archives Nationales and Bibliothèque Nationale in Paris, it is possible to analyze Russia's exploratory concerns of the time. Moreover, we can find the names of many Russian scientists and aides who participated in the geographical surveys and expeditions alongside renowned foreign experts, and who were never mentioned in the main academic publications.[60] Providing information on roads, settlements, and populations, these documents reveal the pivotal importance of the creation and organization of territorial control. The Delisle manuscripts include accounts of expeditions, maps, astronomical calculations, memoirs, and histories of the European and Asiatic regions of Russia as well as Sweden, Finland, and Lapland from the seventeenth century onward, by a variety of different authors. There is, for instance, a *Relation de la Laponie russe* by Salomon Varnesobre, the director of the Imperial Company of Greenland, created by Peter I, which proposed a relation between the Lapps and the Samoyeds and referred to Russian attempts to convert the supposedly ignorant and savage inhabitants.[61] There are interesting excerpts from Joseph de Guignes's work on Tartary and from G. F. Müller's work on the history of the navigation of the Russians in the northern seas.[62]

Ethnographic and linguistic concerns were sometimes evident, although without systematic and thematic attention. The Samoyeds seemed to be of particular interest to the explorers. The structure of nomadic habitations and caravans was cited as a distinctive criterion to distinguish between different tribes. The earlier role of Nicolas Witsen emerges clearly from the unpublished writings on Russia and Siberia that Delisle had collected. The Dutchman Nicolas Corneliszoon Witsen (1641–1717) had first visited Moscow between 1664 and 1665 as a member of J. Boreel's embassy. He spent almost fifty years of his life in the Russian Empire drawing maps and studying populations. He was one of the first to undertake ethnographic investigation. Joseph Nicolas Delisle's own work was scattered among the manuscripts of various authors. His interest in populations and popular culture is evident, for example, in a memoir on the Samoyeds. He was not only interested in such issues as the origin of languages and ethnic groups, but also showed an unusual willingness to investigate the knowledge and perception that these populations had of the world and of their own community. He established, by interviewing them, that they possessed some notions of arithmetic and physics, and some ideas of the geography of the earth and world populations. The absence of pejorative remarks or of the traditional dismissal of native populations as "savages" is noteworthy.[63]

RESURGENCE UNDER RUSSIAN LEADERSHIP: THE GREAT SCIENTIFIC AND ETHNOGRAPHIC EXPEDITIONS (1761–1802)

However biased Western contemporaries may have been in their analysis of Russia, Catherine II herself was well aware that Western criticism was grounded in fact. By the middle of the eighteenth century, the divide between western Europe and Russia had become even wider than it had been in Peter's time.[64] Western Europe had quickly progressed in the amelioration of its material and social life. Even those areas, such as the Holy Roman Empire, which were moving at a slower pace, seemed far ahead of Russia, which, after the period of Peter the Great, had relapsed into a state of incomplete reform. Peter's descendants proved unable either to fully grasp the motivations behind his reform or to complete his tasks. The transformation of Russia impetuously carried out by Peter was irreversible. Yet the country had been left with the characteristics of a hybrid body, certain limbs of which resembled Western structures, albeit joined to a social organization that differed totally from its Western models. With a German upbringing and familiarity with Western ideology, Catherine II was the first monarch after Peter with the persona and capacity to even think of building on his reforms.[65] Foreign criticism certainly added to the urge for development, which was channeled by Catherine into a variety of initiatives. The expeditions patronized by the Academy of Sciences of St. Petersburg from 1768 onward represented the tangible and highly scientific objective of a state that was seeking international recognition, but also needed to enhance its own research domains and organization.

Catherine's interest in the empire and her dream of giving laws to its various tribes is well known. She drew her ideas from ancient examples and important legal theorists, exchanged views and reports with her proconsuls, and met with native delegates. Many requests from indigenous peoples were presented to the Legislative Commission. The delegates from Siberia, for instance, lamented that their ignorance of the Russian language made them vulnerable to abuse by Russian peasants and landlords. Moreover, observing the ethnic variety of Kazan, Catherine speculated on the possibility of a "whole world . . . (to) be created, unified and preserved."[66] Kazan became a strategic base for the discovery of the East, and Catherine endowed it with appropriate institutions, such as Russia's second university, secondary schools, and Orthodox academies. Hers was, however, a paternalistic approach whose humanitarian goals also clashed with the attitudes of Russians toward the natives. Russian political practices continued to deny the complex reality of the multiethnic empire and to emphasize centralization and standardization. Nevertheless, ethnographers showed an altogether opposite tendency, suggesting a multiplicity of national traits that could not be organized around a universal axis. Linguistic categories became the official criteria for ethnographic classification.

Despite the intense and concerted program of exploration carried out in the Asiatic provinces of the empire in the 1730s, many questions were still left unanswered. The vast territories under Russian control or protection were a central ground for the search for unknown linguistic and ethnic relationships between eastern Europe and Asia. Research began to be published in Russia, and then translated into some of the main European languages, from the 1740s onward, when exploration encouraged a comparative approach to linguistic and ethnographic studies.[67] A conviction of the strong connection between languages and the origins of populations dictated the direction that such studies would take. The most significant achievements of fieldwork investigation were to be accomplished thanks to the support of the Russian Academy of Sciences and the direct involvement of Catherine II. Interestingly, it was not uncommon to find in these sources criticism of superficial and incorrect data disseminated by western Europeans, such as widespread confusion between Samoyeds and Lapps.[68]

Although Fischer's *Recherches historiques* concerning Siberia was not published until 1768, it was the fruit of the so-called first academic expedition of 1733–43 and of intense fieldwork that the German historian carried out in the following decades; his hypothesis of a linguistic relationship between Siberia and Hungary paved the way for the future compilation of a series of dictionaries and grammars. Fischer cited in the book his own Siberian dictionary, comprising more than forty languages spoken in Siberia and presenting comparisons among them.[69] A large number of linguistic tables substantiated his argument. The importance of Siberia was evident in Fischer's speculations on geographical, linguistic, and ethnic domains, to such an extent that he felt compelled to provide a comprehensive designation of the term "Siberia" at the very start. He stated that "by having fixed these frontiers, the *Iughorique* Mounts and the whole of Siberia belong to Asia." With an even more precise explanation, "Siberia" designated the regions of the lower Ob River conquered by the Russians under the reign of Tsar Ivan Vasilievich, which had the real name Sibir. But Fischer added that, in general, the denomination was used to designate all the lands conquered by Russia in that vast part of Asia.[70]

The peoples whose origins were in Siberia could be designated as "indigenous." The traits that united them were idolatry, hunting as the prevalent means of subsistence, and a history of mobility and extinction, related to the fragility of their nomadic organization. The Kyrgyz, for example, inhabited Siberia several centuries previously, but had been forced to flee when they became the victims of Russian territorial expansion. The Buryats, Teleutes, Tungus, Samoyeds, Ostyaks, and Tatars still lived there, while the southern Siberian frontiers were inhabited by the Mongols and Kalmyks. Fischer acknowledged Abul-Ghazi's contribution to the improvement of the knowledge of certain populations such as the Kalmyks, Uriats, Kyrgyz, and Aleuts. Generally, the crucial ethnological issue to be solved through the combined examination of physical traits and varied linguistic surveys was whether specific populations were of Tatar or Mongol origins.[71] Fischer used the comparative method extensively to identify the origins, as well as the relationships between languages and dialects, thus establishing their ethnic correlations. Etymology on its own, however, was not enough to offer a coherent set of proofs;[72] it needed to be corroborated by geographical and historical investigation.

Müller himself called for the organization of other voyages and for the destruction of remaining myths and fables contained even in the most authoritative sources.[73] In 1759 he nominated Piotr Ivanovich Rychkov to the academy and, against Lomonosov's will, managed to have him made a corresponding member. Rychkov then organized an Orenburg expedition under the guidance of a series of famous Russian experts, such as Kirilov, Tatishchev, Prince Urusov, Soymonov,[74] and Neplyuyev. Their fieldwork produced a wealth of detailed maps of the region and a number of documents that were written by Rychkov himself. In 1762, he published *The Orenburg Topography,* then a history of the kingdom of Kazan (1767), and an introduction to the topography of Astrakhan (1774).[75] Important ethnographic data on the populations of Cheremises, Chuvash, and Votyaks inhabiting the region of Kazan were published by Müller and Fischer in the *Monthly Composition* edited by Müller himself for the purpose of making information about the empire available to a wider public in Russia.[76] Articles were devoted to administrative divisions, the juridical system, industry, trade, and agriculture.

Scientific enterprises of the size and importance of the expeditions of 1761 and 1768, organized to observe the transit of Mercury and Venus across the sun, certainly reflected a rise in governmental efforts to support missions of geographical and astronomical study. Northeastern Asia offered a particular advantage for astronomical observations, as there were periods in which constant darkness allowed a clear observation of astronomical phenomena even by day. A renowned astronomer of the eighteenth century, Christian Mayer, affirmed that "a clear vision of the complete passage of Venus crossing the Sun, from the rising phase to the setting phase, is possible in those northern countries positioned under 67° and 33' latitude."[77] The astronomical event has a pattern of recurrence at intervals. In the eighteenth century, it occurred in 1761 and 1769. On both occasions, academicians moved away from their European headquarters to pursue astronomical observations all over the globe.[78] In 1761, during the Seven Years' War, conditions did not seem favorable, and Joseph-Nicolas Delisle, for example, had to make strenuous efforts to mobilize the French government, the Academy of Sciences of Paris, and the Compagnie des Indes. In 1769, however, participation was wider and international. An impressive number of articles in the principal European journals kept public opinion well informed about the missions.[79] The reason for this scientific interest was that it represented an astronomical phenomenon relevant to the calculations of the distance between the earth and the sun, to the estimation of the position of the planets, and to the study of the solar system.

The French astronomer Chappe D'Auteroche traveled to Siberia under the patronage of Louis XV and the Royal Academy of Sciences of Paris in 1760–61. The observation of the transit of Venus across the sun in 1761 was the principal aim of his voyage. Yet, Chappe's *Voyage en Sibérie,* published in 1768, was far from being a purely scientific work, and his observations on Russian customs and life provoked debate and rancorous counterattacks both in western and eastern Europe. Although Chappe's mission was not the only one undertaken in Russia, the publication was perhaps the most widely read. Gnucheva's belief that the phenomenon was ignored in Russia has been disproved by several documents of the Academy of Sciences.[80] Astronomical expeditions to Siberia were supported by Lomonosov, I. I. Tambert, and J. J. Stehlin and carried out in Irkutsk and Yakutsk in 1761. We know, for example, that Popov was in Irkutsk and in Selenginsk and that Stepan Rumovskii[81] successfully determined the longitude at Selenginsk, while Andrei Krasilnikov pursued his observations in St. Petersburg. Among the documents of the St. Petersburg Academy of the period from 1767 onward, there are reflections written by the academicians and presented to the director, V. G. Orlov, concerning the organization of the astronomical expeditions of 1769. One of the preoccupations of the team was the appointment of a natural historian who would study those areas chosen for the astronomical observations. In 1769, Islenev was sent to Yakutsk with instructions and scientific questionnaires embracing astronomical issues as well as matters of natural history, infectious diseases, and local remedies.[82]

In 1768–69 Russia's academic enterprises reached a high point. After several years of preparations and with the assistance of prior data and expertise, of which Müller's and Lomonosov's were probably the most crucial, the so-called Second Academic Expedition was set up. As in the case of Cook's or Chappe's travels, the official scientific reason was the astronomical survey of Venus crossing the sun (1769). In addition, however, and maybe most important, Catherine II wanted to combat the bad impressions spread by Chappe's *Voyage*, and she entrusted Pallas, Lepekhin, Rychkov, Samuel Gottlieb Gmelin (nephew of Johann Georg), Falk, Guldenstoedt, Georgi, and many others with an ambitious and unprecedented program of exploration.[83] News about the Russian expeditions was to be found in all European gazettes and journals, as well as in travel literature. Pallas's report published in 1776 turned out to be one of the most valuable pieces of work on this kind of ethnographic and naturalistic research. As a patron, Catherine enjoyed wide success in encouraging important enterprises and the publication of their data. Her expeditions helped to promote a favorable image of the Russian state abroad as well as a parallel process of Russian self-discovery and self-definition at home.

Johann Gottlieb Georgi opened his *Description de toutes les nations de l'empire de Russie* (1776) with an introduction on Siberia, in which he voiced criticism of the European habit of confounding the Mongol and Tatar populations; he showed a meticulous concern for ethnographic-linguistic matters.[84] In Georgi's view, some of the populations of Russia were so intermixed that it was no longer possible to trace their origins. Georgi's book comprised four main sections, corresponding to four different "nations": the Finns, Tatars, Samoyeds, and Mongols. Given that his objective was the ethnographic description of all the populations of the Russian Empire, the population groups into which the "nations" were subdivided were far more detailed and numerous than in all preceding studies. Not only can his work be considered a contemporary encyclopedia of Asiatic peoples, it can also be noted for its remarkable sensitivity toward folklore and popular culture, an interest increasingly common in the late eighteenth century. Georgi provided insights into religion and superstitions, everyday life and domestic utensils, cuisine, social organization, political status, economy, clothing, physical traits, temperament, education, and music and arts. His interests went beyond those of a purely scientific enterprise, demonstrating a genuine passion for other cultures, which allowed him to explore and appreciate dialects, rites, songs, and dances, and through them offer a multifaceted representation of the Asiatic world and the regions beyond the Urals.[85] Georgi, not entirely free from patronizing perspective, introduced the Russians as the ruling nation of the empire, but also provided proof of the drastic disruption that Russian domination brought into the life of some native populations.

The easternmost peoples of Siberia were those who, by all standards, seemed the most "savage" of all and the closest to the "state of nature."[86] Accordingly, the ethnic proximity to northern Americans encouraged descriptions comparable to those of Native Americans. One finds speculations about the geographical proximity of the two continents, the unknown origins of such peoples as the Yukagirs, Chukchi, and Kamchadals, and the savage state of the Koryaks, who bore "a very near resemblance to beasts" and had sexual relations in public.[87] After a detailed and informative description of these peoples and their culture, Georgi could not help expressing a personal judgment: "it would disgust the enlightened mind to pursue the detail of all their scenes of magic and enchantments of which the ceremonies are so egregiously absurd, and so similar to one another, that it will be sufficient to give a succinct account of the most striking and remarkable."[88] From this viewpoint, Russian domination seemed the lesser evil for Asiatic peoples. Georgi stated:

The Tartars, in the neighborhood of Russia, like all the orientals, are more inconstant and desirous of change than the Europeans; and the reason of it is, because they depend on the caprice and despotism of their masters, and are often exposed to the violence of their neighbors: such of them, therefore, as join themselves to the Tartar nations in subjection to Russia see so many real advantages in the secure and quiet happiness in which they live.[89]

There is no doubt that Georgi was one of Catherine's spokesmen and that he had been asked to support the Russian case for eastward expansion. As in Pallas's account, we therefore find also a separate section devoted to the Russian colonies in New Russia that illustrates the life and administration of these settlements, as well as the privileges enjoyed by the newcomers.

Georgi's ethnographic speculations were grounded in the search for similarities and differences among peoples, in an attempt to establish the validity of his ethnic classifications. Nomadic shelters (*kibitki*) were, for instance, built according to the tradition of each population group. The arrangement of the Chuvash villages, their houses, their economic organization, and their funeral ceremonies, were very similar to those of the Cheremises, a population also grouped under the main division of the Finnish nation.[90] Non-Russian peoples were often compared with the "least civilized" groups of the Russian population itself, the peasantry, sometimes even with gypsies and vagabonds. Interestingly, the appellation given by certain populations to their neighbors sometimes showed equal contempt.[91] The lack of written sources, of historical traditions, a life tuned in to the rhythms of nature, superstition, and magic rites, were all attributes of the primitivism of these "savage nations"; especially shamanism, toward which Georgi showed a mixture of fascination and scorn. One should note, however, that these preconceptions were also accompanied by a note of admiration for ancient and powerful civilizations, the forefathers of modern nomads, and the subject of so many contemporary histories, such as those of Abul-Ghazi, d'Herbelot, and Joseph de Guignes.[92] The first archaeological excavations aimed at discovering the remains of these ancient civilizations had already been successfully undertaken under Peter the Great and continued afterward as part of a general program of research into these populations' allegedly glorious Asiatic past.[93]

By using a similar comparative approach and studying ethnolinguistic affiliations, Pallas too investigated the Asiatic and European population groups of the Russian Empire. His account was not limited to ethnographic information, but offered a variety of geographical, historical, botanical, and mineralogical descriptions, and often made reference to the works of Gmelin, Buffon, Müller, Rychkov,[94] Lepekhin, Georgi, and Coxe. The pages devoted to the flora and fauna offered an occasion for tackling topics like the cuisine and dietary habits of the local inhabitants and, for example, the use they made of herbs for therapeutic purposes.[95] Because of its unique and intriguing characteristics, the nomadic world overshadowed all the other subjects discussed and, as in Georgi's account, one of the subtle distinctions portrayed was that between the independent peoples and those subjected to Russian administration. In some instances, Russian influence extended from mere commercial links to the choice of the khan, as in the case of the Kyrgyz, and it had certainly become an integral part of certain societies, as their oaths of allegiance demonstrated.[96] The contacts with foreigners, for instance, had mitigated the barbarism of the customs and laws of the Cossacks in Orenburg and made them more docile (*douce*).[97] Nevertheless, the evils of conquest were not covered up. Pallas documented the large-scale fatalities suffered by the Ostyaks from diseases (smallpox, for example) hitherto totally unknown to them and spread by the Russians, and the disruption brought to their life by Russian hegemony.[98]

In Pallas's account, there are sections that describe the route and the plans followed by the different teams of explorers, including the one led by himself, and those by Falk and by Georgi. Moreover, he enclosed excerpts of various books, such as a memoir on the Glacial Sea by the zoologist Soloviev, a historical sketch of the cities of Ekaterinburg and Perm by Lepekhin,[99] and the history of the Cossacks of Yaik by Müller. Having crossed over to the east of the Urals, he offered a strikingly different ethnic and linguistic picture of a region that, in his view, hardly resembled that of Russia and from which one could draw an extensive glossary.[100] The first population encountered in Asia, the Voguls, seemed wilder than those previously observed. Despite the existence of a variety of different dialects, Pallas, with the help of a dictionary, retraced many connections between their language and Finnish. Although remarkably advanced in its ethnographic perspective, Pallas's account was not devoid of remarks on the primitivism and barbarism of certain customs. He laid frequent stress on superstition, shamanism, or sacrifices, the consumption of raw meat, and other objectionable features of the Asiatic peoples' cultures. He observed the mistreatment of women in nomadic communities in which, however, women also carried out duties that the Western world considered as masculine.[101]

Pallas's exploratory activity was directly linked to the preparation of the last great Russian expedition in the eighteenth century, that of Joseph Billings[102] and his Russian aide, Sarychev (1785–94). This was also known as the "oriental expedition" and, although ranging over a vast variety of scientific objectives, had a predominant geographical and astronomical character. The Academy of Sciences was actively involved in its preparation, but it is likely that the major impetus came, variously, from Cook's voyages, from the publication of Coxe's *Account of the Russian Discoveries Between Asia and America*, and from the announcement in the French press of the forthcoming voyage of Jean-François de la Pérouse.[103] The English report on the expedition, entitled *An Account of a Geographical and Astronomical Expedition to the Northern Parts of Russia* (1802), was actually written by the secretary of the voyage, Martin Sauer, on the basis of Billings's journal.[104] According to Sauer, it was Coxe and Pallas who encouraged Catherine II to set up an expedition that would "complete the geographical knowledge of the most distant possessions of that Empire, and of such northern parts of the opposite continent as Captain Cook could not possibly ascertain."[105]

The instructions were based on an *Ukaz* of Catherine II to the Admiralty College (August 1785)[106] and the "Instruction of the State Admiralty College to the fleet of Captain-Lieutenant Billings."[107] The naturalist research had been, for instance, planned by Pallas and assigned to Patrin, a naturalist and a botanist, for whom Merk was later substituted. An "Instruction" from Pallas to Merk (1786), approved by Catherine, disclosed further scientific goals, such as the description of the customs and languages of the northeastern populations of Asia, and the collection of botanical, zoological, and mineralogical specimens together with written documents of local idioms. Pallas also drew up Article x of the "Instruction," which called for the compilation of accurate charts of the Aleutian isles and other islands, and for evidence of the existence of ports and of little-known or unknown islands. Moreover, this enterprise aimed at settling all the pending disputes between Russia and the Koryaks and the Chukchi. Since the discovery of Kamchatka, Russia had been incapable of keeping in "due subjection" these people, who, according to Georgi, "were the most savage, the most barbarous, the most intractable, the least civilized, the most rugged and cruel people of all Siberia."[108] Yet, when the expedition arrived at the river Omolon, it discovered that a certain Major Shmailev had accomplished this difficult diplomatic task and had reconciled these peoples with the Russians.[109] Perhaps the most substantial achievement of this expedition was the compilation of the first complete work on the ethnography and languages of this population.[110] The sections on popular culture and local traditions were illustrated through a series of engravings. The cartographic work was also unparalleled for that time and the result of meticulous geographical surveys.

The nomadic world was again the dominant theme and was portrayed through its most intrinsic characteristics: tribal life, skirmishes with other population groups, migrations, precarious forms of sustenance, perceptions of territory and time, rituals, and superstitions. Although, at first sight, this account seemed to avoid disparaging comments toward the natives, it is possible to discern the observer's innate sense of superiority when he, for instance, hints at the "inharmonious" sound of certain songs, the stupidity of a man who could not count how many children he had, or "the savage barbarity" of the Cossacks toward their wives.[111] Yet, we are far from the all-encompassing Eurocentrism of earlier works and can undoubtedly sense the presence of a conscious attempt to avoid bias and be more sympathetic toward Otherness. In a Rousseauist vein, Billings appeared to be moved by the hospitality and kindness of these "simple" people and, at the same time, he feared that "progress" and "refinement" would eventually end up spoiling such good qualities.[112] Moreover, there are several examples in the book that prove that advancing Russification was contributing to a deterioration in the condition of these minorities, and disrupting their societies, for example, turning nomads into settlers.[113]

CONCLUSION

The eighteenth century marked an era of unrelenting exploratory activity throughout the lands belonging to the Russian Empire and those that became Russia's targets of conquest and eventually tributary provinces. The investment of significant amounts of money and human resources reflected very ambitious political and administrative plans that became increasingly substantial, especially under the reign of Catherine II. Her program for the enhancement of a well-organized state and clear-cut internal administrative units, the ultimate goal of such expeditions, responded to the need to improve Russian control of this gigantic territory and its heterogeneous ethnic mix. In this light, it is significant to notice the passage of the "scientific" baton from a mainly foreign-dominated elite to a Russian one. Ethnographic exploration was part of a multifaceted project of self-discovery, intrinsically linked to literary and historical debates, which allowed the development of a sense of the Self based on the knowledge of Russia's own territorial domains and cultural resources, including both its Asiatic and European characteristics. Despite the undeniable imperialist designs that stood behind the Russian exploratory process, eighteenth-century ethnographic research was still free from what in the nineteenth century became a systematic attack on non-Russian minorities. As in the rest of Europe, late eighteenth-century Russian ethnographers and thinkers were increasingly sensitive to folk and national cultures, and to a certain extent also voiced some concern for the frailty of nomadic societies.

APPENDIX: A KALMYK LOVE SONG

From Johann Gottlieb Georgi, *Russia, or A Compleat Historical Account of All the Nations Which Compose That Empire*, vol. 4 (London: Printed

for J. Nichols: T. Cadell, in the Strand; H. Payne, Pall-Mall; and N. Conant, Fleet-Street, 1780–83), p. 63.

> Ah thou, mine unparalleled darling!
> How elegant is thy quiver of arrows, O thou, my darling!
> The only food of my soul art thou, my darling!
> Without anger, without falsehood, and full of mildness art thou,
>   my darling!
> Without pride, without any ridiculous restraint, art thou, my
>   darling!
> Thou, whose heart with mine is but one kernel!
> Who has any thing to reproach thee with?
> Any one that does it must do it from jealousy.
> Ah let them say what they will,
> The reproach will lie upon their own taste.
> Let the glorious sun and moon dart their light from the heavens,
> And let all men upon earth see thee and me, both of us alone;
> And even then would we never remove from one another,
> But enjoy the deliciousness of life together.

CHAPTER ELEVEN

Love in the Time of Hierarchy

Ethnographic Voices in Eighteenth-Century Haiti

Jean-Philippe E. Belleau

To Jean-Charles Grégory, Carline Saint-Louis, and all students of anthropology, whose campus was attacked on December 5, 2003, by government-backed gangs, the chimè.

And to Roger Gaillard in memoriam

"*L'amour égale tout.*"
—Alexandre-Stanislas Wimpffen,
*Voyage à Saint-Domingue pendant
les années 1788, 1789 et 1790*

ANTHROPOLOGY BEFORE ANTHROPOLOGY

For most of the eighteenth century, the colony of Saint-Domingue (today's Haiti) figured in the itineraries of most French voyagers traveling in the New World. A Spanish possession until the 1697 Treaty of Ryswick, which officially ceded the western third of the island of Hispaniola to the French Crown, Saint-Domingue had been originally settled by French buccaneers in the early seventeenth century before turning to sugarcane and growing into a plantation colony. During the course of the eighteenth century, the slave population increased exponentially, from fewer than fifty thousand in 1720 to close to half a million in 1788,[1] outnumbering the whites eleven to one. At the dawn of the French Revolution, Saint-Domingue was nicknamed "the pearl of the Antilles," because it produced more sugar than all the colonies of the Americas combined and had acquired a reputation in the *métropole* as a place for quick profit and extravagance. Cap François (today's Cap-Hatien), nicknamed "the Paris of the Antilles," was in 1788 as populous as Boston (the largest town in coastal America at that time) and prided itself on its theater.[2] This eighteenth-century society of Saint-Domingue was undermined by the impact of the Declaration of the Rights of Man, during the French Revolution in 1789, as that text did not recognize any racial categories and was appropriated by free blacks and mulattos, and then by the slaves.

As a plantation colony, Saint-Domingue produced several racial identities that solidified through the eighteenth century: whites, Negroes (synonymous with slaves), and mulattos. The writers considered in this study recognized and integrated the same racial categories invented by the colonial world of France, as well as Spain and Portugal before. To this racial hierarchy, another has to be added, based on property. The Black Code of 1685 recognized two legal categories—owners and slaves. The colonial society was thus one of massive discriminations and prejudices, racial and social, while each racial group in itself was tense with internal discriminations. The whites were divided into three categories: the *grands blancs*, owners of large plantations; the administrators and soldiers; and the mass of artisans, shopkeepers, overseers, and other poor whites, called the *petits blancs*.[3] The whites actually constituted a class of subaltern rulers. As in any colony of this time, the royal companies held a trade monopoly on all exports, a trade imbalance that made white Creoles resentful. The mulattos were referred to as free people of color, although this category also included a significant number of free blacks. The slave population was divided into two socially hierarchized categories: the *Creoles* and the *Bossales*. The former were slaves born in the colony, who usually performed domestic functions and enjoyed higher status, both within and outside the slave sector, while the latter defined slaves born in Africa, who usually worked in the fields. The ethnogenesis of black Creoles was already accomplished by the early eighteenth century, and newly arrived Africans had to join that class in order to survive. Voodoo religion, Creole language, and other cultural patterns were all products of *métissage* (cross-breeding). The tensions implicit in these racial hierarchies eventually brought the colony to civil war, and finally to the victory of the alliance of free men and rebel slaves, proclaiming Haiti independent in 1804.

This study considers the ethnographic conceptions of travelers, thinkers, government officials, soldiers, priests, and explorers who participated in the production of identities throughout the eighteenth century. Can these writers be qualified as ethnographers? Would the term "anthropology" be anachronistic for the Age of Enlightenment? Anthropology is historically bounded, its emergence associated closely with nineteenth-century European imperial expansion into Africa and Asia. Can we then speak of anthropology in the eighteenth-century "age of revolution," preceding the anthropology of the nineteenth-century "age of empire"? The imperial paradigm for anthropology has been often noted by scholars: colonial conquests brought about a need to extract and organize coherent data on non-Western cultures; thus anthropology emerged. Anthropology has, accordingly, been seen as the product of colonialism and as serving colonialism.[4] The founding father of French anthropology, Marcel Mauss, noted this one century after Haitian independence: "The knowledge of peoples, their languages, religion, mores, economic and technical resources is, together with geographic knowledge of their habitat, the necessary condition of good administration."[5]

The texts examined in this study support the theory that anthropology emerged as the intellectual arm of colonial administration. According to their own authors, the ethnographies of Hilliard d'Auberteuil and Moreau de Saint-Méry had one main function: to correct and guide public policies in the colonies. Moreau asked: "But where are those who know the Colonies? I do not mean those who have seen them, or lived there, but those who have studied them under any angle and are able to enlighten the public about them."[6] Hilliard was so upset with colonial mismanagement and ignorance that he compared the legislation in Saint-Domingue to medieval laws and embarked on an ethnographic exercise to educate the metropolis's decision makers about the anthropological realities in the colony.

Saint-Domingue was very different from the other French colonies of the Americas, such as Québec or Louisiana; on Saint-Domingue there was no "frontier," and the island was not populated with "savages"—but still, it was America. It was both a white and a black America, devoid of American savages, an America inhabited and shaped by Europeans, Africans, and their mixed offspring, a unique place where Africa met Europe. The philosophes of the Enlightenment created a discourse of difference in writing about savage society. The xenology of the Enlightenment included, among others, the American savage, the Turk, the Slav, and the African. But the African slave and then the Creole slave occupied a particular place; they were seen as subjugated, domesticated, no longer in their original society. Eighteenth-century xenology further struggled to provide a place for the mulatto. Thus, Saint-Domingue stood apart. Its space was not an American *espace* and there was no unknown, threatening, and mysterious wilderness; instead, there were plantations.

If we recognize that it is indeed difficult to talk about anthropology *sensu stricto* prior to the nineteenth century, it is nevertheless true that the texts studied here constitute more than an accidental or *avant la lettre* proto-anthropology. This is because, notwithstanding the absence of many of the generally accepted characteristics of modern anthropology, the production of knowledge and the mediation of identities by authors who attempted to make sense of cultural differences in the colony of Saint-Domingue constituted a scientific effort to classify and explain social practices, and demonstrated a human sympathy that was often lacking in nineteenth-century anthropology. In these attempts, one may indeed discern an "anthropology of the Enlightenment" and an enlightened ethnographic discourse.

The rationality of enlightened anthropology marked a considerable improvement over earlier ethnographic works. The studies of Saint-Domingue did not describe unicorns or sea monsters, but instead attempted to be rational and logical. Anthropological writers on Saint-Domingue explored the general identity of their subjects, but also offered detailed descriptions and explanations of their customs and social relations. Charlevoix explained that he used letters and reports from missionaries in the field. Hilliard mentioned his archival work in the colonial records and described in detail how he attempted to understand each racial group of the island.[7] A pre-Malinowskian Girod explained how he relied on observation to understand peoples' characters.[8] Descourtilz, Girod, Moreau, and Hilliard associated their work with watching, listening, and writing, the three "moments" of the *métier* of the anthropologist.

What was most prejudicial to truly scientific and valid anthropology here was less the recurrent judging, moralizing, and hierarchizing, or the obvious lack of awareness of Western ethnocentrism, than the constant *enchanting* of the Other by the attribution of magical exoticism. If eighteenth-century ethnography anticipated academic anthropology's organization around the binary distinction Self/Other, the ethnographic works examined here did not simply pose the ethnographic subject as Other, but enchanted, ethnicized, racialized, eroticized, and even loved this Other to the extent that there was no ethnic classification without fantasy. We must therefore examine the question of sexuality as part of proto-anthropology's episteme. The discourse of difference appears as inseparable from the enchanted discourse on magic sexuality: the Other was eroticized by the attribution of a sexuality seen not only as extravagant, but also as "enchanted" or magical.

Interracial love, an idiosyncrasy of the plantation world with little acknowledgment in the Enlightenment classics, was ideologically complicated by the debate about slavery. Ethnographic attention to this subject challenged not only colonial order and racial philosophy but also the epistemological foundation of anthropology itself, for it blurred the opposition Self/Other. The colony was a remarkable concentration of differences, and the attempts to make sense of the cultural diversity encountered in the island were inevitably followed by ethnicization, racialization, and the attribution of Otherness—which also worked the other way around, with ethnicization inventing cultural difference.

An analysis of the white, black, and mulatto identities produced should be placed within the framework of the intellectual questions of the time and of the American *imaginaire* in Europe. Most of the ethnographic texts reflected the debates on slavery, the economic ideas of the physiocrats, and an "environmentalism" that emphasized the causal influence of climate and geography on human behavior. As Hodgen showed, the idea of the hierarchy of cultures and races was in place by the end of the seventeenth century. Attempts at scientific explanations for the inequality of races clearly appeared in these texts. Hilliard d'Auberteuil, for instance, evoked the "natural and organic character of the negro race."[9] Earlier, the influential Voltaire had written about "the internal constitution of the organs of negroes."[10] The major works of the Enlightenment on the Other considerably conditioned ethnographies written by intellectuals. Characteristic of the French Enlightenment was the figure of the "philosopher-traveler."[11] Moreau de Saint-Méry, de Wimpffen, Girod-Chantrans, and Hilliard d'Auberteuil often compared their findings with the great philosophical works of the time. However, Saint-Domingue was such a peculiar place that it obliged each of these writers to articulate an individual reading of the Enlightenment. Furthermore, Saint-Domingue, with its large number of mixed-race inhabitants, presented a situation that challenged eighteenth-century assumptions about race.

This chapter focuses on three aspects of eighteenth-century ethnography on Saint-Domingue. The first part assesses the Othering of the white population. A striking element of these texts remains indeed the inclusion of the white colonists of Saint-Domingue in the island's exoticism, within the sphere of radical alterity to which the West ordinarily assigns nonwhite peoples. The second section examines the ethnicization and racialization of black peoples and their correlated mentalities and mores. The questions of miscegenation, intimate interracial relations, and mulatto identities are the subject of the third part of this chapter. For love often challenges not only the establishment of patterns of correlations between the individual and society, but also what was then the entrenched belief in a hierarchy of races. Love affairs are of particular interest because their ethnographic translation reflected the tensions between two intertwined moralities regarding intimate interracial relations: the official morality stigmatized anyone engaged in such relations, while the practical morality was more accommodating and resulted in complex family structures.[12]

The historical moment of these accounts was significant, for racial identities appear to have considerably solidified during the course of the eighteenth century—and then virtually disappeared. Blacks, whites, and mulattos: these groups were anthropologically, and to a large extent physically, extinct by the beginning of the nineteenth century. Even the Negro ceased to exist, the category reconstructed entirely by ideas about ethnogenesis and the theory of the Haitian nation. The first Haitian constitution actually recognized all Haitians as blacks, even the Polish and German troops who sided with the rebel slaves and eventually settled in Haiti.

THE ANTHROPOLOGISTS

The Dominican missionary Jean-Baptiste Labat (1664–1738) wrote the first ethnography of the French colonies in the West Indies: six volumes published in 1722 with descriptions and illustrations of plants, geography, and people. While most of his work focused on Martinique and Guadeloupe and only one volume on Saint-Domingue, the general descriptions of Africans and slaves offered an ethnography of the French colonies in the Caribbean. Labat's account reflected the greater fluidity of racial identities at the beginning of the century.

The history of Saint-Domingue, written by the Jesuit Pierre François-Xavier Charlevoix (1682–1761) and published in 1730, involved archival research at the Ministry of the Marine (Dépôt de la Marine). The description of the contemporary colony was also based on notes and *mémoires* sent to Charlevoix by a Jesuit missionary in Saint-Domingue, Jean-Baptiste Le Pers.

Michel René Hilliard d'Auberteuil (1740–89) was a jurist from Rennes who advocated autonomy of the colony for the white colonists. Hilliard d'Auberteuil, anticipating nineteenth-century anthropology, had a "professional" connection with colonial authorities. His controversial *Considérations* were written for the Ministry of the Colonies. However, the distribution of his book was forbidden in Saint-Domingue,[13] for it represented a direct attack on colonial rule and advocated more autonomy for the planter class. He described his methodologies in the introduction: "I stirred the dust of public archives of Saint-Domingue . . . I thought I had found in (these) Rules . . . the old Statutes of the *Chevalerie*."[14] An "environmentalist," he believed in the influence of climate, dedicating an entire chapter to climate and customs.[15]

Louis Méderic Élie Moreau de Saint-Méry (1750–1819) was the author of the most exhaustive study of the colony of Saint-Domingue: more than twelve hundred pages in two large volumes describing the people, the economy, and the geography of the colony, written between 1785 and 1788 and published in 1797 in Philadelphia. He was a white Creole, born in Martinique in 1750 and later educated in Paris. He lived in Saint-Domingue for a few years, when the colony was at the height of its economic prosperity. In Paris, he convinced the minister for the colonies to commission from him reports and legal texts. Politically and ideologically close to the rich planters, he played an important role during the French Revolution; in Paris, as a member of the Club Massiac, he was opposed to the Société des Amis des Noirs, who were favorable to abolition. After the execution of the king, he fled to Philadelphia, where he published his work on Saint-Domingue.

The colonial and institutional context that induced Moreau de Saint-Méry's oeuvre anticipated the nineteenth-century anthropology evoked by Mauss. In 1786, the Maréchal de Castries, minister of the colonies, commissioned a study for an overhaul of the legislation of Saint-Domingue,[16] which became the *Description topographique, physique, civile, politique et historique de la partie française de Saint-Domingue.* He intended "to show what the French genius had created two thousand miles from the Métropole, . . . to explore in detail what this genius had been able to produce almost in an instant and with a superiority that left far behind all that other nations had similarly endeavored."[17] The methodological advantage Moreau had over most of the other ethnographers of his time was that, having been born and raised in Martinique, he was most certainly fluent in Creole, the language spoken by slaves, free people of color, and probably many white Creoles. This must have allowed him considerably more access to his subjects of study. Let us also note that about eighty years separate Labat's study from that of Moreau, a period during which racial identities hardened and ideological discourses penetrated ethnographies.

Justin Girod-Chantrans (1750–1841) was a naturalist from the Jura region; he is often described as Swiss, even though be was born and died in Besançon and served the French government his whole life. He traveled in Saint-Domingue between May 1782 and July 1783, and his observation of the plantation society resulted in a book published in 1785, highly polemical in its opposition to slavery and support for the equality of blacks. Alexandre-Stanislas de Wimpffen (1748–1819) belongs to the category of the traveler-philosopher. After a career as a French officer, then as an employee in a trade company, Wimpffen traveled extensively in the West Indies and Mexico. His *Voyage à Saint-Domingue pendant les années 1788, 1789 et 1790* was published in Paris in 1797.[18] An aristocrat from Württemberg, he clearly had literary ambitions and was influenced by the literary style and the wit as much as by the ideas of his time. He affected a literary posture reminiscent of Voltaire.[19]

Thomas Phipps Howard, in the British cavalry, was brought to Saint-Domingue by the war between revolutionary France and England in the 1790s and wrote letters describing not only the military events but also the colonial society he encountered, in the final stage of its existence. Bryand Edwards (1743–1800), another British writer on Saint-Domingue, witnessed some of the revolutionary events in the north of the country. The book he published in 1797 in London on the ill-fated British military expedition on the island was refuted by an exiled French planter in London, Venault de Charmilly. The latter text was a detailed response to Edwards's account of the revolutionary events and his portrayal of the Creole class. The *Voyages* of Michel Etienne Descourtilz offer another late ethnographic discourse about Saint-Domingue. Descourtilz was a naturalist who traveled through the French colonies in the last years of the century. He arrived in Saint-Domingue in 1794 immediately after the collapse of the plantation system.

COLONIAL ENCOUNTERS: AFTER LANDING, ANTHROPOLOGISTS MEET THE WHITES

To most travelers in the late eighteenth century, Saint-Domingue appeared as a society of extreme contrasts, where wealth and luxury coexisted with a dreadful climate and a system of slavery profoundly offensive to the ideals of the Enlightenment. This environment created the intellectual framework for affirming the Otherness of the whites. Notwithstanding their racial resemblance to the dominant minority of the island, the ethnographers assigned to the whites well-defined, essentialized characteristics, many of them negative, that resulted in including the white colonists in the sphere of alterity. The criticisms of our anthropologists often focused on poor whites or *petits blancs*. According to the English officer Howard,[20] the poor whites were "gamblers, tradesmen, mechanics, pimps, felons . . . [and] young Men of Families who have committed crimes,"[21] and are living such "a train of debauchery [that] most of them die after a year," in short, "the very Dregs of the Nation."[22] In Wimpffen's view, these men had migrated from Europe to Saint-Domingue because of their "misery, shame, misbehavior, despair, or the hope of becoming wealthy."[23] But Wimpffen was even more unsympathetic to the female component of this sector: "They sent them trollops from the *Salpêtrière*, trash taken from the muck, shameless whores."[24] Then, quoting the French explorer Bougainville, Wimpffen compared Saint-Domingue to Rome, "whose original founders were nothing but an undifferentiated bunch of brigands and whores led by two mongrels."[25] For Hilliard d'Auberteuil, European immigrants came to Saint-Domingue "moved by needs or vice" and found their place "in obscure gambling dens, or among slaves: wandering and without resources."[26] He also examined the link between the social origins and social practices of the migrants and excused the cruelty of the Creoles: "those who exercise cruelty [against their slaves] are usually villainous refugees or born in the mud of the European cities; the vilest men are also the most barbarous."[27] Hilliard located those who mixed (socially and romantically) with nonwhites in this group and linked miscegenation (which he condemned) to poverty: "Every day, pale men, dying of hunger, who do not dare beg for charity, can be seen on the ocean front (of Cap): several were born in opulence and *mollesse* . . . some sacrifice themselves for pleasure with free Negresses."[28] Moreau de Saint-Méry blamed France for having sent forth "its useless ones, its reckless persons, its credulous children, its dangerous men perhaps."[29] He especially criticized the military troops[30] stationed in the colony, warning of the threats posed by "soldiers, sailors, adventurers . . . since the corruption of morals is a real source of evils."[31] Relations between soldiers and Creole women were frequently judged harshly by our writers. Lieutenant Howard criticized French soldiers who "worst of all marry women of color."[32] Another British officer critically noted the romantic practices of French soldiers: "It is quite the fashion here for everyone to have one of these princess's to live with as housekeepers or nurses."[33]

The negative characteristics assigned to the white population increased considerably over the course of the century. The whites were described as greedy, selfish, ignorant, tasteless, uneducated, sexually obsessed, unfaithful to their spouses, impious, racist, immoral, and capable of the worst cruelty. There is even one account of an incestuous planter, related by Girod-Chantrans :

A white man of about 50 years, unmarried, father of several mulattos and mulatto women had among them one daughter he was in love with. He lived in his plantation house where, in the middle of an already large family, he pressured his daughter to comply with his wishes; every day he was refused. Initially, he used caresses; but not being able to overcome the repugnance of his daughter, he tried threats and finished with cruelties. Nothing could shatter the confidence of this poor girl . . . Her brothers, witnesses of the horror of which she was the victim, eventually overcome by compassion and indignation, strangled the father in his bed. They simply did not think about fleeing and they were arrested . . . They were all executed, as well as the girl who was part of the plot.[34]

This story illustrated the corruptive effects of slavery on morals and also contradicted the conventional image of the mulatto woman. The mulatto daughter was virtuous; the white father was a psychotic pervert.

Violence, a stigma typically applied to non-Western Others, became a central characteristic of white identities. Their violence was predominantly directed at the black population and the slaves in particular. Even Hilliard, the writer most favorable to the white planter class, made frequent allusions to the widespread violence of the whites: "In Saint-Domingue, whoever is white mistreats blacks with impunity."[35] He offered a psychological explanation of such generalized behavior: "The habit of being obeyed renders the master proud, tough, unfair, cruel, and makes him lose all moral virtues."[36] All writers of the second half of the century mentioned violence and, in several cases, presented detailed scenes of cruelty. Girod even provided examples of gratuitous sadism: "In the past, when they (the planters) invited each other for dinner, the host entertained his guests after the meal with the spectacle of a negro whipped to the point of blood. If none could be found to deserve it at the time of the party, a victim was randomly chosen in the mill, and the spectators often exercised their skills on the patient."[37]

Racist violence against free people also was noted. Ethnographies deplored the abuse, insults, and occasionally the physical attacks mulattos endured. The non-owning whites were recognized as the main perpetrators of racial hatred.[38] The French revolutionary envoy Sonthonax denounced them as "aristocrats of the skin," while the French general Pamphile de Lacroix later wrote that the "fanaticism of the prejudice of color" was prevalent among the Creoles.[39] Wimpffen, Moreau, Hilliard, and Edwards also emphasized the prejudices of this social group.

The "little whites" (*petits blancs*) originally constituted a socioeconomic category,[40] probably conceived by the blacks themselves, to designate the Europeans without property and slaves—which would suggest that subalterns could also produce identity. This identity evolved into a political and anthropological category, the *petit-blancs*. The petty white mentality, which would be stigmatized during the decolonization struggles of the twentieth century in Africa as the main obstacle to independence, already appeared as a construction of these eighteenth-century ethnographies.[41]

The characteristics of the white population became increasingly negative over the course of the eighteenth century. Two main reasons were identified by our anthropologists: slavery and the climate, both very important issues during the Enlightenment. First, as the ideology of "environmentalism" grew to be more and more rationalized, the climate of the island was identified as corrupting the whites. By increasing the blood temperature, the climate supposedly rendered the whites unable to control their violence—or their sexual appetite.

Second, with the debate on slavery growing in importance, the ethnographic discourse became increasingly moralistic. The reliability of ethnographic work was affected by the ideological agenda of the writers.[42] With the question of slavery moving to the heart of eighteenth-century anthropological debate, customs and practices were seen as "consequences." By contrast, the earlier description of Labat, dating back to the very beginning of the eighteenth century, as well as that of Charlevoix in 1728, did not present slavery in a controversial manner and offered a more "factual" anthropology than their counterparts in the decades that followed.

Moreau, more politically engaged by the issue, observed that "the habit of being surrounded by slaves, and needing only one look to make everything yield," made Creole children "tyrannical."[43] He insisted on the childhood experience as conditioning the character of adults. White Creoles' greed, he argued, was shaped during childhood by their despotic power over both adult and children slaves.

Moreau came to the same conclusion about white women: "The habit of ruling the slaves and finding nothing but submission necessarily make one's character haughty."[44] However, Moreau's large section on Creole women offered more tribute than criticism. He praised their generosity, beauty, compassion and devotion to their children. Creole women were also eroticized, as Moreau emphasized their languorousness, their appeal, and their talent as dancers and singers. Hilliard's text equally eroticized Creole women, noting that "voluptuousness is in their eyes, and seduction in their hearts."[45]

Creole women, however, were viewed negatively in their dealings with their slaves, particularly house slaves. The violence of the Creole woman was typically provoked by her husband's infidelities. Moreau described melodramatic moments ("awful scenes"[46]) in which wives killed themselves on account of their husbands' behavior. Anger, however, was usually taken out on slaves: "Nothing compares with the wrath of a Creole wife who punishes the slave that her husband had maybe forced to dishonor the conjugal bed."[47] (Paradoxically, Moreau also stated that the main target of the Creole woman's jealousy was the free mulatto woman, therefore not her domestic slave.) These ethnographies reflected both the increasing condemnation of slavery and the insistence on emphatic racial distinctions.

To climate and slavery, as factors of white racial hatred and violence, Bryan Edwards and Lieutenant Howard added a third cause: "the French character." The upper third of the racial hierarchy was, for them, not only white but French, and we believe that their construction of identities of the French whites took place within a larger debate. When framed in national European terms, denunciations of racism should often be interpreted as criticisms of foreign imperialisms, whether French, British, Dutch, or Spanish. Many of the texts examined in this study often compare the condition of slavery in Saint-Domingue to other Caribbean colonies. Notwithstanding their trenchant attacks on slavery, Wimpffen, Hilliard, and Moreau believed that in Saint-Domingue the treatment of the slaves was considerably better than in the British colonies (which none ever visited). To that assertion, Bryan Edwards responded that "[t]he prevalent notion that the French planters treat their negroes with greater humanity and tenderness than the British, I know to be groundless."[48]

The revolutionary events of Saint-Domingue provided evidence for the arguments of each party. Throughout his book, Bryan Edwards related in gruesome detail several executions and lynchings, almost systematically relating them to a French "disposition." The execution of Ogé, a Paris-educated leader of the mulatto class by the authorities in Cap, provided an example of both French barbarity and French racism. Edwards also explained the lynching of the French military commander, Colonel Mauduit, by his own (French) troops in anthropological terms: "The attachment of his regiment towards his person appeared to exceed the usual limits of obedience and duty. The massacre of this man by those very troops . . . affords so striking an instance of that cruel and ungovernable disposition, equally impetuous and inconstant, which prevailed, and I am afraid still continues to prevail, amongst the lower classes throughout the French dominions."[49]

Edwards then gave (not in English, but with discreet Puritanism in Latin) the full details and context of Maduit's lynching, during which the genitals of the officer were severed and then inserted in his mouth. Edwards added: "Such indeed was the baseness of these wretches [the French soldiers], that no modern language can describe, except in terms that could not be endured, the horrible enormities that were practiced on the dead body of their unfortunate commander. It was reserved for the present day to behold, for the first time, a civilized nation exceeding in feats of cruelty and revenge the savages of North America."[50]

The description of the execution of a rebel slave allowed Edwards to contrast the two national characters in regard to the treatment of the colonized:

When the executioner, after breaking his legs and arms, lifted up the instrument to give the finishing stroke on the breast, and which (by putting the criminal out of his pain) is called *le coup de grâce*, the mob, with the ferociousness of cannibals, called out *arrêtez*! and compelled him to leave the work unfinished. [The victim] seemed perfectly conscious, but uttered not a groan. At the end of forty minutes, some English seamen, who were spectators of the tragedy, strangled him in mercy. As to all the French spectators (many of them of fashion, who beheld the scene from the window of their upper apartments), it grieves me to say, that they looked on with the most perfect composure and sang froid. Some of the ladies, as I was told, even ridiculed, with a great deal of unseemly mirth, the sympathy manifested by the English at the suffering of the wretched criminals."[51]

For Lieutenant Howard, the revolutionary events made Saint-Domingue into what Joseph Conrad would later call the "Heart of Darkness":

The French Revolution in Europe acted over again in the Colonies in Miniature: Murder, Assassination, Rape and Robbery was the order of the Day and the Cruelties that were committed in St. Domingo are scarcely to be believed. As revenge is the ruling Passion of a Negro, and as I am much Afraid cause suffic[i]ent existed from the inhumanity of some Whites to their Slaves, the whole Island was immediately filled with Murder and Atrocit[i]es of every kind. What ever the most fancy could im[a]gine was put into Execution Against the Inhabitants and hundred[s] of them, Men, Women and Children, were made to expire in most excruciating Agonies. Instance may be quoted of Men absolutely skin[n]ed alive and those roasted to death before a Slow fire. Women after having suffered every Indignity brutality could suggest, [were] miserably put to death or maimed to live as Examples of terror to others. [And] Children [were] cut out of their Mothers' Womb and dashed to pieces before their faces. In fact Language wants words to Express the Enormities committed in honor of the *Rights of Man*.[52]

British engravings of that time also offered representations, with scenes of violence and torture committed by French soldiers, against whom England had been at war since 1792. Others depicted scenes of "revenge taken by the Black army for the cruelty practiced on them by the French."[53] When Bryan Edwards stated that "[i]t was no longer a contest for victory, but a diabolical emulation [as to] which party could inflict the most abominable cruelties on the other,"[54] he clearly regarded the French as in no way superior to the stigmatized Other, the black African.

PORTRAIT OF THE ANTHROPOLOGIST
AS AN ETHNICIZER

In the colonies, people quite like to characterize the various African
nations: one thus says *Arada dog-eater* or *Greedy as an Arada*.
—Moreau[55]

In his vast *Description* of the social groups of the island, Moreau dedicated an entire section[56] to the "African Slaves," the most exhaustive piece of the ethnographic literature considered here. Interestingly, he said little about the slaves' condition and their work on the plantation. Rather, Moreau focused on their mentalities and customs, in a fashion that contributed to the ethnicization and the racialization of "African Slaves." Moreau identified and characterized no fewer than thirty-seven ethnic groups: Sénégalais, Maures, Yoloffes, Cap-Verd ou Calvaires (not Cap Verde), Foules, Bambaras, Quiambas, Mandigues, Bissagots, Sosos, Bouriquis, Mesurades ou Cangas, Aradas ou Ardras, Caplaous, Mines, Agouas, Socos, Fantins, Cotocolis, Popos, Fidas ou Foedas, Fonds, Maïs, Aoussas, Ibos, Nagos, Mokos, Galbar, Mayombés, Congos ou Franc-Congos, Mousombés, Mondongues, Malimbes, Mozambiques, Quiloi, Quiriam, and Montfiat.

Moreau emphasized both race (generic characteristics of all "blacks" and "Africans") and ethnicities (cultural differences distinguishing these "Africans"). After landing in Saint-Domingue, the newly enslaved subjects were conceived as black (or Negro), African, and ethnic (Arada, Congo, and so forth). Interestingly, the double process of ethnicization and racialization of Africans happened thousands of miles away from their original societies, but the ethnographers observed their subjects as if they had preserved their original cultural qualities.[57] Girod explained that the slaves from various nations had come with the "prejudices of their country,"[58] while Hilliard stated that "[t]he Negroes in Guinea have a particular character according to their Nation, their needs, their commerce."[59] Thus, the intellectual process of ethnicization attributed an ethnic identity to individuals, and gave that identity priority over all other collective identities. Each ethnic group was explicitly named, and was endowed with specific characteristics: "one thus says *Arada dog-eater.*"

Ethnicization was also colonial in nature, for it related characteristics to labor. For Charlevoix, the Senegalois were not only the most handsome but also the most appropriate for domestic work. The Bambaras were taller than the Senegalois but were inclined to steal. The Congos were the shortest but the best at fishing. The Aradas were the most expert at working the land and also the proudest. The Nagos were the most humane, the Mondongos the cruelest, and the Mines the most capricious.[60]

For Hilliard, the Congos were skilled at cultivating the fields, but could learn all professions. To counter their inclination to *marronnage*[61] and bind them on the plantation, he believed that they should be given wives, be encouraged to raise animals, and be encouraged in their appetite for luxury. The Negroes from the banks of the Niger were tall and handsome, skilled at riding horses, and courageous, but unfit for working the land; their wives were very hardworking and thus ideal for domestic work. Hilliard also believed that the Negroes from the Gold Coast were robust, righteous, versatile, humane, and joyful. But there was a problem with Gold Coast Negroes: they superstitiously believed that once dead, they would go back to their country, a belief that encouraged them to commit suicide.[62] To counter this belief, Hilliard recommended gentle treatment, not forced conversion, as nothing was for this people "more revolting than proselytism."[63]

Moreau offered the most extensive attribution of ethnic characteristics of the African slaves in Saint-Domingue. His description of each ethnic group also established specific characteristics for women. For instance, he asserted the following about Arada women's sexuality:

These women are cantankerous and querulous; they can be physically recognized by their hips and buttocks whose sizes have become the standard for comparison. A more advanced study would identify other features all the more particular in that they evidently suppose contradictory uses; the circumcision of the nymph [clitoris] or their dilation in astonishing proportion; dilation accompanied by that of another part, so much so that one sex could to some extent fulfill the role of the other."[64]

The sexuality of the black Other became enchanted, but was also ethnicized; and the ethnicized body became a site of magic sexuality. Moreau also believed that, while all African women were inclined to libertinage, the Congo women were most inclined, and thus became most sought after.[65]

Moreau's command of the Creole language allowed him to discuss a kind of anthropology practiced by the slaves themselves. He quoted several proverbs affirming identities: Bambara could be accused of being turkey robbers, Aradas of eating dogs and being stingy, Congos of being banana eaters, and Ibos of hanging themselves.[66] In addition, Moreau noticed that slaves from the same ship self-identified as *Batimens*; African women who shared the same lover self-identified as *Matelotes*; and the Creole slaves called Africa-born slaves "baptised standing" (*baptisés debout*) or "horses" (*chevaux*), although *Bossales* was the only term that persisted.

The "anthropology" of the subalterns also extended to their masters. What most surprised the Negroes who observed the whites, Moreau asserted, was writing, an invention that they believed the whites obtained from a demon. Moreau also mentioned two opposite black theories of whites. According to the first one, God created man and made him white. After having observed God from afar, the devil attempted to create a similar being, but he turned out black. Irritated, the devil pushed his creation face to the ground, which flattened his nose and swelled his lips. The second theory was articulated by "less modest Negroes": the first man created by

God was black, and the white man was only a black man whose color had degenerated.[67] Both theories resemble what Brazilian anthropology calls an anti-myth: a myth that attempts to integrate and explain the "contact" with whites and, often, with the colonial state.[68]

What are today recognized as forms of resistance to slavery, such as suicide, abortion, poisoning, and *marronnage*, were ethnicized in these ethnographic works. For Descourtilz, Arada men were most likely to poison, while Amina women were inclined to practice abortion.[69] Charlevoix believed that the Mines were subject to desperation and suicide;[70] according to Hilliard, the slaves from the Gold Coast were likely to consider suicide. For Hilliard, Moreau, and Charlevoix, the Congos were inclined to *marronnage*, to whom Moreau added the Bouriquis and the Cangas.[71]

Marronnage, fleeing the plantation, was a phenomenon often described in the literature. Moreau gave an exhaustive anthropological and historical description of a community of marrons that survived for eighty-five years in the mountains of Bahoruco, at the French-Spanish border.[72] We learn that the marrons, who also practiced slavery, had developed guerrilla war tactics, raided small farms to acquire goods and slaves, developed relations with the Spaniards, and had their own beliefs and power structure.

Moreau delineated a particular identity for this community, which he repeatedly designated as a *peuplade* (tribe):

Among them were men of 60 years who never lived anywhere but in the forests where they were born. The true character of them all is anxiety and it was apparent on their faces; fear agitates them all . . . They were cruel if they wanted to intimidate or obtain revenge, they abducted other negroes to turn them into real slaves. They only admitted those who had freely come to them.[73]

The constructivist approach among both Africanists[74] and Americanists[75] in recent years has helped us rethink ethnicity as a category imposed from the outside. Colonial nation-states exported and imposed this category in Africa. Upon arrival in Saint-Domingue, African ethnicities (that had been previously coined and characterized through the exo-definitions of European agents) were assigned to slaves. Coming from African societies probably structured by kingship and kinship rather than ethnicity,[76] "tribal" and ethnic identities were partly constructed by Europeans who ethnicized the cultural differences among slaves in order to dominate and domesticate them. To paraphrase Barth, identities can be assigned *then* self-assigned. African slaves hence found themselves with ethnic identities assigned by the colonial state and its agents (traders, administrators, overseers, and ethnographers). The colonial and illusory nature of the process of ethnicization was suggested by Moreau when he admitted that "[t]here are many places in the Colony, where the nomenclature which I gave is more extensive; but this difference comes only from that Negroes, questioned about the place of their birth, cite the canton, that is then transformed into a kingdom, as if one distinguished Havrais from Norman and from French."[77] Hilliard too recognized that assigning an ethnic origin was an uncertain business and that often the true identity was missed or lost.[78]

Eighteenth-century ethnographers played a major role in the ethnicization process as they rationalized and organized identities according to the hierarchies of the time. Ethnicization, not just identity assignment, is, as we know, the business of anthropological discourse. The characteristics of race and of each ethnic group therefore appeared indispensable to this rationalization, and the resulting identities were neatly bordered. Whether described systematically or mentioned in passing, the qualities of the ethnic man were not only fundamental and essential, but also magically extraordinary, to the point that ethnicity was almost inevitably enchanted.

With racialization, beyond ethnicization, the assignment of enchanted characteristics turned "Africans" into general objects of fascination. While ethnicization implied distinct identities, the construction of blackness and African-ness induced a generic one. Ethnicity gave way to characteristics supposed to be common to all blacks. Both Hilliard and Moreau believed that the body temperature of Africans was higher than that of other races. For that reason, Hilliard recommended that slaves should not be given fish since it was presumed to increase body temperature. Moreau deduced the carefree attitude, "everywhere . . . the characteristic of the Negro,"[79] from the body temperature that rendered physical needs more demanding. Girod believed that the blood of Negroes was so thick that it made them sleep very deeply. Some continued to sleep, he observed, even while they were shaken and screamed at.[80] Blacks sometimes appeared as barbaric, but not necessarily as threatening: fear was rarely evoked in these ethnographic texts, except in those written during the Revolution. Allegations of cannibalism were made, but rarely and anecdotally.[81] Indeed, many writers offered humanizing representations.

Charlevoix believed that blacks were good-natured, humane, humble, generous, and incapable of hatred, envy, or bad faith. Their main flaws, he believed, were credulousness and superstition.[82] For Hilliard, blacks were good-natured, obedient, hardworking, sober, and patient. They only stole when forced to work at night or if the fields assigned to them for gardening were of bad quality.[83] Hilliard even composed a sort of ode to the integrity of blacks, the guardians of their masters' secrets: "the confidant of our weaknesses, the guardian of our money, everything in our houses is in their hands; they respect our trust; they are good to each other; a Negro never endures hunger when his friend has food."[84] Moreau cited the highest moral virtues in constructing black identities. Cleanliness, he asserted, was a fundamental characteristic of the Negroes, especially the women.[85] His sociological impulse led him to wonder whether the aptitudes of blacks were limited not by race, but by their lack of education.[86] Even the flaws he ascribed, such as indolence, fearfulness, prejudices,[87] jealousy, and marital infidelity,[88] were relatively benign.

Why so much praise? One should notice here that these writers who humanized black identities were not abolitionists. They were not advocates of slavery, but believed in the value of the society of Saint-Domingue and that it could only survive with the plantation system. On the other hand, the most negative black identities were attributed by Wimpffen and Girod, the most radically opposed to slavery. The paradox thus is that the humanizing of blacks did not come from abolitionists but from the most conservative (and least ideological) writers in our study. I believe that in order to support the plantation system and the civilization of Saint-Domingue (notwithstanding their criticisms of it), Hilliard and Moreau praised blacks living under the most extreme subjugation, and insisted that they still preserved their humanity. Implicitly, they advocated a gentler, kinder slavery. On the other hand, abolitionists did not always recognize the human qualities of those who were oppressed and dehumanized by the unnatural practice of slavery.

Girod did not attribute to blacks any general racial character. Influenced by Montesquieu, the naturalist from Besançon believed that laws and governments played an essential role in shaping customs and mentality. He believed, however, that the condition of slavery actually prevented slaves from developing common characteristics: "[Society] does not exist for them; what character, what distinct mores could they have? It is the constant relations that bind us to one another, and to our various governments, that compose what is called a national character. But there are no such constant relations for the Negroes, except that of slavery, which brings about the universal fear of the whites."[89] Discussions of the cruelty of slave owners and the inhumanity of slavery nevertheless suggested an identity of victims common to all blacks. At the same time, the recurrent emphasis on indolence, inclination to pleasure, and carefree spirit made representations of blacks far from frightening. The only fear described, from Moreau to Girod, was the black fear of the whites.

VOODOO AND ACCULTURATION

Moreau included in his work a lengthy description of voodoo practices, while other ethnographers only mentioned it.[90] Moreau's study was so detailed that it became an important source for twentieth-century anthropologists of Haitian religions, such as Métraux (1977) and Hurbon (2002).

For Moreau, Vaudoux was a supernatural and all-powerful being worshipped mainly by the *Arada* Africans. That being was incarnated in a nonvenomous snake. Moreau believed that the African religion was being acculturated in Saint Domingue, as he distinguished the voodoo cults with "primitive purity" from others. He described in detail the scenario of a Vaudoux ceremony, occurring secretly at night. The ritual was led by a king and a queen, and had two distinct parts: first the followers expressed solemn requests, then they danced, drank, and fell into trances.[91] The requests to the Vaudoux gods varied: many slaves asked to control the minds of their masters, others wanted money or longer life. Many demands were related to love: to become attractive, to summon an unresponsive lover, to make one's lover faithful, or place a curse upon a rival. The participants sometimes drank goat blood to seal their pact of secrecy, promising to risk or give death rather than revealing Vaudoux's secrets.[92]

The dance began after the pact was made. The "beneficiary" of the ceremony was the first to dance and eventually to experience a trance, followed by the other practitioners and the queen. Alcoholic beverages increased the "delirium." The description of trance by Moreau attempted to be realistic:

[T]he delirium keeps rising. The use of liquors augments its effect even further . . . Some faint and rave while others fall into a kind of furor; but all are seized by a nervous shaking they do not seem able to control. They spin around ceaselessly. And while some tear their clothes apart and bite their own flesh in this sort of bacchanal, others who are deprived of their senses and have fallen on the spot, are transported, still in the dance, to an adjacent and dark room, where a disgusting prostitution sometimes exercises a most hideous empire.[93]

The other descriptions of the voodoo religion, that of Descourtilz and of Malenfant (a planter and colonel during the military events), were far more negative. Both were written with the Haitian revolution as background (and published shortly after). Descourtilz first called Vaudoux a sect of *convulsionnaires* (convulsive people), making the trance the central part of the religious practice.[94] In his third volume, Descourtilz insisted on the negative aspects (vengeance, spell casting, idolatry).[95] He also related voodoo to the Revolution: according to him, Toussaint used the service of a voodoo priest to cast a spell on the French forces. Similarly, Malenfant cast voodoo in a negative light, as he emphasized fanaticism, irrationality, and drinking, and described the voodoo priests as leaders of the rebel slaves.[96]

For Girod and Moreau, there was evidence of cultural miscegenation in Creole, the language spoken primarily by the Creole slaves and which André Marcel d'Ans[97] later called the only true linguistic creation produced by the colonization of the Americas. The earliest controversy about the origin and quality of this language occurred in the second half of the eighteenth century between Girod and Moreau. Girod believed it was an inferior language, not because people of color were incapable of learning French, but, on the contrary, because the whites were stupid enough to believe in the stupidity of their slaves and spoke in a simplified, infantile French to them. The whites imagined and spoke a version of the French language that they thought the Africans would understand. Creole was therefore invented not by the subalterns but by their masters.[98]

Moreau gave a lengthy response to Girod, probably the earliest praise of the Creole language and, interestingly, one that came from an advocate of the white planters and French rule: "There are thousands of small things that one would not dare say in French, a thousand voluptuous images that French would not succeed in portraying, and that Creole expresses or renders with infinite grace."[99] In their own words, most ethnographers clearly identified what is today designated by sociology as the acculturation process. This process appeared to them both physical and cultural. By migrating to Saint-Domingue, Africans lost some of their physical features and acquired new customs and mentalities. Moreau took these transformations for granted, since the climate made changes inevitable: "Such are the various inhabitants of Africa gathered in Saint-Domingue, which becomes their country, and where they acquire a way of being that can neither resemble the one they had in their place of origin nor absolutely differ from it."[100] Hilliard found that those born in Africa acquired, once on the island, a "general character" that erased the characters of each African nation.[101]

LOVE AND PREJUDICE: MISCEGENATION
AND THE HIERARCHY OF RACES

By the beginning of the eighteenth century, the Western belief in a hierarchy of races was established.[102] Saint-Domingue, with its increasing number of mixed people, presented a situation that challenged this view and therefore attracted considerable interest from our ethnographers. The "mulatto" was not an unknown category to the Enlightenment. As Jack Forbes has shown, the mulatto became part of the Spanish, Portuguese, and French conceptual vocabulary with the conquest (of America) and the reconquest (of Moorish Spain).[103] The *Encyclopédie*, the most emblematic work of the Enlightenment, included a short definition of "Le Mulâtre" by Jaucourt in 1765, while in the *Suppléments* to the *Encyclopédie*, in 1777, M. de Bellecombe wrote a longer article on the subject with moralistic and racist arguments against miscegenation. On the whole, however, the mulatto received minimal attention in France and greater consideration in colonial societies. Both Labat, at the dawn of the century, and Moreau, at the other end of it, dedicated entire chapters to mulattos.[104] So did Hilliard, while Wimpffen, Girod, and Descourtilz wrote lengthy descriptions of the origins, mentalities, and habits of this racial class. The mulattos posed two important and related issues: that of intimate relations between individuals of two races, and that of the nature of their offspring, the mulattos themselves.

The topic of sexual exploitation was, with very few exceptions, absent from ethnographies: intimate relations between whites and blacks were usually represented as consensual, and rape was almost invisible. The ethnographic literature does indicate the occurrence of consensual relations, legitimate unions, and love.[105] Yet some writers, recognizing sex, still refused to accept the existence of interracial love.[106] Lieutenant Howard, for instance, explicitly stigmatized intimate interracial relations: "I'll not say Love, for that would be disgracing the Passion."[107] In Saint-Domingue, such relations were seen as entirely sexual, influenced by the climate, lust, ethnic origin, power, or calculation—but not motivated by love. Hilliard described white men legally married to women of color as fortune seekers.[108] Similarly, black female slaves "maneuvered" to seduce their "deadened" masters either for financial profit or to be emancipated: "To obtain their wealth, how many negresses have not profited from masters deadened by libertinism and incapable of removing themselves from its empire over weak and seduced souls, who indulged in it without blushing. Family riches were sacrificed to passion, became the price of debauchery, and respectable names with the best land fell to legitimized mulattos."[109] Love, as such, was an impossibility. Hilliard, who hated the mulattos and despised the white men responsible for their existence, even quantified the number of white men living with their concubines ("vivant concubinairement"): three thousand.[110] Hilliard later specified that three hundred white men were legally married with women of color.[111]

The racial hierarchy of the island became explicit when Hilliard explained that: "A White who legitimately marries a *Mulâtresse* falls from the rank of the Whites and becomes the equal of the free (people of color). The latter even look at him as inferior to them: indeed this man is despicable."[112] The specific "affairs" described or mentioned in the literature were all used by the authors to illustrate the effect of the climate on the instincts and the depravation of either white males or women of color. Love indeed, like slavery, was ideologized.

One of the most remarkable intimate interracial relations, narrated from very different viewpoints and used for political purposes, involved a French aristocratic planter and a mulatto woman in the city of Petit-Goâve. This is how Bryan Edwards recounted the affair of Ferrand de Baudière:

> Mons. *Ferrand de Beaudierre* (sic), a magistrate at *Petit Goâve*, was not fortunate. This gentleman was unhappily enamored of a woman of color, to whom, as she possessed a valuable plantation, he had offered marriage. Apprehensive that by this step he might be displaced from the magistracy, and being a man of a warm imagination, with little judgment, he undertook to combat the prejudices of the whites against the whole class. He drew up, in the names and behalf of the mulatto people, a memorial . . . wherein, among other things, they were made to claim, in express words, the full benefit of the national declaration of rights. Nothing could be more ill-timed or injudicious than this proceeding: it was evident that such a claim led to consequences of which the mulattoes themselves (who certainly at this juncture had no wish to enfranchise the slaves) were not apprized. This memorial was considered as a summons to the negroes for a general revolt. The parochial committee seized the author, and committed him to prison; but the mob took him from thence by force, and in spite of the magistrates, who exerted themselves to stop their fury, put him to death.[113]

In his response to Edwards, Venault de Charmilly gave a different version of the affair. The mulatto lady involved was not rich, although, Venault conceded, "quite pretty," and as for the gentleman: "generally, we did not look at him as a man with much sense. Only love for this *Quarteronne* made him write the memoir he gave to the Men of Color."[114]

Jean-Philippe Garran-Coulon, a revolutionary and an abolitionist who authored a four-volume report on the revolutionary events in Saint-Domingue for the convention in Paris, gave the most detailed account of the last days of Ferrand de Baudière and the political dimensions of his lynching. But the love affair was not mentioned once. According to Garran-Coulon, free men of color presented a moderate petition to the assembly of Petit-Goâve, which provoked a violent reaction from the petty whites, who then arrested and forced the mulatto delegates to admit that the text had been written by a local and respected judge, Ferrand. The same day, the judge was summoned and arrested for having written a request on the behalf of the mulattos. A white mob dragged him out of his cell, had him guillotined, and paraded his head around town on a pike. Thus fell "the first defender of human rights in Saint-Domingue," victim to the same enemies the Revolution was fighting in France.[115]

Garran-Coulon's account provided strikingly distinct racial identities. The Creole whites committed a barbarous crime and generally terrorized the nonwhite population; the free people of color were humble and appeared as victims. Garran-Coulon, like Sonthonax and Polvérel, the envoys of the Jacobins in Saint-Domingue in 1792, used categories that were less racial than political for the revolutionary worldview and recognized two categories that dominated all others, including those who were for the Revolution and those who were against it. It seems improbable that Garran-Coulon did not know about the relation between Ferrand and the beautiful mulatto. He mentioned that the Massiac Club later used "various pretexts" to justify the murder. The relation between the old judge and a young mulatto woman appeared either irrelevant or, probably, would have discredited the judge and therefore weakened Garran-Coulon's attack on the counterrevolutionaries. Love thus fell victim to politics and ideology.

Labat mentioned two interracial marriages he personally knew of. The first one, between a Provençal and a black woman, produced no children and ended in a separation, the husband no longer able to endure the gossip of his compatriots. But in the other one, Monsieur Liétard, "a good man who had married a truly beautiful negresse out of a principle of conscience . . . got handsome little mulattos from his black spouse."[116]

In these eighteenth-century texts, there appeared only one love story—in Labat's account—involving a white woman and a black man.[117] Significantly, the story, in which the Dominican friar was himself an actor, happened at the very beginning of the century, at a time when racial identities had not yet crystallized and stigmas did not render such intimate relations overwhelmingly difficult. The young woman was seventeen, white, and the daughter of a local artisan. The young man was her father's slave. Labat explained that the young woman had taken the initiative, not the slave. After his daughter became pregnant, the father sought the missionary for advice. Labat told him to sell the slave and send his daughter to Guadeloupe or La Grenade to have her deliver in secret. The artisan ignored the advice, and in a state of rage went to see the *intendant* (colonial government official), dragging the slave along to have him punished. But the *intendant* had the girl summoned and questioned her about the violence to which she allegedly had been subjected. Because "she had too much honor and conscience," the adolescent admitted to having initiated the affair. The artisan returned home with his daughter, who risked spending an entire life "in opprobrium." (The slave, meanwhile, was sold away to a Spanish trader.) The story, however, ended well, at least from Labat's perspective. A Pole, named Casimir, suddenly appeared and asked for the hand of the pregnant daughter. Labat celebrated their union, and Casimir later officially recognized the child. "It is rare to find such charity in our century," concluded Labat.[118]

Since races were organized in a vertical hierarchy, the white man "fell" when he became involved with a woman of color. These men were called "*mésalliés*" (literally, misallied) and their stigmatization increased as the century continued.

For Moreau, as well as for Hilliard, the climate was responsible for libertinism, and interracial relations were consensual: "There are physical needs that are felt in hot countries in a very pressing way. There, the need to love degenerates into fury, and it is fortunate that in a colony such as Saint-Domingue, black women can be met to appease a passion that would otherwise cause great devastation."[119] Girod agreed on both counts, for desires are "provoked by the climate and fulfilled and satisfied with acknowledgment by women of color."[120] Most of these writers believed that the climate warmed the blood, which, in effect, rendered white males incapable of controlling their sexual instincts.

Colonial authorities attempted to legislate these relations. The Louisiana Code (1754) penalized interracial unions. A royal ordinance in 1779 prohibited mulatto men and women from attending balls organized by white planters in too ostentatious dresses (which could seduce white men). But Moreau believed that the climate and desires were stronger than the laws: "The heat of the climate, which excites desires and the facility to satisfy them will always render legislative prescriptions useless."[121] This facility was corroborated by Howard, for whom:

There is no Country in the World where the Inducements to Dissipation and Libertinism are greater . . . In the first place Morality is scarcely known. The Heat of the Climate tends so evidently to raise the Passions to their highest Pitch, and the gratifications of them rather looked upon as meritorious, than otherwise: all kind of female modesty being generally unknown [so much so] that a Man inclined to Libertinism finds here perhaps the largest field in the World to gratify himself in.[122]

When examining the representations of women of color in eighteenth-century ethnography on Saint-Domingue, one discovers a radical sexual obsession on the part of ethnographers. The extreme eroticization of the black female body developed to the point that blackness appeared to be associated with sexuality as much as with slavery.

But it is not the black female body in general or that of the mulatto woman but that of the *free* woman of color that was most radically conceived as an object of fascination. Girod-Chantrans summed up the situation when he clearly stated that white men were not attracted to the slaves in the sugarcane field, or even the domestic slaves:

The empire of these subaltern creatures does not extend beyond the savannas . . . They do not make the silly pretense of captivating the delicate whites . . . It is from the class of the free women and more often in that of the *mulâtresses* that they (the whites) seek to supply themselves. Their ease, together with a more elaborate education, bring them closer to the European condition.[123]

Indeed, there are few examples of the eroticization of African women. On the other hand, the essentialization of the mulatto woman centered on her sex appeal. We therefore face a contradiction: if the white men were predominantly attracted to free women of color and if most of them were *mulâtresses*, how did the mulatto "happen" in the first place? The very existence of the attractive mulatto woman suggests relations with black women slaves in the first place. That inconsistency appears not to have been addressed. Clearly emphasized, however, was the sexual extravagance of the island, recurrently condemned and accentuated in the literature.

Even the clergy was allegedly tempted. Labat told of a friar accused by his slave of having fathered her child. During the trial, the woman brandished the baby in the friar's direction and said *"toi papa li"* (you father her), which could well be the oldest written phrase in Creole.[124]

MULATTO IDENTITY AND RACIAL NOMENCLATURE

Labat insisted on the normality of mulatto children: they proved that the color of a child was not transmitted by the mother, as with chickens, but came from both parents.[125] Labat identified three categories of mixed people: the mulatto proper, the *quarteron* (one black grandparent), and the *métis* (white and Indian). The paucity of this categorization contrasts with that of Moreau, written a century later, a difference that reflects the evolution of the question of color and race.

Moreau's *tableau* offered the most comprehensive and specific nomenclature of miscegenation composed about people of mixed descent. In no less than ten pages, Moreau attempted to make sense of the diversity of color of the mixed people on the island. The intriguing classification (more than 128 detailed types of miscegenation offering thirteen types of color, what he calls distinct classes, with both genders combined) was based on a rigorous mathematical logic: a continuum of 128 combinations, with the pure white and the pure black as the two extreme poles. For instance, a *Sacatra* has 16 white parts and 112 black ones; the *Mamelouc* has 120 white parts and 8 black ones. To each "class," Moreau assigned distinct and precise characteristics. The continuum of color was also a continuum of physical features, intelligence, and toleration of the climate.[126] The mulatto—strictly speaking, an offspring of a white and a black—represented the best combination possible for Moreau: "to the sobriety and the force of the Negro, he joined the intelligence and the grace of physical appearance of the White."[127] He was also best suited to the climate of the island. For that reason, the mulatto was supposedly more successful than the *quarteron* (the offspring of white and mulatto).

This nomenclature preserved the ideology of racial hierarchy, as each new group invented by colonization was integrated into the pyramid. It also provided evidence of the increasing solidification of scientific racism in the late eighteenth century. But while reading this nomenclature, one cannot help imagining Moreau scrutinizing people's noses and pigmentation, especially when he specified that "expert eyes are needed to recognize the (lightest) mixing," to the point that he resorted also to "oral and written tradition" to determine people's categories.[128] Thus, racial identity became increasingly precise over the course of the century. Labat assigned very few characteristics, while later ethnographers elaborated well-defined, essentialized identities of mixed people.

These assigned identities of the mixed people oscillated between negative and positive qualities and were marked by contradictions. Their essentialization inevitably made the study of the mentalities and mores of the mulattos an exercise in ethnographic discourse. Hilliard asserted that the mulattos were more pious than the whites; they were also respectful and generally loved the whites, hating only those who had done them considerable harm.[129] Indeed, Hilliard proposed many positive qualities:

People of mixed blood have, like Negroes, considerable filial piety; they have a superstitious respect for their godmother, they are very considerate with the oldsters and never dare contradict them; they are generally very faithful . . . Mulattos were seen cutting down on their luxury to buy some Mulatto children whose fathers could not have emancipated them before dying, and to give to these forsaken children the most precious gift, that of freedom.[130]

But Hilliard d'Auberteuil believed the mulattos and their growing number to be a threat to the colonial order and recommended restrictions in the legal framework for emancipating the slaves.

Moreau believed that the mulattos had agreeable physical forms, were intelligent, lived long, and made excellent soldiers. Unfortunately, they had inherited many of the character flaws of the Negroes, such as indolence and laziness.[131] Moreau was also very specific about mulatto mores: "The Mulatto loves pleasure; it is his only master, but it is a despotic one. To dance, to ride a horse, to indulge in pleasure, here are his three passions. He is the equal of the [white] Creole in the first, and is far superior (to him) in the last one."[132] Girod's examination of the free people of color contrasted considerably with his contemporaries, as he avoided most moralistic judgments about their origins. He stressed that this racial sector was socially differentiated, with mulatto people engaged in very different professions. An entire class of mulattos formed "the urban bourgeoisie" in Saint-Domingue; moreover, "their ways [were] very respectable." He also implied the centrality of family structure for mulattos, and added that many of these families had ancient roots in the island.[133]

But Girod was an exception. For most ethnographers, the mulatto woman was mainly reduced to a sexual identity. Moreau, in his chapter on mulattos, wrote an entire section on *mulâtresses* that solely focuses on their sex appeal:

The whole being of a *Mulâtresse* is delivered to pleasure and the fire of this Goddess burns in her heart to die out only with her life. This cult, that is all her code, her wishes, her happiness. To charm all the senses, to deliver them to the most delicious ecstasies, to surprise them by the most tempting refinements; here is her only intention; and nature, in a way an accomplice of pleasure, gave her charms, appeal and sensitivity; and what is even more dangerous, the ability to feel even more than the one with whom she shares them, the joys of which the code of Paphos itself did not have all the secrets.[134]

Moreau insisted that the almost exclusive profession available to mulatto women was as *courtisane* (prostitute).[135] His very long description of the theater of Cap François, an artistic institution that was central to Creole pride, gave an impression that this establishment was less cultural than sexual. The *théâtre* was a public place that allowed both genders to meet and therefore, according to Moreau, attracted the *courtisanes*. Conversations, explained Moreau, were vertical, as the women of color were located (and segregated) in the upper loges of the amphitheatre and the young Creole and military men were seated below.[136]

Hilliard believed that the "empire" of the *mulâtresses* over the whites made them far more indocile than mulatto men and that "[a]ll their actions are moved by voluptuousness."[137] Wimpffen wrote that they were "the most fervent priestesses of the American Venus. They have turned voluptuousness into a mechanical art to the point of perfection."[138] Thus, the free woman of color was the principal object of fantasy: a category defined not exclusively in racial terms but also in legal and social ones. Did freedom make the woman of color more attractive? Did freedom allow these women some degree of economic power that resulted in greater social exposure? Were long-term relations more likely with free women than with slaves? As Wimpffen and Descourtilz both judged, "Love equalizes everything."[139] Love reduced the distance between the Self and the Other and challenged ethnicization itself. Is the Other still Other when beloved and loving? The "handsome little Mulattos" of Monsieur Liétard, recalled by Labat, were children of a legitimate union that implied banality (the banality of a long-term interracial relation) and challenged ideology.

Girod-Chantrans's sociology of the free people of color included a theory of interracial love that, possibly for the first time, linked miscegenation to the reduction of society's racism and prejudices:

> I see in these liaisons a reason for gentleness in the behavior of the masters, because it is not natural to mistreat the woman who provides us with and shares with us the greatest of all pleasures, because an invincible inclination (*penchant*) makes us care for her, because this kindness to the individual who charms us extends to her kind, who then appear to us much closer and more respectable.[140]

Girod attributed an improvement in the treatment of slaves in the eighteenth century precisely to the increase of interracial unions.[141] He contrasted this improvement to the continuous mistreatments and cruelty against slaves committed by white women, precisely because the latter could not engage in such relations and therefore could not experience the humanity of blacks.

The identities of mulattos in colonial ethnographies (written between 1789 and 1810) were to be "shaken" by revolutionary events and by the rise of the mulattos as political and military actors. Unlike blacks, for whom the War of Independence signified an even greater solidification of assigned identities, mulatto identities became more fluid during that period. The descriptions of Descourtilz exemplified the conflicting representations. He repeatedly cast several mulatto characters in a negative light while portraying others in a very romantic manner. The former type were generally individuals grabbing land away from white owners, including their own siblings. The latter were often military figures. Interestingly, in his *Histoire des deux Indes*, Raynal[142] evoked a black savior who would avenge his fellow blacks. One may wonder whether Descourtilz had read and remembered this passage when he described Toussaint L'Ouverture galloping with his troops in Napoleonic uniforms across the Haitian landscape.

PART THREE

Human Nature and Enlightened Anthropology

CHAPTER TWELVE

The Dreaming Body

Cartesian Psychology, Enlightenment Anthropology, and the Jesuits in Nouvelle France

Mary Baine Campbell

I interpose everywhere admonitions and scruples and cautions with a religious care to reject, repress, and, as it were, exorcise every kind of phantom.—Sir Francis Bacon, *Advancement of Learning*, 1605

"What are those poor souls hunting during the night?" "They hunt for the souls of Beavers, Porcupines, Moose, and other animals, using the soul of the snowshoes to walk upon the soul of the snow."
—Paul Le Jeune, "Relation de ce qui s'est passé en la Nouvelle France . . . 1634."

Finally, it has to be considered that forgetting dreams is aided by the fact that most people show little interest in their dreams anyway.
—Sigmund Freud, *The Interpretation of Dreams*, 1900

TELOS: *LES MOEURS DES SAUVAGES AMERIQUAINS*

All across the seventeenth century, American men and women, young and old, dreamed dreams and saw visions, while appalled Jesuits in New France listened to those dreams, wrote them down, and tried to tell the Americans that their oracles had ceased.[1] It was clearly a difficult experience for a Jesuit, wintering in a small Quebec village full of vivid dreamers who might be told in their sleep by demons to kill you, though more often the dreams took a wish-fulfillment form that led to culturally irresistible requests the next day for one's precious objects: pen, book, or cat.[2] The Jesuit missionaries felt there was more at stake than their own skins, but there was also evident panic afoot in their theological disapproval of these didactic and even oracular dreams. What was at stake for the inhabitants of Nouvelle France was also very high: a relation of 1673, speaking of a "Father [who] has daily received new insults from those who will not be converted," reports that "an elder reproached him publicly with destroying their country, because he destroyed dreams and superstitions [*les songes et les superstitions*]."[3] The contemporary Québec historian Denys Delâge agrees with this elder, and goes further: "by attacking native medicine, shamans, religion, and beliefs [for all of which the dream was central—MBC], the Jesuits would not only throw a whole society into disarray but would shake the entire structure of the . . . Amerindian personality."[4]

The Jesuits had all been through a training that included the visualizations of the *Spiritual Exercises* of St. Ignatius Loyola, and knew from experience as well as books what a powerful force the imagination was in molding the spirit.[5] But they also believed in *training* the imagination, as they had trained their own: in particular, they believed from experience in the human power to *discern* the visual and aural images of the demon from among those of the "good spirit."[6] They discerned a good many demons in the religious and psychological life of seventeenth-century Huronia and Iroquoia, as they underwent not only religious but economic and social conversion processes that disintegrated their cultural worlds and decimated their communities. I am interested in the contribution of the Jesuits' challenging imaginative and physical environment to the anthropology in the making of their field notes and reports, and use as grounding text the important synthesizing and theoretical work of their inheritor and successor, the erudite Cartesian missionary and philosophe Joseph Lafitau, who spent six years among the Iroquois near Montréal in the first decade of the eighteenth century and has been called by some the "father of modern anthropology."

The Jesuit missions of course played their facilitating part—however resistant it may often have seemed to them—in a larger project of economic conquest that sought to bring North America, via the fur trade, into a world market dominated, in the heart of the seventeenth century, by the French, English, and, most successfully, the Dutch. Christian converts had better access to European goods, and in particular after 1640 to guns, as well as receiving better prices for their furs. And Christian missionaries, who spread out farther than and preceded colonial settlers, were the major disease vector for the smallpox and influenza epidemics that halved (in some places wiped out entirely) the populations of the territories in which they operated. The pressures of economic dependency and mortality, and the transformation of productive activities among the Huron and Iroquois tribes (for example, from subsistence farming, fishing, tanning, and pottery to long-distance trapping expeditions and their support) combined to render spiritual matters of exceptional importance, and may well have stimulated a more than usual level of significant dreaming. This importance was experienced as practical and immediate, as well as a long-term issue of cultural survival. A sick woman in Huronia in 1639 who dreamed that she needed presents from everyone in the village could not be cured because the Jesuits, alone among the villagers, refused the blanket she had seen in her dream.[7]

At other times there have come, it is said, certain news that there has appeared in the woods a phantom of prodigious size, who bears in one hand ears of Indian corn, and, in the other, a great abundance of fish, who says that it is he alone who has created men, who has taught them to till the earth, and who has stocked all the lakes and seas with fish . . . and that . . . upon rendering him the honors which he deserves, he would increase both his love and his cares for them . . . He also said that to believe that any one of them was destined to a place of torments and to the fires . . . were false notions, with which, nevertheless, we [Jesuits] treacherously strive to terrify them.[8]

If his native informants and the Jesuit *Relations* offer Lafitau a literal "field of dreams," his own majestic *Moeurs des sauvages ameriquains* is itself readable as a dream, and a foundational one for the nascent discipline of anthropology.[9] Cultural historians have been considering the "imaginary" America of colonial explorers, missionaries, and ethnologists for some thirty years now, and we are possessed of something like a consensus as to the needs filled by the "*sauvages ameriquains.*" Michel de Certeau has investigated Lafitau himself as an imaginative crafter of the structure of the American territory of space-time, and I have analyzed the diplomatic, world-welding function of his excruciating collection of intra-Iroquois torture descriptions.[10] The practices of literary and cultural studies permit us to read any text, even or perhaps especially one that is not primarily a *representation*, as an interpretable dream. Indeed the very origins of our practice lie, earlier than the Midrashic commentary to which Hillis Miller credits it, in the oral deciphering activities of haruspication and dream reading (represented in the extremely ancient book of Genesis, itself put together from oral traditions, by Joseph's dream interpretations in the Egyptian pharaoh's court).

What kind of dream then, did Lafitau's synthesized collection of seventeenth-century Jesuit dreams about dreams bequeath to European study of culture—which for so long meant "other cultures"? As a serious figure in the *siècle des lumiéres*, with its ardent efforts to tame, regulate, and even repudiate the powers of imagination, did Lafitau have a monster or two to contribute from the sleep of his Cartesian reason? I take it as axiomatic that a Jesuit missionary to America, trained in the Ignatian spiritual exercises, would respond to the journey, the disorientation by change of place and diet, the long dark night of the soul of those solo winters, the sensualization of the imagination and, particularly for the martyrs, the "dismembering" of the sensorium, as to a literalization of his initial self-confrontation in seminary.[11] In his village outside of Montréal, Lafitau (like his predecessors) was in a "grotto," another world where the communally supported strictures of home were not available or even, to the people around him, conceivable: the kind of distant, isolating, and sacralized place to which members of ancient Mediterranean mystery cults would travel for "incubation," particularly when in need of healing.[12] The experience of the spiritual exercises is repeated in a literalized, externalized form, as for those Jesuits before him, but it is not overseen, nor encouraged through an absence of worldly stimulation. Ignatius in the sixteenth century knew about the New World, but did not perhaps imagine that world so *totaliter alter.*

For obvious reasons, the influences of Descartes and Ignatius, both of them important in the formation of Lafitau's thought, have not usually been seen as harmonious—the one devoting himself to the liberation of the human mind, especially in its quest for secular knowledge, from the occluding power of the imagination, and the other developing means to harness that same power in pursuit of a surer spiritual truth ("for it is not so much knowledge that fills and satisfies the soul, but rather the intimate feeling and relishing of things"[13]). On the other hand, there is a debate over whether one finds traces of Ignatius in Descartes—such as whole sentences in the *Notebooks* that are verbatim lines from the *Spiritual Exercises.* A recent article in *Critical Inquiry* by Matthew Jones argues against our finding those traces; he points out, however, that the *Geometry* appended to the *Discourse on Method* as a demonstration of the method and its intended function is—*explicitly* so—a set of spiritual exercises itself. Of the new geometrical tools offered there, Descartes says: "I stop before explaining all this in more detail, because I would take away . . . the utility of cultivating your *esprit* in exercising yourself with them, which is the key thing . . . one can [obtain] from this science."[14]

Trained in the Jesuit-formed disciplines both of Ignatius and Descartes (a graduate of the Jesuit college of La Flêche, which Lafitau also attended), Father Lafitau offers in his major work of comparative ethnology not only the readerly training in cross-cultural identification I've written about elsewhere, but more generally an anthropological discipline designed as yet another form of *spiritual discipline*: and this is indeed how many modern practitioners experience the lonesome craft of estrangement from familiar cultural surrounds in which an ethnography is incubated. I am not interested in early ethnology as yet another form of self-fashioning, but rather in the fact that imagination in its service is to be found at the root of modern disciplines that so highly value their egolessness and abstraction as to have forgotten, in theory, some of their original social function. Not every Repressed must return, or should return, but this is a big one. Theoretical ethnology is based on the written traces of fieldwork, and fieldwork is something isolated individual persons *do*, under conditions of high social stress and profound language barriers. A perfect setup for hysteria.

DESCARTES, JESUIT MISSIONARIES, AND HURON AND IROQUOIS DREAMING

Ils . . . me demandoient á quoy crois-tu donc, si tu ne crois pas a tes songes?

—Paul Le Jeune, 1634

The most interesting object on which to concentrate for my purposes is the treatment of dream, first because it is itself a message produced in the context of a profound language barrier, and because it is, potentially, the most solipsistic and incommunicable of all symbolic transactions. Hard to read, even for the dreamer, it becomes an extraordinary object of imaginative trade in the hands of a missionary from another world, and another language family! Second, the dream is interesting because it was, historically speaking, in the cultural home of the anthropologist, undergoing a severe reduction of authority, of epistemological status and of meaning, while in the Huron and Iroquois villages reported on by Jesuits in Quebec, Ontario, and New York, it was still understood as both divine and pragmatic. We might almost contrast the cultures in encounter here as "anthropology cultures" versus "sociétés á rêves," as the French say.[15] But finally because the dream, at least as far into the modern dispensation as the Jesuit-trained Descartes, is also a model for the experience of knowing (*vide*, e.g., the tradition of beginning a philosophical career with a revelatory dream), as is the image-obsessed meditation or reverie of Ignatius's *Spiritual Exercises*.[16]

Descartes' famous dream of 1619—actually three dreams in one night—belongs to the same half century as the American dreams recorded in the *Jesuit Relations*, on which Lafitau based his early eighteenth-century discussion.[17] Those dreams are the dreams of Huron, Ottawa,

Seneca, Montagnais, Iroquois, and sometimes Algonquin "sauvages," or what the French missionaries understood and reported as their dreams.[18] "There are superstitions in the old world as well as in the new," in the words of the most incurious and sarcastic of the Jesuits, the nonetheless intellectually active Paul Le Jeune, who lived among the Huron for many years, starting in 1632, and never evinced any attitude toward their culture but dismissive ridicule and fastidious distaste.[19] The dislike Le Jeune displays for the Hurons' deep conception of dreaming (something like Freud's conception—in contrast to Le Jeune's literalistic and indeed superstitious phobia) is one worth thinking about.[20] For the moment, though, it will be sufficient to note that the founder of modern epistemology, the man back in "old France" who produced an idea of thought that would permit a total break with religious and mythological cognition of the sort both the Huron and Le Jeune take refuge in, began his career with a career-shaping prophetic dream he considered important enough to write a tract about (the now-lost *Olympica*).[21]

The second of Descartes' three dreams, of a loud noise followed by a brilliant *éclarcissement* of many "seeds" ("étincelles") of light in his dark room, is the dream of most concern here.

> There came to him immediately a new dream, in which he believed he heard a sharp explosive noise, that he took for a peal of thunder . . . Eyes open he perceived many sparks of fire spread around the room. [During the interpretations Descartes says that] the bolt of which he heard the clang was the signal of the Spirit of Truth that descended upon him to possess him.[22]

This dream posits for the first time an image consistent throughout Descartes' writing career: the image of knowledge as a sudden flash or clang, an all-at-once weirdly reminiscent of mystical intuition (akin to the Neoplatonic "splendor"); this idea was free of what Matthew Jones describes as the fatal dependence on memory that made Descartes so scornful of contemporary (pre-algebraic) mathematics and geometric proofs.[23] The "clear and distinct perception" as obvious register of truth bespeaks the epistemological desire to know instantly and without mediation, the desire of the mind to move at the speed of light. For the dream-crazy phenomenologist of science Gaston Bachelard, the dream of flight is the quintessential dream because *motion* is the fundamental condition of the imagination: or, as a seventeenth-century English translation of Artimedorus' dream manual put it, "a dream is a *motion or fiction* of the soul."[24] And after all, the theatricalized presentation of Descartes' intuition of the *cogito* takes for its form a series, not of logical deductions, but of "meditations," performed over six days like the Creation. In this it mimics the *haeptamerae*, a Renaissance genre that organized, as commentary on the Genesis creation account, the presentation of all empirical knowledge of the natural or phenomenal world.[25] The parallels with both Creation and the traditional encyclopedic genre of natural knowledge might indicate, as does the account of his dream-induced *hammartia* in the lost *Olympia*, how strongly Descartes felt the power of imagination—to create, to "in-form" as well as to imprint.

For the seventeenth-century Jesuit missionaries, dreaming is linked to (true) religion negatively: according to Father Fremin, "The Iroquois have, properly speaking, only one Divinity—the dream," and according to Father Jean de Quens, "Dreams form one of the chief hindrances to their Conversion."[26] Dreams are what the Amerindians have *instead* of religion; they must be stopped, in order to make the all-important *tabula rasa* for conversion.[27] But in Iroquois and Huron understandings, the dream seems often to be a wish-fulfillment fantasy that directs dreamers to the medically necessary object of their hidden desire, which they will do anything to obtain.[28]

In the *Relations*, a major sign of success in the conversion process comes when the Native American person stops dreaming, or at least stops "believing" (and obeying) or narrating his or her dreams: of the important Mohawk elder Assendasé, one Jesuit writes, "On the day following his baptism, [he] gave a public feast, at which he declared to all the guests that he had renounced dreams";[29] a child convert complains to his novice father that "you . . . have sinned, for this morning you related a dream that you had during the night."[30] The Jesuits of the *Relations* routinely tell their superiors that they have "explained the truth about dreaming" to "these people," though that truth is never recapitulated.[31] We can certainly extrapolate from this moment in Catholic and European intellectual history the understanding that the supernatural guidance of pagan dreams was highly suspect, and the dreamers' moral freedom from dream compulsions considered much greater by the missionaries than by the Iroquois. But the interesting issues for me are the *meaning*—and the *capacity* for meaning—of dreaming, and its imaginary function in European constructions of the New World as "other world"—the Land Where Dreams Come True—and thus in the discipline of anthropology, born in fascination with both America and dreams.

BODY AND SOUL, FRANCE AND NEW FRANCE

Lafitau likens the Iroquois' belief in the transmigration of souls, as reported in the *Relations*, to Descartes' sense of the noninvolvement of body and soul, and praises them for it, going on immediately to laugh at them for believing that animals have souls as people do: "If they express themselves very much as Descartes does on the subject of man's soul," he says, "they are very far from thinking as he does about that of beasts"[32]— Descartes did not believe in the souls of animals (though, of course, Leibniz and other atomists did).[33] Lafitau finds the Iroquois and Huron practice of lucid dreaming, with its attendant beliefs, "absurde,"[34] but delivers them in indirect discourse as if he were passing on the truths that he claims (with Bossuet and Fénelon—not to mention Edward Tylor!) it is the main business of his nascent ethnology to make available: "people should study customs only in order to form customs. Everywhere there is something from which we can profit."[35]

Elsewhere I have paid particularly close attention to Lafitau's interest in the movable, indeed the *transportable* soul, which makes itself felt most forcefully in discussions of lucid dreaming and, especially, of torture; in discussions of torture, the word Lafitau uses for the Iroquois and Mohawk torturers and their audience is *furieux*, recalling the key seventeenth-century term for inspired imagination in French and Italian poetics and art theory, *furor*.[36] Unlike his seventeenth-century precursors in the missions, Lafitau was not deeply interested in the Christian conversion of the people among whom he had come to missionize. He emphasized especially their bigger and yet more parochial agenda—he wanted to prove, against the drift in France of theism, atheism, and libertine thinking, that the religious impulse *per se* was universal in humankind. His Mohawks, Iroquois, and Huron are the noblest of all noble savages; indeed, they are no more savage than Homer's heroes, to whom they are frequently compared and from whom Lafitau traces their lineage.[37] There is a drive in his gigantic tome to invoke not only admiration but empathy in his reader's imagination. He manages this most effectively (as I can attest from readerly marginalia) through quotation and elaboration of sensational passages of torture from the earlier Jesuit letters, during which victims taunt their captors and sing their "death songs" as their nerves are pulled out of their bodies and twisted on redhot iron bars.[38] He may not elicit full-fledged compassion from this technique, but he certainly gets fellow-feeling at the most visceral level. His excruciated Amerindians have become so many American Jesuses, and his European readers participate through identification in the *passio* of their death scenes. At the same time, the singing and taunting are evidence of the American singers' uncanny ability to dissociate from the adventures and constraints of the body.[39]

For all we know, bodily suffering—the unbearable damp chill of the Dutch winter in an unheated house—had something to do as well with Descartes' acts of dissociation in his almost Ignatian *Meditations* of

1641: the prerequisite imaginings preparing the way for the *cogito*. But his great bibliographer, Gregor Sebba, attributes the *cogito* to the work of the much earlier 1619 night of dreams: "He had to make a *tabula rasa*, he had to start with a clean slate, and this is not easily done."[40] The early seventeenth-century secular traveler Marc Lescarbot uses this same image, explaining that the Canadian Indian, who is without even idolatry, is closer to salvation, "being like a bare table, which is ready to receive what[ever] colour . . . one will give to it."[41] Sebba goes on:

The Descartes of the *Meditations* no longer knew as a living experience the darker, deeper strata of human existence; what mattered was knowledge, hardened into propositions that fulfilled the ineluctable demands of the physio-mathematico-philosophical mind that tolerates no contradiction. . . .

Long before Descartes arrived at the method for guiding the mind safely to certainty in all questions that the mind is capable of solving, the inner conflicts that could not be rationally solved were wiped off the slate without any conscious effort of his own. This is what he had expected to happen during the night of dreams and visions.[42]

Sebba interprets Descartes' dreams as delivering him from the burden of the unconscious, so that he could thenceforth live in a mind of pure rational cognition. I wonder if (unprovably) neoclassical and Enlightenment theologians and intellectuals in general were not indulging themselves in a dream of America that unburdened them through displacement of any sense of their own troubling unconscious (or uncontrolled image-making faculty), "the affliction of [Macbeth's] terrible dreams."[43] Certainly we have contributed to a sense of that as indeed the collective mental action going on, in coining terms like "the Sleep of Reason," writing books about "the return of the Repressed," and blaming the French Terrors on the Enlightenment. Perhaps when Goya told us that "the sleep of reason produces monsters," the monsters he referred to included European fantasies about native peoples of the Americas, imaged in the *Jesuit Relations* as great sleepers, great dreamers—and losers in every philosophical battle. (The bitter Paul Le Jeune signifies this incapacity by attributing to various Hurons with whom he has debated theology the defeated, if ambiguous, imprecation "Tu n'as point d'esprit," a suggestive wording in this context.[44])

The Jesuit missionaries, unlike many Franciscan Récollets, believed from the start in the full humanity of the Americans.[45] But given the long European history of conscious and unconscious attempts to dehumanize the natives of America in order to gain access to their lands and resources, it is possible to see that effort at work in the construction of the Indians of New France as ventriloquized puppets:

The *jongleur* . . . shook the tent at first without violence; then becoming animated little by little, he commenced to whistle in a hollow tone, and as if it came from afar; then to talk as if in a bottle; to cry like the owls of these countries . . . then to howl and sing . . . disguising his voice so that it seemed to me I heard those puppets which showmen exhibit in France.[46]

Despite the strong tendency toward dualism in Christian thought, its extreme forms remained and still remain heresy: the body whose resurrection spells the perfection of salvation must be one's own—a dimension of the profoundly personal soul, not a motel room.[47]

Lafitau's admiration for the Cartesian dualism of his potential converts hovers curiously close to the Manichean, the oldest and most dangerous heresy of all for a Christian theology and ritual born in the ecstatic culture of the Greek mystery cults. In his seventeenth-century Jesuit sources, this approval was not forthcoming, especially because the behavior of those in dream quests is so similar to the behavior of the intoxicated, and the two are similarly understood by Indian villages.[48] But Lafitau and his predecessors are very interested in the theatrics of Mohawk and Iroquois culture. In the 1650s, Pere Dablon, for instance, likens their dream rituals to European Carnival and the masquerade "des mauvais Chretiens."[49] As Descartes in the *Meditations* looked out his window and wondered if he saw robots passing on the street disguised by human clothing, so the Jesuits often seem to see Iroquois in ritual situations and scenes of public torture as bodies possessed by external spirits who wear and move them and even speak from within them instrumentally: "The foreign spirit appears to take possession of them in a palpable and corporeal manner and so to master their organs as to act in them immediately . . . It speaks from the depths of their chests thus causing the fortune tellers to be considered ventriloquists. It raises them up sometimes in the air or makes them greater than their real stature."[50]

It is very easy to see people animated by other cultural systems in this way. Indeed, ethnologists now finally turning to the study of their own cultures—for example, Bourdieu—are often led to see their own as similarly mechanized: ethnology is "from above." If Lafitau tends to write (albeit in the displacement of "indirect discourse") as though he *believes* that the Indian bodies are inhabitable by spirits not "their own," as though he believes that their "own" spirits can wander from them in sleep, he certainly does not believe this about Europeans; European witchcraft and its flying dreams are never even mentioned (although comparison and what Certeau calls "copulation" are the dominant structures of the work).[51] In the Europe of his text, it is only *jongleurs* and stage actors who can send their spirits elsewhere and open themselves to possession by an alien spirit—and then only the consciously produced "possession" of the performer's craft (with which Descartes was so fascinated in his later years).

These dreams and dream powers that Catholic Europeans by definition do not have include, along with the immortality Westerners cannot leave unthought: (1) the power of flying and crossing long distances out of the body—in his 1674 *Recherches de la verité*, Malebranche described witches who claimed this power as delusional; (2) both the power of *internal* seeing—knowing one's own desire (a major desideratum of the Ignatian exercises), and the power of *external* seeing—prophecy and prediction; (3) the power of direct, nonpriestly contact with the supernatural; and (4) the power, in some cases, of material causation itself.[52] The dreams even of regular, uninspired New World people are reported as having great consequence in the community: the Récollet friar Sagard tells this story from his journey among the Huron:

It happened that a sick woman dreamed that if the chief's cat had been given to her she would soon be cured. The chief was informed of this and immediately sent her his cat, although he was very fond of it and his daughter even more so; and when the latter saw herself bereft of the animal . . . she fell sick and died of regret . . . although she did not wish to fail in . . . helping her neighbor.[53]

The bitter amusement of many Jesuits at the "greedy" dreams of people who want a necklace or bracelet, even at the door of death,[54] seems a response to the triviality of object inspiring so potentially powerful and consequential an event of consciousness.

As I mentioned at the outset, a frequent, panicked comment about these powerful dreams of desire is that the Frenchmen live in daily fear of being wished dead in a dream, with fatal consequences: "If a savage dreams that he will die if he does not kill me, he will take my life the first time he meets me alone"; "our lives depend upon the dreams of a Savage."[55] Stranded and powerless, the early missionaries see powers in the people around them that they envy, and also fear. They postulate these powers into existence in written words, as their *relations* "stand in for" their personal presence in testimony; for the hierarchy back home (as well as the "pious donors" who supported their publication, and the anthropological theorists who use their texts), they *are* the world of Quebec. The missionaries may also be disoriented by living out what was meditative, imaginative, entranced in their initiation experience of Ignatius's "Exercises." This collective enactment is oddly mirrored in the habit reported by some of whole villages who will (prophylactically) act out wishfulfillment dreams of individuals whose wishes are dark or dangerous—especially cannibalistic dreams taken as foreboding the end of the world.[56] But their rather artificial sense of separateness from all this dream activity

is a part of the vexed transition in the history of European dreaming, often demonstrated in the *Jesuit Relations* by a bizarre inability to recognize and read metaphor or to recognize allegory. The missionaries learn
natural languages well, but seem deaf to what Lacan called, restrictively, the
"language of the unconscious." Lafitau's forefather, Descartes, can "read"
the metaphors of his dreams while inside the dream itself![57] Descartes' contemporary, Pére Le Jeune, on the other hand, after decades in Quebec, sees
Huron dreams only as false actualities, or scripts for actualities that will
be all too real.[58] Even the later Lafitau, in a somewhat less unpredictable
situation than Le Jeune, sees spirits *in* bodies rather than the bodies *of*
spirits.

Descartes' notion of a detachable soul contained in the vessel of the
body makes a nice fit with the Counter-Reformation cult of the Transubstantiation, the violently controversial doctrine that had Protestants accus-
ing Catholic Europeans of ritual cannibalism. In yet another example of
early modern displacements with regard to America, the model of the Eu-
charistic host is applied (implicitly) in the *Jesuit Relations*, and by Lafitau
in their wake, to the very Americans who, by the Spanish, had been almost
inversely imagined as eaters of ensouled Spanish bodies, and whom now
Jesuits were being "martyred" for trying to convert in New France. For
these educated Catholics, the doctrine of the Transubstantiation was making it more difficult than perhaps it was for the English Protestants Bacon
or Sprat to take metaphor metaphorically—and therefore to experience the
flight of fancy, the *motion* of thought, the *leap* of the imagination, without
a paralyzing fear.[59] With hindsight, and the privilege of our own distance
from certain literalisms of belief, it is nonetheless a fearful and sobering
thing to read this image from Le Jeune's account of Huron religious intox-
ication: "[The wife of the Manitou] has a robe made of the most beautiful
hair of the men and women she has killed; she sometimes appears like a
fire; she can be heard roaring like a flame, but her language cannot be understood" (*"elle a une robe des plus beaux cheveux des hommes et des
femmes qu'elle tue, elle paroist quelquefois comme un feu, on l'entend
bien bruire comme une flamme, mais on ne sçauroit distinguer son lan-
gage"*). We might remember that several Jesuits died in that fire, still unable to understand.[60]

What are the Indians of Quebec doing for the eighteenth-century missionary ethnologist Lafitau, in that historical moment Foucault once described as "the very moment Christian reason rid itself of the madness that
had so long been a part of itself" (which "folie" includes the sacred, the
holy)?[61] For this early eighteenth-century theorist, the dream is linked not
so much to the *practice* of Iroquois religion as to the theology and epistemology of American cultures: it is clustered in his book-length chapter on

"Religion" with treatments of divination, prophecy, and the soul, the soul's powers and destiny—a spiritual and cognitive psychology of the Other. Though the increasing loss of epistemological status of dreams in Europe can account in part for the distancing identification of *sauvage* American "sociétés à rêve," it participates in a culture-wide rejection of and fascination with metaphorical discourse and promulgation of enlightened criteria for belief.[62] How much does America itself, Land of Dreams Come True and potentially immense colonial resource, play a part in the fascinated and ambivalent European rejection of dream? How important had it become to educated Europeans to unread their own dreams, their own metaphors? One sees here a profound and elaborate wriggling: "madness" (and its ancient venue, religion) must now belong to the overimaginative and underrational world of Europe's deepest longings (utopian, economic, sexual, and epistemological). That way, Reason can, and should, master the continent and its destabilizing value. The science that emerged from the dynamics of colonial expansion—early anthropology—must then be a science of desire and dehumanization both. Who wishes is mad, who dreams is mad, whose imagination is powerful is mad. For Reason has reasons that the reason must know nothing about.

CHAPTER THIRTEEN

The Anthropology of Natural Law

Debates About Pufendorf in the Age of Enlightenment

Michael Kempe

To define the nature of man was one of the greatest projects of the Enlightenment. Man, for instance, was defined as a complex machine in the new mechanical philosophy, or as a *homo oeconomicus* in economy and politics. In several ways, "man" was reconceptualized in different sciences in the seventeenth and eighteenth centuries. This can be seen also in moral philosophy and jurisprudence. There, man was discovered in a new way as an object of natural law. I would like to show that *one* starting point of that discovery was the discussion concerning German scholar Samuel Pufendorf's theory of natural law. This discussion was one of the major disputes of scholars and intellectuals in Europe in the early Enlightenment, especially in Germany. It was mainly triggered by Pufendorf's definition of the nature of man, from which natural law was supposed to be derived. Pufendorf's definition, I argue, implied a manifold and multiform image of man and thus became the starting point for a controversial debate about the nature of man. This controversy over the anthropology of natural law revealed important aspects of early modern thought concerning the nature of a human and moral being.

The term "anthropology" does not refer to a specific scientific discipline; here it is taken more generally, as an analytical term to investigate different concepts of human nature that can be found in the basic assumptions of scientific theories. Concepts of human nature are cultural constructions. While in other scientific disciplines these constructions are often hidden or unarticulated, in the case of natural law they are the explicit objects of the theory. In this sense, the following analysis can be seen as an investigation into the anthropology of natural law in the early Enlightenment. I begin with an analysis of Samuel Pufendorf's theory of natural law and its anthropological basis. Then, I give some examples of how Pufendorf's theory of natural law was discussed in the early Enlightenment in Germany around 1700. Finally, I say a few words about how the anthropological concept of natural law was transformed in the translation of Pufendorf's theory by the French jurist Jean Barbeyrac. This translation brought Pufendorf's system of natural law to the broader public of the European and American Enlightenment.

PUFENDORF'S "PATCHWORK" ANTHROPOLOGY

With the strict separation of moral theology and natural law in *De jure naturae et gentium* (1672) and *De officio hominis et civis* (1673), Samuel Pufendorf claimed a new start in the tradition of natural law thinking.[1] The *ius naturae* was consequently to be developed as the origin of the law from the nature of man. It thereby referred more to the obligations than to the rights of man.[2] Pufendorf suggests the distinction of three scientific disciplines: (1) the science of natural law common to all people, (2) the discipline of positive rights of individual states, and (3) moral theology. In contrast to the other two disciplines, natural law, according to Pufendorf, was to be deduced entirely from the nature of man.

At the heart of the definition of man's nature lay the natural state theorem. The *status hominem naturalis* was considered according to three criteria: (1) in relation to God (*in ordine ad Deum Creatorem*), (2) in relation of the individual human beings to themselves (*in ordine singulorum hominum ad seipsos*), and (3) in relationship with other human beings (*in ordine ad alios homines*).[3] The natural state itself was characterized as a state of liberty and equality.[4] For Pufendorf, however, this state did not represent an empirical fact, but was—as something achieved by an abstraction—a hypothetical and universal fiction, which transcended all historical reality as a construction that was logically necessary.[5] Empirical material, as, for example, from travel stories about foreign peoples of the New World—such as "De originalibus americanis libri quator" (1652/1669) by George Horn or "Die Unbekannte Neue Welt" (The Unknown New World) (1673) by Arnoldus Montanus and Olfert Dapper—was not considered as a proof, but only as contributions for the observation of human nature. In order to achieve a general, irreducible definition of man, Pufendorf, like Thomas Hobbes, used the geometrical method from contemporary natural science.[6] With the help of this procedure, he at first arrived at a result similar to that of Hobbes, and diagnosed *amor sui*, that is, self-love, and its corollary self-preservation, as a central characteristic of human nature.[7] This human nature represents the *statum hominem* after the Fall of Man. Pufendorf thus contradicted the Protestant doctrine, which sought to deduce natural law from the nature of man *before* the Fall of Man. As another feature, Pufendorf indicated *imbecillitas*, the weakness and distress of man.[8] Furthermore, according to Pufendorf, man also possessed an inclination to harm others, to maliciousness, which was even greater than that of wild animals.[9] He finally diagnosed the capacity for self-perfection, that is, *nobiliores facultates*, as a specific characteristic of man.[10] *Entia moralia* and *entia physica* differentiated two kinds of existence, thus differentiating man from animals.

This "mosaic" or "patchwork" anthropology reflected Pufendorf's methodological eclecticism, which combined different philosophical traditions and which—apart from the mathematical-geometrical method—also brought aspects of the history of moral philosophy to the explanatory structure of natural law. In relation to the Protestant anthropology of original sin, however, here a crucial shift of emphasis took place. Although Pufendorf presupposed the fallen state of man, he stressed human frailty and weakness rather than sinfulness and moral depravity. In contrast to Luther, Pufendorf also had greater confidence in the cognitive capacity of postlapsarian man. He rejected at the same time a derivation of natural law from the *status integritatis* of prelapsarian man, as postulated by Valentin Alberti from Leipzig in his orthodox Protestant doctrine of natural law. As Pufendorf rejected such a derivation, the binary anthropology of the theological natural law was removed from a timescale and was thus detemporalized. Natural law was not to be referred to the past state of man, as it was before the Fall of Man, but rather referred to man in his present condition, as he actually was. The contingency of the present became the starting point for the explanation of natural law. Thus, removing natural law from the connection of theology really meant the separation of anthropology from sacred history—which provoked a storm of indignation among Protestant theologians from the 1670s onward; and Pufendorf remained the subject of controversy for many years.

In the center of Pufendorf's multifaceted anthropology were the characteristics of *amor sui* or *conservatio sui* as well as *imbecillitas*. From them, Pufendorf deduced the principle that man in order to survive must lead a life in community (*necessum esse, ut sit sociabilis*).[11] Thus, *socialitas*, with its anthropological implications, was the centerpiece of Pufendorf's definition of human nature. From this principle, the basic rule of natural law was derived. Here the formula *colendam et servandam esse socialitatem*, signifying the cultivation and preservation of sociability, formed the fundamental standard of natural law.

In contrast to the Aristotelian *zoon politicon* or the Grotian *appetitus societatis*, Pufendorf did not understand *socialitas* as an ultimate *telos* of nature or an actual characteristic, but as a necessary disposition in behavior, which only correlatively resulted from the natural condition of man. This approach united the central theorems of natural law by Thomas Hobbes and Hugo Grotius and at the same time—originally—combined them in such a way that they result in a new theorem. By attributing sociability to *amor sui* and *imbecillitas*, Pufendorf contradicted Hobbes's view that individual self-preservation and self-interest would exclude any sociability, and at the same time Pufendorf contradicted Grotius's assumption that *socialitas* was a natural faculty or impulse. Thus, the controversy—still ongoing in recent research[12]—over whether Pufendorf was a pupil of Hobbes may be answered: yes and no. As Pufendorf's anthropology of natural law did not offer simple clarity, it stimulated further controversies over the nature of man within the debates on natural law. Especially because of its underlying multidimensional image of man, Pufendorf's doctrine of natural law offered enough friction for disagreement and thus sufficient encouragement for further theoretical discussions on natural law.

THE GERMAN DEBATE ABOUT PUFENDORF

At the end of the seventeenth and beginning of the eighteenth century, we can observe in Germany a great debate about Pufendorf's *socialitas* as the basic principle of natural law. Many of the numerous interventions that argued critically, as well as affirmatively, over Pufendorf's theory of natural law were written as academic theses, as dissertations (also called disputations). An early example was the disputation thesis by Jacob Thomasius, "De societatis civilis statu naturali ac legali," published in Leipzig in 1670.[13] Thomasius was one of Pufendorf's teachers.[14] The fact that this dissertation was republished in 1675 makes clear that the text was not only prepared for a certain occasion but also addressed to a larger public. Furthermore, the republication, including detailed notes, increased the length of the work substantially from eighteen to twenty-eight pages.[15] In a comparison of the two editions, it appears that an important shift of the anthropological premises occurred under the influence of Pufendorf's concept of *socialitas*. The thesis, which—by referring to Grotius—dealt mainly with the relationship of the *status naturalis* and the *status legalis* in politics, began with a definition of man: "*Homo per naturam aptum animal est ac destinatum ad societatem.*" The definition of man as an animal equipped from nature and destined for society still clearly referred to a teleological term of human nature with an Aristotelian character.

This definition was slightly modified by a few words in the second edition; while the meaning, however, was modified in a crucial way. Here, we can read: "*Homo per naturam fertur et aptus est ad societatem.*"[16] This was annotated with a detailed argument in reference to Pufendorf's writings on natural law against the thesis of Hobbes, that is, against the assumption that man in his natural state was unsociable, egoistic, and warlike. Thus, by referring to Pufendorf's concept of *socialitas*, and by the omission of the words *animal* and *destinatum*, the classical Aristotelian position was clearly modified. The derivation of the natural law, though, remained unaffected by the reorientation of the anthropological background since Jacob Thomasius—like Pufendorf's main theological opponent, Valentin Alberti—attributed the *ius naturae* not to *socialitas*, but to the *status integritatis* of man before the Fall of Man. Most important, however, was that Pufendorf with his concept of sociability became the main authority for Jacob Thomasius in rejecting Hobbes's thesis of *bellum omnium contra omnes*.

The reception of the Pufendorf theorems in relation to Hobbes was evident—this time the other way round—in the dissertation "De Socialitate, Primo Naturalis Juris Principio," published by Johann Nicolaus Hertius in 1694.[17] It had not escaped Hertius's attention that Pufendorf came dangerously close to Hobbes by attributing *socialitas* also to the necessity for self-preservation. Hertius, on the other hand, derived *socialitas* from the natural *cognatio*, the kinship between human beings, and referred to Richard Cumberland, who had already argued in this way against Hobbes in his own work on natural law.[18]

The Leipzig philosopher Immanuel Proeleus, in his dissertation "De Origine diversorum Juris Naturalis principiorum" of 1703, took up the issue of whether obligations to God and to one's own self could be derived directly from the principle of sociability. Although he approved of Pufendorf's *jus naturae methodo mathematica*, he was also indebted to Hobbes's anthropological premises. Later, in the work "Grund-Sätze Des Rechts der Natur Nebst einer kurtzen Historie und Anmerckungen über die Lehren Des Hrn. Barons von Pufendorf" (General Principles of the Law of Nature Together with a Short History and Notes on the Theories of Baron von Pufendorf) of 1709, Proeleus resumed this line of reasoning, and did use, at least to a certain extent, Pufendorf's explanations to return to Hobbes's *conservatio sui*, which was now explained as the first actual *principium juris Naturae*.[19] For Proeleus, however, unlike Hobbes, this did not result in social pessimism. In the course of this reinterpretation, self-preservation could be made socially acceptable as an ethical principle. Legal dissertations on self-preservation as the basic principle of natural law were published in Wittenberg in 1682 and 1687, as well as in Tübingen in 1707 and in Giessen in 1742.

Within the anthropological model of human nature, Pufendorf brought about a shift of emphasis. While this shift of emphasis only concerned a readjustment of the balance between sociability and self-preservation, this relation was radically challenged in the dissertation "Status naturalis Hobbesii in Corpore Iuris Civ. defensus et defendendus" of 1706 by Nicolaus Hieronymus Gundling.[20] Gundling's teacher, Christian Thomasius, son of Jakob, had already questioned the relevance of Pufendorf's principle of sociability as the basis of a comprehensive doctrine of obligation, because of the separation of law and ethics. In that version, approximately since 1700, Thomasius had given up the principle of "reasonable love" in favor of a more pessimistic anthropology. Gundling, even more radical in his conclusions than Thomasius, also limited natural law to the standard of compulsory social behavior. Sociability was an illusion, and only national obligation made men into socio-compatible human beings. Wherever possible, one should aim for peace, but be ready for war, argued Gundling, with a clear affinity to Hobbes's *bellum omnium contra omnes*. Thereby the way was smoothed for adopting Hobbes more readily, as, for instance, in the dissertations of Johann Heinrich Hombergk von Vach, "Pacem et societatem hvmani generis natvra constitvtam ex ipsis principiis T. Hobbii probatam" (1722), and of Gottlieb Sturm, "Hobbesivs Socialis, hoc est de genvino principio ivris natvralis hobbesii" (1724).

Thus, the Pufendorf debate provided shelter for an intensive discussion about Hobbes. This was made possible by the peculiar tension between sociability and self-preservation in Pufendorf's definition of man's nature: a tension that provoked controversial reactions, rejections, and agreements. One could argue, for instance, *with* Pufendorf *against* Hobbes, like Jacob Thomasius, or *against* Pufendorf's Hobbesian affinities, like Hertius; one could change *from* Pufendorf *to* Hobbes, like Proeleus, or favor Pufendorf *instead of* Hobbes, like Gundling. So Pufendorf's anthropology became more and more a "filter" and "transmitter" of Hobbes's theorems. By mediating Hobbes's concept of self-love, Pufendorf's theory of natural law softened and neutralized the classical Christian verdict on *amor proprius* as a vice. At the same time, self-love—as shown in Gundling's example— could be reestablished as a negative term in the context of a secular, socio-pessimistic anthropology of natural law.

The debate about Pufendorf's *socialitas* rapidly turned into a broad controversy. The dissertations offered a suitable medium for these disputes. Here Pufendorf's supporters as well as opponents expressed themselves and exchanged views; here, the controversial positions encountered one another. Pufendorf's supporters were later also called "socialists."[21] Within their camp there were quite a number of differences. Thus, it remained disputed, for example, whether or not polygamy offended the principle of sociability. More radical critics of the principle of *socialitas*, like Proeleus, argued in particular that not all three circles of obligation (God, Self, neighbor) could be derived from *one* principle. Johann Franz Budde suggested formulating these three basic principles according to their three objects: to honor God, to live moderately, to live socially (*DEUM cole, temperanter vive, socialiter vive*).[22] Others put forward the objection that these principles would contradict or compete with one another. Meanwhile, Heinrich Ernst Kestner, professor of jurisprudence in Rinteln, absolutely objected to *socialitas* in his disputation thesis "Ius naturae et gentium, ex ipsis fontibus Ad ductum Grotii, Pufendorffii et Cocceji Derivatum."[23] He said that a principle in which the unchanging natural law emphasized social use would be too indefinite, that is, too variable in the long run, because what society needed today could be harmful at other times.[24] Kestner consistently rejected a derivation of the *ius naturae* of the intelligible or material sphere of human existence. Following Heinrich and Samuel Cocceji, he attributed natural law to divine will alone. Embedding natural law in the will of God, that is, reverting to a theistic voluntarism, could also be understood as a reaction to the unsatisfactory efforts to derive basic principles from the nature of man in order to explain natural law.

There were many publications that sought to discover a first principle of natural law; among them were dissertations with titles such as "De primo principio legis naturalis" or "De principio primo iuris naturalis."[25] Because of all the different competitive approaches, it was not long before fundamental criticism arose as to whether one could methodically deduce natural law from one universal basic principle. Such a methodologically fundamental criticism was found in the thesis of Johann Ernst Philippi, "Proton pseudos circa principium iuris naturae" published in Halle in 1731.[26] Most, if not all *Doctores Juris naturalis*—whom Philippi divided into *Puffendorfianos, Anti-Puffendorfianos,* and *Philosophos Eclecticos*—would decide in favor of a *Principium Juris Naturae* as *propositionem quandam unicam generalem*, under which all remaining *leges naturales* could be summarized. The criteria that should be fulfilled by primary principles according to deductive logic, were *verum, primum, unicum, adaequatum, et evidens*, as, for example, in Johann Joachim Heinrich Sibrand's "Disputatio Circularis, exhibens Problema Morale" of 1703.[27]

Philippi, however, accused the doctors of natural law of simply stating the fundamental proposition without proof by argumentation, in order to be able to derive from it all other propositions of the *ius naturae* as they wished. The foundation of natural law would then be only a fiction. Philippi mockingly designated all those who proceeded from such a *primum falsum suppositum* as the *Supponentos*, the ones who attribute or suppose falsely.

Philippi mentioned the second edition of Johann Lorenz Fleischer's "Institutiones juris naturae et gentium" in 1730. Fleischer's basic principle was that men would do whatever was necessary for a long and happy life, and avoid whatever made life unfortunate and brought death. This principle was now dismantled by Philippi in a detailed analysis of its inadequacy as a deductive axiom. Philippi's critical analysis made clear that the controversy over the anthropological basis of natural law, which had been sparked by Pufendorf, had now opened up a controversy over the *primum principium*, and finally over methodological matters in general. The later criticism of natural law in the high Enlightenment was already partly anticipated in Philippi's dissertation. At the same time, the efforts to establish a sound and coherent image of man as the firm ground of natural law had collapsed.

PUFENDORF AND THE FRENCH ENLIGHTENMENT

Besides the debate in the German dissertations, the discussion was also continued in the comments and annotations of the many editions of Pufendorf's two major works on natural law. After all, these works experienced an outstanding publishing history in Europe. Up until the beginning of the nineteenth century, "De jure naturae et gentium" was republished in forty-three editions and "De officio hominum et civis" in one hundred fifty editions. Most of the published editions of the eighteenth century were supplemented by annotations and comments. Among the most famous commentators were Jean Barbeyrac (1674–1744) and Gershom Carmichael (1672–1729).

Barbeyrac was a French Protestant who immigrated in 1685 to Berlin, where he translated "De jure naturae et gentium" and "De officio hominis et civis" in several editions in French. These French editions led to a broad dissemination of Pufendorf's ideas about natural law all over Europe. Barbeyrac supplemented his translations with detailed and comprehensive commentaries in many footnotes. These commentaries were also reproduced in many other editions during the eighteenth century, for instance, in the English translations. Carmichael, predecessor of Francis Hutchinson as professor of moral philosophy in Glasgow, edited "De officio hominis et civis" in 1718 and 1724, adding many annotations and supplements of his own.[28] In this way, he brought Pufendorf's theory into the Scottish Enlightenment. The commentaries were praised by many and sometimes even preferred to the text itself. Many other editions and translations also included these annotations, commenting on the commentators. Sometimes the main text was overwhelmed by the huge mass of footnotes that constituted a special medium of communication about Pufendorf and his commentators. For instance, Carmichael and Barbeyrac established an ongoing dialogue in this little universe of footnote commentaries on Pufendorf.

The activities of Barbeyrac as an editor of the works of Pufendorf, as well as the works of Grotius, were more than mere commentary and translation. In his long supplementary footnotes, the French theorist of natural law began a conversation with Pufendorf (and Grotius). From the perspective of Barbeyrac, the theory of Pufendorf represented a synthesis of Grotius and Hobbes, and in Barbeyrac's commentaries, Grotius and Pufendorf were integrated as complementary perspectives. In the words of Giulia Maria Labriola: "We may conclude, on this point, by observing that if, for Barbeyrac, Pufendorf was the author of the only possible synthesis between Grotius and Hobbes, so in our opinion Barbeyrac seeks to present himself as he who makes possible a synthesis between Grotius and Pufendorf."[29]

Central, however, to the annotations of the commentators like Barbeyrac or Carmichael was the discussion of the anthropological premises of natural law. While Carmichael maintained that *socialitas* was not subordinated to self-love, Barbeyrac criticized Pufendorf's ambivalent view of Hobbes, especially his affirmation of the Hobbesian state of nature as a state of war. In the second chapter of "De jure naturae et gentium," Pufendorf wrote: "Hobbes has been lucky enough in painting the Inconveniences of such a State [that is, the state of nature] . . . To conclude, out of Society we have the Tyranny of Passions, War, Fear, Poverty, Filthiness, Barbarity, Ignorance, and Wilderness."[30] In his footnotes on this passage, Barbeyrac argued against Pufendorf's reception of the Hobbesian idea of the *status naturae*: "This is founded upon the false Hypothesis of Mr. Hobbes, that A State of Nature is a State of War."[31]

On the other hand, however, Barbeyrac picked up Pufendorf's concept of natural religion as a universal religion by *ratio*. The idea of overcoming confessional borders by establishing republican virtue on a common religious foundation that was based on the *religio naturalis* gave Barbeyrac, as an exiled Huguenot, the decisive link to connect Pufendorf's theory of natural law with his own concept of tolerance. Besides the concept of natural religion, Pufendorf's principle of *socialitas* was important to Barbeyrac for imagining a society that would be held together more by underlying principles of human sociability than by religious loyalties, so that the coexistence of religions would not affect the secular integrity of the state. Thus, Pufendorf's system of natural law in "De officio hominis et civis" was—in the words of Tim Hochstrasser—"particularly useful here as an account of how such a society, premised on a basic principle of sociability, had historically emerged, and would now function."[32] In this way, Barbeyrac transformed Pufendorf's theory of natural law into a theory of society based on the idea of religious tolerance. Moreover, Barbeyrac's theory was reconceptualized in the liberal political theory that was further developed by his school of natural law in Lausanne ("Westschweizer Natur-rechtsschule"), in particular by Jean-Jacques Burlamaqui and Emmerich de Vattel during the eighteenth century. Finally, through the mediation of the Calvinist Louis de Jaucourt, Barbeyrac's theory of natural law entered into the heart of the French Enlightenment, in the *Encyclopédie*.[33] Pufendorf's theory of natural law, based on an anthropological concept of human nature in relation to society and sociability, thus powerfully influenced the basic assumptions of the anthropology of the Enlightenment.

CHAPTER FOURTEEN

"Animal Economy"

Anthropology and the Rise of Psychiatry from the 'Encyclopédie' to the Alienists

Philippe Huneman

Physiologists in the eighteenth century often made use of the phrase *économie animale* or "animal economy." This came to denote a very precise scheme in the vitalistic context, widely spread by the vitalist physicians of the *Encyclopédie*—among them, Ménuret de Chambaud (1733–1815), Henri Fouquet (1727–1806), and the Chevalier de Jaucourt (1704–79). This scheme supplanted both the old vision of the living creature as composed of a body and a soul—and the Hippocratic humoristic tradition of the soul-body unity in medicine. It yielded a structured research program, based on an anthropological view of man in his milieu, and led to a new conception of mental illness. The first psychiatrists, or "alienists," Philippe Pinel (1745–1826) and Jean-Etienne Dominique Esquirol (1772–1840), were well aware of animal economy, which to some extent enabled them to conceive madness as an illness, characterized by a specific etiology and a specific cure, called moral treatment (*traitement moral*).

SENSIBILITY AND "ANIMAL ECONOMY"

We cannot establish a precise meaning of "animal economy," since in most medical schools—Boerhaavian, Hallerian, or Scottish—it was used with reference to the particular organism. But in some of these traditions, it encompassed a research program in the life sciences—this was the case in French vitalism, and in English and Scottish physiology, after the middle of the century.[1] The main vitalistic thesis, first formulated by Louis de Lacaze (1703–65; *Idée de l'homme au physique et au moral*, 1755) and Théophile de Bordeu (1722–76; *Recherches sur les glandes*, 1751), asserted that life was essentially the "sensibility" of the fibers that constituted the organism. For Bordeu, each organ possessed its own sensibility, hence its "particular life," the life of the organism being the sum of all these lives— which was called an "animal economy"—the term "economy" here really denoting a collection of individual entities.[2] The eighteenth century witnessed a major dispute over the essential life properties: the French vitalists contested the Hallerian thesis, equating life with irritability, and reducing sensibility to a property of the nerves.

This debate developed in a Newtonian framework: Newtonian method, for all these scientists, consisted of defining an irreducible property (for example, gravity) and then explaining phenomena by writing the laws of this property's manifestation. The question was then: which properties were essential to life? Vital properties were something paradigmatic in Enlightenment physiology, with its so-called Newtonian methodology.[3] Of course, the debate on their real nature persisted throughout the century. And as late as in Crichton's *Inquiry into the Nature and Origin of Mental Derangement* (1798), or in Bichat's *Recherches physiologiques sur la vie et la mort* (1801), we find a discussion of the relationships between irritability and sensibility, and the possibility of reducing one to the other. However, due to the wide diffusion of Montpellierian vitalism, French physicians and physiologists were often committed to Bordeu's sensibility monism. A typical discussion of the irritability-sensibility controversy can be found in Lordat's dissertation:[4] the word "sensibility" did not have the same meaning for Haller (for whom it meant the transmission of the impression to the sentient principle) and for the vitalists (for whom it meant the organ's capacity for impression)—but, as the transmission supposed the organ's receptivity, the two sides in the debate, in fact, discussed two related sorts of sensibility.[5]

"Animal economy" gained a more precise meaning in English physiology. A major preoccupation in this tradition was the distribution and effects of the nervous system. William Cullen (1712–90), for instance, tried to substitute his "nervous power" for Hallerian irritability. For him, sensibility and irritability excluded each other, since receiving an impression implied a *weakness* of the nervous power, though to propagate the impression required *strength* of nervous power.[6] This universal causal role of nervous power yielded the famous thesis that "almost all diseases considered from a certain point of view could be called nervous."[7] This explained the importance of nervous problems, which, under the newly forged title "neurosis," became one of the Cullenian classes of illness.

However, two major sources of this "nervous" physiology were Robert Whytt's *Essay on the Vital and Other Involuntary Motions of Animals* (1751) and George Cheyne's famous *English Malady* (1733). By establishing an identity between the living principle and the nervous influence,[8] Whytt not only played a role in the genesis of the concept of reflex,[9] but also contributed to focusing the physician's attention on the links between nervous troubles and madness. Here we find the idea of vaporous illnesses,[10] first worked out by Bernard Mandeville;[11] in France, there followed the work of Pomme[12] and Beauchesne.[13] This notion carried a manifest social component, since vaporous diseases were known to occur among people who did not have to earn their livings, such as scholarly men or aristocratic women.

However, *économie animale*, for the French physiologists, was less a concept than a scheme used to understand the phenomenon of life; therefore, it covered a research program that Ménuret's definition in the *Encyclopédie* can help us to grasp. "This name, taken in the most common and most exact meaning, concerns only order, mechanism, and the whole of the functions and movements that sustain the life of animals, whose perfect exercise . . . constitutes the most flourishing state of *health*, and whose least disturbance is in itself illness, and finally whose entire cessation is the diametric opposite of *life*, i.e. death."[14] An "economy" implies order and exchanges among parts. Such exchanges were ensured by the sensibility inherent in each part. According to Bordeu's model in the *Recherches sur les glandes*, each living fiber had its own way of being sensitive to some particular substances, and this kind of discriminative power created a circulation of fluids throughout the body. But, extended to the whole organism, this model encouraged the search for the "sympathies" linking distant parts of the body, such as the vocal and genital organs during puberty.

Looking for sympathies was the first part of "animal economy" as a vitalistic research program. Although those sympathies were often connected with nerves, they were not identical with nervous connections, as Beauchesne explained it.[15] This was a consequence of the principle that sensibility was more than just nerves.[16] The great nosologist François Boissier de Sauvages (1706–67), who firmly defended vitalistic teaching at the University of Montpellier, from the 1740s, and whose fame contributed to the diffusion of the doctrine, emphasized the correlation between sympathies and *économie animale*: "Hence we see that laws of sympathies that, according to many people, are mere empty names, are in fact properties conforming to reason, and according to which the motor powers, such as nature and freedom, operate in animal economy."[17]

The second part of the program consisted in identifying the main centers of this economy. Following Ménuret, who based his article on Lacaze's and Bordeu's works, there were three centers, ruled by the "universal law of action and reaction": (1) the gastric center (that is, the diaphragm and other organs placed around it); (2) the head—center of the nervous system; and (3) the skin, called *organe extérieur*, which constituted the external milieu of the organism.

Ménuret, writing about the head, claimed that it must be "seen as an organ immediately altered by the affections of the soul, the sensations, the passions" ("considérée comme organe immédiatement altéré par les affections de l'ame, les sensations, les passions").[18] For this reason, "animal economy" was both a medical and a psychological concept, because it dealt with the human organism as a whole, with a psychic as a well as an organic life. Bordeu's sentient principle, invested in the scheme of an animal economy, avoided a dualistic schema of the living thing as a complex of body and soul. Medicine was not by nature dualistic, since the Hippocratic tradition emphasized the equilibrium of humors as the definition of health with no commitment to any action of a soul; this new medicine thus inherited the critique of humoralist medicine by mechanists and iatrochemists, and therefore could not mean, by its rejection of dualism, the same thing as a Hippocratic humoralist holism. Moreover, by identifying the organic sensation of the organ, and the psychic sentiment or feeling of the mind, animal economy could serve as the foundation for the project of the "natural history of man," that is, an *anthropology* treating man "au physique et au moral"—according to Cabanis's famous locution, which was the title of his major work in this field. The science of the soul (moral) and the science of the body (medical) dissolved, making way for an integrated anthropology of man. The fundamental novelty in this emerging program was that an affective element, such as a passion, was no longer seen as acting on humors—facilitating or restraining their motion—but shared the same sensitive nature as the organic elements. Like money for political economy, sensibility or sensitivity was a general force, within a whole economy, and the psychical or physical nature of the economic instances was less significant than their transcription as sensibility.

ILLNESS AND MADNESS IN THE ANTHROPOLOGY
OF ANIMAL ECONOMY

Animal economy inspired new conceptions of disease, and implied new consequences for medical care. According to Boissier, the understanding and classification of symptoms presupposed an inquiry into sympathies.

"Since nothing occurs without sufficient reason, it must be one which implies that some symptoms concur, i.e. co-exist . . . This reason is nothing else than the connection of organs affected by the illness."[19] In this schema, the cause of disease could be either psychical or physical, because the essence of disease was a perturbation of the economy, with its circulating sensibility. Thus, Beauchesne wrote that, in a *maladie vaporeuse*, "the defect of an organ, produced by any moral or physical cause, acts powerfully enough on the nerves to change the order of their usual sensibility."[20] Fevers, according to Pinel's *Nosographie*, were determined in the same way: "A sequence of physical or moral causes, coming from outside or developed inside, can concur in producing fevers."[21] The cure did not have to be alternatively either physical or moral, because restoring a healthy and functional state of the economy meant creating new conditions of sensibility, hence acting on any sensible element: whether the passions or the mind, whether thirst or temperature.

Physicians of the Enlightenment wrote many treatises on the mental etiology and therapeutics of ideas, as well as on the physical therapeutics of mental problems. In France, Tissot published in 1798 *De l'influence des passions de l'âme dans les maladies*. Acknowledging the duality of any therapeutics, and the organismic sense of passion as an affect of the sentient fiber, Tissot sought remedies for the negative influence of passions on diseases, and ways to support their healthy effect, as in the case of joy. In spite of professing a dualistic metaphysics, and believing in the "animal spirits," his project and his method clearly made use of the "animal economy" scheme. When an etiology was unknown, he suggested examining whether "there is any extraordinary incursion of the soul which sustains the disorder of the functions."[22] A few years earlier, Antoine Le Camus established a symmetrically corollary program:[23] medicine should know both minds and bodies, so that it may know how to perfect the mind by acting on the body. Although phrased in terms of the dualism of Descartes and Malebranche, the conception of medicine and use of therapeutics, for Le Camus, belonged to the anthropology of "animal economy."[24] His and Tissot's views were strictly complementary. In England, at the same period, John Gregory's *Comparative View of the State and Faculties of Man with Those of the Animal World* (Edinburgh, 1777) endorsed a similar kind of medical anthropology.[25] In his program, medical knowledge of the "animal economy" was to be brought together with the new science of the mind, or psychology of ideas, first developed by Locke, then by Hume and Hartley.[26]

Passions, in the context of the animal economy, were etiologically and therapeutically relevant. They could either provoke a disease, or help or delay its cure. Raimond Laroque's dissertation was entitled *De l'influence des passions sur l'économie animale considérée dans les quatre âges de la vie* (Montpellier, an VI [1797–1798]), and G. Royer's dissertation, in Paris (1803), had this title: *De l'influence des passions considérées sous le rapport médical.* In the English-speaking medical world, William Falconer published at the same time *The Influence of Passions on the Disorders of the Body* (1788). Tissot's work was just one element in a wide medical literature devoted to the role of the passions, which was slowly being passed from the moralists to the physicians. According to Laroque, each period of life had its peculiar passions,[27] which during puberty constituted a "radical change (*bouleversement*) of the laws of animal economy."[28] So, by following the sympathies, one could understand how passions caused diseases.[29] Of course, Esquirol's thesis, *Des passions*,[30] would be supported by this tradition, which saw passions no longer as effects upon the soul, but as phenomena of animal economy caught in a general circulation of impressions and affections.

THE EQUIVOCAL STATUS OF MADNESS IN THE *ENCYCLOPÉDIE*

The articles dealing with mental illness in the *Encyclopédie* represented the vision of madness in this anthropological and medical tradition at the middle of the century. In this work, multiple approaches to madness coexisted, without any attempt to synthesize them. The entries included *folie, manie, mélancolie, fureur, démence, phrénésie,* and *délire.*

There was some contrast between *folie (morale)* and *folie (médecine)* by d'Aumont, and *manie* by Ménuret. Only the latter was presented in the animal economy scheme. In the article "Folie (morale)," d'Aumont acknowledged an essential relativity in the concept of madness, which prevented it from being seen as real illness. Madness meant to depart from reason—not consciously, as a "slave of a violent passion" (this would be "weakness")—but "confidently and, firmly persuaded that one is following reason." People locked up in hospitals seemed, then, to have "a less common sort" of madness—lunacies that "do not fit with social order" ("elles n'entrent pas dans l'ordre de la société").[31] D'Aumont was skeptical about the etiology of madness: "Madness seems sometimes to stem from an alteration of the soul, communicated to the body's organs; sometimes from perturbation of the body's organs, which influence the soul's operation: this is difficult to separate (*démêler*). No matter which is the cause, the effects are the same." Consequently, the classical dual division of madness between a "moral" and a "physical" aspect was of no validity. Madness was essentially an excess ("every excess is madness"). This vocabulary of "excess" pervaded the whole literature on madness; here it suggested that madness depended upon a point of view.[32] D'Aumont subscribed to the Christian relation between lunacy and wisdom: what seemed mad to the world could be reasonable to the wise man. The world was insane: the order of society was a "combination of human madness," such that madness "enters into the order of society." Pascal conceived something similar: "Les hommes sont si nécessairement fous que c'est être fou d'un autre tour de folie que d'être sage." Men are so inevitably mad that to be wise would be to give a mad twist to madness.[33]

The article "Folie (morale)" was followed by "Folie (médecine)." D'Aumont here presented madness as "a species of lesion in the animal functions."[34] Madness was compared to mania, melancholia, and delirium. The classification was not strict, and in the whole *Encyclopédie* it was difficult to trace a real classification of mental illnesses. D'Aumont distinguished delirium and phrenesia, the latter being accompanied by fever; this was the classical distinction of *mania* and *phrenesis*, inherited from ancient medicine. But, while the first article on "moral madness" insisted on the importance of "excess," this one on "medical madness" stated that madness was "a depravation of the thinking faculty." Depravation and excess were the two main dimensions of an ancient, nonmedical conception of madness.

In the *Encyclopédie*, in the articles "Mélancolie" and "Manie," Ménuret offered a somewhat different conception of madness, sharply marked by the scheme of animal economy. This was evident in the article "Mélancolie":

Considering all those observations, and the most ordinary causes of this illness, one would be close to believing that all of its symptoms are most of the time excited by some defect in the lower stomach (*bas-ventre*), mostly in the epigastric region. It is likely that here lie usually the immediate causes of *melancholia*, and that the brain is only sympathetically affected; to be convinced that some disturbance in those parts can excite a melancholic delirium, one has only to pay attention to the simplest laws of animal economy, and to remember that those parts are pervaded by a great quantity of extremely sensitive nerves, to consider that their lesion induces trouble and disorder within the whole machine, sometimes followed by death . . . and finally, to know that the bearing and influence of the epigastric region upon the rest of the body, and principally on the head, is very considerable.[35]

Here, the French physician Ménuret made use of the same concepts as William Cullen, the Scottish adherent of "animal economy" medicine, who wrote in the opening of his *Lectures in the Materia Medica*: "Nothing affects more the mind than the state of the stomach, and nothing induces more the stomach into sympathy, than the affections of mind."[36] So according to those two medical traditions, in mania, moral causes and physical alterations are both at work in a reciprocal way: while (a) the sympathy between the brain and other centers of the "economy" explains the production of psychical symptoms, conversely (b) the moral affections clearly are possible causes of diseased organs.

The question of a seat of "madness" was treated in a very cautious way by Ménuret in the article "Manie":

All of those causes are established by a great number of observations; but it has not yet been possible to find out what is the defect, the internal disturbance, which is the origin and the proximate cause of the symptoms constitutive of this disease. In general, the etiology of the diseases of the head, and above all those diseases during which operations of the head have complications, is extremely obscure; anatomical observations are in no way illuminating in this matter; the brains of some maniacs have shown no manifest defects to the most perspicacious researchers, while some others have been found full of yellow serum.[37]

In the "animal economy" system, the question of a localization, or a physical seat, of madness—like the brain—was of no importance: more essential was the circulation of those affects that explained the disease. Such an emphasis on circulation was inherited from Herman Boerhaave and Friedrich Hoffmann, with their iatromechanical models; but in the scheme of animal economy the circulation of fluids was reinterpreted through the concept of sensibility. Eventually, animal economy—whether constituted in a nervous-centered approach in the Whytt-Cheyne tradition, or in a kind of sensibility monism, as in the vitalistic approach— offered a descriptive and etiologic scheme of disease, which made it possible to classify the forms of insanity among the disorders, and understand them as *specific forms of global economical perturbation*.

HEALING THE INSANE: ANTHROPOLOGY AND THE REASSESSMENT OF PSYCHIATRIC PRACTICE

The therapeutics of *économie animale* involved a wide diversity of practices, ranging from philosophical admonishments to sudden cold baths or astringents. Nothing was really new and the authors' examples often referred back to the remedies of the ancients. Ménuret wrote thus about melancholia: "One must begin by curing the mind, then apprehending the defects of the body, when one recognizes them, which implies that the physician has already won the patient's confidence, enters into his ideas, adapts to his delirium, seems convinced that things are as the melancholic imagines them." The treatment entails peculiar remedies: "when a lunatic believes that he has some animal alive inside his body, one must act as if one takes it out of him."[38] About the cure of mania: "It seems to me that in order to cure mania, one must violently and suddenly disturb the body, hence creating a considerable change."[39]

Basically, treatments of the insane could be classified along two axes: distract the insane patient from his diseased idea or passion, or change his way of life by a sudden shock. Whether moral or physical, medical practice pursued one of those two approaches: "substitute new ideas" or "violently stress the body," as proposed in the *Encyclopédie*.[40] According to Cullen, "the cure consists in interrupting the patient's attention, or making him pay attention to other objects than the ones he's used to dealing with."[41] Travel and walking were always suggested in the literature, because, as Beauchesne said, they vary the objects of attention.[42] This purpose was emphasized in the English tradition, encouraged by Locke's emphasis on the association of ideas.[43] It is important to note here that this diversity of means was made somewhat more unified and consistent by the scheme of animal economy, especially in its French vitalistic version.

Ways of influencing insanity were, along the two axes, either moral or physical. In the framework of vitalistic animal economy, however, the two series of means could be conflated. The same target had to be reached by all operations: the sensibility. The two axes were two ways of changing the economy, by globally disturbing its form, or locally modifying the circulation of a sensitive element. A cold bath or a violent emotion, like a sudden joy or a surprise—as related in Ménuret's accounts of melancholics—were essentially the same approach of global disturbance. Going for a ride or having a philosophical conversation were also two closely related therapeutic means, modifying the circulation of sensibility. "Moral" or "physical," in such a scheme, were not really relevant categories for describing therapeutic actions.

The essential purpose of the physician was to redress the animal economy. That was why the relationships between the economy and the milieu—the exchanges—would seem more and more important. Acting on the milieu—"managing the milieu," to use Roselyne Rey's word[44]—would appear as a major therapeutic parameter in the treatment of insanity, a parameter then further qualifying all the methods included in the previous treatment and reassessed in the animal economy scheme. In his famous *Mémoires sur les hôpitaux*, published in 1788, Jacques Tenon (1724–1816) wrote: "Man is not sufficiently considered as a sentient being, and, if I am not mistaken, in the hospitals he should be apprehended mostly according to this perspective. Sad experience tells us how much he is sensible to pain."[45] Here, the vitalistic concept of sensibility was used—"sensibility" meaning both the physical sensation of pain and the moral sentiment of suffering. Hospitals had to be reconceived according to the *économie animale* of man as a sentient being. Tenon explained his interest in specifically psychiatric hospitals: "The ordinary hospitals are intended to host the diseased patient; the ones which treat insanity are at the same time intended as remedies; and the first remedy is to give to the lunatics some freedom, to make it possible for them to follow with the right measure the inclinations that nature imposes on them."[46] In short, the "animal economy" scheme allowed Tenon to think of the asylum as a place of healing, because curing insanity meant acting on the animal economy of the insane by managing their milieu.

If we look at the multiple therapies of madness in this period, if we consider Tenon's definition of the madhouse, we seem very near to the Pinellian "moral treatment." It is as if, under this new term, Pinel presented to the world a unified synthesis of practices that the scheme of animal economy helped to conceive. We know that Pinel admired the English madhouses, particularly Haslam's Bedlam, Battie's St. Luke and, above all, the Retreat at York.[47] However, he deplored the English preference for preserving the secrecy of their method.[48] In fact, the emphasis placed on the "milieu," and importance of managing this milieu, hence creating a special place adapted to insane pathologies, was a principle of the Retreat. Samuel Tuke's famous *Description of the Retreat*, in 1813, seemed to develop the idea enunciated in a vitalistic context by Tenon. Tuke claimed that the moral management of the insane was more important, therapeutically, than the etiological theories of madness.[49]

To better appreciate the shift in approaches to healing the insane at this period, one can compare Boissier's statement in 1739 to Pinel's later therapeutic program. In mania and melancholia, according to Boissier, we must first correct the vices of the blood, and then "also use the help provided by the moral (*la morale*)."[50] Where Boissier added "les secours de la morale" to the medical actions upon madness, Pinel spoke of "traitement moral." The substitution of *traitement* for *secours* expressed the idea that mental disease was now entirely caught in the medical realm. What was usually labeled by Boissier as "medical," things like emollients, baths, or bleedings— as opposed to *secours moraux*—became only a part of a wholly medical attitude that included relationships, talks, exchanges, moral exhortations, and little manipulations. As Pinel claimed in his *Nosographie philosophique*, it was time for a "straight union, reciprocal dependency between moral philosophy and medicine."[51]

THE RISE OF PSYCHIATRY AND THE NATURAL
HISTORY OF MAN

The career of Philippe Pinel has been well studied, especially with such recent works as those of Jacques Postel,[52] Jackie Pigeaud,[53] and Dora Weiner,[54] while Gladys Swain's thesis has examined the philosophical meaning of Pinel's famous gesture of liberating the insane.[55] For the purposes of this study, it is important to appreciate and situate Pinel's theory of madness relative to "animal economy" medicine.

If the legitimization of moral treatment was partly to be found in the "animal economy" scheme, Pinel's definition and etiology of madness—called "mental alienation"—were rather confusedly entangled with this scheme. "Animal economy" helped Pinel to bring about a double synthesis, both between the pathological and the physiological, and between mania and ordinary illness. Pinel wrote that "the constant laws of the animal economy, considered in lunacy (*manie*) as in other diseases, impressed me with their uniformity."[56] Pinel's *Médecine clinique* stated the general relationship between *économie animale* and disease: "A disease can be conceived only through its symptoms, either contemporary or successive; according to these views, it constitutes a kind of complex idea, a result of many simple ideas; it represents a peculiar modification of the animal economy, with a certain duration; considered from its beginning until its end, it constitutes an indivisible and unique whole."[57] With regard to insanity, his commitment to the animal economy scheme enabled him to recognize laws of madness.

The knowledge of animal economy formed the basis of a medical approach to mental alienation for Pinel. This was evident in relation to three topics. First, there was the place of the passions. To understand the alienation, he says, "presupposes a medical history of the passions," because those provoke most of the lunacies, when exacerbated.[58]

Second, there was the use of the sympathies. Mania manifests a "reaction of epigastric forces upon the functions of understanding," which can either increase or oppress those functions.[59] Pinel refers to Bordeu and Lacaze, concerning the major influence of the epigastric source on "sympathetic tuning," in order to explain effects in the crisis of mania. The etiology of mania does not necessarily involve the brain, if we keep in mind the epigastric priority in the order of centers in the animal economy.[60] In the "animal economy" scheme, circulation of affects between the centers matters in fact more than the alleged sources of the affects. So within the "animal economy" scheme, Pinel could undertake a definition of madness as a disease—correlated with a reappraisal of moral therapeutic practice in medicine—but without identifying madness as a brain disease, and therefore without assigning it to an already constituted branch of medicine. On the other hand, if the etiology of madness has to be stated in terms of "sympathies" in an animal economy, we see that epigastric affects are more relevant to the cause of insanity than errors of judgment. "It is much more the motions of an irascible nature, than the disturbance of ideas or the weird singularities of judgement, that constitute the true nature of those events"[61]—which thereby definitively neutralizes the traditional equation between madness and error.

Third, there was the sense of the "milieu." Concerning medicine in general, Pinel states this point in his *Médecine clinique*, while he presents the medical method of settling a case. After having described the current state of a disease, and having traced it back to its origin, the physician must "find out the exciting and predisposing causes." These were to be found: "1. in the profession and way of life of the patient; 2. in accidents previous to the present illness, in the preceding healthy state; 3. sometimes, in the diseases which occurred in the patient's relatives."[62] At this point, medicine articulates an anthropological consideration of ways of life, together with medical notions of health and disease. The growing movement of "hygienism" would vindicate such an approach, which later led to the works of Villermé.[63] Through the idea of predisposing causes, medicine became committed to a conception of illness that extended both beyond the current state of an ill body (since it refers to its past), and beyond its individual person (since it is grounded on a way of life shared with others and based on social conditions).

Pinel was therefore fundamentally receptive to appreciating the social components of madness. He would have remembered Cheyne's *English Malady*, which he considered important; and he would have connected his clinical experiences, in Bicêtre and in La Salpêtrière, to the French Revolutionary tornado. The fragility of social positions and the rising of violent passions were apt terrains for creating alienations.[64] This argument, studied by Rosen,[65] suggests the junction of two major trends in anthropology during the last decades of the eighteenth century—namely, the trend toward a "natural history of man" here investigated and the simultaneous trend toward a more naturalistic anthropology. The major philosophical references for such an anthropology were Rousseau's discourses and Buffon's *Histoire naturelle de l'homme*, and its main materials were the reports from non-European countries, such as the Jesuits' travel relations (Lahontan, Lafitau, and so forth).[66] This anthropological tradition, essentially created by naturalists—and whose last major achievement was Jules Joseph Virey's *Histoire naturelle du genre humain* (1817)—insisted on the forging of man's character by his milieu: climate, customs, and institutions. Such works traced the relationships between races, and addressed the conflicting positions of polygenesis (defended by Lord Kames, for instance) versus monogenesis (defended by Buffon, among others). Therefore, some questions arose spontaneously, such as the pervasive influence of social life on man: after Buffon and Rousseau, Bichat's *Recherches*, for instance, questioned the impact of civilized life on the average duration of individual human lives.[67] According to the Rousseauist perspective, society was always seen as disadvantageous for individual men and women. As in Bichat, Pinel's treatise conflated the two anthropological traditions—namely, he conflated the issues of civilization and nature with the animal economy problem of the "milieu" as a condition of health. Concerning mental health, there were anthropological circumstances, which had to be understood in the context of social life, and particularly with regard to the rise of sentiments and passions unknown in a less-civilized state. These issues came to Pinel as part of the intellectual legacy of the Enlightenment.

The shift that Pinel brought to this legacy—as the later French alienists like Esquirol would receive it—was the vindication of a specific status and role for this new scientist and therapist, the "psychiatrist" (using the name forged a few years later by Johann Christian Reill). Pinellian *aliénation mentale* was an autonomous category, requiring an independent therapy.[68] Pinel's creation was less conceptual or theoretical than, let us say, topical: under the phrase *aliénation mentale*, he created the locus for a new vision and understanding of all mental perturbation—between moral/metaphysical "folie" and physiological "neurosis." That is precisely where he departed from the scheme of "animal economy." Indeed, as an autonomous disease not reducible to the mind's error or to the brain, mental alienation stems from what Pinel called the "principe de la manie." About a lunatic, he writes: "through the incoherency of his ideas one grasps the principle of his mania."[69] From this principle—which is neither physiological (such as a nervous lesion) nor intellectual (such as a kind of error)—derived the symptoms of alienation; it was hidden behind those symptoms, though wholly individual, since always embedded in a singular subject's disease. This enabled the doctor to classify the subject's lunacy, and at the same time, to develop a therapeutic dialogue. We see here the difference between moral practices used by *économie animale* physicians, and by Pinel in his moral treatment: whereas the former referred to a general knowledge of animal economy, Pinel stressed the "principle of the mania," belonging to the autonomous psychiatric space postulated by the *Traité médico-philosophique de l'aliénation mentale ou la manie*. Such a conception of mania required a medical specialist, the *aliéniste* of the nineteenth century.

Esquirol, in "De la folie" (1818), further pursued Pinel's anthropological concerns. Esquirol addressed the question of whether there were more insane people since the Revolution than there were before. His answer invoked a sort of statistical bias, according to which precisely the birth of psychiatry and the construction of asylums—both following the Revolution, if we consider that even Pinel's Bicêtre was still a madhouse within a general hospital—discovered and classified great numbers of insane people who were not registered before as such; hence, the increasing numbers for alienation in this period. Esquirol analyzed the relations between alienation and milieu. In the same text, he stated that there was the "most manifest dependence of mental illness on public and private *mœurs*";[70] as an example, he mentioned the decline of religion.[71] Therefore, one could conclude that the origins of modern anthropology—as developed by Durkheim and Weber in the nineteenth century[72]—lay partly in the conflation of the anthropological traditions of the naturalists and physiologists. This conflation was articulated by Pinel when he first addressed this topic of the social-historical conditions of lunacy as a disease.

CONCLUSION

"Animal economy," especially in vitalistic thought, was a scheme for conceiving of the whole man, "au physique et au moral." This scheme enabled Pinel to attribute to mental illness an etiological and therapeutic specificity. We are accustomed to seeing the history of psychiatry as a succession of dialectically opposed stages: the "mental" approach of Pinel's disciples; then the "somatic" psychiatry, emerging from A. L. J. Bayle's thesis on general paralysis (1822) and culminating in Griesinger's treatise and Morel's theory of degeneration; then another "mental" stage represented by psychoanalysis.[73] The history of psychiatry, in this conception, is a struggle between an organogenic vision of mental illness and a psychogenic conception of alienation. Today, this same struggle appears in the rivalry between psychotropic medication and more or less Freudian psychotherapies. However, this distinction was not relevant during the emergence of psychiatry in France in the late eighteenth century. In fact, Pinel had been able to specify a kind of illness called *alienation mentale*, to vindicate a mode of therapy, and to institute a new kind of medical specialty, because he did not raise the question of the mental or physical nature of this problem and its etiology. He was in a position to formulate it, because he was thinking within the anthropological framework of "animal economy," which treated the distinction between mental and physical events with indifference. The great division between the organogenic and psychogenic positions within psychiatry occurred later, and this could happen only because psychiatry was at first essentially indifferent concerning those positions. Emerging psychiatry was, therefore, not concerned, metaphysically speaking, with the mind-body problem, and this formative indifference was rooted in the proto-anthropological perspective of animal economy.

CHAPTER FIFTEEN

Metamorphosis and Settlement

The Enlightened Anthropology of Colonial Societies

Jonathan Lamb

There has always been a fear abroad, at least in what might widely be termed the West, that to travel too far is dangerous, because travelers might suffer from changes of air, diet, health, and scenery. These changes would so far transform them that they would no longer be fit to perceive the world as it truly is, and could therefore no longer claim to be the persons they were. Portuguese in the Pacific called the coordinates of their dead reckoning the *punto de fantasia*, anticipating Diderot, who named the whole region the ocean of fantasy. Upon its bosom, enchanted islands—the Encantadas—were seen to float and change their places, much to the annoyance of mapmakers such as Herman Moll. The witnesses of such miracles were often described as mendacious, deceived, infatuated, and beside themselves. "People are like Wire," observed John Trenchard, the censor of the collapsed South Sea speculation. "The more they are extended, the weaker they become."[1] Buffon warned that degeneration can produce "effects equal to a new nature." Central Africa had such a disturbing effect on the personalities of its European explorers that they began to talk of themselves in the third person, to write memoranda to themselves as follows, "Come, decidedly I must undouble myself."[2] On her trip to what she thinks is the Antipodes, Lewis Carroll's Alice declares, "There is hardly enough of me left to make up *one* respectable person."[3]

The traditional method of dealing with the testimony of these unreliable travelers was simply to call them liars, and their reports the grossest fictions. In the eighteenth century, when voyage literature was beginning to outstrip divinity as the most popular genre of printed literature, it attracted routine denunciations from the arbiters of taste, who believed that the appetite for stories of monsters made monsters of readers. David Hume compared "the miraculous accounts, wonderful events, strange men, and uncouth manners" to be found in travelers' tales with the "monstrous and improbable fictions" of Ariosto.[4] Having shown that Desdemona was a culpable fool to believe Othello's stories of anthropophagi and men whose heads grow beneath their shoulders, Lord Shaftesbury went on to condemn the public appetite for "the barbarian customs, savage manners, Indian wars, and wonders of the terra incognita" that were to be lapped up from accounts of the New World and the Pacific, foisted on unwitting readers by "friars and missionaries, pirates and renegades, sea-captains and trusty travelers." He added that "the study and relish [of such rarities] becomes at last in reality monstrous," leaving polite consensus in ruins and the "Antipodes of Good Breeding" enshrined in public opinion.[5]

It was rather more difficult to deal with settlement in the New World, for in that case, the unsteadiness of travelers and their monstrous imaginings took root in a place and were confirmed by time; it became the character of a community, and its narrative became a wholly new kind of history. The changes affecting these people could no longer be ascribed to mendacity or temporary infatuation. There had to be another explanation. Among the French philosophers, Montesquieu and Buffon advanced theories of environmental determinism, arguing that changes of climate and soil affected the organisms of plants, animals, and humans, and that acclimatization was accompanied by significant changes of body and temperament. In Britain there was some attempt to develop these ideas, but David Hume decisively rejected them in his essay, "Of National Character." He doubted if physical causes made any alteration to the bodies and complexions of travelers and colonists, "nor do I think, that men owe any thing of their temper or genius to the air, food or climate." Moral causes, on the other hand, such as government, revolution, wealth, and penury could make a substantial difference to the development of national character, but once formed, "the same set of manners will follow a nation and adhere to them over the whole globe."[6] Johann Gottfried Herder took up a position somewhere between, defending the distinctness of national cultures, but at the same time allowing for a principle of change that would render a colony not a mixture of identifiable cultural parts—part indigenous and part exotic—but a wholly new entity that (like other cultures) would grow over time into an untransferable and inexplicable phenomenon, with a history so unique it could be represented only in myth.[7] Although there were Englishmen, such as Joseph Ritson, who embraced

Continental theories of change, and likewise Frenchmen such as the Marquis de Sade who agreed with Hume,[8] it was from this division of opinions that distinct national botanical practices can be dated, with the French favoring acclimatization and the English hothouse gardening.

The earliest postrevolutionary accounts of North American settlement neatly divide between these two enlightened positions, with Hector St. John Crevecoeur (born a Frenchman) arguing powerfully for environmental factors in the makeup of that brand new national character, the American; while Thomas Jefferson challenged Buffon's and D'Aubenton's theses of New World degeneracy, citing George Washington, Benjamin Franklin, and Joseph Rittenhouse as specimens of a transatlantic and transhistorical Saxon civic virtue. Crevecoeur wrote, "Dayly Experience Teaches us that the force of the Climate assimilates everything to itself, not only with regard to Vegetation but even with regard to the bodies, Minds and affections of men."[9] Even on the issue of the so-called degeneracy of African slaves, Jefferson denies the efficacy of the environment: "It is not their Condition then, but nature, which has produced the distinction."[10] Typically, Crevecoeur dedicated his *Letters from an American Farmer* to the Abbe Raynal, whereas Jefferson explicitly opposed in his *Notes on the State of Virginia* Raynal's account of the degraded condition of transplanted whites in North America.[11]

Representations of colonies in the New World span these rival views of change and constancy. Aphra Behn says the English colonists of Surinam were scum with an unlimited opportunity under the system of chattel slavery to become scummier. In her *Oroonoko*, she calls the council, "such notorious Villains as Newgate never transported . . . who understood neither the Laws of God or Man, and had no sort of Principles to make them worthy the Name of Men."[12] In a similar vein, Ned Ward calls Jamaica, "The Place where Pandora fill'd her Box . . . the Receptacle of Vagabonds, the Sanctuary of Bankrupts, and a Close-stool for the Purges of our Prisons."[13] Lemuel Gulliver gives a short history of a modern colony: "Ships are sent with the first opportunity, the natives driven out or destroyed, their Princes tortured to discover their gold, a free license given to all acts of inhumanity and lust, the earth reeking with the blood of its inhabitants, and this execrable crew of butchers, employed in so pious an expedition, is a modern colony sent to convert and civilize an idolatrous and barbarous people."[14] On the other hand, in these terrestrial paradises there was an opportunity to build golden cities on the hills and to declare a new order of society. Sir Humphrey Gilbert perished in his ship off the coast of Newfoundland with a copy of More's *Utopia* clutched in his hand. Vasco de Quiroga founded towns modeled on Utopia near Mexico City and Michoacan.[15] Andrew Marvell's *Bermudas* and Gonzalo's speech in *The Tempest* are anticipations of settlement as the perfection of European humanity, subsequently attempted in the buccaneer camps and the slave rebellions of the Caribbean, as well as in the patriotic revolutions of the Americas.

Somewhere in between these extremes of good and bad, of utopian humanity and colonial degeneracy, settlers themselves wondered what changes they were undergoing, and why. In New Zealand, William Yate asked Dr. Lushington to give a legal opinion on the status of eighty children of missionaries born in what was not yet a colony, and he could get no clear description of their status, whether they remained subjects of the Crown or whether they had evolved into clients of the equivalent of sovereign power in the country of their birth.[16] Crevecoeur reported that on the frontier there had sprung up "a New Breed of people neither Europeans nor yet Natives."[17] In *The History of Jamaica*, Edward Long gives a description of settler government not far short of Behn's in contempt ("artifice, duplicity, haughtiness, violence, rapine, avarice, meanness, rancour, and dishonesty, ranged in succession"), but at the same time he is eager to establish a link between them and the English; and thanks to the gracious intervention of Charles II, he is able to call Jamaican settlers "free denisons of England." That is to say, they are like freeborn subjects of England insofar as they enjoy rights of entry to the mother country; but they are never more than only *like* them, since a denizen is a resident alien, never truly at home.[18] In the third letter of the Drapier, Swift is troubled by the quality of denizen that he acquires when sailing westward on the Irish Sea: "I am a free Man in England, and do I become a Slave in six hours by crossing the Channel?"[19] However, his definition of the Anglo-Irish as "the True English People of Ireland" doesn't quite hit the mark, for why would the true stock bear a double name?[20]

What turns an English person into a denizen? What stops an English identity from being true in another place? Anthony Pagden has observed that all Creole elites in the Americas knew by the end of the eighteenth century that they were no longer English, Spanish, French, or Portuguese. Even by the end of the sixteenth century, the *gachupines* (peninsular Spanish) noticed in the *criollos* characteristics peculiar to them, such as their love of ostentation, the liberties accorded women, their passion for tobacco, their highly figurative modes of expression, and the different shapes and caparisons of their saddles.[21] At the same period in Ireland, the so-called New English settlers noticed symptoms of corruption in the Old English so vivid and numerous that they argued a people "degenerated from all manhood and humanity," "worse than dogs," as Andrew Trollope told Sir Francis Walsingham.[22] In his *A View of the State of Ireland*, Spenser posed the question of the Old English, "Are not they that were once English, English still?" The answer seemed to be no, for these settlers had forgotten their English names and taken Irish ones, spoke Erse, and had succumbed to a "most dangerous lethargie" of spirit.[23] Similarly, in the eighteenth century, Long spoke of white Jamaican Creoles becoming languid, careless in their dress, and inclined to talk the language of mulattos, the gibberish of a "degenerate breed of mongrels."[24] Mexican Creoles took native titles, wore Indian clothes, spoke Quechua or Nahuatl, and were accused of deriving their origins from parrots, monkeys, and dogs;[25] thus, in Behn's *The Rover*, Don Vincente was pointed out as a Creole who, because of his "Indian breeding . . . loves it in the dog days."[26] William Douglass wrote that the British settlers in North America were "like the wild Irish, they dread labour more than poverty; like dogs they are always either eating or sleeping."[27] Along the same lines, Jefferson and John Adams abused Alexander Hamilton (born on the island of Nevis) as a Creole bastard.

Speculation about the reasons for such changes went in the two directions distinguished by Hume as physical and moral causes. Among the physical causes there was perhaps some distinctive quality in the condition, soil, or climate of the New World that caused indigenes and settlers alike to develop characteristics wholly un-European; or possibly the passage itself from one world to another occasioned a deficit or alteration in the animal and moral economy that could not be made up or reversed, even though the circumstances of the new place might be exceedingly propitious. Moral causes could be found in the customs and institutions of the new colony, possibly so imperfect they destroyed the integrity of the people. Robert Boyle received a report from Virginia that stated, "People do not look so well here as in England wch may proceed from the nature of the food, their salt meats and unwholesome drinkes as much as from ye Climate."[28] Ned Ward said that New Englanders aged prematurely, "It is usual for the Men to be Grey at Thirty; and look as Shrivel'd in the Face, as an old Parchment Indenture pasted down upon a Barbers Block. . . . The Women have done bearing of Children by the time they are Four and Twenty."[29] For his part, Spenser found that the degeneration of the Old English in Ireland could not be ascribed to the soil or climate, for Ireland "is yet a most beautiful and sweet countrey as any is under heaven."[30] In the New World, chattel slavery was widely blamed for the degeneracy of slaves and slave owners alike. The one urgent and undeniable reason Jefferson proposed for emancipation was the unhappy influence of slave owning upon the manners of patriots.[31] Crevecoeur reserved his highest praise for the Vineyarders and Nantucketers, who thrived without slaves and without a fertile soil.

Whatever the outcome, the inevitability of change in settlers—either for the better or the worse—was more widely acknowledged as the eighteenth century advanced. "For even though they might adhere to the customs of their fathers with an obstinacy equal almost to the instinct of animals, and even though they named their new mountains, rivers, cities and institutions after those of their original country, the great change in climate and soil made eternal sameness in everything impossible."[32] Perhaps the most vivid and various accounts of the enigmas of colonial change are to be found in Raynal's and Diderot's *Histoire des deux Indes* (1772–87). On the one side are the buccaneers who established utopian communities for brief periods of time on the islands of Catalina, Providence, Tortuga, and Santo Domingo, exhibiting a glorious "energy of soul" that had never been seen before. "The principle which actuated these extraordinary and romantic men," they add, "is not easily discovered."[33] On the other side, appalled by the effects of slavery in the New World, Raynal and Diderot pose the question of change in its most acute and unpleasant forms as an unaccountable and terrible metamorphosis:

Is it possible that civilized men who were brought up in the midst of polished cities, is it possible that all such men, without exception, should pursue a line of conduct equally contrary to the principles of humanity, to their interest, to their safety and to the first dawnings of reason; and that they should continue to become more barbarous than the savage? This change of character in the European who quits his country is a phenomenon of so extraordinary a nature, the imagination is so deeply affected with it, that while it attends to it with astonishment, reflection tortures itself in endeavoring to find out the principle of it, whether it exist in human nature in general, or in the peculiarities of navigators, or in the circumstances preceding or posterior to the event.[34]

In his study of the Creole history of Jamaica, Edward Brathwaite is still asking the same question of settler culture: "Was it the influence of slavery? . . . Was it some factor in eighteenth-century Britain and Europe, creating this disposition? Or was it the action of an as yet undiscovered 'law' which operates when groups or cultures come into contact with each other?"[35]

In any event, it was conceded on all sides that irreversible changes had occurred. In Jean Rhys's *Wide Sargasso Sea* (1966)—which revisits the characters of *Jane Eyre* (1847) in a Creole Caribbean scenario—Rochester gazes into Antoinette's sad, dark, alien eyes, and thinks, "Creole of pure English descent she may be, but they are not English or European either."[36] Antoinette says, "I often wonder who I am and where is my country and where do I belong and why was I ever born at all."[37] There was much at stake in trying to identify and master this force for change. If it could be understood and resisted, then one had access to Jefferson's brand of diasporic yet immutable virtue. If such changes were for the better, then they might be embraced as the means of perfecting the human species, and rising from mere humanity toward humanity squared, or what the humanist Carolus Bovillus called *homo-homo*.[38] If, on the other side, these changes lead to the sink of human depravity, to the level of a dog, or below a dog—a condition Giorgio Agamben has defined as *homo sacer*, "a threshold of indistinction and of passage between animal and man,"[39] and actually identified by Spenser as lycanthropy among the Irish shamans who "make the wolfe their gossip"[40]—then it was best to have it clearly exhibited so that it might be more certainly avoided. These issues were compendiously reviewed in the fourth book of *Gulliver's Travels*, where it was not certain whether the Yahoos were the degenerate offspring of European castaways, or autochthonous humans. Gulliver was never sure how to express this, whether it was a perfectly original human figure that aroused his horror and astonishment, in all its native nastiness, or whether he beheld its defaced and corrupt descendant, with its sins inscribed on its body. The satire, if satire it was, constantly pointed to the connections between the gestures of these apelike creatures and the behavior of courtiers, lawyers, and politicians, posing the question of degeneracy both as the loss and the acquirement of culture. Are the beastlike humans the original of humanity, or the repulsive end of it; are members of civil society the perfection of human nature, or its scandal? Or is there no difference, and is one as bad as the other? And if so, are animals such as horses better than humans?

The enigmas of migration and settlement were handled anciently, as Anthony Pagden has pointed out, by the poets.[41] Homer's story of Circe was an allegory of the changes that overtake mariners in distant landfalls. Plutarch wrote a dialogue called *Gryllus*, about the man in Odysseus's crew who liked the life of a pig on Circe's island, and disliked the prospect of being changed back into a man. That was not an option in Lucretius's treatment of mutability, where he wrote, "Whatever is changed, and breaks the Bounds of its first Nature, instantly dies, and becomes another thing." Unimpressed by the national teleology and stability of Virgilian epic, Ovid produced a narrative of the perpetual and confusing metamorphoses incident to changing place in which he dates the flux and uncertainties of the world from the Age of Iron, when the unhappy conversion of pine trees into ships' keels, and decent human beings into sailors, precipitated the subsequent transformations of humans into beasts, gods, and plants, and of gods into humans and beasts. These confusions of shape and function are always most dramatically presented when the leading character is transplanted from his or her homeland (such as Medea, Jason, or Europa), or when a new settlement is being made, such as Cadmus's foundation of Thebes. In his *Republic*, Plato has no major city near the sea, in order that these mutabilities might never threaten the immortal symmetry of his commonwealth.

Plutarch's Gryllus, who thought it not such a bad life being a pig in a strange country, challenged Ulysses as a failed colonist: "You have shied away from the change from one shape to another . . . you are a man who boggles at the simple matter of changing worse for better." Change struck Edmund Spenser as the most obvious and odious example of the failure of colonization. With the barbarities of the Old English of Ireland in mind, he instanced Gryllus as an animal in more senses than one ("Let Grill be Grill, and have his hoggish mind"). Not enchanted by mutability, Spenser nevertheless believed like Ovid that a world filled with changing shapes, changing more rapidly and shockingly under the influence of travel and transplantation, might only be controlled by managing change, not preventing it. His Garden of Adonis in *The Faerie Queene* draws on two potent fictions reimported into the Old World from the New, the terrestrial paradise and Utopia. In botanic gardens such as those at Leyden and Oxford, which sought to reestablish the ancient paradise on the basis of plant specimens taken from newly discovered territories, the system of beds or *pulvilli* bear a distinct resemblance to the arrangement of gardens, houses, and families in More's island of Utopia whence, we are told, surplus population is transplanted to the Utopian colonies and, in times of a low birthrate, recalled home. The seeds of the Garden of Adonis are arranged in the same utopian fashion, and sent out by the genius of the place for transplantation, and then after a term resumed into the beds:

> After that they againe returned beene,
> They in that Gardin planted be againe;
> And grow afresh, as they had never seene
> Fleshly corruption, nor mortall paine,
> Some thousand yeares so doen they there remaine;
> And then of him are clad with other hew,
> Or sent into the chaungefull world againe,
> Till thither they return, where first they grew:
> So like a wheele around they runne from old to new.[42]

Spenser's botanic garden, then, is like those at Padua, Leyden, Oxford, and Montpellier, to the extent that it conserves the paradisal or utopian promise of the New World in a metropolitan setting, curing the degeneration of species there, at the center. It is so positioned in the circuit that the worst excesses of transplantation are corrected at home, be they conceived as the cruelty of the invading European or the loss of identity that afflicts Gryllus and Gulliver in the course of their travels. The garden of Adonis is not like those gardens planted at the rim of discovery, such as Pierre Poivre's in Mauritius, van Riebeeck's at the Cape, Helenus Scott's at Bombay, or the botanic garden of the medical faculty at the University of Mexico, where Creole naturalists such as Jose de Alzate y Ramirez tackled theories of degeneration and taxonomy with equal zeal in the eighteenth century.[43] These were planted to encourage the understanding of exotic species and to renovate fallen European stock at the furthest reach of their susceptibility to change. Bernardin de Saint-Pierre's eighteenth-century novel *Paul et Virginie* is based on his botanical researches with Poivre at the garden of Pamplemousse on Mauritius, and it writes the story of the Garden of Adonis back to front, for it tells of Creole innocence, the pure and unanticipated result of transplantation, thriving in the remote woods of the island until it is sacrificed in a futile attempt to fetch it home and improve it in Paris.

This difference between botanic gardens at the rim and at the center suggests a difference between Creole and metropolitan/republican conceptions of virtue, one depending on environmental determinism and the fluidity of national character, and the other on the stability of nature, difference, and condition. In Spenser's picture of the centripetal movement of planted things, where corruption is acquired at the colonial edge then thrown off at the metropolitan center, there is a homogeneous sense of place and time, with cycles completed when the corruptions of traveling and plantation are abolished by coming home. Centrifugal excellence in a colonial context, on the other hand, defies explanation, as Raynal says, and can be accounted for only by supposing that indigenous strengths, previously unrecognizable to European eyes, can be imparted to those like Gryllus, who do not boggle at changing worse for better. Tacitus, Thomas More, and the Creole intellectuals of Mexico agreed that such strengths originally depended upon important absences of things—of luxuries, taverns, iron, horses—but the truly Creole element in this radical change for the better, or for the worse, is its causelessness, its exorbitance to any stable point of view, its resistance to the conception of change as a diasporic interlude between exodus and return, and its belief that only Creoles can write or understand a Creole history.

It is strange how quickly Ovid was creolized in New Spain. He was first published in Mexico City in 1577; and when the figures of Perseus, Actaeon, and Daphne emerged in the frescoes of Ixmiquilpan as centaurs, severed heads, and shrubs, a blend of pre-Hispanic and Ovidian imagery, it was not as allegories of hybrid Christianity but as the proofs of the perpetual force of metamorphosis.[44] Crevecoeur is alternately enchanted and overwhelmed by "this surprising metamorphosis" of American settlers, as he calls it: "In Europe they were as so many useless plants, wanting vegetative mould and refreshing showers. They withered; and were mowed down by want, hunger, and war; but now, by the power of transplantation, like all other plants, they have taken root and flourished!"[45] Nevertheless he notices that the desire to manipulate this change, and to construe metamorphosis as a patriotic inheritance of immutable virtue and a revolutionary destiny, turns citizens into animals. "We must perish, perish like wild beasts,"[46] he cries now that he has become the prey of "Man who eats not Man, yet kills Man and takes a singular Pleasure in shedding his Blood."[47] Crevecoeur is talking of terrible things that happened in the War of Independence, a cause for which he was no partisan; and in the process he establishes a crucial difference between Americans, who he sees have evolved into two types. On the one hand are settlers and Creoles, intimate with the land that they have shaped and been shaped by, but largely ignorant of how this has happened and of whom they have become; and on the other are republicans and patriots who pretend to be perfectly well aware of the Machiavellian moment they inhabit. As one of the former, Crevecoeur is so implicated in the surprising metamorphosis of settlement, that he cannot handle it objectively. He says, "I am too deeply concerned, to examine this Subject with Impartiality."[48] His enemies are fast-talking ideologues with explanations for everything, intent on controlling and directing the metamorphoses that have befallen them: "callous, pushing Country saints."[49]

The same fatal division between settlers and republicans is the theme of Euclides da Cunha's Brazilian novel of 1902, *Rebellion in the Backlands* (*Os Sertoes*). He tells the remarkable story of a war that was fought in the latter part of the nineteenth century in the arid region of Brazil around Canudos between the inhabitants, the *sertanejos*, and the new republic of Brazil. The *sertanejos* were people who had grown back into this unfriendly land, covered with caatinga scrub, to become its effectual autochthons. Their houses were tumbledown, their religion was messianic, their cathedral a projection of their wild imaginations, with its "impossible volutes, its capering delirium of incorrect curves, its horrible ogives and embrasures,"[50] and their history, insofar as they could tell it, a series of incomprehensible miracles. Their opponents were actuated by the kind of republican patriotism typical of other insurgent Creole elites in the Americas, characterized as follows by da Cunha in the first person plural:

Deluded by a civilization which came to us second hand; rejecting, blind copyists that we were, all that was best in the organic codes of other nations, and shunning, in our revolutionary zeal, the slightest compromise with the exigencies of our own national interests, we merely succeeded in deepening the contrast between our mode of life and that of our rude native sons, who were more alien to us in this land of ours than were the immigrants who came from Europe. For it was not an ocean which separated us from them, but three whole centuries.[51]

There are strong lines of this division between autochthony and republicanism in the cult of patriotism among the *criollos* of Mexico, who regarded its ancient history as theirs by virtue of conquest, and preferable to the history of Europe. They distinguished *nacion*, or racial inheritance, from *patria*, a culture of indigenous and settler heroism, assigning to the latter the real political importance of Creole communities in Mesoamerica, which were linked together, as they understood it, in a kind of universal monarchy that had nothing in common with republics, being a patriotic federation with a history that was unique.[52] If Creoles seemed like beasts to peninsular Spaniards, that was because the Spanish had tried to make them so, either by willfully misreading their singular history or by hindering the formation of institutions and archives that might have fostered and expressed it.[53] When republicanism came to the continent, it had to ignore a Creole politics that didn't fit the European templates that members of the insurgent elite such as Bolivar were using: his heroes among the Spanish and the Indians were those who had not been tainted by the history of conquest and its aftermath. These issues were fought out with shrubs and flowers too. The Royal Botanical Garden was founded in Mexico to challenge the Creole hegemony in the faculty of medicine at the university, and to establish the primacy of the Linnaean system, with its exclusively sexual emphasis on the process of reproduction, and its taxonomic hostility to the blurrings of metamorphosis.[54] But as Bernardin de Saint-Pierre, the *sertanejos*, and the *criollo* intellectuals variously point out, if acclimatization is the only way to call exotic soil one's own, of what earthly use is a hothouse plant, which can only thrive if it is taken back home, like the specimens in the Garden of Adonis, or the settlers of More's Utopia?

This is a problem whose solution is still being debated. In postcolonial studies there is some reluctance to deploy terms such as Creole and settler other than in a historical context because their associated attributes of undirected change and metamorphosis are regarded as extraneous or even hostile to a concept of difference better served by words such as *diaspora*, *exodus*, and *hybridity*. The word *diaspora* is widely in use now in the United States. The only people who need settlement here are the erstwhile nomads, who cannot find a remedy at law unless they are settled. Everyone else—at least everyone with a stake in the migrations and displacements belonging to a mobile, multicultural, and global economy—emerges from a diaspora. The word has been wrenched, as James Clifford has pointed out, from its specific reference to the dispersal of communities of Jews, Greeks, and Armenians over the last two millennia, in order that it might comprehend the Asians, South Asians, Russians, Hispanics, Filipinos, Polynesians, and Arabs who comprise the latest migrant additions to the

American melting pot.[55] Of course melting pot is no longer the right word, for all diasporas command attention as unique events. The history of the Jews who escaped first the pogroms and then the Holocaust is preceded by the account of twenty million Africans shipped into slavery. These are injustices so unimaginable they can be framed only by the carefully preserved history of each forced removal. So every minority must add its narrative of exile to the national quilt of distinctive sufferings. Even the descendents of the WASP elite claim diasporic status on account of religious persecution, as Scots and Irish claim it on grounds of clearances and famines. Tom Hayden, doyen of the New Left in the days of the Vietnam protests, has recently discovered his Irish blood and the trauma of his people's diaspora and has asked all Americans to attend to the history of such injustices in order to avoid assimilation and self-hatred.[56]

James Thomson, in his eighteenth-century patriot poem, *Liberty*, which is often cited as a classic articulation of British imperialism, deftly joins the idea of a colony to the theme of diaspora when he glosses it as "the calm Retreat / Of undeserved Distress, the better Home / Of those whom Bigots chace from foreign Lands." Now people write books and articles about the diaspora of law, the diaspora of knowledge, and even the diaspora of terror, as if ideas along with communities are simply on a circuit, with home and "better home" apparently at opposite ends of the compass. But like the utopian drift of Homi Bhabha's hybrid word "unhomely," the "better home" relies upon an idea of home in order to call home a foreign land. There cannot be a diasporic community without a dream of return and a residual sense of identity that entails a strong susceptibility to nostalgia.[57]

Like diaspora, the word "hybridity" accuses the monolith of colonial power and its servant, the immutable metropolitan subject, of precipitating the migrations of peoples and the destruction of local cultures. It comprehends the vast involuntary upheavals and anomies of mobile folk, no longer sure who they are, acting at the instigation of those who are perfectly certain of their identity and their place. Strung between two worlds, dispersed but longing for home, these victims confront their masters as diasporic hybrids, "neither one thing nor the other." Out of that amphibian condition their resistance to oppression grows by virtue of mimicry that, according to Homi Bhabha, transforms "neither one thing nor the other" into "almost the same but not quite," and converts the loss of home into a community of the unhomely.[58] These transformations unsettle the imperialist subject so confident of his identity and his cause, and breed a set of doubts the hybrid can exploit.

This postcolonial modification of the dialectic has been questioned from both the historical and the political sides. Robert Young has doubts about the origin of this agonistic tension between Self and Other: "If there is one consistent misrepresentation in colonial writing it is that the subject of Europe, the European self, was a single, unquestioning imperially minded entity."[59] In his book *Colonialism's Culture* (1994), Nicholas Thomas demonstrates how variously, unpredictably, and often unsuccessfully Europeans settled in the Pacific; and I have tried to show in *Preserving the Self in the South Seas* (2001) that settlement in New Zealand was, and still is, by no means a one-sided struggle between settlers and Maori. From the political side, Michael Hardt and Antonio Negri challenge the efficacy of hybridity, not by denying a conflict between colonial Self and diasporic Other in the period following the Berlin Conference, but by showing that it is entirely insufficient for theorizing the realities of contemporary global power, which result from the consummation of the logic of indefinite expansion preached by Jefferson's republic. They argue that an ever-expanding frontier and a policy of almost unrestricted immigration gave to nineteenth-century America the characteristics of a utopic empire, in which sovereign power was immanent in a people perpetually altered by immigration, themselves citizens of a patria whose boundaries were indefinite. It was at once the best place and a no-place, eu- and outopia; a scene of immutable Saxon virtue in an unstable environment. Even in the eighteenth century, this mobile state of affairs caused a frisson of ontological angst: no definite patria, no definite people: "It made men aware that they were centaurs," says J. G. A. Pocock in a teasing phrase.[60] There is no diaspora from the diaspora. The only exodus possible from such a republic, once its western frontier has been used up, has to be from the species itself, Hardt and Negri suggest; from *homohomo* to *homo sacer*, or what they term an "anthropological exodus." Of course, this is the same exodus already noted with distaste by Spenser and others in the doggish or hoggish features of unregenerate Creoles.

In the settler metamorphoses I have been trying to illustrate, and which Crevecoeur most dramatically represents, there is no effectual loyalty to home, or any ground of a previous identity on which to anchor alterations of the Self, and make them obedient to will and intention. The irrefutable fact of change prevents any turning back, or any strategic deployment of the changes affecting the Self. I think this is why Ovidian metamorphoses are for the most part inexplicable and unallegorizable, and almost always accompanied by the loss of speech, the readiest instrument of memory, and the surest sign of origin, species, and home. Writing survives (in the story of Philomela, for example) only to promote the next steps in the process of change: infanticide, cannibalism, and transformation into a bird. Very seldom is metamorphosis reversed, like Io's, and even then she finds it impossible to speak of what it was like to be a cow. Ovid himself, and Arachne his other Self, prove upon themselves how dangerous it can be to write the record of metamorphosis. The change from human to animal, or from human to plant or stone, is radical and unambivalent. Actaeon is not a hybrid. When, in *The Golden Ass*, Lucius is changed from an ass back into his human form, he is not the same Lucius that he was before, nor does he claim any continuity with his previous Self.[61] Like Thrasyleon the bandit in the same story, who was attacked while disguised as a bear and resolutely chose to die in role, growling and snarling, Lucius tries to keep pace with what he has become, and to renounce what he was. There is no nostalgia in undirected metamorphosis, which is why Hardt and Negri choose the word to describe the challenge presented by the era of the posthuman, when human labor will be so revolutionized that we shall find the model for the change in Donna Haraway's fable of the cyborg, that hybrid of machine and organism subsisting on the anthropological frontier between nature and technology.[62]

But the cyborg fable is not uniquely expressive of the anthropological exodus from the human, for it never parts company from the notion of a managed resistance and a consciously adapted hybrid form. America has never found that kind of future particularly disturbing. Prosthesis is a national addiction. Haraway herself has suggested the cyborg fable is the junior partner in a much more significant pairing of humans and dogs.[63] But the metamorphosis of settlement that creates people such as Crevecoeur's Americans, da Cunha's *sertanejos*, and Plutarch's Gryllus is not half so appealing. It is for the same single reason that Jefferson rejected Buffon's and Raynal's descriptions of change in the New World, that the republican Brazilians were determined to suppress the eccentricities of the inhabitants of Canudos, and that Spenser despised any mutability that was irreversible. The reason is that none of them could tolerate an idea of change independent of human control, as Herder says it always must be. For them, change has to be rerouted through the metropole to make it recognizable and useful, even if the destiny of the people thus changed should lead to war with the motherland.

Apparently, nobody wants to be like Gryllus the pig, or those dogs of Old English, but it is the Aesopian fable, exploring the animal side of the nonhuman, rather than the cyborg fable with its machinate and prosthetic supplements, that gives the best account of an anthropological exodus. Aesop's fables of cats that turn into ladies, and ladies into cats, foreshadows Mandeville's *Fable of the Bees*, where a commonwealth of anthropomorphic insects unaccountably metamorphose into real bees and swarm into a hollow tree. The shame that attaches to settlers who exit from the species to become like animals has been touched upon by J. M. Coetzee in his South African novel, *Disgrace* (1999). It is a story about David Lurie and his daughter, Lucy, white South Africans who arrive from different routes at the limit of the fantasy of patria. For Lurie, it comes while working in a dog shelter, where he advances from the experience of ostracism to understand the disgrace a dog feels when it knows it is going to die. Then he shares with the animal the most alarming premonition of extinction, "that immense alteration," as David Hume calls it. His daughter arrives at her limit when she understands on what very narrow terms she can go on living on her farm in the Eastern Cape after she has been raped there. Her father thinks she has alternatives, such as going back "home" to Holland, a Garden of Adonis. She refuses his offer, and decides to accept the terms, saying, "It is humiliating. But perhaps that is what I must learn to accept. To start at ground level. With nothing. Not with nothing but. With nothing. No cards, no weapons, no property, no rights, no dignity." "Like a dog." "Yes, like a dog."[64] It is a bleak picture of metamorphosis, but at least it is an acknowledgment that change—unmanaged and irreversible—is the groundwork of all other change. The same message is delivered in a jollier way in the famous Irish bull collected by the Creole novelist Maria Edgeworth. "I was a beautiful baby, but they changed me." Crevecoeur's eighteenth-century shamanic meditation on the Aesopian prospects of life on the frontier, recorded in one of the American farmer's unpublished letters, opens up the same abyss as the last book of *Gulliver's Travels*. Crevecoeur writes:

If man had not receiv'd the gift of Speech, the only Advantage that sets him above the rest of beings, what would he be?—imagine 100 Families plac'd in the midst of our Forests, without being able to communicate any Ideas to each other, they would dwindle below the Rank of Animals—their Neighbours the wolves and the Foxes, would soon become the Geniusses of the Land, the honest Beavers the Philosophers . . . and man would in a little time, make Room for those strange and more sagacious Animals.[65]

Whatever the history destined to be written of the metamorphosis whose symptoms Crevecoeur, Herder, and Darwin noted, it is not going to be a chronicle of what Coleridge called in his *Constitution of Church and State*, "the harmonious development of those qualities and faculties that characterize our humanity."[66] I think it would be more likely to illustrate the truth of Terry Eagleton's gloss on that phrase, in which he suggests that humanity is the fabulous idea that metropolitan culture attaches to certain powerful political interests. At least a pig or a dog, or the dwindled human being who has a wolf for his gossip, or the Creole reduced to admiring the philosophy of the beaver, perpetrate no such fiction about the changes that have overtaken them. And that is a decent thing, although it may not, in the common acceptation of the word, be a proof of their humanity.

CONCLUSION

CHAPTER SIXTEEN

The Old Wor(l)d
and the New Wor(l)ds:

A Discursive Survey from Discovery to Early Anthropology

Marco Cipolloni

Let Observation with extensive view survey Mankind from China
to Peru.—Samuel Johnson

SPAIN, MODERN EUROPE, THE ATLANTIC OCEAN,
AND SOME OTHER NEW WOR(L)DS

In settling an island, the first building erected by a Spaniard will be a
church; by a Frenchman, a fort; by a Dutchman, a warehouse; and
by an Englishman, an alehouse.

—Eighteenth-century proverb

We began thinking about this book in 2002. At that time, the issue of the
links between the European Renaissance and the Atlantic Enlightenment
(that is, between the early modern framework called "discovery" and the
eighteenth-century beginnings of a new comparative approach to cultural
life) were being reconsidered for various reasons and from many different
points of view. All over the world, globalization, multiculturalism, and the
phenomenon of international terrorism brought new attention and emphasis to the idea, the experience, and the limits of cultural difference, and
this was also evident in academic discourse. At the same time, this book has
been made possible by the longstanding and ongoing scholarship of its
contributors concerning both the European Enlightenment and its origins.

The diverse perspectives of their contributions provided me, writing this final chapter, not only with new knowledge but also with new nuances of insight into the crucial passage from discovery to anthropology (through imperial settlement and ethnography).

The main purpose of this concluding chapter is to connect the early modern epic of the great discoveries with the gradual emergence of a positivist approach to the comparative variety of human cultures. Substantial elements of this positivist approach, today called anthropology, were produced in the intellectual harvest of the eighteenth-century European rediscovery of the Americas, a collective project that involved several generations of colonial officers, travelers, scientists, sailors, Jesuits, and (after 1773) former Jesuits. Thanks to the personal prestige of some leading figures, such as Alexander Von Humboldt, Alexis de Tocqueville, and Charles Darwin, the most relevant achievements of their work, including a substantial revision of all the most important sources concerning the New Worlds, reached the nineteenth-century European public, changing our cultural consciousness forever.

During the previous fifty years, the intellectual communities of eighteenth-century Europe had explored, described, and revised the written and the living memory of the Atlantic experience, both as a body of writings and as a real New World. Taking their sources seriously, the savants, the gazetteers, the members of the salon circles and of the scientific societies made philology a great adventure. They invented a new language (with new words) in order to recapitulate, on maps and in texts, the polemically aggressive conquest techniques successfully used by the early explorers of the transatlantic world. The reconsideration of the Atlantic corpus as a whole and the dawning mythology of the tropics engaged the intellectual elites and selected publics of Europe in the project of defining and transcending (through reading, traveling, and rewriting) the limits of their own identity and civilization. In the eighteenth century, an open series of "new worlds" were included in the discussion—and made marginal and peripheral. The most effective arguments and topics of this Atlantic westward perspective (for example, the Black Legend of Spain, the Caribbean pirates, the climatic theory, the Indian tribes, or the Jesuit missions in Paraguay) became very popular, were widely circulated all over Europe, and left a profound mark on the public style and polemic rituals of the enlightened intellectual community. For better or worse, Spain and the Spanish West Indies became a useful model for many future new worlds (including those of science fiction[1]), and the eighteenth-century rediscovery of the Americas inspired the ideological occupation of many other "marginal regions," such as Eastern Europe, the Arctic North, and the South Seas.

The Spanish contribution was important for obvious historical reasons,[2] but also added a theatrical effect, highlighting the difference between the way we "look" or "seem" Western and the way we actually "feel" or "act" as westerners. The famous American writer Richard Wright, a typical long-term product of the "double consciousness" of the so-called Black Atlantic, captured this baffling effect in 1960, in his travel book *Pagan Spain*: "Even in Asia and Africa, I had always known where my world ended and where theirs began. But Spain was baffling; it looked and seemed western, but it did not act/feel western."[3] In Spain the historical origins and the cultural limits of the Atlantic exploration and settlement were anthropologically closer than anywhere else.

I am consciously filtering my contribution to this volume through a Spanish lens, even if I regard it as part of the contemporary historical and anthropological debates about the imperial origins of Western civilization[4] and the modern limits of European identity.[5] In my opinion, the eighteenth-century restyling of the Spanish Atlantic world was perhaps the first serious attempt at a sophisticated mechanism of sociocultural recording, concerning the dialectics between present and past.[6] Over the last fifteen years, since the end of the Cold War in 1989, since the Maastricht Treaty in 1991 (ratified in 1993), since the quincentennial of the Discovery of America in 1992, more and more scholars have been focusing on the links between the beginnings of modern consciousness and self-consciousness (during the Renaissance period) and the development of both the Euro-Atlantic identity and the East-West opposition.[7]

Logically and geographically, the East and the West are a pair of relatively well-defined positions, the Eastern and the Western margins of a self-asserted focus. Historically, in the modern consciousness of Europe and the Atlantic West, East and West have also marked the opposition between the Continent and the Ocean, Asia and the Americas, India and the West Indies. The continental image of modern Europe as a cultural vehicle for the living tradition of the Ancient World has its roots in Europe's sense of itself as an Atlantic peninsula, a *cul de sac*, or a *finis terrae*. Along the Atlantic shores and coastlines, the historical and geographical notion of background (the historical past, the memory of Indo-European traditions) encountered the seductive and dangerous possibilities offered by the ocean and the overseas islands (representing prophecy, the future, Christian promise).[8] Even more than in the maps of the Renaissance, the continent and the islands of the Enlightenment became (and in tourist literature still are) something more than a pair of complementary horizons. They implied two different perspectives upon the peninsula called Europe. On the one hand, there was the westward- and forward-oriented adventure, which made the Spanish, the Portuguese, and the British colonial enterprises and empires the first real examples of global politics.[9] On the other hand, there was the eastward- and backward-oriented tradition, connected to the meaningful symbols of the Christian world and the Roman Empire.[10]

At the beginning of the modern period, the all-encompassing empire of Charles V represented an encounter between the long-term memory of the continent and its dreaming about the islands, a bridge between the eastern-continental roots and the western-oceanic new basis of the European Self. According to Jean-Frédéric Schaub, after Charles V, the transatlantic scale of the Spanish Empire became a key element for the better understanding of the heritage and mental mapping of the imperial tradition: the symbols of the Holy Roman Empire found continuity in Vienna, in a "regional dimension," but only the transoceanic dominions of the Iberian powers could update and fulfill the prophetic dreams concerning the historical possibility of a universal Christian monarchy.[11] All the courts of seventeenth-century Europe were fully aware of this. Schaub's interpretation, focused on France and the French Golden Age, is not explicitly East-West oriented, but his vision of the dual continuity of the Holy Roman Empire, in Vienna and in Madrid, indirectly highlights the reemergence of the East-West polarization as a crucial element for the development of the modern European mind.

As Alain Corbin emphasizes in the opening methodological remarks of his *Le territoire du vide* (1988), the waves of the Atlantic Ocean overwhelm the myth of the "*longue durée*," making room for a new approach, focused on "representations, desires, curiosity, perceptions and discourses." The European rediscovery of the Atlantic world and the invention of the "tropics" meant passing from a precolonial imagination to a consciously colonial world. In this Atlantic-centered system, almost everything (towns, courts, rituals, names, maps) existed twice, as a European model and as a transoceanic copy or a tropical version. According to Carlo Galli's recent edition of Francisco de Vitoria's *De iure belli*, during the sixteenth century, the cultural consequences of the geographical discoveries made European intellectual elites more and more conscious that the so-called *respublica christiana* "is ever more clearly just a part of the world."[12]

Following the evolution of this consciousness, on the path from discovery to anthropology, from prophecy to natural selection, we may reconsider—as a matter of discourse, genre, and representation—the historical relationship between the center and the margins, the Old World and the New Worlds, Europe and its own frontiers. Any description is really a self-portrait of the descriptor, the subject author, and of his public, rather than a portrait of the descript, the object described.[13] As Bachelor Tomás López Medel wrote from South America to the Habsburg sovereigns in 1551:

Please don't trust any message or personal memory received from here, nor the ones from our most perfect saints, because our life here is defined by passions, ambition and personal interests . . . and anyone of us always writes according to the opinions and projects he supports . . . I know that, as our kings and masters, it is your obligation to read and mind the arguments proposed by each one of us, but, please, mistrust us all.[14]

"Here" and "there," the periphery and the center, the "apoderado" and the sovereigns, the empowered and the remote sources of any colonial power—in fact, the defining elements of the center, its power, and its position—are the relations among the parts and not the parts in themselves or their subjectivities. Any center depends upon perspective and can be identified, seen, and described from various points of view. In the imperial tradition of modern Europe, the historical center has never been a precise geographical point. In spite of the propaganda and the mapping activities promoted by the royal courts to support the myth of their own centrality, in Europe and later in the Americas, the center always has been a horizon, a matter of perspective, defined by a shifting frontier.

During the *ancien régime*, the fascination of the year 1492 was enormous.[15] From Montaigne's famous essay *Des Cannibals* (1580) to Lahontan's *Dialogues avec un sauvage* (1703), the face-to-face encounter between Selfness and Otherness was narrated many times and always as a meaningful experience.[16] Most of the different versions (including those of utopia, the state of nature, cannibalism, and ritual sacrifice) have included a moral dimension. During the late Renaissance, or Golden Age, the cultural shock of the New World was used as a mask (as in Shakespeare's *The Tempest*), in order to elude censorship or to describe other things: the non-utopian present of England (More), the violent youth of the market economy (Hobbes), and the religious civil wars in France (Montaigne). The reference to the New World became a fascinating instrument to focus on other conflicts. As Alain Corbin suggests, during the seventeenth century and the first half of the eighteenth century, the Holy Bible and the Latin and Greek traditions still dominated the book market, the popular imagination, and the making of the European mind.[17] Only after 1750 (and the publication of Diderot's *Encyclopédie*) did the empirically based representation of the Atlantic world become relatively free from the moral legacy of the past.

THE EAST, THE WEST, AND MANY PLACES IN
BETWEEN: BARBARIANS AND/OR SAVAGES

If the Eastern lands are famous because of their peculiarities and
wonders, even Western margins are to be mentioned because of their
natural marvels. Sometimes Nature, tired of being serious and real,
keeps herself a little aside and here, feeling free because of the re-
moteness of marginal regions, plays the game of transgression, with
shy and secret excess.
—Giraldus Cambrensis, *Topographia Hibernica*, 1188

After World War II, the Iron Curtain, cutting the body of Europe in two
parts, polarized the continent and created the complementary myths of a
Western Euro-American and an Eastern Euro-Asiatic Europe. When the
Iron Curtain fell, along with the Berlin Wall, in November 1989, the European Community, which had grown from the ruins of World War II as
a typical product of enlightened cosmopolitanism and pacifism, was
restyled as the European Union. It rediscovered the enlightened roots of
the project, but also drew elements from a different and earlier tradition,
making the Union's universalism a composite one. The institutional network, originally conceived to include potentially any European and
democratic nation-state, and to control and dissolve any authoritarian
nationalism, was now becoming a container of national identities and a
mechanism to orient the transitional phases of peripheral nation-states
toward modernity and Western democracy.

In this contemporary context, we may reconsider the links between the
universalism of the Enlightenment and the historical expansion of the
colonial empires previously created by the so-called composite monarchies. These links conditioned the beginnings of anthropology as a scientifically based activity of observation and recording about human societies
and manners (a science of culture and of men, rather than a science of Man
or a science of Mankind). Such observation and recording occurred in the
context of an extension (a westward, oceanic, and scientifically oriented
extension) of the antisystematic attitude defined by the word "essay." The
written discourse of the "essay" was something more than a new genre.
Diderot's *Encyclopédie* was the project whose framework offered the "essay" a new role in the Age of Enlightenment, as the meaning of the word
shifted from Montaigne's ideal of variety (of arguments and topics) toward
a more complex notion.[18]

The essay's traditional key elements (the use of a modern language for
works of erudition, an urgent curiosity about novelty of any kind, a new
style and more than a touch of methodological skepticism) established the

basis for the exhibition of a rhetorical mix of pride and modesty. Like their authors, the essays were audience-oriented and antiauthoritarian, a nonsystematic alternative to the scholastic tradition.[19] The opposition "essay" *versus* "treatise" encouraged the emergence of the anthropological mythologies of the Atlantic world. The essay became the vehicle for the rediscovery of the Americas. From the Renaissance to the Age of Enlightenment, the dialectics between the centers and the margins, and the relation between ruling power and organized knowledge concerning the so-called New Worlds, indicate the path that we are going to follow to reconstruct the transition from discovery to rediscovery or, in other terms, from discovery to anthropology. This retrospective exercise concerned the modern origins of the Western wor(l)d-wide science and technique we call anthropology. It depended upon the New Worlds, but also upon a new grammar and some new words.

Over the last three centuries, the Western identity of both Europe and the Atlantic world has always been produced by semantic exercises of cultural and political defining, sketching, and reframing. The linguistic nature of this problematic iconology meant a mythical coincidence between the complementary horizons of naming and mapping.[20] For instance, within the changing borders of Poland, the name "Poland" was preserved. Likewise, the towns of Buenos Aires, La Havana, Mazagão (a Portuguese North African settlement that, according to Laurent Vidal [2005], "crossed the Atlantic" between 1769 and 1771), and even Avezzano (the small mountain village of central Italy, where my family name originates) are not located where they existed originally, when and where their history began. Many other urban settlements (for example, Constantinople or Saint Petersburg) remain in the same place, but their name has changed through history. If the same town can be renamed and if the same name can follow the changing identity of an urban community, it is because the world of semantics is not organized in terms of coincidence, but in terms of memory, perspective, continuity, and limits. As the epigraph from Giraldus Cambrensis suggests, reality itself sets a limit for the shifting of limits. The borders of Poland shifted eastward and westward a number of times, but never so often as those of the mythical kingdom of Prester John!

After November 1989, the cultural nature (memory, perspectives, continuity, and a concrete series of historical limits) of Europe and the Western world became more evident than ever before, defying the previously accepted geographical conventions. The Euro-Atlantic cultural perspective, called the Western world, was clearly expanding eastward, in a theater of evolving geopolitics, reoriented according to the reframing of the Euro-Atlantic Self. A series of crises became the mirror for the changing perspective of self-definition in post–Cold War Europe, as experienced in new relations with Latin America, Russia, the Balkans, and the Middle East. Many of the contributors to this volume were soon to become involved in the 1990s, directly or indirectly, in this academic reframing of the modern Western identity of Europe and the Atlantic.

From the age of the great discoveries on, Europe began looking eastward, westward, and backward for a better definition of its own historicity and identity. Greek culture, the Roman Empire, and the Christian tradition defined the maps of the past, but it was during the eighteenth century that Europe made its own West into "the West" and its own East into "the East." The European continent itself, seen through the modern lens of global perspectives created by the anthropologists of the Enlightenment, became a meeting point, an intermediary area where Nature and Art converged, a landscape garden, a theatrical stage of moralized knowledge, a copy of Eden. By mapping the communitarian savageries of the naked Indians and of the barbarians in terms of tribes (like biblical Israel) and primitivism (like the Christian Apostles), the imagination of European civilization combined the Great Code of the Holy Bible[21] with the Western myth called Nature and the Eastern one called Barbarism. European consciousness shifted toward the Atlantic to become more modern (from Italy to Spain during the sixteenth century, and later from France to England).[22] Barbarism and savagery, the barbarians and the savages, the primitives and the natural men, defined the cultural limits of evolving European identity, making European civilization and its composite tradition a space in between. Europe and its modern mind defined the evolving center of a chronological continuum called Western civilization, a link between memory and project, the background and the promised land. It was the homeland of the present and of presence, self-defined in opposition to the remote margins of the Eastern past (the Barbarians) and the Western future (the Savages).

During the seventeenth century, the savage world became a symbol. Native Americans, Africans, and African Americans entered modernity representing an absolute idea of Nature and mythical Innocence. As Aphra Behn wrote in *Oroonoko, or The Royal Slave* (1688):

And these People represented to me an absolute *Idea* of the first State of Innocence, before Man knew *how to sin:* And 'tis most evident and plain, that *simple Nature* is the most harmless, inoffensive and vertuous Mistress. 'Tis she alone, if she were permitted, that *better instructs the World, than all the Inventions of Man:* Religion wou'd here but destroy that Tranquillity they possess *by Ignorance*; and Laws wou'd but teach'em to know Offence, of which they have no Notion.[23]

The eastern borders of Europe were a different and more artificial primitive space. This was not a landscape of Nature, but a stage for naturalization.

When he visited Poland in the first half of the seventeenth century, Marc-Antoine de Saint-Amant summarized the rules and the sequence (dress, fashion, manners, language, translation, renaming) of this role-playing game:

> The thought comes to me . . .
> To dress as a proud and noble Sarmatian . . .
> To follow the Polish fashion in everything . . .
> I am named the fat Saint-Amantsky.[24]

The building of an Atlantic and Euro-American vision of the world made continuity with the Indo-European tradition of the barbaric invasions less evident and even unconscious. The westward epic of the Portuguese, the Spanish, and the British transatlantic expansions were not recounted as a new wave of Indo-European invasions. On the one hand, the Christian prophetic legacy and, on the other hand, the ambiguous category of "the Indians"—adopted in the Renaissance to describe the native populations of the New Worlds—made this myth of continuity impossible.[25] The Indians of the so-called West Indies slowly evolved into "natives," "aboriginals," and "indigenous" peoples, but during the long coda of the Renaissance they also remained "Indians." It was a matter of geography, but it was, even more, a matter of history. Eastward and westward were space horizons, but at the same time they were parts of a discourse (rather than territories and lands) connecting the past (the background) and the future (the New World) in a single narrative, in a single world and in a single word (as Indians).[26]

Jack Goody has pointed out[27] that techniques of writing have been crucial for the taming of non-European minds. Jorge Cañizares-Esguerra has suggested that they have been even more important for the making of the European mind itself. Through language and grammar Europe exported the logic of progress and colonized the future. In this New World of authorized and printed words, Father Antonio Vieira, a Portuguese Jesuit and missionary of the seventeenth century, wrote a book whose title can be considered a manifesto of this forward-looking historical consciousness: *Prolegomenos da história do futuro.*

UNIVERSAL DICTIONARIES AND ENCYCLOPEDIAS,

DATA AND DOCUMENTS

ART: a Portion of Science, or general Knowledge, considered not in it-self, as Science, but with relation to its Circumstances, or Appendages.

—Ephraim Chambers, *Cyclopaedia*, 1728, Preface

The first explicit mention of the word "anthropology" to name a conscious project of organized knowledge about Man is in Chavannes's works—*Essai sur l'education intellectuelle, avec le projet d'une science nouvelle* (1787) and *Anthropologie, ou science générale de l'homme* (1788)—but the origins of the notion lay in the new attitude encouraged by the style of the essay. Before Chavannes, before Diderot's *Encyclopédie*, organized knowledge about Man (like Medicine)[28] was practical rather than theoretical, an Art more than a Science, a field for aphorisms, essays, dialogues (about *sauvagerie*: from Lahontan and Buffier to Voltaire and Diderot), and even *Lettres édifiantes et curieuses* (the Jesuits, from 1702) rather than the subject matter of treatises. It always involved history and contexts, even in the present tense, which is typical of any dictionary.

From the beginnings of missionary ethnography, medicine offered metaphors to describe the making of this new field and style. Fray Bernardino de Sahagún opened the prologue of his *Historia general de las cosas de Nueva España* as follows:

> The physician cannot accurately prescribe medication to the ill person without knowing the origins or cause of the illness. Thus, a good physician must be knowledgeable in terms of medications as well as in regard to illnesses in order to appropriately apply to each illness its opposite medication . . . The sins of idolatry, idolatrous rites, idolatrous superstitions, ceremonies, omens, and abuses have not been completely lost. In order to preach against them, and even to determine if they indeed still exist, one must know how they were used by the Indians during the period of idolatry, etc.[29]

We know Sahagún was a Franciscan friar who described the pagan rituals of the Mexican Indians in order to organize their destruction and make them disappear, but the text also contained a radical program, conceived to efface any form of superstition.

For Sahagún, the first and the best "remedio" against superstition was a new model of curiosity and of practical and universal knowledge. The entry into this early anthropology was through language. New words were the keys of access to the New World: "This work is like a net which brings up to light all the words of this language, with their own meanings, their metaphoric meanings and manners of speech, most of the ancient ones, the good and the bad."[30] For this reason, Fray Bernardino describes his mission as medicine and his own work as a general dictionary or, in his own terms, as an unauthorized "Calepino":

> When this work was started, those who heard about it began saying that it would be like a Calepino . . . Indeed it would be very beneficial to write such a useful book for those who wish to learn this Mexican language. That is what Ambrosio Calepino did for those who wanted to learn the Latin language and the meaning

of its words. However, the same cannot be done in this case. Calepino extracted the Latin words, their meanings, difficulties, and metaphors from the works of poets, orators, and other Latin writers. Thus, he was able to back up all of his statements with their texts. I do not have such an opportunity, for these people do not have letters or writing. This is why it was impossible for me to write a Calepino.[31]

Fray Bernardino collected oral materials recorded by transcription and through images. He used language and linguistics (grammars and dictionaries) as the provisional framework for field anthropology. The manuscript of his Indian Calepino, called *General History of the Things of New Spain* (including divine, human, and natural things), was a catalogue of words in context, whose "glosas" were short articles or essays.

At the beginning of the eighteenth century, with the general crisis of *auctoritas* and the new wave of the "*querelle des anciens et des modernes,*" the model of sixteenth-century missionary linguistics and the logic of Sahagún's unauthorized and unpublished Calepino were still the best available format for the collecting and organizing of universal knowledge. The key elements of this attitude were "art" and the "universal dictionary." Art, in Latin and in Spanish, was still at that time a synonym for grammar (we have many "Artes" of various languages). Universal, in combination with Dictionary, meant at the same time "worldwide" and "complete."

To become a useful imperial instrument of practical and universal knowledge, any historical language required an Art. From Calepino, to Technical Dictionary, to Universal Dictionary, to Encyclopaedia, in historical sequence, the new "Art" (that is, grammar) of the essay used words to conquer the world. The early eighteenth-century English universal dictionaries included *Lexicon Technicum, or A Universal English Dictionary of Art and Sciences* by John Harris (1704) and the *Cyclopaedia, or An Universal Dictionary of Arts and Sciences: Containing the Definitions of the Terms, and Accounts of the Things Signify'd Thereby, in the Several Arts, Both Liberal and Mechanical, and the Several Sciences, Human and Divine,*[32] by Ephraim Chambers (1728).[33]

All Science (human and divine!) was, in itself, a matter of "relation" between Theory and Practice; any Art (including grammar), however, could be defined as the medium of such a "relation," a combination of Experience, Observations, and Skill. According to Chambers, Art was the key to the passage from catalogue to perspective, from *Universal Dictionary* to *Cyclopaedia*. The word "Art" does not define a complete, worldwide, and autonomous body of knowledge, but just: "a Portion of Science, or general Knowledge, considered not in it-self, as Science, but with relation to its Circumstances, or Appendages." So "Science" was still a synonym for the all-involving notion of general knowledge. "Art," however, was what we now call a system (a notion defined by Condillac in 1749, in a *Traité*, not in an *Art*). The most characteristic framework of Art defined "with relation to its circumstances, or appendages" was centrality, a notion always assumed and supported by the Arts.[34]

The new "Arts" of the Enlightenment, including eighteenth-century anthropology (which before Chavannes's 1787 project was not a "Science"), had their roots in the imperial imagination of the Renaissance and the Baroque period. "Artistically" considered, the lights of the Enlightenment were instruments of theatrical technique, parts of a staging machine conceived to produce shadows and dark sides, like, for instance, the famous Black Legend, *leyenda negra*.[35] The "Sciences," however, in the Age of Enlightenment, supported the ideal of a pure and full light, with little room left for shadows or dark sides.

The myth of the present and the center, imposed by the perspective of the Arts, offered the framework of a progressive and entirely civilized living tradition, whose activities—copying and describing life—should link the legacy of the past to any possible perspective on the future. From the early Renaissance to the end of the Enlightenment (from discovery to anthropology, from Columbus's navigation to Darwin's circumnavigation, from a caravel named *Santa María* to a brigantine named *The Beagle*), a new world project called modern identity was prophetically conceived and shown as European and Atlantic. The Renaissance and, later on, the Enlightenment made possible a "universal" discourse about human and natural life.[36] It marked a turning point in the intellectual history and tradition of Europe, the Atlantic, and the West. Man, life, and nature, classified in their variety, became parts of the same development and characters in the same story, elements of a single frame, recorded in a single file, ordered according to the stages of a single progress. The idea of progress emerged in the second half of the eighteenth century as a central theme of the Enlightenment. This story, supported by the material documents recorded in the huge body and archive of the earth, was larger and more dramatic than any mythical narrative about origins ever told before. Progress was seriously moral, but it could not be easily moralized (any longer). Each tradition, whether bequeathed, revealed, or "invented," had a part in it. Everything was real and existing as part of the same narrative, but nothing could be considered true "in it-self," because truth was always a matter of perspective, of art and shadows—to be defined, as for any other aspect of civilization, "with relation to its circumstances and appendages."

Columbus in 1492 offered a prophetic fantasy about the possibility of using the gold of the New World to fund the conquest of Jerusalem. Two centuries later, in 1762, the Capuchin Ilarione da Bergamo visited Mexico:

"to seek alms for the maintenance of our missionaries in the realm of Tibet and other adjacent realms."[37] The worldwide expansion of Jesuit missions, the circumnavigations of Anson, Cook, and Bougainville, and the Siberian and Mexican travels of Chappe d'Auteroche, transformed the market logic of this East-West connection and of its instruments and techniques (sciences and arts) into the first useful framework of Western modernity, a global bridge across cultures. Between 1540 and 1773, to use a chronological frame that is obviously meaningful for studies concerning the Society of Jesus,[38] "Cultures, Sciences, and the Arts" explored the global horizons of this new scenario. Early anthropologists learned from the late Jesuits, just as early Jesuits had once learned from the Franciscans.

Sixteenth-century Franciscans, seventeenth-century Jesuits, and the early anthropologists of the eighteenth century mixed and combined the three levels of cultures, sciences, and arts. They pursued the great adventure of intellectual geography as a strategic instrument for changing perspective, in historiography as well as in linguistics and in the natural sciences. They described the basic experience of Western modernity: the face-to-face encounter with Otherness.

The series of key words for the American New World has been: Discovery, Conquest, Mission, Colony, Ethnography, Anthropology, and Scientific Anthropology. The first part of the sequence—Discovery, Conquest, Colony—suggests a quest for law and order, perceived and conceived as useful principles for any ongoing and overseas expansion of the Euro-Atlantic notion of "*Ordem e Progresso*" (according to the slogan that still appears on the Brazilian flag). The second part of the sequence—Ethnography, Anthropology, Scientific Anthropology—suggests the public dimension of language, description, and perspective, considered as possible instruments of cultural hegemony.

Ever since the eastern campaigns of Alexander the Great, the westward building of modern transatlantic empires has been perhaps the first serious project directed toward progressive world unification. The Spanish encounter with the New World fed upon many cultural elements, including the reconquest of medieval Spain, the Christian humanism of Erasmus, and the imperial crown of Charles V. The early modern consciousness of Europe and of Western civilization emerged as a new ideal of world order. That order included a new order for words: the modern style of the essay, and the systematic production of "Arts" and "Universal Dictionaries," devoted to normalizing many modern and ancient languages, including those of the Amerindians. From the beginning, anthropology would be a part of this westward expansion and would also offer a critical perspective on it.[39]

During the Age of Enlightenment, most of the best documented European crossings of the Pacific Ocean (for instance, Anson's, 1740–44;

Bougainville's, 1766–69; and, later, Darwin's, 1831–36) were completed by sailing westward as part of a "*Voyage autour du monde*" (which became the title of Bougainville's account). Even when it included new data based on direct experience, eighteenth-century anthropological work was intellectually a two-step process, the product of a reassessment that left anthropology chronologically and critically separated from its sources, from its basis in fieldwork, and deeply influenced by personal and national interests, markets, and polemics. Diderot's dialogic *Supplément* (1772) to Bougainville's *Voyage autour du monde* (1771) offers one of the most explicit examples of this anthropology of critical reassessment. Direct observations were often set in dialogue with recent and ancient sources, in order to check, to confirm, or to disprove their authority. The effort involved in collecting, translating, and publishing old documents and prophecies, most of them concerning the so-called West Indies, was enormous. Juan Bautista Muñoz, a lawyer from Valencia whom the Court of Madrid made "Cosmógrafo Mayor de Indias," collected and revised the whole corpus of Spanish documents concerning the Atlantic to offer a basis for a Spanish edition of Robertson's *History of America* and, ultimately—when this idea was abandoned—for a completely new book.

The early anthropologists were the children of the "end of the Renaissance";[40] they believed in philology and they employed it on the composite corpus of their tradition. While looking backward and westward, they recycled textual techniques of the Renaissance to reshape the textual legacy of the Renaissance itself. At the same time, they were also members of the intellectual elite of the transitional society of the Enlightenment. Eighteenth-century anthropologists experienced the collapse of the *ancien régime* from within. In the second half of the eighteenth century, Europe itself was becoming a New World.

Most of the eighteenth-century European crossings of the Pacific Ocean were made and recounted according to the westward geographical epic of the Renaissance. The encounter with the eastward expansion of the Russian Empire (the voyages of Bering in the first half of the eighteenth century, and the so-called secret expedition promoted by the Russian governor of Siberia, Vassilj Miatlev, in 1753) was a shock for the Spaniards. This shock was echoed in the book *I Moscoviti nella California (The Muscovites in California)*, published in Rome by the Franciscan José Torrubia in 1758.

More than a century would pass after Bougainville's and Cook's travels, until a new constellation of scientific authorities, travelers, and artists—such as Melville and Taylor, Livingstone and Stanley, Verne and Salgari, Stevenson and Conrad, Amunsen and Nansen, Boas and Malinowski,

Benedict and Mead, and Gauguin and Flaherty—explored the new horizons of the Arctic and the Antarctic, of Africa and the islands of the South Seas, reorienting the anthropological imagination of the Western world toward a rediscovery of the polarity of North and South. The centrality of the Euro-Atlantic nations was reasserted, but the new peripheries would lie along a North-South rather than an East-West axis. The gap between the North and the South became the framework for both imperialism and the end of colonization; it would be used to explain the underdevelopment of the Third and the Fourth Worlds, but also to investigate a concrete series of regional, national, and even local paths toward modernization.

THE REBIRTH OF THE ATLANTIC COMMUNITY
IN THE AGE OF THE COLD WAR

> From different Parents, different Climes we came. At different periods. Fate still rules the same Unhappy Youth while bleeding on the ground; 'It was Yours to fall—but mine to feel the Wound.'
> —J. G. Stedman, frontispiece of *Narrative of a Five Years Expedition Against the Revolted Negroes of Surinam*, 1794

After the end of World War II, when Europe was under reconstruction, the Iron Curtain revealed the renewed importance of East and West and of imperial ideology. The postwar reorienting of world geopolitics recycled the mapping, the language, and the symbols of older empires and older polemics. The making of the historical discourse rediscovered perspective and prophecy, concerning the "rise and fall" of new and old imperial powers.

Already before the war, Silvio Zavala studied the institutional basis of the Atlantic world, describing the modified and "modernized" American *encomienda* as an Indian version of the frontier institution of the Spanish Reconquista.[41] During the war, in 1943, the Italian scholar Antonello Gerbi renewed the tradition of intellectual history, publishing in Peru the book that became famous as *La disputa del Nuovo Mondo: storia di una polemica (1759–1900)*, and in 1948, at the moment of the reemergence of the East-West logic of the Cold War, J. A. Manzano y Manzano, the biographer of Columbus, summarized in a single word, "incorporación,"[42] the imperial and colonial strategy of the Castillian Crown. Later, Edmundo O'Gorman, a Mexican colleague of Zavala, combining intellectual and institutional history, proposed another crucial concept: "invention."[43] The object of the "incorporación"/"invención" was named "Indias" (the West

Indies) in Zavala's and Manzano y Manzano's titles and "America" (later, the Americas) in O'Gorman's perspective.

During this period of early Cold War historiography, the transition from discovery to anthropology began to be described as the transition from a religious or missionary ethnography (mostly Catholic) to a scientific model of internationally organized knowledge concerning humankind:[44] anthropology became the discourse of colonial self-consciousness. Meanwhile, the Western world was experiencing two overlapping intellectual perspectives: strategy, ideology, and politics were again strictly East-West oriented, but the North-South orientation prevailed for business, culture, postcolonial transition phases, and international cooperation.

The worldwide success of the Latin American novel, from the late 1960s on, was at the same time a cultural and a political event. Nobody interpreted it as a Western phenomenon. In Europe as well as in the United States, the international cultural industry saw it as a counter-conquest movement by which a group of very well-promoted young writers from the deepest South, a region of poverty and oppression, dramatically broke onto the best-seller lists of the rich North. Despite the Marxist ideology of many of the authors (they were considered Communists, and most of them have been and still are close friends of Castro and the Cuban Revolution), their literature was essentially global and absolutely Western.

Yet, the epic of the overwhelming impact of the "Indians" on the sleepy Spanish cultural market of late Francoism has been recounted according to a completely different imagery: Joaquín Marco and Jordi Gracia[45] have explicitly compared the arrival of the new Latin American literature in Spain and Europe with the older barbarian invasions from the East. Very Western in many personal and professional regards, García Márquez and Vargas Llosa, Fuentes and Cortázar, and Donoso and Carpentier lacked all the basic characteristics of historical barbarism: they were extremely polite (even cosmopolite), they were cultural sons of the empire they were invading, and they perfectly mastered the Latin of their Romans. The Catalan publishing industry opened the European market to their works, and converted their success and political radicalism into a powerful instrument to modernize and renew Spanish culture. Extremely Western and modern, these writers were not the "Indians" they pretended to be, nor the "barbarians" the book market and Spanish cultural industry wanted them to be. Still, they were perceived "mythically" as Indians and, in Spain, as invaders and barbarians.

After 1989, when glasnost politics dissolved the Iron Curtain and the quick *decline and fall* of the "Evil Empire" became complete, forty years of symbolic mapping strategies also collapsed, leaving the Western world all alone, face to face with the "buried mirror" of 1992, the fifth centennial of the Great Discovery; in 1992, when Carlos Fuentes published *The Buried Mirror: Reflections on Spain and the New World*,[46] the ambiguous nature and the distorting effects imposed by Cold War logic were becoming more and more evident and cried out for a revision. So, when I first met Larry Wolff, in Paris, on the occasion of the "East-West Seminar" of 1994, organized by Robert Darnton, many subjects concerning East and West, Eastern Europe and Western Europe, and the rediscovery of America and the West Indies in the Age of Enlightenment were ready to be reexamined, in cultural history as in geopolitics. Our respective academic books, *Tra memoria apostolica e racconto profetico: il compromesso etnografico francescano in Nuova Spagna (1524–1621)* and *Inventing Eastern Europe: The Map of Civilization on the Mind of the Enlightenment*, were both published in 1994 and both focused on problems of European identity and its modern formation. A set of cultural questions was then reemerging on the agenda of the political present and the economic future. Most of these questions had been asked first during the Renaissance, and some of them had even been answered, later on, during the eighteenth century. The Atlantic skyline of our common and contradictory cultural past contained the narrative and the memory of when and where the Center and the West became one and the same.

Now, thirteen years later, the present project and volume, collecting different voices and papers, can be seen as a bridge, constructed in order to communicate across the cultural, historical, geographical, and even genre gaps that separate, in their different relationships with Europe and the European mind, the two peripheral worlds whose invention we described in our 1994 books: the Latin American and the Slavic, the Spanish dominions and the Russian Empire, Iberia and the Balkans, the intellectual communities of the Spanish friars and of the French philosophes, the rhetoric of ethnographic description and the rhetoric of travel writing, and the Christian Renaissance and the secular Enlightenment.

Meanwhile, most of the countries of Latin America and of Eastern Europe were entering into a new phase of their history. Making the so-called third wave of democratization complete and concrete, they experienced both the network of the new global economy and the violent impact of its contradictory social effects. The international controls on debt and on public banking policies supported the advent of transnational companies. Market deregulation made the recent democracies the first explorers of the limits and the contradictions that are peculiar to any transitional phase.

From Gibbon to Spengler, the East and the West have been rhetorically invoked as representational reference points for the rise, the decline, and the fall of civilizations, for looking backward and looking forward. The rhetorical counterpoint and dialogue between East and West are related to the fact that they are both defined with respect to a common center: Europe and/or the Atlantic. East and West exist as two counterparts of the modern European discourse, as two different accents of the same voice. All the basic patterns of our classical historical perspectives over time are present here: the parable and the cycle, memory (to be preserved) and prophecy (to be accomplished), the destiny mythically revealed and the progressive imagination of the secularized mind, the past and the future, the mountains where we think we originate and the wide open sea we dream of crossing. From this point of view, the contents of this volume also sketch a collective portrait of the intellectual framework that made this project of transatlantic cooperation possible and based on common ground. It includes echoes and fragments from more than ten years of personal and professional conversations between me, a European specialist about the Americas, and Larry Wolff, an American specialist about Continental and Eastern Europe.

Lewis Carroll's Alice entered Wonderland because the book of history she peeped into (her sister's book) seemed too poor to her in pictures and conversations. Most of my conversations with Larry and even some pictures of our respective families (sent across the Atlantic in order to escape from the boredom that, according to Alice, is characteristic of us historians and our books) made the United States and Italy (Southwestern Europe!) a personal extension of our professional dialogue concerning Eastern Europe and Latin America. Mixing these two levels, we could identify and explore four different forms of the contemporary postcolonial West. The two Wests we lived in—Southwestern Europe and the East coast of the United States—were relatively more central and similar; the two we worked on—Latin America and Eastern Europe—were relatively more peripheral and different. But wherever we were—at home and in our respective professional fields, in Mexico and in Berlin, in Venice and in Las Vegas (and even more so visiting the Las Vegas version of Venice!)—we never felt lost. Always and everywhere we could clearly perceive the all-embracing shadow of a deep continuity: in some way, our professional and personal worlds and words (which do not include the whole of the world and of words) were one (or different parts of the same thing). Through a sophisticated mechanism of partial exclusion, the universal imagination of the Enlightenment defined each of our four worlds as modern, Western, European, and Atlantic, making each one of them a fragment of a wider unity. The intellectual project of the Western tradition was at work all around us and worked surprisingly well, everywhere and anytime. Mixing hegemonic ambitions and ethnocentric self-promotion with the possibility of an insightful critical revision of its own basis, the cultural character of the West was demonstrating an impressive capacity for inclusion and adaptation.

Being two, Larry Wolff and I, and also four (because of the added perspectives of our respective fields), our multiple consciousness and the fond memory of the Republic of Letters has conditioned our cooperation and helped us to negotiate the competing intellectual currents that constitute the modern and postmodern academic discourse of the West.

THE "END" OF THE ENLIGHTENMENT: DARWIN, TOCQUEVILLE, AND THE PUBLIC

> Je m'assure que ceux qui n'ont pas tant voyagé que moi et qui ne savent pas toutes les raretés de la nature, pour les avoir presque toutes vues comme j'ai fait, ne seront point marris que je leur aprenne quelque particularité.
> —Marc-Antoine de Saint-Amant, *Moïse sauvé*,
> "Préface," Leyden, 1654

Our academic dialogue became possible and could make sense because of two elements: the Ocean in between and the bridging tradition of the Enlightenment, which offered us a common background and intellectual framework. The historical reciprocity between the geographical legacy of the Renaissance and the intellectual tradition of the Enlightenment remains meaningful in a transatlantic context.[47] By mixing maps and prophecies, the epic of the Great Discovery defined and explored the image and the idea of a moveable West. The anthropology of the Enlightenment would redefine and classify it according to intellectual principles and formulas, concerning the interpretation of the transition from discovery to anthropology.

Over the last three centuries, various formulas inspired by the same logic have been at work in any transoceanic encounter between the self-limited free will of individuals and the intellectual measure of universal reason, wherever and whenever the Enlightenment and the Atlantic world have met each other, within the Western tradition. The shift from discovery to anthropology (that is, invention through rediscovery) became possible in the Age of Enlightenment. During the eighteenth century, the curiosity of early anthropologists was potentially overwhelmed by the access to an increasing quantity of data and observations (collected by travelers and scientists all over the world). Old and new information and data required a new intellectual framework to be organized in a coherent network. The "philosophes" interested in anthropology needed criteria of selection, useful principles of analysis, and a methodical attitude. They needed to be "oriented" or "reoriented" (in all the Western languages, the concept of orientation is linguistically Eastern). They needed to rely on a useful set of formulas and principles. All this did occur when Eastern Europe was invented, when the Atlantic world and the Americas were rediscovered.

During the eighteenth century, in the Age of Neoclassicism, the first Renaissance discipline to be redeployed was philology. The systematic comparison between the Ancients and the Moderns (the famous "querelle") juxtaposed the dead and the living, documents and direct experiences, reading and traveling. From the Peruvian expedition organized by the French Scientific Academy in 1735–44 until the 1831–36 journey of Charles Darwin, the idea of understanding difference *versus* sameness according to the principles of a universal logic has been *the* framework for articulating relations between history and life, the past and the present, the Old World and the New Worlds. This was a matter of ideas, but also of attitude, language, and personal style. The renewal of the scientific arena and the understanding of the New Worlds required a complicated mix of *ancien régime* and democracy, aristocracy and public opinion, empires and free trade, court rituals and gazettes, salons and magic lanterns.

Darwin's *Journal of Research*, the self-portrait of a naturalist as a young man, can be considered among the last of the enlightened wor(l)d adventures and, at the same time, a memoir of the last scientific westward travel of the Enlightenment. The *Journal* (first published in 1839 as part of the complex memory of the *Beagle* expedition, edited by Captain Robert Fitz-Roy) presents the experiences and memories of Darwin and the way he recorded and absorbed the "shock" of the New World. In a recent article entitled "Darwin's Savage Mnemonics," Cannon Schmitt insists on this crucial dimension, comparing the *Beagle* papers with other writings of the famous naturalist to underline how and why the first encounter with "an untamed savage" became "unforgettable" for Darwin. According to Schmitt, in Darwin's mind, the heritage of the Scottish Enlightenment (the savage seen as a contemporary primitive or barbarian) was paving the way for something new: the savages become "memorable" because "they are themselves instigation to memory, living mnemonic devices."[48]

For us, the most interesting aspects concern, on the one hand, the legacy of Alexander Von Humboldt, and on the other hand, the fact that the first meeting with some untamed savages of Tierra del Fuego and the observations made in the Galapagos Islands seem to divide, both psychologically and scientifically, the sea adventures of the young Darwin into two parts. The *Beagle* made a complete circumnavigation, from England to England (from Davenport to Falmouth), but, after the Galapagos Islands, Darwin's *Journal* is as flat and uninteresting as a conventional chapter of travel literature.[49] The Pacific Ocean (that is, the coral formations, the extreme isolation of the islands, and the good savages of the South Seas) impressed Darwin as a scientist and inspired his revolutionary notes on natural selection, but, from a more personal point of view, the Pacific offered him only a long way home. On the other hand, the Atlantic, the continental excursion, and the circumnavigation of Latin America (visited between 1832 and 1835) changed him forever. An enlightened traveler became a "patient man," ready for boredom and suffering (as he wrote in various letters and in the pages of his *Autobiography*, written many years later). Darwin landed in Falmouth, after almost five years spent traveling around the globe on the famous brigantine, on October 2, 1836. As he wrote in a letter to captain Robert Fitz-Roy, this day was a sort of new birthday: a "second life" was beginning for him. Like Voltaire's Candide, after visiting the whole of the world, Darwin retired to Downe, Kent, southwest of London, and spent most of his "second life" raising his own roses in his own garden, as a quiet man, a family gentleman, and a cabinet anthropologist. But his own roses would become famous because of their revolutionary aroma: in July 1837, a few weeks after the beginning of the Victorian Age, he began the first draft of his *On the Origin of Species by Means of Natural Selection*. The new formulas proposed in this book, first published 1859, revolutionized science and even helped make anthropology a new science—influenced by Darwinism—so that enlightened anthropology became a closed chapter in intellectual history. In fact, Darwin's personal style and attitude as a traveler in the 1830s had perfectly embodied the mix of science, politics, and adventure that were characteristic of the Enlightenment. In 1830, before he traveled on the *Beagle*, Darwin read some of the memoirs and travels of Alexander von Humboldt.

It was Humboldt who brought the style of enlightened travel into the nineteenth century—travel as an adventure lived to be told—and both Darwin and Alexis de Tocqueville continued to travel in that style. Tocqueville's famous travels in the United States began in April 1831 and ended in March 1832 (meanwhile, the *Beagle* had left Davenport in December 1831). Between 1832 and 1835, when Darwin was discovering and exploring the coasts and the continent of South America, Tocqueville published the results of his voyage: *Du système pénitentiaire aux Etats-Unis et de son application en France*, in 1833, and the two volumes of *De la démocratie en Amérique*, between 1832 and 1835. This work can be compared with Humboldt's *Essai sur la Nouvelle Espagne du Méxique*, published in 1808 and based on the 1803–1804 visit. In these books we can recognize the nobleman and intellectual whose curiosity was seduced by the nature and the institutions of the New World. Dependence and inequality (Humboldt) and independence and equality (Tocqueville) deeply impressed the aristocratic mind of these two authors.

Of all the face-to-face encounters between the Old and the New World, Tocqueville's personal discovery of American democracy can be considered one of the most representative. The dialogue between two traditions, perceived as the old and the new one, was for Tocqueville's mnemonics a seminal experience, something as "unforgettable" as Darwin's first encounter with the "untamed savages," a few months later, in December 1832. The whole of Tocqueville's life and work, including *L'ancien régime et la révolution*, first published 1856, three years before Darwin's *Origin of Species by Means of Natural Selection*, emphasizes this same pattern.

Many other authors used the sophisticated technique of memory building mastered by Antonio de Ulloa, Humboldt, Tocqueville, and Darwin: among them the Spanish and the Spanish American Jesuits, banned in 1767 and exiled in Italy; the court cosmographer Juan Bautista Muñoz, who collected documents concerning the Spanish Indies for the projected Spanish edition of Robertson's *History of America*; and the Spanish nobleman Ramón de la Sagra, who, in 1836, published in Paris a complete report on his *Cinco meses en los Estados-Unidos de la América del Norte: Diario de viaje desde el 20 de Abril al 23 de Setiembre de 1835*. Theirs was more than a technique for making observations; it was a technique for remaking observations and managing information, writing about the experience of the new in different times and for different audiences. In order to understand this attitude we should focus on:

  a. *the chronological gap between the scientific experience and the writings it inspired*: Ulloa, Humboldt, Tocqueville, and Darwin reorganized their notes throughout their lives; the Jesuits and Muñoz had made this into an institutional technique, which Ramón de la Sagra transformed into a personal "reading" of the American reality; and
  b. *the issue of the audience*: Ulloa divided his work into two different reports, one for the public and another, called "secret," for his king; the Jesuits and Humboldt did the same thing, though in a different way, by reorganizing their observations at different levels; the Muñoz collection is still divided: half in the public library of the Real Academia de la Historia, and half in the less public space of the Palacio Real.

Despite their old-fashioned personal styles, authors such as Darwin, Tocqueville, and de la Sagra were extremely self-conscious and modern when they organized their arguments in order to reach their audiences. It was an act of theoretical violence, by which they assumed that modern authors are compelled to stress every argument, making it extreme and pushing it "to the limit of untruth"—as Toqueville himself suggests in the introduction to *Democracy in America*—and not because of logic, but because of democracy, communication, and language.

In this New World, the rules of everything are different and have to follow a different logic. Western issues of writing and reading shape the problem of Indian languages. According to Tocqueville: "The languages spoken by the savage tribes of America differ among themselves in their words, but all are subject to the same grammatical rules. These rules diverge at several points from those which have seemed to preside over the formation of language among men. The idiom of the Americans seems to be the product of new combinations."[50] Tocqueville, seduced by his own argument, added a footnote "*Sur les langues américaines,*" on the American languages, considered as a single family of languages and a recent field of study:

The languages spoken by the Indians of America, from the North Pole to Cape Horn, have all been formed, people say (*dit-on*), on the same model . . . It is only recently that the American languages, and especially the languages of North America, have attracted the serious attention of philologists. It has been discovered, for the first time, that this idiom of a barbarous people was the product of a very complicated system of ideas, of very erudite combinations. It has been noticed that these languages were very rich.[51]

A stated use of the sources ("dit-on"!), a strategy of presentation based on the relationship between text and notes, and a clear idea of the limits of Western logic: the cultural codes of eighteenth-century anthropology (the complementary myths of the savages and the barbarians) required a complex process of writing and rewriting to reach different audiences with different degrees and portions of the same information. Anthropology required a sophisticated perception of the social world (seen as a network) and of its theatrical organization. From the end of the Renaissance to the late Enlightenment, Europe became self-consciously modern, exploring its West and its East, but also exploring the variety of its public spheres.

THE ATLANTIC WORLD AND THE TRANSATLANTIC
RULES OF ACADEMIC DISCOURSE:
A READING-TRAVELING-WRITING MODEL FOR THE
ANTHROPOLOGY OF THE ENLIGHTENMENT

Your Lordship has read innumerable Volumes of Men and Books; not
Vainly for the gust of Novelty, but Knowledge, excellent Knowledge.
                —Aphra Behn, *Oroonoko, or The Royal Slave*,
                        "Epistle Dedicatory," 1688

The Atlantic world offers an interesting model of discursive transformation, because it was discovered (in the sixteenth century) and rediscovered
(in the eighteenth century). In the same period, the East of Europe was
explored (in the seventeenth century) and Eastern Europe invented (in the
eighteenth century). The Atlantic world was Europe's first New World,
and because of this priority mastered all of the later inclusions in European modernity. The distance between discovery in the sixteenth century and
rediscovery in the eighteenth century, newly discovered and discovered
again, is crucial for understanding the beginnings of anthropology.

Focusing on the epic history of cod fishing, Mark Kurlansky has written a brilliant antiacademic book about the logic that inspired the first
discovery of the Atlantic Ocean: *Cod: A Biography of the Fish That
Changed the World*, published in 1997. Four years later, in 2001, Jorge
Cañizares-Esguerra, in *How to Write the History of the New World*, focused on the changing perspectives of historiography in describing the rediscovery of the Atlantic world.[52] His work, based on a Ph.D. thesis, follows the academic standards and describes more how the history of the
New World was rewritten, rather than how it was originally written. The
protagonists of both books—cod, dried or salted; and the old geographical documents, philologically edited and collected or translated—widely
circulated all over Europe, offering "high-quality nutrition" to both the
material and the spiritual hungers of the European mind and imagination.
Traveling eastward and bringing the aroma and the image of the ocean to
the continent, fish and philology inspired a great cultural adventure that
actually "changed the world," as Kurlansky's subtitle suggests.

The reinvention of the Atlantic and the invention of Eastern Europe
were, therefore, almost contemporary. For Eastern Europe and the Americas, the rediscovery of the Atlantic became a point of reference and a
model of methodological identity. Europe itself disappeared, transformed
into pure perspective: the Atlantic world was not a "land" West, but
rather a "water" West, by which some European principles began to circulate all over the world.

The Atlantic rediscovered was not the "space of time" (according to the metaphor of Thomas Mann in his 1934 book *Meerfahrt mit Don Quijote*) that Larry Wolff and I were looking for in 1994, but it was the space of time we crossed (and we still need to cross) whenever we needed (and we need) a closer perspective on our respective research fields (Eastern Europe and Latin America). Three centuries of enlightened cultural history made the Atlantic shores into the shores of the West and its waters a borderland between mentalities, which reflect the differences between the public style of the academic communities and the teaching institutions the two of us have been involved in and working for in the last twenty years.

From this point of view, it is curious and maybe ironic that Larry Wolff's field (Eastern Europe and the Enlightenment) is usually considered to belong to the European discipline and my own field (Spanish American Literature and Linguistics) a mostly American one. The transatlantic dimension of our perspectives makes the ocean itself a perfect symbol of the different vistas that, in Western academic discourse concerning the Enlightenment, still separate the West of the Eastern (European) studies from the West of the Western (American) studies. Summarized and ordered in a single East-West sequence, the series mapped by the Enlightenment concerns: Eastern Europe, Europe, the Atlantic, America and Latin America, and marginally the Far North and the islands of the South Seas.

The Atlantic Ocean is neither my field, nor Larry Wolff's, but it has been the medium of the friendship and cooperation out of which this book was born. In spite of our friendship and personal goodwill, however, the ocean in itself would not have been enough. Our scientific dialogue would have never had a chance without the tradition of the *siècle des lumières*. Just like our first encounter and meeting in 1994 (at the East-West seminar for "young scholars," sponsored by the International Society for Eighteenth-Century Studies), the topic, the possibility, and the list of the contributors of this book are also an integral part of the intellectual legacy of the Enlightenment in its modern academic forms. Arguments and proposals have grown out of a complicated network of conversations, books, and travels, crossing the ocean in both directions, through geography and history. Meanwhile, the time has passed and we are no longer "young scholars," as we were in 1994. Some of our respective perspectives and opinions about identity, modernity, and the West have probably changed, but the family life and the conversational patterns of the academic field called Eighteenth-Century Studies have remained with us.

Over the last thirteen years, each of us has explored, from the personal and professional West he lived in, the opposite periphery of the cultural continent called the West, crossing the Atlantic world to approach its margins and to map the coastline of modern Western consciousness. From a discursive point of view, we traveled toward and inside the self-consciousness that

those margins redefined during the eighteenth century. Some shifts from discovery to anthropology (from the Renaissance to the Enlightenment, from
Otherness revealed to Selfness redefined) are now an accepted part of the
genres and rules of academic discourse and community. Academic discourse,
organizing the dialectics of topic and comment, the given and the new, is in
itself a representation of the institutional making of contemporary professional memory.[53] It is a theatrical mix of philology and nostalgia, and the
consequent critical self-consciousness is one of the most typical products of
the contemporary European mind.

The contributors to this volume on the anthropology of the Enlightenment have offered us, their editors, some part of their own critical self-
consciousness in this academic discourse. We would like to thank all the
authors for making this experiment in academic and personal archaeology possible and meaningful. Together with them we have explored the
"sources" that the philosophes of the Enlightenment selected, read, cut,
quoted, translated, organized, and bequeathed to us, as part (and possible
counterpart) of their anthropological heritage. At the same time, we offer
our interpretations of this legacy that they collected according to a particular chronology and/or a concrete series of references and preferences.
Both levels of discussion—sources and interpretations—allow us to focus
on a complex communication system that includes the reading, rewriting,
drawing, traveling, lecturing, translating, demonstrating, mapping, and
printing strategies and techniques that, in the Age of Enlightenment, encouraged the beginnings of modern anthropology.

Newly collected travel writings with new printed images and new rules
to select and identify citations transformed the book trade of the eighteenth century and the mind of the European public, recasting curiosity
about the world from the earlier mix of superstition, fear, and geographical gossip in the seventeenth century. The rediscovery/invention of New
Worlds (eastward and westward) in the Age of Enlightenment was the
product of a combination between synchronicity and history. It was a retrospective act of cultural colonization, a landscape gardening technique
expanded to the scale of transoceanic world geography and applied with
an element of exoticism. It can be compared with the rediscovery/inven-
tion of the classical world in the Renaissance.

As the humanists did with the manuscripts of the Latin and Greek
legacy, the early anthropologists of the eighteenth century collected, selected, revised, translated, and published travel documents and papers
produced by traders, soldiers, and missionary men from the late Middle
Ages on. For institutional and critical reasons, these early anthropologists
checked both the information and the narrative of their sources. This revival of the geographical imagination of the Renaissance made the travel

compilations of the seventeenth century and the corpus of the so-called *Annuae Litterae*, sponsored and produced by the members of the Society of Jesus, a more concise and convenient equivalent of the copying tradition of medieval monks. Within this critical revision, the Golden Age of both the Spanish Empire and French absolutism began to appear as dark centuries, the new and condensed Atlantic and American "Middle Ages." These modern "Middle Ages," including the so-called Black Legend, were rhetorically distorted to produce a sophisticated series of retrospective effects.

During the fifteenth and sixteenth centuries, the invention of focal depth and the historical formulation of the real Middle Ages introduced a thousand years of chronological chasm between the time of the Ancients and the time of the Moderns. During the eighteenth century, the authors of the neoclassical discourse repeated the same pattern in an accelerated version, in order to articulate modernity and reorient its logic. The Ancient and the Modern could be contemporary. The possibility of being or becoming modern with different rhythms, and not necessarily all at once and all together, permitted the historical coexistence of different degrees of modernity, of different paths to modernity, even of different kinds of modernity. With the new conception of progress, the image and narrative of our history became elements of a serial drama. The enlightened rediscovery of the Atlantic world deified and secularized the historical process at the same time. Modernity was transformed into a path toward the future, a transparent representation of our destiny.

Adapting a famous slogan of Marshall McLuhan's (*Understanding Media*, 1964), we can say that for the early anthropologists of the eighteenth century, "the medium was the message." Polemics, propaganda, and market techniques were important elements for defining the mechanism of the new modernity. The complementary strategies of traveling by reading and of reading by traveling (the portable books in octavo and sextodecimo became popular in the eighteenth century!) made the anthropologists of the Age of Enlightenment into an intellectual community of readers. At the same time, any reader could become involved, as a spectator, in the exciting social enterprise of horror and wonder, mastered by cabinet anthropologists. Some experiences concerning Otherness and some intellectual categories as new and stimulating as the *sauvage* and the *bizarre* could be directly experienced by any "amateur" or "dilettante." The spectacle of the Other's world received an increasing degree of publicity thanks to the scientific rituals sponsored and promoted by the courts, the circles of salon society, and the activities of the booksellers and the gazetteers. Through anthropology, a select public entered the circles of the philosophes. It was not (yet) a question of the modern public sphere, but it was something more than a simple matter of sociability. Such institutions as the Royal Society, Société des Sciences de l'Homme, Sociedades de Amigos del País, emphasized even in their names the social nature of observations. Travelers and writers were individuals, but their individual eyes were an extension of society, the sophisticated technology of a collective and artificial body. The limits of this body and of its perceptions were defined by the "*sociedad letrada*," the readers-and-writers intellectual community, but other sectors of society soon became involved, thanks to the propaganda effect produced by a sophisticated staging machine and network of illustrations, speeches, tales, magic lanterns, exhibitions, and even reality shows (with real savages and/or a believable imitation of their mythical image).

Two complementary sequences were at work in this process. The first one, based on the "practice of reading,"[54] transformed the reading-rewriting and the reading-illustrating sequences into a powerful mechanism of selection, translation, and explanation, oriented toward the public recycling of a considerable amount of previous information. The second sequence, directly based on the "practice of traveling,"[55] focused on the traveling-writing and the traveling-illustrating sequences, considered as a complementary set of reproduction techniques, useful for increasing the social value of any personal travel.

The formulation of this mechanism offers an opportunity to reconsider and revise the framing strategy that traditionally separates the scientific and positivist anthropology of the nineteenth century from the *anthropologie philosophique* or *science de l'homme* of the eighteenth century. Most of the research devoted to reconstructing the origins of academic anthropology highlights the difference between "science" and "opinion" as the key point. However, in my opinion, the real change involved the modification of the market-oriented intersections between pure science, "considered in it-self," and the environmental totality of culture (the "Circumstances or Appendages" by which the eighteenth-century concept of "Arts" was defined).

During the Age of Enlightenment, topics such as observation, identity, and Otherness were never perceived as neutral or descriptive. Consciousness was a social business, a role-playing game, a style more than a discipline. Technology and science were useful (to "mediate" whenever communication was difficult or distorted), but, just because of their usefulness, they could never be abstracted from their environment, that is, from history and culture.

Working with previous sources as well as their personal notes, traveler-reader anthropologists of the eighteenth century reoriented the techniques of philology. One of the main differences between the humanist philology of the Renaissance and the neoclassical attitude of the Enlightenment was that the culture of the Enlightenment conserved both Science "in it-self" and the "Circumstances or Appendages" of Art. The anthropology of the Enlightenment could be considered, adapting the logic and terminology of early technical dictionaries, as "the Portion of Art in which a series of Circumstances or Appendages are considered in themselves, as Science."

In the eighteenth century, a better-defined conception of both Science and the complementary Arts of reading, traveling, and writing produced, in between, an extended fuzzy area of "double consciousness" and multiple identity.[56] This area included most travel writing. Frequently, the writing and the reading of travelers' reports involved polemics. Especially when published, travel accounts contributed to arguments in scientific and artistic debates, because the accounts mixed observation techniques with narrative strategies, information with rhetoric, description with presentation, and perspective with staging. In the anthropology of the Enlightenment, marvels and wonders appeared natural rather than supernatural, matters of difference and freakishness rather than miracles.

When the logic of discovery became public, and rediscovery began to evolve toward anthropology, it happened through—rather than against— the impressionistic tradition of travel papers and ethnographical diaries and documents. The evolution of publishing and the book market reshaped the activities of traveling, writing, and reading as a continuum, influencing the origins of contemporary scientific anthropology.

In these regards, the French-German *soi-disant* baron Alexander von Humboldt embodied late eighteenth-century intellectual lifestyle and cosmopolitanism. Between 1799 and 1804, he organized a five-year personal Grand Tour throughout the Americas. He visited the territories of Venezuela, Ecuador, Peru, Mexico, and the United States. Back in Europe, he began to edit his notes and papers, paying for their publication in many volumes during the first half of the nineteenth century. For almost fifty years, in Europe as well as in Latin America, he was considered an authority on any kind of American topic; during the years 1848–52, Alfred Russel Wallace conceived his own four-year South American scientific adventure as a copy of the model created by Humboldt fifty years before, and declared it explicitly it in his book, *A Narrative of Travels on the Amazon and Rio Negro*, first published 1853. Since Humboldt had lived in Paris and in Berlin, and had explored the Spanish "Ultramar" and later the Russian Empire, he was also representative of the newborn European consciousness (and self-consciousness). He had direct knowledge and experience of both the transatlantic West and the European East and he was so perfectly bilingual that he wrote his personal notes either in German or in French.

Humboldt died in 1859 at the age of ninety. In the same year, Darwin published the first edition of *On the Origin of Species*, which sold out in less than a week. The *Bildung* phase of the "*science des autres*" was over. The field and the market of scientific anthropology were experiencing a new beginning. Just like the Atlantic world during the Age of Enlightenment, anthropology too would now be rediscovered, as a British (and later as an American) experimental science, based on fieldwork expeditions and on the systematic exploration of new territories. The Colonial Office of the British Empire took an interest in Africa, South Asia, and the South Seas, during the Golden Age of Victorian imperialism.

As a traveler and even as a travel writer of journals and notebooks, Darwin may be considered one of the last practitioners of enlightened anthropology. As a scientist, however, and as the author of *The Origin of Species* (1859) and *The Descent of Man* (1872), he also explored the boundaries between anthropology and natural science. Considering the chronology of Darwin's writing, we can observe the following: in the late 1830s and the 1840s, Darwin frequently introduced his arguments as "*Observations on*" or "*Journal of.*" During the 1850s and 1860s, the predominant formats were: "*A Monograph of*" and "*On the.*" Later, the most typical strategy of presentation was a simple article: "*The.*" This series of introductions highlights the shifting of scientific consciousness from a rhetoric of subjectivity toward a rhetoric of objectivity, from the legacy of Montaigne's essay toward a rediscovery of treatises and authority.

The East-West anthropology of the Enlightenment was an updated version of the *geographical notion of discovery* (and rediscovery), typical of the Renaissance period, and the North-South anthropology of the late nineteenth century was an updated version of the *scientific notion of discovery* (and rediscovery), typical of the Baroque Age. For the geographical imagination of the Renaissance, the idea of discovery always required a discoverer, someone who found something new. For Baroque science, the idea of discovery was different. What was found and revealed was a law, a representation, a prevision, a no-longer-secret connection, rather than an authentic portion of reality or a vision to be told and interpreted. The rise of the nineteenth-century positivist approach was the twilight of reading-traveling-writing anthropology, but, for Eastern Europe and Russia, for the Americas, for the Arctic, and for the Far East (China and Japan)—that is, for the regions discovered and explored during the Renaissance, the regions studied in the Baroque Age and the Age of Enlightenment—this sunset, and the subsequent scientific updating of the maps, would be extremely gradual.

Most of the contributions in this volume explore the European mind in relation to these regions, as they were described by the reading, traveling, and writing of the early anthropologists. The making of this intellectual framework began in the second half of the seventeenth century, and its evolution continued for several decades into the nineteenth century. When Darwin, whose theories would change the natural history of life forever, began his westward circumnavigation of the globe and his exploration of the South American coastline, from Salvador to El Callao, the international prestige of the great "savants" of the late Enlightenment was still intact. When the *Beagle* left Davenport on December 27, 1831, Darwin intended to present himself to the community of Latin-American scientists with a very formal letter of introduction signed by Alexander von Humboldt, who had crossed the Atlantic in June 1799, more than thirty years before.

This intellectual and ritual continuity may be dated back to the Renaissance, for it was then, and later during the well-known "querelle" of the Ancients versus the Moderns, that a double intellectual framework emerged: On the one hand, the transatlantic New Worlds recently discovered versus the Old World (Europe and the terrain of the Indo-European invasions in the regions of India and the Middle East); and on the other hand, separated by the dark centuries of the Middle Ages, the Modern World of the European expansion (westward and eastward) versus the limited *Cosmopolis* of the Ancient World (the geopolitics of Alexander the Great and of the Roman Empire). The former framework was the most impressive, but the latter had deeper consequences. The Modern World is not only the New World: it includes both the Old and the New, Europe and its new East and West, inhabited by "peuplades" (to use Tocqueville's expressive term for "tribes") of barbarians and savages. The modern idea of progress could be identified with the European capacity for inclusion and with the savages-and-barbarians' capacity for being included, both aspects depending upon the dialectics between the old center of modernity (Europe) and its traditional and/or new margins (the transatlantic Western and the Eastern margins of the old continent).

The so-called Old World was not the only Ancient World. The West Indies also had their "antiquities," which could be discovered, studied, imported, and collected. Being modern and ancient at the same time, Europe could become the center and the engine of modernity, ready to export its history as modernization and to absorb many different manifestations of Otherness. The "New Worlds" were not modern in themselves. On the contrary, they were peripheral and relatively primitive areas, discovered in order to be included and modernized, invented and classified, to be brought into the new discipline of anthropology (and to be named by its new words). Defined by discovery (according to Pagden, through a series of "encounters," in which the serial effects made each encounter something

more than an episodic circumstance), these regions made modernity possible as a relationship, through their inclusion in a network of different
relationships. Modernity was not an attribute of Europe, nor of the
Americas; modernity was the consciousness of the connection between
European centrality and the discovered/invented marginality of the New
Worlds. The European discourse about chronology, history, and tradition
could be exported, in order to transform the Americas and the Slavic
world into the West and the East of modern consciousness and modern
geography. This development brought about the birth of both modernity
and anthropology.

The myth of modernity is like the myth of love: to be modern, every-
body needs somebody. Nobody can live modernity all alone and on his
own. Prospero, the famous shipwrecked scientist of Shakespeare's *The
Tempest*, met a savage named Caliban, but he didn't need the meeting.
Defoe's Robinson Crusoe, probably the most independent, self-reliant,
and famous character of shipwreck created by the eighteenth-century
imagination, needs the good savage he names Friday, and needs to transform Friday's unlimited freedom into a pale copy of his own self-limited
free will. Modernity and humanity cannot be considered "in them-
Selves," as Sciences, but always "with relation to their Circumstances or
Appendages," as Arts (the art of being culturally modern and the art of
being culturally human).

The anthropological icons of both the promised land of the future
and the most remote past could coexist in a series and inhabit the same
framework. The possibility of a new beginning and the fascination with
primitive societies were more than similar: they offered two parallel versions of the same myth. During the Age of Enlightenment, the making
of the Eastern and the Western worlds renewed Europe's intellectual
identity. The old continent and even the idea of a continental perspective
shifted, becoming as new as the notions of the European East and the
Atlantic West.

CONCLUSION: ROBINSON AND FRIDAY

The contributions to this volume, from several generations of scholars
and specialists, explore the reshaping produced by the reciprocity implicit in any kind of "encounter" (including the most violent clash). As
the *ancien régime* was coming to an end, Eurasian Russia and Spanish
America were the paradoxically peripheral centers of two great peripheral empires. To explore the huge bodies of such empires, scientific expeditions generally required the authorization of the state. The travelers

and anthropologists of the Enlightenment, like Jean Chappe d'Auteroche and Alexander von Humboldt, had a special relation to the imperial ruling elites of Russia and Spain. Most of the data collectors had been and still were missionary or military men. Most of the scientists were members of the aristocracy. The Old World rediscovered the New and renewed its own Self thanks to the imperial tradition of the *ancien régime*, rather than the shock of revolution. Even the archaeologists, who rediscovered the Egyptian legacy with Napoleon, did it according to the forms of the Empire Style!

From the linguistic point of view, adjectives such as Eastern, associated with Europe, or Latin and/or South, added to America, introduced a double specification. At the origins of Atlantic modernity, the odd couple of Europe (as the center) and the Indies (as the margins), also known as the Old World and the New Worlds, involved an epic narrative concerning the mythology and public memory of the Atlantic discovery. A global world of mutual dependence was born. As Raynal wrote in the first volume of his *Histoire philosophique et politique des établissements et du commerce des Européens dans les deux Indes* (1770):

There has been no event more interesting for the human species in general and for the peoples of Europe in particular than the discovery of the New World and the passage to the Indies by the Cape of Good Hope. Then began a revolution in commerce, in the power of nations, in the manners, industry, and government of all peoples. It was at this moment that the men of the most remote countries become necessary to one another . . . and everywhere men communicated their opinions, laws, customs, remedies, maladies, virtues, and vices.[57]

The legacy of the great discoveries and the Golden Age became the first subject that the early anthropologists were supposed to revise. Raynal's work was a great success (with three different editions in ten years: 1770, 1774, and 1780, completed with *Atlas* in 1772 and *Suppléments* in 1780). Yet, the label "*les deux Indes*"—the two Indies—was culturally unconvincing. The importance of the distinction—(East) Indies versus West Indies—practically ended with Raynal's book.

During the last third of the eighteenth century, two new conceptual pairs began to reframe European notions of centrality and marginality: (1) (Western) Europe/Eastern Europe; and (2) (North) America/Latin (or South) America.[58] The Cold War idea of Europe as Western Europe and of America as North America, still identifies clearly the composite center of the Atlantic-centered West. The cultural centrality of both areas is still perceived as self-evident, even if the self-consciousness they represent is probably one of the most typical products of the eastward-westward oriented anthropology of the Enlightenment this book describes. Two complementary

processes made it possible: the invention of Eastern Europe and the rediscovery of America (the basis for the invention of Latin America). The fact
that America and North America, like Europe and Western Europe, have
been and are still used as synonyms can be considered as linguistic evidence
of this mechanism of invisible reciprocity: Europe has become "Western"
through and because of the invention of Eastern Europe, and America has
been made "Northern" through and because of the invention of Latin
America. The twilight of the Enlightenment reoriented the European mind
toward a new self-consciousness concerning East and West, and introduced, with the notion of Latin America, the complicated idea of the South
of the West of the West.

The inner ambiguity of the new labels and the intermingling of diplo-
macy and violence (explored during the nineteenth century by the geopo-
litical parables of the Austro-Hungarian Empire and North American
Manifest Destiny) is perhaps the clearest evidence of the cultural modernity of the Enlightenment. If we really want a more realistic approach to
eighteenth-century anthropology, we should highlight the quest for space
and for different perspectives that was typical of this period. Intellectuals
such as Humboldt or Tocqueville were members of the traditional aristocracy. Their experience and curiosity about the collapse of the *ancien
régime*, and their description of the decline of the Spanish Empire and the
speedy rise of the United States reflected the first wave of so-called globalization.

The making of anthropology was the transition from the "*Agricoltura
christiana*" (the biblical metaphorical tradition of "the Lord's vineyard")
to a project of human landscape gardening in which a planned network
of "circumstances or appendages" should resolve the opposition between the New World (which was obviously unknown) and the *société
des savants* (whose membership and prestige depend upon a remarkable
level of previous knowledge). The tribes of the *untamed* "savages" were,
for the new tribe of the *libertine* "savants," a problematic mirror. As an
intellectual community of free men and free-thinkers based on ritual and
codified practices like reading and writing, the *société des savants*, the
sociedad letrada, was not so utterly remote from the ritual communities
of the savage world.[59] In the fictions of Swift and Voltaire, in Defoe's
face-to-face encounter between Robinson and Friday, we can see this
mirroring effect at work.[60] The movies have amplified it: if each cinematic Friday is an almost naked savage, most of the cinematic Robinsons
(that is, Dan O'Herlihy in Luis Buñuel's *The Adventures of Robinson
Crusoe*, 1952, and Peter O'Toole in Jack Gold's, *Man Friday*, 1975) actually look like barbarians.[61] Robinson's recreated civilization is a
sophisticated adaptation to the "Circumstances or Appendages" of the

shipwreck. Western identity, reconstructed after a collapse, became the setting of old-fashioned newness, a theater of tradition-based novelty. Robinson's island is the perfect model of what I have called human landscape gardening, a place where anthropology can meet, name, and describe Friday, but also a place where the public must confront Robinson's own spiritual condition.

The logic of enlightened anthropology has a great cinematic potential also because it works as a zoom effect. In order to perceive and describe complexity and Otherness, the Western Self needs a double focus: on the one hand, there is the closed-up perspective (even an interior view); on the other hand, there is the broad survey, "from China to Peru." Only by instruments and techniques and within an imperially ruled territory could this kind of game be played seriously. The power structure of the *ancien régime*, and some sophisticated lens systems such as the telescope and the microscope, were essential to the deep logic (and the remote logistics) of the transition from discovery to anthropology and from landscape to life.

Twentieth-century literature offers us the possibility of using a similar technique to understand what exactly happened when the newness of the West was first apparent. I would like to conclude this book by using, as retrospective points of reference, the famous ending and the famous beginning of two novels. First the ending of F. Scott Fitzgerald's *The Great Gatsby*:

I became aware of the old island here that flowered once for Dutch sailors' eyes— a fresh, green breast of the New World. Its vanished trees, the trees that had made way for Gatsby's house, had once pandered in whispers to the last and greatest of all human dreams; for a transitory enchanted moment man must have held his breath in the presence of this continent, compelled into an aesthetic contemplation he neither understood nor desired, face to face for the last time in history with something commensurate to his capacity for wonder . . . So we beat on, boats against the current, borne back ceaselessly into the past.

Then, the beginning of Gabriel García Márquez's *Cien años de soledad* (*One Hundred Years of Solitude*, translated into English by Gregory Rebassa):

Many years later, as he faced the firing squad, Colonel Aureliano Buendía was to remember that distant afternoon when his father took him to discover ice. At that time Macondo was a village of twenty adobe houses, built on the bank of a river of clear water that ran along a bed of polished stones . . . The world was so recent that many things lacked names, and in order to indicate them it was necessary to point.

In both texts, the point is how deeply the feeling of something new can mark our memory and our capacity for wonder, collective or individual.

Fitzgerald imagines the marvel of geographical discovery through which a new continent revealed its beauty to European eyes. García Márquez's fantasy concerns a circus parody of a "scientific" and experimental discovery, the endlessly repeated experience of newness. Through ice, Europe reveals a useful truth to America. The peripheral Macondo discovers a cool metaphor for the center. Both passages describe a level of experience immune to change. The marvel of the bay of New Amsterdam/New York, the islands and the waters, and the childish emotion of old colonel Aureliano Buendía are there, still now and forever after, as strong as they were when the original experience took place, stronger than fear, than any tempest or firing squad.

As in mystical poetry or in encounters of the third kind, the experience of newness is in itself extreme, powerful, and absorbing. Face to face with the sudden advent of a New World, the frontier between fantasy and memory sometimes vanishes. Fitzgerald's experienced narrator and García Márquez's inexperienced child were both obviously overwhelmed. No previous experience could make them ready to understand what they were feeling. The whole of their identity was absorbed, renewed, and involved in a new beginning, in a real copy of a mythical experience of origins. The past becomes present, the discourse concrete, the told tales real. It's a kind of magic, a dream of gentle cruelty, claiming an escape from history and historicity in order to avoid the collapse of consciousness.

The shift from discovery to anthropology, from the Old to the New Worlds, began with nostalgia for this kind of experience. The desire to preserve and transform the overwhelming feeling of discovery into a narrative and a discourse seems to be even stronger than the will to create a critical mirror or to increase general knowledge. Humboldt's prose offers an example of this mix of passions and details (which was not simply a passion for details). The euphoria of the ascent to the mountains, in Venezuela as well as in Ecuador or Peru, or the sadness that Lima inspired in him, were obviously matters of subjective sensibility. It was the same subjective sensibility that enabled him to compare the New Worlds of Latin America and Eastern Europe.

In his first great book, the *Essai politique sur le royaume de la Nouvelle-Espagne du Mexique*, published in 1811, Humboldt directly compared the demographic growth of the American New World, with that of the regions of Eastern Europe:

The parts of Europe in which culture only began very late and in the last half of the past century, presents some very striking examples of this excess of births. In Western Prussia . . . in the Russian empire . . . the same causes produce everywhere the same effects. The newer the culture of a country, the easier is the subsistence on soil newly reclaimed, and also the faster the progress of population . . . I regard as very probable that in 1808 the population of Mexico will surpass 6,500,000. In the Russian empire, *of which the political and moral state has several striking relations with the country that occupies us*, the increase of population due to the excess of births is much faster than we concede for Mexico . . . However, what great obstacles nature itself sets against the progress of population in the more northern parts of Europe and Asia! What a contrast between the fertility of the Mexican soil, enriched by the most precious vegetable productions of the torrid zone and these sterile plains which lie buried under snow and ice for more than half of the year![62]

At the turn of the century, the two new worlds—the Eastern and the Western—were closer than ever before. Among the "several striking relations" there was also the actual case of economic competition. The Mexicans were seriously worried about the consequences of Bering's explorations and about the settlements of some Russian traders along the coasts of Alaska and Northwestern America. Europe and the Atlantic world could be bypassed. What Humboldt tells about this peculiar "Circumstance or Appendage" can be understood in terms of "general knowledge" from the point of view of the newborn "*science des hommes*," the anthropology of the Enlightenment: "The Spanish government, since 1788, has shown uneasiness about the appearance of the Russians on the northwest coasts of the new continent . . . Two nations who, occupying the opposite extremities of Europe, find themselves brought together in the other hemisphere, on the eastern and western borders of their vast empires. The interval that separates these borders is becoming progressively smaller."[63]

Notes

CHAPTER ONE

1. Montesquieu, *Persian Letters*, trans. C. J. Betts (New York: Penguin Classics, 1985), pp. 63, 76.

2. Montesquieu, *Persian Letters*, p. 124.

3. Sir Edward Evans-Pritchard, *A History of Anthropological Thought*, ed. André Singer (New York: Basic Books, 1981), pp. 3, 11; see also Thomas Hylland Eriksen and Finn Sivert Nielsen, *A History of Anthropology* (London: Pluto Press, 2001), pp. 1–15.

4. Jonathan Swift, *Gulliver's Travels*, ed. Peter Dixon and John Chalker (New York: Penguin Classics, 1985), p. 10.

5. Swift, *Gulliver's Travels*, p. 93.

6. Swift, *Gulliver's Travels*, pp. 272, 327.

7. Lady Mary Wortley Montagu, *Selected Letters*, ed. Robert Halsband (New York: Penguin Books, 1986), p. 118.

8. Swift, *Gulliver's Travels*, p. 339.

9. Montaigne, *Essays*, trans. J. M. Cohen (New York: Penguin Classics, 1983), p. 108.

10. Tzvetan Todorov, *Nous et les autres: la réflexion française sur la diversité humaine* (Paris: Seuil, 1989), pp. 69, 468; see also Anthony Pagden, *European Encounters with the New World: From Renaissance to Romanticism* (New Haven: Yale University Press, 1993); Stephen Greenblatt, *Marvelous Possessions: The Wonder of the New World* (Chicago: University of Chicago Press, 1991).

11. Peter Gay, *The Enlightenment, An Interpretation*, vol. II, *The Science of Freedom* (1969; New York: Norton, 1977), p. 319.

12. Michèle Duchet, *Anthropologie et histoire au siècle des lumières: Buffon, Voltaire, Rousseau, Helvétius, Diderot* (Paris: François Maspero, 1971); Hans-Jürgen Schings, ed., *Der ganze Mensch: Anthropologie und Literatur im 18. Jahrhundert* (Stuttgart and Weimar: Verlag J. B. Metzler, 1994).

13. Edward Said, *Orientalism* (New York: Vintage Books, 1979).

14. Tzvetan Todorov, *La conquête de l'Amérique: la question de l'autre* (Paris: Seuil, 1982).

15. Norbert Elias, *The History of Manners* (*The Civilizing Process*, vol. I), trans. Edmund Jephcott (New York: Pantheon Books, 1978), pp. 40–50; Larry Wolff, *Inventing Eastern Europe: The Map of Civilization on the Mind of the Enlightenment* (Stanford: Stanford University Press, 1994), pp. 12–13, 48–49; Samuel P. Huntington, *The Clash of Civilizations and the Remaking of World Order* (New York: Simon & Schuster, 1996).

16. *Encyclopédie ou dictionnaire raisonné des sciences, des arts et des métiers*, vol. I (Paris: Chez Briasson, David, Le Breton & Durand, 1751), p. 497.

17. Samuel Johnson, *Dictionary of the English Language* (London: Strahan, 1755).

18. Voltaire, *Age of Louis XIV and Other Selected Writings*, trans. J. H. Brumfitt (New York: Twayne Publishers, 1963), p. 148; see also Jochen Schlobach, "The Concept of Culture and Its Genesis in the 18th Century: The Case of Voltaire," *Frihetens århundre*, vol. III, *Litteratur, kunst og filosofi i Frankrike*, ed. Knut Ove Eliassen and Svein-Eirik Fauskevåg (Kristiansand, Norway: Høyskoleforlaget, 2000), pp. 149–65.

19. Voltaire, *Micromegas* in *Candide, Zadig, and Selected Stories*, trans. Donald Frame (New York: Signet Classics, 1963), pp. 177, 184.

20. Voltaire, *Essai sur les moeurs et l'esprit des nations*, ed. René Pomeau (Paris: Garnier Frères, 1963), vol. I, pp. lxvii–lxxi, 6–9.

21. Voltaire, *Essai sur les moeurs*, vol. I, pp. 22–25.

22. Voltaire, *Essai sur les moeurs*, vol. II, p. 803.

23. Voltaire, *Essai sur les moeurs*, vol. II, pp. 804–7.

24. Claude Lévi-Strauss, *Tristes tropiques*, trans. John Weightman and Doreen Weightman (New York: Atheneum, 1975), p. 390.

25. Jean-Jacques Rousseau, *Discourse on Inequality*, trans. Maurice Cranston (New York: Penguin Classics, 1984), p. 79.

26. Rousseau, *Discourse on Inequality*, p. 103.

27. Rousseau, *Discourse on Inequality*, p. 136.

28. Rousseau, *Discourse on Inequality*, p. 135.

29. Rousseau, *Discourse on Inequality*, p. 159.

30. Rousseau, *Discourse on Inequality*, p. 161.

31. Evans-Pritchard, *A History of Anthropological Thought*, p. 20.

32. Gay, *The Enlightenment, An Interpretation*, vol. II, p. 337.

33. Christian Marouby, *L'economie de la nature: essai sur Adam Smith et l'anthropologie de la croissance* (Paris: Seuil, 2004).

34. George Stocking, "Scotland as the Model of Mankind: Lord Kames' Philosophical View of Civilization," in *Toward a Science of Man: Essays in the History of Anthropology*, ed. Timothy Thoresen (The Hague: Mouton, 1975), pp. 77, 83.

35. David Spadafora, *The Idea of Progress in Eighteenth-Century Britain* (New Haven: Yale University Press, 1990), p. 285.

36. Lisbet Koerner, *Linnaeus: Nature and Nation* (Cambridge: Harvard University Press, 1999), pp. 56–81; see also Gunnar Broberg, "Homo Sapiens: Linnaeus's Classification of Man," in *Linnaeus: The Man and His Work*, ed. Tore Frängsmyr (Sagamore Beach, Mass.: Watson Publishing/Science History Publications, 1994), pp. 156–94.

37. Duchet, *Anthropologie et histoire au siècle des lumières*, pp. 232–44.

38. Larry Wolff, *Venice and the Slavs: The Discovery of Dalmatia in the Age of Enlightenment* (Stanford: Stanford University Press, 2001), p. 160.

39. Wolff, *Venice and the Slavs*, pp. 162–63.

40. James Cook, *The Journals of Captain James Cook on His Voyages of Discovery*, vol. I, *The Voyage of the Endeavour, 1768–1771*, ed. J. C. Beaglehole (Cambridge: Cambridge University Press, published for the Hakluyt Society, 1955), pp. 125–27.

41. Cook, *Journals*, vol. I, pp. 395–99.

42. Ganath Obeyesekere, *The Apotheosis of Captain Cook: European Mythmaking in the Pacific* (Princeton: Princeton University Press, 1992); Marshall Sahlins, *How "Natives" Think: About Captain Cook, for Example* (Chicago: University of Chicago Press, 1995); Nicholas Thomas, *Cook: The Extraordinary Voyages of Captain James Cook* (2003; New York: Walker & Company, 2004), p. 65.

43. Denis Diderot, "Supplement to Bougainville's Voyage," in *This Is Not a Story*, trans. P. N. Furbank (Oxford: Oxford University Press, 1993), pp. 102–9.

44. P. J. Marshall and Glyndwr Williams, *The Great Map of Mankind: British Perceptions of the World in the Age of Enlightenment* (London: J. M. Dent, 1982), p. 7.

45. Edmund Burke, *Correspondence*, vol. III, ed. George Guttridge (Cambridge: Cambridge University Press, 1961), letter to William Robertson, June 9, 1777, p. 351.

46. Johann Gottfried von Herder, *Reflections on the Philosophy of the History of Mankind*, ed. Frank Manuel (Chicago: University of Chicago Press, 1968), pp. 3, 62, 71; Wolff, *Inventing Eastern Europe*, p. 310.

47. Immanuel Kant, *Anthropology from a Pragmatic Point of View*, trans. Mary Gregor (The Hague: Martinus Nijhoff, 1974), pp. 3–5, 60–61, 151–93; John Zammito, *Kant, Herder, and the Birth of Anthropology* (Chicago: University of Chicago Press, 2002), p. 345.

48. Wolff, *Inventing Eastern Europe*, p. 300.

49. Wolff, *Inventing Eastern Europe*, pp. 312–13.

50. Isaiah Berlin, *Three Critics of the Enlightenment: Vico, Hamann, Herder*, ed. Henry Hardy (Princeton: Princeton University Press, 2000), pp. 220–21.

51. Wolff, *Inventing Eastern Europe*, p. 348; Larry Wolff, "Between the Eastern and Western World: John Ledyard in Central Europe," in *Images of Central Europe in Travelogues and Fiction by North American Writers*, ed. Waldemar Zacharasiewicz (Vienna: Stauffenburg Verlag, 1995), pp. 10–26; James Zug, *American Traveler: The Life and Adventures of John Ledyard, the Man Who Dreamed of Walking the World* (New York: Basic Books, 2005).

52. Wolff, *Inventing Eastern Europe*, p. 345.

53. *John Ledyard's Journey through Russia and Siberia 1787–1788: The Journal and Selected Letters*, ed. Stephen Watrous (Madison: University of Wisconsin Press, 1966), p. 228.

54. Wolff, *Venice and the Slavs*, pp. 193–94.

55. Marquis de Sade, *Justine*, in *Three Complete Novels*, ed. Richard Seaver, trans. Austryn Wainhouse (New York: Grove Press, 1966), pp. 648–49.

56. Sade, *Philosophy in the Bedroom*, in *Three Complete Novels*, p. 253.

57. Sade, *Philosophy in the Bedroom*, in *Three Complete Novels*, p. 324.

58. Sade, *Philosophy in the Bedroom*, in *Three Complete Novels*, p. 327.

59. Sade, *Juliette*, trans. Austryn Wainhouse (New York: Grove Press, 1968), p. 182.

60. Sade, *Juliette*, pp. 182, 189–90.

61. Sade, *Juliette*, pp. 183, 189, 507; Wolff, *Venice and the Slavs*, pp. 165–66.

62. Voltaire, *Philosophical Dictionary*, ed. and trans. Theodore Besterman (New York: Penguin Classics, 1983), p. 397.

63. George Stocking, *Race, Culture, and Evolution: Essays in the History of Anthropology* (New York: The Free Press, 1968), pp. 15–21.

CHAPTER TWO

A version of this chapter was delivered as the W. F. Church Memorial Lecture at Brown University in 2005.

1. Edward Gibbon, *The History of the Decline and Fall of the Roman Empire*, vol. I, ch. 9; David Womersley, ed., *Edward Gibbon: The History of the Decline and Fall of the Roman Empire* (London: Allen Lane, The Penguin Press, 1994), vol. I, p. 230.

2. Gibbon, *Decline and Fall*, vol. VI, ch. 71; Womersley, *Edward Gibbon*, vol. III, p. 1068.

3. This distinction is drawn in Gibbon, *Decline and Fall*, vol. I, ch. 8; Womersley, *Edward Gibbon*, vol. I, p. 213.

4. Womersley, *Edward Gibbon*, vol. I, pp. 238–39.

5. Womersley, *Edward Gibbon*, vol. I, pp. 230–31.

6. Joseph de Guignes, *Histoire generale des Huns, des Turcs, des Mogols, et des autres peuples Tartares occidentaux* (Paris: Chez Desaint et Saillant, 1756–58, in four volumes). See Rolando Minuti, *Oriente barbarico e storiografia settecentesca: rappresentazioni della storia dei Tartari nella cultura francese del XVIII secolo* (Venice: Marsilio, 1994); J. G. A. Pocock, *Barbarism and Religion IV: Barbarians, Savages and Empires* (Cambridge: Cambridge University Press, 2005), part 2.

7. Adam Smith, *An Inquiry into the Nature and Causes of the Wealth of Nations*, ed. R. H. Campbell and A. S. Skinner (Indianapolis: Liberty Classics, 1981), vol. II, pp. 711–15.

8. Gibbon's favored source for stadial theory seems to have been Antoine-Yves Goguet, *De l'origine des loix, des arts, et des sciences: et de leurs progrès chez les anciens peuples* (La Haye: P. Gosse, 1758). See Pocock, *Barbarians, Savages and Empires*, ch. 3.

9. Gibbon, *Decline and Fall*, vol. I, ch. 10; Womersley, *Edward Gibbon*, vol. I, pp. 255–60.

10. Snorri Sturluson, *Edda*, ed. Anthony Faulkes (London: Dent, 1987), pp. 3–5.

11. Gibbon, *Decline and Fall*; Womersley, *Edward Gibbon*, vol. I, pp. 256–57. See also Gibbon, *Decline and Fall*, vol. VI, ch. 71, n. 20; Womersley, *Edward Gibbon*, vol. III, p. 1068.

12. For Gibbon's account of these provinces, see Gibbon, *Decline and Fall*, vol. I, ch. 1; Womersley, *Edward Gibbon*, vol. I, pp. 50–52.

13. Gibbon, *Decline and Fall*, vol. I, ch.10; Womersley, *Edward Gibbon*, vol. I, pp. 274–81, 300–302.

14. Gibbon, *Decline and Fall*, vol. III, ch. 29; Womersley, *Edward Gibbon*, vol. II, p. 98.

15. Gibbon, *Decline and Fall*, vol. III, ch. 30; Womersley, *Edward Gibbon*, vol. II, p. 145.

16. Womersley, *Edward Gibbon*, vol. II, p. 142.

17. Womersley, *Edward Gibbon*, vol. II, p. 145.

18. Womersley, *Edward Gibbon*, vol. II, p. 149.

19. Ibid.

20. Gibbon, *Decline and Fall*, vol. I, ch. 10; Womersley, *Edward Gibbon*, vol. I, p. 255.

21. Gibbon, *Decline and Fall*, vol. III, ch. 27; Womersley, *Edward Gibbon*, vol. II, p. 45.

22. Gibbon, *Decline and Fall*, vol. III, ch. 31; Womersley, *Edward Gibbon*, vol. II, pp. 231–34, 493–507.

23. Gibbon, *Decline and Fall*, vol. III, ch. 36; Womersley, *Edward Gibbon*, vol. II, pp. 381–91.

24. Gibbon, *Decline and Fall*, vol. III, ch. 33; Womersley, *Edward Gibbon*, vol. II, p. 281.

25. Gibbon, *Decline and Fall*, vol. III, ch. 36; Womersley, *Edward Gibbon*, vol. II, p. 360.

26. Gibbon, *Decline and Fall*, vol. III, ch. 35; Womersley, *Edward Gibbon*, vol. II, p. 345.

27. Gibbon, *Decline and Fall*, vol. III, ch. 34; Womersley, *Edward Gibbon*, vol. II, p. 302.

28. Gibbon, *Decline and Fall*, vol. III, ch. 35; Womersley, *Edward Gibbon*, vol. II, p. 352; "Geougen" is de Guignes's spelling, and Gibbon's, for the Chinese "Juan-juan."

29. Gibbon, *Decline and Fall*, vol. IV, ch. 42; Womersley, *Edward Gibbon*, vol. II, p. 691.

30. Gibbon, *Decline and Fall*, vol. I, ch. 10; Womersley, *Edward Gibbon*, vol. I, p. 260.

31. Gibbon, *Decline and Fall*, vol. III, ch. 37; Womersley, *Edward Gibbon*, vol. II, pp. 433–44.

32. Gibbon, *Decline and Fall*, vol. V, ch. 49; Womersley, *Edward Gibbon*, vol. III, p. 109: "The mutual obligations of the popes and the Carlovingian family, form the important link of ancient and modern, of civil and ecclesiastical, history."

33. But see Gibbon, *Decline and Fall*, vol. V, ch. 54, where the origins of the Reformation are traced through medieval heresies of Greek and dualist origin.

34. Gibbon, *Decline and Fall*, vol. III, ch. 38; Womersley, *Edward Gibbon*, vol. II, pp. 501–4.

35. Louis-Gabriel, Comte de Dubuat-Nançay, *Histoire ancienne des peuples de l'Europe* (Paris, 1772), twelve volumes.

36. Johann Jakob Mascov, *The History of the Ancient Germans, Including That of the Cimbri, Celtae, Teutones, Alemanni, Saxons and Other Ancient Northern Nations, Who Overthrew the Roman Empire, and Established That of the Germans, and Most of the Kingdoms of Europe . . . Now Translated into English by Tho. Lediard, Esq.*, in two volumes (London: J. Mechell, 1737–38). Gibbon did not read German and cannot have consulted the original Leipzig edition of 1726.

37. Jean-Baptiste du Bos, *Histoire critique de l'établissement de la monarchie française dans les Gaules* (Paris: Didot, 1742).

38. Gabriel Bonnot de Mably, *Observations sur l'histoire de France* (Geneva: par la Compagnie des libraires, 1765).

39. Note, however, Gibbon's varying judgments of Montesquieu; du Bos has "less genius than his successor Montesquieu" (Gibbon, *Decline and Fall*, vol. VI, ch. 69, n. 1); Mably has "a merit to which even Montesquieu is a stranger" (Edward Gibbon, *Decline and Fall*, vol. III, ch. 38, n. 90).

40. Montesquieu, *Esprit des Lois*, vol. XI, p. 6. Quoted but dismissed by Gibbon, *Decline and Fall*, III, ch 38, n. 119, and the text to which this note is attached.

41. Womersley, *Edward Gibbon*, vol. I, pp. 238–39.

42. J. G. A. Pocock, *The Ancient Constitution and the Feudal Law* (Cambridge: Cambridge University Press, 1957, 1987), chs. 1, 4; Donald R. Kelley, *The Foundations of Modern Historical Scholarship* (Princeton, N.J.: Princeton University Press, 1970).

43. Goguet, *De l' origine des loix, des arts, et des sciences*, especially on this.

44. For Gibbon's debt to Lodovico Antonio Muratori, see Womersley, *Edward Gibbon*, vol. III, pp. 1243–44; J. G. A. Pocock, *Barbarism and Religion II: Narratives of Civil Government* (Cambridge: Cambridge University Press, 1999), pp. 384–85.

45. Gibbon, *Decline and Fall*, vol. V, ch. 49; Womersley, *Edward Gibbon*, vol. III, p. 144.

46. Gibbon, *Decline and Fall*, vol. III, ch. 38; Womersley, *Edward Gibbon*, vol. II, p. 512. For Voltaire on the same subject, see Pocock, *Barbarism and Religion II*, pp. 117–18.

47. This point is energetically made in a review of Ferguson's *Essay on the History of Civil Society*, which Gibbon certainly edited and may have written; see Pocock, *Narratives of Civil Government*, pp. 353–54.

48. Larry Wolff, *Inventing Eastern Europe: The Map of Civilization on the Mind of the Enlightenment* (Stanford, Calif.: Stanford University Press, 1994); *Venice and the Slavs: The Discovery of Dalmatia in the Age of Enlightenment* (Stanford, Calif.: Stanford University Press, 2001).

49. Norman Davies, *Heart of Europe: A Short History of Poland* (Oxford: Oxford University Press, 1984); *Europe: A History* (Oxford: Oxford University Press, 1996); *The Isles: A History* (London: Macmillan, 1999).

50. Pocock, *Narratives of Civil Government*, chs. 5–10, 16–19.

51. For this as the history of European historiography, see Pocock, *Barbarism and Religion III: The First Decline and Fall* (Cambridge: Cambridge University Press, 2003), ch. 12.

52. For the role of David Hume in this, see Pocock, *Narratives of Civil Government*, chs. 11, 13–15, and Karen O'Brien, *Narratives of Enlightenment: Cosmopolitan History from Voltaire to Gibbon* (Cambridge:Cambridge University Press, 1997).

53. Robert Bartlett, *The Making of Europe: Conquest, Colonization and Cultural Change, 950–1350* (Princeton, N.J.: Princeton University Press, 1993).

54. Gibbon, *Decline and Fall*, vol. V, ch. 48 ("Plan of the Succeeding Volumes"); Womersley, *Edward Gibbon*, vol. III, pp. 23–27.

55. Gibbon, *Decline and Fall*, vol. V, ch. 55; Womersley, *Edward Gibbon*, vol. III, pp. 455–60.

56. Womersley, *Edward Gibbon*, vol. III, p. 1229, for Gibbon's references to Jones.

57. John Burrow, *Evolution and Society: A Study in Victorian Social Theory* (Cambridge: Cambridge University Press, 1966).

58. Gibbon, *Decline and Fall*, vol. I, ch. 8; Womersley, *Edward Gibbon*, vol. I, p. 228.

59. Gibbon, *Decline and Fall*, vol. V, ch. 50; Womersley, *Edward Gibbon*, vol. III, pp. 154–70.

60. Womersley, *Edward Gibbon*, vol. III, p. 178.

61. Gibbon, *Decline and Fall*, vol. VI, chs. 64–65.

62. Womersley, *Edward Gibbon*, vol. III, pp. 809–18.

CHAPTER THREE

1. Volney's account of Palmyra is in *Voyage en Syrie et en Égypte*, (1787–1799), ed. Anne Deneys-Tunney and Henry Deneys in *Oeuvres* (Paris: Fayard, 1998), 3 vols., III, 474–80. His account of his vision, however, occurs in what was to become his most celebrated work, *Les ruines ou méditation sur les révolutions des empires* in *Oeuvres*, ed. Anne et Henry Deneys (Paris: Fayard, 1989), 2 vols., I, 171–73, 232–34.

2. Voltaire, *Essai sur les moeurs et l'esprit des nations*, ed. René Pomeau (Paris: Garnier Frères, 1963), II, 772. For a detailed if somewhat eccentric view of Voltaire's "sinophilia," see Étiemble, *l'Europe chinoise* (Paris: Gallimard, 1989), II, 205–93.

3. Voltaire, *Essai sur les moeurs*, I, 59.

4. Quoted by Girolamo Imbruglia, "Tra Anquetil-Duperron e *L'histoire de deux Indies*. Libertà, dispotismo e feudalismo," in *Rivista Storica Italiana*, CVI (1994), 141.

5. "The Fourth Anniversary Discourse, Delivered 15 February," 1787 [to the Asiatic Society of Calcutta] in *The Collected Works of Sir William Jones* [1807], facsimile edition (New York: New York University Press, 1993), III, 36.

6. Montesquieu, *L'esprit des lois*, book XIX, chap. 12.

7. Montesquieu, *Lettres persanes* (Letter 131), ed. Roger Caillois (Paris: Bibliothèque de la Pléiade, 1949), 327.

8. Montesquieu, *L'esprit des lois*, X, 14.

9. Plutarch, *The Fortunes of Alexander*, 329.

10. *Les ruines ou méditation sur les révolutions des empires*, 171–72, and *Voyage en Syrie et en Egypte, pendant les années 1783, 84 et 85*, ed. Anne Deneys-Tunney and Henry Deneys (Paris: Fayard, 1998), 133–42.

11. Voltaire, *Essai sur les moeurs*, I, 821–22.

12. "L'Islamisme et la science," in *Oeuvres complètes de Ernest Renan*, ed. Henriette Psichari (Paris: Calmann-Lévy, 1947), 947–49.

13. Voltaire, *Essai sur les moeurs*, I, 832.

14. Voltaire, *Essai sur les moeurs*, I, 818.

15. Voltaire, *Essai sur les moeurs*, II, 415–16.

16. *Législation orientale: ouvrage dans lequel, en montrant quels sont en Turquie, en Perse et dans l'Indoustan, les principes fondamentaux du gouvernement, on prouve* (Amsterdam, 1778), 161–67.

17. Quoted in Uday Singh Mehta, *Liberalism and Empire: A Study in Nineteenth-Century British Liberal Thought* (Chicago: University of Chicago Press, 1999), 186.

18. Voltaire, *Essai sur les moeurs*, II, 773.

19. Voltaire, *Essai sur les moeurs*, I, 268.

20. Voltaire, *Essai sur les moeurs*, I, 203.

21. "De la Chine," in *Dictionnnaire philosophique*, in *Les Oeuvres complètes de Voltaire*, ed. Christiane Mervaud et al. (Oxford: Voltaire Foundation, 1994), 538–39.

22. "Reflections on the Philosophy of History," in *On World History: An Anthology*, ed. Hans Adler and Ernst A. Menze (Armonk, N.Y., and London: M. E. Sharpe, 1997), 235.

23. *New Essays*, quoted in Franklin Perkins, "Leibniz and Chinese Morality," *Journal of the History of Ideas* 63 (2002): 447–64, 460.

24. "Preface to the *Novissima Sinica*," in Gottfried Wilhelm Leibniz, *Writings on China*, ed. Daniel J. Cook and Henry Rosemont Jr. (Chicago and La Salle: Open Court), 51.

25. Quoted in Perkins, "Leibniz and Chinese Morality," 455.

26. "Preface to the *Novissima Sinica*," 46.

27. *Despotisme de la Chine*, in *Ephémérides du citoyen, ou bibliothéque raisonée des sciences morales et politiques* (Paris: 1767), I, 3.

28. *Depotisme de la Chine*.

29. "Preface to the *Novissima Sinica*," 46–47.

30. Montesquieu, *L'esprit des lois*, VII, 21.

31. Voltaire, *Essai sur les moeurs*, I, 216.

32. "État de la Chine selon ses détracteurs," part of Raynal's *Histoire* in *Oeuvres*, ed. Laurent Versini (Paris, Robert Laffont, 1995), III, 652.

33. Voltaire, *Essai sur les moeurs*, I, 215.

34. Voltaire, *Essai sur les moeurs*, II, 783.

35. Voltaire, *Essai sur les moeurs*, I, 231.

36. Montesquieu, *L'esprit des lois*, XVII, 3.

37. "Reflections on the Philosophy of History," 247.

38. "Two Letters Addressed to a Member of the Present Parliament on the Proposals for Peace with the Regicide Directory of France," in *The Writings and*

Speeches of Edmund Burke, ed. Paul Langford et al. (Oxford: Oxford University Press, 1981–1991), IX, 248–49.

39. *Journal of the Proceedings of the Late Embassy to China* (London: 1817), 491.

40. "Reflections on the Philosophy of History," 241–43.

41. Voltaire, *Essai sur les moeurs*, II, 767.

42. Voltaire, *Essai sur les moeurs*, I, 231.

43. Voltaire, *Essai sur les moeurs*, I, 271.

44. *Les ruines ou méditation sur les révolutions des empires*, 232.

45. *Discours préliminaire de l'Encyclopédie*, in *Oeuvres complètes de D'Alembert*, 5 vols. (Paris: 1821–22), I, 17–99, 67.

46. *Essai sur les éléments de philosophie ou sur les principes des connaissances humaines* (Paris: Fayard, 1996), 19.

47. *Les ruines ou méditation sur les révolutions des empires*, 179.

CHAPTER FOUR

A version of this chapter was presented in April 2002, at the Center for European Studies, Harvard University, where I received very helpful comments from Emma Rothschild and Talal Asad. A grant from the John Carter Brown Library was indispensable for consultation with many sources cited in this paper. I would also like to thank Gauri Viswanathan and Gayatri Spivak for their support and comments. Ninon Vinsonneau ensured that the French passages were not nonsensical. The late Yves Benot provided stimulating conversation around these ideas. Remaining errors are my own.

1. "Arrêtons-nous ici et plaçons-nous au temps où l'Amérique et l'Inde étaient inconnues. Je m'adresse au plus cruel des Européens et je lui dis: Il existe des régions qui te fourniront de riches métaux, des vêtements agréables, des mets délicieux. Mais lis cette histoire et vois à quel prix la découverte t'en est promise. Veux-tu, ne veux-tu pas qu'elle se fasse? Croit-on qu'il y eût un être assez infernal pour dire: JE LE VEUX. Eh bien! il n'y aura pas dans l'avenir un seul instant où ma question n'ait la même force." From a chapter entitled "Réflexion sur le bien et le mal que la découverte du nouveau-monde a fait à l'Europe" (Reflections on the good and evil which the discovery of the New World has done to Europe). Guillaume Thomas Raynal, *Histoire philosophique et politique des établissemens et du commerce des Européens dans les deux Indes* (Geneva: Jean-Léonard Pellet, 1782), bk. 19, chap. 15, p. 298. (I have used the octavo edition, hereafter: *Histoire*, 19:15, 298.) Translations of passages and chapter headings from this work are mine throughout.

2. "Qu'attestent ces forts dont vous avez hérissé toutes les plages? Votre terreur et la haine profonde de ceux qui vous entourent. Vous ne craindrez plus, quand vous ne serez plus haïs. Vous ne serez plus haïs, quand vous serez bienfaisant. Le barbare, ainsi que l'homme civilisé, veut être heureux." From a chapter entitled "Principes que doivent suivre les Français dans l'Inde, s'ils parviennent à y rétablir leur considération et leur puissance" (Principles which the French should follow in India, if they succeed there in reestablishing their esteem and presence). Denis

Diderot, *Oeuvres*, "Bouquins," ed. Laurent Versini, 5 vols. (Paris: R. Laffont, 1994), 3:699.

3. I have in mind several recent studies on the South Pacific by scholars such as Jonathan Lamb, *Preserving the Self in the South Seas, 1680–1840* (Chicago: University of Chicago Press, 2001); and Alex Calder, Jonathan Lamb, and Bridget Orr, eds., *Voyages and Beaches: Pacific Encounters, 1769–1840* (Honolulu: University of Hawai'i Press, 1999). Roy Porter's focus in this area has been more on the relation of this work to later anthropological writing, as both of these reflect forms of the traveler's nostalgia. See "Circumnavigation: Bougainville and Cook" in Roy Porter, *Haunted Journeys: Desire and Transgression in European Travel Writing* (Princeton: Princeton University Press, 1991), 86–122. For another discussion of Cook and Bougainville, see "Enlightenment and Beyond" in Roy Porter, *The Enlightenment* (London: Humanities Press International, 1990), 61–63.

4. Edward W. Said, *Orientalism* (New York: Pantheon Books, 1978).

5. From the famous entry "Encyclopedia" in Denis Diderot, *Rameau's Nephew and Other Works* (Indianapolis: Bobbs-Merrill, 1964), 277. "En effet, le but d'une encyclopédie est de rassembler les connaissances éparses sur la surface de la terre." Diderot, *Oeuvres*, 1:363.

6. It is worth noting that while an extended discussion of the philosophes is not present in Edward W. Said's *Orientalism*, they do figure in his *Culture and Imperialism* (New York: Vintage Books, 1994). See pp. 240, 246 et passim for a discussion of Raynal and Diderot in relation to French anticolonialism.

7. I use this term as elaborated by Antonio Gramsci, *Selections from the Prison Notebooks of Antonio Gramsci* (New York: International Publishers, 1985), and developed by Ranajit Guha, *Dominance Without Hegemony* (Cambridge, Mass.: Harvard University Press, 1997).

8. A literal translation of the title: *Philosophical and Political History of the Settlements and of the Commerce of Europeans in the Two Indies.* (Note that "établissements" in French can mean both a settlement and a commercial enterprise or "comptoir.")

9. Although I primarily refer to the 1780 edition, in some instances—due to limited availability—I refer to Guillaume Thomas Raynal, *Histoire philosophique et politique des établissemens et du commerce des Européens dans les deux Indes* (Paris: A. Costes et cie, 1820).

10. Denis Diderot, *Political Writings*, Cambridge Texts in the History of Political Thought (Cambridge: Cambridge University Press, 1992), 165–214. I also refer to the selection in vol. 3 of Diderot, *Oeuvres*, 581–759.

11. French scholarship upon the *Histoire* began in earnest in the 1970s after a proper catalogue of the documents in the Fonds Vandeul had been undertaken. Michèle Duchet, among the earliest of scholars to write on Diderot's relation to the *Histoire*, focuses primarily upon the New World, and more particularly upon the debates around slavery among the physiocrats, the administrators, and the philosophes. Michèle Duchet, *Anthropologie et histoire au siècle des lumières: Buffon, Voltaire, Rousseau, Helvétius, Diderot*, Bibliotheque d'anthropologie (Paris: François Maspero, 1971); Michèle Duchet, *Diderot et l'histoire des deux Indes ou, l'écriture fragmentaire* (Paris: A.-G. Nizet, 1978). Almost contemporary

with her first work is Yves Benot, *Diderot, de l'athéisme à l'anticolonialisme* (Paris: François Maspero, 1970). One other comprehensive study that precedes these is Hans Wolpe, *Raynal et sa machine de guerre: l'histoire des deux Indes et ses perfectionnements* (Stanford: Stanford University Press, 1957). Important recent articles include Anthony Pagden, "The Effacement of Difference: Colonialism and the Origins of Nationalism in Diderot and Herder," in *After Colonialism: Imperial Histories and Postcolonial Displacements*, ed. Gyan Prakash (Princeton: Princeton University Press, 1995), and Sankar Muthu, "Enlightenment Anti-Imperialism," *Social Research* 66, no. 4 (1999), elaborated in Sankar Muthu, *Enlightenment Against Empire* (Princeton: Princeton University Press, 2003). The series *Studies on Voltaire and the Eighteenth Century* has dedicated several volumes to different aspects of the *Histoire*. These include: Hans-Jürgen Lüsebrink and Manfred Tietz, eds., *Lectures de Raynal: l'histoire des deux Indes en Europe et en Amérique au XVIIIe siècle* (Oxford: Voltaire Foundation, 1991); Hans-Jürgen Lüsebrink and Anthony Strugnell, eds., *L'histoire des deux Indes: réécriture et polygraphie* (Oxford: Voltaire Foundation, 1995).

12. One nineteenth-century British reader tellingly bound his English translation of the *Histoire*, by Justamond, with his own abbreviated translation of the title on the spine: "The History of *Both* the Indies." Guillaume Thomas Raynal, *A Philosophical and Political History of the Settlements and Trade of the Europeans in the East and West Indies*, trans. J. Justamond, 3rd ed. (London: T. Cadell, 1777), in the possession of the John Carter Brown Library.

13. Anthony Pagden, *Lords of All the World: Ideologies of Empire in Spain, Britain and France, 1500–1800* (New Haven: Yale University Press, 1995). A similar distinction between the "first" British Empire that was focused on the Atlantic and the "second" British Empire that focused on Asia has, however, been the subject of much dispute among imperial historians. See "Britain Without America—A Second Empire?" in P. J. Marshall, ed., *The Oxford History of the British Empire: The Eighteenth Century* (New York: Oxford University Press, 1998). For a comparative study of the Spanish, French, and British empires, which effectively deploys this distinction, see D. K. Fieldhouse, *The Colonial Empires: A Comparative Survey from the Eighteenth Century*, 2nd ed. (London: Macmillan Press, 1982).

14. This is done with regard to the Levant in chapter 4 of Srinivas Aravamudan, *Tropicopolitans: Colonialism and Agency, 1688–1804*, Post-Contemporary Interventions (Durham: Duke University Press, 1999). Chapter 7 of this work concerns Raynal. See also Srinivas Aravamudan, "Progress Through Violence or Progress from Violence? Interpreting the Ambivalences of the *Histoire des deux Indes*," in *Progrès et violence au XVIIIe siècle*, ed. Valerie Cossy and Deirdre Dawson (Paris: Honoré Champion Éditeur, 2001).

15. Alexis de Tocqueville, *Democracy in America* (New York: Penguin, 1984), 132.

16. More specifically, Voltaire praises the Quakers for winning over *land* from the Indians by means of trade. By this and other inducements they were able to procure territory in a less-violent manner than the Jesuits. Duchet, *Anthropologie et histoire au siècle des lumières*, 211.

17. For a discussion of *doux commerce*, see "Money Making and Commerce as Innocent and *Doux*," in Albert O. Hirschman, *The Passions and the Interests: Political Arguments for Capitalism Before Its Triumph* (Princeton: Princeton University Press, 1981). See also his discussion of Montesquieu, 70–80.

18. See Duchet, *Anthropologie et histoire au siècle des lumières*. The most comprehensive biography of Diderot—Arthur McCandless Wilson, *Diderot* (New York: Oxford University Press, 1972), 591—also describes him as a "populationist."

19. Michel Foucault, *The History of Sexuality* (New York: Vintage Books, 1980), vol. 1, 77. Foucault does not, however, comment on the role of the Levant in Diderot's novel. Nonetheless, appreciating the significance of Diderot's later participation in the *Histoire des deux Indes* can allow for a reading of his work that does more than simply note that he made use of an exotic locale.

20. Anthony Strugnell, *Diderot's Politics: A Study of the Evolution of Diderot's Political Thought After the Encyclopédie*, International Archives of the History of Ideas (The Hague: Nijhoff, 1973), 115. In discussing Diderot's response to Dom Deschamps's *Lettres sur l'esprit du siècle*, Strugnell writes: "Dom Deschamps had succeeded in striking a hidden chord in Diderot. He had aroused in him an anarchic trait which three years later would find its full expression in the *Supplément au Voyage de Bougainville*." However, Strugnell is presently involved in the project to issue a critical edition of the *Histoire*, and is likely to have modified his thoughts since the writing of this study. For more recent work, see Anthony Strugnell, "La voix du sage dans l'histoire des deux Indes," in *Diderot, les dernières années, 1770–84: colloque du bicentenaire, 2–5 septembre 1984 à Edimbourg*, ed. Peter France and Anthony Strugnell (Edinburgh: Edinburgh University Press, 1985).

21. "Orou . . . We have a circulation of men, women, and children . . . which is of far greater importance than the circulation of commodities, which are no more than the product of people's work." Diderot, *Political Writings*, 60.

22. His relationship to Abbé Galiani needs to be addressed in order to develop an answer to this question.

23. Diderot, *Political Writings*, 64.

24. Diderot's early translation of Shaftesbury introduced him to the ideas of sensualism, which influenced his early novel, *Les bijoux indiscrets*. We see echoes of that view here; namely, that the body and sensual experience are the basis for knowledge. Here the impediments to the progress of European society have to be overcome by transforming the sexual and social relationships that encompass the human body.

25. For the reference to "mine and thine," see Diderot, *Political Writings*, 42.

26. Diderot, *Political Writings*, 66.

27. Diderot, *Political Writings*, 46.

28. Diderot, *Political Writings*, 69.

29. Diderot, *Political Writings*, 64.

30. Diderot, *Political Writings*, 64.

31. Wilson, *Diderot*, 590.

32. Diderot, *Political Writings*, 70.

33. Diderot, *Political Writings*, 71.

34. Diderot, *Political Writings*, 65.

35. In the character of Orou can be seen many of the "naturalist" attitudes toward sex defined by the physician Charles Vandermonde in his *Essai sur la manière de perfectionner l'espèce humaine*, published in 1756. For an examination of this work, with a brief reference to Diderot, see Kathleen Wellman, "Physicians and Philosophes: Physiology and Sexual Morality in the French Enlightenment," *Eighteenth-Century Studies* 35, no. 2 (2002), 271. Diderot refers to Vandermonde often in the *Histoire*, as in his entry "Créoles," Diderot, *Oeuvres*, 3:706.

36. Raynal, *Histoire*, 1780, 10:134; "Le vœu de chasteté répugne à la nature et nuit à la population; le vœu de pauvreté n'est que d'un inepte ou d'un paresseux; le vœu d'obéissance à quelqu'autre puissance qu'à la dominante et à la loi, est d'un esclave ou d'un rebelle." Cited by Strugnell, *Diderot's Politics*, 225, in relation to Diderot's views on the church.

37. Diderot, *Political Writings*, 178.

38. Diderot, *Political Writings*, 178; "N'aurait-il pas été plus humain, plus utile et moins dispendieux, de faire passer dans chacune de ces régions lointaines quelques centaines de jeunes homes, quelques centaines de jeune femmes? Les hommes auraient épousé les femmes, les femmes auraient épousé les hommes de la contrée. La consanguinité, le plus prompt et le plus fort des liens, aurait bientôt fait des étrangers et des naturels du pays une seule et même famille." Diderot, *Oeuvres*, 3:693.

39. Edmund Burke, *Reflections on the Revolution in France*, Pelican Classics (Baltimore: Penguin Books, 1969), 140. Burke makes this remark with regard to heritable property as an institution and means to pass on virtue.

40. "des étrangers et des naturels du pays"; "une seule et même famille," Diderot, *Oeuvres*, 3:693.

41. "Le commerce s'établit sans trouble entre des hommes qui ont des besoins réciproques, et bientôt ils s'accoutument à regarder comme des amis, comme des frères, ceux que l'intérêt ou d'autres motifs conduisent dans leur contrée." Diderot, *Oeuvres*, 693.

42. "In dealing with subjects that are important for human happiness, your first concern and duty must be to rid your soul of all hope and fear. There, lifted up above all human considerations, you float above the atmosphere and look at the earth beneath you. . . . There, finally, as I see at my feet these beautiful lands where the arts and sciences are flourishing, and which lay for so long under the darkness of barbarism, I have wondered: who is it who dug these canals, drained these plains, founded these towns, brought together, clothed and civilized these people? And the voices of all enlightened men among them have answered: 'It is commerce; it is commerce.'" Diderot, *Political Writings*, 170.

43. The movement of goods is presented in the *Histoire* as reciprocal, rather than in one direction. "Les productions des climats placés sous l'équateur, se consomment dans les climats voisins du pole; l'industrie du Nord est transportée au Sud; les étoffes de l'Orient sont devenue le luxe des Occidentaux." Raynal, *Histoire philosophique et politique des établissemens et du commerce des Européens dans les deux Indes*, 1:2. Marx's distinction between commercial capitalism and industrial capitalism is obviously absent from the *Histoire*; the absence enables the

paean to commerce. But even within the decades of the 1780s and 1790s, one finds a darker and more brooding view of colonial commerce in such a figure as Edmund Burke, whose familiarity (initially through his relation William Burke, as well as through parliament) with the East India Company would lead to the famous trial of Warren Hastings. Diderot's view of commerce remains more optimistic, provided one was able to rein in the destructiveness of missionaries evidenced in the South American example.

44. Strugnell, *Diderot's Politics*, 223 and passim.

45. Diderot, *Oeuvres*, 693; "Les Indiens auraient adopté le culte de l'Europe, par la raison qu'une religion devient commune à tous les citoyens d'un empire, lorsque le gouvernement l'abandonne à elle-même, et que l'intolérance et la folie des prêtres n'en font pas un instrument de discorde."

46. In trying to relate these fascinating writings from Diderot to contemporary scholarly discussions on colonialism, we should at least take note of his awareness that modernity arrives with colonialism, and is thereby tainted in a manner that is quite different than within Europe itself. The *douce colonisation*, or the fantasy of a noncoercive colonial encounter, is a response to this awareness.

47. "Le dernier mot de Diderot dans le dialogue permanent entre l'homme sauvage et l'homme civilisé dont le XVIIIe siècle n'arrive pas à se tirer? On notera d'abord que Diderot compare les 'nations sauvages' et 'les nation civilisées' pour donner l'avantage aux premières en 1770, aux secondes en 1780." Diderot, *Oeuvres*, 3:585–586. Versini argues that in the later editions of the *Histoire*, Diderot became more and more convinced by Hobbes over Rousseau. He cites several lines from the *Réfutation d'Helvétius* in support of this, and concludes, "Diderot est profondément, résolument et religieusement l'homme de la sociabilité et du progrès." This seems too strongly to negate the ferocity and irony of the early Diderot regarding clerics, the destruction of primitives as a result of their encounter with Europeans, etc. (cf. the first epigraph to this article). Moreover, it overlooks the fact that Diderot, perhaps unlike Rousseau, already mocked the idea of a wholly innocent natural man, which some might accuse Rousseau of vaunting. Diderot was never fully persuaded by this illusion, and revealed this awareness in other discursive forms, such as the philosophical dialogue of the *Supplément*. In this sense, it is crucial that Diderot turned to these other genres. In a philosophical or political treatise, he might not have been as flippant, humorous, or incautious. In literature, that form of writing in which anything can be said (to paraphrase Jacques Derrida's definition), he is willing to take a thought to its extreme, even when it negates his initial impulse.

48. Strugnell, *Diderot's Politics*, 216.

49. It may have been this excessive focus upon internal European debates that contributed to a lack of interest in the *Histoire*. I would have to disagree with the judgment that Diderot, when asked by Raynal in 1765 to contribute to the *Histoire*, "[a]t first . . . seems to have taken no great interest in it and his contributions to the first edition . . . are generally unremarkable; they are mostly concerned with the bad effects of colonization and religion, the injustice of slavery and reflections about *sauvages*." John Hope Mason, *The Irresistible Diderot* (London: Quartet Books, 1982), 343.

50. Robert Darnton, *The Forbidden Best-Sellers of Pre-Revolutionary France* (New York: W. W. Norton, 1995). Darnton discusses the *Histoire des deux Indes* as a crucial text in reconsidering the Enlightenment, based on the disparity between texts currently considered canonical and those that in reality were the most widely read and circulated.

51. The omitted paragraph would be the final one to a section given the title "National Character at Home and Overseas," Diderot, *Political Writings*, 177–79.

52. Diderot, *Oeuvres*, 693; "Tels seraient les heureux effets que produirait, dans une colonie naissante, l'attrait du plus impérieux des sens. Point d'armes, point de soldats: mais beaucoup de jeunes femmes pour les hommes, beaucoup de jeunes hommes pour les femmes."

53. Raynal, *Histoire*, 1780, 1:2; "L'Europe a fondé par-tout des colonies; mais connoît-elle les principes sur lesquels on doit les fonder? . . . Ne peut-on découvrir par quels moyens et dans quelles circonstances?"

54. Diderot, *Political Writings*, 86; "L'empire de Russie occupe une étendue de 32 degrés en latitude et de 165 en longitude. Civiliser à la fois une aussi énorme contrée me semble un projet au-dessus des forces humaines, surtout lorsque je me promène sur la lisière et que je trouve ici des déserts, là des glaces, ailleurs des barbares de toute espèce." Diderot, *Oeuvres*, 511.

55. "If in the whole reign, the Empress were to civilize only this district, she would have achieved a great deal," Diderot, *Political Writings*, 96.

56. Diderot, *Political Writings*, 86; "La troisième, ce serait d'accepter une colonie de Suisses; de la placer convenablement; de lui assurer ses privilèges et la liberté; d'accorder les mêmes privilèges et la même liberté à tous ceux de ses sujets qui entreraient dans la même colonie. Les Suisses sont agriculteurs et soldats; ils sont fidèles. Je sais par cœur toutes les objections qu'on peut opposer à ces moyens; elles sont si frivoles que je ne me donne pas la peine d'y répondre." Diderot, *Oeuvres*, 3:512.

57. "Idée systématique sur la manière d'amener un people au sentiment de la liberté et à l'état policé."

58. "Si j'avais à civiliser des sauvages, que ferais-je? Je ferais des choses utiles en leur présence, sans leur rien ni dire, ni prescrire. J'aurais l'air de travailler pour ma seule famille et pour moi.

"Si j'avais à créer une nation à la liberté, que ferais-je? Je planterais au milieu d'elle une colonie d'hommes libres, très libres, tels, par exemple, que les Suisses, à qui je conserverais bien strictement ses privilèges, et j'abandonnerais le reste au temps et à l'exemple." Diderot, *Oeuvres*, 3:326.

59. In this sense, the colonized are in a state not much different than one Jean-Jacques Rousseau observes among animals. Though the context is quite different, developing this thought requires consideration of an episode where Rousseau presumes that pongos, an "anthropomorphic animal" seen in the Congo, push wood into a fire more to imitate the action of a man rather than from any deeper knowledge. "I remember seeing a monkey perform the same maneuver that it is denied [by a traveler's account] a pongo can do. It is true that my ideas not then being directed to this problem, I myself committed the error for which I reproach our

travelers, and I neglected to examine whether the monkey's intention was in fact to sustain the fire, or simply, as I believe, *to imitate the action of a man*. Whatever the case, it is well demonstrated that the monkey is not a variety of man" [emphasis mine]. *Discourse on Inequality*, n. J, collected in Jean-Jacques Rousseau, *The First and Second Discourses* (New York: St. Martin's Press, 1964), 208. For the original French passage, see Jean-Jacques Rousseau, *Oeuvres complètes*, Bibliothèque de la Pléiade, vol. III (Paris: Gallimard, 1964), 211.

60. Diderot, *Oeuvres*, 3:693.

61. Diderot, *Oeuvres*, 3:705; "L'avantage physique de croiser les races entre les homes comme entre les animaux, pour empêcher l'espèce de s'abâtardir, est le fruit d'une expérience tardive, postérieure à l'utilité reconnue d'unir les familles pour cimenter la paix des sociétés."

62. Diderot, *Oeuvres*, 3:706; "Les Créoles sont en général bien fait. À peine en voit-on un seul affligé des difformités si communes dans les autres climats. . . . L'histoire ne leur reproche aucune de ces lâchetés, de ces trahisons, des ces bassesses, qui souillent les annales de tous les peuples. À peine citerait-on un crime honteux qu'ait commis un créole."

63. Uday Singh Mehta, *Liberalism and Empire: A Study in Nineteenth-Century British Liberal Thought* (Chicago: University of Chicago Press, 1999).

64. Duchet, *Anthropologie et histoire au siècle des lumières*, 215.

65. Raynal, *Histoire*, 1820, 1:25; "fait honneur à la religion chrétienne de l'abolition de l'esclavage. Nous oserons n'être pas de son avis. C'est quand il y eut de l'industrie et des richesses dans le peuple que les princes le comptèrent pour quelque chose. C'est quand les richesses du peuple purent être utiles aux rois contre les barons que les lois rendirent meilleure la condition du peuple."

66. Diderot, *Oeuvres*, 3:689; "Dans ces sociétés mercantiles, la découverte d'une île, l'importation d'une nouvelle denrée, l'invention d'une machine, l'établissement d'un comptoir . . . la construction d'un port, deviendront les transactions les plus importantes; et les annales des peuples demanderont à être écrites par des commerçants philosophes, comme elles l'étaient autrefois par des historiens orateurs."

67. Diderot, *Oeuvres*, 3:689; "Il s'établit en Europe un esprit de trocs et d'échanges." Adam Smith's reflection upon Greek and Roman colonies in relation to those of modern Europe merits closer attention. See Donald Winch, *Classical Political Economy and Colonies* (Cambridge: Harvard University Press, 1965). Emma Rothschild, *Economic Sentiments: Adam Smith, Condorcet, and the Enlightenment* (Cambridge, Mass: Harvard University Press, 2001), proposes a more interesting context for some of Smith's thought, such as the much-cited (if rarely used) image in his work of the invisible hand.

68. Smith frequently refers to a 1773 edition of the *Histoire des deux Indes* in bk. IV, chap. VII, "Of Colonies" in *The Wealth of Nations*. For a consideration of Adam Smith and Raynal in relation to larger questions of commerce, see Emma Rothschild, "Global Commerce and the Question of Sovereignty in the Eighteenth-Century Provinces," *Modern Intellectual History* 1, no. 1 (2004).

69. Diderot, *Oeuvres*, 3:689–90; "La découverte d'un nouveau monde pouvait seule fournir des aliments à notre curiosité. Une vaste terre en friche, l'humanité réduite à la condition animale, des campagnes sans récoltes, des trésors

sans possesseurs, des sociétés sans police, des hommes sans mœurs: combien un pareil spectacle n'eût-il pas été plein d'intérêt et d'instruction pour un Locke, un Buffon, un Montesquieu! Quelle lecture eût été aussi surprenante, aussi pathétique que le récit de leur voyage! Mais l'image de la nature brute et sauvage est déjà défigurée. Il faut se hâter d'en ressembler les traits à demi effacée, après avoir peint et livré à l'exécration les avides et féroces chrétiens qu'un malheureux hasard conduisit d'abord dans cet autre hémisphère."

70. Rousseau, *The First and Second Discourses*, 210. "Depuis trois ou quatre cens ans que les habitans de l'Europe inondent les autres parties du monde et publient sans cesse de nouveaux recueils de voyages et de rélations, je suis persuadé que nous ne connoissons d'hommes que les seuls Européens; encore paroît-il aux préjugés ridicules qui ne sont pas éteints, même parmi les Gens de Lettres, que chacun ne fait guéres sous le nom pompeux d'étude de l'homme, que celle des hommes de son pays. Les particuliers ont beau aller et venir, il semble que la Philosophie ne voyage point." Rousseau, *Oeuvres complètes*, 212. This footnote from Rousseau also contains a prolonged consideration of the orangutan in the Congo, whose place in the later history of evolutionary arguments and scientific racism requires more consideration than I can give it here. Rousseau refers to several observers who point to similar social characteristics shared by Blacks (les Nègres) and the orangutan. His remark also serves to qualify the assertion that much eighteenth-century thought is free from the racial views more prevalent in the nineteenth-century. And yet it is not clear from note X whether Rousseau agrees with this observation; in effect, he cites it primarily to note that its reliability cannot be verified given the current impoverished state of knowledge on these places. See pp. 208–11, and the conclusion on 214.

71. Rousseau, *The First and Second Discourses*, 212; "non toûjours des pierres et des plantes, mais une fois les hommes et les mœurs." Rousseau, *Oeuvres complètes*, 213.

72. Rousseau, *The First and Second Discourses*, 210.

73. "Il n'y a guéres que quatre sortes d'hommes qui fassent des voyages de long cours; les Marins, les Marchands, les Soldats, et les Missionnaires; or on ne doit guéres s'attendre que les trois premiéres classes fournissent de bons observateurs . . . et quant à ceux de la quatriéme, occupés de la vocation sublime qui les appelle . . . on doit croire qu'ils ne se livreroient pas volontiers à des recherches qui paroissent de pure curiosité." Rousseau, *Oeuvres complètes*, 212.

74. Translation modified. Rousseau, *The First and Second Discourses*, 212. "Les Académiciens qui ont parcouru les parties Septentrionales de l'Europe et Méridionales de l'Amérique avoient plus pour objet de les visiter en Géometres qu'en Philosophes . . . nous ne connoissons point les Peuples des Indes Orientales, fréquentées uniquement par des Européens plus curieux de remplir leurs bourses que leurs têtes. . . . Supposons un Montesquieu, un Buffon, un Diderot, un Duclos, un d'Alembert, un Condillac, ou des hommes de cette trempe voyageant pour instruire leurs compatriotes, observant et décrivant comme ils savent faire, La Turquie, l'Egipte, la Barbarie . . . les Malabares, le Mogol, les rives du Gange . . . puis dans l'autre Hemisphére, le Méxique, le Perou. . . . Supposons que ces nouveaux Hercules, de retour de ces courses mémorable, fissent ensuite à loisir

l'Histoire naturelle Morale et Politique de ce qu'ils auroient vu, nous verrions nous mêmes sortir un monde nouveau de dessous leur plume, et nous apprendrions ainsi à connoître le nôtre." Rousseau, *Oeuvres complètes*, 213–14.

75. Walter Benjamin, *Illuminations* (New York: Schocken Books, 1986), 83–110.

76. "Où est-il, ce grand homme, que la nature doit peut-être à l'honneur de l'espèce humaine? Où est-il, ce Spartacus nouveau, qui ne trouvera point de Crassus? Alors disparaîtra le Code Noir." Guillaume Thomas Raynal, *Histoire philosophique et politique des établissemens et du commerce des Européens dans les deux Indes* (Maestricht: chez Jean-Edme Dufour imprimeur & libraire, 1774), vol. III, 204. The passage is altered in the later edition, cf. Raynal, *Histoire philosophique et politique des établissemens et du commerce des Européens dans les deux Indes*, 11:24, 139. The passage calling for an "avenger of the New World" is itself a reworking of an episode from the 1771 novel by Louis Sébastien Mercier, *L'an deux mille quatre cent quarante* (Geneva: Slatkine Reprints, 1979), chap. 22, p. 178.

77. The notion that Toussaint had read Raynal's *Histoire*—suggested by C. L. R. James, *The Black Jacobins: Toussaint L'Ouverture and the San Domingo Revolution*, 2nd ed. (New York: Vintage Books, 1989), 24–25; and by Aimé Césaire, *Toussaint Louverture: la révolution française et le problème colonial* (Paris: Présence Africaine, 1981), 197—is vividly conveyed in the painting of the Haitian captain Jean-Baptiste Belley, painted by Anne-Louis Girodet in 1797, which portrays him leaning against a bust of Raynal. Belley had fought alongside Toussaint before joining the French revolutionary army. For a discussion of this painting, see Viktoria Schmidt-Linsenhoff, "Male Alterity in the French Revolution—Two Paintings by Anne-Louis Girodet at the Salon of 1798," in Ida Blom, Karen Hagemann, and Catherine Hall, *Gendered Nations: Nationalisms and Gender Order in the Long Nineteenth Century* (New York: Berg, 2000); and Darcy Grimaldo Grigsby, *Extremities: Painting Empire in Post-Revolutionary France* (London: Yale University Press, 2002).

78. See Jennifer Pitts, *A Turn to Empire: The Rise of Liberal Imperialism in Britain and France* (Princeton: Princeton University Press, 2005), and the chapter on "The Crisis of Liberal Imperialism," in Karuna Mantena, *Alibis of Empire: Social Theory and the Ideologies of Late Imperial Rule* (Princeton: Princeton University Press, forthcoming).

CHAPTER FIVE

1. Meek's own summary of the theory in his introduction is the following: "In its most specific form, the theory was that society 'naturally' or 'normally' progressed over time through four more or less distinct and consecutive stages, each corresponding to a different mode of subsistence, these stages being defined as hunting, pasturage, agriculture, and commerce." Ronald Meek, *Social Science and the Ignoble Savage* (Cambridge: Cambridge University Press, 1976), p. 2.

2. Adam Smith, *An Inquiry into the Nature and Causes of the Wealth of Nations*, vol. I, Glasgow edition (Oxford: Clarendon Press, 1979), p. 10.

3. Bonar, James: *A Catalogue of the Library of Adam Smith*, 2nd ed. (London: Macmillan, 1932).

4. François-Xavier Charlevoix, *Journal d'un voyage fait par ordre du roy dans l'Amérique septentrionale* (Paris, 1744); R. P. Joseph-François Lafitau, *Moeurs des sauvages Américains, comparées auz moeurs des premiers temps* (Paris, 1724).

5. Adam Smith, *Lectures on Jurisprudence*, vol. V, Glasgow edition (Oxford: Clarendon Press, 1978), p. 201.

6. Dugald Stewart, in his famous "Account of the Life and Writings of Adam Smith," in *Essays on Philosophical Subjects*, vol. III, Oxford edition (Oxford: Clarendon Press, 1980), p. 293. In addition to the several illuminating "introductions" in the Glasgow edition of the *Essays*, Stewart's "Account" is also discussed by W. P. Wightman's "Adam Smith and History of Ideas" and Andrew S. Skinner's "Adam Smith: An Economic Interpretation of History," both in *Essays on Adam Smith*, ed. Andrew S. Skinner and Thomas Wilson (Oxford: Clarendon Press, 1975), as well as by Meek.

7. A point extensively discussed and recognized, in particular by T. D. Campbell in *Adam Smith's Science and Morals* (London: George Allen and Unwin, 1971), pp. 79–80. For a broader discussion of Smith's epistemology and empiricism, see in addition to the essays already mentioned: David A. Reisman, *Adam Smith's Sociological Economics* (London: Croon Helm, and New York: Harper and Row, 1976), particularly p. 37; and, among others, Frans Planck in "Adam Smith: Grammatical Economist," in *Adam Smith Reviewed*, ed. Peter Jones and Andrew S. Skinner (Edinburgh: Edinburgh University Press, 1992).

8. Adam Smith, *Lectures on Jurisprudence*, p. 497.

9. Adam Smith, *Lectures on Jurisprudence*, p. 213.

10. Adam Smith, *Lectures on Jurisprudence*, p. 214.

11. Adam Smith, *Wealth of Nations*, p. 691.

12. See Henry F. Dobyns: *Their Numbers Become Thinned* (Knoxville: University of Tennessee Press, 1983).

13. Arthur Dobbs, *An Account of the Countries Adjoining to Hudson's Bay in the North-West Part of America* (London, 1744), pp. 27–28.

14. William Douglass, *A Summary, Historical and Political, of the First Planting, Progressive Improvements, and Present State of the British Settlements in North America, Boston, New-England (1747–1750)* (London: E. Baldwin, reprint 1755), pp. 180, 187.

15. In *Adam Smith's Discourse; Canonicity, Commerce and Conscience* (London: Routledge, 1994).

16. Adam Smith, *Lectures on Jurisprudence*, p. 14.

17. Adam Smith's scenario is here again exemplary: "The most naturally [*sic*] contrivance they [the hunters] would think of, would be to tame some of those wild animalls they caught . . . They would more probably begin first by multiplying animalls than vegetables, as less skill and observation would be required." Adam Smith, *Lectures on Jurisprudence*, p. 14.

18. See Richard B. Lee and Irven de Vore, eds., *Man the Hunter* (Chicago: Aldine Publishing Company, 1968), particularly the introduction and chapter 4, and

Richard B. Lee's essay, "The Hunters: Scarce Resources in the Kalahari," as well as Marshall Sahlins, *Stone Age Economics* (New York: Aldine de Gruyters, 1972).

19. Douglass, *Summary*, pp. 173–74.

20. "Of vegetables they plant corn, wild kidney beans (*Phafeoli*) of several kinds, pumpkins of different sorts, squashes, a kind of gourd, watermelons and melons (*Cucumis melo* L.). All these plants have been cultivated by the Indians long before the arrival of the Europeans. They likewise eat various fruits which grow in their woods. Fish and meat constitute a very large part of their food. And they like chiefly the flesh of wild cattle, roe-bucks, stags, bears, beavers and some other quadrupeds. Among their dainty dishes they reckon the water taregrass (*Zizania aquatica* L.), which the French call *folle avoine*, and which grows plentifully in their lakes, in stagnant waters, and sometimes in rivers which flow slowly. They gather its seeds in October, and prepare them in different ways, and chiefly as groats, which taste almost as good as rice. They make also many a delicious meal of the several kinds of walnuts, chestnuts, mulberries, acimine (*Annoma muricata* L.), chinquapins (*Fagus pumila* L.), hazel nuts, peaches, wild prunes, grapes, whortleberries of several sorts, various kinds of medlars, blackberries and other fruits and roots." Pehr Kalm, *Travels to America*, English translation 1770 (New York: Dover Publications, 1937), p. 533.

21. A problem also commented on by J. G. A. Pocock, even if it is with a different emphasis, in the fourth volume of his *Barbarism and Religion* series. The absence of soil cultivation based on deep plowing, itself dependent on the domestication of large animals that only appears with the second (pastoral) stage, made it difficult for Europeans to recognize American agricultural practices—later described as "horticulture" to distinguish them from the former—as a true form of agriculture. Hence the dismissal of their importance and contribution as a mode of subsistence, and the overwhelming temptation, as Pocock writes, "to relegate all American Peoples before settlement to the category of 'savages' defined as the first stage of development." J. G. A. Pocock, *Barbarism and Religion*, vol. 4, *Barbarians, Savages and Empires* (Cambridge: Cambridge University Press, 2005), pp. 171–75. What Smith and his contemporaries must now contend with in their better-informed sources is the flip side of this misrecognition: having defined the first stage as that of hunters, they are confronted with the scandalous evidence of the universal presence of some form of agriculture among American "savages."

22. Adam Smith, *Lectures on Jurisprudence*, p. 15, my emphasis.

23. Lafitau, *Moeurs des sauvages Américains*, p. 90.

24. As does, for example, Monboddo in *Of the Origin and Progress of Language*, vol. I (Edinburgh, 1773–1792), pp. 258–59.

25. Adam Smith, *Wealth of Nations*, p. 363.

26. Adam Smith, *Wealth of Nations*, pp. 206, 237.

27. "Adam Smith's Master Narrative: Women and the *Wealth of Nations*," in *Adam Smith's* Wealth of Nations: *New Interdisciplinary Essays*, ed. Stephen Copley and Kathryn Sutherland (Manchester, UK: Manchester University Press, 1995).

28. Charlevoix, *Histoire*, p. 330. "Outre le soin du ménage, et la provision du bois, les femmes sont presque toujours chargées seules de la culture de leurs champs."

29. Charlevoix, *Histoire*, 334. "Pour les hommes, ils font gloire de leur oisiveté, et passent en effet plus de la moitié de la vie sans rien faire, persuadés que le travail journalier dégrade l'Homme, et n'est d'obligation que pour les femmes."

30. Adam Smith, *Lectures on Jurisprudence*, p. 521.

31. Adam Smith, *The Theory of Moral Sentiments*, vol. I, Glasgow edition (Oxford: Clarendon Press, 1976), p. 210.

32. Adam Smith, *Theory of Moral Sentiments*, p. 205.

33. Douglass, *Summary*, p. 153.

34. Lafitau, *Moeurs*, vol. II, pp. 1–2. "ils sont les gens du monde les plus des-oeuvrez; et si l'on excepte certaines petites choses qui ne leur demandent pas beaucoup de temps, moins encore de sujettion et d'application, ils sont presque toûjours les bras croisez, ne faisant autre chose que tenir des assemblés, chanter, manger, joüer, dormir, et ne rien faire."

35. Adam Smith, *Essays on Philosophical Subjects*, p. 187.

36. Adam Smith, *Wealth of Nations*, p. 697.

37. Jean-Jacques Rousseau, *Discours sur l'origine de l'inégalité* (Paris: Garnier-Flammarion, 1971), p. 151, "qui n'existe plus, qui n'a peut-être point existé, qui probablement n'existera jamais."

38. Adam Smith, *Lectures on Jurisprudence*, p. 334.

39. Adam Smith, *Lectures on Jurisprudence*, my emphasis.

40. Adam Smith, *Lectures on Jurisprudence*, p. 335.

41. Adam Smith, *Lectures on Jurisprudence*.

42. Adam Smith, *Lectures on Jurisprudence*, p. 336.

43. Adam Smith, *Lectures on Jurisprudence*, pp. 336–37.

CHAPTER SIX

The author would like to thank Thomas Ahnert for the opportunity to contribute this chapter.

1. Gabriel Honoré Bonnot, Abbé de Mably, *De la manière d'écrire l'histoire* (Paris: Société Littéraire-Typographique Kehl, 1784), 225–33.

2. *Annual Register* (1777): 214–15. Edmund Burke to William Robertson, June 9, 1777, National Library of Scotland (NLS) MS 3943, ff. 17–18.

3. *Annual Register* (1777): 214–15.

4. William Robertson, *The History of America*, in *The Works of William Robertson*, 3 vols., ed. Richard B. Sher (London: Thoemmes, 1996), 2: 50.

5. Anthony Pagden, *European Encounters with the New World: From Renaissance to Romanticism* (London: Yale University Press, 1993), 1–15.

6. Bryan Edwards, *History of the West Indies; Political and Commercial Survey of the West Indies* (London: G. and W. B. Whitaker, 1819), I: xxix. Nicholas Hudson, "From 'Nation to Race': The Origin of Racial Classification in Eighteenth-Century Thought," *Eighteenth-Century Studies* 29, no. 3 (1996): 247–62, esp. 250–51.

7. Cornelius de Pauw. *Récherches philosophiques sur les Américains, ou mémoires intéressants pour servir à l'histoire de l'espèce humain* (Berlin: J. G. Baerstecker, 1772). P.J. Marshall and Glyndwyr Williams, *The Great Map of Mankind: British Perceptions of the World in the Age of Enlightenment* (London: Dent, 1982), 219. D. A. Brading, *The First America: The Spanish Monarchy, Creole Patriots, and the Liberal State* (Cambridge: Cambridge University Press, 1991), 431–32, 436–38. Antonello Gerbi, *The Dispute of the New World: The History of a Polemic*, trans. Jeremy Moyle (London: University of Pittsburgh Press, 1973), 52–56.

8. E. Adamson Hoebel, "William Robertson: An Eighteenth Century Anthropologist-Historian," *American Anthropologist* 16 (1960): 648–55.

9. Jefferson to Chastellux, June 7, 1785, in Thomas Jefferson, *Writings*, ed. Merrill D. Peterson (New York: Library of America, 1984), 800–801. Lewis Morgan, "Montezuma's Dinner," *North American Review* 122 (1876): 265–309.

10. *Monthly Review* 57 (1777): 47.

11. David Armitage, "The New World and British Historical Thought: From Richard Hakluyt to William Robertson," in *America in European Consciousness*, ed. Karen Ordahl Kupperman (Chapel Hill: University of North Carolina Press, 1995), 52–75.

12. Bruce P. Lenman, "'From Savage to Scot' via the French and Spaniards: Principal Robertson's Spanish Sources," in *William Robertson and the Expansion of Empire*, ed. Stewart J. Brown (Cambridge: Cambridge University Press, 1997), 196–209. Mark Duckworth, "An Eighteenth-Century Questionnaire: William Robertson on the Indians," *Eighteenth-Century Life* 11 (1987): 36–49. Christopher J. Berry, *Social Theory of the Scottish Enlightenment* (Edinburgh: Edinburgh University Press, 1997), 92–93.

13. John Playfair to William Robertson *secundus*, July 10, 1777, National Library of Scotland (NLS) MS 3943, ff. 26–27.

14. See Pierre Berthiaume, "*Raynal: rhétorique sauvage, l'Amerindien dans l'Historie des deux Indes*," *Studies in Voltaire and the Eighteenth-Century* 333 (1995): 234.

15. *Critical Review* 43 (1777): 401–16.

16. Juan Nuix, *Reflexiones imparciales sobre la humanidad de los Españoles en las Indias, contra los pretendidos filosofos y politicos* (Madrid: Joachin Ibarra, 1782), xxxix–xl. For Clavigero, Robertson was "mas que Raynal en la desconfianza de la historia, y mas proveido de libros y manuscritos espanoles": Francisco Javier Clavigero, *Historia Antigua de México* (Mexico City: Editorial Porrua, 1945), I: 48. See also Girolamo Imbruglia, "*Les premières lectures italiennes de l'Histoire philosophique et politique des deux Indes: entre Raynal et Robertson*," *Studies in Voltaire and the Eighteenth Century* 286 (1991): 235–51, on the perceived superiority of Robertson as a *historian* over Raynal the propagandist.

17. Jeffrey Smitten, "Impartiality in Robertson's *History of America*," *Eighteenth-Century Studies* 19 (1985): 56–77.

18. Josiah Tucker, *A Treatise Concerning Civil Government* (London: T. Cadell, 1781), 169–70; James Dunbar, *An Essay on the History of Mankind* (London: W. Strahan, 1781), 217–18.

19. Louis Van Delft, *Litterature et anthropologie: nature humaine et caractère à l'age classique* (Paris: Presses Universitaires de France, 1993).

20. Van Delft, *Litterature et anthropologie*, 118.

21. Van Delft, *Litterature et anthropologie*, 257–62. See also Henri Coulet, "La notion de caractère dans l'œuvre de Beaumarchais," *Revue de l'université de Moncton* II (1978).

22. Van Delft, *Litterature et anthropologie*, passim.

23. On this issue, see Neil Hargraves, "The 'Progress of Ambition': Character, Narrative and Philosophy in the Works of William Robertson," *Journal of the History of Ideas* 63 (2002): 261–82.

24. Wilcomb E. Washburn and Bruce Trigger, "Native peoples in Euro-American historiography," in *The Cambridge History of the Native Peoples of the Americas: Vol. 1, North America*, ed. Bruce Trigger and Wilcomb E. Washburn (Cambridge: Cambridge University Press, 1996), 61–124, esp. 74–87.

25. Knud Haakonssen, "James Mill as Conjectural Historian," *Natural Law and Moral Philosophy: From Grotius to the Scottish Enlightenment* (Cambridge: Cambridge University Press, 1996), 295–304.

26. William Robertson, *The History of America*, 1: 253–55.

27. Edwards, *History of the West Indies*, 1: xxix–xxxii.

28. Alexander Du Toit, "Who Are the Barbarians? Scottish Views of Conquest and Indians, and Robertson's *History of America*," *Scottish Literary Journal* 26 (1999): 29–47.

29. William Robertson, *The History of America*, 1: 348.

30. William Robertson, *The History of America*, 2: 278–79.

31. William Robertson, *The History of America*, 3: 193–94.

32. William Robertson, *The History of America*, 3: 195; on de Solis, and Robertson's reaction to him, see the "Prologo" by José de la Revilla to Antonio de Solis, *Historia de la Conquista de Méjico* (Paris: Baudry, 1844), 5–9.

33. William Robertson, *The History of America*, 3: 194.

34. Brading, *The First America*, 433–34.

35. William Robertson, *The History of America*, 2: 261

36. William Robertson, *The History of America*, 2: 246, 250, 252, 266.

37. William Robertson, *The History of America*, 2: 306, 314. On sentiment and historical character, see Karen O'Brien, *Narratives of Enlightenment Cosmopolitan History from Voltaire to Gibbon* (Cambridge: Cambridge University Press, 1996), 115–22.

38. William Robertson, *The History of America*, 2: 279.

39. William Robertson, *The History of America*, 2: 283.

40. Du Toit, "Who Are the Barbarians?"; William Robertson, *The History of America*, 2: 364, 385–86. See also Neil Hargraves, "Enterprise, Adventure and Industry: The Formation of 'Commercial Character' in William Robertson's History of America," *History of European Ideas* 29 (2003): 33–54.

41. Jeffrey Smitten, "Robertson's History of Scotland: Narrative Structure and the Sense of Reality," *Clio* 11 (1981): 29–47.

42. William Robertson, *The History of America*, 2: 248, 267, 271.

43. David Hume, *The Natural History of Religion*, ed. H. E. Root (Stanford: Stanford University Press, 1967), 56.

44. Compare Tzvetan Todorov, *The Conquest of America: The Question of the Other*, trans. Richard Howard (New York: HarperPerennial, 1992); and Urs Bitterli, *Cultures in Conflict: Encounters Between European and Non-European Cultures, 1492–1800* (Cambridge: Polity Press, 1993), 25–26.

45. On Robertson's "romanticism" here, see D. J. Womersley, "The Historical Writings of William Robertson," *Journal of the History of Ideas* 47 (1986): 497–506, esp. 503–6.

46. William Robertson, *The History of America*, 2: 308, 314.

47. William Robertson, *The History of America*, 2: 387–88.

48. William Robertson, *The History of America*, 2: 310.

49. William Robertson, *The History of America*, 2: 379.

50. William Robertson, *The History of America*, 2: 341.

51. William Robertson, *The History of America*, 2: 346.

52. William Robertson, *The History of America*, 2: 348–50. The term "multitude" occurs frequently, for example: 2: 308, 311, 342–43, 353, 377, 384.

53. William Robertson, *The History of America*, 2: 248–49.

54. William Robertson, *The History of America*, 2: 380.

55. William Robertson, *The History of America*, 3: 64.

56. William Robertson, *The History of America*, 3: 24.

57. William Robertson, *The History of America*, 3: 38.

58. William Robertson, *The History of America*, 3: 42.

59. William Robertson, *The History of America*, 3: 46.

60. William Robertson, *The History of America*, 3: 31.

61. William Robertson, *The History of America*, 3: 66.

62. William Robertson, *The History of America*, 3: 42.

63. William Robertson, *The History of America*, 3: 76.

64. William Robertson, *The History of America*, 2: 253. In some ways, Robertson's explanation of Montezuma's inaction and consequent imprudence is similar to that of Hume concerning Charles I, although of course in a vastly different context.

65. William Robertson, *The History of America*, 3: 160–61.

66. For instance, William Robertson, *The History of America*, 3: 367, 418–23.

67. Berry, *Social Theory of the Scottish Enlightenment*, 96.

68. William Robertson, *The History of America*, 3: 154.

69. William Robertson, *The History of America*, 3: 151.

70. William Robertson, *The History of America*, 3: 151.

71. William Robertson, *The History of America*, 3: 161.

72. Jose de Acosta, *Historia Natural y Moral de las Indias*, ed. Barbara G. Beddall (Valencia: Valencia Cultural, 1977), 395–449. Anthony Pagden, *The Fall of Natural Man: The American Indian and the Origins of Comparative Ethnology* (Cambridge: Cambridge University Press, 1982), 146–97.

73. William Robertson, *The History of America*, 3: 198.

74. On Robertson's handling of Mexican and Peruvian religion, see Nicholas Phillipson, "Providence and Progress: An Introduction to the Historical Thought

of William Robertson," in Brown, *William Robertson and the Expansion of Empire*, 55–73; esp. 66–68.

75. William Robertson, *The History of America*, 3: 199.
76. William Robertson, *The History of America*, 3: 198.
77. William Robertson, *The History of America*, 3: 199–200.
78. William Robertson, *The History of America*, 3: 183.
79. William Robertson, *The History of America*, 3: 206.
80. William Robertson, *The History of America*, 3: 208.
81. William Robertson, *The History of America*, 3: 208, 210, 225.
82. William Robertson, *The History of America*, 3: 226.
83. William Robertson, *The History of America*, 3: 60–61.
84. Berry, *Social Theory of the Scottish Enlightenment*, 140–41.
85. Hargraves, "Enterprise," 48.

CHAPTER SEVEN

1. Raymond Schwab, *The Oriental Renaissance: Europe's Rediscovery of India and the East, 1660–1860*, trans. Gene Patterson-Black and Victor Reinking (New York: Columbia University Press, 1984).

2. Ulrich Gaier, *Herders Sprachphilosophie und Erkenntniskritik* (Stuttgart: Frommann-Holzboog, 1988); Robert Mayo, *Herder and the Beginnings of Comparative Literature* (Chapel Hill: University of North Carolina Press, 1969).

3. Robert Reinhold Ergang, *Herder and the Foundation of German Nationalism* (New York: Octagon Books, 1976).

4. The phrase "mythical image" comes from A. Leslie Willson, *A Mythical Image: The Ideal of India in German Romanticism* (Durham, N.C.: Duke University Press, 1964).

5. See John H. Zammito, *Kant, Herder, and the Birth of Anthropology* (Chicago: University of Chicago Press, 2002), 18–41.

6. Johann Gottfried Herder, *Selected Early Works, 1764–1767*, ed. Ernest A. Menze, trans. Ernest A. Menze and Michael Palma (University Park: Pennsylvania State University Press, 1992), 69–84.

7. Frederick Beiser, *Enlightenment, Revolution, and Romanticism: The Genesis of Modern German Political Thought, 1790–1800* (Cambridge: Cambridge University Press, 1992), 193–94. Compare also Susan Shell, *The Embodiment of Reason: Kant on Spirit, Generation, and Community* (Chicago: University of Chicago Press, 1996), 46–76.

8. Herder, *Selected Early Works*, 102.

9. Ibid.

10. Zammito, 155–60.

11. Thomas R. Trautmann, *Aryans and British India* (Berkeley: University of California Press, 1997), 131–89.

12. Johann Gottfried Herder, *Herders Werke in Fünf Bänden*, Vol. 2, ed. Wilhelm Dobbek (Berlin: Aufbau-Verlag, 1969), 11.

13. Zammito, 157.

14. For example, compare Thomas Hariot, *A Briefe and True Report on the New Found Land of Virginia* (1592) (New York: Dover Publications, 1972).

15. Herder, *Selected Early Works*, 106.

16. Ibid.

17. Ibid., 115.

18. Ibid.

19. Ibid., 116.

20. Ibid., 134.

21. Ibid.

22. Ibid., 163.

23. Ibid., 169.

24. Ibid., 178.

25. Ibid.

26. Ibid., 186–87.

27. Ibid.

28. *Herders Sämmtliche Werke, Vol. VI*, ed. Bernhard Suphan (Berlin: Weidmannsche Buchhandlung, 1883), 347.

29. Ibid., 356.

30. Ibid., 347–48.

31. Ibid., 350.

32. Schwab, *The Oriental Renaissance*, 7–8. Anquetil-Duperron's French and Latin translations of the Upanishads, the *Oupnek'hat* (1787, 1801–1802), inspired Arthur Schopenahauer's fascination with Indian thought.

33. Edwin Bryant, *The Quest for the Origins of Vedic Culture* (Oxford: Oxford University Press, 2000), 14–21; Martin Lewis and Kären Wigen, *The Myth of Continents; A Critique of Metageography* (Berkeley: University of California Press, 1997), 55–68; Trautmann, *Aryans and British India*, 41–52.

34. *Herders Sämmtliche Werke, Vol. V*, ed. Bernhard Suphan (Berlin: Weidmannsche Buchhandlung, 1891), 487.

35. Ibid., 483.

36. Ibid., 485.

37. Wilhelm Halbfass, *India and Europe: An Essay in Understanding* (Albany: State University of New York Press, 1988).

38. *Herders Sämmtliche Werke, Vol. V*, 483–84.

39. *Herders Sämmtliche Werke, Vol. XIV*, ed. Bernhard Suphan (Berlin: Weidmannsche Buchhandlung, 1909), 28–29.

40. *Herders Sämmtliche Werke, Vol. XVIII*, ed. Bernhard Suphan (Berlin: Weidmannsche Buchhandlung, 1883), 238.

41. Ibid., 500.

42. Ibid., 549.

43. Beiser, *Enlightenment*, 210.

44. *Herders Sämmtliche Werke, Vol. XVIII*, 516.

45. Willson, *A Mythical Image*, 60.

46. *Herders Sämmtliche Werke, Vol. V*, 514. The Northern European *Wilden* consisted of the Goths, Vandals, Burgundians, Anglos, Huns, Franks, Bulgarians, and Slavs, as well as others.

47. *Herders Sämmtliche Werke, Vol. V*, 514.
48. Cited from Leon Poliakov, *The Aryan Myth: A History of Racist and Nationalist Ideas in Europe*, trans. Edmund Howard (New York: Basic Books, 1974), 192–93.
49. Susanne Zantop, *Colonial Fantasies: Conquest, Family, and Nation in Precolonial Germany, 1770–1870* (Durham, N.C.: Duke University Press, 1997).
50. *Herders Sämmtliche Werke, Vol. XVIII*, 212. The first two stanzas were translated by me. The following stanza is translated by Zantop, *Colonial Fantasies*, 95.
51. *Herders Sämmtliche Werke, Vol. XIV*, 383–85.
52. *Herders Sämmtliche Werke, Vol. XVIII*, 222.
53. *Herders Sämmtliche Werke, Vol. XIV*, 28, 39.
54. Ibid., 389.
55. Ibid., 27.
56. Ibid., 28–29.
57. *Herders Sämmtliche Werke, Vol. XIII*, ed. Bernhard Suphan (Berlin: Weidmannsche Buchhandlung, 1887), 415–16.
58. *Herders Sämmtliche Werke, Vol. XVI*, ed. Bernhard Suphan (Berlin: Weidmannsche Buchhandlung, 1887), 67–68.
59. *Herders Sämmtliche Werke, Vol. XIV*, 34.
60. Ronald Inden, "Orientalist Constructions of India," *Modern Asian Studies* 20, no. 3 (1986): 401–408.
61. *Herders Sämmtliche Werke, XIV*, 31.
62. The title of the play has various renderings, as does the spelling of the title character's name and the use of accent marks over the letters. Compare W. J. Johnson's introduction to *The Recognition of Sakuntala*, trans. W. J. Johnson (Oxford: Oxford University Press, 2001), ix–xxix.
63. Schwab, *The Oriental Renaissance*, 57–64.
64. Ibid.
65. Willson, *A Mythical Image*, 65–66; Schwab, *The Oriental Renaissance*, 138–40.
66. *Herders Sämmtliche Werke, Vol. XVI*, ed. Bernhard Suphan (Berlin: Weidmannsche Buchhandlung, 1887), 88.
67. Ibid., 98.
68. Ibid., 91.
69. Ibid., 88.
70. Schwab, *The Oriental Renaissance*, 60.
71. *Herders Sämmtliche Werke, Vol. XVI*, 88–90.
72. Ibid., 91.
73. Ibid., 68, 78.
74. Ibid., 85–86.
75. Ibid., 68.
76. Schwab, *The Oriental Renaissance*, 60.
77. *Herders Sämmtliche Werke, Vol. XVI*, 71.
78. Ibid., 72.
79. Ibid., 74.

80. Ibid., 77.

81. Ibid.

82. *Herders Sämmtliche Werke, Vol. XVI*, 82.

83. Ibid.

84. Ibid., 79.

85. George S. Williamson, *The Longing for Myth in Germany: Religion and Aesthetic Culture from Romanticism to Nietzsche* (Chicago: University of Chicago Press, 2004), 74–120.

CHAPTER EIGHT

1. Alan Frost, "The Pacific Ocean: The Eighteenth Century's 'New World,' " in *Captain James Cook: Image and Impact*, ed. Walter Veit, 2 vols. (Melbourne: Hawthorn Press, 1972 and 1979), II, pp. 5–49.

2. John Locke, *Two Treatises of Government*, ed. Peter Laslett (New York: Mentor, 1965), II, p. 343, sec. 49.

3. Peter Hulme and Ludmilla Jordanova (eds.), *The Enlightenment and Its Shadows* (London: Routledge, 1990), p. 10.

4. James Sheehan, "Germany," in *Encyclopedia of the Enlightenment*, ed. Alan Kors, 4 vols. (New York: Oxford University Press, 2003), II, pp. 119–25.

5. Peter Reill, *The German Enlightenment and the Rise of Historicism* (Berkeley: University of California Press, 1975), p. 216; Jonathan Knudsen, *Justus Möser and the German Enlightenment* (Cambridge: Cambridge University Press, 1986), p. 186.

6. Joachim Whaley, "The Protestant Enlightenment in Germany," in *The Enlightenment in National Context*, ed. R. S. Porter and M. Teich (Cambridge: Cambridge University Press, 1981), pp. 106–17.

7. Reill, *German Enlightenment*, p. 133.

8. Nickolaus Jacquin, *Plantarum Rariorum Hortii Caesearei Schoenbrunnensis Descriptiones et Icones*, 4 vols. (Vienna: C. F. Wappler, 1797–1804), vol. 1, *Praefatio*, pp. iii–v. (I owe this reference to Robert King.)

9. Morris Berman, " 'Hegemony' and the Amateur Tradition in British Science," *Journal of Social History* 8 (1974–75): 30–43.

10. Charles McClelland, *State, Society, and University in Germany 1700–1914* (Cambridge: Cambridge University Press, 1980), pp. 39–45.

11. Mareta Linden, *Untersuchungen zum Anthropologiebegriff des 18, Jahrhunderts* (Frankfurt: Peter Lang, 1976), pp. 41, 62; John Zammito, *Kant, Herder, and the Birth of Anthropology* (Chicago: University of Chicago Press, 2002), p. 28.

12. Manfred Urban, "Cook's Voyages and the European Discovery of the South Seas," in *James Cook, Gifts and Treasures from the South Seas*, ed. Brigitta Hauser-Schaüblin and Gundolf Krüger (Munich: Prestel, 1998), pp. 30–55 (esp. 51).

13. Han Vermeulen, "Origins and Institutionalisation of Ethnography and Ethnology in Europe and the USA," in *Fieldwork and Footnotes, Studies in the History of European Anthropology*, ed. Han Vermeulen and Arturo Alvarez Roldan (London: Routledge, 1995), pp. 39–59 (esp. 25).

14. Urban, "European Discovery," pp. 51–52.

15. Vermeulen, "Origins," p. 42.

16. Michael Harbsmeier, "Towards a Prehistory of Ethnography: Early Modern German Travel Writing as Traditions of Knowledge," in *Fieldwork and Footnotes*, pp. 19–38 (esp. 22–23).

17. Lisbet Koerner, "Daedalus Hyperboreus: Baltic Natural History and Mineralogy in the Enlightenment," in *The Sciences in Enlightened Europe*, ed. William Clark, Jan Golinski, and Simon Schaffer (Chicago: University of Chicago Press, 1999), pp. 389–422 (esp. 414).

18. Katherine Faull, "Introduction" to *Anthropology and the German Enlightenment: Perspectives on Humanity*, ed. K. Faull (Lewisburg, Pa.: Bucknell University Press, 1995), pp. 11–19 (esp. 12).

19. J. R. Forster, "Specimen Historiae Naturalis Volgensis," *Philosophical Transactions of the Royal Society* 57 (1767): 312–57.

20. Z. Fedeorowicz, "Zoology in Danzig in the XVII and XVIII Centuries," *Memorabilia Zoologica* 19 (1968): 187–93 (English translation from the Polish at Alexander Turnbull Library, Wellington, MS 1486).

21. Ruth Dawson, "Collecting with Cook: The Forsters and their Artifact Sales," *Hawaiian Journal of History* 13 (1979): 5–16.

22. Ilse Jahn, "Forster (1729–1798) und die Konzeption einer 'Allgemeinen Naturgeschichte'—Zum Gendenken an seiner 200, Todestag," *Sitzungsberichte der Gesellschafte Naturforschender Freunde zu Berlin* 37 (1998): 1–12 (esp. 2).

23. Michael Hoare (ed.), *The* Resolution *Journal of Forster*, 4 vols. (London: Hakluyt Society, 1982), I, p. 107.

24. G. Forster, *Werke; Sämtliche Schriften, Tagebücher, Briefe*, ed. Akademie der Wissenschaften, 18 vols. (Berlin: Akademie Verlag, 1958–2003), XIV, p. 299; G. Forster to [Countess] Maria Wilhelmine von Thun (French), March 6, 1785.

25. G. Forster, *A Voyage Round the World in His Britannic Majesty's Sloop, Resolution*, ed. Nicholas Thomas and Oliver Berghof, 2 vols. (Honolulu: University of Hawai'i Press, 2000), I, p. 9.

26. J. R. Forster, *Observations Made During a Voyage Round the* World, ed. Nicholas Thomas, Harriet Guest, and Michael Dettelbach (Honolulu: University of Hawai'i Press, 1996), p. 9.

27. In his "Der Brodbaum" ("The Breadfruit Tree") of 1784. Thomas Saine, *Georg Forster* (New York: Twayne Publishers, 1972), p. 30.

28. Erwin H. Ackerknecht, "George Forster, Alexander von Humboldt, and Ethnology," *Isis* 46 (1955): 83–95 (esp. 85).

29. John Lyon and Phillip Sloan, *From Natural History to the History of Nature: Readings from Buffon and His Critics* (Notre Dame, Ind.: Notre Dame University Press, 1981), p. 121.

30. Muséum National d'Histoire Naturelle, MS 189, "Catalogue d'un Herbier rapporté des Isles de la Mer Australe par M. Forster et cédé à M. le Comte de Buffon pour le Cabinet du Roy, en November 1777."

31. L. C. Rookmaker, "The Zoological Notes by Johann Reinhold and Georg Forster Included in Buffon's *Histoire Naturelle* (1782)," *Archives of Natural History* 12 (1985): 203–12.

32. Robert Wokler, "From L'Homme Physique to L'Homme Morale and Back: Towards a History of Enlightenment Anthropology," *History of the Human Sciences* 6 (1993): 121–38.

33. J. Forster, "Lectures on Natural History and Especially on Mineralogy . . . Begun to Be Read and Composed 1767 and 1768" (Berlin: Staatsbibliothek), MS germ. oct. 22a, folios 3–4, 9–12, 18.

34. J. R. Forster, "Lectures on Entomology: Drawn Up 1786 and Delivered from Jan.–June 1769" (Berlin: Staatsbibliothek), MS germ. oct. 21, folios 3–4.

35. J. R. Forster to D. Barrington, Peabody Museum, Salem, Mass., December 12, 1768.

36. Charles Withers, "Geography, Natural History and the 18th Century Enlightenment: Putting the World in Place," *History Workshop Journal* 39 (1995): 137–63.

37. J. R. Forster, "Nota rélativement aux Curiosités Artificielles, qu'on a rapports de la Mer du Sud" (Wellington, MS: Alexander Turnbull Library), 3497 (printed in M. Hoare, *The* Resolution *Journal*, IV, pp. 780–82).

38. J. R. Forster, "Anmerkungen über die beste Methode mit Nutzen zu Reisen" (Berlin: Staatsbibliothek), MS germ. quart. 246.

39. Michael Hoare, *The Tactless Philosopher: Johann Reinhold Forster (1729–98)* (Melbourne: Hawthorn Press, 1976), p. 76.

40. J. Forster, *Observations*, p. 185.

41. For example, the "surprisingly accurate" vocabulary list recorded in Balad. J. Hollyman and A. G. Huadricourt, "The New Caledonian Vocabularies of Cook and the Forsters," *Journal of the Polynesian Society* 69 (1980): 215–27 (esp. 226).

42. Karl Rensch, *The Language of the Noble Savage: The Linguistic Fieldwork of Reinhold and George Forster in Polynesia on Cook's Second Voyage to the Pacific 1772–1775* (Canberra: Archipelago Press, 2000), pp. v, 23, 77–80.

43. J. R. Forster, "Vocabularies of the Languages Spoken in the Isles of the South Sea . . . 1774" (Berlin: Staatsbibliothek), MS or. oct. 62, folio 4.

44. Janet Browne, *The Secular Ark: Studies in the History of Biogeography* (New Haven: Yale, 1983), p. 38.

45. Britta Rupp-Eisenreich, "Aux 'Origines' de la 'Völkerkunde' Allemande: De la "Statistik" à l' 'Anthropologie' de Georg Forster," in *Histoires de L'Anthropologie (XVIe–XIXe Siècles)*, ed. Britta Rupp-Eisenreich (Paris: Klincksieck, 1984), pp. 89–115 (esp. 104). On the extent to which Forster's concern with a "total" local history embodied an interest in the forces that shaped history as a whole, see Jörn Garber, "Anthropologie und Geschichte," in *Georg Forster in Interdisziplinärer Perspektive*, ed. Claus-Volker Klenke (Berlin: Akademie Verlag, 1994), pp. 193–210 (esp. 203).

46. Hoare, *The Tactless Philosopher*, p. 143. See, for example, George Forster's critical remarks on those who would explain the character of a society solely in terms of climate in his description of New Caledonia. G. Forster, *Observations*, II, p. 592.

47. Hans Böedeker, "Aufklärerische Ethnolologische Praxis: Johann Reinhold und Georg Forster," in *Wissenschaft als Kulturelle Praxis 1750–1900*, ed. Hans Böedeker (Göttingen: Vandenhoeck and Ruprecht, 1999), pp. 227–53 (esp. 236).

48. Adrienne Kaeppler, "Die Ethnographischer Sammlungen der Fosters aus dem Südpazifik. Klassische Empirie im Dienste der Modernen Ethnologie," in *Georg Forster in Interdisziplinärer*, pp. 59–75.

49. J. R. Forster, *Observations*, pp. 9–10.

50. G. Forster, *Voyage*, p. 6.

51. "Noch Etwas," in G. Forster, *Werke*, VIII, pp. 130, 131, 137.

52. Ibid., p. 141; Thomas Strack, "Philosophical Anthropology on the Eve of Biological Determinism: Immanuel Kant and Georg Forster on the Moral Qualities and Biological Characteristics of the Human Race," *Central European History* 29 (1996): 285–308 (esp. 302).

53. Second edition of 1785, entitled *Über die körperliche Verschiedenheit des Negers vom Europäer* (*On the Bodily Difference Between Negroes and Europeans*).

54. "Noch Etwas," in G. Forster, *Werke*, VIII, pp. 143, 153.

55. Ibid., pp. 153–54.

56. Rupp-Eisenreich, "Aux 'Origines,' " p. 103.

57. Saine, *Georg Forster*, p. 35.

58. J. R. Forster, *Observations*, p. 172.

59. Ruth Dawson, *Georg Forster's* Reise um die Welt: *A Travelogue in Its Eighteenth-Century Context*, University of Michigan PhD, 1973, p. 86.

60. G. Forster, *Voyage,* I, p. 171.

61. Ibid., I, p. 256.

62. Ibid., I, pp. 400–401.

63. J. R. Forster, *Observations*, p. 329.

64. Hoare, *The Tactless Philosopher*, p. 14.

65. Hoare, Resolution *Journal*, IV, p. 613.

66. J. R. Forster, *Observations*, p. 339.

67. Hoare, Resolution *Journal*, III, p. 395.

68. Paul Hazard, *European Thought in the Eighteenth Century* (Harmondsworth: Penguin, 1965), pp. 51–52, 80–81.

69. Hoare, Resolution *Journal*, I, p. 278.

70. J. R. Forster, "On the Human Species in the Isles of the South Seas" (Berlin: Staatsbibliothek), MS germ. oct. 79, folio 3.

71. J. R. Forster, *Observations*, p. 200.

72. Ulrich Kronauer, "Rousseaus Kulturkritik aus der Sicht Georg Forster," in *Georg Forster in Interdisziplinärer*, pp. 147–56; Rupp-Eisenreich, "Aux 'Origines,' " p. 103. On George Forster and Rousseau, see also Eberhard Berg, *Zwischen den Welten. Anthropologie der Aufklärung und das Werk Georg Forsters* (Berlin: Reiner Verlag, 1982).

73. G. Forster, *Voyage*, II, p. 481.

74. Muséum National d'Histoire Naturelle, MS 186 (Foster MSS, section on "sago").

75. H. West, "The Limits of Enlightenment Anthropology: Georg Forster and the Tahitian," *History of European Ideas* 10 (1989): 147–60.

76. J. Forster, *Observations*, pp. 205, 195–96.

77. Ibid., pp. lxxviii, 196, 235.

78. G. Forster, *Voyage*, II, p. 684.

79. G. Forster, *Werke*, VIII, pp. 65–68 (French).

80. Ackerknecht, "Forster," p. 84.

81. G. Forster, *Werke*, XIV, p. 599; G. Forster to Sömmering, Dec. 1786.

82. I. Jahn, "Scientia Naturae—Naturbetrachtung oder Naturwissenschaft? Georg Forsters Erkenntnisfragen zu biologischen Phänomenon in Vorlesungs-Manuskripten aus Wilna und Mainz," in *Georg Forster in Interdisziplinärer*, pp. 159–77 (esp. 166).

83. Muséum National d'Histoire Naturelle, MS 188, *Rudimenta Scientiae Naturalis* (1786), fol. 7.

84. Timothy Lenoir, "Kant, Blumenbach, and Vital Materialism in German Biology," *Isis* 71 (1980): 77–108 (esp. 86).

85. Stefano Bertoletti, "The Anthropological Theory of Johann Blumenbach," in *Romanticism in Science: Science in Europe, 1790–1840*, ed. Stefano Poggi and Maurizio Bossi (Dordrecht: Kluwer, 1994), pp. 103–25 (esp. 110).

86. Niedersächisische Staats—und Universitätsbibliothek [Göttingen], Blumenbach MSS, IV.

87. J. Forster, *Observations*, p. 1.

88. Jahn, "Forster," p. 6.

89. Hoare, *Tactless Philosopher*, p. 311.

90. Frost, "The Pacific Ocean," pp. 35–36.

91. H. Plischke, "Die Malayaische Varietät Bluemenbachs," *Zeitschrift für Rassenkunde* 8 (1938): 225–31 (esp. 229).

92. Hoare, *Tactless Philosopher*, pp. 317–18, 327.

93. J. Forster, *History of the Voyages and Discoveries in the North*, translated into English (London: G. G. J. Robinson & J. Robinson, 1786), p. xiv.

94. G. Forster, "Neuholland und die brittishche Colonie in Botany-Bay," in his *Werke*, V, pp. 163, 174, 176, 161–62. Cited from the English translation by Robert King, Australian National Library, SR 909.7/S768, pp. 1, 7–8, 10–11.

95. G. Forster, "Cook der Entdecker," in Forster, *Werke*, V, pp. 191–302. Cited from the English translation by P. Klarwill, Alexander Turbull Library, Wellington, MS—Papers—1485, pp. 1, 5, 8, 20, 83, 86–89. M. E. Hoare, "Cook the Discoverer": An Essay by Georg Forster," *Records of the Australian Academy of Science* 1 (1969): 7–16 provides a summary of this important essay.

96. G. Craig, "Engagement and Neutrality in Germany: The Case of Georg Forster, 1754–94," *Journal of Modern History* 41 (1969): 1–16 (esp. 4, 12–13).

97. Saine, *Georg Forster*, p. 134.

98. G. Forster, *A Letter to the Right Honourable, The Earl of Sandwich*, in G. Forster, *Voyage*, II, pp. 790, 799.

99. British Library, Add. MS 8098, fol. 436, Blumenbach to Banks, Jan. 19, 1799.

100. Ibid., fol. 486, Wilhelmina Sprengel to Banks, June 4, 1799.

101. Hoare, *Tactless Philosopher*, p. 310.

102. J. S. Gordan, *Reinhold and Georg Forster in England, 1766–1780*, PhD thesis, Duke University, 1975, p. 62.

103. Forster, *Werke*, XIV, pp. 642–43; G. Forster to Pennant, March 5, 1787.

104. Urban, "European Discovery," p. 55; Manfred Urban, "The Acquisition History of the Göttingen Collection," pp. 60–70 (both in Hauser-Schäublin and Krüger, *James Cook*).

105. Eva Raabe, Eberhard Schlesier, and Manfred Urban (eds.), *Verzeichnis der Völkergundlichen Sammlung des Instituts für Völkerkunde der Georg-August-Universität zu Göttingen*, Teil 1: *Abteilung Ozeanien* (Göttingen: Das Institut, 1988), p. 49.

106. Urban, "Acquisition History," pp. 70–71.

107. Urban, "European Discovery," p. 53.

108. Included in Klaus-Georg Popp (ed.), *Cook der Endecker* [Schriften über James Cook] (Leipzig: Reclam, 1980) along with G. Forster's writings on Cook.

109. Forster, *Werke*, XIII, p. 291; Forster to Banks, May 27, 1780.

110. Robert Leventhal, "The Emergence of Philological Discourse in the German States," *Isis* 77 (1986): 243–60 (esp. 250).

111. Urban, "European Discovery," p. 53.

112. Niedersächisische Staats—und Universitätsbibliothek, Cod. Mich. 327, fol. 229, Pringle to Michaelis, May 6, 1766; folios 239–40, June 1769; fol. 260, Sept. 23, 1771; fol. 314, July 9, 1774; fol. 319, Dec. 30, 1774; fol. 324, July 18, 1775; fol. 335, May 16, 1777.

113. Paul Raabe and Wilhelm Schmidt-Biggemann (eds.), *Enlightenment in Germany* (Bonn: Hohwacht Verlag, 1979), pp. 175–76.

114. John Gascoigne, "Blumenbach, Banks, and the Beginnings of Anthropology at Göttingen," in *Göttingen and the Development of the Natural Sciences*, ed. Nicolaas Rupke (Göttingen: Wallstein Verlag, 2002), pp. 86–98; and *Joseph Banks and the English Enlightenment: Useful Knowledge and Polite Culture* (Cambridge: Cambridge University Press, 1994), pp. 149–59.

115. Niedersächisische Staats—und Universitätsbibliothek, Blumenbach MSS, VI: 12, Andrew Halliday to Dr. Clarke, Jan. 27, 1821.

116. Ibid., V: 20, Isaac Buxton to Blumenbach, n.d. [ca. 1820].

117. Ibid., I, iii: 14, 35; V: 42 (includes John Bigge to Blumenbach, April 16, 1822).

118. Ibid., V: 43, William Davison to Blumenbach, Dec. 6, 1822.

119. Ibid., V: 45, Alex Caldeburgh to Blumenbach, August 30, 1825.

120. Ibid., V: 58, Thomas Traill to Blumenbach, May 12, 1829.

121. Ibid., V: vi, John Crawford to Charles König, May 3, 1832.

122. Ibid., V: 28, Benjamin Barton to Blumenbach August 12, 1796. An undated letter (V: 15 from Michaelis to Mrs. Blumenbach [French]) refers to having "received the head of an Indian chief from a very distinguished anatomist from Philadelphia."

123. Ibid., V: 40, John Sullivan to Blumenbach, October 4, 1824.

124. Ibid., VI, Edward Everett to Blumenbach, November 9, 1835.

125. Georgette Legée, "Johann Reinhold Friedrich Blumenbach, 1752–1840. La Naissance de L'Anthropologie à L'époque de la Révolution Française," *Histoire et Nature* 28–29 (1987–88): 23–45 (esp. 30).

126. British Library, Add. MS 8098, Blumenbach to Banks, May 8, 1792.

127. Niedersächisische Staats—und Universitätsbibliothek, Blumenbach MSS, V: 34; F. P. to Blumenbach, March 24, 1826.

128. Urban, "Acquisition History," p. 74.

129. Legée, "Blumenbach," p. 33.

130. Urban, "Acquisition History," p. 74.

131. Johann von Herder, *Outlines of a Philosophy of the History of Man*, English trans. T. O. Churchill (London: Printed for J. Johnson by Luke Hansard, 1800), p. 153.

132. Herder, *Reflections*, edited by Frank Manuel using the Churchill translation (Chicago: University of Chicago Press, 1968), pp. 4, 6, 51, 62.

133. Immanuel Kant, *Anthropology from a Pragmatic Point of View*, trans. and ed. Mary Gregor (The Hague: Martinus Nijhoff, 1974), p. 4.

134. Emmanuel Eze, "The Color of Reason: The Idea of 'Race' in Kant's Anthropology," in *Anthropology and the German Enlightenment*, pp. 200–41 (esp. 228).

135. Strack, "Philosophical Anthropology," p. 293.

136. Emmanuel Eze, *Race and the Enlightenment: A Reader* (Oxford: Blackwell, 1997), p. 70.

137. Hoare, *Forster's* Resolution *Journal*, I, p. 114.

138. Michael Dettelbach, "Global Physics and Aesthetic Empire: Humboldt's Physical Portrait of the Tropics," in *Visions of Empire: Voyages, Botany, and Representations of Nature* (Cambridge: Cambridge University Press, 1996), pp. 258–92 (esp. 266).

139. Ackerkneckt, "George Forster," p. 85.

140. Ludwig Uhlig, "Georg Forsters Horizont," in *Georg Forster in Interdisziplinärer Perspektive*, pp. 3–14 (esp. 11).

141. Alexander von Humboldt, *Cosmos: A Sketch of a Physical Description of the Universe*, trans. C. E. Otté, 4 vols. (London: Henry Bohn, 1849–52), I, pp. 362, 365.

For a recent work which includes an illuminating discussion of the German response to the Pacific, see Harry Liebersohn, *The Travelers' World: Europe and the Pacific* (Cambridge, Mass.: Harvard University Press, 2006), which appeared while this chapter was in press.

CHAPTER NINE

1. For a more substantial account of these and other Greenlanders' accounts of their visits to Denmark, see Michael Harbsmeier (ed.), *Stimmen aus dem äussersten Norden. Wie die Grönländer Europa für sich entdeckten*, vol. 11 (Sigmaringen: Fremde Kulturen in alten Berichten, 2001). A shorter English version concerning Pooq is published in Michael Bravo and Sverker Sörlin (eds.), *Narrating the Arctic: A Cultural History of Nordic Scientific Practices* (Canton, Mass.: Science History Publications, 2002).

2. Quoted and translated from Alfred Bertelsen, *Grønlænderne i Danmark, bidrag til belysning af grønlandsk kolonisationsarbejde fra 1605 til vor tid*, vol. 145, no. 2 (Copenhagen: Meddelelser om Grønland, 1945), p. 41.

3. Quoted from Bertelsen, *Grønlænderne i Danmark*, p. 34.

4. Hans Egede, *Relationer fra Grønland 1721–36 og Det gamle Grønlands ny Perlustration 1741: Udgivne af Louis Bobé*, vol. 54 (Copenhagen: Meddelelser om Grønland, 1925), p. 184.

5. Quoted from Johannes Balle, *Grønlænderen Pôk hvorledes han kom til Danmark, hans oplevelser der, og hvad han fortalte sine landsmænd derom, da han kom tilbage*, in *Tidsskriftet Grønland*, 12. årg. 1964, p. 328.

6. Quoted from Egede, *Relationer fra Grønland*, p. 184; Balle, *Grønlænderen Pôk*, p. 323.

7. Poul Egede, *Grammatica Grönlandica Danico-Latina* (Copenhagen, 1760), pp. 214–19.

8. Poul Egede, *Grammatica*, pp. 219–23.

9. Poul Egede, *Grammatica*, pp. 225–31.

10. Poul Egede, *Grammatica*, pp. 233–37.

11. Poul Egede, *Grammatica*, pp. 237–39.

12. See Gian Carlo Roscioni, *Sulle tracce dell' "esploratore turco." Letteratura e spionaggio nella cultura libertina del Seicento* (Milan, 1992).

13. Winfried Weisshaupt, *Europa sieht sich mit fremden Blick : Werke nach dem Schema der "Lettres persanes" in der europaischen, insbesondere der deutschen Literatur des 18. Jahrhunderts* (Frankfurt am Main: P. Lang, 1979).

14. *En Grønlænders Beskrivelse over København med Betænkning over de Ti Buds Helligholdelse*, trykt hos Herman Höecke (Copenhagen, 1771), p. 10.

15. See Johann Ernst Gründler and Bartholomäus Ziegenbalg, *Die Malabarische Korrespondenz. Tamilische Briefe an deutsche Missionare. Eine Auswahl*, ed. Kurt Liebau, vol. 5 (Sigmaringen: Fremde Kulturen in alten Berichten, 1998).

16. Norman Doiron, *L'art de voyager* (Paris: Sainte-Foy, 1995).

17. See Michael Harbsmeier, "Kadu und Maheine. Entdeckerfreundschaften in deutschen Weltreisen um die Wende zum 19. Jahrhundert," in Wolfgang Gried (ed.), *Sehen und Beschreiben. Europäische Reisen im 18. und frühen 19. Jahrhundert*, vol. 1 (Eutin: Eutiner Forschungen, 1991), pp. 150–78.

18. Michael Alexander refers more than once to Omai's predecessors in his reconstruction of Omai's stay in London; see his *Omai: Noble Savage* (London: Collins Harvill Press, 1977), 69, 75, 106. Discussing the reception of James Bruce as well as of Omai in London in 1774, Nigel Leask has arrived at a much more sophisticated description of what he calls "the problem of credit" in London. See Nigel Leask, *Curiosity and the Aesthetics of Travel Writing 1770–1840* (Oxford: Oxford University Press, 2002), pp. 54–101.

19. This did not prevent Cartwright from bringing another boy, Noozelliackk, with him to England in 1773; he died from smallpox only three days after an attempt at vaccination. "So fatal is that disorder to this race of mortals," says Cartwright. George Cartwright, *Journal of Transactions and Events, during a residence of nearly sixteen years on the coast of Labrador; containing many interesting particulars, both of the country and its inhabitants, not hitherto known*, 3 vols. (Newark, 1792), vol. I, p. 286.

20. See Helge Kleivan, *Eskimoer på besøk i England i 1772. Fra George Cartwrights dagbok fra Labrador* (Oslo: Polarboken, 1957), p. 140.

21. Cartwright, *Journal of Transactions and Events*, vol. I, p. 267.

22. Cartwright, *Journal of Transactions and Events*, vol. I, pp. 266–67.

23. Cartwright, *Journal of Transactions and Events*, vol. I, p. 269.

24. Cartwright, *Journal of Transactions and Events*, vol. I, p. 270.

25. Cartwright, *Journal of Transactions and Events*, vol. I, p. 271.
26. Cartwright, *Journal of Transactions and Events*, vol. I, p. 272.
27. Cartwright, *Journal of Transactions and Events*, vol. I, pp. 268–69.

CHAPTER TEN

1. Compare M. Khodarkovsky, "From Frontier to Europe," in *Russian History, Special Issue: The Frontier in Russian History* (Los Angeles: Charles Schlacks Jr., 1992).

2. M. Khodarkovsky, "Ignoble Savages and Unfaithful Subjects," in D. R. Brower and E. J. Lazzerini (eds.), *Russia's Orient: Imperial Borderlands and Peoples, 1700–1917* (Bloomington-Indianapolis: Indiana University Press, 1997), p. xvi.

3. R. P. Geraci, *Window on the East: National and Imperial Identities in Late Tsarist Russia* (Ithaca, N.Y.: Cornell University Press, 2001).

4. The same fate was in store for the Kazakhs. Compare M. Khodarkovsky, *Russia's Steppe Frontier: The Making of the Colonial Empire, 1500–1800* (Bloomington-Indianapolis: Indiana University Press, 2002), pp. 182–83.

5. On the seventeenth-century Russian exploratory process: L. Bagrow, *A History of Russian Cartography Up to 1800* (Ontario: Walker Press, 1975), pp. 19–38.

6. V. M. Kabuzan, *Narodi Rossii v XVIII veke. Chislennost' i etnicheskii sostav* [The Russian Population in the Eighteenth Century. Figures and Ethnic Composition], Akademiya Nauk CCCP-Institut Istorii CCCP (Moscow: "Nauka," 1990), p. 15.

7. Ibid., p. 6.

8. M. Khodarkovsky, *Russia's Steppe Frontier*, p. 186.

9. M. Khodarkovsky, "Ignoble Savages and Unfaithful Subjects," p. 25.

10. Compare Geraci, *Window on the East*, pp. 21–22.

11. Abul-Ghazi, *Histoire généalogique des Tartares, traduit du manuscrit tartare d'Abulgasi Chan par M. D.* (Leyden: Abram Kallewier, 1726). The document was discovered and brought to Europe from Siberia by Strahlenberg. It was published in Holland in 1726. It would be published in Russia only in 1768. J. T. Strahlenberg (von), *Description historique de l'empire de Russie, traduite de l'ouvrage Allemand de M. le Baron de Strahlenberg,* 2 vols. (Amsterdam: De Saint and Saillant, 1757), p. ix.

12. Both Montesquieu and Voltaire availed themselves of this book. C. L. Montesquieu de Secondat, *De l'esprit des lois* (Paris: Garnier-Flammarion 1979), book XIII, pp. 367–68; F. M. A. Voltaire, *Essai sur les mœurs* (1756, reprint Paris: Garnier Frères, 1963), p. 17.

13. A nomadic population of Mongolian origins, the Kalmyks migrated to eastern Europe, in an area situated westward of the river Volga and northward of the Caspian Sea, between the seventeenth and eighteenth centuries.

14. Abul-Ghazi, *Histoire généalogique des Tartares,* p. 88; compare Geraci, *Window on the East*, p. 17.

15. Abul-Ghazi, *Histoire généalogique des Tartares,* pp. 88, 104. Among his sources, he mentioned the French author Petis de la Croix, whose work could be

found in the Bibliothèque du Roy, and the discoveries of Major Ismailov, a Russian envoy to the Chinese court in 1719–21.

16. Ibid., pp. 20–21, 42–43.

17. Ibid., pp. 30–31.

18. Ibid., pp. 241–43.

19. Ibid., p. 485.

20. R. H. Fisher, *Bering's Voyages: Whither and Why* (London: University of Washington Press, 1977), Appendix I.

21. Compare *Du voyage fait par le Capitaine Beering, au Kamtschatka depuis 1725 jusqu'en 1730; ou Abrégé de son Journal*, in Strahlenberg, *Description historique de l'empire de Russie*, vol. II, pp. 267–71.

22. Gottfried Siegfried Bayer (1694–1738) was a German Sinologist and philologist who was appointed as a professor of Greek and Roman in St. Petersburg in 1726 and participated in the activities of the Academy of Sciences. Among his numerous works: *De origine et priscis sedibus Scytharum*, in *Commentarii Academiae Scientiarum Imperialis Petropolitanae* (Petropoli: Typis Academiae, 1726).

23. Strahlenberg, *Description historique de l'empire de Russie*, vol. I, pp. 255–59. The French translation is shorter than the German original, and does not follow the structure of the original edition, in which, for instance, the "Vocabolarium Calmucko-Mungalicum" is situated in the first volume. Although entirely bilingual (German and Swedish), Strahlenberg wrote his book in German, likely because it would reach a wider public.

24. Ibid., vol. II, pp. 166–67.

25. Ibid., vol. II, pp. 206–207.

26. Contrary to the original, in the French translation, the words are listed in alphabetical order.

27. Strahlenberg, *Description historique de l'empire de Russie*, vol. II, p. 311.

28. J. R. Krueger, *The Kalmuck-Mongolian Vocabulary in Strahlenberg's Geography of 1730, Asiatica Suecana. Early Eighteenth-Century Documents and Studies*, vol. I (Stockholm: Almqvist & Wiksell International, 1975), pp. 28–30.

29. *Encyclopédie ou Dictionnaire raisonné des sciences, des arts et des métiers* (Lucques: Giuntini, 1758–76), vol. XIV, "La Russie," pp. 375–78; F. M. A. Voltaire, *Histoire de l'empire de Russie sous Pierre le Grand*, in *Oeuvres historiques. Texte établi, annoté et présenté par R. Pomeau* (Paris: Gallimard, 1957), p. 367; G. J. Georgi, *Russia, or A Compleat Historical Account of All the Nations Which Compose That Empire*, 4 vols., English trans. W. Tooke (London: Printed for J. Nichols: T. Cadell, in the Strand; H. Payne, Pall-Mall; and N. Conant, Fleet-Street, 1780–83), vol. I, p. xvi.

30. F. Müller, *Voyages et découvertes faites par les russes* (Amsterdam: C. G. F. Dumas, 1766), p. 2.

31. Müller stressed the importance of Peter's written instructions to the first general-admiral of the Russian navy, F. M. Apraksin, which were never carried out, however, due to Peter's engagement in warfare and reformist activity. Compare G. F. Müller, *Sochineniya po istorii Rossii. Izbrannoe, sostavlenie, stat'ya A. B. Kamenskogo* [Writings on the History of Russia, a Selection, Edition, and

Articles]. Footnotes by A. B. Kamenskogo and O. M. Medushevskoy (Moscow: "Nauka," 1996), p. 420.

32. S. Krasheninnikov, *Histoire de Kamschatka des Iles Kurilski and c., traduite de la langue Russienne par Eydos, avec deux cartes*, 2 vols. (Lyon: Benoit Duplain, 1767).

33. His travel diary is *Reise von Kamtschatka nach Amerika mit den Commander Captain Bering*, St. Petersburg, 1793, which was translated and is fully contained in F. A. Golder (1877–1929), *Bering's Voyages: An Account of the Efforts of the Russians to Determine the Relation of Asia and America* (New York: American Geographical Society, 1922–25).

34. The German J. E. Fischer was not only a keen historian but also an antique dealer and a voyager under Russia's service. As a professor in Petersburg and a member of the Academy of Science, he investigated the populations and history of Siberia, also producing a number of written works either in German or in Latin.

35. Compare Y. Slezkine, "Naturalists Versus Nations: Eighteenth-Century Russian Scholars Confront Ethnic Diversity," in D. R. Brower and E. J. Lazzerini (eds.), *Russia's Orient*, p. 30.

36. G. F. Müller, *Voyages et découvertes*, vol. I, pp. 5–7.

37. Ibid., p. 8.

38. Ibid., p. 24.

39. Ibid., pp. 62–81.

40. Ibid., p. 142.

41. Müller cited Abul-Gazhi, *Kaempfer's Histoire du Japon* (1727–28), Strahlenberg, Du Halde, maps by d'Anville, Buache, Guillaume Delisle, Kirilov, Witsen, Linnaeus, and so forth. Ibid., pp. 155–61, 316.

42. S. Bayer was the only historian of the academy and helped Müller to learn Russian as well as to become interested in Siberia. Johann-Werner Paus was the director of translators at the academy and an expert on church Slavonic. He acted as translator for both Müller and Bayer, and introduced them to some ancient sources.

43. J. L. Black, *Müller and the Imperial Russian Academy* (Kingston-Montreal: McGill-Queen's University Press, 1986), pp. 56–57.

44. Compare Strahlenberg, *Description historique de l'empire de Russie*, p. 262.

45. F. Müller, *Voyages et découvertes*, vol. I, pp. 335–37, 340.

46. From 1731 to 1741, he was assisted by a senior official, Alexei L'vovich Pleshecheev, anxious to cooperate, who was also author of a historical-geographical manuscript on Siberia. J. L. Black, *Müller and the Imperial Russian Academy*, p. 58.

47. The first four chapters were probably completed in 1742, before going back to St. Petersburg. The first part was submitted to Elizabeth in 1744, and in 1746 Razumovskii assigned to Golubtsov the task of translating it into Russian. He gathered inscriptions, genealogical information on noble families and the Romanovs, old rolls (*stolbtsy*) and books that he ordered chronologically, archaeological remains, coins, and so forth.

48. A very useful questionnaire was, for instance, that of Tatishchev, which was found by Müller and employed for the preparation of his own questionnaires.

49. F. Müller, *Voyages et découvertes*, vol. I, pp. 350–54.

50. Yet, the translator admitted to having reedited the original in order to eliminate some boring sections, which he attributed to Gmelin's style. J. G. Gmelin, *Voyage en Sibérie, contenant la description des mœurs et usages des peuples de ce Pays, e cours des rivières considérables, la situation des chaînes de montagnes, des grandes forets, des mines, avec tous les faits d'Histoire Naturelle qui sont particulières a cette contrée. Fait aux frais du Gouvernement Russe, par M. Gmelin, Professeur de Chymie et de Botanique, Traduction libre de l'original allemand, par M. de Keralio, premier Aide-Major, à l'Ecole Royale Militaire, et chargé d'enseigner la Tactique aux Elèves de cette Ecole,* 2 vols. (Paris: Chez Desaint, Libraire, rue du Foin Saint Jacques, 1767), pp. vi–viii.

51. Ibid., p. 143.

52. Ibid., pp. 10–14.

53. D. Dahlmann, *Als schwäbischer Pietist unter Schamanen*. Johann Georg Gmelin in Sibirien's *Damals*, no. 27 (1885), issue 12, pp. 74–79.

54. J. B. Müller, *Les mœurs et usages des Ostiakes, et la manière dont ils furent convertis en 1712, à la Religion Chrétienne du rit Grec, avec plusieurs remarques curieuses sur le Royaume de Sibérie, et le Détroit de Weygatz or de Nassau, par Jean Bernard Müller, Capitaine de Dragons au service de la Suède, pendant sa captivité en Sibérie* [no place or date of publication (1727)].

55. Ibid., pp. 147–51. Compare G. L. L. Buffon (de), *Histoire naturelle, générale et particulière avec la description du Cabinet du Roy* (1749–88), vol. III (Paris: de l'Imprimerie Royale, 1750), pp. 375–78. Buffon used J. B. Müller's book as a source.

56. Gmelin, *Voyage en Sibérie,* pp. 77, 91.

57. Ibid., p. 391.

58. On Russo-German relationships in the eighteenth century, see *Russkie i Nemtsi v XVIII veke. Vstrecha kultur* [Russians and Germans in the Eighteenth Century. A Cultural Encounter], ed. S. Ya. Karp (Moscow: "Nauka," 2000). There is a long section devoted to science on pp. 92–159, which includes an essay on the Russo-German dispute within the Academy of Sciences.

59. J. L. Black, *Müller and the Imperial Russian Academy,* pp. 118–20.

60. Marine 2/JJ/89, Manuscrits de M. Delisle de la Croyère, Observations astronomiques (1733–41), vol. 36, no. 4 in the Archives Nationales (Paris: Dépôt du Service Central Hydrographique; Marine).

61. Marine 2/JJ/72, vol. 115–19, no. 11.

62. Ibid., vol. 19, no. 16.

63. Ibid., vol. 19, no. 25.

64. M. Raeff, *The Well-Ordered Police State: Social and Institutional Change Through Law in the Germanies and Russia, 1600–1800* (New Haven: Yale University Press, 1983), pp. 223–24.

65. V. O. Kliuchevsky, *A Course in Russian History: The Time of Catherine the Great,* trans. and ed. S. Marshall Shatz (London and Armonk, N.Y.: M. E. Sharpe, 1997), p. 90.

66. W. F. Reddaway (ed.), *Documents of Catherine the Great. The Correspondence with Voltaire and the Instruction of 1767 in the English Text of 1768* (Cambridge: Cambridge University Press, 1931), pp. 17–18.

67. Compare M. O. Kosven, *Etnograficheskie resul'taty Severnoy ekspedicii 1733–1743 gg.* [The Ethnographic Results of the Northern Expedition 1733–1743] (Moscow: S. I., 1961); cited in D. A. Shirina, *Peterburskaya Akademiya Nauk i Severo-Vostok 1725–1917 gg.* [The Academy of Sciences of Petersburg and the Northeast, 1725–1917] (Novosibirsk: Vo "Nauka," 1994), p. 28.

68. J. E. Fischer, *Recherches historiques sur les principales nations établies en Sibérie et dans les pays adjacents lors de la conquête des russes . . . , ouvrage traduit du russe* (Paris: De l'Imprimerie de Laran et Cie., 1774), p. 183.

69. Ibid., p. 247.

70. Ibid., pp. 1–9.

71. Ibid., pp. 161–69.

72. On this matter, as well as on other purely methodological issues, Fischer was opposed to Strahlenberg. Compare ibid., pp. 147, 183.

73. F. Müller, *Voyages et découvertes*, vol. 1, pp. 376–79.

74. On the secret topographic activity carried out by Feodor Ivanovitch Soymonov in the Oby region in 1738, see Marine 2/JJ/72, vol. 115—19, no. 26.

75. His history of Orenburg first appeared as a series in Müller's periodical, *Ezhemesyachniya Sochineniya* in 1759. *Ezhemesyachniya Sochineniya k Pol'ze i Uveseleniyu Sluzhashchiya* [Monthly Composition for Profit and Entertainment], 20 vols. (St. Petersburg: Academy of Sciences, 1755–64).

76. Ibid., St. Petersburg: 1756, pp. 33–53.

77. D. A. Shirina, *Peterburgskaya Akademiya Nauk*, pp. 50–51. Mayer was a participant in one of the numerous 1769 astronomical expeditions. Compare *Expositio utriusque observationis et Veneris et eclipsis solaris factae Petropoli in specula astronomica die 23 mai 1769. Illustrissimo ac excellentissimo domino comiti de Orlow, . . . a Christiano Mayer* (Petropoli: Typis Academiae Scientiarum, 1769).

78. J. Bertrand, *L'Académie des Sciences et les académiciens de 1666 et 1793* (Paris: J. Hetzel, 1869), p. 298. On the French and British preparations for the transit of Venus in 1761 and 1769, see H. Woolf, *The Transit of Venus: A Study of Eighteenth-Century Science* (Princeton: Princeton University Press, 1959), pp. 23–97, 150–99.

79. *Le Journal des savants pour l'année MDCCLXI* (A Paris . . . avec privilège du Roi, Avril 1761), pp. 250–52; *Le Journal des savants* (Avril 1761): 835–37.

80. V. F. Gnucheva, *Geograficheskii departament Akademii nauk XVIII veka* [The Department of Geography of the Academy of Sciences in the Eighteenth Century] (Moscow: Izd-vo Akademii Nauk SSSR, 1946), p. 71; P. Cazzola, *Russia-Bologna: tre secoli di rapporti, incontri e viaggi* (Bologna: CLUEB, 1990), p. 55; compare D. A. Shirina, *Peterburgskaya Akademiya Nauk*, p. 50.

81. Rumovskii was later entrusted with the supervision of the Geographical Department. His calculations of astronomical points served as a corrective to data that had been previously gathered by Delisle de la Croyère.

82. I. Islen'ev, *Collectio omnium observationum quae occasione transitum Veneris per solem a MDCCLXIX . . . Petropoli, Academiae scientiarum 1770. Extrait du journal d'observations faites à l'occasion du passage de Vénus* (S. Pétersbourg quarto).

83. P. S. Pallas, *Voyage de M. P. S. Pallas en différentes provinces de Russie et dans l'Asie septentrionale*, 5 vols. (Paris: Gautier de la Peyronie, 1788–93), vol. I, pp. iii–iv. The German original is published in 1776, while the French translation came out only in 1788–93 as a new expanded edition with an attached atlas, published by Gautier de la Peyronie in 8 volumes.

84. G. J. Georgi, *Russia*, vol. I, p. xxxv; compare P. S. Pallas, *Voyage de M. P. S. Pallas*, vol. I, pp. 485–86.

85. G. J. Georgi, *Russia*. In vol. IV, for instance, there is a series of texts of Kalmyk songs; compare vol. IV, pp. 61–68 (appendix).

86. Ibid., vol. III, pp. 203–29.

87. Ibid., vol. III, pp. 194–229. Compare Bougainville, *Voyage autour du monde, par la frégate du Roi La Boudeuse et la Flûte l'Etoile; en 1766, 1767, 1768, et 1769* (A Paris: Chez Saillant et Nyon), p. 48.

88. G. J. Georgi, *Russia*, vol. III, p. 290.

89. Ibid., vol. I, pp. 155–56.

90. Ibid., vol. I, pp. 94–104.

91. Ibid., pp. 113, 62, 173.

92. Ibid., vol. IV, pp. 69–120, 181–82.

93. This information has also been drawn from the exhibition *Siberia: The Men of the Frozen Rivers*. Exhibition at the Stables of Miramare Castle, Trieste, March 5–July 29, 2001. The State Museum Hermitage, St. Petersburg; City of Trieste, Department of Culture; Monuments of Fine Arts for Friuli-Venezia Giulia. Peter's Siberian collection was initially preserved in his *Kunstkamera* (1717) and later moved to the Hermitage in 1859. It comprises pieces of animalistic art, totems, golden statues, jewelry, and carpets.

94. Pallas used Rychkov's data, especially for the region of Orenburg. P. S. Pallas, *Voyage de M. P. S. Pallas*, vol. I, p. xiii.

95. Ibid., vol. I, pp. 93, 354–80.

96. An Ostyak oath; ibid., vol. IV, pp. 75–76. For a biography of Pallas, see F. Wendland, *Peter Simon Pallas, 1741–1811: Materialien einer Biographie* (Berlin: W. de Gruyter, 1992).

97. Ibid., vol. I, p. 445.

98. Ibid., vol. IV, pp. 52, 74–75.

99. I. I. Lepekhin, *Drevnye zapiski puteschestviya po raznym provinciyam Rossiyskogo gosudarstva v 1768–1772 godu* [Old Notes of a Journey Through the Various Provinces of the Russian Empire], 4 vols. quarto, St. Petersburg Academy of Sciences, 1795–1814.

100. P. S. Pallas, *Voyage de M. P. S. Pallas*, vol. II, p. 187.

101. Ibid., vol. IV, pp. 57–61, 71, 94. Pallas reported that both the Samoyeds and the Ostyaks treated women as impure beings and slaves.

102. The Englishman Joseph Billings had been the assistant astronomer on Cook's last voyage.

103. M. Sauer, *An Account of a Geographical and Astronomical Expedition to the Northern Parts of Russia, for Ascertaining the Degrees of Latitude and Longitude of the Mouth of the River Kovima; of the Whole Coast of the Tshutski, to East Cape . . . Performed by Command of Her Imperial Majesty Catherine the*

Second, Empress of All the Russias, by Commodore Joseph Billings, in the Years 1785, etc., to 1794. The Whole Narrated from the Original Papers by Martin Sauer, Secretary to the Expedition (London: T. Cadell, Jun and W. Davies, 1802), pp. vii–xiii.

104. Ibid., p. xiii.

105. Quoted in A. G. Cross, *"By the Banks of the Neva": Chapters from the Lives and Careers of the British in Eighteenth-Century Russia* (Cambridge: Cambridge University Press 1997), pp. 216–18.

106. M. Sauer, *An Account of a Geographical and Astronomical Expedition,* Appendix V.

107. D. A. Shirina, *Peterburskaya Akademiya Nauk,* p. 53.

108. G. J. Georgi, *Russia,* vol. III, p. 176.

109. M. Sauer, *An Account of a Geographical and Astronomical Expedition,* p. 69.

110. Ibid., Appendixes I and II include, respectively, a "Vocabulary of the Yukagir, Yakut, and Tungoose (or Lamut) languages" and a "Vocabulary of the languages of Kamtshatka, the Aleutan Islands, and of Kadiak."

111. Ibid., pp. 60–61, 66.

112. Ibid., p. 18.

113. Ibid., pp. 112–14, 160, 170, 222, 251.

CHAPTER ELEVEN

I am indebted to Professors Alex Dupuy and Thomas Doughton for their help in this research. I thank the Houghton Library and the David Rockefeller Center for Latin American Studies at Harvard.

1. These were the official data of the census conducted by colonial authorities. Moreau de Saint-Méry, *Description topographique, physique, civile, politique et historique de la partie française de Saint-Domingue,* vol. 1 (Paris: chez Dupont, 1797–1798). Several historians believe they were underestimated because the planters understated the number of their slaves to avoid taxes. See Gabriel Debien, *Les esclaves aux Antilles françaises, XVIIème–XVIIIème siècles* (Basse-Terre: Société d'Histoire de la Guadeloupe, 1974).

2. Laurent Dubois, *Avengers of the New World: The Story of the Haitian Revolution* (Cambridge, Mass.: Harvard University Press, 2004).

3. The Spanish and Portuguese colonies tended to discriminate between whites born in the colonies, the Criollos, and those from Spain, which created a rigid and resented hierarchy that did not exist in Saint-Domingue.

4. Gérard Leclerc, *Anthropologie et colonialisme* (Paris: Fayard, 1972); Jean Copans, *Anthropologie et impérialisme* (Paris: Maspéro, 1975).

5. Marcel Mauss, letter to the minister of colonies, 1907, in Marcel Fournier, *Marcel Mauss* (Paris: Fayard, 1994), p. 195. Claude Lévi-Strauss believed that there was anthropological discourse as soon as a colonial situation existed. He located this correlation not in the nineteenth century, as did most historians of anthropology, but in the conquests of the Americas. In the last section of his inaugural lecture to the College de France in 1960 (*Discours de réception au Collège de*

France, Paris, 1960, p. 27), Lévi-Strauss regretted that the chair of social anthropology that was then being created and offered to him had not been established first in the sixteenth century for Jean de Léry, a French Huguenot who traveled to Brazil in 1556.

6. Moreau, *Description*, vol. I, p. x.

7. Hilliard, *Considérations sur l'état présent de la colonie Française de Saint-Domingue* (Paris: Grangé, 1776–1777), vol. I, p. 132.

8. Justin Girod-Chantrans, *Voyage d'un Suisse dans differentes colonies d'Amérique pendant la dernière guerre* (Neuchatel: Imprimerie Typographique, 1785), p. 116.

9. Hilliard, *Considérations*, vol. II, p. 94.

10. Voltaire, *Traité de métaphysique* (Manchester: Manchester University Press, 1967), p. 74. In the same volume, Voltaire compared Negroes to animals.

11. Michèle Duchet, *Anthropologie et histoire au siècle des lumières* (Paris: Flammarion, 1977), p. 111.

12. The eighteenth-century structures of mulatto kinship, as analyzed by Stewart King, *Blue Coat or Powdered Wig: Free People of Colour in Pre-revolutionary Saint-Domingue* (Athens: University of Georgia Press, 2001) in his spectacular study of free people of color, prove the alliances between mulatto families and French migrants.

13. Charles Frostin, *Les révoltes blanches à Saint-Domingue* (Paris: L'École, 1975), p. 329.

14. Hilliard, *Considérations*, vol. II, p. 313.

15. Hilliard, *Considérations*, vol. II, pp. 19–49.

16. Georges Jean-Charles, "Moreau de Saint-Méry," in Claude Moïse, ed., *Dictionnaire historique de la Révolution Haitienne* (Montréal: CIDIHCA, 2003), p. 233. See also Dubois, *Avengers*, chap. 2.

17. Moreau, *Description*, vol. I, p. v.

18. Baron de Wimpffen, *Haiti au XVIIIème siècle: richesse et esclavage dans une colonie française* (Paris: Karthala, 1993); the original edition appeared in Paris in 1797 under the title *Voyage à Saint-Domingue pendant les années 1788, 1789 et 1790*; all references that follow refer to the 1993 edition.

19. Pluchon, "Introduction," in Wimpffen, *Haiti*.

20. Thomas Phipps Howard, *The Haitian Journal of Lieutenant Howard, York Hussars*, ed. R. N. Buckley (Knoxville: University of Tennessee Press, 1985).

21. Howard, *Journal*, p. 101.

22. Howard, *Journal*, pp. 101–102.

23. Wimpffen, *Haiti*, p. 102.

24. "On leur envoya des catins de la Salpétrières, des salopes ramassées dans la boue, des gaupes effrontées." Wimpffen, *Haiti*, p. 103. The Salpétrière is a hospital in Paris.

25. "dont les premiers fondateurs n'étaient qu'un ramas confus de brigands et de putains, conduits par deux bâtards." Wimpffen, *Haiti*, p. 103.

26. Hilliard, *Considérations*, vol. II, pp. 55–56.

27. Hilliard, *Considérations*, vol. I, p. 144.

28. Hilliard, *Considérations*, vol. II, p. 276.

29. Moreau, *Description*, p. 9.

30. In 1788, about one-fourth of the white population was composed of soldiers.

31. Moreau, *Description*, p. 9.

32. Howard, *Journal*, p. 101.

33. Johnston Letters, Johnston to his wife, August 29, 1796, Martinique, quoted by R. N. Buckley, in "Introduction," Howard, *Haitian Journal*, p. 181 (footnote 1).

34. Girod, *Voyage*, pp. 158–59 (Lettre VIII).

35. Hilliard, *Considérations*, vol. I, p. 145.

36. Hilliard, *Considérations*, vol. I, p. 136.

37. Girod, *Voyage*, p. 135. Let's note here that cruelty rarely appeared in earlier accounts. Paradoxically, mistreatments probably declined during the course of the eighteenth century, as shown by Debien in *Les esclaves*. What probably increased was the visibility and awareness of physical violence that became increasingly unacceptable in the eyes of the "intellectuals," particularly, but not only, those opposed to slavery.

38. The controversial descriptions of the lynching of the aristocrat Ferrand de Beaudière by a mob of petty whites, which constitute evidences of the portrayal of racial hatred, are analyzed in the final part of this essay.

39. Pamphile de Lacroix, *La révolution de Haiti*, ed. Pierre Pluchon (Paris: Karthala, 1995), p. 55.

40. The Black Code of 1685 distinguished only owners and nonowners rather than using racial categories.

41. Indeed, these eighteenth-century categories survived the anthropological extinction (and to a large extent, this was also a physical extinction) of the whites in the colony of Saint-Domingue, as they were used in the twentieth century by André Gide and Frantz Fanon, among others.

42. Pierre Pluchon, *Nègres et Juifs au 18ème siècle* (Paris: Taillandier, 1984).

43. Moreau, *Description*, vol. I, p. 13.

44. Moreau, *Description*, vol. I, p. 22.

45. Moreau, *Description*, vol. I, p. 31.

46. Moreau, *Description*, vol. I, p. 22.

47. Moreau, *Description*, vol. I, p. 22.

48. Bryan Edwards, *An Historical Survey of the French Colony in the Island of St. Domingo Comprehending a Short Account of Its Ancient Government, Political State, Population, Production and Exports* (London: John Stockdale, 1797), pp. 11–12.

49. Edwards, *Historical Survey*, pp. 54–55.

50. Edwards, *Historical Survey*, p. 57.

51. Edwards, *Historical Survey*, p. 78. Colonel Venault de Charmilly, *Lettre à M. Bryan Edwards en refutation à son ouvrage* (London: T. Baylin, Greville-Street, Holborn, 1797), p. 61, denied that the seamen had been ridiculed.

52. Howard, *Journal*, p. 78 (italics and parentheses are from the Roger Buckley edition).

53. Michèle Oriol, *Images de la révolution à Saint-Domingue* (Port-au-Prince: Deschamps, 1992), p. 126.

54. Edwards, *Survey*, p. 91.

55. Moreau, *Description*, vol. I, p. 30

56. Moreau, *Description*, vol. I, pp. 23–67.

57. Let's note here that none of the ethnographers traveled to Africa, with the exception of Labat, who visited the coast of West Africa late in his life, but only after having written his work on Saint-Domingue.

58. Girod, *Voyage*, Lettre X, p. 165.

59. Hilliard, *Considérations,* vol. II, p. 59.

60. Pierre François Xavier Charlevoix, *Histoire de l'Isle Espagnole ou de Saint-Domingue, ecrite sur des mémoires manuscrits du p. Jean-Baptiste Le Pers* (Paris: F. Barois, 1730–1731), p. 498.

61. *Maronnage*, a term of Spanish origin, referred to the action of fleeing the plantation to live in the mountainous areas.

62. This representation of the slaves' religion was widespread among whites. Mutilations of rebelled slaves during public executions by colonial authorities (mentioned above by Bryan Edwards) aimed at preventing blacks from rebelling, as it was believed that they would not dare present themselves to their ancestors with missing body parts.

63. Hilliard, *Considérations*, vol. I, pp. 59–62.

64. Moreau, *Description*, vol. I, p. 31.

65. Moreau, *Description*, vol. I, p. 33.

66. Moreau, *Description*, vol. I, pp. 27, 30–31, 33, 37.

67. Moreau, *Description*, vol. I, p. 63.

68. Roberto da Matta, "Mito e anti-mito entre os Timbira," in *Mito e linguagem social* (Rio de Janeiro: Tempo Brasileiro, 1970).

69. Michel Etienne Descourtilz, *Voyages d'un naturaliste et ses observations* (Paris: Dupart, 1809), vol. I, p. Liij.

70. Charlevoix, *Histoire*, p. 498.

71. Hilliard, *Considérations*, vol. II, p. 60; Moreau, *Description*, vol. I, p. 33; Charlevoix, *Histoire*, p. 498.

72. Moreau, *Description*, vol. II, p. 497–502.

73. Moreau, *Description*, vol. I, p. 502.

74. See, among others, Jean-François Bayard, *L'illusion identitaire* (Paris: Fayard, 1996); and Carola Lentz and Paul Nugent, *Ethnicity in Ghana: The Limits of Invention* (New York: Saint-Martin's Press, 2000).

75. See, among others, Eduardo Viveiro de Castro, "Etnologia Brasileira," in *O que ler na ciência social brasileira (1970–1995)* (Água Branca, SP: Edutora Sumaré, 1999) for a discussion on the topic.

76. Ribeiro, work in process, in which he asserts that "there was no ethnic group whatsoever in Africa before European colonization" (personal communication, São Paulo, 2004).

77. Moreau, *Description*, vol. I, p. 35. Legal acts of that time almost systematically included the ethnic origin of the slave, often without any other characteristics, except gender. Although the demographic numbers are probably accurate, the African ethnic identities may well have been assigned without direct dialogue or contact with those listed. In the eighteenth-century colonial world, most of the

data on slaves came from interviews with administrators and overseers, not from the slaves themselves.

78. Hilliard, *Considérations*, vol. I, p. 62.

79. Moreau, *Description*, vol. I, p. 25.

80. Girod, *Voyage*, p. 173 (Letter XI). (Slaves were sleep deprived. Most of the field slaves slept less than five hours a night, a factor in the mortality rate. See Gabriel Debien, *Les esclaves*.)

81. I found cannibalism mentioned only once, in Moreau, *Description*, vol. I, p. 33.

82. Charlevoix, *Histoire*, pp. 499–501.

83. Hilliard, *Considérations*, vol. I, pp. 132–33.

84. Hilliard, *Considérations*, vol. I, pp. 140–41.

85. Moreau, *Description*, vol. I, p. 44.

86. Moreau, *Description*, vol. I, p. 62.

87. Moreau, *Description*, vol. I, p. 25.

88. Moreau, *Description*, vol. I, p. 56.

89. Girod, *Voyage*, p. 165.

90. Moreau, *Description*, vol. I, pp. 46–51.

91. Moreau, *Description*, vol. I, p. 46.

92. Moreau, *Description*, vol. I, pp. 47–48.

93. Moreau, *Description*, vol. I, pp. 49–50.

94. Descourtilz, *Voyages*, vol. I, p. Liij.

95. Descourtilz, *Voyages*, vol. III, pp. 180–87.

96. Colonel Malenfant, *Des colonies, et particulièrement de celle de Saint-Domingue* (Paris: Audibert, 1814), chap. VIII.

97. André-Marcel d'Ans, *Le Créole français d'Haiti* (The Hague: Mouton, 1968).

98. Girod, *Voyage*, Lettre XIII.

99. Moreau, *Description*, vol. I, p. 65.

100. Moreau, *Description*, vol. I, p. 35.

101. Hilliard, *Considération*, vol. II, pp. 59–62.

102. Margaret T. Hodgen, *Early Anthropology in the Sixteenth and Seventeenth Centuries* (Philadelphia: University of Pennsylvania Press, 1964).

103. Jack D. Forbes, *Africans and Native Americans: The Language of Race and the Evolution of Red-Black Peoples* (Urbana and Chicago: University of Illinois Press, 1993), pp. 131–89.

104. Jean-Baptiste Labat, *Nouveau voyage aux isles de l'Amérique* (Paris: Giffart, 1722), vol. II, chap. VI; Moreau, *Description*, vol. I, chap. 3.

105. Stewart King (2001) enumerates many such situations, even if his text did not focus on "love" as a category.

106. Intimate interracial relations of that time cannot be reduced only to abuse, forced relations, and matters of power. To argue that power is "the only game in town" fails to explain the diversity of human experience. See M. Brown ("On Resisting Resistance," *The American Anthropologist*, 1996, vol. 98, no. 4) and M. Sahlins ("Good-Bye *Tristes Tropes*: Ethnography in the Context of Modern World History," *Journal of Modern History*, 1993, vol. 65, n. 1). Love

happens, and its Tocquevillian dimension is particularly interesting in a hierarchical context.

107. Lieutenant Howard, *Journal*, p. 104.

108. Hilliard, *Considérations*, vol. II, pp. 78–79.

109. Hilliard, *Considérations*, vol. II, p. 81.

110. Hilliard, *Considérations*, vol. I, p. 41.

111. Hilliard, *Considérations*, vol. II, p. 79.

112. Hilliard, *Considérations*, vol. II, pp. 78–79.

113. Bryan Edwards, *Historical Survey*, p. 21.

114. Venault, *Lettre*, p. 52.

115. Jean-Philippe Garran-Coulon, *Rapport sur les troubles de Saint-Domingue* (Paris: Imprimerie Nationale, 1798–1799), vol. I, p. 110.

116. Labat, *Nouveau voyage*, vol. II, p. 127.

117. Labat, *Nouveau voyage*, vol. II, p. 129.

118. Labat, *Nouveau voyage*, vol. II, p. 129.

119. Hilliard, *Considérations*, vol. II, pp. 90–91.

120. Girod, "Lettre XII," *Voyage*, p. 180.

121. Moreau, *Description*, vol. II, p. 187.

122. Howard, *Journal*, p. 101.

123. Girod, *Voyage*, pp. 181–82.

124. Labat, *Nouveau*, vol. II, p. 124.

125. Labat, *Nouveau*, vol. II, p. 127.

126. Moreau, *Description*, vol. I, p. 78.

127. Moreau, *Description*, vol. I, p. 76.

128. Moreau, *Description*, vol. I, p. 79. Moreau specified that "[i]f the evidence can not be found in the color, it can be found in the 'assemblage' of the features, in the flat nose, in the thick lips that too often denounce the origin. . . . There are surely some *quarteron*, twice as white as a Spaniard or an Italian." Moreau, *Description*, vol. I, pp. 86–87.

129. Hilliard, *Considérations*, vol. II, p. 74.

130. Hilliard, *Considérations*, vol. II, p. 78.

131. Moreau, *Description*, vol. I, pp. 90–91.

132. Moreau, *Description*, vol. I, p. 90.

133. Girod, *Voyage*, pp. 182–83. Stewart King's (2001) research using notary acts corroborates Girod's study.

134. Moreau, *Description*, vol. I, p. 92. The Greek island of Paphos was a center for the cult of Aphrodite, the goddess of love.

135. Moreau, *Description*, vol. I, p. 95.

136. Moreau, *Description*, vol. I, pp. 364–65.

137. Hilliard, *Considérations*, vol. II, p. 77.

138. Wimpffen, *Haiti*, p. 120.

139. "L'amour égale tout." Wimpffen, *Haiti*, p. 17; Descourtilz, *Voyages*, vol. I, p. 52.

140. Girod, *Voyage*, p. 185.

141. Girod, *Voyage*, p. 186. This assertion is corroborated by Debien (1974), for whom slavery gradually became less cruel in the course of the eighteenth century.

142. Guillaume-Thomas Raynal, *Histoire philosophique et politique des établissements et du commerce des Européens dans les deux Indes* (Geneva: Jean-Léonard Pellet, 1782), vol. VII. Michèle Duchet, in *Anthropologie et histoire au siècle des lumières* (Paris: François Maspero, 1971), believes that Diderot actually wrote the chapters on slavery.

CHAPTER TWELVE

Earlier drafts of this chapter benefited from discussions at Birkbeck College (University of London), the Max Planck Institute for the History of Science ("The Sleep of Reason" and "Knowledge and Belief"), and the 2003 International Society for Eighteenth-Century Studies panel on "Anthropology and the Enlightenment." I'm especially grateful to Marie-Noelle Bourguet, Luca Codignola, Lorraine Daston, Mary Fuller, Alan Gabbey (whose challenges I have not met yet), Fernando Vidal, Susan Wiseman, and Larry Wolff, as well as my research assistant, Emily Bernhard Jackson, swift in every sense. The research and writing was funded and otherwise enabled by the Guggenheim Memorial Foundation and the Max Planck Institute for the History of Science.

1. On the related topic of the "cessation of the oracles," there was considerable discussion in the century covered by this chapter: see, e.g., Lord Herbert of Cherbury, *De religione gentilium* (London, 1645), and the international controversy begun when Bernard Bovier de Fontenelle translated and expanded the Dutch scholar Antonius van Dale's *De oraculus ethnicorum* (Amsterdam, 1683) as *L'histoire des oracles* (Paris, 1686): Aphra Behn in turn translated and further expanded Fontenelle's French into the English *History of Oracles, and the Cheats of the Pagan Priests* (London, 1688); the 1707 and 1709 pamphlets of refutation by the French Catholic Jean Francois Baltus were translated and expanded in 1709 and 1710 by "a priest of the Church of England" and George Hickes (also a Church of England minister).

2. "They have . . . great faith in their dreams, imagining that what they have seen in their sleep must happen, and that they must execute whatever they have thus imagined. This is a great misfortune, for if a Savage dreams that he will die if he does not kill me, he will take my life the first time he meets me alone" ["Ils ont outre vne grande croyãce à leurs songes, s'imaginans que ce qui'ils ont veu en dormant doit arriuer, et qu'ils doiuent executer ce qu'ils ont resué: ce qui est vn grand malheur, car si vn Sauuage songe qu'il mourra s'il ne me tue, il me mettra à mort à la premiere rencontre à l'escart"] (Le Jeune, *Jesuit Relations* 6 (1634): 181–83). For the example of the cat, see p. 249 of this essay. Le Jeune doesn't always believe these dreams: "on the 27th, a woman, who had been baptized the day before, died in our Village. The same day her father came to us to relate a very amusing dream ("un songe tout á fait agreeable") that she had, according to his story, a little while before her death. The sole purpose of this imaginary dream ("songe supposé") was to get a few strings of beads" (Le Jeune, *Jesuit Relations* 13 [1637]: 149). All quotations, in French and English, are drawn from the bilingual edition of Ruben Gold Thwaites, *The Jesuit Relations and Allied Documents* (Cleveland: Burrows Brothers, 1896), 73 vols., and cited by author, date, vol. and p. number; those

whose libraries do not have that edition may be able to consult in French Lucien Campeau's (better and more inclusive) *Monumentae Novae Franciae*, 9 vols. (Rome: Monumenta historica Societatis Iesu, 1967–2003. The manuscript originals of the published *Relations* do not survive, though some letters and "journaux" are printed in Felix Martin's *Relations inédits de la Nouvelle-France, 1672–79*, 2 vols. (1860; rpt. Montréal: Éditions Élysées, 1972), and in vol. 9 of Campeau: most available manuscript material is in Rome at the Archivum Romanum Societatis Iesu. See Luca Codignola, Fernand Hervey and Pierre Hurtebise, eds., *L'Amérique du Nord francaise dans les archives religieuses de Rome, 1600–1922* (Québec: Éditions de l'IQS and Les Presses de l'Université Laval, 1999); also Luca Codignola, "The Battle Is Over: Campeau's *Monumenta* vs. Thwaites' *Jesuit Relations, 1602–1650*," *European Review of Native American Studies* 10, no. 2 (1996): 3–10. Prof. Codignola, pointing out the hurry with which the *Relations* proper were printed, gives the opinion that there was little time for censorship of their original manuscripts (personal communication, Feb. 20, 2004). I am grateful for his generous help during my perplexities on this point.

3. Dablon, *Jesuit Relations* 58: 177.

4. Denys Delâge, *Bitter Feast: Amerindians and Europeans in Northeastern North America, 1600–64 (Le Pays renversé)* (Vancouver: UBC Press, 1993), p. 77.

5. These exercises constitute a lengthy program of daily meditation, prayer, self-examination, and the "diligent search for what one's heart desires" (288/20), divided into four "weeks," performed under the supervision of a guide and preferably in a state of withdrawal from the world. Ignatius describes the stage called "composition" thus: "contemplation about visible things . . . consists in seeing through the gaze of the imagination the material place where the object I want to contemplate is situated. . . . Where the object is invisible, . . . the composition will be to see with the gaze of the imagination and to consider that my soul is imprisoned in this body" (295/45). The guide must not say too much in introducing objects for meditation: "for it is not so much knowledge that fills and satisfies the soul but rather the intimate feeling and relishing of things" (283/Annotation 2). Dating the Exercises is tricky, as Ignatius believed in the importance of their being transmitted orally. André des Freux's Latin translation of Ignatius's original Spanish manuscript was commissioned for papal approval in 1548. I quote both page and paragraph numbers from Joseph A. Munietz and Philip Endean, trans., *Saint Ignatius of Loyola: Personal Writings* (London: Penguin Books, 1996); the editors have provided the standard paragraph numbers.

6. This was the purpose of the Inquisition's 1431 trial of Joan of Arc for heresy. "According to a psycho-physiology that was still current in the 18th century, when we sleep, the imagination is left to function by itself. In the standard seventeenth- and eighteenth-century view, the imagination is the faculty that the soul has to form images by altering the fibers or the substance of the brain. The anatomo-physiological mechanism is part of the definition; and that makes the imagination not a disembodied psychological process, but a physical process which acts on the so-called 'animals spirits' in such a way as to produce not only dreams, but also phenomena such as sleepwalking. So in fact, even for Nicolas Malebranche, who was not a Jesuit but was a Cartesian, it is the body, not the mind that dreams"

(Fernando Vidal, commentary on a draft of this article, delivered October 2003 at the Max Planck Institut für Wissenschaftsgeschichte colloquium "Knowledge and Belief"). I was lucky to be in residence at the MPIWG while Fernando Vidal and Lorraine Daston were writing papers for the conference on the imagination hosted by Vidal and Claudia Swann at Northwestern University, Dec. 2003, "Interior Temptations" (sequel to the 2002 MPIWG conference, "The Sleep of Reason," for which I drafted this chapter). Daston's "Material Powers of the Imagination" and Vidal's "Imagination and Canonization" have educated me in the corporeality of fantasy, dreaming, and visualizing; I hope they will soon be published.

7. *Jesuit Relations* 17 (1639): 169–201.

8. *Jesuit Relations* 30 (1645–46): 27; this matter can be illuminated comparatively. In a study of the sociology of religious experience (mostly dreams and visions, both pagan and Christian) in late antiquity, Frank Trombley suggests that in times of religious transition—such as that of the Christianization of the Mediterranean littoral—both agitated discourse about the supernatural and demonization of spiritual presences in the losing cosmology become prominent: the victors are exorcists, needed more than ever in the density of ambivalence and anxiety invoked by the replacement of familiar gods. Victors "discern" devils, projections of the previous divinities as not only ugly but malevolent in their dethronement. He offers a wonderful and more ancient example of conversion ambivalence from the Psalms, in which the Lord appears as an angry Zeus/weather god: "He bent heaven downward and descended and there was darkness under his feet. He rode on the back of an angel and he flew, he dropped on the wings of the wind. He shall make darkness his hiding place and clouds of dark water his tent" (Psalm 18 [17]: 9–11); Frank R. Trombley, "Religious Experience in Late Antiquity: Theological Ambivalence and Christianization," *Byzantine and Modern Greek Studies* 24 (2000): 12.

9. Fernando Vidal points out in his commentary that the frontispiece of Lafitau's huge work represents a vision (a subcategory of dream for the early modern intellectual) shown to the writer by Time, "which in the long run makes all things known, [and] shows that all cultural artifacts are connected 'to the first origin of humanity, to the essence of our religion, and to the entire system of revelation,' and he makes that truth palpable and evident by means of 'a sort of mysterious vision.'" I quote from the annotated edition (definitive for French as well as English scholarship) of William Fenton and Elizabeth Moore (1977); the edition conveniently provides, as do I here, volume and page numbers for the 1724, 2-vol. French edition (there is also a 4-vol. edition of 1724). An annotated French edition is under way under the direction of Réal Ouelle and Laurier Turgeon at the Presses de l'Université de Montréal.

10. Certeau, "Writing vs. Time"; Campbell, "Faith, Flesh, and Science: Anthropology Made in America, 1724" and chap. 9, "E pluribus unum," of *Wonder and Science*.

11. See Antonio T. de Nicolás, "Mysticism as Biology and Educational Foundation in Ignatius de Loyola," in Christopher Chapple, ed., *The Jesuit Tradition in Education and Missions: A 450-year Perspective* (Scranton: University of Scranton Press; and London: Associated University Presses, 1993), 34–51.

12. Victoria Nelson offers a succinct account of "grottos" in *The Secret Life of Puppets* (Cambridge: Harvard University Press, 2001); on incubation and prophetic

or therapeutic dreams, see Trombley, "Religious Experience in Late Antiquity," 2–60, esp. 38–40.

13. *St. Ignatius of Loyola: Personal Writings*, 283.

14. René Descartes, *Oeuvres de Descartes*, ed. Charles Adam and Paul Tannery, 11 vols. (Paris: Léopold Cerf, 1908), 6: 374; the translation is on p. 53 of Matthew Jones's "Descartes's *Geometry* as Spiritual Exercise," *Critical Inquiry* 28 (Autumn 2000): 40–71; on the debate over Ignatian influence, see citations in his n. 46. I have found at least one identical sentence myself, and am not yet convinced on this point.

15. See, e.g., Sophie Jama, *Anthropologie du rêve* (Paris: Presses universitaire de France, 1997), or anthropologist Giordana Charuty of the École Pratique des Hautes Études on "les sociétés à rêves" at, e.g., www.sommeil.univ-lyon1.fr/articles/savenir/societe/societe.html.

16. For example, Proclus, Cardanus, and Descartes himself in his lost *Olympica*.

17. These cluster especially in the middle third of the century. War broke out between the French and the Iroquois in the late 1650s and New France was taken over as a Royal Province in 1663, unsettling the symbiotic organization of traders for the Compagnie des Cents Associés and mostly Jesuit missionaries (who were turned on by the Iroquois in the years following the epidemics of 1657–58, for which they were rightly suspected as the major disease vector). For a good account of the imbrication of trading and missionary interests until that time, see Denys Delâge, *Bitter Feast: Amerindians and Europeans in Northeastern North America, 1600–64 (Le Pays renversé)* (Vancouver: UBC Press, 1993).

18. Usage is confusing in identifying indigenous groups, as sometimes Iroquois means the "language family" that includes, e.g., both the Huron and Iroquois confederacies, and within the Iroquois confederacy we also find the Iroquois tribe. Most of the tribes with whom the Jesuits spent time were of the Huron and Iroquois confederacies, competing within the larger Iroquoian "family," except for the Algonquian Abenaki and Montagnais tribes of Maine and the Gulf of St. Lawrence.

19. "Il y a des superstitio[n]s en l'ancienne France aussi bien qu'en la nouuelle." Le Jeune, *Jesuit Relations* 16 (1639): 194.

20. Father Paul Rageneau is more respectful: "Beyond the desires which we generally have that are free, or at least voluntary in us, [and] which arise from a previous knowledge of some goodness that we imagine to exist in the desired thing, the Hurons believe that our souls have other desires, which are, as it were, inborn and hidden. These, they say, come from the depths of the soul, not through any knowledge but by means of a certain blind transport of the soul towards certain objects; these transports might be called in philosophical terms 'innate desires' [*Desideria innata*] to distinguish them from 'elicted desires' [*Desideria Elicita*]. . . . Now they believe that our soul makes these desires known by means of dreams, which are its language," 1647–48 (33: 189). He goes on to describe the Huron understanding of psychosomatic events: "if it be not granted what [the soul] desires, it becomes angry, and . . . revolts against the body, causing various diseases, and even death" (33: 189).

21. Although Descartes' little tract has not survived intact, much of it is quoted and/or paraphrased in the *Vie de Monsieur Des-Cartes* of his near-contemporary, Adriene Baillet: it can be found, among other places, in vol. 10 of Adam and Tannery, *Oeuvres de Descartes*.

22. Descartes, *Oeuvres* 10: 182, 186; "Il lui vint aussitôt un nouveau songe, dans lequel il crût entendre un bruit aigu et éclatant, qu'il prit pour un coup de tonnére. . . . [A]yant ouvert les yeux, il apperçût beaucoup d'étincelles de feu répandues par la chambre. . . . [l]a foudre dont il entendit l'éclat, etoit le signal de l'Esprit de Vérité qui descendoit sur luy pour le posséder."

23. Jones, "Descartes' Geometry," 57–59.

24. Bachelard, *Air and Dreams: An Essay on the Imagination of Movement* [*L'Air et les songes*, 1943] (Dallas: The Dallas Institute Publications, 1988); Artemidorus, *The Judgement, or Exposition of Dreams* [Oenicriticon], trans. Robert Wood (London, 1606); I quote from p. 1 of the 4th ed. (London, 1644).

25. See, e.g., Arnold Williams, *The Common Expositor: An Account of the Commentaries on Genesis, 1527–1633* (Chapel Hill: University of North Carolina Press, 1948).

26. *Jesuit Relations* 54 (1669–70): 97 and 42 (1656): 135; in 1642, during the period of the Huron missions, and more specifically during a virulent influenza epidemic, we find "Dreams are indeed the God of these poor infidels" (23: 171).

27. The term "religion" is Lafitau's, and means what we mean by it generally today: a system of ritual practices and beliefs based on faith in and submission to a powerful supernatural being or beings.

28. See Anthony F. C. Wallace's interesting and informative article, "Dreams and Wishes of the Soul: A Type of Psychoanalytic Theory Among the Seventeenth-Century Iroquois," *American Anthropologist* 60 (1959): 234–48.

29. Claude Deblon, *Jesuit Relations* 58 (1670): 173.

30. *Jesuit Relations* 23 (1643): 113.

31. Such announcements can be found elsewhere: "The Father [Superior] instructed her as to the nature of dreams, and explained to her the Catechism" (Le Jeune, *Jesuit Relations* 15 [1638]: 73); "I prepared some for Baptism, and disabused them of their errors regarding dreams [j en (*sic*) desabusois de leurs réveries]" (Fremin, *Jesuit Relations* 54 [1669–70]: 183).

32. *Jesuit Relations* 1: 230 [I, 360].

33. See, e.g., Leibniz: "Each living body has a dominant entelechy [substantial form] which is the soul in the case of an animal, but the members of this living body are full of other living beings, plants, and animals, each of which also has its dominant entelechy or soul" (Gottfried Wilhelm Leibniz, "The *Monadology*," par. 70, in Leibniz, *Philosophical Papers and Letters*, ed. and trans. Leroy E. Loemker, 2nd ed. (Dordrecht and Boston: D. Reidel, 1969). Thanks to Erica Fudge.

34. *Jesuit Relations* 1: 231 [I, 362].

35. *Jesuit Relations* 1: 28 [I, 5]. The still-continuing spiritual plunder of the colonized peoples of the New World is another and related story I hope to discuss elsewhere in the larger project of which this chapter will form a part. The indirect discourse used by Lafitau on this subject remains a trope for Freud, when, e.g., he

discusses a father's atavistic dream, sleeping in the next room to where a candle was burning his just-deceased child's arm, that his child came to him to say "I'm burning": "If the father had woken up first and then made the inference that led him to go into the next room, he would, as it were, have shortened his child's life by that moment of time" (*Interpretation of Dreams*, ed. James Strachey, in *The Standard Edition of the Complete Psychological Works of Sigmund Freud*, vol. 5 (London: Hogarth Press and Institute of Psycho-Analysis, 1958), 509–10.

36. See citations in n. 6; for "furieux," see, e.g., II, 271 in French 1724 ed.

37. George R. Healy quotes Voltaire's amusement from chap. 8 of the *Essai sur les moeurs*: "Il fait venir les Américains des anciens Grecs et voici ses raisons: les Grecs avaient des fables, quelques Américains en ont aussi. Les premiers Grecs allaient à la chasse, les Américains y vont. Les premiers Grecs avaient des oracles, les Américains ont des sorciers. On dansait dans les fêtes de la Grece, on danse en Amérique. Il faut avouer que ces raisons sont convainçantes." Actually, Lafitau's arguments are much more sophisticated, and Voltaire's sarcasm cheap. See Healy, "The French Jesuits and the Noble Savage," *William and Mary Quarterly*, 3rd ser., 15, no. 2 (April 1958): 143–67.

38. For example, the 2-vol. first edition at Harvard's Houghton Library, which belonged to Massachusetts lieutenant governor William Dummer, for whom the northern frontier of Massachusetts during the 1720s was a zone of armed conflict with Penobscot, Míkmaq, Wabenaki, and other nations during the French and Indian Wars.

39. See chap. 9 of Campbell, *Wonder and Science*, 295–310. In an article on (Protestant) conversion and nativist revival in Moravian Pennsylvania, Jane T. Merritt says: "Nanticoke and Shawnee warriors, visiting Bethlehem in March 1753, examined pictures of the crucified Christ . . . and responded with awe: 'do but look, how many wounds he has, how much blood flows forth!' . . . The warriors' awe at the number of wounds, the powerful image of the man sweating blood, and their own ideals of stoicism under torture all suggest that they saw Christ as the ultimate warrior captive." "Dreaming of the Savior's Blood: Moravians and the Indian Great Awakening in Pennsylvania," *William and Mary Quarterly*, 3rd ser., 54, no. 4 (October 1997): 723–46, 742.

40. Gregor Sebba, *Dream of Descartes*, ed. Richard A. Watson (Carbondale: Southern Illinois University Press, 1987), 34.

41. Mark Lescarbot, *Nova Francia: A Description of Acadia, 1606*, trans. P. Erondelle, 1609, ed. H. P. Biggar (London: George Routledge, 1928), 156.

42. Sebba, *The Dream of Descartes*, 34–35.

43. *Macbeth*, III, ii, 18. On understandings of the unconscious during the period covered here, and generally before Freud, see L. L. Whyte, *The Unconscious Before Freud* (New York: Basic Books, 1960) esp. chaps. 4 and 5 and, more specifically, Genevieve Rodis-Lewis, *Le problème de l'inconscient de la cartesianisme* (Paris: Presses universitaires de France, 1950).

44. See, e.g., Le Jeune, *Jesuit Relations* 6 (1638): 172, 178.

45. According to the affable and urbane Baron Lahontan: "The Récollets brand the Savages for Stupid, gross and rustick Persons, uncapable of Thought or Reflection: But the Jesuits gave them other sort of Language, for they intitle them

to good Sense, to a tenacious Memory, and to a quick Apprehension season'd with a solid Judgement. The former allege that 'tis to no purpose to preach the Gospel to a sort of People that have less Knowledge than the Brutes." *New Voyages to North-America*, 1703; rpt., ed. Reuben Gold Thwaites, 2 vols. (Chicago, 1905; rpt.: New York: Benjamin Franklin, 1970), 2: 413.

46. Le Jeune, *Jesuit Relations* 6 (1634): 165.

47. See Fernando Vidal, "Brains, Bodies, Selves, and Science: Anthropologies of Identity and the Resurrection of the Body," *Critical Inquiry* 28, no. 4 (July 2002): 930–74; also Carolyn Walker Bynum, *Fragmentation and Redemption: Essays on Gender and the Human Body in Medieval Religion* (New York: Zone Books, 1992), esp. "Material Continuity, Personal Survival, and the Resurrection of the Body."

48. See R. C. Dailey, "The Role of Alcohol Among North American Indian Tribes as Reported in the *Jesuit Relations*," *Anthropologica* N.S., 10, no. 1 (1968): 45–57. "Liquor greatly facilitated the attainment of dreams which was for the Indian his most valued experience. Through alcohol he was able to achieve a degree of ecstasy never possible in prehistoric times" (Dailey, 57).

49. *Jesuit Relations* 42 (1655–1656): 154. See Normand Doiron, "Songes sauvages: De l'interprétation jésuite des songes amérindiens au XVIIe siècle," *L'Esprit Créateur* 30, no. 3 (Fall 1990), 59–66, esp. 63–64. He is quoting Dablon's journal from Jean de Quen's "Relation . . . de 1655–1656," chap. 9 (*Jesuit Relations* 42: 145–69).

50. Lafitau, I, 243. For accounts of the Enlightenment and post-Enlightenment future of the idea of ventriloquism, closely tied with the concept of the oracle—and "the cheats of the pagan priests," see Leigh Eric Schmidt's article (which also attends to later seventeenth-century discourse), "From Demon Possession to Magic Show: Ventriloquism, Religion and the Enlightenment," *Church History* 67, no. 2 (June 1998): 274–34; and Clarcke Garrett's *Spirit Possession and Popular Religion: From the Camisards to the Shakers* (Baltimore: Johns Hopkins University Press, 1987). Schmidt quotes a brief passage of ambivalence more like Lafitau's from the entry on "ventriloquist" in Thomas Blount's 1656 *Glossographia*: "one that has an evil spirit in his belly, or one that by use and practice can speak as it were out of his belly."

51. See "Writing vs. Time: History and Anthropology in the Works of Lafitau," *Yale French Studies* 59 (1980): 37–64.

52. "In this state of withdrawal, with one's mind not divided amongst many things but entirely taken up with one thing alone . . . one is able to use one's natural powers all the more freely in the diligent search for what one's heart desires." Ignatius, "Annotations" to the *Spiritual Exercises*, 288.

53. The account of his travels by Récollet friar Gabriel Sagard-Théodat is available in both English and French in *The Long Journey to the Country of the Hurons*, ed. George W. Wrong, trans. H. H. Langton (Toronto: Champlain Society, 1939), vol. 25. The passage quoted here is found on pp. 118–19.

54. For instance, Le Jeune, *Jesuit Relations* 13 (1637): 149.

55. Le Jeune, *Jesuit Relations* 6 (1634): 183; 5 (1633): 161.

56. See Wallace, "Dreams and Wishes of the Soul," 240.

57. Baillet: "il décida, en dormant, que c'étoit un songe, [et] il en fit encore l'interprétation avant que le sommeil le quittat. Il jugea que le *Dictionnaire* ne

voulait dire autre chose que toutes les Sciences ramassées ensemble" etc. (Adam and Tannery, *Oeuvres de Descartes* 10: 284).

58. This was the tendency of contemporary secular dream manuals, such as the reeditions of Artemidorus cited above: dreams are concerned with the future, not the past, and usually in rather practical ways.

59. On the relation of metaphor to the debates on transubstantiation, see Judith H. Anderson's admirable and exhaustive essay, "Language and History in the Reformation: Cranmer, Gardiner, and the Words of Institution," *Renaissance Quarterly* 54 (2001): 20–51.

60. Le Jeune, *Jesuit Relations* 6 (1634): 174–75. The eight "Saints Martyrs" were Fathers Antony Daniel, Charles Garnier (whose reports, along with those of Brébeuf, were especially important to Lafitau), Noel Chabanel, Isaac Jogues (with his lay companions Jean La Lande and René Goupil), and most famously Jérôme Lalemont and Jean de Brébeuf: all died between 1642 and 1649, mostly during the Iroquois genocide of the Huron in the late 1640s. Only some of the famous eight died by fire. On the Eurocanadian founding myth of the martyrs, see Guy Laflèche's spirited deconstruction in "La spiritualité des Jésuites de la Nouvelle-France: L'interpretation des *Visions* de Jean de Brébeuf," *Voix et Images* 33 (Spring 1986): 464–74, a preview of the first volume of his 5-vol. *Les saintes martyrs canadiens* (Laval: Éditions du Singulier, 1988–95).

61. Michel Foucault, *Madness and Civilization: A History of Insanity in the Age of Reason*, trans. Richard Howard (New York: Random House, 1965), 79. Foucault's long sentence is suggestive in our context. It continues: at that very moment, "the madman, in his abolished reason, in the fury of his animality, received a singular power of demonstration: it was as if scandal, driven out of that superhuman region where it related to God and where the Incarnation was manifested, reappeared, in the plenitude of its force and pregnant with a new lesson, in that region where man has a relation to nature and to his animality" (79–80)—in New France? Writing around the same time as Foucault, sociologist Peter Berger says: "One of the essential qualities of the sacred, as encountered in 'religious experience,' is otherness, its manifestation as something *totaliter aliter* as compared to ordinary, profane human life," *The Sacred Canopy: The Social Reality of Religion* (1967; rpt. Hammondsworth: Penguin, 1973), 94. Freud describes the impression produced by a dream upon the just-waking mind as one "of something alien, arising from another world" (*Interpretation of Dreams*, 4).

62. This is the general topic of my book in progress, from which an article ("Dreaming, Motion, Meaning") is forthcoming in K. Hodgkin, M. O'Callaghan, and S. J. Wiseman, eds., *Reading the Early Modern Dream* (Routledge); see also Peter Holland, "The Interpretation of Dreams in the Renaissance," in Peter Brown, ed., *Reading Dreams: The Interpretation of Dreams from Chaucer to Shakespeare* (Oxford: Oxford University Press, 1999).

CHAPTER THIRTEEN

For critical, helpful comments, I owe many thanks to Marie Theres Fögen and Michael Stolleis. Special thanks to Britta Wöplern (Köln) for her help in preparing an English text. The chapter is based on a paper from the roundtable "The Anthropology of the Enlightenment" at the Eleventh International Congress of the Enlightenment, Los Angeles, August 3–10, 2003; the chapter also continues the preliminary work of my research published in "Geselligkeit im Widerstreit. Zur Pufendorf-Kontroverse um die socialitas als Grundprinzip des Naturrechts in der Disputationsliteratur in Deutschland um 1700," in *Jahrbuch für Recht und Ethik* 12 (2004): 57–70.

1. Samuel Pufendorf, *De jure naturae et gentium* (1672), ed. Frank Böhling (Berlin: *Gesammelte Werke*, 1998), Bd. 4.1 and 4.2; ders., *De officio* (1673), ed. Gerald Hartung (Berlin: *Gesammelte Werke*, 1997), Bd. 2.

2. Pufendorf, *De officio*, Preface.

3. Ibid., book 2, chap. 1, § 2.

4. Ibid., § 8.

5. See Samuel Pufendorf, *De statu hominem naturali* (1678): Samuel Pufendorf's *On the Natural State of Men*. The 1678 Latin edition and English translation, trans. and comm. by Michael Seidler (Lewiston, N.Y.: Edwin Mellen, 1990). See also Hans Medick, *Naturzustand und Naturgeschichte der bürgerlichen Gesellschaft. Die Ursprünge der bürgerlichen Sozialtheorie als Geschichtsphilosophie und Sozialwissenschaft bei Samuel Pufendorf, John Locke und Adam Smith* (Göttingen, 1973), pp. 30–63.

6. For this transfer of method, see Wolfgang Röd, *Geometrischer Geist und Naturrecht. Methodengeschichtliche Untersuchungen zur Staatsphilosophie im 17. und 18. Jahrhundert* (Munich: Verl. d. Bayer. Akad. d. Wiss., 1970).

7. Pufendorf, *De officio*, book 1, chap. 3, § 2.

8. Ibid., § 3.

9. Ibid., § 4.

10. Ibid., § 6.

11. Ibid., § 7.

12. See Fiametta Palladini, *Samuel Pufendorf discepolo di Hobbes. Per una reinterpretazione del giusnaturalismo moderno* (Bologna, 1990); and Thomas Behme, "Pufendorf—Schüler von Hobbes?" in *Denkhorizonte und Handlungsspielräume. Historische Studien für Rudolf Vierhaus zum 70. Geburtstag* (Göttingen, 1992), pp. 33–52.

13. Jacob Thomasius, *De societatis civilis statu naturali ac legali dissertatio politica* (Leipzig, 1670).

14. See Gertrud Schubart-Fikentscher, *Untersuchungen zur Autorenschaft von Dissertationen im Zeitalter der Aufklärung* (Berlin: Akademie Verlag, 1970).

15. Jacob Thomasius, *De societatis civilis statu naturali ac legali dissertatio politica* (Leipzig: Georg, 1675).

16. Ibid., § I.

17. Johann Nikolaus Hertius, *De Socialitate, Primo Naturalis Juris Principio. Occasione l. 3. D. de justitia & jure* (Gießen, 1694).

18. Ibid., § IX, p. 17: *Cum hac nostra quoque sententia non difficulter componemus Richardum Cumberlandum, disquisitione philosophica de legibus naturae statuentem, benevolentiam latissimè diffusam (cum Deo sc. & hominibus) officiorum principium, mensuram, regulam, unicamque legem. Quandoquidem*

benevolentia illa, quà alios homines complecitur, socialitas est, de qua heic agimus.

19. Immanuel Proeleus, *Grund-Sätze Des Rechts der Natur Nebst einer kurtzen Historie und Anmerckungen über die Lehren Des Hrn. Barons von Puffendorff Wie auch einem Beweiß/ Daß die Pacta nicht des Interesse, sonder ihrer Natur und Eigenschafften wegen zuhalten* (Leipzig: Georg, 1709), p. 145.

20. Nicolaus Hieronymus Gundling, *Status naturalis Hobbesii in Corpore Iuris Civ. defensus et defendendus* (Halle: Saale, 1706).

21. Gottlieb Hufeland, *Lehrsätze des Naturrechts und der damit verbundenen Wissenschaften* (Jena, 1790), p. 17.

22. See Johann Heinrich Zedler, "Natur-Rechts (Grund-Satz des)," in *Grosses vollständiges Universal-Lexikon aller Wissenschafften und Künste* (Halle/Leipzig: Johann Heinrich Zedler, 1740), Bd. 23; ND Graz: Akademische Druck-und Verlagsanstalt, 1995), Bd. 23, columns 1205–24, here column 1222.

23. Heinrich Ernst Kestner, *Ius naturae et gentium, ex ipsis fontibus Ad ductum Grotii, Pufendorffii et Cocceji Derivatum* (Rinteln, 1705).

24. Ibid., p. 8, § XI: *Deinde hoc principium valdè indefinitum est, nam societas multis & variis, imò contrariis modis promovetur, quin si Ju N. Ex hoc principio flueret, sequeretur illud jus infinitum posse mutari, nam quod hodie utile est ad societatem colendam, alio tempore noxium esse potest.*

25. For example: Johann Wilhem von der Lith, *De primo principio legis naturalis* (Haale, Saale: Zeitler, 1699). See also Merio Scattola, "Models in History of Natural Law," in *Ius Commune. Zeitschrift für Europäische Rechtsgeschichte* 28 (2001): 91–159, here 144–45.

26. Johann Ernst Philippi, *Proton pseudos circa principium juris naturae; seu primum falsum suppositum, communiter hactenus receptum, quasi totum jus naturae ex unica quadam propositione generali, omnes reliquias leges naturales sub se comprehendente* [Respondent: Ernst Gottlob Philippi] (Halle, 1731).

27. Johann Joachim Heinrich Sibrand, *Disputatio Circularis, exhibens Problema Morale, an detur principium Juris naturalis verum, primum, vnicum, adaequatum, et euidens, nec ne?* (Rostock, 1703).

28. See James Moore and Michael Silverthorne (eds.), *Natural Rights on the Threshold of the Scottish Enlightenment: The Writings of Gershom Carmichael* (Indianapolis: Liberty Fund, 2002).

29. Giulia Maria Labriola, *Barbeyrac interprete di Pufendorf e Grozio. Dalla costruzione della sovranità alla teoria della resistenza* (Naples, 2003), p. 565. "*Possiamo concludere, su questo punto, osservando che se per Barbeyrac Pufendorf è stato l'autore dell'unica sintesi possibile fra Grozio e Hobbes, così a nostro avviso Barbeyrac stesso cerca di porsi come colui il quale rende possibile una sintesi fra Grozio e Pufendorf.*"

30. Samuel Pufendorf, *Of the Law of Nature and Nations . . . To Which Are Added All the Large Notes of Mr. Barbeyrac, Translated from the Best Edition, the Fourth Edition, Carefully Corrected* (London, 1728), book II, chap. II, p. 105.

31. Jean Barbeyrac, in ibid., footnote 12.

32. Tim Hochstrasser, "Conscience and Reason: the Natural Law Theory of Jean Barbeyrac," in *The Historical Journal* 36, no. 2 (1993): 289–308, here 291.

33. See Simone Zurbuchen, *Naturrecht und Natürliche Religion. Zur Geschichte des Toleranzbegriffs von Samuel Pufendorf bis Jean-Jacques Rousseau* (Würzburg, 1991).

CHAPTER FOURTEEN

1. The frequency of the doctoral dissertations devoted to some aspects of this concept is evidence that thinking of an organism as an "animal economy" was taken for granted at the end of the eighteenth century: we can see that, after following vitalistic teaching, students wrote theses with the following titles: Pierre Philippe Ferrier, *Dissertatio medico physica, an possibile influences imaginationis in oeconomia animale, et alienum corpus* (Montpellier, 1786, directed by P. J. Barthez); N. Jauber Boisnerf, *Influence des saisons sur l'économie animale* (Montpellier, an VI [1797–1798]); Jacques Guitard, *Influence des corps célestes sur l'économie animale* (Montpellier, an VI [1797–1798]); Raimond Laroque, *De l'influence des passions sur l'économie animale, considérée dans les quatre âges de la vie* (Montpellier, an VI [1797–1798]), etc.

2. The organism as a collection of individual lives was a commonplace in the eighteenth-century French medical literature—e.g., Mr. D. G.'s thesis, "Essai sur l'irritabilité" (Avignon, 1776): "The life of each organ of the animated body is not only a simple life, but it is really the product of as many particular lives as there are organic molecules that enter into this organ's constitution" (p. 12). The author, here, created a synthesis between Buffon's *molécules organiques* (which was an embryological concept) and Bordeu's medical thesis, arguing that a life was constituted by particular organic lives.

3. "In so far as there were trans-national models for medical theorists during the later Enlightenment, they were provided by Haller's work, and the ideal of Newton. Sensibility, the capacity to feel, and irritability, the capacity to react to stimuli, were presented as the basic biological properties, and Haller's conceptual framework was assimilated by many concerned with all aspects of the life sciences." From W. F. Bynum, "Health, Disease and Medical Care," in *The Ferment of Knowledge: Studies in the Historiography of Eighteenth Century Science*, ed. R. Porter, and G. S. Rousseau (New York: Cambridge University Press, 1980), p. 221; Pinel noticed that Haller's memoir on irritability "constitutes another remarkable epoch in the medical sciences" ("Méthode d'étudier la médecine," *Médecine clinique, ou la médecine rendue plus précise et plus exacte par l'application de l'analyse ou recueil et résultats d'observations sur les maladies aigues, faites a la Salpetriere*. Paris: J. A. Bronson, 1804, xxxvi).

4. Lordat, *Réfléxions sur la nécessité de la physiologie dans l'étude et l'exercice de la médecine* (Montpellier, an V [1796–1797]).

5. Lordat, *Réfléxions*, pp. 20–21.

6. William Cullen, *Lectures on Materia Medica* (Dublin: Whitestone, 1761), p. 12.

7. William Cullen, *First Lines in the Practice of Physick* (London: Cadell, 1784), § 1090. Cullen followed a Whyttian suggestion, as Robert Whytt wrote about "vaporous diseases": "All the diseases can, in a way, be called affections of

the nervous system, because, in each disease, the nerves are more or less struck, and that yields the diversity of sensations, motions, changes, which . . . makes it difficult to know them. However, we must call 'nervous symptoms' or 'nervous disease,' properly speaking, only the illnesses which, in the case of . . . an unusual sensibility of the nerves, or in some counternatural states, are produced by causes, which would not have had similar effects in a well constituted patient, or would have them at a much less degree." Whytt, *Observations on the Nature, Cause, and Cure of Those Disorders Commonly Called Nervous, Hypochondriac or Hysteric* (Edinburgh: Hamilton, 1765), chap. 2, § XVII. Cullen replaces Whytt's "nervous system" with "nervous power," thereby giving a wider generality to the theses.

8. Robert Whytt, *Essay on the Vital and Other Involuntary Motions of Animals* (Edinburgh: Hamilton, 1751). "Upon the whole," wrote Whytt, "there seems to be in man one sentient and intelligent principle, which is equally the source of life, sense and motion, as of reason, and which, from the law of its union with the body, exerts more or less its power or its influence, as the different circumstances of the several organs actuated by it may require. That this principle operates upon the body, by the intervention of the brain or nerves is, I think, likewise probable . . . in consequence of which it may determine the nervous influence variously in different organs, and so become the cause of all the vital and involuntary motions, as well as of the animal and voluntary" (p. 300).

9. See Georges Canguilhem, *La formation du concept de réflexe* (Paris: Vrin, 1972).

10. Whytt, *Observations*. The word "vaporous" belongs to a century-lasting metaphor, which associates melancholia to the effects of evaporating bile into the brain. Hence, diseases akin to melancholia, such as hypochondria or hysteria, have been settled in terms of vapors, clouds, etc. On this point, see Stanley Jackson, *Melancholia and Depression: From Hippocratic to Modern Times* (New Haven, Conn.: Yale University Press, 1986), p. 397.

11. Bernard Mandeville, *A Treatise of the Hypochondriack and Hysterick Passions, Vulgarly Called the Hypo in MEN and Vapours in WOMEN* (London: Tomson, 1711). See commentary by Jackson, *Melancholia and Depression*, pp. 287ff.

12. Pierre Pomme, *Traité sur les affections vaporeuses des deux sexes* (Lyon: Benoît Duplain, 1763).

13. Pierre Beauchesne, *De l'influence des affections de l'âme dans les maladies nerveuses des femmes, avec le traitement qui convient à ces maladies* (Montpellier: Méquignot, 1781). We find, in 1766, by Lebesgue, an *Essai théorique et pratique sur les maladies des nerfs*, dealing with the same topics. The question of gender was important here, too—in fact, it was entangled with the nervous disease theme; the author asked "why women are more disposed to this illness than men."

14. "Oeconomie animale," *Encyclopédie ou Dictionnaire raisonné des sciences, des arts et des métiers* (Paris: Librairies Le Breton, Durand, David et Briasson, 1752–77), vol. X, p. 362.

15. "It is impossible to explain all the phenomena of nervous sympathies by mere mechanical means, by the actions of organs which often have no other links

between them than general connections designed to unify a part within the whole from which it emanates. I think that it is possible that sensation is perpetuated in an organ distant from the one which received the first impression, as the effect of a perfect analogy between nerves of those two organs" (Beauchesne, *De l'influence des affections de l'âme*, p. 63).

16. Compare J. F. Hedelhofer, *De la sensibilité et des sensations en general* (Paris, 1803): "Sensibility does not need to be restricted to the nervous fibers" (p. 21).

17. François Boissier de Sauvages, *Nosologie méthodique, ou distribution des maladies en classes, genres et espèces selon l'esprit de Sydenham et la méthode botanique*, (Lyon: Mercier 1772), § 287, p. 276. On Boissier's influence on the Montpellier school and vitalistic thinking, see Julian Martin, "Sauvages's Nosology: Medical Enlightenment in Montpellier," *Medical Enlightenment of the 18th century*, ed. A. Cunningham and R. French (Cambridge: Cambridge University Press, 1990), pp. 111–37.

18. "Oeconomie animale," *Encyclopédie*, XI, p. 362.

19. Boissier, *Nosologie méthodique*, § 207, p. 215.

20. Beauchesne, *De l'influence des affections de l'âme*, p. 47.

21. Philippe Pinel, *Nosographie philosophique*, I, 6th ed. (Paris: Richard, Caille et Ravier, 1813), p. 3.

22. Samuel-Auguste Tissot, *De l'influence des passions de l'âme dans les maladies* (Paris: Armand Koenig, 1798), § 113, p. 168.

23. Antoine Le Camus, *Médecine de l'esprit, où l'on traite des dispositions et des causes physiques qui sont des conséquences de l'union de l'âme avec le corps, influant sur les opérations de l'esprit; et des moyens de maîtriser ses opérations dans un bon état ou de les corriger quand elles sont viciées* (Paris: Ganeau, 1765).

24. Very significant is the fact that Le Camus treated in the same manner "virtues" and "passions," since "virtues and passions in nature belong as much to the body as to the soul" (p. 170).

25. According to Kathleen M. Grange, the writers undertaking this approach included the later revolutionary leader Marat, in *De l'homme, ou des principes et des lois de l'influence de l'âme sur le corps et du corps sur l'âme* (Amsterdam: Chez M. Rey, 1775); see Grange, "Pinel and XVIIIth Century Psychiatry," *Bull. Hist. Med.* 35 (1961): 450.

26. John Gregory, *Comparative View of the State and Faculties of Man with Those of the Animal World* (Edinburgh: Dodsley, 1777). "Most of those who studied the human mind, have been too less acquainted with the structures of the human body (i.e. anatomy) and the laws of animal economy (i.e. physiology); and mind and body are so intimately connected, and have such a mutual influence on one another, that the constitution of each of them could not be understood if examined separately" (p. 5).

27. The importance of age for animal economy was great; in the same year as Laroque, it was also addressed by Joseph Franchet's dissertation, entitled *Maladies affectées aux divers âges* (Montpellier, an VI [1797–1798]).

28. See Philippe Huneman, *Bichat. La vie et la mort* (Paris: Puf, 1998).

29. On this point, see Grange, "Pinel and XVIIIth Century Psychiatry," p. 451.

30. J. E. D. Esquirol, *Les Passions considérées comme causes, symptômes et moyens curatifs de l'aliénation mentale* (Paris: Didot, 1805).

31. It is strange to note that this text, written at the very moment of the medicalization of madness, included a few themes that would become major weapons in the critique of psychiatry after the 1960s (Goffmann, Szaz, Foucault, etc.). This further suggests how much was at stake in the definition of madness as a disease.

32. Boissier also shared the lexicon of excess—among the classes of "vesania," he counted hallucinations, delirium, and a third class of names, "*bizarreries—morositates,*" characterized by a peculiar mistake: little things are appreciated with *too much* pleasure, or the reverse; *bizarrerie* is a "*too great* desire or aversion for something" (*Nosologie méthodique*, VIII, p. 192). Excess and depravation were linked in this class of madness. Among this class, we find disturbed appetites of pregnant women, bulimia, and also nymphomania and satyriasis.

33. *Pensées,* frag. 412 (Lafuma edition), *Oeuvres complètes* (Paris: Seuil, 1963).

34. *Encyclopédie*, VII, p. 47.

35. *Encyclopédie*, X, p. 389.

36. Cullen, *Lectures on Materia Medica*, p. 7.

37. *Encyclopédie*, X, p. 22.

38. *Encyclopédie*, X, p. 391. Classical example, already mentioned by Cullen.

39. *Encyclopédie*, X, p. 23. According to d'Aumont ("Délire"), this change, which aims at "always opposing affects contrary to the dominant affects," should use "musical instruments, songs, dance, sudden noises, regular noises, light, etc." (*Encyclopédie*, IV, p. 788).

40. d'Aumont, "Délire," *Encyclopédie*, III, p. 86.

41. Cullen, *First Lines*, § 1245.

42. Beauchesne, *De l'influence des affections de l'âme*, p. 160. See also Cullen, *First Lines*, §1573: "constrained attention required by the direction of some corporal exercise is a way to distract the mind from any chain of ideas."

43. See George Cheyne, *Natural Method of Curing the Diseases of the Body, and the Disorders of the Mind Depending on the Body* (London: Strathan, 1742).

44. Roselyne Rey, "Vitalism, Disease and Society," in *Medicine in the Enlightenment*, ed. R. S. Porter (Amsterdam: Clio Medica, 1995), pp. 275–88.

45. Jacques Tenon, *Mémoires sur les hôpitaux* (Paris: Pierres, 1788), p. XXVI.

46. Ibid.

47. Among several occurrences, see Pinel, "Observations sur le régime moral qui est le plus propre à guérir, dans certains cas, la raison égarée des maniaques," *Gazette de santé* (1789): 4; published in Postel, *Genèse de la psychiatrie—les premiers écrits de Philippe Pinel* (Paris: Synthelabo, 1981), p. 194.

48. Pinel, "Mémoire sur la manie pour servir l'histoire naturelle de l'homme" (1794), § II; published in Postel J., *Genèse de la psychiatrie*, p. 240.

49. Samuel Tuke, *Description of the Retreat, an Institution Near York, of the Society of Friends, Containing an Account of Its Origin and Progress, the Modes of Treatment, and the Statement of Cases* (York: Alexander, 1813); "Whatever theory we maintain in regard to the remote causes of insanity, we must consider moral treatment, or management, of very high importance" (p. 131).

The word "management" typically belongs to the conception of the "milieu" in the scheme of animal economy. Tuke's description of this "moral treatment," although published in 1813, i.e., after Pinel's book was well-known, related the Retreat's practices from the beginnings; Tuke's description (p. 162) can be compared to Georget's description in *De la folie* (Paris: Crevot, 1820; reed. Toulouse: Privat, 1972), chap. 5, § I). Concerning the therapeutic achievement in the Retreat, from its foundation to its redefinition by the medical powers, see Anne Digby, "Moral Treatment at the Retreat, 1796–1846," in *Anatomy of Madness*, I, ed. R. S. Porter, W. F. Bynum, and J. Shepherd (London: Tavistock, 1985), pp. 55–72.

50. Boissier, *Nosologie méthodique*, VIII, p. 28.

51. Pinel, *Nosographie philosophique*, 2nd ed., vol. II, § 9, p. 12.

52. Jacques Postel, *Genese de la psychiatrie: les premiers écrits psychiatriques de Philippe Pinel* (Paris: Le Sycomore, 1981).

53. Jackie Pigeaud, *Aux portes de la psychiatrie. Pinel, l'ancien et le moderne* (Paris: Flammarion, 2002).

54. Dora Weiner, *Comprendre et soigner* (Paris: Fayard, 2001); Weiner, "Observe and Heal: Philippe Pinel's Experiment at the Salpêtrière Hospice, 1802–1805," in *Knowledge and Power: Perspectives in the History of Psychiatry*, ed. E. J. Engstrom, M. M. Weber, and P. Hoff (Berlin: Verlag für Wissenschaft und Bildung, 1999)..

55. Gladys Swain, *Le sujet de la folie* (Paris: Payot, 1976); Swain, *Dialogue avec l'insensé* (Paris: Gallimard, 1993).

56. Pinel, *Traité médico-philosophique de l'aliénation mentale ou la manie* (Paris: Richard, Caille et Ravier, 1802), I, § 25, p. 104.

57. Pinel, *Médecine clinique*, § II, p. 387.

58. Pinel, *Traité médico-philosophique*, § 18, p. 80.

59. Pinel, *Traité médico-philosophique*, § 9, p. 27.

60. See also Pinel, *Nosographie philosophique*, § 7, p. 12.

61. Pinel, *Traité médico-philosophique*, § 7, p. 18. In the *Nosographie philosophique*, Pinel defines *vesaniae* as constituted by "a more or less pronounced lesion of the functions of the understanding, *or* of the affective faculties." (III, chap. I (*classe des névroses*), p. 36, 6th ed.) The disjunction, here, proves that madness is not *essentially* an intellectual trouble.

62. Pinel, *Médecine clinique*, p. 5.

63. On this point, see William Coleman, *Death Is a Social Disease: Public Health and Political Economy in Early Industrial France* (Madison: University of Wisconsin Press, 1982).

64. Pinel, *Traité médico-philosophique*, p. 161.

65. George Rosen, *Madness and Society: Chapters in the Historical Sociology of Mental Illness* (London: Routledge, 1968).

66. On this anthropology, see *Inventing Human Science*, ed. C. Fox, R. Porter, and R. Wokler (Berkeley: University of California Press, 1995); and on Buffon, Diderot, and Rousseau, see the classic work, Michèle Duchet, *Anthropologie et histoire au siècle des Lumières* (Paris: Albin-Michel, 1971).

67. Note that Bichat was acquainted with Pinel's medical practice.

68. The reality and results of moral treatment in Bicêtre and La Salpetrière have been addressed by Dora Weiner, *Comprendre et soigner*, chap. VII, pp. 217–57; and J. Postel and C. Quêtel, *Nouvelle histoire de la psychiatrie* (Paris: Dunod, 1994), pp. 152–60, 314–24.

69. Pinel, *Traité médico-philosophique*, § 23, p. 98.

70. "De la folie," in Esquirol, *Des maladies mentales* (Paris: Baillière, 1838), I, pp. 23–25.

71. Esquirol's concept of *monomanie* (alienation focused on a single topic, whether accompanied by a sad passion or a happy one) is tied to the acknowledgment of an interaction between milieu and alienation: some *monomanies* are epidemic, as the one depicted in Don Quixote ("De la monomanie," *Des maladies mentales*, I, p. 343).

72. For instance, Esquirol undertook the first study of suicide from a psychiatric perspective.

73. Wilhelm Griesinger, *Die Pathologie und Therapie der psychischen Krankheiten*, (Stuttgart: Grabbe, 1845); Pierre-Marie Morel, *Traité des dégénerescences physiques, morales et intellectuelles de l'espèce humaine* (Paris: Baillière, 1857). This conception can be found in the excellent Postel and Quêtel, *Nouvelle histoire de la psychiatrie*, or in Theodore Brown's paper, "Psychiatry," in R. S. Porter and W. F. Bynum (eds.), *Companion Encyclopaedia of the History of Medicine* (London: Routledge, 1993).

CHAPTER FIFTEEN

1. John Trenchard, *Cato's Letters: Or, Essays on Civil Liberty*, 4 vols. (London: J. Walthoe, 1725), 3:70.

2. Johannes Fabian, *Out of Our Minds* (Berkeley: University of California Press, 2000), 64.

3. Lewis Carroll, *Alice's Adventures in Wonderland*, ed. Roger Lancelyn Green (Oxford: Oxford University Press, 1971), 15.

4. David Hume, "Of Miracles," in *The Essays of David Hume* (London: Grant Richards, 1903), 528.

5. Earl of Shaftesbury, Anthony Ashley Cooper, *Characteristics of Men, Manners, Opinions, Times, etc.* (Indianapolis: Bobbs Merrill, 1964), 1:222.

6. David Hume, *Essays and Treatises* (London: A. Millar, 1758), 123.

7. Johann Gottfried Herder, *On World History*, ed. Hans Adler and Ernest A. Menze, trans. Ernest A. Menze and Michael Palma (New York and London: M. E. Sharpe, 1997), 36–38; Anthony Pagden, "The Effacement of Difference: Colonialism and the Origins of Nationalism in Diderot and Herder," in *After Colonialism*, ed. Gyan Prakash (Princeton: Princeton University Press, 1994), 141–46.

8. See Julia Douthwaite, *The Wild Girl, Natural Man and the Monster: Dangerous Experiments in the Age of Enlightenment* (Chicago: Chicago University Press, 2002).

9. J. Hector St. John de Crevecoeur, *More Letters from the American Farmer*, ed. Dennis D. Moore (Athens: University of Georgia Press, 1995), 90.

10. Thomas Jefferson, *Notes on the State of Virginia* (New York: Harper Torchbooks, 1964), 137.

11. Jefferson, *Notes*, 64.

12. Aphra Behn, *Oroonoko: Or, The Royal Slave*, ed. Lore Metzger (New York: Norton, 1973), 69.

13. Ned Ward, *Five Travel Scripts* (New York: Columbia University Press, Facsimile Text Society, 1933), 13.

14. Jonathan Swift, *Travels into Several Remote Nations of the World* (Oxford: Oxford University Press, 1902), 372.

15. Carlo Ginzburg, "The Old World and the New Seen from Nowhere," *No Island Is an Island*, trans. John Tedeschi (New York: Columbia University Press, 2000), 19.

16. William Yate, "Correspondence of William Yate," William Alexander Turnbull Library, Micro MS 239, 1808–40, January 12, 1836.

17. Crevecoeur, *More Letters*, 183.

18. Edward Long, *The History of Jamaica*, 3 vols. (1774; London: T. Lowndes; New York: Arno Press, 1972) 1:4, 9–13.

19. Jonathan Swift, *The Drapier's Letters*, ed. Herbert Davis (Oxford: Oxford University Press, 1935), 40.

20. Swift, *Drapier's Letters*, 83.

21. Anthony Pagden, "Identity Formation in Spanish America," in *Colonial Identity in the Atlantic World, 1500–1800*, ed. Nicholas Canny and Anthony Pagden (Princeton: Princeton University Press, 1987), 83–88.

22. Nicholas Canny, "Identity Formation in Ireland," in *Colonial Identity in the Atlantic World, 1500–1800*, ed. Nicholas Canny and Anthony Pagden (Princeton: Princeton University Press, 1987), 168.

23. Edmund Spenser, *A View of the State of Ireland*, ed. Andrew Hadfield and Willy Maly (Oxford: Blackwell, 1997), 53.

24. Long, *History of Jamaica*, 2:278, 427, 327.

25. Anthony Pagden, *Spanish Imperialism and the Political Imagination* (New Haven: Yale University Press, 1990), 106; Jorge Canizares-Esguerra, *How to Write the History of the New World* (Stanford: Stanford University Press, 2001), 286.

26. Aphra Behn, *The Rover*, ed. Janet Todd (London: Penguin, 1992), 161.

27. William Douglass, *A Summary of the Present State of the British Settlements in North America* (London: E. Baldwin, 1755), 153.

28. Robert Boyle, Papers 39, Library of Royal Society, London (n.d.), 182.

29. Ward, *Five Travel Scripts*, 11.

30. Spenser, *A View of the State of Ireland*, 11.

31. Jefferson, *Notes*, 155.

32. Herder, *On World History*, 271.

33. Guillaume Raynal, *A History of the East and West Indies*, 10 vols., trans. J. O. Justamond (London: W. Strahan and T. Cadell, 1783), 5:79–82.

34. Raynal, *History of the East and West Indies*, 5:2.

35. Edward Kamau Brathwaite, *The Development of Creole Society in Jamaica, 1770–1820* (Oxford: Clarendon Press, 1971), 297.

36. Jean Rhys, *Wide Sargasso Sea* (New York: Norton, 1966), 67.

37. Rhys, *Wide Sargasso Sea*, 102.

38. Carolus Bovillus, *Il libro del sapiente*, ed. Eugenio Garin (Turin: Einaudi, 1987), 73; Michael Hardt and Antonio Negri, *Empire* (Cambridge: Harvard University Press, 2000), 72.

39. Giorgio Agamben, *Homo Sacer: Sovereign Power and Bare Life,* trans. Daniel Heller-Roazen (Stanford: Stanford University Press, 1998), 104.

40. Spenser, *A View of the State of Ireland*, 64.

41. Pagden, "Effacement," 18, 61.

42. Edmund Spenser, *Faerie Queene* (London: W. Faden, 1758), 161.

43. Canizares-Esguerra, *How to Write the History of the New World*, 282–85.

44. Serge Gruzinski, *The Mestizo Mind* (New York: Routledge, 2002), 88–90.

45. J. Hector St. John de Crevecoeur, *Letters from an American Farmer,* ed. Susan Manning (Oxford: Oxford University Press, 1997), 43.

46. Crevecoeur, *Letters*, 201.

47. Crevecoeur, *More Letters*, 159.

48. Crevecoeur, *More Letters*, 156.

49. Crevecoeur, *More Letters*, 215.

50. Euclides da Cunha, *Rebellion in the Backlands,* trans. Samuel Putnam (Chicago: University of Chicago Press, 1944), 155.

51. da Cunha, 161.

52. Pagden, *Spanish Imperialism*, 95, 109.

53. Pagden, *Spanish Imperialism*, 125.

54. Canizares-Esguerra, *How to Write the History of the New World*, 284.

55. James Clifford, "Diasporas," *Cultural Studies* 9, no. 3 (August 1994): 302–38.

56. Tom Hayden, *Irish on the Inside: In the Search of the Soul of Irish America* (New York: Verso, 2001).

57. Nicholas Thomas, *Colonialism's Culture* (Princeton: Princeton University Press, 1996), 11.

58. Homi Bhabha, *The Location of Culture* (London: Routledge, 1994), 33, 89.

59. Robert Young, *Postcolonialism: An Historical Introduction* (Oxford: Blackwell, 2001), 74.

60. J. G. A. Pocock, *The Machiavellian Moment* (Princeton: Princeton University Press, 1978), 532.

61. Apuleius, *The Golden Ass*, trans. P. G. Walsh (Oxford: Oxford University Press, 1995).

62. Hardt and Negri, *Empire*, 218.

63. Donna Haraway, *The Companion Species Manifesto* (Chicago: Prickly Paradigm, 2003), 11.

64. J. M. Coetzee, *Disgrace* (New York: Viking, 1999), 205.

65. Crevecoeur, *More Letters*, 155.

66. Samuel Taylor Coleridge (1830, 42–43), cited in Terry Eagleton, *The Idea of Culture* (Oxford: Blackwell, 2000), 7.

CHAPTER SIXTEEN

1. The movie *Gattaca* (1997), with a remote planet to be colonized only by genetically purified settlers, according to new "*estatutos de limpieza de sangre*," is a recent example.

2. See David Brading, *Orbe indiano. De la Monarquía Católica a la República criolla (1492–1867)* (Mexico City: Fondo de Cultura Económica, 1993); and Frank Holl, *Humboldt y el Colonialismo*, in Thomas Gomez, ed., *Humboldt et le monde hispanique* (Paris: Université de Paris X, Centre de Recherches Ibériques et Ibéro-Américaines, 2002), pp. 59–66. Close to my perspective are also Leopoldo Zea, *La huella de Humboldt* (Mexico City: FCE, 2000); Jean Paul Duviols and Charles Minguet, *Humboldt, savant-citoyen du monde* (Paris: Gallimard, 1994); and the series by Jonathan Hart, *Representing the New World: English and French Uses of the Example of Spain* (New York and London: Palgrave, 2001), *Columbus, Shakespeare and the Interpretation of the New World* (New York and London: Palgrave, 2002), and *Comparing Empires: European Colonialism from Portuguese Expansion to the Spanish-American War* (New York and London: Palgrave, 2003).

3. Richard Wright, *Pagan Spain* (London: The Bodley Head, 1960), p. 165; see Paul Gilroy, *The Black Atlantic: Modernity and Double Consciousness* (Cambridge, Mass.: Harvard University Press, 1993).

4. The works of John Pocock and of Anthony Pagden are essential references, but I am also considering alternative perspectives such as Mary Louise Pratt's *Imperial Eyes: Travel Writing and Transculturation* (London: Routledge, 1992); and Jorge Cañizares-Esguerra, *How to Write the History of the New World* (Stanford: Stanford University Press, 2001).

5. A useful bibliographical survey concerning both the anthropological and the historical aspects of this controversial point is *Fare memoria, costruire identità*, a recent monographic issue of the journal *Novecento* 10 (January–June 2004). Four of its contributions are especially relevant to my paper's perspective: Fabio Dei, "Antropologia e memoria. Prospettive di un nuovo rapporto con la storia," pp. 27–46; Luca Scuccimarra, "Frammenti di memoria: l'Europa, l'identità, la storia," pp. 61–75; Stefano Petrungaro, "L'Est europeo, o a est dell'Europa: in margine al dibattito su mental maps, confini e balcanismo," pp. 77–86; Patrick Hyder Patterson, "Sull'orlo della ragione," pp. 87–106, the Italian translation of the 2003 article "On the Edge of Reason: the Boundaries of Balkanism in Slovenian, Austrian and Italian Discorse," *Slavic Review* 62 (2003): 110–41.

6. Two classic studies are Hayden White, *Metahistory: The Historical Imagination in Nineteenth Century Europe* (Baltimore: John Hopkins University Press, 1973); Eric J. Hobsbawm and Terence Ranger, *The Invention of Tradition* (Cambridge: Cambridge University Press, 1983). A more interdisciplinary approach could include medical suggestions concerning the treatment and the cultural origins of some important diseases of memory. See Daniel L. Schacter, ed., *Memory Distortion: How Minds, Brains and Societies Reconstruct the Past* (Cambridge, Mass.: Harvard University Press, 1995); and Paul Antze and Michael Lambeck, eds., *Tense Past: Cultural Essays in Trauma and Memory* (New York and London:

Routledge, 1996). See also Jorge Cañizares-Esguerra, *How to Write the History of the New World. Histories, Epistemologies, and Identities in the Eighteenth-Century Atlantic World* (Stanford: Stanford University Press, 2001).

7. The idea of Eastern Europe was consolidated in the Age of Enlightenment according to Larry Wolff, *Inventing Eastern Europe: The Map of Civilization on the Mind of the Enlightenment* (Stanford: Stanford University Press, 1994); or even later according to Hans Lemberg, "Zur Entstehung des Osteuropabegriffs im 19. Jahrhundert. Vom "Norten" zum "Osten" Europas," *Jahrbücher für Geschichte Osteuropas* 33 (1985): 48–91; and Frithjof Benjamin Schenk, "Mental Maps: Die Konstruktion von geographischen Räumen in Europa seit der Aufklärung," *Geschichte und Gesellschaft* 28 (2002): 493–51; Maria Todorova reframed the question of the Balkans in terms of Southeastern Europe in her *Imagining the Balkans* (New York: Oxford University Press, 1997) and later, in analytical terms, in the article "Der Balkan als Analysekategorie: Grenzen, Raum, Zeit," *Geschichte und Gesellschaft* 28 (2002): 470–92.

8. According to Alain Corbin, *Le territoire du vide* (Paris: Aubier, 1988), the intellectual attitude of the Western world toward the shores changed positively between 1750 and 1840. Giorgio Triani, *Pelle di luna pelle di sole. Nascita e storia della civiltà balneare (1700–1946)* (Padua: Marsilio, 1988), describes some long-term effects of this transformation. In "Il linguaggio delle isole" and in "L'isola-continente come donna," the first two variations of his book, *L'isola, la donna, il ritratto. Quattro variazioni* (Turin: Bollati Boringhieri, 1996), Sergio Perosa highlights the ambiguity of the islands and of their dialectics with the continent, from the Renaissance on. According to Perosa, the identity of the islands has always been attributed as female, and, because of its insularity, the New World has been frequently referred to as a She-World. Mark Kurlansky used the continent-versus-islands opposition to define the Caribbean cultural space in *A Continent of Islands: Searching for the Caribbean Destiny* (Reading, Mass.: Addison-Wesley, 1992). From a different and more anthropological point of view, Marshall Sahlins, in his *Islands of History* (Chicago: University of Chicago Press, 1985), studied Captain Cook's encounter with the Hawaiian Islands in 1778.

9. For an updated map of the practical and the ideological consequences of this colonial expansion during the eighteenth century, see Byron Wells and Philip Stewart, eds., *Interpreting Colonialism* (Oxford: SVEC-Voltaire Foundation, 2004); and Jonathan Hart, *Comparing Empires*. Hart, conscious that "The mythology of history is a potent force" (p. xi), explicitly insists on the context represented by the "Atlantic basin," where "the expansion of western European nations beyond Europe" (p. 1) took place: "A major rationale for this study is to follow the first great expansion of the western European empires and, while concentrating most on the New World, to place the colonization of the western Atlantic in the wider context of the Atlantic world, including Africa, and the connections with Asia through the Pacific and the Indian Oceans" (p. 5).

10. According to Hart, *Comparing Empires*, when Spain and Portugal began to "expand offshore and later overseas" (p. 2) they founded "western European and seaborne" empires, but culturally connected with the legacy of the Roman Empire, used by the modern Europeans "as a measure of their own empires"

(p. 3). On this basis, "Portugal and Spain became the 'empires' that other kingdoms would emulate, criticize and seek to displace, sometimes at once" (p. 4).

11. Jean-Frédéric Schaub, *La France espagnole: les racines hispaniques de l'absolutisme français* (Paris: Seuil, 2003); I quote from the Spanish version, *La Francia española* (Madrid: Marcial Pons, 2004), p. 18.

12. Francisco de Vitoria, *De iure belli*, ed. Carlo Galli (Bari: Laterza, 2005), p. vi; on the evolution of this geographical consciousness, see also the letters published and studied by Mary Pedley, *The Maps Trade in the Eighteenth Century: Letters to the London Map Sellers Jefferys and Faden* (Oxford: SVEC-Voltaire Foundation, 2000); see also Corbin, *Le territoire du vide*.

13. Marco Cipolloni, *Il sovrano e la corte nelle "cartas" della Conquista* (Rome: Bulzoni-CNR, 1991).

14. Tomás López Medel, *Colonización de America: informes y testimonios 1549–1572* (Madrid: Corpus Hispanorum de Pace, CSIC, 1990), pp. 71–72.

15. Schaub, *La France espagnole*, p. 17.

16. Cannon Schmitt recently updated this framework, studying Darwin's voyages in the article "Darwin's Savage Mnemonics," *Representations* 88 (Fall 2004): 55–80.

17. See Corbin, *Le territoire du vide*. In Italy the links between utopia and post-Renaissance classicism have been studied by scholars such as Domenico Consoli, *Dall'Arcadia all'Illuminismo* (Bologna: Cappelli, 1972); and Sergio Bartolommei, *Illuminismo e utopia: temi e progetti utopici nella cultura francese (1676–1788)* (Milan: il Saggiatore, 1978). The interpretation of Hobbes's state of nature as a mask of the totally free market has been elaborated by Crawford Brough Macpherson, *The Political Theory of Possessive Individualism. From Hobbes to Locke* (Oxford: Oxford University Press, 1962).

18. The original idea of bookseller Le Breton was a "translation" of Chambers's *Cyclopaedia*, 1728, but Diderot, as the supervisor of this "translation," transformed the French version in a revolutionary project, centered on the idea of a new series of essays. The broad eighteenth-century notions of translation are essential for understanding this process, as I recently pointed out, for the eighteenth-century Spanish book market and stage, in M. Cipolloni, "Il Secolo d'Oro delle traduzioni o la nascita di una *nación traducida*: il mercato della medazione linguistico-culturale nella Spagna del secondo Settecento e dello Entresiglos," in H. Honnaker, ed., *Dieci incontri per parlare di traduzione, Materiali di discussione* 3 (2005): 88–100.

19. Juan Marichal spoke of the essay's "voluntad de estilo." Marichal, *La voluntad de estilo: Teoría e historia del ensayismo hispánico* (Barcelona: Seix Barral, 1957; reprinted Madrid: Revista de Occidente, 1971; updated edition, Madrid: Alianza, 1984).

20. Graham Burnett, *Masters of All They Surveyed: Explorations, Geography and a British El Dorado* (Chicago: Chicago University Press, 2000). A Spanish and Spanish American perspective can be reconstructed with José Espinosa y Tello, *Memorias sobre las observaciones astronómicas hechas por los navegantes españoles en distintos lugares del globo* (Madrid: Imprenta Real, 1809); M. A. Dóbrigny and J. B. Eyriés, eds., *Viaje pintoresco a las dos Américas, Asia y*

Africa. Resumen jeneral de todos los viajes y descubrimientos de Colón, Magallanes, Las Casas, Gómara, La Condamine, Ulloa, Jorge Juan y Humboldt (Barcelona: Imprenta Olivares, 1842); Francisco Vindel, *Mapas de América en los libros españoles de los siglos XVI al XVIII (1503–1798)* (Madrid: s.i., 1955–59); and Antonio Lafuente and Antonio Mazuecos, *Los caballeros del punto fijo. Ciencia, política y aventura en la expedición geodésica hispanofrancesa al virreinato del Perú en el siglo XVIII* (Madrid: CSIC-Serbal, 1987). A Portuguese paradox is described by Laurent Vidal, *Mazagão, la ville qui traversa l'Atlantique. Du Maroc à l'Amazonie (1769–1783)* (Paris: Flammarion, 2005).

21. Northop Frye, *The Great Code: The Bible and Literature* (New York: Harcourt, 1982); Giuliano Gliozzi, *Adamo e il Nuovo Mondo: la nascita dell'antropologia come ideologia coloniale: dalle genealogie bibliche alle teorie razziali* (Florence: La Nuova Italia, 1977).

22. It is the epic of the Portuguese, the Spanish and the British Empires, an overseas prophetic enterprise made of guns and sails or of swords and crosses, according to the brilliant metaphors proposed by Carlo M. Cipolla, *Guns and Sails in the Early Phase of European Expansion, 1400–1700* (London: Collins, 1965); and Charles A. Truxillo, *By the Sword and the Cross: The Historical Evolution of the Catholic World Monarchy in Spain and the New World, 1492–1825* (Westport, Conn., and London: Greenwood Press, 2001). A less-epic image of the same period is offered by Jonathan Hart, *Columbus, Shakespeare* (2002) and *Comparing Empires* (2003), and also by J. H. Parry, *The Establishment of the European Hegemony, 1415–1715: Trade and Explorations in the Age of the Renaissance* (New York: Harper and Row, 1966; first edition 1949); and Pierre Leon, *Histoire economique et sociale du monde* (Paris: Colin, 1978), whose volume devoted to the period 1580–1730 has the following title: *Les hesitations de la croissance*. A few years ago, Jocelyn Hillgarth, a specialist on medieval Spain, published a big book, *The Mirror of Spain, 1500–1700: The Formation of a Myth* (Ann Arbor: The University of Michigan Press, 2000), a very original survey on the period we are interested in. Hillgarth's theory concerns the foundations and emergence of a negative epic, perceiving and representing (or vice versa) Spain as a different, peripheral, and even relatively remote, un-European and primitive country. Hillgarth's book offers an updated version of Richard Kagan's "Prescott's Paradigm," concerning the "understanding of Spain as America's antithesis," a new geohistorical version of the famous "querelle des Anciens et des Modernes." See Richard Kagan, "Prescott's Paradigm: American Historical Scholarship and the Decline of Spain," *American Historical Review* 4 (1966): 423–46, republished in R. Kagan, ed., *Spain in America* (Urbana and Chicago: University of Illinois Press, 2002), appendix, pp. 247–76. The myth of the colonial period as an American Middle Age, recently studied by Amanda Salvioni, *L'invenzione di un medioevo americano: rappresentazioni moderne del passato coloniale in Argentina* (Reggio Emilia: Diabasis, 2003), can be considered a Latin-American equivalent of Kagan's "Prescott's Paradigm." Barbara Fuchs, *Mimesis and Empire: The New World, Islam, and European Identities* (Cambridge: Cambridge University Press, 2001), includes Islam and the pirates in the role-playing game of this imperial and retrospective fantasy, where "the Moors are played by the Indians" (p. 1). See also

M. Cipolloni, "Nota introduttiva," in William Hickling Prescott, *La Conquista del Messico* (Turin: Einaudi, 1992), Italian trans. by Pietro Jahier and Maria Vittoria Malvano, pp. v–xiv.

23. Aphra Behn, *Oroonoko, or The Royal Slave/Oroonoko schiavo di sangue reale* (Turin: Einaudi bilingual series, 1998), pp. 17–19 (italics are mine).

24. Marc-Antoine Saint-Amant, *Epistre diversifiée à M. Des-Noyers secretaire des commendements de la Serenissime Reine de Pologne*, in *Les Oeuvres* (Paris: J. de Luyne, 1661), p. 343.

25. Hart, *Comparing Empires*.

26. Johannes Fabian, in his study *Time and the Other: How Anthropology Makes Its Object* (New York: Columbia University Press, 1983), underlines the "tendency to place the referent(s) of anthropology in a Time other than the present of the producer of the anthropological discourse," p. 31.

27. Jack Goody, *The Domestication of the Savage Mind* (Cambridge: Cambridge University Press, 1977).

28. See E. Lonati, "Scienza medica e tradizione enciclopedica nell'Inghilterra del Settecento: testi a confronto," *MPW—Mots Palabras Words* (Milan), 2 (2002): 29–59.

29. Fray Bernardino de Sahagún, *Historia general de las cosas de la Nueva España*, ed. Juan Carlos Temprano, 2 vols. (Madrid: Historia 16, 1990), vol. I, p. 1.

30. Sahagún, *Historia general*, vol. I, p. 3.

31. Sahagún, *Historia general*, "Al sincero lector," vol. I, p. 6.

32. Sahagún divides the "things" of New Spain similarly ("divinas, humanas, naturales").

33. Chambers's *Cyclopaedia* was the model on which Diderot's *Encyclopédie* was based. The universal dictionaries of Harris and Chambers were recently studied by E. Lonati, "Scienza medica."

34. Art critic Rudolph Arnheim, *The Power of the Center* (Berkeley, Los Angeles: University of California Press, 1982), interpreted this "power" of the center as a possible bridge to connect the theory of the Art with the history of the Arts.

35. It was the so-called Black Legend, concerning Spain and the Spanish conquerors and settlers, based on the apologies written by fray Bartolomé de las Casas in the sixteenth century and echoed, during the eighteenth century, by many authors: among them Robertson, Raynal, and De Pauw. About the blackness of the Legend and its long-term consequences, see Richard Kagan, "Prescott's Paradigm," Walter D. Mignolo, *The Darker Side of the Renaissance: Literacy, Territoriality and Colonization* (Ann Arbor: University of Michigan Press, 1999), and recently María de Guzmán, *Spain's Long Shadow: The Black Legend, Off-Whiteness, and Anglo-American Empire* (Minneapolis: University of Minnesota Press, 2005).

36. *Raynal: de la polémique à l'histoire*, ed. Gilles Bancarel and Gianluigi Goggi (Oxford: SVEC-Voltaire Foundation, 2000); and Jeff Loveland, *Rhetoric and Natural History: Buffon in Polemics and Literary Context* (Oxford: SVEC-Voltaire Foundations, 2001).

37. Ilarione da Bergamo, *Viaggio al Messico* (Bergamo: Secomandi, 1976), p. 20.

38. The proceedings of the 1997 Jesuit Conference at Boston College have been published in 1999 by Toronto University Press in the volume *Cultures, Sciences and the Arts, 1540–1773,* edited by J. O'Malley, G. Bailey, S. Harris, and T. F. Kennedy. On Jesuits and natural science, see also Luis Millones Figueroa and Domingo Ledesma, eds., *El saber de los Jesuitas, historias naturales y el Nuevo Mundo* (Frankfurt: Vervuert-Iberoamericana, 2005).

39. See Hart, *Columbus, Shakespeare* (2002); Hart, *Comparing Empires* (2003); Claudio Esteva Fabregat, "Sobre el origen indiano de la Antropología cultural," *Etnohistoria* I, 2 (1998); and Mario Hernandez Sánchez-Barba, "Culminación intellectual de una cultura hispanoamericana: Antropología y Filosofía de la Historia," chapter VII of Idem, *La época dorada de América: pensamiento, política, mentalidades* (Madrid: Biblioteca Nueva, 2003).

40. John M. Headley, *Tommaso Campanella and the Transformation of the World* (Princeton, N.J.: Princeton University Press, 1997).

41. Silvio Zavala, *La encomienda indiana* (Madrid, 1935; reprinted Mexico City: Porrúa, 1982).

42. Juan Antonio Manzano y Manzano, *La incorporación de Indias a la Corona de Castilla* (Madrid:Cultura Hispánica, 1948). Antonello Gerbi, with the standard Italian editions of his *La disputa del Nuovo Mondo* (Naples and Milan: Ricciardi, 1955; revised 1983) opened a long-term debate that, during the late 1960s and the early 1970s, echoed the crisis of colonialism and connected anthropology with the colonial discourse, involving, among others, Vittorio Lanternari, *Occidente e terzo mondo* (Bari: Dedalo, 1967); Charles Minguet, *Alexandre de Humboldt, historien et géographe de l'Amérique espagnole* (Paris: Maspero, 1969); Sergio Moravia, *La scienza dell'uomo nel Settecento* (Bari: Laterza, 1970); Stefano Landucci, *I filosofi e i selvaggi* (Bari: Laterza, 1972); Giuliano Gliozzi, *La scoperta dei selvaggi: antropologia e colonialismo da Colombo a Diderot* (Milan: Principato, 1971); and Michèle Duchet, *Anthropologie et histoire au siècle des Lumières* (Paris: Maspero, 1971).

43. Edmundo O'Gorman, *The Invention of America* (Bloomington: Indiana University Press, 1961).

44. In Italy, this comparative analysis of the differences between the ethnographic aspects of missionary work and the anthropological perspective inspired various meetings and discussions, whose proceedings have been published: *Antropologi e missionari a confronto,* ed. U. Casalegno (Rome: LAS, 1988); *Missioni: percorsi tra antropologia e storia,* ed. C. Mattalucci-Yilmaz, *Etnosistemi,* 9 (2002); and *In nome di Dio: l'impresa missionaria di fronte all'alterità,* ed. F. Cuturi (Rome: Meltemi, 2004).

45. Joaquín Marco and Jordi Gracia, eds., *La llegada de los bárbaros: la recepción de la literatura hispanoamericana en España (1960–1981)* (Barcelone-Buenos Aires: Edhasa, 2004).

46. Carlos Fuentes, *The Buried Mirror, Reflections on Spain and the New World* (1992; New York: Mariner, 1999).

47. Numa Broc, *La géographie de la Renaissance 1420–1620* (Paris: CTHS, 1986); Numa Broc, *La géographie des philosophes. Geographes et voyageurs français au XVIIIe siècle* (Paris: CTHS, 1969). Jean Chappe d'Auteroche and

later the Spanish members of the La Condamine expedition transformed geography and mapping, and science and politics, in a great intellectual adventure (see Antonio Lafuente and Antonio Mazuecos, *Los caballeros del punto fijo. Ciencia, política y aventura en la expedición geodésica hispanofrancesa al virreinato del Perú en el siglo XVIII* [Madrid: CSIC-Serbal, 1987]).

48. Cannon Schmitt, "Darwin's Savage Mnemonics," *Representations* 88 (Fall 2004): 55–80.

49. Janet Browne, *Charles Darwin: Voyaging* (New York: Knopf, 1995); Patrick Tort, *Darwin et le darwinisme* (Paris: Presses Universitaires de France, 1997). The case of Darwin can be compared with the case of Wallace, studied by Alfredo Bueno Hernández and Jorge Llorente Bousquets, *L'evoluzione di un evoluzionista. Alfred Russel Wallace e la geografia della vita*, ed. M. Zunino (Turin: Bollati Boringhieri, 2004), new and revised Italian edition of a previous book (*El pensamiento biogeográfico de Alfred Russel Wallace*, Bogotá: Academia Colombiana de Ciencias Exactas, Físicas y Naturales, 2003), esp. chaps. 1 and 2.

50. Alexis de Tocqueville, *De la démocratie en Amérique*, ed. François Furet (Paris: Garnier-Flammarion, 1981), vol. I, p. 81.

51. Tocqueville, *De la démocratie en Amérique*, vol. I, note C, p. 564.

52. Mark Kurlansky, *Cod: A Biography of the Fish That Changed the World* (New York: Walker and Company, 1997); Cañizares-Esguerra, *How to Write the History of the New World*.

53. On this special topic, I have been oriented by some of my colleagues at Modena University and especially by the contributions included in a volume recently edited by Marina Bondi, Laura Gavioli, and Marc Silver, *Academic Discourse, Genre and Small Corpora* (Rome: Officina Edizioni, 2004).

54. The bibliography about reading as a social practice is enormous. A good critical synthesis concerning the most important theories of the 1970s (Roland Barthes, Wolfgang Iser, Robert Jauss, Michel de Certeau, Harald Weinrich, Robert Winmann, etc.) is offered by Carlo Arcuri, ed., *Saggi sull'estetica della ricezione, L'immagine riflessa*, 1986, vol. I, and by Robert C. Holub, ed., *Teoria della ricezione* (Turin: Einaudi, 1989).

55. Traveling can be considered as a social practice in the same way and as an extension of reading.

56. Paul Gilroy, *The Black Atlantic: Modernity and Double Consciousness* (Cambridge, Mass.: Harvard University Press, 1993).

57. Guillaume Thomas Raynal, *Histoire Philosophique et politique des Établissemens et du Commerce des Européens dans les deux Indes* (Geneva: Chez J. L. Pellet imprimeur, 1781), vol. I, book 1, chap. 1, pp. 1–2.

58. During the nineteenth century, many authors offered historical and even anthropological arguments to explain and/or justify and support the idea of the difference between the two Americas, among them Ramón de la Sagra, *Cinco meses en los Estados-Unidos de la América del Norte* (Paris: Pablo Renouard, 1836). According to Humboldt, U.S. independence could be an example but not a model for the anticolonial struggle of the Creole elites of Latin America. The myth of Latin American difference was summarized recently by Howard J. Wiarda, *The Soul of Latin America: The Cultural and Political Tradition* (New

Haven: Yale University Press, 2001). The North American perspective on Spain and Spanish culture and language is deeply influenced by such a myth. James D. Fernández treated this well in his study, "Longfellow's Law: The Place of Latin America and Spain in U.S. Hispanism, circa 1915," in *Spain in America: The Origins of Hispanism in the United States*, ed. Richard L. Kagan (Urbana and Chicago: University of Illinois Press, 2002), pp. 122–41. (Fernández's "Longfellow's Law" says: "U.S. interest in Spain is and has always been largely mediated by U.S. interest in Latin America," p. 124.)

59. *Ritualidades iberoamericanas: un acercamiento interdisciplinario*, ed. Martin Lienhard (Madrid-Frankfurt: Iberoamericana-Vervuert, 2003) underlines this continuity in ritualism (in terms of representations concerning nature, society, and words); see also Daniel Brewer and Julie Candler Hayes, eds., *Using the Encyclopédie: Ways of Knowing, Ways of Reading* (Oxford: SVEC-Voltaire Foundation, 2002).

60. See Ian Watt, *Myths of Modern Individualism: Faust, Don Quixote, Don Juan, Robinson Crusoe* (Cambridge: Cambridge University Press, 1996).

61. See Robert Meyer, *Three Cinematic Robinsonades*, in Robert Meyer, ed., *Eighteenth-Century Fiction on Screen* (Cambridge: Cambridge University Press, 2002), pp. 35–51.

62. Alexandre de Humboldt, *Essai politique sur le royaume de la Nouvelle Espagne du Mexique*, 2 vols. with uninterrupted page numeration (Thizy-Paris: Utz, 1997), vol. I, p. 97 (italics are mine).

63. Humboldt, *Essai politique*, vol. I, p. 348.

Index